Writers and Revolution

The revolution of 1848 has been described as the revolution of the intellectuals. In France, the revolution galvanized the energies of major romantic writers and intellectuals. This book follows nine writers through the revolution of 1848 and its aftermath: Alphonse de Lamartine, George Sand, Marie d'Agoult, Victor Hugo, Alexis de Tocqueville, Pierre-Joseph Proudhon, Alexander Herzen, Karl Marx and Gustave Flaubert. Conveying a sense of the experience of 1848 as these writers lived it, this fresh and engaging study captures the sense of possibility at a time when it was not yet clear that the Second French Republic had no future. By looking closely at key texts in which each writer attempted to understand, judge, criticize or intervene in the revolution, Jonathan Beecher shows how each endeavoured to answer the question posed explicitly by Tocqueville: Why, within the space of two generations, did democratic revolutions twice culminate in the dictatorship of a Napoleon?

Jonathan Beecher is Professor Emeritus of History at the University of California at Santa Cruz. A European intellectual historian, with a special interest in France and Russia, his previous publications include *Charles Fourier: The Visionary and His World* (1986) and *Victor Considerant and the Rise and Fall of French Romantic Socialism* (2001). His works have been translated into French, Italian and Japanese.

T0371522

Writers and Revolution

Intellectuals and the French Revolution of 1848

Jonathan Beecher

University of California, Santa Cruz

CAMBRIDGE
UNIVERSITY PRESS

CAMBRIDGE
UNIVERSITY PRESS

Shaftesbury Road, Cambridge CB2 8EA, United Kingdom

One Liberty Plaza, 20th Floor, New York, NY 10006, USA

477 Williamstown Road, Port Melbourne, VIC 3207, Australia

314–321, 3rd Floor, Plot 3, Splendor Forum, Jasola District Centre, New Delhi – 110025, India

103 Penang Road, #05–06/07, Visioncrest Commercial, Singapore 238467

Cambridge University Press is part of Cambridge University Press & Assessment, a department of the University of Cambridge.

We share the University's mission to contribute to society through the pursuit of education, learning and research at the highest international levels of excellence.

www.cambridge.org
Information on this title: www.cambridge.org/9781108829373

DOI: 10.1017/9781108909792

First published 2021
First paperback edition 2024

A catalogue record for this publication is available from the British Library

Library of Congress Cataloging-in-Publication data
Names: Beecher, Jonathan, author.
Title: Writers and revolution : intellectuals and the French Revolution of 1848 / Jonathan Beecher, University of California, Santa Cruz.
Description: First edition. | New York : Cambridge University Press, 2021. | Includes bibliographical references and index.
Identifiers: LCCN 2020046737 (print) | LCCN 2020046738 (ebook) | ISBN 9781108842532 (hardback) | ISBN 9781108829373 (paperback) | ISBN 9781108909792 (epub)
Subjects: LCSH: France–History–February Revolution, 1848–Literature and the revolution. | France–History–February Revolution, 1848–Influence. | France–History–1848-1870. | French literature–19th century–History and criticism.
Classification: LCC DC272 .B37 2021 (print) | LCC DC272 (ebook) | DDC 944.07–dc23
LC record available at https://lccn.loc.gov/2020046737
LC ebook record available at https://lccn.loc.gov/2020046738

ISBN   978-1-108-84253-2   Hardback
ISBN   978-1-108-82937-3   Paperback

In memory of three inspiring teachers:
Edward P. Morris
Stanley Hoffmann
Judith Nisse Shklar

Contents

Figures

Preface

This is a book that I have been thinking about, imagining and rehearsing for much of my life as a historian. It was in my sophomore year in college that Ted Morris steered me in the direction of 1848: we were reading Fromentin's novel *Dominique*, and he kept asking me to think about the relation between this apparently apolitical work and 1848. Two years later I wrote a senior thesis with Valentine Boss on the critique of political religions developed by Alexander Herzen in 1848. I went on to do several years of graduate work in Russian intellectual history, and my original idea was to study the rise of socialism in the Russia of Nicholas I. But I took a long detour into the life and thought of Charles Fourier and the reverberations of his thought in July Monarchy France. This turned into two large books. It was only when I was well embarked on the present book that I began to see it as part of a single story: a trilogy. The first two parts of the trilogy were my intellectual biographies of Charles Fourier and Victor Considerant. Both of these books were attempts to reach a sympathetic yet critical understanding of the extraordinary flourishing of radical ideas and utopian visions that marked the 1830s and 1840s in France, and the present study of European writers and 1848 is centrally concerned with the collapse of such dreams after 1848.

When I began, I saw myself as writing contextual history. My goal in the first book, *Charles Fourier: The Visionary and His World*, was to get beyond the conventional view of Fourier as a sort of inspired lunatic who lived in a self-contained mental universe. I wanted to look at him and his ideas in relation to his experience and against the background of the various "worlds" that he traversed. My hope was that by grasping the interplay between Fourier's ideas and the circumstances in which he lived, I could present a richer account of his theory than those offered by commentators who saw Fourier as a "precursor" of Marx or Freud and whose main concern was with his "modernity." In the second book, *Victor Considerant and the Rise and Fall of French Romantic Socialism*, my task was different. Victor Considerant was a largely derivative thinker who found an audience for Fourier's ideas in the 1840s but flattened

them out, turning Fourier's call for the liberation of instinct into a
scheme for the organization of labour. It seemed to me that the best
way to approach him was to relate him to the larger movement of which
he was a part – not the Fourierist movement but something broader and
more pervasive: what I called "the rise and fall of French romantic
socialism."

I continue to see myself as a contextual historian, but a large part of
this book consists of the close reading of texts – inspired in part by the
work of Hayden White and by French textual analysis. The book could
be described as an exercise in comparative storytelling – an attempt to
get at the revolution of 1848 and its aftermath by comparing the itineraries and writing of my nine intellectuals. The point of the book is, as
I make clear in the Prologue, to explain what contemporary intellectuals –
liberals, republicans, democrats and socialists – understood as a failure.

I have benefitted greatly from the opportunity to present versions of
my "book project" to colleagues as it evolved over the years. My thanks
go first to George Sheridan and Jeremy Popkin for inviting me to join
them in a French Historical Studies conference panel on 1848 at
Rutgers. Thanks also to Carol Harrison for a searching comment at that
session. A Pierson lectureship at the University of Oregon gave me the
chance to work out my ideas more extensively. More recently I have had
the opportunity to participate in conferences on 1848 at Cambridge and
Paris and to meet so many fine scholars working on 1848. I have greatly
enjoyed exchanges growing out of these conferences with Gareth
Stedman Jones, Douglas Moggach, Emmanuel Fureix, Sylvie Aprile,
Fabrice Bensimon, Romy Sanchez, Jorge Myers, Christopher Clark
and Miles Taylor. I want particularly to thank Gareth for the contribution his work on Marx, on early socialism and on the link between
socialism and religion has made to our understanding of the history of
nineteenth-century European radicalism.

In recent years I have been able to present overviews of and chapters
from my book at conferences at Vanderbilt and UN Reno, and talks at
Stanford and UC Santa Cruz. I am particularly grateful to my colleagues
in Cultural Studies here at UCSC and especially to Gail Hershatter,
James Clifford, Donna Haraway, Gopal Balakrishnan and Jerome Neu.
Their encouraging response to my Cultural Studies talk a few years ago
meant a lot to me. I also thank Keith Baker and Dan Edelstein and J. P.
Daughton, generous and welcoming colleagues at Stanford.

Over the years colleagues and friends have generously taken the time to
read my chapters as they slowly appeared. I am especially grateful to Gary
Miles, Peter Kenez and the late John Dizikes, each of whom read just
about everything. I thank Jeremy Jennings for a very helpful reading of

the finished manuscript. Several of my colleagues have given me much needed critical readings of specific chapters. For this I especially want to thank Ruth MacKay, Dominica Chang, Naomi Andrews, Mary Pickering, Christopher Johnson, Irina Paperno, Joseph Butwin and Mark Traugott. Along the way, Mark has helped me with any number of problems, large and small. And I would like to indicate here how lucky I feel to have had as a colleague for more than four decades as fine a scholar of 1848 and as generous a friend as Mark Traugott. I also want to acknowledge a number of fellow travellers who have encouraged me in various ways and taught me by example, sometimes without knowing it: Terry Burke, Patrice Higonnet, Temma Kaplan, Biliana Kassabova, Lloyd Kramer, Kristin Ross, Bali Sahota, Alan Spitzer, Bruce Thompson, Steven Vincent, John Womack and my dear friend Buchanan Sharp.

My thanks to longstanding French colleagues and friends. I owe a lot to Michèle Riot-Sarcey who has taught me much through both her work and our talks about nineteenth-century French radical thought. I am very grateful to Ludovic Frobert who has organized fascinating colloquia on early French socialism and on the *canuts* of Lyon and has had the kindness to invite me to participate in several of them. Thanks also to Nicole Edelman, Chantal Gaillard, Chantal Guillaume, Philippe Hamon, François Jarrige, Pierre Mercklé, Philippe Régnier, Loïc Rignol, René Schérer and Anne Verjus. I have a particular debt of gratitude to my longstanding Besançon friends – especially to my "brother," Gaston Bordet, who has introduced me to so many different facets of the history of French radicalism, past and present, and to Thomas Bouchet who has written so much and so well about 1848 and social movements of the 1830s and 1840s. Thanks also to my comrade Michel Cordillot and to Marc Veuilleumier whose meticulous scholarship has meant so much to all of us working on 1848. And thanks to Edward Castleton, a Bisontin by adoption, who is now playing a central role in the reorientation of Proudhon scholarship and whose unpublished and about-to-be-published papers have been so helpful to me and many others in our efforts to make sense of Proudhon's thought. Finally, my thanks for numerous kindnesses over the years to my friends of sixty years standing (!), Catherine Vourc'h and Anne Vourc'h and their families, to the late Michel and Colette Cotté, and to my friends-in-Fourier, Philippe and Danielle Duizabo and Jean and Monique Adam for the warmth of their welcome at Paris and Condé-sur-Vesgre.

Closer to home, I am grateful to my university for the award of multiple Academic Senate Research Grants for work on this book. I also want to thank Alice Yang and Alan Christy, provosts respectively

of Stevenson and Cowell Colleges here at UCSC, for providing me with
an office – shared with my friend Gildas Hamel – long after my formal
retirement. Given my peculiar study habits and my need to be within
walking distance of our wonderful library, it would have been hard –
perhaps impossible – for me to complete this book without the office and
without all the help I have received from colleagues at the McHenry
Library, notably Beth Remak-Honeff, from the Interlibrary Loan staff,
and from Jay Olson and Kim Hwe in the Humanities Division. And now
that my book has migrated to England, I want to thank Elizabeth Friend-
Smith, Atifa Jiwa and Lisa Carter for welcoming the book at Cambridge
and for the help and encouragement they have given me as I have
attempted to adapt myself to the conventions of publishing in a digital
age. Thanks also to Tanya Izzard for a fine index and to Benjamin
Johnson, a patient, supportive and resourceful copyeditor.

Unlike my biographies of Fourier and Considerant, which were largely
based on archival sources, this book has grown to a significant degree out
of my teaching – out of courses in French history, nineteenth-century
European intellectual history, and seminars on 1848, on the history of
Paris and *Les Misérables*. I have learned much through exchanges with
students in these courses, and I want to acknowledge at least a few of
them: Naomi Andrews, Bob Andrus, Bob Brauneis, Alexandra Carter,
Kukui Claydon, Sarah Johnson Doenmez, Carolyn Eastman, Jennifer
Heyneman, Sarah Leonard, Ruth MacKay, Laura Mason, José Orozco,
Kathryn Paisner, Grace Phelan, Dianne Williams Pitman, Paul Pitman,
Clay Ramsay, Doug Reed, Carina Scott, Amy Stewart, Anthony Von der
Muhl, Virginia Ward and Janna Wicklund.

I am dedicating this book to the memory of three people: Edward
Morris, Stanley Hoffmann and Judith Nisse Shklar. Although each of
them is remembered in many other ways, I knew them first as teachers.
Ted Morris got me started in French studies, taught me how to read
critically and helped me to acquire a love of French literature that
continues to enrich my life. Stanley Hoffmann's amazing lecture course
on French Society and Politics, with all the wonderful novels on its
impossibly long reading list, opened up new worlds for me. And the
experience of meeting with Dita Shklar once a week to discuss a graduate
field in Ancient Political Theory left me not only with a deeper understanding of Plato, Aristotle, Thucydides and Polybius, but also with a
lifelong admiration for her lucidity and humane skepticism. She remains
for me a model of moral seriousness and intellectual generosity.

Finally, I want to thank my family. Over the past decade, Merike and
I have both been absorbed by work on ambitious projects – hers even
more ambitious than mine. Now she is finishing work on the third

volume of her translation of Jaan Kross' great historical novel, *Between Three Plagues*, an attempt to recreate the life of Balthasar Russow, the author of *The Livonian Chronicle* (1578), a work regarded by some as the first history of Estonia. As we both worked away on our grand projects, I came to feel a wonderful sense of intellectual comradeship with Merike. Our boys have also become intellectual comrades: David, the historian, with whom I have discussed many of the issues that this book raises, and Lembit, the composer, from whom I am expecting a musical appreciation of 1848 to rival his Oratorio for male chorus, two horns and harp on Fourier's *New Amorous World*.

Chronology

Political Regimes in France 1789–1848

French Revolution:
Constitutional Monarchy 1789–1792
First Republic 1792–1804
Revolutionary Government by the Convention 1792–1795
Directory 1795–1799
Consulate 1799–1804: Dictatorship of Napoleon Bonaparte
Napoleonic Empire 1804–1814: Napoleon I
First Bourbon Restoration 1814–1815
Napoleon's Hundred Days 1815
Second Bourbon Restoration 1815–1830
Louis XVIII 1814–1824
Charles X 1824–1830
July Monarchy 1830–1848
Constitutional Monarchy: Orleanist King Louis-Philippe

Second French Republic: February 24, 1848 to December 2, 1851

1848

February 22	Crowds protest cancellation of reformist banquet.
February 23	National Guard defects. Guizot dismissed.
February 23	Protest culminates in shooting on the Boulevard des Capucines.
February 24	Barricades rise all over Paris. Street fighting. King abdicates.
February 24	Insurgents seize Tuileries and Hôtel de Ville.
February 24	Provisional Government formed.

February 25	Provisional Government proclaims the "right to work."
February 25	Lamartine defends tricolor flag.
February 26	National Workshops set up.
February 26	Abolition of death penalty for political crimes. Mobile Guard created.
February 28	Luxembourg Commission established to study organization of work.
February 29	Abolition of salt tax and municipal customs duties.
March 4	Abolition of slavery in French colonies. Freedom of press and assembly.
March 4	Lamartine's Manifesto to the European Powers proclaims non-intervention.
March 5	Proclamation of universal (male) suffrage.
March 8	National Guard opened to all adult males.
March 14	Dissolution of elite companies of National Guard.
March 16	Special 45 centimes surtax on each franc of direct property taxes.
March 16	Demonstration by elite National Guard units.
March 17	Massive republican counter-demonstration.
April 15	George Sand's *Bulletin de la République* calls for a democratic assembly.
April 16	Worker demonstration dwarfed by massive counter-demonstration.
April 20	*Fête de la Fraternité*
April 23	Election of National Constituent Assembly: Massive conservative majority.
April 27–28	Repression of workers' protest at Rouen.
May 4	National Assembly meets. Republic proclaimed.
May 10	Provisional Government replaced by Executive Commission.
May 15	Crowd invades Assembly. Abortive coup.
May 16	Luxembourg Commission dissolved.
May 20	Assembly opens debate on National Workshops.
June 4	By-elections to National Assembly: Proudhon and Hugo elected.
June 5–10	Unrest among Paris workers. Arrests.
June 21	Decree on National Workshops.
June 22	Worker demonstrations at Paris.
June 23–26	"The June Days." Civil War in Paris.

June 24	Executive Commission resigns. Power to Cavaignac. State of siege.
June 26	Insurrection crushed. Shooting of prisoners.
June 28	Cavaignac forms a ministry. National Workshops abolished.
July–August	Reaction, Red Scare, Emergence of the Party of Order.
July 5	Carnot removed as Minister of Public Instruction.
July 28	Decree on clubs.
July 31	Assembly condemns Proudhon.
August 9–11	Decrees on the press.
August 25–26	Prosecution and flight into exile of Blanc and Caussidière.
September 4	National Assembly begins to discuss the Constitution.
September 17	By-elections. Winners include Louis-Napoleon Bonaparte.
November 4	Constitution approved 739:30. Hugo and Proudhon vote against.
November 24	Pope Pius IX flees into exile with Austrians at Gaeta.
December 10	Louis-Napoleon Bonaparte elected President of the Republic.

1849

April 16	French troops sent to Rome.
April 30	First attack by French troops on Roman Republic.
May 7	Constituent Assembly protests attack on Rome.
May 13	Legislative Assembly elected. Gains for Right but "Red France" emerges.
June 3	French troops begin siege of Roman Republic.
June 11	Assembly rejects Ledru-Rollin's demand for no-confidence vote.
June 13	Paris demonstration against government broken up. Radicals arrested.
June 19	New law banning clubs.
July 3	Roman Republic falls to French troops. Pope can return to Vatican.
July 27	New law on the press.
October	Trial of those implicated in June 13 demonstration.

1850

March 10	By-elections result in radical victories.
March 15	Falloux Law gives Catholic Church control of education.
May 31	New electoral law eliminates three million voters.
June 9	Law forbidding clubs and public meetings.
July	President Louis-Napoleon tours the provinces.

1851

July 19	Assembly rejects constitutional revision to permit re-election of president.
October– November	Louis-Napoleon fails to restore universal male suffrage.
December 2	Coup d'état of Louis-Napoleon: National Assembly dissolved.
December 3–4	Limited resistance in Paris.
December 5–10	Extensive resistance in the provinces is crushed.
December 21	Plebiscite gives massive approval to Louis-Napoleon.

1852

November 21	Second plebiscite approves Empire.
December 2	Louis-Napoleon becomes Emperor.

1   Prologue

The year 1848 was the great revolutionary year of the nineteenth century – the year when barricades appeared on the streets of all the major European capitals and people demonstrated all over Europe against arbitrary, autocratic government. No one outside of Italy paid much attention in January when rebels in Palermo forced Ferdinand II, the King of the Two Sicilies, to grant a liberal constitution. But then in February Parisians overthrew King Louis Philippe. During three days of street fighting, barricades went up all over Paris (see Figure 1.1), soldiers refused to fire on demonstrators, the National Guard went over to the insurgents, and, on February 24, the king abdicated and fled to England. That afternoon the insurgents proclaimed the Second French Republic, and a Provisional Government established itself at the Paris city hall.

In the next few weeks, a revolutionary wave swept across Europe: from the Atlantic to the Ukraine, from the Baltic to the Black Sea. "This was," writes Christopher Clark, "the only truly European revolution that there has ever been."[1] Its echoes were felt far beyond Europe: in Latin America and North Africa and even in Tsarist Russia. To begin with, the Parisian scenario of banquets and barricades, mass meetings and street demonstrations, played out in the capitals of the two great central European powers: Prussia and Austria. By the end of March, liberal constitutional governments had been proclaimed not only in Berlin and Vienna, but also in Milan, Budapest, Prague and Cracow, and there were stirrings of nationalist revolt throughout the great, sprawling Habsburg Empire.

In Paris, on February 25, the Provisional Government issued a decree calling for elections for a Constituent Assembly to be held by universal male suffrage. Other decrees established freedom of the press, assembly and association, opened the National Guard to all adult male citizens, and abolished the death penalty for political crimes. Under pressure from

---

[1] Christopher Clark, "Why Should We Think about the Revolution of 1848 Now?," *London Review of Books* (March 7, 2019), 12.

Figure 1.1 Photo taken by Hippolyte Bayard from the steps of the
Madeleine late February 1848, looking down the rue Royale toward the
Place de la Concorde and the Palais Bourbon. The remains of two
barricades are visible in the foreground. Hulton Archive via Getty

a huge crowd gathered in front of the Hôtel de Ville, the Provisional
Government also issued a decree guaranteeing all citizens the right to
work (*le droit au travail*). To expedite this decree a program of National
Workshops was organized and a special Commission of Labour established under the direction of the socialist Louis Blanc. In a gesture of
obvious symbolic importance, it was decided that the Commission would
meet in the Luxembourg Palace, the former seat of the Chamber of
Peers. The National Workshops were regarded by the moderate majority
of the Provisional Government as a temporary expedient to provide relief
to unemployed workers. But by treating the workshops as a means of
implementing a basic human right, the right to work, and by designating
the workshops as "National," the Provisional Government seemed to
suggest that this revolution would do more than establish a democratic
republic. Its aim would not only be to extend the right to vote to all adult
males, but also to confront what had come to be known as "the social
question" – the problem of endemic poverty and unemployment among
the labouring poor. This, at any rate, is how the declaration of the right to
work was understood by many members of the working class. In their
eyes, the National Workshops represented a permanent commitment

and the recognition of a right. They saw the Workshops, as William Sewell has put it, as "a first step in the direction of a state-aided system of producers' associations."[2]

The confrontation with the social question was largely absent from revolutionary outbreaks outside of France in 1848. These revolutions were directed against autocratic regimes established or reinforced in 1815 by the Congress of Vienna. In most of them, the goal was liberation from subservience to Austria or Prussia. They began with working-class agitation in the cities, with the attempts of peasants to reclaim traditional rights, and with student demonstrations in university towns. But leadership generally fell into the hands of middle-class liberals. And these revolutions culminated not in the overthrow of existing monarchies but in the abolition of vestiges of feudalism and in liberal reforms including a widening of the suffrage and promised constitutions granting freedom of speech, the press, association, assembly and religion. Some of these reforms were short-lived; and outside of France, as the saying went, "revolution stopped at the foot of the throne." Nonetheless and taken as a whole, the revolutions of 1848 constituted the most widespread and sustained burst of revolutionary activity of the whole nineteenth century. They touched all of Europe, and they raised the hopes of liberals and radicals like nothing since 1789. Many 'forty-eighters were writers and intellectuals, and their activities during this revolutionary springtime became infused with messianic dreams, heroic impulses, and a seemingly limitless faith in the power of ideas to change the world.

The initial period of revolutionary euphoria lasted just a few months. In France it was marked by a flood of radical newspapers and pamphlets, and by the creation in Paris alone of some 450 revolutionary clubs. It was punctuated by two *journées* or popular interventions. In the first, on March 17, 100,000 workers took to the streets to protest the assertion of special prerogatives by elite National Guard units. The second intervention, on April 16, began as a democratic election rally, but turned into a conservative triumph when, fearing a radical coup, leading democrats withdrew their support. When elections for a national Constituent Assembly were held on Easter Sunday, April 23, the enthusiasm of democrats and radicals cooled. For the French provinces strongly favoured conservative candidates, and traditional elites did well everywhere. Of 900 new representatives, 700 were wealthy enough to have served in the Chamber of Deputies during the July Monarchy, and most

---

[2] William H. Sewell, Jr., *Work and Revolution in France: The Language of Labor from the Old Regime to 1848* (Cambridge, 1980), 243–253. See also Rémi Gossez, *Les Ouvriers de Paris* (Paris, 1968), 10–14.

of these were royalists. *La Revue des deux mondes* summed up the attitude
of conservatives in noting that they could hardly complain about universal suffrage "since it gives our principles such wise defenders."[3]

After the elections the Provisional Government gave way to a more
conservative Executive Committee, and conflict developed between
Paris and the provinces and between the radical democrats and the
conservative majority in the National Assembly. The social question
was put on hold. In newspapers and club meetings radicals talked about
overthrowing the Assembly and proclaiming a revolutionary dictatorship.
In May an attempt was made to do just that. But the only result of the
abortive insurrection of May 15 was to get some radical leaders arrested,
to compromise others, and to strengthen the position of what was
becoming known as the "Party of Order." By June, the conservative
majority in the Assembly had had enough of the radical social experiment
initiated in February. This meant the end of the National Workshops. On
June 21, a decree put all members of the Workshops on call for army duty
in the provinces.

This decree was understood by many Parisian workers as a declaration
of war. On June 22, barricades rose in the working-class quarters of
Paris – the whole Eastern and Central parts of the city. What followed
was four days of the bloodiest street fighting that Paris had ever known.
Regular army troops and bourgeois National Guard units were called in
to combat the insurrection, and these were followed by trainloads of
provincial militia units. Finally, after four days of fighting, the insurrection was put down. About 1,500 insurgents were executed without
trial, and the number killed in the fighting was probably two or three
times greater.

The insurrection of June 1848 was remarkable on many counts. The
most extraordinary thing to contemporary observers was that some
50,000 working-class insurgents fought entirely on their own, without
the leadership or even the help of the middle-class democrats and socialists who had long been claiming to speak on behalf of "the people." The
rebels fought, in Tocqueville's words, "without a war-cry, without chiefs
or a standard, and yet with a cohesion and a military skill that surprised
the oldest officers ... Women took part as much as men ... It was not a
political struggle ... but a class war, a kind of slave war."[4] Tocqueville's
verdict, which was echoed by Karl Marx, surely exaggerates the clarity
with which many of the participants saw the situation. The workers who

[3] "Revue des deux mondes, September 30, 1848" in Pierre Rosanvallon, *Le sacre du citoyen: Histoire du suffrage universel en France* (Paris, 1992), 299.
[4] Alexis de Tocqueville, *Souvenirs* (Paris, 1978), 212–213.

put down the insurrection believed they were defending democracy and constitutional government. Class lines were shifting in 1848, and there were workers on both sides of the barricades. But the outcome of the June insurrection was clear. It smashed the hopes of the socialists and romantic intellectuals who had greeted the February Revolution as the start of a new era. It also inaugurated a period of political repression and red-baiting that lasted through the fall. Censorship was restored, radical clubs shut down and leftist leaders brought to trial. It was in this atmosphere of reaction that a constitution was drafted and a new election organized, this time for the presidency of the Republic. The leading candidate who soon emerged was none other than Louis-Napoleon Bonaparte, a nephew of the great Napoleon.

Until 1848 Louis-Napoleon had led the life of an unsuccessful political adventurer. He was a failed conspirator who had spent most of the 1840s in prison or in exile. Still, he had three things going for him. First, there was the magic of his name. The Napoleonic legend still resonated in France, especially among peasants. Secondly, he had a negative appeal to members of the working class, because he had not even been in France at the time of the June insurrection and had had nothing to do with its repression. Finally, his apparent mediocrity seemed to make him an attractive figurehead for the designs of the royalist politicians. When the presidential elections were held in December, they threw the weight of their influence behind Louis-Napoleon, expecting that his election would prepare the way for the restoration of monarchy in France.

In fact, Louis-Napoleon Bonaparte proved to be a shrewder politician than anyone expected. He won the presidential election of December 1848 by a 4:1 margin over his nearest rival. In the three years that followed – in the course of some complicated political jockeying – he managed to frustrate the designs of the royalists as well as those of the democrats and socialists. Then, on December 2, 1851, the anniversary of his uncle's coronation as emperor, after failing to persuade the National Assembly to revise the constitution to permit his reelection, he staged a carefully planned coup d'état, suspended the republican constitution, and assumed dictatorial powers. A year later, he had himself proclaimed Emperor and began a reign that would last until 1870.

The revolution of 1848 has been described as the revolution of the intellectuals.[5] In France especially the revolution served to galvanize the energies of many of the major romantic writers and intellectuals of the time. The poet Lamartine became the leader of the Provisional

---

[5] Lewis Namier, *1848: The Revolution of the Intellectuals* (London, 1962).

Government and its foreign minister. The novelist George Sand wrote electoral bulletins for the Interior Ministry. Victor Hugo, Tocqueville, Lamennais, Proudhon, the poet Béranger and the popular novelist Eugene Sue were all elected to the National Assembly. Even Baudelaire – who was subsequently to express contempt for all forms of political action – formed his own club and edited his own journal. And the painter Courbet designed the illustration for Baudelaire's short-lived journal.

The outcome of the revolution of 1848 in France was to destroy the hopes that many writers and intellectuals had come to place in politics and in collective action in the public sphere. Some of the 'forty-eighters were thrown into exile, others into silence. Some continued to look forward to an ideal Republic, others to a great revolutionary event in the distant future. Many came eventually to believe that there could be no lasting republic without universal education and a universal appreciation of civic virtues. A few, like Victor Hugo, became more fervent advocates of social change after 1851. But to most of the writers and intellectuals who had invested their energies in the revolution and identified with its aims, the collapse of the Second Republic seemed to demonstrate the futility of political involvement and the collective pursuit of social ideals. This withdrawal of intellectuals from politics and political commitment was a striking outcome of the revolutionary upheavals of 1848–1851. It was accompanied in literature by the triumph of the doctrine of "art for art's sake" and in political theory by the recourse to the critical, ironical and elitist stance that has been described as "Parnassian liberalism."[6] It was also accompanied by attempts on the part of many intellectuals to look critically at the ideals and practices of 1848 and to explain what had "gone wrong."

While the Second French Republic lasted almost four years, elsewhere in Europe things went more quickly. Just as in France, there was an initial period of euphoria marked, in Central Europe, by the overthrow of absolutist regimes, the abolition of remaining seigneurial privileges, the proclamation of constitutions, and the organization of elections. In the Rhineland, the Palatinate, and throughout Southern Germany, there were instances of peasant unrest that contemporaries compared to the Peasants' War of 1525. But, except in Hungary where an established gentry elite took control, the radical movements were not durable. Within a few weeks, nationalist rivalries, emerging social conflicts and unresolved political issues brought political activists down to earth.

[6] George Armstrong Kelly, *The Humane Comedy: Constant, Tocqueville and French Liberalism* (Cambridge, 1992), 221–255.

The reversal in Vienna, the capital of the Austrian Empire, was particularly rapid. On March 13 and 14, demonstrations in Vienna forced the resignation of Metternich, the creation of a Civic Guard, and the promise of a constitution. Two months later the future of the Empire was in doubt. The North Italian provinces of Lombardy and Venetia were in revolt. Effective authority was divided between three centres of power: German Vienna, Hungarian Budapest and Croatian Zagreb – each claiming sovereign authority. Half a dozen other national movements – Polish, Romanian, Slovenian, Serb, Czech and Slovak – were aspiring to sovereign status. The state was virtually bankrupt and, on May 17, the feeble-minded Emperor Ferdinand I and his court fled the capital.

Yet by August everything had changed. Most of North Italy had been reconquered. The emperor was back in Vienna. His government was now discussing the future shape of the monarchy with a pliant constituent assembly. Financial problems remained, Venice still clung to a shaky independence and the Hungarians remained defiant, but steps were being taken to restore Habsburg authority throughout the Empire. In October radicals took control of Vienna, killing the Austrian Minister of War and seeking to prevent Austrian troops from joining the effort to suppress the revolution in Hungary. Ferdinand and his court fled the capital for a second time. In response a force of 70,000 imperial troops, led by Prince Alfred Windischgrätz, "the very epitome of the feudal and absolutist regime that had been overthrown in March 1848," put Vienna to siege and crushed the insurgency.[7] In November Prince Felix von Schwarzenberg, the brother-in-law of Windischgrätz, became Austrian prime minister, persuaded the Emperor Ferdinand to abdicate in favour of his nephew, Franz Josef, and reestablished autocratic rule over the empire, returning Austria to "a form of centralism and absolutism even more severe than under Metternich."[8]

The revolt of Czech nationalists in the Austrian province of Bohemia followed a similar course. In Prague radical students, intellectuals and artisans took to the streets in March demanding political and social reform and Czech autonomy. But the initial euphoria soon gave way to conflict between German and Czech nationalist movements, both of which were strong in Bohemia. In early June Czech nationalists organized a Slavic Congress in Prague to discuss the reorganization of the Habsburg Empire as a federation of relatively autonomous South

---

[7] Jonathan Sperber, *The European Revolutions, 1848–1851* (Cambridge, 2005), 216–225.
[8] Alan Sked, "The Nationality Problem in the Habsburg Monarchy and the Revolutions of 1848: A Reassessment" in Douglas Moggach and Gareth Stedman Jones (eds.), *The 1848 Revolutions and European Political Thought* (Cambridge, 2018), 344.

German and Slavic states. The leaders of the Czech nationalist movement were, like their German counterparts, constitutional monarchists,
loyal to the Habsburg Emperor. But on June 12 a radical insurrection
broke out at Prague. This gave Windischgrätz, who wanted a confrontation, the opportunity to subdue the Czech insurgency with an
artillery bombardment of Prague. Thereafter, while young Czech
radicals continued to talk of revolution, the chief spokesmen for Czech
nationalism were moderates like the historian Frantisek Palacky for
whom the goal was not independence but autonomy within a reformed
Austrian Empire.

It was in Hungary that the most significant challenge to Austrian
sovereignty emerged. In the spring of 1848, Hungary acquired a constitution, a charismatic leader, a national army and a parliament elected by
a broad suffrage but dominated by the gentry. The leader, Lajos Kossuth,
was an eloquent and tireless orator and an ardent patriot who rose from
the lesser nobility to the status of a national icon.[9] The constitution,
which included the abolition of serfdom and all manorial obligations,
called for the annexation of Croatia and Transylvania and it left Hungary
essentially self-governing. But it also privileged the Magyar language and
limited the rights of non-Hungarians. By the end of the summer,
Hungary was ringed by hostile nationalities including Croats, Serbs,
Slovaks and Romanians, whom Austria could play off against Hungary.
Soon Hungary was at war not only with Austria, but also with Croatia
and Romania. In the fall of 1848, Kossuth tirelessly travelled over the
Hungarian countryside, rallying the Hungarian people and calling on
them to defend their country. After a series of defeats, including the
occupation of Budapest by Windischgrätz in January 1849, the
Hungarians won victories in the spring, recapturing Budapest and
driving the Austrians out of Transylvania. On April 14, 1849, the
Hungarian Diet made Kossuth president of the Hungarian Republic.
For four months Hungary was an independent state. The Austrians,
fearing a Hungarian attack on Vienna, requested aid from the Russia of
Nicholas I. The Tsar responded by dispatching 200,000 Russian troops
to Hungary. Finally, in August 1849, with Russian help, the Austrians
crushed the independent Hungarian Republic.

The situation in the Prussian capital of Berlin was complicated by the
fact that the revolution of 1848 produced two elected assemblies. The
first was a Prussian parliament charged with writing a constitution for
Prussia. The second was the German Constituent National Assembly,

---

[9] Istvan Deak, *The Lawful Revolution: Louis Kossuth and the Hungarians, 1848–1849*
(London, 2001).

otherwise known as the Frankfurt Parliament, which met at Frankfurt to draw up a constitution for a united Germany. Both of these assemblies were created in the aftermath of the March 18 Revolution, and both were dissolved within a year. As it turned out, Frederick William IV had second thoughts and German liberals proved more adept at discussing first principles than at initiating significant reforms. The task facing the Frankfurt Parliament was not made easier by the fact that the "Germany" for which its members were writing a constitution did not yet exist.

In the fall of 1848, a royalist reaction took shape in Prussia. Facing an uprising of hungry workers, the King declared a state of siege, dissolved the Prussian assembly and decreed a new conservative constitution. In other German states, liberal ministers were dismissed and autocratic rule was restored. It soon became clear that, lacking the power to raise an army and impose taxes, the Frankfurt Parliament could exist only as long as the King of Prussia wished it to exist. In April 1849, when the parliament completed its work and offered the throne of a united Germany to Frederick William IV, he simply refused. He would not accept an office created by a democratically elected legislature claiming popular sovereignty. Later that spring, when revolutionary governments were proclaimed in Saxony, Baden and the Bavarian Palatinate, they were crushed by Prussian troops. Rebels held out in the fortress of Rastatt in Baden until July 23, 1849. With their surrender, the German revolution of 1848 was over.

Revolt also broke out in 1848 in the North Italian states under Austrian control and in the Papal States. Insurgents in Milan and Venice expelled the Austrians from the provinces of Lombardy and Venetia. Their initial victories on the barricades led to the creation of liberal governments which then sought aid from the Piedmontese king Charles-Albert. But the Piedmontese army was soundly defeated in July by Austrian troops under Field Marshal Joseph Radetzky. By late August the Austrians had reconquered all the Empire's possessions in Northern Italy, except for Venice.

The radical movement in the Papal States got underway later and lasted longer. When Pius IX became Pope in June 1846, his first act was to amnesty political prisoners. Italian liberals initially had high hopes for him but were disappointed by his opposition in 1847 to constitutional reforms and his refusal in 1848 to support the nationalist struggle against Austria. By summer he faced the opposition of a robust liberal movement supported by refugees from all over Italy. The assassination on November 15 of his advisor, Pellegrino Rossi, ended any last hope for a liberal Papal State. Ten days later Pius IX fled into exile at Austrian-held Gaeta, and radical republicans took control in Rome. In January

1849 elections were held by universal male suffrage for a Roman Constituent Assembly. The outcome was a Roman Republic led by a Triumvirate including Giuseppe Mazzini. This republic lasted less than five months. It was, as we shall see in Chapter 6, crushed by French troops in a military operation overseen by Alexis de Tocqueville during his brief tenure as French Foreign Minister.

By the summer of 1849, it was apparent that there was no solidarity among the non-German nationalities that revolted against Austrian and Prussian rule. National self-consciousness was often restricted to particular social classes, and nations at different levels of development competed with each other within the old empires instead of joining forces against them. It also became clear that – outside the cities – there was little support for the constitutional reforms and governments established in the spring of 1848 in Prussia and Austria. When universal male suffrage was applied in the framework of the old state and the old social order – and among a population still largely illiterate – the result was to return traditional elites. And the chaotic deliberations of the French National Assembly and the Frankfurt Parliament in Germany demonstrated that European liberals were not only too inexperienced but also too divided to develop parliamentary institutions capable of satisfying the aspirations of the people they represented. Thus, a main result of the revolutions of 1848 was to discredit parliamentary government. During the 1850s and 1860s, a new political order emerged in Europe. It was dominated – not by liberal or radical intellectuals, but rather by leaders like Bismarck and Louis-Napoleon, whose authoritarian rule was backed up by strong armies and large bureaucracies.

Overview of the Book

This book considers the experience and the writings of nine European writers and intellectuals who lived through the revolution of 1848 in France and wrote about it. Some of their writings on 1848 are very well known. Tocqueville's *Souvenirs*, Marx's two essays, *Class Struggles in France* and *The Eighteenth Brumaire of Louis Bonaparte* and Flaubert's great novel *L'Education sentimentale* are, in their different ways, classic commentaries on 1848. Less well known are the formal histories of 1848 by Alphonse de Lamartine and Marie d'Agoult, who wrote under the name of Daniel Stern. I will also consider the memoirs and essays on 1848 written by the anarchist Pierre-Joseph Proudhon and the radical Russian émigré Alexander Herzen. Finally, there are the writings of Victor Hugo and George Sand. Hugo wrote two polemical essays and a volume of poetry alternately ridiculing and chastising "Napoléon le petit." No less interesting for my purposes are Hugo's speeches as a member of the National Assembly. George Sand wrote little in retrospect about the revolution of 1848 – and why this should have been so is a question worth pondering. But her correspondence, lovingly edited by Georges Lubin, is a magnificent guide to the hopes and disappointments of those who celebrated the February Revolution as the dawn of a new day.

My chapters on these writers will have a double focus. I want, first of all, to convey a sense of the experience of 1848 as each of them lived it. By following them through the history of the Second French Republic, I hope in part simply to "situate" them with reference to the important political events of the period – the *journées* of March, April and May 1848, the insurrection of June and its crushing, the election of Louis-Napoleon Bonaparte as President of the Republic in December and finally the coup d'état December 2, 1851. A related aim – more difficult to achieve but also more important – is to recover the sense of *possibility* felt by contemporaries at a time when it was not yet obvious that the Republic had no future – when, to use Samuel Hayat's expression, "the Republic was revolutionary."[10] On March 30, 1848, in a Bulletin issued by the new Interior Ministry, French voters were told that in the elections soon to be held by universal male suffrage they would experience "a new birth, a baptism, a regeneration."[11] Three months later such language would have sounded hollow. As we think and write about the February Revolution, there is no way we can erase our knowledge of how things turned out. What we can do, however, is to try to imagine ourselves in the place of people who lacked that knowledge. In doing this – in seeking to "give the past back its present" in Pierre Rosanvallon's words – I will be drawing extensively on the correspondence, the journalism, and (when possible) the diaries, notebooks and daily jottings of my nine individuals.[12]

The sources are of course different for each writer. For Flaubert, the experience that matters is not his contemporary reaction to the events of 1848–1851 but rather his attempt to grasp the passions and energies of the period vicariously two decades later. But five of our writers did leave fascinating records of their hopes and fears as they varied from day to day

---

[10] Samuel Hayat, *Quand la République était révolutionnaire: Citoyenneté et représentation en 1848* (Paris, 2014).

[11] *Bulletin de la République*, March 30, 1848 in Françoise Mélonio, "1848: la république intempestive" in François Furet and Mona Ozouf (eds.), *Le Siècle de l'avènement républicain* (Paris, 1993), 391.

[12] Javier Fernández Sebastián, "Intellectual History and Democracy: An Interview with Pierre Rosanvallon," *Journal of the History of Ideas*, 68(4) (October 2007), 710.

during the course of the Second Republic. This is just what George Sand's extraordinary correspondence offers. Marx's correspondence has also been carefully edited; and while not as voluminous as Sand's, it can be supplemented by Marx's journalism to give a detailed depiction of Marx's changing states of mind. Proudhon's notebooks, now available to scholars in their entirety, constitute a rich record of Proudhon's inner life during this period – his judgments on his fellow radicals, his ideas for newspaper articles and his doubts about his own activities. For Marie d'Agoult, a key source is the engagement calendars that she kept throughout her life – calendars in which she sometimes jotted notes and reflections that went well beyond names and dates and convey a sense of her ambitions, her pride and her deep insecurities. Finally, a wonderfully rich, if problematic, source concerning Victor Hugo's attitudes is the trove of daily jottings (often undated) published after his death under the title *Choses vues*.

It is well worth taking a close look at the day-to-day experience of our writers in the aftermath of the February Revolution because this was a time when anything seemed possible. For a few weeks, Michèle Riot-Sarcey has written, "utopia seemed to become real" and there appeared to be no limit to the creation of clubs, associations, journals, experiments in the organization of labour and new forms for the exercise of popular sovereignty.[13] Obviously, the ways in which our writers experienced 1848 varied enormously. At one extreme we have Lamartine who led the Provisional Government at the outset. At the other extreme there is Flaubert who witnessed the February Revolution but thereafter kept his distance from Paris, devoting the next few years to work on a novel set in third-century Egypt and then to what we might describe as sexual tourism in the Middle East. Only in the 1860s, as he set about writing *L'Education sentimentale*, did Flaubert throw himself into the effort to reach a vicarious understanding of the mentality of the generation that made (and combatted) the revolution of 1848.

There is a striking contrast between the experience of our two female writers. Both George Sand and Marie d'Agoult were journalists in 1848. Both were at odds with the emerging feminist movement and its focus on the right to vote. But Sand experienced the revolution on the streets and in the Left Bank café that was her headquarters in the spring of 1848. She was closely connected to the Provisional Government and wrote articles for the Interior Minister's *Bulletin de la République*. On one occasion

---

[13] Michèle Riot-Sarcey, *Le Réel de l'utopie: Essai sur l'histoire politique du dix-neuvième siècle* (Paris, 1998) and *Le Procès de la liberté: Une histoire souterraine du dix-neuvième siècle en France* (Paris, 2016).

(April 16) she was also involved in the planning of a revolutionary *journée* that, in the end, did not happen. Marie d'Agoult, on the other hand, experienced the revolution as a spectator – first as a *salonnière* and a journalist, then as a historian, observing, interviewing and taking notes.

Tocqueville, Hugo and Proudhon were elected to the National Assembly in 1848. But in 1849 their paths diverged. Tocqueville was appointed Foreign Minister by Louis-Napoleon on June 3, 1849, just in time to oversee the French military intervention in Italy that brought down the Roman Republic and restored papal power in Rome. In response to this intervention Hugo delivered a fiery speech that heralded his emergence as a leader of republican resistance to the Party of Order. Proudhon, the self-proclaimed anarchist who emerged in July 1848 as a spokesman for the poor of Paris and a defender of the June insurgents, was arrested on June 5, 1849, and spent the rest of the Second Republic in prison. This did not prevent him from marrying, fathering a child and writing three books during his prison years.

Finally, Karl Marx and Alexander Herzen were both radical émigrés drawn to the City of Light in the 1840s. For both of them the experience of Paris was seminal. During his fifteen months in Paris, Marx was profoundly influenced not only by his study of the French Revolution, French philosophical materialism and British political economy and its French socialist critics, but also by his encounter with the Parisian working class. Finding in Paris and in French thought the "earthly world" that German philosophy ignored, Marx deployed the weapons of French materialism to criticize Hegelian idealism in *The Holy Family* and brought the Hegelian concept of alienation to bear on the analysis of labour under capitalism in the *Economic and Philosophical Manuscripts of 1844*. As Lloyd Kramer has written, it was in Paris in 1844 that Marx ceased to be a German philosopher and became a European social theorist.[14] Herzen's experience of Paris was different but no less important. By his own account, it was at Paris in 1847 that Herzen began to see through the idealized vision of the West that had enabled him to survive Nicholaevan Russia. For almost two decades prior to his emigration in 1847, Herzen had been living vicariously in the West, and for him the word "Paris" was intimately connected with memories of the French Revolution and what he called "the colossal struggle for thought, for rights, for human dignity." He was initially disappointed to find in France a deeply bourgeois civilization, obsessed with money, property and profit. Then he was devastated to witness the collapse of all his hopes

---

[14] Lloyd Kramer, *Threshold of a New World: Intellectuals and the Exile Experience in Paris, 1830–1848* (Ithaca, 1988), 175.

in "those painful, ghastly, degrading June Days." Marx and Herzen travelled in the same circles in Paris and had common friends – the Russian anarchist Mikhail Bakunin and the German poet Georg Herwegh, among others. Both may have marched on June 13, 1849, in an abortive demonstration, protesting the French military intervention in Rome, and both were obliged to leave France shortly thereafter. Although they both lived in London during the 1850s and 1860s, they never met and clearly did their best to avoid meeting.[15]

In considering the experience of these nine individuals during the revolution of 1848, I do not want to limit myself to their actions – to what they did during the life of the Second Republic. I also want to consider their hopes and fears. Two things especially need to be recalled. First, the enormous sense of *hope* built up among writers and journalists prior to the February Revolution and during its first weeks. Many liberals, democrats and socialists genuinely believed at the outset of the revolution that they were participating in the inauguration of a new age of class harmony and social justice. Secondly, we need to understand the sense of confusion that many of these same people felt in June when 50,000 Parisian workers revolted against the republic intended to be the instrument of their liberation. The insurrection of June 1848 forced many self-proclaimed radicals to reconsider their longstanding and unquestioning admiration of "the people."

Why these writers and these texts? I've chosen them because I find them interesting and because they reveal important aspects of the period 1848–1851 – not because they constitute a representative spectrum of views. I could have chosen others. Dolf Oehler has written a fine book on writers and 1848 focusing on a somewhat different cast of characters including Baudelaire and Heine.[16] I have left out some individuals who played an important role in 1848 – Louis Blanc is the obvious example – because I believe their writings on the revolution lack the depth and insight to be found in the work of other less important figures, like Marie d'Agoult, whom I have included.[17] If this book had a wider focus, fascinating chapters might have been written on Wagner, Bakunin and the Dresden uprising of May 1849 and on the American intellectual

---

[15] Michel Mervaud, "Le Conflit avec les 'marxides'. Note sur les rapports de Herzen et de Marx," *Revue des études slaves*, 83(1) (2012), 163–175.

[16] Dolf Oehler, *Le Spleen contre l'oubli, juin 1848: Baudelaire, Flaubert, Heine, Herzen* (Paris, 1996).

[17] Louis Blanc's voluminous writings on 1848, including his *Histoire de la Révolution de 1848*, published long after the events described, are devoted largely to the settling of scores with other members of the Provisional Government.

Margaret Fuller and the Roman Republic of 1849.[18] There are also conservative thinkers from the margins of Europe who would be well worth considering – the Spaniard Donoso Cortés, for example, whose articles and speeches in 1848–1851 made him famous as "the oracle of the counter-revolution," and the Russian poet, Feodor Tyutchev, who saw Christian Russia as the only answer to the challenge posed by the revolution of 1848 to existing authorities and to the idea of authority itself.[19]

I would particularly like to have included in this book a chapter on Auguste Blanqui who had come by 1848 to personify revolution in the bourgeois imagination but whose actions prior to his arrest on May 22 were marked by prudence and pragmatism. The problem is that the sources simply don't exist for a study of Blanqui and 1848 comparable to those I have written about other figures. His correspondence, preserved in the Moscow archives, is largely familial.[20] And his testimony under police questioning was clearly marked by the desire to say as little as possible. What I have tried to do in the final chapter has been to bring together the radically different images of Blanqui that appear in our texts. In the absence of sources that might enable us to get inside Blanqui's head, I believe that the view of Blanqui "from outside" has value.

My second aim in this book, in addition to tracking my writers' experience of 1848, will be to look closely at a series of texts in which each of them attempted to understand, judge, criticize, celebrate, or intervene in the revolution and its aftermath. Here I will adopt a literary approach, taking account of the narrative structure and formal content of my texts. One book which has helped me work out an approach of my own is Hayden White's *Metahistory*.[21] Hayden White's work – including the essays written since *Metahistory* – has been, and continues to be, a

---

[18] Ellen Dubois, "Margaret Fuller in Italy," *Women's Writing*, 10(2) (July 2003), 287–305 is an excellent account of this final phase in Margaret Fuller's career. On Bakunin see Jean-Christophe Angaut, "Revolution and the Slav Question: 1848 and Mikhail Bakunin" in Moggach and Stedman Jones (eds.), *The 1848 Revolutions*, 405–428.

[19] Carolina Armenteros, "Le 1848 de Juan Donoso Cortés (1809–1853)" in *Revue d'études proudhoniennes*, V (2019), 233–253; Feodor Tyutchev, "La Russie et l'Occident," with drafts and commentary, *Literaturnoe Nasledstvo*, 97 (Moscow, 1988), I, 183–230.

[20] The Blanqui archive at the Russian State Archive for Social and Political History in Moscow consists of 90 files and 241 documents. It includes over 100 letters from Blanqui to his sisters, but also letters to lawyers, journalists and friends, and drafts of articles on political, philosophical and religious themes. Rossiskie Gosudarstvennie Archiv Sotsialno-politicheskoe Istorii, Fond 228, opis 1. Letters prior to 1848 have been published in Louis-Auguste Blanqui, *Oeuvres*, Dominique LeNuz (ed.) (Nancy, 1993), I.

[21] Hayden White, *Metahistory: The Historical Imagination in Nineteenth-Century Europe* (Baltimore, 1973).

wake-up call to historians, alerting us to the importance of studying history as writing and not only as experience.[22] It certainly was that for me. And the more recent essays on narrative discourse and historical representation have sharpened our awareness of the choices made by all historians, consciously or not, in translating knowing into telling.[23] This said, my concern in the present book is more with the surface features of texts than with their deep structures – more with voice, imagery, tone, diction and point of view than with basic tropes and "modes of employment." And I will raise questions familiar to literary critics like: Who is speaking? To whom? In what circumstances? To what end? With what authority? Using what rhetorical strategies? What (literary) conventions shape the texts? What questions are, and are not, raised in these texts?

Two books, each inspired by the work of Hayden White, that I have found helpful in addressing such questions are Larry Shiner's study of "literary form and history in Tocqueville's *Recollections*" and Philippe Carrard's *Poetics of the New History*.[24] Carrard elegantly illustrates the way in which the focus on language and rhetoric can illuminate our reading of contemporary historical writing. And Shiner's illuminating and unjustly neglected work has been helpful to me not only as a study of Tocqueville but also as a model of a rhetorical approach to a historical text. No less important to me as a source of inspiration and guidance are T. J. Clark's two wonderful studies of painters and 1848: *The Absolute Bourgeois* and *The Image of the People*. I read these books when they first appeared over forty years ago. In the preface to a later edition Clark situates them at a particular historical moment, a moment long gone, when the radical hopes of the 1960s were still alive.[25] But I still feel the excitement conveyed by my initial reading of *The Absolute Bourgeois*. And I believe that the attempt to explain what went wrong in 1848 and how a clownish imposter could appear as a saviour to both the impoverished small peasantry and the affluent bourgeoisie has lost none of its relevance today.

[22] Dominick LaCapra, "A Poetics of Historiography: Hayden White's *Tropics of Discourse*" in *Rethinking Intellectual History: Texts, Contexts, Language* (Ithaca, 1983), 72.

[23] Hayden White, *The Content of the Form: Narrative Discourse and Historical Representation* (Baltimore, 1990). See also *Tropics of Discourse: Essays in Cultural Criticism* (Baltimore, 1985) and *The Fiction of Narrative: Essays on History, Literature and Theory, 1957–2007* (Baltimore, 2010).

[24] L. E. Shiner, *The Secret Mirror: Literary Form and History in Tocqueville's "Recollections"* (Ithaca, 1988); Philippe Carrard, *Poetics of the New History: French Historical Discourse from Braudel to Chartier* (Baltimore, 1992).

[25] T. J. Clark, *The Absolute Bourgeois: Artists and Politics in France 1848–1851* (Berkeley, 1999), 5–8. See also *Image of the People: Gustave Courbet and the 1848 Revolution* (Berkeley, 1999). Both originally published in 1973.

What texts will we consider? In the chapters on Lamartine (Chapter 2) and Marie d'Agoult (Chapter 4) the main texts will obviously be their histories of the revolution of 1848. These are radically different works. D'Agoult's history is carefully researched, elegantly structured and impressive for its considered and nuanced judgments. It communicates brilliantly the perspective of the moderate republicans who led the revolution during its first four months. These were people who had devoted themselves for twenty years to the emancipation of the working class, but who found themselves supporting the crushing of the June insurrection on the ground that, however justified it may have been, it was an attack on the republic. Lamartine's history is a slapdash work – a celebration of himself, apparently intended to revive his flagging political fortunes but shedding little light on his motives and actions in 1848. I will argue that to understand the part played by Lamartine in the spring of 1848 another text must be considered. This is the immensely popular (and immensely long!) *Histoire des Girondins* that he published in 1847. Far from being the encomium to the Girondins that this book is sometimes taken for, I think it can (and should) be read as an instruction manual for the making of a moderate revolution, with the Girondins exemplifying how not to do it.

George Sand's novels did much to shape the ideas and sensibilities of the young people who welcomed the February Revolution; and during March and April she helped prepare the elections by writing *Bulletins de la République* to be sent out by Ledru-Rollin's Interior Ministry. Her voluminous correspondence illustrates vividly the enormous enthusiasm of many romantic writers – and their readers – during the first weeks of the revolution. Her rejection of the proposal by a group of feminist journalists that she herself stand for election opens a window on divisions among feminists in 1848. But from my perspective the primary importance of George Sand lies in the fact that her correspondence is a remarkably illuminating guide both to the flowering of the cult of "the people" in the spring of 1848 and to the causes of the disillusionment that set in even before the elections of April 23. Sand's relations with the worker-poet Charles Poncy are considered at length because they can stand as an epitome of both the success and the failure of Sand's attempts to get close to "the people."

Alexis de Tocqueville's *Souvenirs* offer a fascinating and acerbic picture of the major actors, the revolutionary *journées*, and his unhappy experience as foreign minister in 1849 during the presidency of Louis Napoleon. One remarkable feature of the *Souvenirs* (which were only published in 1893) is the brutal clarity of Tocqueville's judgments. He excels at revealing hidden motives and unmasking pretensions (especially those of his political allies). By his own account, it was not a work of history, but a memoir written "for myself alone." In prose marked by a somewhat archaic elegance, Tocqueville vividly conveys a sense of the hopes and fears of the propertied classes who identified themselves with the Party of Order that came to dominate the political life of the Second Republic after the massive conservative victory in the April elections. At the same time, he takes a dark view of both the July Monarchy and the republicans and socialists who brought it down. He argues that by limiting politics to a narrow stratum, the July Monarchy had fatally impoverished the notion of public interest; but he also argues that the radicals who had a chance at power in 1848 were so lacking in political experience that they could only play at revolution, mimicking the roles and gestures of the revolutionaries of 1789–1794.

With the chapter on Victor Hugo (Chapter 5), we enter the world of the opposition to the Party of Order. I will have much to say about *Napoléon le petit*, the first work published by Hugo after the coup d'état. But the focus will be on his political evolution – on the process by which this peer of France and adornment of the July Monarchy became the embodiment of democratic and republican resistance to Louis-Napoleon. In this chapter I will track the developing radicalism of Hugo's speeches to the National Assembly. My main question will be: how do we explain the fact that Hugo was energized by the failures of the Republic between 1848 and 1851 whereas most of his contemporaries gave up on politics and retreated into silence?

Pierre-Joseph Proudhon wrote his *Confessions d'un révolutionnaire* in six weeks. The writing is vigorous, argumentative and colloquial. It abounds in imaginative riffs and mock-heroic epithets that remind one of Marx's *Eighteenth Brumaire*. It is full of pithy one-liners, mostly directed against Proudhon's fellow democrats and socialists. Proudhon later claimed that he was writing "under the influence of an intuition" that made him "speak with the vehemence of an oracle."[26] But the oracle's tone keeps changing. He is bombastic at times, at other times lyrical. And the book concludes with an earnest – and thoroughly *unironic* – celebration of irony. In his one genuinely confessional chapter, Proudhon criticizes himself for failing to foresee the June insurrection. For four months, he tells us, he was simply a spectator. Employing the seemingly irresistible theatrical metaphor, he explains that in the wake of the June disaster, he left his place in the audience and became an actor. This meant carrying on the struggle against the Party of Order single-handedly – taunting, provoking, attacking, playing the fool when necessary. The great problem

---

[26] Proudhon to Charles Edmond, July 9, 1854, *Correspondance de P.-J. Proudhon*, vol. VI (Paris, 1875), 39.

in writing about this text, and more generally about Proudhon's experience of 1848, is to find a "bottom line" – an interpretation that does justice to the changing views of this contrarian thinker without losing all coherence.

The Russian radical émigré, Alexander Herzen, left three works that focus on the revolution of 1848. Two of these are volumes of essays. The third is Herzen's great autobiography, *My Past and Thoughts*, in which his life story pivots around 1848. In these works, Herzen – who left Russia in 1847 – describes himself as arriving in Paris as pilgrims once arrived in Jerusalem or Rome. By his own account, he rapidly discovered the fundamentally bourgeois character of French civilization, and this discovery was followed by the crushing of the June insurrection. Then the political debacle was compounded by personal tragedy – the deaths of his mother and son and his wife Natalie, her death preceded by her seduction by a German poet whom Herzen had considered his best European friend. In all his writing on 1848, we find Herzen trying to come to terms with his own bitter experience and at the same time looking for a perspective from which the collapse of his pre-revolutionary ideals and dreams would make sense. The most powerful essays are jeremiads in which he laments the loss of his ideals, replays the June insurrection, seeks to purge his own feelings of anger and despair, and reflects on the powerlessness of historical actors to change the world according to a plan. In his attempt to explain what went wrong in 1848, Herzen returns repeatedly to the dogmatism of the revolutionaries and their inability to get beyond paradigms drawn from the first French Revolution. For Herzen, as for Proudhon (whom he greatly admired) and for Marx (whom he did not admire) the fatal weakness of the left lay in its inability to emancipate itself from memories that, in the end, served to justify and cloak the return of repressive centralized government.

Of all the commentaries on the revolution of 1848 and its aftermath, the best known, surely, are the two brilliant essays by Karl Marx, *Class Struggles in France* and *The Eighteenth Brumaire of Louis Bonaparte*. In these works, Marx seeks to draw lessons for the German working class from the defeats of the French proletariat between 1848 and 1851. He does so by systematically contrasting the world of historical reality – the class struggle – and the realm of shadow and illusion in which historical actors fancy that their speeches and parliamentary manoeuvres make a difference. He explains brilliantly how Louis-Napoleon could have appeared as a saviour to the impoverished small peasantry. He raises questions concerning the relations of class, politics and ideology. But what is most striking about these essays is their rhetorical power – the literary skill with which Marx evokes the ghosts and shadows that constitute the realm of ideology and illusion. Throughout there are dozens of literary allusions and buried quotations from the *Iliad* and the *Bible* and Shakespeare and Goethe's *Faust*. "What is the point of all this?" one might ask. Why in a work intended not for intellectuals but to raise the consciousness of German workers, should Marx indulge himself with so many literary references and rhetorical flourishes? This is a key question that I will address in my chapter on Marx (Chapter 9).

Finally, we get to Flaubert and *L'Education sentimentale*. There are many ways of considering this novel. It is a novel about love – the unconsummated love of a young man, Frederick Moreau, for a married woman: Madame Arnoux. It is also a novel about politics and society: it offers a vast satirical fresco of Parisian life under the July Monarchy and culminates with a long final section on 1848. More centrally, it's a novel about illusions – romantic illusions and political illusions. It focuses on the experience and the imaginative life of the generation of young people who came to maturity around 1840 and whose lives were either broken or redirected by the revolution of 1848. Here Flaubert subsumes an unsparing critique of the sentimental humanitarian radicalism of the 'forty-eighters within a broader dissection of the mentality of the whole generation of romantic idealists to which the revolutionaries belonged.

The political world, as Flaubert describes it, is a world in which people are constantly mimicking the heroes of 1789. It is also a world in which ideological discourse is essentially meaningless – a world in which people rarely mean what they say, and often don't know what they mean. Flaubert is no less hard on the conservative aristocrats, merchants and functionaries; and the conversation at the receptions of the wealthy banker Dambreuse is just as inane as the talk in the revolutionary clubs. This sense of the triviality and emptiness of the mental world of the elite is reinforced by the picture that Flaubert paints in his last novel, *Bouvard et Pécuchet*, of the response to the revolution of 1848 in a small town in Normandy. It is worth asking then if we should accept the insistence of the narrator of *L'Education sentimentale* on the essential similarity of the zealotry of the Right and the Left. Are we to take as Flaubert's final word his narrator's comment that the June insurrection culminated in "an equality of brute beasts, a common level of bloody atrocities" in which "the fanaticism of the rich counterbalanced the frenzy of the poor"[27]? I don't think so, and I will try to show why at the conclusion of the chapter on Flaubert (Chapter 10).

[27] Gustave Flaubert, *L'Education sentimentale* (Paris, 1961), 338.

A word about how one might read this book. In writing it, I have tried to reach a relatively wide audience; and I would like to think that the book will be of interest to readers who come to it with little prior knowledge of 1848. I have written the first dozen pages of this introduction and have provided a chronology of events with such readers in mind. But I have not included a detailed narrative of the revolutionary year because I want to focus on the way in which each text illustrates a particular perspective and not on its contribution to a "correct" understanding of the revolution and its aftermath. Because some of my writers are not well known to English readers – notably Marie d'Agoult and Alexander Herzen – I have included substantial biographical information in those chapters. For those who want to read some chapters and not others, I have tried to write each chapter so that it can stand by itself. This has meant some repetition in background information and in the definition of terms. But I believe the book hangs together as a whole and presents a coherent picture of the intellectual response to 1848.

Having offered a brief overview of the book, I want to comment on some features of French political culture (1815–1848) that are important for an understanding of 1848.

The Shadow of the French Revolution

In the years between the fall of Napoleon and the revolution of 1848, French political and cultural life never got out of the shadow of the first French Revolution.[28] This is true in two senses. First, the revolution created a vacuum of power and authority. The revolutionaries did not succeed in permanently suppressing monarchy, aristocracy, and the established Catholic Church. Napoleon brought back aristocracy and the Church, and the Bourbon monarchy was restored after his fall. But none of these institutions was the same after 1815. The great problem confronting the Bourbons and their supporters was how to confer legitimacy on a regime that had been imposed by foreigners on a defeated nation. The Bourbons claimed to rule by divine right, and Louis XVIII liked to refer to 1815 as the "twenty-second year of our reign." But as contemporaries observed, the Bourbons had been brought back to France "in the baggage-train of the allies." After the Hundred Days and the enthusiastic response of the French to the return of Napoleon, it was difficult to take seriously the claim of Louis XVIII that he had been

---

[28] For excellent studies on the legacy of the French Revolution see François Furet and Mona Ozouf (eds.), *The French Revolution and the Creation of Modern Political Culture, III, The Transformation of Political Culture 1789–1848* (Oxford, 1989).

"recalled by the love of his people to the throne of his fathers." The problem of legitimacy was to plague the Bourbons down until their overthrow in 1830.

Aristocracy was also restored in post-revolutionary France – first by Napoleon who created his own "imperial nobility" and then by the Bourbons – though without the tax exemptions and other fiscal privileges enjoyed by the Old Regime nobility. The years after 1815 were also marked by the return of émigré nobles to France and by the revival of the old seventeenth-century traditions of etiquette and precedence and deference to rank. The salon once again became a space in which literary and political topics could be discussed relatively freely and in which women could exercise a kind of authority denied them in the Revolutionary and Napoleonic periods. At the same time a great deal was said and written about the importance of blood and aristocratic lineage. But much of this was no longer taken seriously outside the nobility. Even within its ranks, there were some like Stendhal's Marquis de la Môle for whom the revived concern with matters of precedence and lineage was simply a game to be played. For others it was, like the revival of duelling during the Restoration, a kind of brave conceit on the part of people who knew very well that insofar as there was a ruling class in France, what its members had in common was not blue blood or family traditions but rather money – invested in land perhaps, but money all the same. These people may have possessed *châteaux* and aristocratic titles, but the titles had lost much of their meaning, and the *château* itself began to lose its symbolic function as the locus of aristocratic political authority and became more like a bourgeois country house – a haven for family and friends.[29]

Finally, there is the question of the role of religion and the Catholic Church in post-revolutionary society. During the Revolution, with the abolition of clerical privilege, the seizure of Church lands, the Civil Constitution of the clergy, dechristianization and the subsequent creation of the cults of Reason and the Supreme Being, the Church had been divided, impoverished, persecuted and marginalized. It survived. But it emerged terribly weakened from the ordeal of the revolutionary and Napoleonic years. In 1814, 42 percent of the active priests in France were sixty or over, and the total number of secular priests was just 36,000

---

[29] Christopher H. Johnson, *Becoming Bourgeois: Love, Kinship and Power in Provincial France, 1670–1880* (Ithaca, 2015), 133. On the integration of the traditional aristocratic honor culture into the bourgeois ethos see also William M. Reddy, *The Invisible Code: Honor and Sentiment in Postrevolutionary France, 1814–1848* (Berkeley, 1997).

compared to 60,000 in 1789. There were 3,345 vacant clerical posts in France, and churches were falling into ruin. The task confronting the Church after the fall of Napoleon therefore was to renew and enlarge the priesthood, to rebuild churches and seminaries, and most importantly to win back to Christianity a population that many observers regarded as lost.[30]

During the Bourbon Restoration the Catholic Church regained its privileged status, enlarged the corps of clerics, and took control of education at all levels, while revival movements and militant lay organizations sought to resacralize public life. Huge outdoor revival meetings or "missions" were organized in towns and cities throughout France, often culminating with the raising of a gigantic cross and the burning of books and revolutionary symbols.[31] In attempting to bring France back to the faith, missionaries resorted to the scare tactics of the Old Regime clergy, threatening lapsed Christians with punishment by an angry God. But especially in rural areas parish priests often found it advisable to present Christianity as the religion of a loving Jesus rather than a harsh and distant God. Thus the years between 1815 and 1848 were marked by a revival of a Christ-centred Christianity on the part of priests and primary schoolteachers.[32] And intellectual life was marked by a series of efforts to imagine a new spiritual power which might take over the role formerly played by the Catholic Church in satisfying the needs and shaping the beliefs of the faithful.

There is a second way in which the memory of the first French Revolution continued to shape French political culture between 1815 and 1848. During this period there were not yet organized political parties. But such groupings as did exist had one common feature: they all defined themselves with relation to the first French Revolution. First, there were the two royalist factions: the Bourbons and the Orleanists. After the fall of the Bourbons in 1830, their partisans were known as the Legitimists; between 1815 and 1830 the more extreme were called "ultras." The Orleanists supported the claim to the French throne of the House of Orleans and King Louis Philippe who came to power with the overthrow of the Bourbon King Charles X. The Legitimists were not

---

[30] Nigel Aston, *Religion and Revolution in France, 1780–1804* (Washington, DC, 2000), 339; Edward Berenson, *Populist Religion and Left-Wing Politics in France, 1830–1852* (Princeton, 1980), 18.

[31] Sheryl Kroen, *Politics and Theater: The Crisis of Legitimacy in Restoration France, 1815–1830* (Berkeley, 2000), esp. 76–108, 121–153, 202–221. See Gaston Bordet, *La Grande Mission de Besançon, janvier-février 1825: Une fête contre-révolutionnaire, néo-baroque ou ordinaire?* (Paris, 1998) for a fine microhistorical study.

[32] Berenson, *Populist Religion*, 22.

all of one mind. Their greatest writer, Chateaubriand, was more liberal than many of the Orleanists. But all the ultras and most of the Legitimists were reactionary in the most literal sense: they regarded the French Revolution as a disaster and would have liked to do away with all the changes introduced by the Revolutionary and Napoleonic regimes. Indeed, their goal was to go back two hundred years to the "feudal monarchy" that they believed had preceded Louis XIV and the rise of "absolute" monarchy. Their political philosophy, which was most fully articulated by the Sardinian diplomat Comte Joseph de Maistre and the Vicomte Louis de Bonald, began with the critique of the French Revolution and the eighteenth-century *philosophes*. They claimed that the French Revolution had been sent by Providence to punish France for faith in Enlightenment rationalism and for the crime of unbelief. They celebrated authority, which they regarded as divine in nature. They particularly idealized paternal authority, claiming that the authority of the father in the family and the noble in his province was ideally similar to that of the monarch in his kingdom.[33]

What distinguished the Orleanists from the Legitimists was that the former accepted the French Revolution as a necessary and important part of French history. The father of Louis Philippe took the name "Philippe Egalité" during the Revolution. He joined the Jacobin Club and served as a deputy in the Convention, where he voted for the execution of Louis XVI before he himself was guillotined during the Terror. His son, the future "citizen king" Louis Philippe, fought in the republican army at Valmy and briefly joined the Jacobin Club before fleeing into exile in April 1793. The Orleanist monarchy of Louis Philippe has commonly been described as France's "bourgeois monarchy." But modern historians have shown that the *grands notables* who effectively governed France during the July Monarchy included both rich businessmen and members of the nobility. Indeed, landed wealth remained the basis of political power under the July Monarchy. Over half the electors derived their wealth primarily from the ownership of land, and in 1840 two-thirds of the 13,000 wealthiest men in France were great landowners.[34]

Unlike the two Bourbon kings, who claimed that they had freely chosen to bestow a constitution on their subjects, Louis Philippe

---

[33] Excellent recent studies are Darrin M. McMahon, *Enemies of the Enlightenment: The French Counter-Enlightenment and the Making of Modernity* (New York, 2001) and Carolina Armenteros, *The French Idea of History: Joseph de Maistre and his Heirs, 1794–1854* (Ithaca, 2011).

[34] Peter McPhee, *A Social History of France 1789–1914*, 2nd ed. (New York, 2004), 115–116; André-Jean Tudesq, *Les Grands notables en France, 1840–1849*, 2 vols. (Paris, 1964).

accepted the principle of national sovereignty. He also agreed to the restoration of the revolutionary tricolor as the national flag and to a slight expansion in the number of eligible voters. The Orleanists saw themselves as the heirs of the *constituants* of 1789. They believed that having established a constitutional and parliamentary monarchy and having recognized the sovereignty of the nation, they had realized the vision of the French revolutionaries of 1789. The task now, argued their leader François Guizot, was to bring an end to the revolution, to construct a stable representative government – "a monarchy surrounded by representative institutions" – and to "establish definitively, not order alone, not liberty alone, but order and liberty at the same time."[35] The problem was that the Orleanists felt that the regime set up in 1830 had no further need of reform.

The failure of the July Monarchy to respond to the economic and social changes of the 1830s and 1840s and to accommodate the demands of a significant portion of the bourgeoisie (including many liberal Orleanists) for a widening of the suffrage created conditions for the establishment of a democratic republic in 1848. But the republican movement had been a conspicuous part of the French political landscape ever since the early years of the Bourbon Restoration. In 1830 republicans played an important role in bringing down Charles X. Inspired by the memory of the overthrow of the Bourbons on August 10, 1792, they regarded the failure to establish a republic in 1830 as an act of thievery. The revolution, they said, had been "filched."[36]

The first four years of the July Monarchy were a time of extraordinary ferment. The electoral law of May 1831 which enlarged the suffrage from 99,000 to 166,000 (out of a total population of 32 million) was widely regarded as inadequate. A vigorous republican movement arose calling for universal male suffrage. This was accompanied by the development of political clubs and associations such as the *Société des Amis du Peuple* and the *Société des droits de l'homme*. Styling themselves after the Jacobins of 1792, the members of the *Société des droits de l'homme* initially believed that an insurrection at Paris – a repeat of the July Revolution – could lead to the establishment of a democratic republic. They soon limited themselves to organizing a network of republican clubs which, by 1833, included a majority of working-class members.[37]

---

[35] Discours de Guizot, Chambre des députés, February 19, 1831, *Histoire parlementaire de France. Recueil complet des discours prononcés dans les Chambres de 1819 à 1848 par M. Guizot*, I (Paris, 1863), 222. On the roots, limits and legacy of Guizot's political philosophy see Pierre Rosanvallon, *Le Moment Guizot* (Paris, 1985).

[36] John M. Merriman (ed.), *1830 in France* (New York, 1975).

[37] Jill Harsin, *Barricades: The War of the Streets in Revolutionary Paris, 1830–1848* (New York, 2002), 65–83; Gabriel Perreux, *Au Temps des sociétés secrètes: La propagande*

Working-Class Organization and Protest

One important consequence of the ferment of 1830–1834 was to energize working-class activism and to provoke a new awareness of "the social question" among republicans. France at this time was still a nation of peasants and the industrial labour force was small. Only about 400,000 French workers worked in enterprises employing twenty or more labourers. A central role was played in the French economy by skilled artisans – carpenters, printers, tailors, shoemakers, who worked in small shops run by a master, a *chef d'atelier*, who was aided by apprentices and often employed a few journeymen or *compagnons*. These skilled artisans dominated the economic life not only of Paris and Lyon but also of new industrial cities like Saint-Etienne. They made decent wages, led respectable lives, were literate for the most part, and in some cases showed a real hunger for culture.[38] Agricol Perdiguier, a journeyman joiner who wrote his autobiography, reported that *compagnons* in the building trades at Bordeaux would meet in the evenings to read aloud the tragedies of Racine and Voltaire and their imitators. "We liked sad and terrible plays especially. The more deaths there were at the end of the tragedy, the more sublime, magnificent and perfect we thought it was."[39] A few groups of skilled artisans created their own unique artistic forms. The silk weavers of Lyon, for example, created their own puppet theatre with characters like Guignol and Gnaffron who were recognizable types from the silk industry and other Lyon trades.

As William Sewell has shown, the forms of organization adopted by skilled workers after 1815 were greatly influenced by the pre-revolutionary past. Although the guild system had been formally abolished in 1791, vestiges lived on. If any kind of working-class

républicaine au début de la Monarchie de Juillet (1830–1835) (Paris, 1931); Alain Faure, "Mouvements populaires et movement ouvrier à Paris," *Le Mouvement Social*, 88 (July–September, 1974), 79–81.

[38] The essential study of the radicalism of skilled workers remains Sewell, *Work and Revolution*, which traces the development of "the idiom of association" from the journeymen's brotherhoods of the Old Regime to the mutual aid societies and producers' associations of the July Monarchy and the workers' corporations of 1848. For a fascinating analysis of the intellectual life of working-class radicals in the 1830s and 1840s and a critical reading of representations of the world of work by writers of working-class origin, see also Jacques Rancière, *La Nuit des prolétaires: Archives du rêve ouvrier* (Paris, 1981). Subsequently Rancière challenged the argument that worker militancy in this period came largely from groups of skilled artisans with a strong collective identity. See Jacques Rancière, "Le Mythe de l'artisan," and responses by Sewell and Christopher Johnson in *International Labor and Working Class History*, 24 (Fall 1983), 1–25.

[39] Agricol Perdiguier, *Mémoires d'un compagnon* (Paris, 1964), 137.

consciousness existed in France before 1830, its truest expression was probably the sectarianism, divisiveness and corporate pride of the *compagnonnages*, associations of artisans which came into being at the end of the Old Regime as the journeyman's alternative to the stultified hierarchy of the trade guilds.[40] But the years after Napoleon were also marked by the emergence of new types of working-class association like the mutual aid societies providing aid and insurance to their members. These societies collected monthly dues and paid out benefits when their members fell sick, retired, or died. Like confraternities under the Old Regime, they were usually named for patron saints whose festivals they celebrated annually. Under the Restoration, mutual aid societies were supported and patronized by both church and state, which regarded them as instruments in the campaign to bring the working-class back to the faith. Bourgeois patrons also played an important role in defining and shaping early French mutual aid societies.[41] But after 1830 workers began to use such societies for their own purposes – to maintain standards of workmanship, to arbitrate disputes, to draw up wage rates and to organize boycotts or strikes when these rates were not observed. Some of these functions were illegal and had to be carried on in secret, Thus, as Sewell observes, the "officially recognized mutual aid societies were commonly only the public face of much more comprehensive workers' corporations."[42]

Another form of association that engaged the energies of skilled workers in the aftermath of the July Revolution was the producers' association or cooperative. The purpose of these associations, which were initially created by Parisian tailors, shoemakers and printers, and by shoemakers at Lyon, was first of all to emancipate skilled craftsmen from the wage system and from dependence on middlemen by enabling them to market their goods for themselves and, secondly, to give producers some control over the introduction of new techniques of production. The idea of the producers' association was first articulated in October 1830 in a short-lived Parisian working-class journal, *L'Artisan, journal de la classe ouvrière*; it was given fuller elaboration in the writings of the socialist Philippe Buchez, who became an advisor to various groups of artisans,

---

[40] Sewell, *Work and Revolution*, 166–172; Emile Coornaert, *Les Compagnonnages en France du moyen âge à nos jours* (Paris, 1966); Cynthia Truant, *The Rites of Labor: Brotherhoods of Compagnonnage in Old and New Regime France* (Ithaca, 1994). For George Sand's encounter with Agricole Perdiguier and *compagnonnage*, see Chapter 3, p.85.

[41] See Carol E. Harrison, *The Bourgeois Citizen in Nineteenth-Century France: Gender, Sociability, and the Uses of Emulation* (Oxford, 1999), 123–139.

[42] Sewell, *Work and Revolution*, 165.

helped found a jewellers' cooperative in Paris in 1834, and oversaw the
creation of a long-lasting worker-run paper, *L'Atelier*, in 1840.[43]

These producers' associations were neither revolutionary nor violent.
Nor were the "philanthropic societies" formed by tailors, shoemakers and
workers in other trades in Paris and the provinces in the early 1830s.[44] But
skilled workers engaged in some forms of action that led to violence.
Strikes were not new, but they became frequent in the July Monarchy.
In 1833 there were seventy-two strikes, most of them undertaken by skilled
workers – privileged and relatively well-paid artisans in Paris and Lyon and
other old urban centres and in industries with longstanding traditions of
collective action. Occasionally strike movements involved different trades
at the same time. The most important of these were the strike waves of
1833 and 1840 in Paris, the latter including 20,000–30,000 workers
throughout the Paris building trades. More typically, strike movements
were confined to particular industries. They were mostly short-lived,
spontaneous and poorly organized reactions to a cut in wages or the
violation of a traditional relationship between masters and men.[45] But
behind the concrete grievances, as Michèle Riot-Sarcey has shown, lay a
call for the recognition of basic human rights, starting with the right to a
measure of control over the conditions of their work.[46]

On one occasion a strike took on huge proportions. At Lyon in
October 1831 the silk weavers or *canuts* obtained the support of the local
Chamber of Commerce and the Prefect of the Rhone and representatives
of the majority of the workshop masters (*chefs d'atelier*) and silk merchants (*maîtres fabricants*) for the establishment of a fixed minimum rate
for finished cloth (*tarif de façon*). But a few merchants refused to accept
the agreement and, with the support of the mayor and Lyon's wealthy
elite, launched a boycott of certain workshops. The *canuts* responded by
calling a strike and holding a mass demonstration on La Croix-Rousse –
the hill overlooking Lyon which, with its 6,000 looms and its *traboules* or

[43] Bernard H. Moss, "Parisian Producers' Associations (1830–1851): The Socialism of
Skilled Workers" in Roger Price (ed.), *Revolution and Reaction: 1848 and the Second
French Republic* (London, 1975) 73–86 and Christopher H. Johnson, "Economic Change
and Artisan Discontent: The Tailors' History, 1800–1848" in Roger Price (ed.),
Revolution and Reaction, 87–114. See also Armand Cuvillier, *Un journal d'ouvriers
"L'Atelier"* (Paris, 1954).
[44] Sewell, *Work and Revolution*, 204–206; Octave Festy, *Le Mouvement ouvrier au début de la
Monarchie de Juillet (1830–1834)* (Paris, 1908), 263–264.
[45] Jean-Pierre Aguet, *Les Grèves sous la monarchie de juillet (1830–1847): Contribution à
l'histoire du mouvement ouvrier français* (Geneva, 1954), 1–125; Alain Faure,
"Mouvements populaires," *Le Mouvement social*, 88 (July–September, 1974), 51–92;
Roger Price, *The Second French Republic: A Social History* (Ithaca, 1972), 72–74.
[46] Riot-Sarcey, *Le Réel de l'utopie*, 217–219.

passageways, was the redoubt of the *canuts*. The strike movement rapidly turned into a full-scale insurrection in the course of which the *canuts* took control of the city, forced the army to evacuate, and set up a provisional government in the Hôtel de Ville on November 23.[47] Once the *canuts* had gained control, it became evident that they were not of one mind. A radical minority consisted mainly of *compagnons* and apprentices, and a moderate majority was dominated by workshop masters who were not interested in revolution. On November 24, the majority reached an understanding with the prefect and established a fragile truce. For ten days Lyon was governed by sixteen *chefs d'atelier* in collaboration with the prefect. But on December 3 Lyon was invested by a force of 20,000 troops sent from Paris, led by Marshall Soult and the Duc d'Orleans. There was no resistance. Soult quickly appointed a new prefect, Antoine Gasparin, who reestablished order, arrested ninety workers, declared an amnesty for the other insurgents, and installed a temporary garrison of 10,000 troops.[48]

Defeat did not reduce the *canuts* to silence. They remained well organized, self-confident and – in the eyes of the government – dangerous. Their newspaper, *L'Echo de la Fabrique*, founded just three weeks before the rebellion, owned and edited by *chefs d'atelier*, was to appear regularly for the next two-and-a-half years.[49] The revolt did have an enormous impact on bourgeois public opinion. On December 8, the journalist Saint-Marc Girardin wrote an article in the *Revue des deux mondes* that framed the issue in the starkest terms. Lyon, he said, had revealed the "grave secret" of the antagonism between the class with property and that without. "The barbarians who threaten society are not in the Caucasus or the steppes of the Tartary, but in the faubourgs of our manufacturing cities."[50] The rebellion was remembered in a different way by the *canuts* themselves and by republican socialists like Louis Blanc who wrote later that the revolt of the *canuts* was "the bloody

---

[47] The classic study of the 1831 insurrection is Fernand Rude, *L'Insurrection lyonnaise de novembre 1831: Le movement ouvrier à Lyon de 1827–1832* (Paris, 1969). Ludovic Frobert, *Les Canuts, ou la démocratie turbulente, Lyon 1831–1834* (Paris, 2009) is an excellent modern study.

[48] For a forceful critique of the view that the *canuts* had no political program, that they "stumbled" into power and were "embarrassed" by their victory, see Riot-Sarcey, *Le Réel de l'utopie*, 167–201. Riot-Sarcey argues that the insurrection was a moment of intellectual awakening in which utopian ideas acquired new life when taken up in the course of a search for concrete solutions to specific social problems. See also Hayat, *Quand la République était révolutionnaire*, 43–45.

[49] Ludovic Frobert (ed.), *L'Echo de la Fabrique: Naissance de la presse ouvrière à Lyon* (Lyon, 2010).

[50] *Journal des débats*, December 8, 1831.

demonstration of the economic vices" of the free market system which "leaves the poor at the mercy of the rich and promises an easy victory to greed."[51] For many republicans this was the moment at which republicanism became identified with the discovery of "the social question."[52]

Another explosion of revolutionary violence occurred in Paris on June 5–6, 1832 at the funeral of the popular General Lamarque.[53] A huge and unruly crowd made its way across Paris to the Pont d'Austerlitz where the ceremony was to take place. During the funeral speeches, shouts of "Vive la République!" rang out; stones were thrown at police and carriages overturned. A horseman appeared, dressed in black and deploying a red flag topped with the Phrygian cap of revolution. Rumours spread that the Hôtel de Ville had been captured by insurgents. A detachment of dragoons was fired upon; in return, another detachment charged the crowd. Quickly barricades began to rise in the centre of Paris, in the narrow streets behind the Hôtel de Ville and around the Place de la Bastille. By mid-afternoon, the insurgents controlled much of Central and Eastern Paris. But on the government side, the Paris garrison of 18,000 troops was augmented by 6,000 National Guards and 2,000 Municipal Guards. That evening, as government troops took back much of Paris, republican leaders, meeting in the offices of Le National, were divided, with a majority reluctant to give full support to the insurgency. The next morning the government declared a state of siege, and the National Guard was reinforced by the arrival of Guardsmen from the suburbs. By noon it was clear that the insurgency would fail. But a pocket of resistance held out around the Eglise Saint-Merry until late afternoon. In the end, the casualties for what Georges Weill described as "the first truly republican insurrection since 1815" came to 800 killed and wounded.[54]

[51] Louis Blanc, *Histoire de dix ans, 1830–1840,* 5 vols. (Paris, 1841–1844), vol. III, 85.

[52] Jean-Claude Caron, "Etre républicain en monarchie (1830–1835): La gestion des paradoxes" in Patrick Harismendy (ed.), *La France des années 1830 et l'esprit de réforme"* (Rennes, 2006), 36–37: "Before the insurrection of the Lyon canuts, the social question properly speaking ... was hardly mentioned in most of the programs, projects, manifestos and other professions of faith of the republican societies ... The insurrection of the Lyon canuts changed the situation totally."

[53] On the funeral as a site of political protest, see Emmanuel Fureix, "La Construction rituelle de la souveraineté populaire: deuils protestataires (Paris 1815–1840)," *Revue d'histoire du XIXᵉ siècle,* 42 (2011), 21–39.

[54] Thomas Bouchet, *Le Roi et les barricades: Une histoire des 5 et 6 juin 1832* (Paris, 2000). See also Charles Jeanne, *"A Cinq heures nous serons tous morts!" Sur la barricade Saint-Merry, 5–6 juin 1832,* Thomas Bouchet (ed.) (Paris, 2011); and Mark Traugott, *The Insurgent Barricade* (Berkeley, 2010), 1–7. For precise figures on the casualties see Harsin, *Barricades,* 60. Blanc, *Histoire de dix ans,* III, 287–342 is a detailed and

The failed republican revolution of June 5–6, 1832 was not forgotten: Victor Hugo devoted over two hundred pages to it in *Les Misérables* (1862).[55] A more rapid response came from the Chamber of Deputies which voted a whole series of repressive laws – laws against the press, against public criers, against the right of assembly, and most importantly laws against the right of association. In March 1834 the Chamber of Deputies began to discuss a law on association that rendered all existing republican groups and workers' organizations illegal and stipulated that members of these organizations should be tried before courts without juries. Within a few days after the passage of this law both Paris and Lyon were literally up in arms. In Lyon, the silk weavers, together with a large contingent from the Société des droits de l'homme, shut down their Jacquard looms and took over the city as they had in 1831. With banners proclaiming "Live free or die fighting!", they held out this time for four days against 13,000 government troops. At least 320 people were killed in the fighting.[56] On the day after the defeat of this second Lyon insurrection, barricades went up in Paris. Bitter street fighting went on for two days between republicans and royal troops. On one occasion, unforgettably depicted in a lithograph by Daumier, in response to shots fired on government troops from a building on the rue Transnonain, the troops massacred a dozen residents of the apartment including a baby. After pacifying Lyon and Paris, the government organized a series of trials – the result of which was to decimate the leadership of the Lyon *canuts* and to destroy the republican movement as a political force for the rest of the decade.

In the face of repression, French republicans turned to the history of the first French Revolution for inspiration. As Georges Weill put it in his classic history of the republican movement, during the July Monarchy republicans sought in the French Revolution "examples, lessons, a doctrine; they relived the revolution in their associations, their newspapers, their projects of reform. Militants savored the speeches and writings of

---

passionately engaged account from a republican perspective. The statement by Georges Weill is from *Histoire du parti républicain en France (1814–1870)* (Paris, 1928), 70.

[55] Victor Hugo, *Les Misérables*, 2 vols. (Paris: Garnier, 1963), vol. II, 266–504. The climax of Hugo's narrative is the terrible and poignant chapter "Gavroche dehors" which describes the "frightening game of hide-and-seek with death" played on a barricade at Saint-Merry by "cette petite grande âme." (458–461) See Thomas Bouchet, "Ecrire l'insurrection. De Charles Jeanne aux *Misérables*" in Charles Jeanne, "*A cinq heures nous serons tous morts!*", 129–162.

[56] See Robert Bezucha, *The Lyon Uprising of 1834: Social and Political Conflict in the Early July Monarchy* (Cambridge, MA, 1974). On the Paris uprising see Harsin, *Barricades*, 84–105.

the great days."[57] There were some – like Auguste Blanqui and Godefroy Cavaignac –whose fathers had been members of the Convention; others knew of the Revolution through the stories of old men who had fought at Fleurus or participated in the Festival of the Supreme Being. And the 1830s and 1840s were marked by the appearance of an abundance of printed sources on French Revolution including the forty volumes of Buchez and Roux's *Histoire parlementaire de la Révolution française* (1834–1838), Albert Laponneraye's edition of the speeches and writings of Robespierre, the *Histoire populaire de la Révolution française* by Etienne Cabet (1839). All of this culminated in 1847 with the virtually simultaneous appearance of three major histories of the French Revolution – by Michelet, Louis Blanc and Lamartine – each of which offered guidance for future revolutionaries.

Republicans and Socialists

In the 1830s republicans did not form a regularly constituted political party with recognized leaders. Rather, they were a collection of groups with similar aspirations. At the conservative extreme there were the elderly republicans around the marquis de Lafayette, who admired the American republic but regarded constitutional monarchy as the best form of government possible in the France of their time. At the other extreme came the revolutionary radicals led by Auguste Blanqui, Armand Barbès and Martin Bernard, who harked back to conspiratorial traditions connected with Gracchus Babeuf's "Republic of Equals" and to the attempts of Carbonarist army officers to overthrow the Bourbon monarchy in the early 1820s. Having created a secret society with a thousand members, Blanqui and Barbès tried and failed to stage a coup d'état in Paris in May 1839.[58] But this did not mark the end of the appeal to revolutionary traditions by republican opponents of the July Monarchy.

Within the republican movement of the 1830s and 1840s there were two main factions, each associated with a newspaper and each harking back to a different strand of the revolutionary tradition. The moderate republicans of *Le National* saw themselves as the heirs of the Girondins,

---

[57] Weill, *Histoire du parti républicain*, 178. See also Claude Nicolet, *L'Idée républicaine en France* (Paris, 1994), 85: "For republicans of different stripes [in the 1830s and 1840s] the French Revolution was more than a point of departure. It was at once a model, a gospel, a historical reference, and especially a mode of being."

[58] See Harsin, *Barricades*, 124–144, and Thomas Bouchet, "Les Sociétés secrètes pendant la monarchie censitaire" in Jean-Jacques Becker and Gilles Candor (eds.), *Histoire des gauches en France*, 2 vols. (Paris, 2005), I, 161–168.

and the more radical republicans of *La Réforme* identified themselves
with the Jacobins and Montagnards who took control of the Revolution
after the expulsion of the Girondins in May 1793. The leaders of *Le
National*, Armand Carrel and Armand Marrast, believed that electoral
reform must precede social change. In economics they were hostile to
state intervention but applauded Jean-Baptiste Say's attack on financial
oligarchies. Similarly, in politics they distanced themselves from the
"excesses" of the Jacobin dictatorship but filled the pages of *Le
National* with spirited attacks on Louis Philippe and Guizot. The founders of *La Réforme*, Godefroy Cavaignac and Alexandre Ledru-Rollin,
regarded electoral reform as a point of departure but were centrally
concerned with social questions and popularized the notions of the "right
to work" and the "organization of labour" which became essential to the
democratic creed in 1848. In the aftermath of the February Revolution
they became advocates of a "democratic *and social* republic" which would
bring an end to the laissez-faire individualism that led to unrestrained
competition and exploitation.[59]

Another movement that flourished in the early 1830s was romantic or
"utopian" socialism. Its French founders – Henri Saint-Simon and
Charles Fourier – both began to write around 1800, published major
works a decade later, but only attracted a significant number of followers
after 1825. These early socialists were not primarily economic thinkers.
They were looking for order and authority in a world torn apart by
revolution, and their ideas were presented as remedies for the collapse
of community. They believed that the French and industrial revolutions
had produced a breakdown of traditional associations and group ties,
that individuals were becoming increasingly detached from any kind of
corporate structure, and that society as a whole was becoming frag-
mented and individualistic. Egoism was the great problem: the Saint-
Simonians called it "the deepest wound of modern society."[60] The
romantic socialists' vision of a better world was the result of a search
for some substitute for the old forms of community that egoism and
individualism were destroying.

The 1840s in France were marked by the emergence of a new generation of romantic socialists who created sects and ideologies of their own.
Étienne Cabet attracted a substantial working-class following with the

---

[59] On early French republicanism Weill, *Histoire du parti républicain* remains valuable. But
see also Pamela M. Pilbeam, *Republicanism in Nineteenth-Century France, 1814–1871*
(London, 1995).

[60] *Doctrine de Saint-Simon. Exposition: Première année, 1829*, Célestin Bouglé and Élie
Halévy (eds.) (Paris, 1924), 148–149.

austere and authoritarian communist utopia described in his novel
Voyage en Icarie (1839). Convinced that inequality was the root of all
evil, Cabet stipulated that goods should be held in common and that all
citizens would eat the same food, wear the same clothes and live in the
same kind of dwelling. The former Saint-Simonian Pierre Leroux pro-
pounded a mystical humanitarian socialism, arguing that social reform
should be guided by a new religion of humanity. Finally, Louis Blanc
gained a wide audience for his version of Jacobin state socialism with the
publication in 1839 of *L'Organisation du travail*.[61]

There was also an important group of feminist socialists who had
initially been attracted to the ideas of Saint-Simon and Fourier but
subsequently found a voice of their own. Désirée Véret, Jeanne Deroin,
Pauline Roland, Suzanne Volquin and Eugénie Niboyet were all drawn
to the Saint-Simonian movement because of its concern with the needs
and aptitudes of workers and women, and then went on to found short-
lived feminist journals in 1832 and the longer-lasting *La Voix des femmes*
in 1848. Véret and Flora Tristan both knew the aged Fourier and
deepened his insight that the emancipation of women is the key to all
social progress. And Tristan's proposal for a workers' union in *L'Union
ouvrière* (1843) can be seen as a kind of early syndicalist utopia.[62] These
early feminist socialists are now often called "precursors," but in their
own time they had to struggle to be taken seriously. Attacks on them
came not only from conservatives but also from republicans like Daumier
(whose cartoons in the *Charivari* ridiculed the "blue-stockings" and "les
Divorceuses"), from misogynist socialists like Proudhon, and even from
George Sand who, when asked by the editors of *La Voix des femmes* to
stand for election in 1848, replied coldly that she did not want to become
"the standard-bearer of a feminist coterie."[63]

Some of these early socialists did not initially ally themselves with the
republican movement. The Fourierist leader Victor Considerant

[61] Christopher H. Johnson, *Utopian Communism in France: Cabet and the Icarians, 1839–1851* (Ithaca, 1974); Armelle Le Bras-Chopard, *De l'égalité dans la différence: Le socialisme de Pierre Leroux* (Paris, 1986); Leo A. Loubère, *Louis Blanc: His Life and his Contribution to the Rise of French Jacobin-Socialism* (Evanston, 1961); Francis Démier (ed.), *Louis Blanc. Un socialiste en république* (Paris 2005).
[62] The literature on early French feminism is rich. Works that I have found particularly valuable include Michèle Riot-Sarcey, *La Démocratie à l'épreuve des femmes*; Susan K. Grogan, *French Socialism and Sexual Difference* (Basingstoke, 1992); Naomi J. Andrews, *Socialism's Muse: Gender in the Intellectual Landscape of French Romantic Socialism* (Lanham, MD, 2006); Joan Scott, *Only Paradoxes to Offer: French Feminists and the Rights of Man* (Cambridge, MA, 1996).
[63] George Sand to the editors of *La Réforme* and *La Vraie République*, April 8, 1848, George Sand, *Correspondance*, Georges Lubin (ed.), 26 vols. (Paris, 1964–1991), VIII, 391–392.

dedicated his major work, *Destinée sociale* (1834–1844), to Louis Philippe and remained a defender of constitutional monarchy down until 1847.[64] In due course the boundary lines between socialism and republicanism became blurred. By 1848, romantic socialism had merged with the other ideologies of the democratic left to form a single movement that was broadly democratic and socialist. The shared beliefs that held this movement together included a faith in the right to work and in universal (male) suffrage, a belief that the differences between classes and nations were not irreconcilable, and a program of "peaceful democracy" which assumed that, if politicians would only appeal to the higher impulses of "the people," a new era of class harmony and social peace would begin.

A striking feature of radical discourse in the 1830s and 1840s was the blending of Christian language and imagery with socialist and republican ideologies.[65] After 1830 arguments for social and political change were increasingly framed in Christian terms. This infusion of radical social thought with Christian ideas and language began with Saint-Simon and Fourier. In 1825 in his final work Saint-Simon called for the creation of a "New Christianity" which would take over the role formerly played by the Catholic Church in shaping the attitudes and beliefs of ordinary people. Fourier included in his *Nouveau monde industriel* (1829) an elaborate exercise in scriptural exegesis demonstrating the concordance of his theory with the New Testament.[66]

Saint-Simon and Fourier were "pragmatic" Christians who adopted Christian language in an effort to engage their readers. But, in 1834, a more fervent voice made itself heard. This was Félicité de Lamennais, who initially saw in the Catholic Church an antidote to the anarchy unleashed by the French Revolution but came to believe that the

---

[64] Jonathan Beecher, *Victor Considerant and the Rise and Fall of French Romantic Socialism* (Berkeley, CA, 2001), 173–180.

[65] On this theme see Berenson, *Populist Religion*, and "A New Religion of the Left: Christianity and Social Radicalism in France, 1815–1848" in Furet and Ozouf (eds.), *The Transformation of Political Culture 1789–1848*, 543–560; Gareth Stedman Jones, "Religion and the Origins of Socialism" in Ira Katznelson and Gareth Stedman Jones (eds.), *Religion and the Political Imagination* (Cambridge, 2010), 171–189; Michael C. Behrent, "The Mystical Body of Society: Religion and Association in Nineteenth-Century French Political Thought," *Journal of the History of Ideas*, 68(2) (April 2008), 219–243; Johnson, *Utopian Communism*, 214–259; Frank Paul Bowman, *Le Christ des barricades 1789–1848* (Paris, 1987); Jonathan Beecher, "Fourierism and Christianity," *Nineteenth-Century French Studies*, XXII (Spring/Summer 1994), 391–403; Miguel Abensour, "L'Utopie socialiste: une nouvelle alliance de la politique et de la religion" in *Le Temps de la réflection* (Paris, 1981), 61–112; and Pierre Pierrard, *L'Eglise et les ouvriers en France (1840–1940)* (Paris, 1984), 123–171.

[66] Henri de Saint-Simon, *Le Nouveau christianisme*, Henri Desroche (ed.), (Paris, 1969); Charles Fourier, *Oeuvres complètes*, 12 vols. (Paris, 1966–1968), VI, 357–380.

Church had forsaken the teachings of Jesus to join the monarchs of Europe in suppressing the strivings of the poor toward a better life. In October 1830 Lamennais founded a journal, *L'Avenir*, which called for freedom of the press, freedom of conscience, and the regeneration of the Catholic Church. Following the condemnation of *L'Avenir* by the Pope in 1832, he left the Church. Two years later he published *Paroles d'un croyant*, an extraordinary prose poem in which he denounced the papacy for having "divorced itself from Christ" and summoned "the people" to revolt in the name of the Gospel against the injustices perpetrated by civil and ecclesiastical authorities. This work which a contemporary described as "an apocalypse touched up with prayer and blasphemy," was soon translated into almost every European language. Abandoned by Catholics, Lamennais became a hero to democrats, one of whom, George Sand, wrote him: "We count you among our saints ... You are the father of our New Church."[67]

The movement of "left-wing religiosity" spread rapidly. Socialists claimed Jesus Christ, a carpenter and man of the people, for the revolutionary movement, arguing that the preacher of the Sermon on the Mount belonged not to the Catholic Church but to the poor and the downtrodden. Republicans filled their pamphlets with tributes to Jesus Christ, "the first *sans-culotte*." Saint-Simonians insisted on the need for a new "spiritual power" that would take over the role formerly played by the Catholic Church in shaping the attitudes and beliefs of the people. Pierre Leroux presented himself as the champion of "religious democracy."[68] And the Christian communist Etienne Cabet called for a return to the traditions of primitive Christianity, abandoned by the Catholic Church. "Communism," declared Cabet, "is Christianity in its original purity."[69] This blending of socialism, communism and radical republicanism with Christian language and imagery became a distinctive feature of revolutionary discourse in 1848.

The Emergence of the Press

The spread of republican and socialist movements took place at the same time as – and under the influence of – the emergence of a new type of

[67] Alfred Nettement, *Histoire de la littérature française sous le gouvernement de Juillet* (Paris, 1859), 347; George Sand to Lamennais, May 10, 1841, *Correspondance*, V, 303.
[68] Pierre Leroux, "De l'individualisme et du socialism (1834)" in David Owen Evans (ed.), *Le Socialisme romantique. Pierre Leroux et ses contemporains* (Paris, 1948), 224.
[69] Johnson, *Utopian Communism*, 215.

mass journalism in France.[70] This was the dawn of the age of the large-circulation daily newspaper. The first two such papers were *La Presse*, founded by Emile de Girardin, and *Le Siècle* of Armand Dutacq. These papers, which lasted well into the twentieth century, were founded on the same day: July 1, 1836. Taking advantage of technical innovations in printing and publishing, Girardin and Dutacq cut costs and lowered subscription rates through the publication of advertising and attracted new readers through the publication of serial novels. In the next dozen years, with novels by Balzac and Dumas leading the way, these two papers and the liberal *Constitutionnel* tripled their sales, their daily circulation rising from under 10,000 to over 30,000.[71] *La Presse* published the first serial novel, Balzac's *La Vieille Fille*, in 1839. Three years later, the huge success of Eugène Sue's sentimental exposé of Parisian street life, *Les Mystères de Paris*, enabled Sue to collect the record sum of 100,000 francs for the publication of his next novel, *Le Juif errant*, in 1844.

During the July Monarchy the number of papers multiplied, both in Paris and the provinces; and a newspaper (whether daily, weekly or monthly) became an important adjunct for any organized group. Thus at Lyon in 1829 there were just two newspapers, but shortly after the July Revolution a reader at Lyon could choose between Legitimist, Orleanist and republican papers, and satirical and artistic journals as well as a woman's journal and the *Echo de la Fabrique*, the weekly newspaper published by and for Lyon's silk weavers.[72] Republicans and socialists quickly became wedded to what Constantin Pecqueur called the "new medium" of journalism. The Fourierist Victor Considerant asserted that "the journal is the pivot of propaganda" and that any new idea must create "its own periodical press." This was "the only way today to acquire publicity, plausibility and power." Likewise, for the socialist Pierre Leroux "no true and legitimate government is possible without the preparatory work performed by the press."[73]

The audience reached by the press grew rapidly after 1830. Newspapers were available in cafés and clubs and reading rooms. Thus each copy could be read by a dozen people, and it has been estimated that

---

[70] On the simultaneous rise of socialism and mass journalism in France see Thomas Bouchet, *et al.* (eds.), *Quand les socialistes inventaient l'avenir. Presse, théories et expériences, 1825–1860* (Paris, 2015).

[71] Charles Ledré, *La Presse à l'assaut de la monarchie 1815–1848* (Paris, 1960), 244. On the history of the press during the July Monarchy see also Claude Bellenger *et al.* (eds.), *Histoire générale de la presse française*, 5 vols. (Paris, 1970), II; and Reddy, *The Invisible Code*, 184–227.

[72] Jeremy Popkin, *Press, Revolution, and Social Identities in France, 1830–1835* (University Park, PA, 2002).

[73] Bouchet *et al.* (eds.), *Quand les socialistes inventaient l'avenir*, 16, 33.

over ten times more people read newspapers in Paris in the early 1830s than were eligible to vote.[74] Readers turned immediately to the *Premier-Paris*, the lead story, which offered critical comment on the day's news from a particular political point of view. The writer of this column was usually anonymous. But he was in Balzac's words the "tenor" of the operatic ensemble that constituted a newspaper staff, and his daily task was, as Balzac wrote in his *Monographie de la presse parisienne*, to express cleverly ideas already held by the paper's readers. Newspapers also contained a judicial section, a column of *faits divers*, a section on the Bourse, and the occasional book review. "The public loves to be served three or four authors, spat upon like dogs and loaded with ridicule each morning," wrote Balzac, who spoke from experience.[75] Finally, parliamentary debates were also reproduced – often with partisan notations concerning audience response: "murmurs," "violent interruptions," "thunderous applause," "explosion of bravos." We shall see in the chapters on Hugo (Chapter 5) and Proudhon (Chapter 7) that this journalistic custom remained alive and well in the Second Republic.

The early years of the July Monarchy were also marked by an explosion of political caricature. This was made possible both by the introduction of lithography, a process invented by Senefelder in 1796 but widely used in France only after 1820, and by a law passed in October 1830 which ended – temporarily as it turned out – the censorship of caricatures, although "offensive" cartoons like Daumier's "Gargantua" could still result in prosecution (see Figure 1.2).

Charles Philipon, a mediocre artist but a brilliant editor and entrepreneur, stepped into the breach. His creation of the image of Louis Philippe as a gluttonous and self-important pear was taken up by more talented artists like Daumier, Grandville and Traviès and served to reduce respect for the monarchy and to reinforce the critique made by republican journalists.[76]

In September 1835, following a failed assassination attempt on Louis Philippe, the government promulgated the so-called September laws, which drastically restricted freedom of the press and had the effect of banning all political satire and political caricature. Thereafter Daumier

---

[74] H. A. C. Collingham, *The July Monarchy. A Political History of France 1830–1848* (London, 1988), 178.

[75] Honoré de Balzac, *Monographie de la presse parisienne* (Paris, 1965), 42–46; Collingham, *July Monarchy*, 173–174.

[76] David S. Kerr, *Caricature and French Political Culture 1830–1848: Charles Philipon and the Illustrated Press* (Oxford, 2000); Laura O'Brien, *The Republican Line: Caricature and French Republican Identity, 1830–1852* (Manchester, 2015).

Figure 1.2 "Gargantua," lithograph by Daumier. Louis-Philippe is
shown consuming sacks of money extracted from the poor and
excreting peerages, decorations and commissions for his fat little
favourites. "Gargantua" was meant to appear in *La Caricature* on
December 16, 1831. The government stopped publication and
sentenced Daumier to six months in prison. Photograph: Alamy

and his peers had to limit themselves to social satire. But social satire
turned out to be corrosive and even more widely influential than the
political. With the figure of the dapper confidence-man Robert Macaire,
drawn for newspapers by Daumier and played on stage by Frédéric
Lemaître, the bourgeoisie laughed at itself and the critique of bourgeois
society acquired life and substance. By 1840, Robert Macaire had
entered the world of the stock market. The small-time swindler had
become a master speculator whose accomplices included corrupt treas-
ury agents and even cabinet ministers.[77] Thus the discrediting of the
government was well advanced by 1847 when Victor Hugo denounced
the ministry of François Guizot as "the narrow and mean government of
interests, expedients, and profit."[78] But the effectiveness of the political

---

[77] Amy Wiese Forbes, *The Satiric Decade: Satire and the Rise of Republicanism in France,
 1830–1840* (Lanham, MD, 2010), 85–124.
[78] Victor Hugo, "Choses vues 1847" in *Oeuvres complètes Histoire* (Paris, 1987), 991.

cartoon between 1830 and 1835 was not forgotten. In 1848, with the renewed abolition of censorship, caricature once again became an important feature of the political landscape. And Robert Macaire lived on. In October 1847, when Proudhon dismissed a speech of Lamartine's as hot air, he called it "a superb joke" worthy of Robert Macaire. Two years later, when Karl Marx was discussing the origins of the February Revolution, it made sense to characterize Louis Philippe as "Robert Macaire on the throne."[79]

Roots of the February Revolution

Newspapers, cartoons and political pamphlets could ridicule authorities, magnify scandals and expose corruption. But they did not by themselves bring the July Monarchy down. Economic hardship also played a role, and the roots of the February Revolution lay in an agricultural crisis – not a "modern" crisis of overproduction, but a crisis of the "traditional" kind originating with bad weather, crop failures and high food prices.[80] To understand this crisis, and the role of the peasantry during the Second Republic, some general remarks are in order.

In the larger European context nineteenth-century French rural society was in some ways unique. Britain was dominated by large-scale commercial farming with labour performed by landless wage earners. Serfdom endured in central and Eastern Europe until mid-century, and the Junkers maintained their ascendancy in East Prussia long after legal emancipation. Italy and Spain had large areas dominated by large landed estates. Independent peasant farming persisted in Southwestern Germany and Northern Spain. But to some outsiders, France was the bastion of an independent and free peasantry.[81] Writing in the 1880s, Thomas Hardy, an unsurpassed chronicler of the lives of the rural poor in the South of England, could contrast the demoralized, deferential agricultural labourer of Dorset, whose land and communal rights had been long since lost, with what he regarded as the sturdy, independent French peasantry across the channel.[82]

---

[79] Pierre Haubtmann (ed.), *Carnets de P-J. Proudhon*, 4 vols. (Paris, 1960–1974), II, 243, 245; Karl Marx, *Class Struggles in France* (New York, 1964), 36.

[80] Roger Price, *The French Second Republic*, 82–90; François Démier, "'Comment naissent les Révolutions' … cinquante ans après," *Revue d'histoire du XIXᵉ siècle*, XIV(1) (1997), 31–49.

[81] Roger Magraw, *France, 1800–1914: A Social History* (London, 2002), 118.

[82] Thomas Hardy, "The Dorsetshire Labourer," *Longman's Magazine* (July 1883).

Viewed at closer range, the condition of the peasants in mid-nine-teenth-century France was less inspiring. Despite the abolition of man-orial dues and other vestiges of feudalism, many French peasants were worse off in the 1840s than their grandparents had been in 1789.[83] The problem was that while the Revolution and Napoleon had given peasants clear title to their land, freed from manorial obligations, the rural popu-lation had grown and many French peasants had lost their traditional rights of usage. The right of the rural poor to cut wood, gather food and graze livestock on common land was restricted under Napoleon and practically eliminated in some areas by the Forest Code of 1827.[84] If there were more peasant property owners than ever before during the July Monarchy, the amount of land that each individual owned had shrunk. The great problem besetting peasants was the subdivision or *morcellement* of land holdings. This was the result of the constantly increasing popula-tion and the absence of primogeniture. During the Old Regime inherit-ance laws varied from one region to another but generally recognized some form of primogeniture, which enabled peasants to keep property intact in a family. These laws were largely abolished during the French Revolution. The Napoleonic Code of 1804 did allow parents to bequeath a double share of property to a single child, but this did not prevent the splitting up of property over time.[85]

The problem of *morcellement* was compounded by the steady increase in population in France from 30 million in 1815, to 32.6 million in 1830, to 35.4 million in 1846. This increase was particularly acute in rural areas like the Lot and the Ardèche in the South and the Haute Marne in the East, which were by 1840 more heavily populated than ever before (or since).[86] How were these rural areas able to support so large a popula-tion? To some extent they weren't. The 1840s were a period of massive movement from the countryside to the city: young men seeking work in the building trades and young women seeking jobs as domestic servants. But still the rural population kept growing at least until 1840. The question remains: How was rural France able to support into the 1840s

---

[83] On this point see the conclusions of Jean Vidalenc, *La Société française de 1815 à 1848, I: Le Peuple des campagnes* (Paris, 1970), esp. 369.

[84] On the effects of the Forest Code and the persistent struggle of peasants in one region, the Var, to reclaim traditional rights of usage, see Maurice Agulhon, *La République au village: Les populations du Var de la Révolution à la IIe République*, 2nd ed. (Paris, 1979), 42–106.

[85] See Magraw, *France, 1800–1914: A Social History*, 118. See also James Lehning, *The Peasants of Marlhes: Economic Development and Family Organization in Nineteenth-Century France* (Chapel Hill, 1980), 115–117.

[86] Gabriel Désert, "L'essor démographique" in Georges Duby and Armand Wallon (eds.), *Histoire de la France rurale*, 4 vols. (Paris, 1976), III, 59–66.

a peasant population vastly greater than at any time before or since? Here two factors were at play. First, families unable to make ends meet through farming or agricultural labour alone could supplement their income by handloom weaving or handicrafts in their homes. The combination of farming and cottage labour had long enabled France to maintain a rural population far larger than agricultural production alone would allow. By the 1840s this system had become widespread, especially in the textile-producing areas of the North and East of France. In Picardie, for example, in 1843 almost 25,000 rural workers were employed in the cotton industry; and in Champagne of the 50,000 workers in the wool industry, three-quarters lived in the countryside. Similar figures could be given for cotton weavers in Normandy and near Mulhouse in Alsace.[87]

Cottage labour in the textile industries enabled peasant smallholders to survive at a time of unprecedented crowding in the countryside because work in these industries could be performed not only by men but by women and children as well. In 1851, over 50 percent of the workers in the textile and clothing industries were women; and most of these women were peasants working at home. However, the economic crisis that began in 1846, cutting into the market for manufactured goods, marked the beginning of the end for cottage industries and hastened the flow of population out of depressed rural areas. In many parts of France, it was not possible for farm workers and their families to supplement their income through cottage industries. Especially in the poor and mountainous areas of Southern and Central France, peasants had to leave home for a part of the year in search of work. A day labourer from the Sarthe could increase his wages by 60 percent by seeking work at harvest time in the great grain-growing area around Chartres. A peasant from Puy-de-Dôme who went to the Gard to do harvest work could earn 50 percent more there than at home. The numbers affected by these patterns of seasonal migration were large. A survey of 1852 estimated that the total number of migrant harvest workers in the preceding year came to 880,000. Migrant harvest workers, of course, worked a short season. But things were different for the very large number of migrant workers who left poor mountainous areas like the Alpes, the Massif Central and the Pyrenees to seek temporary work in the cities either in the building trades or else to hire themselves out as porters, water carriers, coachmen or knife grinders. For these people the time away from home could amount to eight or ten months.[88]

---

[87] Désert, "Symptômes de surpeuplement," *Histoire de la France rurale*, III, 66–79. Roger Price, *A Social History of Nineteenth-Century France* (London, 1987), 164.

[88] Désert, "Migrations saisonnières," *Histoire de la France rurale*, III, 71–74. See also Gérard Noiriel, *Une Histoire populaire de la France* (Marseille, 2018), 327–366.

So, cottage industries and patterns of seasonal migration made it possible for the French countryside to support a rural population that was greater in the 1840s than ever before or since. But it did not support them well. In fact, a large part of this population lived in a state of extreme poverty. The amount of land they owned was not adequate to see them through years of bad weather and bad harvest. Unable to rely on customary rights of usage, peasants fell into debt in unprecedented numbers during the 1840s. This is dramatized in Balzac's great novel *Les Paysans* (1844) which presents a picture of widespread peasant indebtedness and the stranglehold that rural bankers and money lenders exercised over much of rural France.[89]

During hard times – notably during the winter of 1846/1847 – the poverty of the countryside was so great that many peasants joined bands of beggars and vagabonds that traversed the countryside in search of food in areas like the Beauce and the Sarthe. Sometimes they would scavenge food; sometimes they would forcibly requisition it; sometimes they would rob grain convoys. Popular price-fixing was also common, as at Cluny in January 1847 where a crowd at a grain market in the former abbey forced merchants to sell at a just price.[90] In regions where customary rights of grazing and gleaning had once been observed, peasants sought to reestablish these rights by force, threatening to burn down the farms and mills of proprietors who resisted them. All of this could, and sometimes did, lead to outbreaks of peasant violence – *jacqueries* – that required the calling in of the National Guard or even of government troops.[91]

What did the poor peasants want? They wanted an end to the long-standing taxes on salt, wine, and tobacco. Most importantly, they wanted land. The land hunger of the French peasant was proverbial, and it was never stronger than in the 1840s when so many family farms were being broken up. Two specific demands lay behind the desire for land and the outbreaks of rural violence: (1) Given their indebtedness and their increasing dependence on village bankers, the mass of poorer peasants desperately needed credit – the ability to borrow money in hard times on terms that were not suicidal. The problem for small farmers was that, while they did well in good years, they had to borrow in the years of bad harvest. Once in debt, it was almost impossible to get out of it, as was

---

[89] See Marx's tribute in *Capital*, III (Moscow, 1959), 39 to Balzac's account in *Les Paysans* of how a small peasant becomes "enmeshed" in "the spider-web of usury."

[90] Pierre Lévêque, *Une Société en crise: La Bourgogne au milieu du XIXe siècle (1846–1852)* (Paris, 1983), 27.

[91] Peter McPhee, *The Politics of Rural Life: Political Mobilization in the French Countryside, 1846–1852* (Oxford, 1992), 56–74.

shown in excruciating detail by the Bourbonnais farmer Emile Guillaumin in his moving fictional biography of a sharecropper, *La Vie d'un simple*. (2) If peasants at the end of the July Monarchy were desperately in need of credit, another thing they wanted with almost equal fervour was the restoration of those customary rights of usage that whole peasant communities had traditionally enjoyed during the Old Regime. In some parts of France these traditional rights had survived the Revolution – only to be suppressed by forest laws and enclosure acts passed during the Restoration and the July Monarchy. In hard times it seemed imperative for peasants to get these rights back.

All of this can stand as background to the revolution of 1848. Peasants in 1848 would attempt in some areas to reclaim customary rights.[92] But initially they did not support the Republican Government. Why? Not simply out of blind conservatism, but rather because the Republic offered them nothing. The socialists and republicans who helped make the February Revolution did not have a peasant policy.[93] Their notion of the "social question" focused on the cities, and for them "the people" were urban workers. The first measure taken by the Provisional Government that directly touched the lives of peasants was to impose a 45 percent increase in property taxes. They could have done nothing else more likely to turn peasant smallholders against the Republic.

Now we must turn to a brief account of the economic crisis – first agricultural and then financial – which set the stage for the February Revolution. The mid-1840s were marked by hard times all over Europe. This was the time of potato famine in Ireland and the "hungry '40s" on the continent. In France the harvest of 1845 was bad, and that of 1846 was worse. In many parts of France, the price of wheat doubled between the Spring of 1846 and the Spring of 1847; and this brought a significant increase in the price of bread. But high bread prices, in an economy where millions lived on the margin and bread was an essential staple, meant that workers and poor peasants had less to spend on clothing and other manufactured goods. And with the collapse of the domestic market for manufactured goods came widespread unemployment.

Along with this agricultural crisis there was a financial crisis, a crisis of credit, provoked by the railroad boom of the 1840s and by speculation stimulated by the rapid industrial and commercial growth of 1840–1846.

---

[92] See for example Agulhon, *La République au village*, 279–284, and McPhee, *Politics of Rural Life*, 80–82.

[93] George Fasel, "The Wrong Revolution: French Republicanism in 1848," *French Historical Studies*, VIII(4) (Autumn 1974), 654–677.

At the time the government did not bail out bankrupt companies. But it did import grain in bad times to sell at artificially low prices. In 1846 it was obliged to draw heavily on the assets of the Bank of France in order to pay for imports of Russian wheat in the winter of 1846/1847. As a result, the gold reserves of the Bank of France fell from 200 million francs in June 1846 to 47 million in January 1847, whereupon, to the consternation of the *bourgeoisie d'affaires*, the Bank raised its lending rate from 4 percent to 5 percent.

Conditions improved in the last few months of 1847. The harvest was better; unemployment fell; and the Bank of France returned to the 4 percent lending rate. Nonetheless the consequences of this crisis were dire. In rural France the whole system of cottage industries, which was essential to the survival of the poorer peasants, had suffered a major blow with the collapse of the domestic market for clothing and other goods produced by peasants working on the putting-out system. At the same time in the cities there had been massive unemployment. During the winter and spring of 1847 workers no longer able to feed their families robbed grain convoys, broke machines, and set upon the houses of the rich. The situation approached anarchy in parts of rural France, and government troops often had to intervene. The most spectacular disturbance occurred in January 1847 at the market town of Buzançais, not far from the residence of George Sand. It began as a case of popular price-fixing when carts were stopped and their contents sold at a just price. But the crowd went on to force the mayor, the justice of the peace and sixty notables to sign a document promising to sell grain at a fixed price until the next harvest. They then attacked mills and châteaux, killing a wealthy landowner. The government response was swift: 400 infantry and 100 cavalry were sent into this town of 4,000 inhabitants, and three ring-leaders were guillotined in the main square of Buzançais.[94]

Finally, with the better harvest of 1847 calm returned. But a result of this whole period of crisis and disorder was that the upper classes – the *notables* who controlled France – lost confidence in the ability of the government both to maintain a climate in which business could prosper and to retain the respect and obedience of the lower classes. This loss of confidence in the ability of the government to maintain order gave added

---

[94] McPhee, *Politics of Rural Life*, 64–65; Roger Price, *The Modernization of Rural France* (London, 1983), 178–181. Cynthia A. Bouton, *Interpreting Social Violence in French Culture: Buzançais, 1847–2008* (Baton Rouge, 2011). See George Sand's commentary on these events: "These are hungry people who are angry at hoarders and speculators. They have displayed a rare discernment in their acts of vengeance which, although quite illegal, were nonetheless just." Sand to René Vallet de Villeneuve, February 5, 1847, *Correspondance*, VII, 608–610.

resonance to the major political development of 1846–1847: a series of scandals that served to discredit both the government and the regime in the eyes of much of the population.

In the parliamentary elections of 1846, the government led by François Guizot had won a big majority in the Chamber of Deputies. Its enemies in the Chamber were the so-called Dynastic Opposition led by Odilon Barrot. For a decade this group had been introducing bills designed to broaden the suffrage. Each time these bills were voted down by Guizot's majority. Finally, in 1847 a series of events revealed to the world at large just how the majority was held together. It became known that two former ministers had accepted bribes for the granting of government concessions. Then Guizot himself was accused of having taken 600,000 francs from government funds to pay off a man who had been "sold" a high government job to which he was never appointed. At the same time, more modest forms of corruption were brought to light – payoffs to deputies who supported the government, bribes to minor officials who could influence the awarding of government contracts. This led Karl Marx and Alexis de Tocqueville to use the same image to describe the July Monarchy. The government, both wrote, resembled a joint stock company organized solely to benefit its principal shareholders.[95] A consequence of these revelations was to create a receptive audience for a number of writers who had begun to identify themselves with democratic and socialist doctrines and to contrast the corruption of the government and the narrowness of its social base with the purity and dignity of the common people. In their writings the celebration of "*le peuple*" became a repeated theme, and along with it came the spread of the idea that if only the people were allowed to express themselves through the ballot – the exercise of universal male suffrage – good government and harmonious social organization would follow.

In the eyes of the parliamentary opposition, which included both moderates like Odilon Barrot and radical republicans like Ledru-Rollin – the main problem with the July Monarchy was the narrowness of its social base. It was the insistence of Guizot and Louis Philippe on keeping the *pays légal* small that fostered the corruption and the spirit of egotism so pervasive among members of the government. Finally, in the summer of 1847 the leaders of the Dynastic Opposition carried the issue to the country by devising a tactic to get around the laws against political associations. They organized banquets which reformist deputies would attend along with electors and local *notables* who could pay a

---

[95] Karl Marx, *Class Struggles in France (1848–1850)* (New York, 1964), 36; Tocqueville, *Souvenirs*, 40.

"subscription" fee high enough to exclude the working poor. After the dinner there would be toasts for electoral reform and criticism of the government's policies.

In all some sixty reform banquets were held between July and December 1847, and they were attended by roughly 20,000 people. The first took place at Paris on July 9. Others followed in the provinces – among them a banquet at Mâcon where Lamartine prophesied that the regime might be overthrown by a "revolution of contempt." The largest banquet at Rouen attracted 1700 people, including Flaubert who wrote afterward that he was "nauseated" by the bombast of the orators.[96] At another banquet in Lille Ledru-Rollin violently attacked the regime and called for universal male suffrage. This was one of several banquets at which republicans played a leading role – much to the distress of Barrot and the Dynastic Opposition. When the last of the provincial banquets took place in December, there was no agreement between republicans and moderate opposition deputies concerning the desired goal of this whole "banquet campaign."

Up to this point, the speech-making had mostly been moderate, and the cost of participation effectively excluded members of the working class. But in January a group of radical National Guard officers decided to challenge the government by organizing a banquet in the quartier Saint-Marcel, one of the poorest districts of Paris. The Paris Prefect of Police refused to authorize the banquet. The organizing committee, which had been taken over by members of the Chamber of Deputies, then issued a series of statements assuring the Prefect of their intention to avoid any kind of provocation or violence. Such statements were echoed by the republican newspaper, *La Réforme*; and the members of the revolutionary group, the Society of the Seasons, were ordered by their leaders, Lucien de La Hodde and Albert, not to take up arms.[97] But as the events of February 22–24 were to show, the leaders – both reformist and radical – had lost control, and they found themselves at the head of a revolution for which they were not prepared. Hippolyte Carnot, soon to become minister of public instruction, put it this way:

If our wishes were for the Republic, our hopes did not extend beyond reform. It was a revolution which occurred, and it gave us the Republic. We accepted gladly, not without a certain uneasiness, for we could not disguise the fact that it took us by surprise.[98]

---

[96] Flaubert to Louise Colet, late December 1847, *Correspondance*, I (Paris, 1973), 491.
[97] William Fortescue, *France and 1848: The End of Monarchy* (London, 2005), 56–65.
[98] Papers of Hippolyte Carnot, Archives Nationales 108AP, carton 3 in Fasel, "The Wrong Revolution," 657–658.

2   Lamartine, the Girondins and 1848

No single individual more clearly epitomizes the hopes, illusions and confusions of February 1848 than Alphonse de Lamartine, the poet who became the leading figure in the Provisional Government created immediately after the overthrow of Louis Philippe. At the time of the February Revolution, Lamartine was fifty-eight years old. Ever since the publication in 1820 of his *Méditations poétiques* he had enjoyed a reputation as one of France's greatest lyric poets. This little volume made Lamartine famous overnight, and for many readers he would always remain what he was for Flaubert's Emma Rouault, the future Madame Bovary: the elegiac poet of refined melancholy whose verses captured ineffable feelings and sad memories of lost loves.[1] But he later claimed that poetry was merely the distraction of his youth and that his true vocation was politics.

In turning from poetry to politics, Lamartine lost none of his romantic confidence in his own intuitions and continued to believe in the power of the word to enrich experience and to create new worlds. In 1834 in a long essay on "the destinies of poetry" Lamartine wrote that the poet had a divine calling to guide a politics that had entered a new age. "My conviction," he declared, "is that we are at one of the great epochs of reconstruction and social renewal." The political task was no longer to decide whether the nobility, the priesthood or the bourgeoisie should rule France; it was to decide if the "moral" and "religious" idea of "evangelical charity" would replace "the idea of egoism in politics." In accents similar to those of Shelley's not-yet-published "Defence of Poetry," Lamartine wrote that the role poetry could play was to liberate individuals from commonplace expectations and to widen the bounds of the thinkable: "to point the way toward

This chapter is based on previously unpublished material in "Lamartine, the Girondins, and 1848" in Douglas Moggach and Gareth Stedman Jones (eds.), *The 1848 Revolutions and European Political Thought* (Cambridge: Cambridge University Press, 2018), 14–38.
[1] Gustave Flaubert, *Madame Bovary* (Paris, 1961), 36–37, Pt I, ch 6.

utopias, imaginary republics and cities of God" and to inspire the courage to seek and attain such ideals.[2]

Elected to the Chamber of Deputies in 1833, Lamartine kept his distance from existing factions and talked of founding his own "parti social." He was no socialist, for he had an unwavering belief in the sanctity of private property. But he recognized the necessity of state intervention "to prevent wealth from being oppressive and poverty from being envious and revolutionary." He was a critic of competition, which he called "selfishness left to itself"; he feared the power of high finance, which he called the feudalism of money; and in February 1835 he warned the Chamber of Deputies that "the question of the proletariat" could cause a "terrible explosion." When pressed to offer solutions, he almost always appealed to a notion of Christian charity. "Let's have other peacemakers than our soldiers, other arguments than our bayonets," he told the Chamber of Deputies in his first major speech. "Let's put charity into our laws."[3]

By the 1840s, Lamartine had adopted republican and democratic positions, and he set himself the task of simultaneously forging the vision of a new world in his speeches and embodying in his own words "the voice of the people."[4] In addressing the Chamber of Deputies he proudly described himself as "a son of revolutions, born in their womb."[5] But he lived the life of a *grand seigneur*, maintaining a splendid Parisian *hôtel* and large estates at Saint-Point and Monceau in addition to his childhood home in the village of Milly. He entertained grandly, kept nine horses, a dozen greyhounds, a multitude of servants, and paid for the education of village children. Acquaintances were divided about him. Marie d'Agoult admired him but regretted that in literature and in life he never had to struggle to achieve success.[6] Others found him vain and self-centred, quick to claim knowledge that he did not possess and endowed with a seemingly unlimited confidence in his own intuitions. Tocqueville wrote that he had "never met a mind more devoid of any thought of the public welfare" than Lamartine's nor "a mind that had a more thorough contempt for the truth." The liberal politician Charles de Rémusat described Lamartine (see Figure 2.1) as a man who "thinks constantly of himself and only of himself":

[2] Alphonse de Lamartine, "Des Destinées de la poésie" in *Oeuvres de Lamartine* (Bruxelles, 1836), 371, 373. See also George Armstrong Kelly, *The Humane Comedy: Constant, Tocqueville and French Liberalism* (Cambridge, 1992), 187–189.

[3] "Speech of May 13, 1834" in Alphonse de Lamartine, *La Politique et l'histoire*, Renée David (ed.) (Paris, 1993), 78. See also Fernand L'Huillier, *Lamartine en Politique* (Strasbourg, 1993), 179.

[4] For a comprehensive, and fine-spun analysis of Lamartine's oratory see Dominique Dupart, *Le Lyrisme démocratique, ou la naissance de l'éloquence romantique chez Lamartine, 1834–1849* (Paris, 2012).

[5] "Speech of March 24, 1840" in Alphonse de Lamartine, *Oeuvres oratoires et écrits politiques, La France parlementaire (1834–1851)*, Louis Ulbach (ed.), 6 vols. (Paris, 1864), II, 318.

[6] Daniel Stern [Marie d'Agoult], *Histoire de la Révolution de 1848*, 3 vols. (Paris, 1850–1853), I, 16.

Figure 2.1 Portrait of Alphonse de Lamartine by Théodore Chassériau, 1844. Photograph: Getty

Wake him suddenly from the deepest sleep, give him the most surprising news, or the most tragic, and he will think of only one thing: the role he might be called upon to play. He will reply speaking only of himself … Lamartine has more elevation than morality, more dignity than rectitude, more honor than conscience, more intelligence than wisdom, more genius than reason.[7]

For Rémusat, Lamartine was "a dangerous man."

Nonetheless, most of Lamartine's contemporaries were impressed by his oratory. Victor Hugo called him "the only orator in the Chamber who surpasses Berryer, Thiers, Guizot [and] Odilon Barrot."[8] Marie d'Agoult admired the nobility of his gestures and his skill at improvisation; and she compared "his rolling periods, which swell and break in their majestic monotony" to waves beating on a cliff.[9] But the fullest description of Lamartine's gifts as a speaker is ironically nuanced. In his *Livre des orateurs*, Louis de Cormenin describes Lamartine's language as possessing "more colour than solidity, more brilliance than profundity, more emphasis than vigour, more sonority than substance."[10] And a few contemporaries found Lamartine's "democratic lyricism" (Rémusat's term) insufferable. For Balzac, Lamartine's talent as a speaker consisted of telling his audience in soothing and "harmonious" tones: "I am just as unhappy as you are. I understand you. Come to me, let us weep together on the banks of this stream, under the willows." For Alexander Herzen, who heard Lamartine speak "in his familiar bombastic style" to the National Assembly in 1848, his speeches were "like whipped cream": "you think you are eating a whole spoonful, and it turns out to be a few drops of sweetened milk. I find him unbearable on the tribune, but the French are amazed by him."[11]

Learning from the Girondins

By the early 1840s, Lamartine found that the well of poetic inspiration had begun to run dry and that his poetry was no longer selling. This created problems for him because, as a man of extravagant tastes who lived beyond his means, he depended on the sale of his books to stay solvent. By 1843, his debts were estimated at 1,200,000 francs. To get

---

[7] Alexis de Tocqueville, *Souvenirs* (Paris, 1978), 176; Charles de Rémusat, *Mémoires de ma vie*, Charles Pouthas (ed.), 5 vols. (Paris, 1958–1967), IV, 31.
[8] L'Huillier, *Lamartine en politique*, 79.   [9] Stern, *Révolution de 1848*, I, 20.
[10] Louis de Cormenin, "Livre des orateurs (1836)" in Thomas Bouchet (ed.), *Un Jeudi à l'Assemblée: Politiques du discours et droit au travail dans la France de 1848* (Québec, 2007), 76.
[11] Honoré de Balzac, *Modeste Mignon* (Paris, 1881), 57; Alexander Herzen, *Letters from France and Italy, 1847–1851*, trans. Judith E. Zimmerman (Pittsburgh, 1995), 123.

out of debt Lamartine decided to write a history of the French Revolution aimed at a wide audience. He began work in August 1843. Two years later, after a lawsuit and lengthy negotiations, he signed a lucrative contract with Balzac's publisher, Furne. Finally, between March 20 and June 19, 1847, the *Histoire des Girondins* appeared in eight volumes and 3,000 pages. Lamartine was no historian, and reviewers had no trouble pointing out his errors, contradictions and omissions. Both Michelet's and Louis Blanc's histories of the French Revolution, which began to appear just prior to Lamartine's, were grounded in a much deeper knowledge of the sources, events and leaders of the revolution. But neither of these works received anything like the enthusiastic response given to the *Histoire des Girondins*. Lamartine's language was sumptuous, and readers like the novelist Delphine de Girardin delighted in "the felicity of his expression" and "the sonorousness of his language."[12]

The verdict of posterity has been less enthusiastic. Today Lamartine's *Histoire des Girondins* is best remembered for the sardonic one-liners it inspired: for Tocqueville's comment that Lamartine's "crude colors besmirched every imagination"; for Chateaubriand's expression of surprise that Lamartine should have wished to "gild the guillotine"; and for Alexandre Dumas' statement that Lamartine had "raised history to the dignity of the novel." (The characterization of the *Histoire des Girondins* as a "novel" was to be repeated dozens of times, but Dumas was the only person who meant it as a compliment!) More generally, after the February Revolution Lamartine's book was seen by many as having "caused" or "set the stage for" the fall of the July Monarchy. Marie d'Agoult wrote that the *Histoire des Girondins* "had a kind of electric reverberation throughout all of France." It was one of the most decisive of the "immediate causes" of the revolution of 1848 "in reviving suddenly, by a magical gift of evocation, the shades of the heroes and martyrs of '89 and '93, whose grandeur seemed a silent reproach to our pettiness and whose ardent convictions disturbed our sleep and put our inertia to shame." Victor Hugo was (for once) more succinct: he wrote in *Choses vues* that the "lively and eloquent" *Histoire des Girondins* "taught Revolution to France."[13]

---

[12] Delphine de Girardin, "Lettres parisiennes du vicomte de Launay" in *Oeuvres complètes de Madame Emile de Girardin, née Delphine Gay*, 6 vols. (Paris, 1860–1861), V, 438; "Liszt to Marie d'Agoult, July 17, 1847" in *Correspondance de Liszt et de Madame d'Agoult*, Daniel Ollivier (ed.), 2 vols. (Paris, 1933–1934), II, 388.

[13] Tocqueville, *Souvenirs*, 100; "Chateaubriand" in Henri Guillemin, *Lamartine et la question sociale* (Paris, 1946), 161. "Alexandre Dumas" in Antoine Court, *Les Girondins de Lamartine*, 2 vols. (Saint Julien-Chapteuil, 1988–1990), I, 83; Stern, *Révolution de*

So widespread was the belief of contemporaries that Lamartine's book was in some way responsible for the outbreak of revolution in France that it comes as a shock actually to read the book. The *Histoire des Girondins* is a historical melodrama which rivals Dickens' *Tale of Two Cities* and Carlyle's *French Revolution* in the attention paid to popular violence and surpasses them in its emphasis on mindless violence. It is a melodrama in which images of "*jeunes et beaux*" victims of the Terror alternate with portraits of vicious revolutionaries ranging from Marat, the personification of the "fury" of the suffering and inarticulate masses, to Antoine Simon, the brutal prison guard and torturer of the dauphin at the Temple.

When the occasion demands, Lamartine invents speeches and imagines poignant scenes for his protagonists – for Louis XVI at Varennes, for Vergniaud at the imaginary "last banquet" of the Girondins and even for Robespierre on the night of the September massacres. He lingers on the executions, repeatedly tracing the route taken by the tumbrils carrying the condemned from the Conciergerie to the Place de la Révolution. He says the historian must have pity, but his pity is generally deployed in support of royalists, starting with the well-meaning, inarticulate Louis XVI and the long-suffering Marie-Antoinette, "légère dans la prospérité, sublime dans l'infortune, intrépide sur l'échafaud."[14] And the most unambiguously positive portrait in the whole book is that of the chaste, angelic Charlotte Corday whose physical beauty, together with "the celestial beauty of her love of country" makes her a "Jeanne d'Arc de la liberté."[15]

Among the revolutionaries, two of the most positive figures – Mirabeau and Danton – are both presented as deeply flawed. Mirabeau, who gave the Revolution "form, passion, and a language," had "sold himself" to the monarchy. And Danton, in whom the "the heart of France" was beating, had everything required of a citizen except for the one thing that really mattered: virtue. Lamartine notes the energy and conviction of the Montagnards but dwells on their weakness and limitations; and except for Madame Roland and Condorcet and (sometimes) Vergniaud, the Girondins are treated critically as lightweights and "intriguers." Insofar as the book has a hero, it is not Vergniaud or any of the Girondins but rather Robespierre, who is presented as engaged in his

1848, I, 13–14; Victor Hugo, *Choses vues: Souvenirs, journaux, cahiers, 1830–1885*, Hubert Juin (ed.) (Paris, 2002), 517.

[14] Alphonse de Lamartine, *Histoire des Girondins*, Jean-Pierre Jacques (ed.), 2 vols. (Paris, 1984), II, 505.

[15] Lamartine, *Histoire des Girondins*, II, 389.

last months in a desperate struggle to contain the radical forces that he himself has done so much to unleash.

Why then were the Girondins interesting to Lamartine? Why did he call his book the *Histoire des Girondins*? The short answer is that when Lamartine chose the title in August 1843, his original plan was to focus on the period running from the opening of the Legislative Assembly (October 1, 1791) to the exclusion of the Girondins from the Convention (June 2, 1793).[16] The more illuminating answer is that for Lamartine the Girondins were negative models. They were revolutionary rhetoricians for whom politics was a matter of public gesture and private intrigue carried on "in the interest of the lettered middle class to which they belonged." They were "men imbued with the republican ideas of antiquity, when the liberty of citizens presupposed the slavery of the masses and when the republics were so many aristocracies." No wonder then that the Girondins "had a poor understanding of the Christian genius of the democratic republics of the future."[17]

The Girondins were also weak and inconsistent. They pushed for a declaration of war in the mistaken belief that it would purge the body politic and consolidate their power. They played a leading role in the overthrow of the monarchy, but they were incapable of establishing a viable republic. And during their months in power, they repeatedly compromised their principles in return for tactical gains that proved to be worthless. They voted for the execution of the king because they wrongly thought that this would gain them popular support. Like Pontius Pilate, they handed over the monarchy to the people without being convinced of its vices and handed over the king to the Jacobins without being convinced of his criminality.[18] Even at the end, on trial for their lives, they failed to confess to the "glorious crime" of having wished to moderate the Revolution but tried instead to defend themselves with individual arguments. "They only became great after having lost all hope."[19]

But what about Robespierre? Why was *he* important to Lamartine? In what ways can he be described as the "hero" of the *Histoire des Girondins*? Here the most important point is that Lamartine's Robespierre is a man of order. What he dreamed of was not the "permanent agitation in the streets" that Danton wanted but rather "the calm and orderly reign of the people personified by its representatives."[20] Far from being bloodthirsty, he was disturbed by the popular violence encouraged by Hébert and

---

[16] Court, *Les Girondins de Lamartine*, I, 63, 197–200.
[17] Lamartine, *Histoire des Girondins*, I, 772.
[18] Lamartine, *Histoire des Girondins*, II, 113.   [19] Ibid, 527.   [20] Ibid, 469.

Chaumette and the Commune de Paris. Lamartine imagines a Robespierre "tortured by the massacres of September" and as someone who saw the imposition of the legal terror as a means of ending the popular and spontaneous terror. But Lamartine's portrayal of a nonviolent Robespierre does not stop there. He represents Robespierre as having doubts – or second thoughts – about the execution of Marie-Antoinette, the Girondins, Danton and many others – though not the violent Hébertistes.

In writing the *Histoire des Girondins* Lamartine was much concerned with the lessons that might be drawn by contemporaries from the French Revolution. He put it this way at the outset of the book:

I am undertaking to write the history of a small number of men who, thrown by Providence into the midst of the greatest drama of modern times, epitomize the ideas, the passions, the errors, the virtues of the times ... This history [which is] full of blood and tears is also full of lessons for the people.[21]

What then were the lessons to be learned from Lamartine"s history?

The first, clearly, was the need to take up once again the work of 1789 – to promote democratic ideas and to establish a more lasting republic than the Republic of 1791, which the Girondins did so much to make – and to compromise. In writing the book Lamartine was consciously focusing the minds of contemporaries on one of the possible outcomes of the gathering political crisis in July Monarchy France: on the overthrow of the monarchy and on the possibilities and problems inherent in republican government.

But if Lamartine wanted to rehabilitate the French Revolution, his book was also clearly a warning against its "excesses" – and a plea to separate Revolution and Terror. He was in a nutshell arguing for a *moderate* republic, which he saw as the strongest bulwark against anarchy and popular violence. He believed that this argument could best be made by depicting the violence of the Revolution in all its horror. Lamartine said all of this – and more – in letters to friends. To Molé for example:

Don't read my [book]. It's written for the people. They are going to play a great role. We must prepare them, make them loathe violence so that the next revolution may be pure of the excesses of the first one. It is my duty to prepare the people, to prepare myself, because I will be the man of a new society.[22]

What is remarkable is that for three months in 1848 Lamartine did play the role for which he had prepared himself. The moderate republic that

---

[21] Lamartine, *Histoire des Girondins*, I, 29.
[22] Jean Lucas-Dubreton, *Lamartine* (Paris, 1951), 228.

Figure 2.2 The Duchesse d'Orléans pleads for a regency, February 24, 1848. *Illustrated London News*, March 4, 1848. Photograph: Getty

emerged from the February Revolution owed more to his efforts than to those of anyone else.

Lamartine in February

Karl Marx was scarcely exaggerating when he wrote that Lamartine "was the February Revolution itself ... with its illusions, its poetry, its imaginary content, and its phrases."[23] During the crucial first days, Lamartine was at the centre of events. On the afternoon of February 24, when word of the King's abdication had spread across Paris and a crowd had broken into the Chamber of Deputies in the Palais Bourbon, Lamartine was preparing to speak. The widow of the Duc d'Orléans, the eldest son of Louis Philippe, had come to the Chamber with her two sons to ask to be appointed regent (see Figure 2.2). A majority of the deputies were sympathetic to her claim. But the crowd was demanding the

[23] Karl Marx, *Class Struggles in France (1848–1850)* (New York, 1964), 39.

proclamation of a republic. Under the circumstances, Alexis de Tocqueville later wrote, Lamartine was the only man who could "withstand the torrent" and save the monarchy. Tocqueville whispered to him: "We are losing ... Go to the rostrum and speak."[24] In his own account of these events, Lamartine asserted that he might indeed have brought the crowd around to monarchy. He even included in his *Histoire de la Révolution de 1848* a portion of the speech he might have given.[25] But he explained that he feared that the proclamation of a regency would provoke violent resistance. In fact, he had already declared his support for a republic.

That morning, at a meeting in the office of *Le National,* an understanding had been reached concerning the formation of a provisional government. Lamartine did not attend this meeting, but with Paris in the hands of insurgents, he let it be known that he was ready to join a provisional government.[26] Thus, once on the rostrum, and after paying tribute to the courage of the duchesse, he called for a government that would bring an end to the "terrible misunderstanding" that had long existed between the different classes and then asked for the constitution of a provisional government.[27] The list of names, which had already been drawn up, was read out, first by the elderly Dupont de l'Eure, who could not be heard, and then by the leather-lunged Ledru-Rollin. The crowd roared: "No more Bourbons! ... We want a republic!" But the Chamber was now overrun with demonstrators, and the noise was deafening. Pikes, guns, and swords were waved; a demonstrator ordered the president of the Chamber to remove his hat out of respect for the people; another aimed his gun at Lamartine, thinking he was Guizot; an apprentice butcher, covered with blood, approached the rostrum brandishing a large cutlass. Finally, Ledru-Rollin declared that seven names had been approved by acclamation, and voices cried out: "To the Hôtel de Ville!"[28]

The Hôtel de Ville, the seat of the municipal government, recently renovated at great expense by Louis Philippe, was located in the heart of working-class Paris just outside the Faubourg Saint-Antoine. It was the one public building in the capital to which the poor were unequivocally

---

[24] Tocqueville, *Souvenirs*, 95. See also L'Huillier, *Lamartine en politique*, 177–178.

[25] Lamartine, *Histoire de la Révolution de 1848*, 2 vols. (Paris, 1849), I, 201–204.

[26] Stern, *Révolution de 1848*, I, 211, 224–225; Tocqueville, *Souvenirs*, 451–452.

[27] Stern, *Révolution de 1848*, I, 223–230.

[28] Lamartine, *Révolution de 1848*, I, 229–231; Hippolyte Castille, *Histoire de la Seconde République*, 4 vols. (Paris, 1854–1856), I, 283–292; William Fortescue, *Alphonse de Lamartine: A Political Biography* (London, 1983), 141–142. See also *Le Moniteur universel, Journal official de la République française,* February 25, 1848, 500–502; and Maurizio Gribaudi and Michèle Riot-Sarcey, *1848, la Révolution oubliée* (Paris, 2009), 61–65.

attached. And it was in the square in front of the Hôtel de Ville, the Place de Grève, that revolutions of Paris had traditionally been ratified.[29] Thus, with the crowd at their heels and preceded by two drummers and a tricolor flag, Lamartine and other members of the self-appointed provisional government hurried along the quays and across the Seine to the Hôtel de Ville. They quickly acquired an escort of about 500 people – National Guards, students, workers, well-dressed bourgeois – many of them armed. When they reached the Place de Grève, they found it packed with a boisterous, agitated crowd and they had difficulty making their way into the Hôtel de Ville.[30]

From the balcony of the Hôtel de Ville Lamartine and his colleagues proclaimed the Provisional Government. Then they barricaded themselves in a conference room with a dozen students from the Ecole Polytechnique standing guard. By candlelight, they allotted cabinet positions. The venerable Dupont de l'Eure, who had served both the Directory and the Bourbon Restoration as a legislator, was unanimously elected president. The radical republican Ledru-Rollin, a founder of the journal *La Réforme*, was given the Ministry of the Interior, while Lamartine was made Minister of Foreign Affairs with the understanding that he would exercise real authority. Other positions were given to the famous astronomer, François Arago, and to the moderate republicans Pierre Marie, Adolphe Crémieux, Louis-Antoine Garnier-Pagès and Armand Marrast.Further negotiations resulted in the addition in subordinate positions of the democrat Flocon, the socialist Louis Blanc and Blanc's protegé, the artisan Alexandre Martin, also known as Albert (see Figure 2.3).[31] The atmosphere inside the Hôtel de Ville was chaotic, and the Provisional Government was repeatedly interrupted by delegations demanding shorter working hours, better wage rates and an end to unemployment and poverty. As the night wore on, they began to issue proclamations, announcing them to the crowd outside on the Place de Grève. The most important, drafted by Lamartine, stated that "a reactionary and oligarchical government" had been overthrown, and declared with studied vagueness that "the republican form" had been provisionally adopted until such time as the nation could be consulted."[32]

The next morning, February 25, a large crowd gathered in front of the Hôtel de Ville calling on the Provisional Government to guarantee the

---

[29] Charles Tilly, *The Contentious French* (Cambridge, MA, 1986), 41–61.
[30] Stern, *Révolution de 1848*, I, 235–238; Castille, *Séconde République*, I, 293–297.
[31] Stern, *Révolution de 1848*, I, 249–250, 254–255.
[32] Stern, *Révolution de 1848*, I, 251–252.

Figure 2.3 The Provisional Government, engraving by Achille Devéria, 1848. Hilton Archive via Getty.
Front (from left): François Arago, Ledru-Rollin, Dupont de l'Eure, Marie, Lamartine.
Rear: Louis Blanc, Flocon, Crémieux, Marrast, Albert (Alexandre Martin), Garnier-Pagès.

rights of workers within the new republic. Shortly after noon, an armed delegation of workers forced their way into the meeting room and demanded that the Provisional Government take concrete steps toward "the organization of labour," the first step being the publication of a decree guaranteeing "the right to work." Marie d'Agoult paints a vivid picture of the ensuing exchange:

A man entered, gun in hand; his face was pale and contorted; his lips trembled with rage. He advanced boldly right up to the work table and, pounding the floor with the butt of his gun, he pointed toward the Place de Grève ... Everyone was silent.[33]

The worker's commanding presence was both an insult and a threat to the members of the Provisional Government. But his brazen challenge

---

[33] Stern, *Révolution de 1848*, II, 38. For the whole episode see Rémi Gossez, *Les Ouvriers de Paris* (Paris, 1967), 10–14.

left them "overcome by astonishment and a certain respect." A group of workers stood behind him without speaking a word. For Lamartine and his colleagues, there was "something solemn" about the situation.

Finally, the worker broke the silence. According to Marie d'Agoult, whose account is the most reliable we have, he declared in a firm voice that he had come, in the name of the people, to call upon the government to proclaim *the right to work*:

While speaking in this way, Marche – that was the name of the working-class orator – stared boldly at Lamartine with his large eyes gleaming. He did this no doubt to make Lamartine understand that he suspected him, more than the others, of betraying the cause of the people. Lamartine understood this. Approaching the worker, he tried to lull him with honeyed words [*caresses oratoires*]. But no sooner had Lamartine begun speaking than Marche interrupted him. "Enough fancy talk, Monsieur de Lamartine [*Assez de phrases comme cela.*]" he exclaimed ironically. "Enough poetry. The people don't want any more of that. They are the masters, and they order you to decree the right to work without delay."[34]

At this point, Lamartine adopted a peremptory tone. His colleagues could do what they wished, he said, but he would never sign a decree that he could not understand. Then, speaking more softly, he put his hand on the back of the worker. Granting that the desires of the people were legitimate, he again turned on the flow of eloquence. The situation of the government was critical, he said, and the problem was complex. It could not be resolved by a simple decree.

This time Lamartine's language found its mark. As the words rolled off his tongue, "Marche, confused, hesitant, moved, agitated, beaten, turned toward the workers who had entered the room with him, as if to seek their advice." And they, more by gesture than by words, urged Marche not to insist. "Well, alright," he exclaimed at last, "we'll wait. We have confidence in the government since it has confidence in us. The people will wait. We will place three months of poverty in the service of the government."[35]

But this was not the end of the discussion of the right to work. For while Lamartine was dissuading the workers from insisting on a premature decree, and while they were expressing their willingness to wait, the socialist Louis Blanc, was drafting a decree with the help of Ledru-Rollin and Flocon:

The Provisional Government commits itself to guaranteeing the livelihood of the worker through work. It commits itself to guaranteeing work to all citizens. It

[34] Stern, *Révolution de 1848*, II, 39.
[35] Ibid, 40; Castille, *Seconde République*, I, 332–336.

recognizes that the workers should form associations among themselves to enjoy the legitimate benefits of their work.[36]

To make good on this commitment the government announced the next day the establishment of a program of National Workshops to provide government-financed work for the unemployed. And, on February 28, in response to demonstrations demanding a government ministry to direct the labour force and intervene in the economy, the Provisional Government agreed to create a commission of workers' representatives which would meet in the Luxembourg Palace under Louis Blanc's direction to discuss workers' grievances and how to remedy them. But the Luxembourg Commission had no budget and no formal legislative powers.

It has often been pointed out that in issuing its decree on the right to work, the Provisional Government was making a promise it could not possibly keep.[37] Lamartine himself admitted later that the creation of the National Workshops was "a temporary expedient, terrible but necessary."[38] It also seems that the moderate majority in the Provisional Government meant the National Workshops to fail. By giving them a name close to Louis Blanc's "social workshops" and by making Blanc the director of a powerless Luxembourg Commission to oversee workers' problems, they apparently intended that the failure of the program would compromise Louis Blanc's socialism.[39] And what about Lamartine? He had spoken fervently against Louis Blanc's ideas. Why did he sign the decree? Was he aware that it placed the government in a difficult position, but counted on the power of his oratory to manage the situation? Did he even read the decree before signing it? Was he, as Marie d'Agoult suggests, so satisfied with his day's work (and his oratorical success) that he would sign anything?[40]

Later on, as night was beginning to fall, Lamartine and his government faced one more serious challenge. A crowd gathered again on the Place de Grève, calling on the Provisional Government to demonstrate its

---

[36] *Moniteur universel*, February 25; Stern, *Révolution de 1848*, II, 41. For Blanc's position see his *Histoire de la Révolution de 1848*, 2 vols. (Bruxelles, 1870) I, 133.

[37] Castille, *Seconde République*, I, 334–335; Stern, *Révolution de 1848*, II, 37–38.

[38] Lamartine, *Révolution de 1848*, II, 123.

[39] Mark Traugott, "Les Ateliers Nationaux en 1848" in Jean-Luc Mayaud (ed.), *1848: Actes du Colloque International du Cent Cinquantenaire* (Paris, 2002), 185–202; Donald McKay, *The National Workshops* (Cambridge, MA, 1933), 11–13.

[40] Stern, *Révolution de 1848*, II, 41. For an interpretation more sympathetic to Lamartine, see Francis Démier, "Droit au travail et organization du travail en 1848" in Mayaud (ed.), *1848: Actes du Colloque*, 159–183.

commitment to the establishment of republican government by adopting a red flag. They asserted that the tricolor flag, first adopted by the revolutionary government in 1792 and then brought back in 1830, had been stripped of its prestige by the corrupt July Monarchy. They were supported by Louis Blanc. Lamartine, on the other hand, argued for the retention of the tricolor and had the support of the moderate majority in the Provisional Government. He then took on the perilous task of persuading the crowd, which was armed and determined not to let the government "steal" the revolution, as it had been stolen from them in1830. At this point, Lamartine's eloquence served him well. Appearing on the balcony of the Hôtel de Ville on five separate occasions, he argued forcefully that the tricolor flag, which had been carried "around the world" by the revolutionary and Napoleonic armies, was their national flag, whereas the red flag was soaked in the blood of civil war. Finally, he won over the crowd.[41]

At the end of the day, surely one of the most gratifying days in his public life, Lamartine was exhausted. But later he found time to write his niece Valentine a detailed account of his role in "founding the Republic" and the "universal adoration" of which he was now the object. And he wrote a letter to an old friend that reads like a battle report written by a victorious general after a spectacularly successful encounter.[42] The task now of course was to give substance to the new Republic.

One vital step in that direction was taken the next day when the Provisional Government issued a decree, proposed and drafted by Lamartine, abolishing the death penalty for political offences. This decree, which reflected his passionate desire to ensure that there would be no terror under the Second Republic, was welcomed by journals of almost all parties. Lamartine played an important role in the drafting of two other documents: a decree issued on March 2 formally established elections by universal manhood suffrage for a National Constituent Assembly, and a directive to French diplomats issued on March 4 simultaneously placated French republicans by denying the validity of the treaties signed at the Congress of Vienna in 1815, and reassured existing governments by adding that as a practical matter the status quo would be respected. France would not attack its neighbours, but would, if appealed to, come to the aid of oppressed people struggling for freedom.

[41] Stern *Révolution de 1848*, II, 16–23.
[42] "To Valentine de Cessiat, February 27, 1848, and to Charles Rolland, February [28 or 29], 1848" in *Correspondance d'Alphonse de Lamartine (1830–1867)*, Christian Croisille (ed.), 7 vols. (Paris, 2000–2004), V, 255–257, 261–262.

Guiding the Revolution: The Failure of a Strategy

For two months Lamartine enjoyed a kind of popularity that had few precedents in the history of French political culture. An admiring crowd followed him home on the evening of February 25 and would not disperse until he was too exhausted to speak. On the 26th admirers mobbed him as he left the Hôtel de Ville; and on the 27th he escaped the crowd only by taking refuge in Victor Hugo's house on the Place des Vosges. A few days later the erection of a column in his honour was suggested for the Place de la Concorde, and the rue Coquenard in the eleventh arrondissement was renamed rue Lamartine. Glowing tributes to Lamartine's "splendid conduct," his "generous ideas" and his "inspired language" appeared in the conservative Le Correspondant; the Fourierist Victor Considerant praised Lamartine as "the living incarnation of harmony"; and the critic Sainte-Beuve wrote on February 29 that Lamartine "has been great during the journées and has done honour to "la nature poétique." Even Marshal Bugeaud, who had commanded the troops defending the July Monarchy on February 24, paid tribute later to Lamartine's "generous sentiments."[43]

This was only the beginning. For the next two months, Lamartine was celebrated for bringing the nation together and keeping the revolution on a moderate course. His apotheosis came on April 23 with the elections for the National Assembly. The electoral system adopted – scrutin de liste départemental – meant that votes were counted by department and each voter could select a number of representatives proportional to the population of his department. There were no residential requirements and no limit was placed on multiple candidatures – with the result that Lamartine's name was placed on the ballot in eleven different departments. The turnout was massive: 84 percent of the eligible voters actually cast ballots. In the end, Lamartine was elected in ten departments, receiving a total of 1,283,501 votes.[44]

What was the basis of Lamartine's extraordinary success in the April elections? He was widely seen as the most prominent moderate republican within the Provisional Government. But his main support came not only from moderate republicans, who favoured democratic political changes, but also from conservatives who believed that he would exert a powerful restraining influence on democrats and socialists. As Tocqueville put it, "To all of those whom the revolution harmed or

---

[43] Fortescue, Lamartine, 162–163; Victor Considerant, Le Socialisme devant. Le vieux monde (Paris, 1848), 92.
[44] For details see Fortescue, Lamartine, 164–165.

frightened," Lamartine appeared "as a saviour." "They were expecting him to put himself unhesitatingly at their head in order to attack and destroy the socialists."[45] Lamartine understood this. When Caussidière urged him to get rid of the moderates in the Provisional Government, he replied: "The 1,500,000 votes that I have just received were given to me only because I offered guarantees of peace and order."[46] But here lay a problem that Lamartine himself was slow to recognize. If he owed his electoral success in part to the fears of conservatives, these fears were greatly reduced by the outcome of the elections. For despite Lamartine's personal triumph, the elections were above all a triumph – not for the moderate republicans but for the conservative *notables* who had tradition-ally dominated French society. The representatives elected in April included 75 nobles or former peers and 439 former monarchists as opposed to just 55 radicals and socialists and 231 moderate republic-ans.[47] What this shows is that after April 23 conservatives no longer needed the check provided by Lamartine against radicals and socialists.

Prior to the election, conservatives already had doubts about Lamartine. His behaviour on the murky *journées* of March 17 and April 16 had raised questions in the minds of both monarchists and moderate republicans about where his real sympathies lay. After the huge popular demonstration of March 17, calling for the postponement of the elec-tions, Lamartine met individually with leading radicals including Blanqui, Barbès, Cabet and Raspail, and he gave help and protection to radical clubs such as Sobrier's Club des Clubs.[48] A month later, as radicals planned a second demonstration, Lamartine sent agents to their clubs to try to moderate their activities; and on April 15 he summoned Auguste Blanqui to the Foreign Ministry on the Boulevard des Capucines at dawn for a second private meeting, which lasted three hours. He was apparently trying (successfully as it turned out) to dis-suade Blanqui from participating in the demonstration. But to conserva-tives it seemed that Lamartine was playing a double game, and he was soon accused of having "conspired" with Blanqui and Sobrier[49]

The suspicions of the Right were reinforced in early May by Lamartine's insistence that Ledru-Rollin be included in the Executive Commission that replaced the Provisional Government after the election

[45] Tocqueville, *Souvenirs*, 174.
[46] Marc Caussidière, *Mémoires de Caussidière*, 2 vols. (Paris, 1849) II, 81.
[47] Frederick A. de Luna, *The French Republic under Cavaignac, 1848* (Princeton, 1969), 107–113.
[48] Fortescue, *Lamartine*, 159.
[49] Guillemin, *Lamartine en 1848* (Paris, 1948), 46–48; Stern, *Révolution de 1848*, II, 161–163; L'Huillier, 186–187, 193.

of the National Assembly. Why did Lamartine insist on including Ledru-Rollin in the Executive Commission? What mystified contemporaries was that Lamartine and Ledru-Rollin had been widely assumed to represent two antagonistic poles within the Provisional Government. Many conservatives supported the moderate republican Lamartine precisely because they saw him as a counter-weight to the radical democrat Ledru-Rollin. They found it hard to interpret Lamartine's support of Ledru-Rollin as anything other than a self-interested political calculation. They saw it as an attempt to guarantee his political future in case the Left gained power, or as an attempt to get republican support in a possible presidential campaign. It is likely, however, that Lamartine was genuinely committed to the idea that the "concord" of widely diverse factions was the only foundation on which a lasting republic could be built in France. As he told a deputation on March 19: "Previous republics were in effect, partisan republics; we want this republic to be the republic of the entire nation."[50]

Lamartine's problem, in the polarized political landscape of May and June, was – as William Fortescue has argued – that he never stopped trying "to be popular among all classes, satisfy practically every shade of opinion, and win the support of nearly all political groups. With equal enthusiasm he sought the approval of Paris *salons* and revolutionary clubs."[51] He attempted simultaneously to please the radical Joseph Sobrier and the conservative British aristocrat Lord Normanby. On April 16, he welcomed National Guardsmen – who were shouting "Death to the Communists! Death to Cabet!" – but the next day he offered Cabet and his wife refuge in his Paris apartment. Likewise, he was constantly at odds with Louis Blanc, but at a Provisional Government meeting on April 19, he vigorously opposed Blanc's arrest. "Altogether," Fortescue concludes, Lamartine "was continually laboring to achieve a general reconciliation." This desire to win the approval of both the salons and the revolutionary clubs "accorded with his belief in social *fraternité* and political harmony."[52] But it compromised him in the eyes of conservatives.

Lamartine was further compromised by his inability to contain popular unrest on May 15. On that day a debate was scheduled in the National Assembly on the question of French support for Polish independence. A march on the Assembly was organized to deliver a petition on behalf of the Poles. But this turned into an attempt to overthrow the newly elected government. The Assembly was invaded by a huge crowd, and in the

[50] *Le Moniteur universel* (March 20, 1848), 644, in Fortescue, *Lamartine*, 172.
[51] Fortescue, *Lamartine*, 172.   [52] Ibid, 173.

ensuing chaos a radical orator named Aloysius Huber, who was subsequently shown to have been employed as a police spy during the July
Monarchy, got control of the rostrum and shouted at the top of his lungs:
"Citizens, the National Assembly is dissolved!" After more confusion,
the crowd poured out of the Assembly and the insurgents headed for the
Hôtel de Ville, the traditional setting for the proclamation of revolutionary governments. Few actually reached the Hôtel de Ville though, for
they were intercepted by the National Guard. The Guard rapidly surrounded the Assembly and arrested the remaining insurgents along with
others whose principal crime was to be known as prominent figures on
the Left.

The abortive insurrection of May 15 played so nicely into the hands of
the reaction that it has been argued that the whole thing was a trap – in
Henri Guillemin's words, "a well-executed police operation."[53] However
that may be, May 15 compromised radicals and got many of their leaders
arrested. By nightfall Barbès, Albert and Raspail were in police custody;
Blanqui was in hiding; and Louis Blanc, who had been unwillingly
carried in triumph by the insurgents, had been deeply compromised.
Lamartine was not implicated in the coup. But May 15 was not a good
day for him either. After trying unsuccessfully to calm the unrest in
the Assembly, he disappeared. Later he joined a National Guard unit
rounding up insurgents near the Hôtel de Ville. Afterwards, returning to
the Assembly, he was recognized and cheered by soldiers and guardsmen. This caused him to believe that his reputation would emerge
untarnished from this episode.[54] He was wrong.

In fact, the Assembly had lost confidence in the Executive
Commission; and Lamartine was now regarded with suspicion by many
leaders of the Party of Order. "You cannot imagine," wrote Thiers to
Bugeaud, "all the vile tricks, the stupid intrigues, and the double games
that Monsieur de Lamartine is up to."[55] The *Revue des deux mondes* shed
crocodile tears over the spectacle of Lamartine's loss of the prestige that
he had enjoyed in February before "turning his back" on "reasonable
people."[56] On May 22, Xavier Marmier summed up the feelings of many
conservatives when he noted in his journal: "We need a leader. M. de
Lamartine could have been this leader, but his alliance with Ledru-Rollin
and his inexplicable attitude toward recent events have cost him his

---

[53] Henri Guillemin, *La Première résurrection de la République*, (Paris, 1967), 352.
[54] L'Huillier, *Lamartine en politique*, 192; Henri Guillemin, *Lamartine en 1848*, 64 and see
62–65 for a comprehensive account of Lamartine's role on May 15.
[55] Cited in Guillemin, *Lamartine en 1848*, 65.
[56] *Revue des deux mondes* in L'Huillier, *Lamartine en politique*, 193.

popularity."[57] Lamartine himself began to lose hope. "I'm going to resign," he wrote the journalist Alphonse Karr on May 18, "because if I don't quit in three days, they will get rid of me in four."

The collapse of Lamartine's support in the National Assembly became evident on June 12, when he attempted to speak about the danger represented by Louis-Napoleon Bonaparte's victory in the by-elections of June 4. The Assembly was much more interested in attacking Lamartine than in listening to his warning about Louis-Napoleon. Hecklers interrupted him to shout out the names of radicals with whom he was accused of conspiring. "Yes, no doubt," replied Lamartine, "I conspired with these men, I conspired with Sobrier, I conspired with Blanqui, I conspired with several other people. Do you know how I conspired? I conspired the way a lightning rod conspires with lightning!"[58] The image was striking. But it was lost on the Assembly.

What brought matters to a head was the question of the National Workshops. By early June it was evident that the leaders of the National Assembly were determined to liquidate the Workshops. Lamartine hoped arrangements could be made to help the dismissed workers. But a majority in the Assembly, led by Falloux, was determined that the liquidation of the Workshops should take place without delay, whatever the consequences might be. Not surprisingly, once the termination of the Workshops was announced on June 21, crowds gathered and barricades began to rise in the working-class quarters of Paris.

There was nothing in Paris' past to equal the ferocity of the fighting that marked the workers' revolt that began on June 23. The "June Days" were all over by noon on June 26, but in the course of those four days, a battle was fought in the streets of Paris that left thousands dead and culminated with the arrest of some 15,000 insurgents. The June Days left a scar on the memory of almost everyone who lived through them. One reason for this was the sheer magnitude of the event. Some 50,000 men and women, the whole of eastern Paris it seemed, took up arms against the government; and the force deployed against them was twice as large by the end of the fighting. What made the June insurrection unforgettable, though, was what contemporaries took to be its class character. It made a mockery of Lamartine's hope that the Second French Republic could transcend class divisions to become "everybody's government."

If the June Days marked the end of the dream of a republic of fraternity and concord, they also marked the end of Lamartine's prominence in French public life. On June 23, the first day of the insurrection and

---

[57] Xavier Marmier, *Journal: 1848–1890*, Eldon Kaye (ed.), 2 vols. (Genève, 1968), I, 128.
[58] Maurice Toesca, *Lamartine ou l'amour de la vie* (Paris, 1969), 451.

Lamartine's last full day in power, a conflict arose between the Executive Commission and General Eugène Cavaignac who had been appointed commander of the government troops in Paris that morning. The Executive Commission wanted every barricade to be attacked as soon as it was built. Cavaignac wanted to wait until the revolt was fully developed and only then to unleash a massive attack on the insurgents. Cavaignac's strategy, which would lead to much higher casualties, meant that there was little actual fighting on June 23. But Lamartine, who with his fellow members of the Executive Commission was still nominally in charge, felt that he had to do something. That evening around 6 pm, accompanied by two *représentants du peuple*, he rode on horseback to the Boulevard du Temple and tried to talk with the insurgents manning the barricades there. He might have been shot, and he later claimed that at that moment he imagined a martyr's death for himself.[59] But when the insurgents recognized him, they put down their arms. He appealed to them to give up the fight, which they refused to do. When he returned home, his secretary described him as "overwhelmed, pale and defeated."[60]

The following day, June 24, the National Assembly voted to declare a state of siege and to give absolute power to General Cavaignac. With this, the Executive Commission ceased to exist. Henceforth Lamartine was just one of 900 representatives. But he suffered from more than a loss of status. As Maurice Toesca has written, "The June Days broke Lamartine's will."[61]

Visitors to Lamartine in July reported that he was passive and fatalistic but not without hope. He and his wife had retired to the outskirts of Paris, renting a villa in the Bois de Boulogne. When the Russian mystic Madame Swetchine visited him there, she found him unaccountably "calm, serene, confidant in the future" – not only the country's future but his own as well. She didn't know whether to attribute this to thoughtlessness, pride, or illusion. For he was now blamed for everything that went wrong from February to June: for the failure to maintain law and order in Paris, for the 45 percent increase in property taxes, and for the ongoing economic crisis. In July he had to testify at length before the commission of enquiry established by the National Assembly to investigate the *journée* of May 15 and the June insurrection. He was also obliged to defend his conduct of foreign policy before the Assembly's foreign affairs committee.

[59] Lamartine, *Révolution de 1848*, II, 484.
[60] Toesca, *Lamartine*, 455; Guillemin, *Lamartine en 1848*, 75–79.
[61] Toesca, *Lamartine*, 456.

Forced repeatedly to justify himself, Lamartine finally took his case to the public with a pamphlet addressed to the voters in the departments that had elected him in April. In this pamphlet (completed August 25) he responded to attacks on his personal ambition, his radical sympathies, and his weakness in defence of law and order. He claimed that the July Monarchy had fallen of its own weight – not as the result of a conspiracy to which he had been a party. He argued that the proclamation of the Second Republic had been essential to maintain order and that he had done everything possible to limit violence.[62]

In his own politics, Lamartine moved to the right after June. The insurrection reinforced his old fears of popular disorder. He broke decisively with Ledru-Rollin and developed a more critical view of France's revolutionary tradition. He continued to think of himself as a moderate republican. But he believed that France had more to fear from continuing popular unrest than from military dictatorship or Bonapartism. So he presented himself as someone who had saved France from a new Terror and the dictatorship of the Paris clubs.[63]

In September Lamartine returned to public life. He participated actively in the National Assembly's debate over the constitution, arguing for a single-chamber legislature and a strong popularly elected executive. He spoke eloquently against the amendment proposed by Jules Grévy which would have given executive power to the head of a council of ministers appointed by the National Assembly. France needed a popularly elected president, he argued, a president who could stand apart from the Assembly and pursue an independent course. Did Lamartine take this view because he had not yet abandoned his own presidential aspirations? Possibly. His enemies, including Falloux, suspected as much. What is beyond doubt is that Lamartine's speeches in support of the popular election of the president helped set the stage for the election of Louis-Napoleon Bonaparte and the eventual overthrow of the Second Republic.[64]

In October, on returning to Mâcon after the legislative session, Lamartine got caught up in a round of receptions, dinners, speeches and visits. His continuing local popularity convinced him that he still had a role to play on the national stage. Thus he allowed himself to become a candidate in December's presidential election. But his candidacy was curiously half-hearted. It was only on November 30 that he made a formal announcement.[65] And he refused to issue a program or

---

[62] *Lettre aux dix départements* in Lamartine, *Trois mois au pouvoir* (Paris, 1848).
[63] Fortescue, *Lamartine*, 244.   [64] Fortescue, *Lamartine*, 241–243.
[65] "A divers journaux, November 30, 1848," *Correspondance de Lamartine*, V, 530–531.

manifesto, or even to campaign in any meaningful way. "I don't desire the presidency of the Republic," he wrote a friend. "I would find the burden too heavy. I pray God to impose it on others." But if he were called upon, he added, "no human consideration would cause me to hesitate."[66] By the end of November it was clear, perhaps even to him, that he would not be called upon. But he could not bring himself to withdraw.

The night before the presidential election Lamartine had dinner with friends at the Restaurant Véry in the Palais Royal. He was recognized by passers-by and a crowd gathered. When he left the restaurant, they burst into spontaneous applause. A few days later, Lamartine proudly described the incident to his niece Valentine. But that evening, as the first results were published, it became clear that he would receive only a pitiful handful of votes. He wrote his niece that he felt "an unspeakable joy" and that he had "feared the presidency more than death itself." But he could not contain himself from inveighing against "the darkest, stupidest and most universal ingratitude" on the part of "the bourgeoisie and the nobility whom I have shielded with my body for three months on end and whom I alone have saved."[67] A visitor on December 15 described him as having "aged frightfully" in just a few weeks.[68]

On December 20, the results were announced to the National Assembly. Louis-Napoleon Bonaparte won 5,534,520 votes. His nearest rival, Eugène Cavaignac, received 1,448,302. Ledru-Rollin, the candidate of the Left, received 371,431, and Raspail got a smattering of votes. At the bottom of the list came Lamartine with a grand total of 17,914 votes. Victor Hugo noted in his journal that when Lamartine's total was read out, the representatives on the Right "burst out laughing."[69]

Although he claimed not to care, Lamartine was bitterly disappointed. He felt humiliated and betrayed by those who had hailed him as a saviour in February. He was apparently offered a post in Louis-Napoleon's government, but this did not interest him. He did try, however, to play a role in politics through political journalism. In April 1849, he began to publish a monthly journal called *Le Conseiller du Peuple* which sought to

[66] "To Marie-Louis de Marcellus, November 1, 1848," *Correspondance de Lamartine*, V, 502.

[67] "To Valentine de Cessiat, December 11, 1848," *Correspondance de Lamartine*, V, 536.

[68] Marie d'Agoult, *Journal*, December 15, 1848: "Petetin vient de voir Lamartine [qui] est affligé de cette ingratitude du people. Il vieillit d'une manière effrayante, s'est fait d'immenses illusions": BNF NAF 14326.

[69] Fortescue *Lamartine*, 247–248. I follow Fortescue for the numbers, taken from *Le Moniteur universel* for December 22. The numbers read out to the Assembly were slightly different.

"enlighten, moderate, instruct and advise" the literate but poorly educated masses. This gave him the opportunity to try his hand at writing fiction for ordinary working people. He also wrote a monthly political editorial in which, assuming the voice of "a simple citizen," he celebrated "the people" and inveighed against "the men of faction and violence" who "wanted to impose on us ... a partisan, vengeful, expropriating and bloody republic, along with the red flag." Although never highly popular, this journal had a modest success, its circulation rising from 5000 in April 1849 to 40,000 in October 1850.[70]

In the legislative elections of May 1849, Lamartine ran on a conservative ticket and lost. Thus, for the first time since 1833, he had no role at all in national political life. He won back his seat in the by-elections of July and remained in the Assembly for the next two years. But his main concern after his fall from power was the writing of a book that would tell his story of the revolution of 1848 and justify the role he played in it.

Autobiography as History

Lamartine wrote the *Histoire de la Révolution de 1848* in just a few months. During his four months in power he had had no time to take notes, and when he sat down to write at his rented villa in the Bois de Boulogne, he had few sources to work with apart from his memories and copies of his speeches and reports. But this hardly mattered to him, as he wanted to move fast. He knew that other histories of 1848 were on the way, and he wanted to get his book out before theirs. (In fact his was the first major history of 1848 to appear.) Of course, he wanted to explain himself and to justify his role. But he still hoped that his political career was not over. If the French only understood how much he had done for them, he believed that he might be called back to a position of leadership. Thus he was generous in his comments about everyone who might be in a position to help him make a political comeback. Thus too he had no desire to make a definitive judgment on the final significance of the revolution of 1848. He preferred to regard the Second French Republic as a work in progress.

In writing his history of the revolution of 1848, then, Lamartine chose not to see the revolution as a failure, and chose not to write in the tragic or pathetic mode that many later historians of the Second Republic would adopt. He had been marginalized after June, and his halfhearted presidential candidacy in December had made him an object of ridicule

---

[70] *Conseiller du peuple*, I, 1, 16, 250.

in some quarters. But he himself saw things differently. In telling his story
of 1848 he focused on his dream of a moderate republic and his effort to
give substance to that dream by channelling the energies of "the people"
in constructive directions. He believed that this effort had not been
irremediably compromised by the June insurrection. It was simply necessary to repeat again and again the story of his own successful efforts to
reach out to the people, to guide them, and to speak for them. There
were "lessons" to be learned from his three months in power, and the
first of these lessons concerned the need to find peaceful, non-violent
means of breaking down the barriers that separated "the people" from
the educated elite in France.

This said, the fact remains that Lamartine's *Histoire de la Révolution de
1848* is a very strange book. This is not because Lamartine takes positions
that are in themselves odd or surprising. What is strange is the disparity
between the book's form and its content. It purports to be a history of
1848; in fact, it is a self-congratulatory memoir. The central figure is
Lamartine himself, and episodes in which he does not appear, or plays a
modest role, are given short shrift. Half the book, the whole first volume,
is devoted to the first three days of the revolution when Lamartine was at
the centre of events. In treating the period after his fall from power he
quickly loses interest. The June Days receive only cursory treatment, and
the book concludes with Lamartine's last official act as a member of the
Executive Commission on June 24. Thus it is a highly personal history,
but at the same time it is written from an Olympian perspective. The
author situates himself above the fray and refers to "Lamartine" always in
the third person, which creates an oddly comic effect in passages describing Lamartine's feats of bravery and his brilliant oratory. In his narrative
of February 25 he pictures himself speaking, "his clothing torn, his head
bare, his forehead covered with sweat," as he wins over the crowd to the
tricolor flag. He records speeches that "Lamartine" might have given,
and he traces the process whereby "the name of Lamartine" acquired "a
sort of inviolability" in the eyes of the people of Paris.[71]

In a somewhat embarrassed preface Lamartine acknowledges the disparity between his desire to write history in "the lapidary and impersonal
style of the Greeks and Romans" and his focus on "the personal role that
I played in events." Perhaps, he admits, he was wrong to call this work a
"history." He claims that he only recognized the problem when he was
halfway through the first volume, but by then it was too late to adopt a
more familiar mode of writing,[72] The text actually includes a number of

[71] Lamartine, *Révolution de 1848*, I, 201–204, 385–386; II, 5.
[72] Lamartine, *Révolution de 1848*, I, "Préface," unpaginated.

the same stylistic and rhetorical features that marked the *Histoire des Girondins*: the remarkable pictoral sense, the impressive *tableaux* of great moments, the use of oceanic metaphors to describe the "storm-tossed," "sinking," and even "drowning" members of the Provisional Government, and the "flood," the "tides," the "torrents," the "undulations" and the "waves" of the crowd as it "inundated" the Place de Grève.[73] What is most surprising about the book is the contrast between the vividness of the language and the ineptness of Lamartine's attempts at explanation. Why the failure of the effort to build a moderate republic? Why his own rapid loss of popularity? He really can't tell us. Why the surge of support for Louis-Napoleon in the summer of 1848? The only explanation that Lamartine gives is that the name of Napoleon was popular in France.[74]

A particularly striking feature of Lamartine's book is the theatrical character of the writing. The metaphor of the theatre – so prevalent in much of the writing on 1848 – is not especially prominent. But Lamartine does offer careful descriptions of décors and clothing, succinct sketches of the actors (minor as well as major), long extracts from speeches (usually his own), snatches of dialogue, and dramatic confrontations. Many scenes are played out in half-darkness – such as the initial meeting of the Provisional Government during which the atmosphere inside the Hôtel de Ville is "thickened" by the smoke from gas lamps and the candles give off a "sinister" light.[75] The character sketches are done with stylish ostentation: the writing is studded with balanced phrases and elegant epigrams that call attention to the cleverness of the writer. But the net effect is often bland and cloying. Thus he writes of Louis Philippe: "Nature made this prince upright and moderate; exile and experience made him politically astute." And we learn that Crémieux was "the tender advisor of the Duchesse d'Orléans in the morning, and of the Republic in the evening." Unlike Tocqueville, whose most wicked comments were reserved for his political allies, Lamartine saved most of his criticism for those with whom he did not agree, but there again the criticism is often banal and vague. Of Louis Blanc, for example, he writes: "The heart of Louis Blanc burst in fraternal sentiments, his speech in images, but his system in darkness."[76]

The blandness and banality of Lamartine's judgments surely derived in part from his desire to write history in the decorous and "somewhat

---

[73] For example: Lamartine, *Révolution de 1848*, I, 214, 251–255, 284, 313, 336, 359, 388; II, 206.
[74] Lamartine, *Révolution de 1848*, II, 462.   [75] Lamartine, *Révolution de 1848*, I, 299.
[76] Lamartine, *Révolution de 1848*, I, 7, 239; II, 60.

solemn manner of antiquity." He did not want to debase himself by attacking his contemporaries or discussing their peccadillos. Nor did he wish to make enemies who might hinder a possible political comeback. Thus he flatters almost everyone – sometimes with what one critic describes as "dithyrambic exaggeration."[77] All the members of the Provisional Government (including Louis Blanc!) are talented, well-meaning, incorruptible and even handsome. Armand Marrast is perhaps "less well endowed by nature," but his wit, eloquence and good heart compensate for his physical shortcomings. Under a rustic exterior Ferdinand Flocon possesses "a heart incapable of yielding to fear, but always ready to give way to pity." Odilon Barrot is "the Lafayette of 1848" whose "character, of an undisputed purity, sometimes weakened by compromises and by indecision but never by a hard heart, made him a serious and almost [!] inviolable idol of the people." Even Adolphe Thiers, whom Lamartine detested, is described as a "mordant and witty speaker" and as "the soul, the intelligence, and the word" of the dynastic opposition.[78]

The historian Jules Gesztesi has observed that in writing history Lamartine was "not a judge but rather a priest who grants absolution." Similar observations were made by contemporary reviewers, such as the Orléanist Eugène Forcade who derided Lamartine's addiction to fulsome praise: "You get sick of this insipid and trite goodwill which doesn't honour anyone because it flatters everyone. You get indignant at the phlegmatic lyricism of this grave Philinte who makes a show of being moved by the Duchess of Orléans and whose sycophancy extends even to Blanqui." One does not have to share Forcade's disdain for Lamartine to appreciate the cogency of his critique of Lamartine's "phlegmatic lyricism."[79]

Taken as a whole, the *Histoire de la Révolution de 1848* is not only a defence of Lamartine's actions in 1848; it is also an argument for his importance, his shaping influence on the course of events. He repeatedly argues that his intervention saved France from falling into a state of anarchy and civil war. A case in point is his account of the *journée* of March 17. The previous day he had been instrumental in persuading the

[77] Alfred-Auguste Cuvillier-Fleury, "M. de Lamartine, héros et historien de la Révolution de février (17 août, 1849)", *Portraits politiques et révolutionnaires*, 2 vols. (Paris, 1852), I, 148.
[78] Lamartine, *Révolution de 1848*, I, 15, 23, 25, 85.
[79] Jules Gesztesi, "Préface" to his edition of Lamartine's *Histoire de la Révolutiuon de 1848* (Paris, 1948), 10; Eugène Forcade, "L'Historien et le héros de la Révolution de février," *Revue des deux mondes*, III (August 1849), 309. In Molière's *Misanthrope*, Philinte was a conciliatory individual who was adept at bestowing compliments.

elite National Guard units to give up their distinctive fur caps (*bonnets à poil*). Then, on March 17, a popular counter-demonstration threatened to turn into something much more dangerous. A minority of radical zealots were plotting, he writes, to make this popular demonstration "the unknowing instrument of their perverse and ambitious designs." Lamartine credits himself with standing firm on this occasion when Blanqui and other club leaders attempted to force on the Provisional Government an indefinite adjournment of the elections, the withdrawal of all government troops from Paris and the proclamation of what amounted to a revolutionary dictatorship.[80]

After March 17, Lamartine was sufficiently worried about the possibility of a radical coup in Paris that he negotiated secretly with General Négrier, the commander of the *Armée du Nord*, concerning the possibility that the Provisional Government might have to quit Paris. At the same time, he attempted to persuade the more tractable radical leaders to join with him in resisting all "tentatives of communism, terrorism and dictatorship." He describes himself as having made overtures to Lamennais, Raspail, Barbès, Cabet, Sobrier, even to Auguste Blanqui. For all of this, and especially for his "secret" 6 am meeting with Blanqui, Lamartine was much criticized. But he believed (or claimed to believe) that his talks with the radicals had spared France "the convulsions" that would have been sure to follow the overthrow of the Provisional Government.[81]

Lamartine describes the *journée* of April 16 as another occasion on which he thwarted a challenge to the authority of the Provisional Government. This case is more complicated, for his actions were by his own account devious and manipulative. In his history of 1848 Lamartine describes himself as having intentionally exaggerated the threat posed to the Provisional Government by the radical demonstration of April 16. The demonstrators' avowed aim was to postpone the parliamentary elections and to create a "Ministry of Progress" concerned with workers' issues. But rumours circulated that they were really plotting to purge the Provisional Government and to turn power over to a committee of public safety. Lamartine claims to have "affected more terror and discouragement than he actually felt" in order to convince Ledru-Rollin to call out the National Guard to put down the "insurrection."[82]

It can be argued that Lamartine was actually *staging* a threat to the authority of the Provisional Government. For Henri Guillemin, April 16 was "an enormous mystification, conceived, prepared and carried out [by Lamartine] with astonishing sang-froid."[83] Be that as it may – and

---

[80] Lamartine, *Révolution de 1848*, II, 204–207, 212, 221–228.   [81] Ibid, 231–232, 235.
[82] Ibid, 309.   [83] Guillemin, *Lamartine en 1848*, 45.

this view is perfectly consistent with Lamartine's own account of the *journée* – it is clear that here, as elsewhere in his *Histoire de la Révolution de 1848*, Lamartine was attempting to persuade conservatives that they owed him thanks for having saved them (and France) from civil war and anarchy. Of course, Lamartine did not get the thanks of conservatives. What he did get was sarcastic comments about incendiaries who turn into firemen.

The Man Who "Taught Revolution to France"

Throughout his *Histoire de la Révolution de 1848* Lamartine systematically plays down his own evolution toward the Left prior to the February Revolution and his alliance, once in power, with Ledru-Rollin and other democratic republicans. In his depiction of the National Workshops Lamartine ignores the efforts made by Marie and others to ensure their failure. Instead, he writes of the Workshops as a redoubt of radicalism, as an "army of 20,000 workers composed in great part of the lazy and of trouble-makers." And he describes his own activities in May and June as motivated by "a single thought: to dissolve if possible or to crush if necessary the insurrection of the National Workshops."[84] His insistence on including Ledru-Rollin in the Executive Committee is not explained. Indeed, it is hardly mentioned. And the impression he creates is that after May 15 his sole concern was to arm the Republic against an attack from within.

In the end, Lamartine's effort to present himself as a conservative and thus win the support of the Party of Order was far from successful. While his book received positive reviews from allies like Eugène Pelletan in *La Presse*,[85] the response of conservatives was hostile and in some cases devastatingly so. Writing in the *Revue des deux mondes*, the Orleanist Eugène Forcade described the book as an "incoherent improvisation" and "a perpetual hallucination" unified only by "the constant praise that M. de Lamartine bestows upon himself."[86] The review by Alfred-Auguste Cuvillier-Fleury was only slightly more nuanced. Lamartine is not a historian or a statesman, writes Cuvillier-Fleury; he is a poet. As the head of the Provisional Government, "he didn't govern; he sang." His book was not about the revolution; it was about Lamartine. It was a monument to his pride."[87]

[84] Lamartine, *Révolution de 1848*, II, 459, 474.
[85] Eugène Pelletan, "Feuilleton: 'Histoire de la Révolution de 1848, par M. de Lamartine'," *La Presse*, XIV (August 12, 1849), 4791.
[86] Forcade, *Revue des deux mondes* (1849), III, 324, 309.
[87] Cuvillier-Fleury, *Portraits politiques et révolutionnaires*, I, 133, 147, 159.

The book sold well at first: 5,000 copies were purchased in the first forty days, and the first edition in two volumes was soon followed by an illustrated edition and a German translation.[88] All this enabled Lamartine to make a lot of money from the book – 200,000 francs according to Sainte-Beuve. But the negative reviews damaged sales in the long term. As other more balanced and credible histories of 1848 appeared, his book lost its appeal to the general reader. A few years later Louis Blanc could write drily about what he regarded as Lamartine's prodigious capacity for self-deception. The *Histoire* was, he wrote:

[A]n inconceivable novel and the more inconceivable in that it was written, I'm sure, in good faith. M. de Lamartine is too decent a man to have the sad power of deceiving others, but he has the power of self-deception ... to a degree that is close to prodigious.[89]

The last two years of the Second Republic were the most difficult period of Lamartine's public life. He continued to sit in the National Assembly until the coup of December 2, 1851. During this period he spoke occasionally, often defending unpopular positions on the suffrage and freedom of the press, on the deportation of *proscrits* and the abolition of the death penalty for political crimes. But the age of oratory was over, and the high hopes that he had articulated for a generation of 'forty-eighters' were dead, When he took the podium he was sometimes interrupted with insults, catcalls and derisive laughter, and his attempts to evoke the ideals proclaimed in February were met with volleys of sarcasm. On February 23, 1850, when Thiers described the February Days as "funestes," Lamartine protested. But it was Thiers whom the Assembly applauded. Two months later, when Lamartine compared the suffering of political deportees to that of Napoleon at Sainte-Hélène, he was accused of "shameful" and even "blasphemous" language.[90]

Although the coup of December 2 was no surprise to Lamartine, it was a bitter blow. Four days later he drew up a declaration to his electors in the Loiret, condemning the coup and urging them to establish "a *cordon sanitaire* of abstention and passive resistance" around the new government. But he never published the declaration; and his fears of popular violence were renewed by the widespread resistance to the coup in Saône-et-Loire. He quickly distanced himself from the movement of active resistance. Within a year he had reconciled himself to a ruler whom

[88] Gesztesi, "Préface," 17.
[89] "Louis Blanc to Marie d'Agoult, January 23, 1862" in Daniel Stern, *Lettres républicaines du Second Empire (documents édits)*, Jacques Vier (ed.) (Paris, 1951), 91.
[90] Dominique Dupart, *Lamartine le lyrique* (Paris, 2011), 89–95.

he came to regard as less dangerous than his uncle. "I look the other way," he wrote, "and I work to earn my bread and pay my creditors."[91]

At the time of the coup d'état Lamartine was sixty-one years old, and he still had seventeen years to live. But his political career was over: he would never again hold public office – not even on the *conseil général* of Saône-et-Loire. For the rest of his life, his great preoccupation was to pay his creditors. His main source of income was, and always had been, his pen. In an effort to get out of debt he wrote unceasingly during the 1850s, producing a whole series of literary and historical pot-boilers. These included an eight-volume *Histoire des Constituents* (1853–1855), a projected companion work to the *Histoire des Girondins* with Mirabeau replacing Robespierre in the starring role. There were also eight-volume histories of Turkey and of the Bourbon Restoration as well as hastily written memoirs and several monthlies including *Le Civilisateur*, which offered "instruction for the masses in history and morality." None of this prodigious output did much to reduce his debt which, by his own estimation, had risen by 1859 to almost two million francs.

In 1858 friends organized a national subscription for Lamartine and secured the support of Napoleon III. This alienated his old republican allies and elicited a ferocious reaction from Legitimists, Orleanists, and the Catholic hierarchy. The Bishop of Belley wrote that if the Faith disappeared from "our dear and Catholic France," it would be Lamartine's fault. In 1860 he attempted to raise money by producing a new edition of his collected works. He sent out personal, handwritten letters to potential subscribers – only to provoke responses like the following from Ferdinand de Wegmann: "Monsieur, You have done incalculable harm to France. Do not hope that she will pardon you! Let the Mountain subscribe to your works. I only give charity to the *good poor.*"[92]

In 1861, Lamartine produced a lengthy "Critique de l'Histoire des Girondins" which was actually less a critique than a panegyric to its author. In it Lamartine admitted to no more than "a few errors of judgment" amounting to "five or six pages" in a book of 3,000 pages.[93] His main concern in this uncritical "Critique" was to reply to the accusations of conservatives like Wegmann that his book had "made" the Revolution of 1848. His response was that his book did not make the

---

[91] Fortescue, *Lamartine*, 260; Toesca, *Lamartine ou l'amour de la vie*, 525–526.
[92] *Souvenirs de Charles de Cussy, 1795–1866*, 2 vols. (Paris, 1909), II, 339 in Guillemin, *Lamartine en 1848*, iii.
[93] Lamartine, "Critique de l'Histoire des Girondins" in *Oeuvres complètes de Lamartine*, 41 vols. (Paris, 1860–1866), XV, 259.

revolution or the republic, but that it "made the republic possible in rendering it innocent." He went on to assert that "without the book on the Girondins, the Revolution of February 24 would have led to terror."[94] His argument convinced no one.

The view that Lamartine had "taught revolution to France" by publishing the *Histoire des Girondins* remained pervasive among conservatives long after 1848. There were many who never forgave him either for the book or for his inept efforts to put out the fire of revolution once it had started. Of course, Lamartine was also viewed critically by radicals. Whereas Wegmann and the Orleanist Eugène Forcade regarded Lamartine as responsible for the February Revolution, Alexander Herzen expressed disgust for "the laudanum of Lamartine," whose frothy speeches concealed his real aim, which was to bar the way to socialism. Similarly, Louis Ménard described him as an *endormeur* who did what he could on February 24 to deny the rights of the people who had made the revolution.[95]

A more discerning contemporary assessment of Lamartine's role in 1848 is provided in another history of the revolution – that of Marie d'Agoult, who wrote under the pen name of Daniel Stern. This work is structured around the contrast between Lamartine, who represents the generous and idealistic aspirations of February, and Adolphe Thiers, who was in his person the "vulgar dénouement" of an abortive revolution. Insofar as d'Agoult's history has a hero, it is Lamartine. But he is a flawed hero, capable of seducing public opinion but not of satisfying it. He is a soaring orator and his powers of intuition are great, but he lacks patience and political skill. D'Agoult writes that Lamartine's "negligent optimism" – his conviction that to achieve his goals, he had merely to proclaim them in lofty language – accounts both for his rise to power and for his rapid fall. She illustrates her critique of Lamartine with a brilliant extended metaphor: "As his star shone in the sky with an incomparable brightness, as he seemed to command the winds that filled his sails and the furious waves that died at his feet, his distracted hand rested on the tiller without guiding it."[96] Thus, while luck and intuition kept Lamartine afloat, he never reached the shore he sought. He sailed on, his hand remaining on the tiller but not steering the ship. Ironically, as d'Agoult herself recognized twenty years later, the politician who finally did bring the moderate republican ship to port was the "vulgar" Adolphe Thiers.

[94] *Cours familier de littérature*, XII, 188 in Court, *Les Girondins de Lamartine*, II, 196.
[95] Louis Ménard, *Prologue d'une révolution* (Paris, 1904), 39.
[96] Stern, *Révolution de 1848*, III, 102–103.

There are other ironies in Lamartine's career as a *quarante-huitard*. For all his clear-sightedness in imagining the role that he was to play in 1848, Lamartine seems to have been mystified by the collapse of his own influence once (with his help) the radicals had been marginalized. And for all his Dickensian brilliance in bringing the first French Revolution to life in the *Histoire des Girondins*, he was totally unable to provide a plausible account of the revolution in which he was a principal actor. He saw himself as the saviour of society – as someone who had for three months given substance to the dream of a moderate republic and who thereafter stood ready, if called upon, to keep that dream alive. In retrospect, we may see him as one of the last of the political romantics who believed in the power of the word – first through poetry and then oratory – to transform the world.

3 George Sand
"The People" Found and Lost

From her death in 1876 until her rediscovery by feminist scholars a century later, George Sand was remembered as a rebel who wore men's clothes and smoked cigars and whose lovers included Chopin and Musset, or else as the author of pastoral novels celebrating the countryside of Berry and the peasants who lived there. More recently, attention has been given to her early novels – *Indiana*, *Valentine* and *Lélia* – which dramatized the struggles of independent women to free themselves from the constraints of marriage and male-dominated society. It is also now recognized that she did much during the 1840s to illustrate the ideas of socialists like Pierre Leroux, and to widen the audience for their ideas. But none of these images goes far to explain the power that George Sand's work exercised over the minds and hearts of her contemporaries – men as well as women – or the role she played in shaping the sensibilities of the generation of young people who welcomed the February Revolution as the dawn of a new age. To cite only one example, the young Alexander Herzen and his fiancée Natalie Zakharova were so steeped in her writings and so influenced by her validation of deep feeling that they took the names of characters in her novels and conducted their epistolary courtship accordingly. Fifteen years later, when Natalie had a Sandian affair with the German poet Georg Herwegh, Herzen could think of no greater insult than to call Herwegh "a *petit bourgeois*, like George Sand's Horace (see Figure 3.1)."[1]

When seen in connection with 1848, what is most fascinating about George Sand is the way her work embodies the cult of "the people" – the aspiration of writers and intellectuals to go to the people, to understand the people, to describe their lives and to help them better themselves. She saw the novel – and she wrote almost sixty novels – as both a celebration of the people and a means of reaching them. "Today's novel," she wrote in *La Mare au diable*, "should replace the parable and the fable of naïve

---

[1] Alexander Herzen, *My Past and Thoughts. The Memoirs of Alexander Herzen*, trans. Constance Garnett, rev. Humphrey Higgins, 4 vols. (New York, 1968), II, 903.

Figure 3.1 Photograph of George Sand by Nadar (Gaspard-Félix Tournachon), 1864. Photograph: Getty.

times."[2] George Sand did not write anything resembling a history of 1848. Nevertheless, much of her later work stands in the shadow of 1848; and the twenty-six volumes of her correspondence, lovingly edited

[2] George Sand, *La Mare au diable* (Paris, 1889), 5.

by Georges Lubin, include a rich record of how the first months of the
Second Republic were experienced by an articulate and thoughtful
writer, deeply committed to the vision of harmony and reconciliation
that inspired the 'forty-eighters and to the belief, shared by many of
them, that the voice of the people is the voice of God. This chapter will
focus on the correspondence. But, to put Sand's experience of 1848 in
perspective, we first need to discuss her political education during the
July Monarchy.

The Emergence of the Writer

In January 1831, at the age of twenty-six, Aurore Dudevant set out for
Paris to become a writer, leaving behind her husband, two children and
her country estate at Nohant in the province of Berry. The break was not
absolute. According to the contract of separation that she had drawn up
with her husband, she would alternate three month periods in Paris and
Nohant and would receive the annual allowance of 3,000 francs allotted
to her by their marriage contract. Her goal was to make herself known as
a writer in a literary world already crowded with young writers such as
Hugo, Musset, Vigny, Balzac and Sainte-Beuve.

In May 1832, having cultivated editors and publishers, having published reviews, articles, satirical sketches, short stories and a novel, and
having in addition encouraged, nursed and supported her lover Jules
Sandeau, Aurore Dudevant became George Sand, the pseudonymous
author of *Indiana*. This novel, with its portrait of an unhappy wife trying
to free herself from the prison of marriage, made her famous. After its
publication her private life became public property, and her works were
read as guides to life. "I cannot read six pages of hers," wrote George
Eliot, "without feeling that it is given to her to delineate human passion ...
with such truthfulness, such nicety of discrimination, such tragic power
and withal such loving gentle humor that one might live a century ... and
not know so much as these six pages will suggest."[3] For the rest of her
life, Sand was to write indefatigably, producing at least a novel a year.

For four years, Sand threw herself into her writing – and into a series of
passionate entanglements with the actress Marie Dorval, the poet Alfred
de Musset, an Italian doctor and (briefly) Prosper Mérimée. Her political
awakening came in 1835. The occasion was the "monster trial" of 121 silk
weavers and their republican allies, accused of having fomented the

---

[3] J. W. Cross (ed.), *George Eliot's Life as related in her letters and journals*, 3 vols. (Boston,
1908), I, 169–170.

revolt of April 1834 when rebels took over the city of Lyon. During the course of the trial, Sand slipped into the Chamber of Peers dressed as a man in order to witness the proceedings. She became acquainted with the celebrated republican defenders – Ledru-Rollin, Garnier-Pagès, Barbès and – most importantly – Michel de Bourges, who became her lover. Sand later wrote of the trial as a transforming experience and of Michel de Bourges as having awakened her to a new life. His eloquence and the intensity of his republican convictions inspired in her the ability "to feel strong emotions that politics had never before awakened in me."[4] The liaison with Michel de Bourges did not last, but it left her with the sense that, while she was "by nature poetic and not legislative," she had a political role to play as a writer.

Ever since 1830, Sand had considered herself a republican; after 1835 she gravitated toward the socialists. She formed ties with Louis Blanc and Pierre Leroux and the renegade Catholic priest Félicité de Lamennais. She particularly valued the friendship of Pierre Leroux. A former Saint-Simonian and a founder of the influential journal *Le Globe*, Leroux entered Sand's life in 1836, at about the same time as Frederic Chopin. No two individuals could have been less alike than the frail, fastidious Chopin and the shaggy, dishevelled, militantly plebian Leroux. But both relationships endured. To Chopin Sand was for almost a decade a lover and a nurse. Leroux, on the other hand, became Sand's philosophical mentor and she became his financial and psychological benefactor.

Pierre Leroux was a seminal figure in the history of French socialism.[5] In his early writings, Leroux had given currency to the opposition between *socialisme* and *individualisme* and had offered scathing criticism of inequalities of wealth and opportunity. When Sand got to know him, he was embarked on the construction of a philosophical system. His fullest elaboration of the system came in 1840 with the publication of *De l'Humanité*, a work too abstract to gain a wide audience but influential, in part, through Sand's success in giving substance, in her fiction, to some of Leroux's central ideas. In particular, Sand found inspiration in Leroux's radical egalitarianism, his belief that Christianity must give way to a more comprehensive "religion of humanity" and his insistence on

---

[4] Georges Lubin (ed.), "Histoire de ma vie" in *Oeuvres autobiographiques*, 2 vols. (Paris, 1971), II, 329.

[5] On Pierre Leroux, see Armelle Le Bras-Chopard, *De l'égalité dans la différence: Le socialisme de Pierre Leroux* (Paris, 1986); and David O. Evans, *Le Socialisme romantique: Pierre Leroux et ses contemporains* (Paris, 1948).

the need to build a society ruled not by egoism, but by the shared consciousness of participation in a common humanity.

Sand's correspondence is full of paeans to Pierre Leroux. She writes that he is her "guide," her "saviour," that he "rescued" her at a time of personal crisis.[6] Her novel *Spiridion* is dedicated to Leroux: "Friend and brother in years, father and master in virtue and science." She claims that Leroux himself wrote the best parts of *Consuelo*.[7] In fact, Sand did at least as much for Leroux as he for her. She gave him money; she helped finance two journals over which Leroux had editorial control – the *Revue indépendante* (1841–1848) and the *Revue sociale* (1845–1848); and when Leroux moved to Boussac, not far from Nohant, she helped Leroux set up a printing shop there. She was, in short, his personal benefactress – a role that she played with tact and sensitivity, disguising her gifts as royalties whenever possible.[8]

Leroux was himself an artisan, a printer and the inventor of a new kind of composition machine called the *pianotype*, and he was able to put Sand in touch with other skilled workers and thus to reinforce the ties that bound her to "the people." Having grown up in Berry, she felt close to peasant France. But she was well aware that she knew little about the growing class of urban artisans, the *peuple des faubourgs*. One great service that Leroux did for her was to introduce her to one of the most articulate working-class intellectuals of nineteenth-century France: Agricol Perdiguier.

Agricol Perdiguier was a journeyman *menuisier* (a joiner or finish carpenter) active in the *compagnonnage* movement.[9] The *compagnonnages* were societies of journeymen that provided shelter, training and employment for itinerant craftsmen on their traditional *Tour de France*. They traced their origin to fraternities of workers on medieval cathedrals. Outlawed by the Chapelier Law of 1791, the *compagnonnages* went underground under Napoleon but resurfaced after 1815. In their heyday, three distinct groups or *devoirs* of *compagnonnage* competed with one another, each with its own myths and traditions. In 1839, Perdiguier published his *Livre du compagnonnage* which revealed rituals and

---

[6] George Sand, "To Sainte-Beuve, January 20, 1842" in *Correspondance*, Georges Lubin (ed.), 26 vols. (Paris, 1964–1991), V, 576.

[7] "To Ferdinand Guillon, February 14, 1844" in *Correspondance*, VI, 431.

[8] See Jean-Pierre Lacassagne (ed.), *Pierre Leroux et George Sand: Histoire d'une amitié (d'après une correspondence inédite 1836–1866)* (Paris, 1973).

[9] On Perdiguier, see Jean Briquet, *Agricole Perdiguier, compagnon du tour de France et représentant du peuple, 1805–1875* (Paris, 1981) and Agricol Perdiguier, *Mémoires d'un compagnon* (Paris, 1964).

"mysteries" associated with the movement and appealed for an end to the sectarian rivalry and violence that beset the movement.[10]

In June 1839, Pierre Leroux gave Sand a copy of the *Livre du compagnonnage*. This book opened up a new world for Sand. She had long been curious about the lives of skilled workers, but she knew nothing about the customs, history and secret rites of *compagnonnage* except that they reminded her of the traditions of masonic lodges and brotherhoods about which she had read. Here was a slice of the life of the people that was unknown to her – and here too was a wonderful topic for a novel. Early in 1840, Sand began working on *Le Compagnon du Tour de France*, a novel which she hoped would make Perdiguier and *compagnonnage* more widely known. Sand set the novel in the Restoration period when Perdiguier had made his own Tour de France as an apprentice joiner. Thanks to his help, most of Sand's information was accurate. But, on its publication, the novel was widely criticized. In the Catholic and conservative press it was attacked as an apologia for socialist and communist ideas, and Sand herself was depicted as a wanton alcoholic who went out to the Paris *faubourgs* on Sundays to get drunk with Pierre Leroux while allegedly studying working-class life.[11] More plausibly, critics of all persuasions – including Sand's lover Frederic Chopin – found her hero, the honest, upright *compagnon*, Pierre Huguenin, just too good to be true. Sand had a response to this criticism. She did not deny that her hero was idealized, but she insisted that, "despite all the obstacles posed by laws, prejudices and customs," a "complete man" would soon emerge from the proletariat. She was not disturbed by the consternation of the "delicate and refined Chopin." For she believed that while Pierre Huguenin might be a fiction, he was a prophetic fiction.[12]

The publication of *Le Compagnon du Tour de France* has been seen as marking Sand's turn to socialism. This is true enough, provided one recalls that Sand, who rarely used the term "*socialisme*" prior to 1849, had in mind something closer to a religious movement than a political ideology. Socialism for her was a cause, an ideal, "*une foi sociale*" in the light of which the social, economic and psychological problems associated with early industrialization could be healed. In this respect, Sand was no different from many other romantic socialists who had, in Edgar

[10] On compagnonnage, see Emile Coornaert, *Les Compagnonnages en France du moyen âge à nos jours* (Paris, 1966); E. M. Saint-Léon, *Le Compagnonnage, son histoire, ses coutumes, ses règlements et ses rites* (Paris, 1983).
[11] Evans, *Le Socialisme romantique*, 115.
[12] "To Charles Poncy, November 24, 1845" in *Correspondance*, VII, 186.

Newman's words, given the language of early French socialism "the flavor of a religious revival."[13]

Getting Close to "the People"

Agricol Perdiguier was just one of many working-class writers with whom Sand corresponded in the 1840s. There were also several "proletarian poets" to whom she gave advice, encouragement, and discrete subsidies. These people were part of a group of worker-poets who flourished during the July Monarchy. They were autodidact artisans who did not limit themselves to the writing of songs; many of them also aspired to write classical verse in the manner of Racine or fables like La Fontaine's. Most were provincials – unknown in Paris but locally admired and associated with the "regionalist renaissance" in post-Napoleonic France.[14] Those whom Sand knew best included the mason Charles Poncy from Toulon, Marie-Eléanore Magu, a half-blind weaver-poet from Lizy-sur-Ourcq and his son-in-law, the locksmith Jérôme-Pierre Gilland.

During the July Monarchy many established French writers – including Hugo, Lamartine and Nodier – "adopted" and encouraged worker-poets. None took this task more seriously than George Sand. She wrote prefaces and introductions to their published work; she offered advice on unpublished manuscripts; she introduced them to other writers; and she celebrated their work in two "Dialogues familiers sur la poésie des prolétaires." The most prolific of Sand's worker-poets was the mason from Toulon, Charles Poncy.[15] They remained in correspondence until Sand's death; and while their relationship took on an intimacy lacking in Sand's relations with any of the other worker-poets, it can stand as an epitome of both the success and the failure of Sand's attempts to get close to "the people."

---

[13] Edgar Leon Newman, "The Historian as Apostle: Romanticism, Religion, and the First Socialist History of the World," *Journal of the History of Ideas*, LVI(2) (April 1995), 239–261. See also Edward Berenson, *Populist Religion and Left-Wing Politics in France, 1830–1852* (Princeton, 1984) and Miguel Abensour, "L'Utopie socialiste: une nouvelle alliance de la politique et de la religion," Le Temps de la réflection, 2 (1981), 61–112.

[14] On the worker-poets, see Edmond Thomas (ed.), *Voix d'en bas: La poésie ouvrière du XIXᵉ siècle* (Paris, 1979); and various articles by Edgar Leon Newman, notably "The New World of the French Socialist Worker Poets: 1830–1848," *Stanford French Review*, III(3) (Winter 1979), 357–368.

[15] On Charles Poncy, see Elzéar Ortolan, "Notice sur Charles Poncy" in *Poésies de Charles Poncy, ouvrier maçon de Toulon: Marines, Le Chantier*, new ed (Paris, 1846), vi–xlix; Maurice Agulhon, *Une Ville ouvrière au temps du socialisme utopique: Toulon de 1815 à 1851* (Paris, 1970), 235–242, 246–254, 328–331; Jean Touchard, *La Gloire de Béranger*, 2 vols. (Paris, 1968), II, 116–118, 131–134, 145–147; and Sewell, *Work and Revolution*, 236–242.

The son of a mason, Charles Poncy was born in 1821. He was thus seventeen years younger than Sand who referred to him from the beginning as "my child" and "my son." At an early age, he began working for his father. He learned to read at a school run by the Frères de la Doctrine Chrétienne, and his interest in poetry seems to have been inspired by Racine's tragedy *Athalie*. His poetry attracted the interest of a liberal jurist at Toulon, Elzéar Ortolan, who paid for the publication of his first small volume of poems.[16] Poncy was just twenty years old when the volume appeared under the title *Marines*. His poems were long on lofty sentiments and trite adjectives – "*ineffables délices*," "*doux parfum*," "*divin zéphyr*," "*chant mélodieux*." But when Poncy sent a copy to George Sand, her response was ecstatic. "My child," she began, "you are a great poet, the most gifted and inspired among all the fine proletarian poets whom we have joyfully seen emerge in recent times." She advised him not to let his success go to his head. He would be feted; he would be offered pensions and decorations. But he must refuse them and keep his "noble heart" free from "the vanity that destroys all our bourgeois poets." Thus, Sand's first letter contained a warning:

Take care, noble child of the people! You have a greater mission than you perhaps believe. Resist, suffer, endure poverty and obscurity if you must rather than abandoning the sacred cause of your brothers.[17]

In subsequent letters, Sand offered shrewd commentary on particular poems, and criticism of Poncy's occasional pomposity, lapses of taste, mixed metaphors and faulty diction. She especially urged him to stop celebrating sirens and *bayadères* and to stick to what he knew. Sand's main theme was that Poncy must remain faithful to his proletarian roots: "Persevere, my noble child, and remain a man of the people."[18] Again, a few months later: "You are never more touching and more original than when you are a mason, a man of the people, and the tender husband of Désirée."[19] This was not the only time during the July Monarchy when an established writer subjected a literary neophyte to lectures about the need to "remain proletarian." Victor Hugo in 1837 was already exhorting a working-class protegé to "be proud of your title as a worker" and to be "patient and resigned" in the face of appeals to revolution.[20] Unlike Hugo, Sand was not calling for patience and resignation; she was asserting that she knew better than Poncy himself what he should be and become.

---

[16] On Elzéar Ortolan, see Agulhon, *Une Ville ouvrière*, 226–251.

[17] "To Charles Poncy, April 27, 1842" in *Correspondance*, V, 641–642.

[18] "To Charles Poncy, May 14, 1842" in *Correspondance*, V, 666.

[19] "To Charles Poncy, February 16, 1843" in *Correspondance*, VI, 46.

[20] Victor Hugo, "Lettre à un ouvrier poète (October 3, 1837)" in *Oeuvres complètes* (Paris, 1967), V, 1126.

Not surprisingly, a tension developed between Poncy's increasingly bourgeois ambitions and Sand's insistence that he remain the proletarian she knew him to be. She often returns to her main theme: "I repeat, be a man of the people in your heart of hearts, and if you protect yourself from the vanity and corruption of the 'middle' and 'upper' classes, as they are called, everything will be fine."[21] To encourage Poncy, Sand sent him a personal, almost confessional, letter in December 1843, telling him that she understood him better than his bourgeois admirers like "le bon Monsieur Ortolan" because she too had known poverty.[22] She said that she was only "apparently" born an aristocrat. "I belong to the people by blood as much as by feeling. My mother was from a lower class than yours ... She came from the vagabond and degraded class of the bohemians of this world." Sand conceded that thanks to her paternal grandmother, the illegitimate daughter of Maréchal de Saxe, she became an heiress at an early age. But at the start, she knew poverty and she had never forgotten her plebian origins.[23]

In 1844, Poncy published a second volume of poems entitled *Le Chantier*. Although the term *chantier* refers to a construction site, the poems were mostly on bucolic themes. But once again, Sand was delighted, and this time it was she who arranged for publication. She sent the manuscript to the poet Béranger (whose enthusiasm was muted); she wrote a preface; and once the volume was published, she circulated copies among her friends and had a dozen copies sent to silk weavers at Lyon. She also gave Poncy blunt advice about possible recipients of his book. Don't bother about Musset, she told him: "the sacred fire that once inspired him to write sublime verse" had been extinguished. "He is deeply scornful of the worker-poets, and unless a miracle occurs, he will spit on your volume." The critic Lerminier should also be ignored: "You don't know that Lerminier has been officially designated to mock and denigrate the worker-poets in the *Revue des deux mondes*." In fact, there was just one bourgeois who really sympathized with working people. That was Louis Blanc, "a young man of admirable talent and great promise."[24]

In 1845, a banquet in Poncy's honour was organized in Paris by the working-class monthly *La Ruche populaire*. In the end, the banquet was cancelled. But the trip to Paris gave Poncy the opportunity to meet well-

---

[21] "To Charles Poncy, January 21, 1843" in *Correspondance*, VI, 20.
[22] "To Charles Poncy, May 14, 1842" in *Correspondance*, V, 664.
[23] "To Charles Poncy. December 23, 1843" in *Correspondance*, VI, 327–328. None of this was absolutely false. But it was, to say the least, a highly selective account of a childhood that was, in most respects comfortable and privileged.
[24] "To Poncy, January 26, 1844" in *Correspondance*, VI, 408–410.

known writers and also to visit Nohant on his return. Sand was anxious about the visit: she feared that this working-class poet in whom she had invested such high hopes, would prove to be a disappointment. Thus she was thrilled to find that Poncy had not been spoiled by Paris or by success. After his departure she wrote him with relief: "I found you in every way after my own heart."[25] Subsequently, the tone of her letters became more intimate. Earlier, she had initiated a correspondence with Poncy's young wife, Désirée, and had begun to address the couple and their daughter as *"mes chers enfants."* Now she *tutoyéd* Poncy and began to take him into her confidence, sharing her worries with the young man. Finally, in August 1847, she sent him a full account of her difficulties with her daughter Solange and asked him to come to Nohant without his family for a heart-to-heart conversation.[26]

The visit did not happen, and within a few months Sand was so deeply caught up in revolutionary politics that her personal problems were forgotten. But she did not forget Charles Poncy: in March 1848, she first "implored" and then "commanded" him "in the name of my maternal friendship" to become a candidate for the National Assembly. Her letter concluded with the hope that "we will all meet in Paris, full of life and action, ready to die on the barricades if the Republic succumbs."[27] Three weeks later she returned to the charge: The time had passed for personal poetry, for rest and retreat. "Poetry is in action now. Anything else is empty and dead." There is only one conceivable subject for a writer now, and that "unique and grandiose subject" is the Republic. "The Republic is life. It is lost if the true friends of the people slumber. It is saved if we are all there. Arise! Arise!"[28]

Poncy tried hard to answer George Sand's call to arms. He allowed his name to be placed in nomination, and on April 2 his candidacy was announced in the local journal *Le Var* and confirmed on April 10 in the Parisian *Le National*, where Poncy's name (alongside that of his mentor Elzéar Ortolan) appeared on a list of nine moderate republican candidates. But his candidacy did not begin to conform to George Sand's high expectations. In his *profession de foi*, dated March 20 and published in the journal *Le Toulonnais*, he spoke of his "profound incapacity" for the position of *représentant du people*:

I will say with the traditional frankness of the proletarian that I don't feel myself equal to the mandate proposed for me. I know how to write for the public more or

---

[25] "To Poncy, November 24, 1845" in *Correspondance*, VII, 185.
[26] "To Poncy, August 27, 1847" in *Correspondance*, VIII, 76–82.
[27] "To Poncy, March 8, 1848" in *Correspondance*, VIII, 330–331.
[28] "To Poncy, March 28, 1848" in *Correspondance*, VIII, 372.

less adroitly, but I am not able to speak well in public, and for these reasons I do not seek the glorious title of representative, given the fact that nothing in me could justify this ambition, and finally I don't even dare to desire it.

On April 12, Poncy took the logical next step and published a letter in *Le Toulonnais* withdrawing his candidacy "irrevocably and forever." It does not appear that he dared to show George Sand either his *profession de foi* or his letter of withdrawal.[29]

When the election results were announced at the end of April, Poncy's total was listed as 1,062 votes, most of them presumably from voters who were, like Sand, not aware of his withdrawal. Writing Poncy on May 5, Sand observed that in his "rapid explanation" of his defeat in the election, he had "forgotten" to tell her what she really wanted to know: "In the name of what ideas were you defeated after having had such good prospects at the outset?"[30] Charles Poncy, in whom she had placed such high hopes, would have found it difficult to answer this question.

In 1850, Poncy published a third volume of poetry entitled *La Chanson de chaque métier.* Each of the poems in this volume described a different craft, and most had been written prior to 1848. In his preface Poncy credited Sand with the idea for the book. Finding himself "lacking inspiration" in 1846, he asked Sand for advice. She urged him to consider writing "a collection of popular songs, at once playful, naïve, serious and grand, above all simple and easy to remember," songs "so flowing and so simply written that the ordinary worker, who barely knows how to read, can understand and remember them." These songs would "poeticize and ennoble each type of work" while at the same time criticizing "the bad social direction" of each craft at present. Poncy writes that this proposal filled him with "a new ardor," and he set to work at once. He was almost done when the February Revolution "was carried out in the name of the ideas that had inspired these couplets." This left his book "like a hammer in the hands of a worker who has nothing left to destroy." After some hesitation, Poncy published the poems without change. He believed that his social criticism remained relevant in 1850 and that the book might later serve "to make known the spirit and the situation of the workers" prior to the February Revolution. In this way, he hoped to "give a new and salutary direction to proletarian poetry."[31]

---

[29] Most of this information comes from George Lubin's splendid annotations in *Correspondance*, VIII, 331n. But see also Agulhon, *Une Ville ouvrière*, 246–254.

[30] "To Poncy, May 5, 1848" in *Correspondance*, VIII, 445.

[31] Charles Poncy, *La Chanson de chaque métier* (Paris, 1850), Préface, vi–xviii. This preface takes the form of a letter to George Sand.

Poncy's poems did not give a new direction to proletarian poetry. The movement expired in the aftermath of 1848. And 1848 marked the end of Poncy's efforts to speak for the proletariat or to identify himself as a manual worker. Giving up his career as a mason, he used his connections at Toulon to acquire a desk job at the City Hall in early June 1848. He lost that job in 1850 during a purge of moderate republicans from the city government. But he quickly landed on his feet, winning a competition for the position of secretary of the Chamber of Commerce of Toulon. He held this position until his retirement. After 1852 he had no trouble accommodating himself to the Second Empire. In the process he turned his poetic talents to new ends, winning the Légion d'honneur for a poem celebrating Napoleon III.[32]

Long afterward Charles Poncy looked back with detachment at his days as a proletarian poet:

I do not see precisely what is to be gained by resurrecting the worker-poets. They had their moment no doubt, their vogue, and they inspired the enthusiasm of generous souls who believed them called to a kind of priesthood or apostolate centering on what was then called the people. Their halo vanished in 1848 with the proclamation of the Republic that they had longed for ... There is a reason for their disappearance from the literary and political scene. It is that their Republic, just like the kingdom of God in the Gospel, was not of this world. They did not want to imitate the charlatans selling universal fraternity, agrarian laws, heavenly dreams and other false panaceas by which workers have been intoxicated ... For thirty years, starting with Béranger, they have all been properly buried; and those like me who have had the sad luck to grow old and outlive the others have become the *bêtes noires* of the reds of the present generation.[33]

Poncy died a rich man in 1891, having made a small fortune in real estate speculation at Toulon.

Charles Poncy's letters to George Sand have not survived. But Poncy carefully saved and numbered Sand's letters to him, and the letters eventually made their way back to her. After Sand's death in 1876, her daughter Solange went through her papers; and on a folder containing a particularly warm letter from her mother to Poncy, Solange wrote a bitter comment about Sand and her worker-poet:

What a fuss she made to support her plebian courtiers. And how strangely things sometimes turned out. Poncy, at heart a *conservative*, was decorated by Napoléon III when the Empress visited Toulon, and for a piece of verse addressed to the

[32] Agulhon, *Une Ville ouvrière*, 235–242, 246–254.
[33] "Charles Poncy to Henry Jouin, January 8, 1884" in Touchard, *La Gloire de Béranger*, II, 133.

sovereign. But G. Sand imagined people in her own image, having absolutely nothing in common with the original.[34]

Sand and Solange had come to detest each other by 1850, and one could discount these comments as the bile of an angry daughter. Yet when one reads them in the light of the story we have just told, it is hard to deny that they contain a certain truth. George Sand wanted to believe the best of the people she cared for, but "the best" as she saw it often bore little relation to what mattered to them. She could not see that Charles Poncy's desires and goals had little to do with her own fantasies. She was to make a similar mistake with regard to "the people" in 1848.

Working with the Provisional Government

The February Revolution took George Sand by surprise. That winter she had much else on her mind besides politics. Her long liaison with Chopin had reached its bitter end; she and Solange were at war; and she was at work on her autobiography. As one who could describe herself as "going through the most painful period of my life," she hardly noticed the banquet campaign. "Don't get mixed up in all that," she wrote her son Maurice in Paris. It was all factional intrigue, and there was no reason to "get beaten up for Odilon Barrot and company."[35] A few days later, with a new republican government in power, she was ecstatic. Arriving in Paris on March 1, she plunged into politics, meeting with Lamartine, Ledru-Rollin, Lamennais and Mazzini; seeking positions in the new government for old friends; getting a guided tour from Louis Blanc of the Palais de Luxembourg, the new "palace of labour"; and sleeping little. "Everything is fine," she wrote a friend. "Personal worries disappear when public life calls us and absorbs us." To another friend she wrote that she felt "young again."[36]

For a few weeks, Sand's enthusiasm knew no bounds. As she told Frédéric Girerd, whom she helped appoint *commissaire de la République* in the Indre, the situation required "not merely dedication and loyalty but also fanaticism." "You must rise above yourself," she wrote, "abjure all weakness, break off your affective ties if they stand in the way ... I cannot insist too strongly on the need to sweep away every trace of the bourgeois spirit." Above all, she declared, "you must be really, *fundamentally*,

---

[34] Undated comment by Solange Dudevant-Sand on a folder containing Sand's letters to Poncy: Annotations by Georges Lubin, *Correspondance*, VII, 191n.
[35] "To Maurice Sand, February 18, 1848" in *Correspondance*, VIII, 299.
[36] "To Frédéric Girerd, March 6, 1848" in *Correspondance*, VIII, 324; "To Charles Poncy, March 8, 1848" in *Correspondance*, VIII, 330.

Figure 3.2 Barricade on the rue Saint-Martin, February Revolution. Its builders pose for a ceremonial picture after the fighting. *Illustrated London News*, March 4, 1848.

revolutionary." This is just the sort of language that Sand would later denounce as the language of zealotry and democratic despotism. But, in the first week of March, she could write confidently that "demagoguery is not to be feared" and that "the people have proved that they are greater and more beautiful than all the rich people and the savants in the world."[37]

The same euphoric tone pervaded the articles published by Sand immediately after the February Revolution. The first began on a triumphal note: "The republic is the most beautiful and best form of modern society," she wrote. "The republics of the past were incomplete sketches. They failed because they had slaves. The republic that we are founding will only have free men, equal in rights" (see Figure 3.2). In this article, written in Paris on March 3 and published in the *Journal du Loiret* on March 8, Sand asserted that the new republic would terminate the conflict between rich and poor that had brought pain and suffering to all classes. The *classe moyenne* had sided with the people in February, and in doing so it had won their trust and their love. But it was important for the middle class to maintain that trust so that the people, who did not yet fully understand the limits to their power, might not be tempted to break with the middle class and even to violate "the sanctuary of the national representation." Sand concluded with a recommendation. Elections should be organized so that in each department in France at least one

[37] "To Frédéric Girerd, March 6, 1848" in *Correspondance*, VIII, 324.

peasant and one urban labourer would be chosen to serve in the future national assembly.[38]

A few days later, Sand wrote the first of two *Lettres au peuple* in which she again insisted on the necessity of maintaining the alliance between the people and the middle class. Here she outdid herself in praising the "bon et grand peuple" – for their "bravery in combat," their "sublime disregard for danger" and their "magnanimity" toward their enemies. Now that they had recovered from "the fatigue of their noble victory," she urged them to wipe away their blood and sweat and to meditate on their destiny. "You are going to reign, oh people! (see Figure 3.2) Reign fraternally with your equals of all classes." And Sand told the people that they could look forward to a time when the Republic would enable them to unite with their brothers in other classes to create a "fraternal union which would destroy all false distinctions and would remove the very word 'classes' from the book of humanity."[39]

Finally, in a letter addressed "To the Rich," Sand attempted to dispel the fear of "communism" among the propertied classes. "You are frightened by a phantom," she told them. You believe its triumph will mean the seizure of your property and the destruction of the family. In fact, you have nothing to fear. The main thinkers associated with communism are pacifists – here Sand mentions explicitly Pierre Leroux and Etienne Cabet. And insofar as there is a communist movement in France, "it has just demonstrated its legal submission to the established order by proclaiming its support of the young republic." But communism is more an ideal than an existing reality. "It is as an aspiration that it attracts followers." It has supporters among the rich, in all nations, and among all classes. Many self-proclaimed communists do not belong to any particular sect or movement because "they prefer to retain in their soul a pure ideal." The faith of these people is indomitable. "If they lived for a hundred years under Louis Philippe, they would die with the same convictions. For communism is true Christianity and the religion of fraternity poses no threat to the pocketbook or the life of anyone."[40]

George Sand's connections in the Provisional Government included both moderates like François Arago, Hippolyte Carnot and Armand Marrast, and radicals such as Ledru-Rollin, Louis Blanc and Marc

---

[38] George Sand, "Un Mot à la classe moyenne" in *Politique et polémiques (1843–1850)*, (Paris, 2004), Présentation Michelle Perrot (Paris, 1997), 223–227. In this article the terms *classe moyenne* and *bourgeoisie* are used interchangeably.

[39] "'Hier et aujourd'hui,' March 7, 1848" in *Politique et polémiques*, 235–243.

[40] "Aux riches" in *Politique et polémiques*, 229–233. This article was first published in *Les Petites Affiches de La Châtre* on March 16. On March 24, it was reprinted in Eugénie Niboyet's journal *La Voix des femmes*.

Caussidière. She was also a long-standing friend of Lamartine. On March 4, when she went to the Foreign Ministry to get a passport for Mazzini, Lamartine invited her to watch from his office the massive procession along the Boulevard des Capucines in honour of the victims of government gunfire on February 23. She was deeply moved:

> I watched the cortege go by from the window of Guizot [the former foreign minister] while I talked with Lamartine. The cortege was handsome, simple and touching: 400,000 people pressed together from the Madeleine to the July Column. Not a gendarme, not a policeman and still so much order, decency, calm and mutual politeness that there wasn't a sprained ankle or a battered hat. It was admirable. The people of Paris are the best people in the world.[41]

Sand's conversation with Lamartine went on "for several hours." By his account, he convinced her that the survival of the Republic required "the sudden, energetic and complete repudiation of the excesses and crimes that had dishonored and destroyed the first revolution," and he asked her to assume the editorship of a "popular paper," to be subsidized by the Provisional Government, which would eradicate the bad memories of 1793 and "sow in the mind of the masses the principles of peace, discipline and fraternity." Lamartine later claimed that she initially accepted his offer but then changed her mind, preferring to ally herself with Ledru-Rollin and to collaborate on the Interior Ministry's *Bulletin de la République*, which evoked the "grim memories of the First Republic" that Lamartine was trying to suppress.[42]

A week in Paris was enough to convince Sand that the Republic had triumphed there. "I saw the people: great, sublime, naïve, generous," she wrote Charles Poncy:

> I spent nights without sleeping, days without sitting down. You are crazy, you are drunk, you are happy to fall asleep in the mire and to wake up in heaven … The Republic has been won. It is assured. We will all perish rather than lose it. The Provisional Government is composed of excellent men for the most part, all of them a bit limited and unready for a task that would call for the genius of Napoleon and the heart of Jesus. But collectively these men … will be equal to the situation.[43]

But what about the provinces? There the cause of the Republic had not yet been won. Thus when she returned to Nohant on March 8, Sand assigned herself the task of mediating between Paris and the provinces. Her role as she saw it was, first of all, to represent the provinces to Paris

---

[41] "To Augustine Brault, March 5, 1848" in *Correspondance*, VIII, 319.
[42] Alphonse de Lamartine, *Histoire de la Révolution de 1848*, 2 vols. (Paris, 1849) II, 137–138.
[43] "To Poncy, March 8, 1848" in *Correspondance*, VIII, 330.

and, secondly, to educate the provinces – to do what she could to incul-
cate democratic values and sympathies among the peasants and workers
of Berry and to break down their suspicion of Paris.

This was a tall order at a time when the Republic was about to
introduce itself to rural France by raising direct taxes by 45 percent.
But Sand saw herself as the representative of the Provisional Government
and, once back in Nohant, she began writing letters to her friends in
which she articulated its "desires" and "wishes." As she told Fréderic
Girerd: "The Provisional Government fervently desires and sincerely
wishes that the people, the real people, be represented in person at the
National Assembly."[44] She discovered, however, that the task of "revolutionizing" (her word) the provinces was more difficult than she had
imagined.[45] Even in Berry, which she knew well, there was a basic
passivity that had to be overcome. "Our rustic population, so grave, so
gentle and so upright, will not resist any good influence. But it has no
initiative, it is passive. It's a lump of earth that is waiting for a ray of
sunshine to germinate." Already on March 9, she was urging that the
election be postponed to give republicans the time to overcome "the dull
and dumb mentality of the provinces."[46]

Seeking to vanquish provincial inertia, Sand published a series of
brochures aimed at the peasantry. Adopting the persona of Blaise
Bonnin, a well-to-do farmer from Berry, she explained to the peasants
why the Republic was a good thing, why its taxes were worth paying, and
why it was important to vote. She also threw herself into local politics. In
the neighbouring town of La Châtre she mobilized democrats for the
coming elections and published articles in the local newspapers. In the
village of Nohant, where her son Maurice had been appointed mayor, she
organized a *cérémonie champêtre* complete with bagpipe and the National
Guard in wooden clogs.[47] On March 17, she wrote Pauline Viardot that
it was hard work "to enlighten the minds of ... 200 electors all of whom
say, 'Vive la République! Down with taxes!' and don't want to hear of
anything else." "The peasants think slowly," she reported in another
letter, "and are suspicious of anyone who wants to widen their
horizons."[48]

As important as this provincial work was to Sand, she could not stay
away from Paris for long. As she wrote Pauline Viardot, she found herself

---

[44] "To Frédéric Girerd, March 8, 1848" in *Correspondance*, VIII, 328.
[45] "To Pierre Bocage, March 11, 1848" in *Correspondance*, VIII, 338.
[46] "To Henri Martin, March 9, 1848" in *Correspondance*, VIII 332–333.
[47] For a description of the *fête* at Nogent, see Karénine, *George Sand*, IV, 37–40.
[48] "To Pauline Viardot, March 17, 1848" in *Correspondance*, VIII, 351; and "To Louis
Vardot, March 17, 1848" in *Correspondance*, VIII, 349.

"revived" and even "electrified" by contact with the poor people of Paris, and she feared losing "not my faith but my enthusiasm" if she stayed too long at Nohant.[49] Thus, on March 21, she returned to the capital and moved into her son's fifth-floor *mansard* at 8, rue de Condé near the Odéon Theatre. For the next two months she remained in Paris, writing feverishly, keeping in touch with her friends in the government – notably Louis Blanc and Ledru-Rollin – and holding court most days *chez* Pinson, a student restaurant on the rue de l'Ancienne Comédie that she had first frequented in the early 1830s. During this period she turned out pamphlets and brochures aimed at peasants and workers (including five brochures entitled *Parole de Blaise Bonnin aux bons citoyens*), drafted circulars and announcements for the Interior Ministry and the Ministry of Public Education and wrote a short political play, *Le Roi attend*, for a free performance at the opening of the new Théâtre de la République on April 6. She founded a weekly newspaper of her own, *La Cause du peuple*, and she also contributed articles to Théophile Thoré's paper, *La Vraie République*. Her aim in all of this was to convince the public of the need for all classes to work together.

If George Sand was close to radical democrats, like Thoré and Ledru-Rollin, her relations with the emerging feminist movement were more complicated. She was an ardent partisan of women's struggle for civil equality – especially equality in marriage and in the family – but she had little sympathy for the movement for women's suffrage, which she regarded as premature. Thus in early April, when she was invited by Eugénie Niboyet and other feminists associated with the journal, *La Voix des femmes*, to stand for election to the National Assembly, her response was strongly negative.[50] They had described her as embodying the virtues of both sexes – as "male in her virility" and "female through her divine intuition, her poetry." She responded bluntly:

A journal published by ladies has proclaimed my candidacy for the National Assembly. If this joke only wounded my self-esteem by attributing to me a ridiculous pretension, I would overlook it … But my silence might lead people to believe that I adhere to the principles that this journal wishes to spread … I cannot allow myself to be taken, without my consent, for the representative of a feminine coterie with which I have never had the least relation, good or bad.[51]

---

[49] "To Pauline Viardot, March 17, 1848" in *Correspondance*, VIII, 350–351.
[50] On this episode and on the feminist movement in 1848, see Michèle Riot-Sarcey, *La Démocratie à l'épreuve des femmes: Trois figures critiques du pouvoir 1830–1848* (Paris, 1994), esp. 181–261.
[51] "To the editor of *La Réforme* and to the editor of *La Vraie République*, April 8, 1848" in *Correspondance*, VIII, 391–392.

She believed that the women's suffrage movement which, even if successful, would only benefit literate and well-educated women, was a distraction from the essential struggle for the rights of poor and under-educated women. The battle that needed to be fought and won, in her view, was the battle not for the vote but for education and against the "lack of schooling, desertion, depravation, and poverty, which weigh on women in general even more than on men."[52] When the journal placed her name on its electoral lists, she replied more fully:

Should women participate in political life one day? Yes, one day, I agree with you. But is that day near? No, I don't think so, and for the political condition of women to be altered, society will have to be transformed radically ... As for you, women, who seek to begin with the exercise of political rights, permit me to tell you that you are playing childish games. [53]

Sand had long believed that the struggle for women's rights should be carried on, initially, on the terrain of marriage and society, and not that of politics. Thus, in her exchange with *La Voix des femmes*, she was returning to the great theme of her earliest novels – the injustice of a system that made divorce an impossibility and marriage a prison for most women.

While Sand believed that the agitation for women's suffrage was premature, she was deeply involved in the effort to influence the outcome of the elections. Indeed, one of her major occupations during her first five weeks in Paris was the drafting of anonymous dispatches, called *Bulletins de la République*, sent out by the Ministry of the Interior to each of France's eighty-six departments in order to raise republican consciousness in the provinces prior to the elections for the National Assembly. Between March 25 and April 29, she drafted nine *Bulletins de la République*. In one she tried to convince "country people" of the importance of paying the grossly unpopular 45 *centime* tax imposed by the government in order to avoid bankruptcy. Another *Bulletin*, which appeared on April 13, reminded all voters of the need to choose candidates who would "work tirelessly to build the edifice of democratic society on a solid foundation." But one of the *Bulletins de la République* went much farther than this; and it caused an uproar all over France. This was *Bulletin* No. 16, which appeared on April 15. The key passage was the following:

If the elections do not bring about the triumph of social truth, if they are the expression of the interests of a caste, torn from the confident loyalty of the people,

---

[52] *Bulletin de la République*, No. 12 (April 6, 1848); *Bulletins de la République émanés du Ministère de l'Intérieur du 13 mars au 6 mai, 1848. Collection complète* (Paris, 1848), 56.
[53] "Aux membres du Comité central [Mid-April 1848]" in *Correspondance*, VIII, 401, 407.

the elections, which ought to be the salvation of the republic, will be its downfall ... There would then be just one means of salvation for the people who built the barricades. This would be to express their will a second time and to defer the decisions of a false national representation.[54]

Sand was saying, in other words, that *if* the elections did not produce a genuinely democratic assembly, then "the people who built the barri-cades" – i.e. the republicans and democrats of Paris – would be justified in overthrowing the democratically elected assembly and in creating some kind of revolutionary dictatorship which would govern France until new elections could produce a more satisfactory outcome. It is worth noting here that while George Sand was later to be held personally responsible for this appeal to revolutionary dictatorship, her views were shared by other radicals at the time, including at least one member of the Provisional Government, Louis Blanc.

Giving Up on Politics

The first major blow to Sand's hopes for the Republic came on April 16, when a workers' demonstration planned by Louis Blanc was followed by a huge conservative counter-demonstration. George Sand's role in the murky *journée* of April 16 is anything but clear. For a week, Louis Blanc had been planning a large peaceful demonstration in which workers would gather on the Champ de Mars and march to the Hôtel de Ville to present the Provisional Government a patriotic contribution and a renewed demand for the organization of work. As the day approached, Sand was, by her own account, involved in intense discussions with radical leaders concerning the need to put pressure on – and possibly purge – the Provisional Government. On April 13, she wrote Maurice that "a political demonstration is being organized in which I must abso-lutely take part. An entirely peaceful demonstration, but one which must remedy much nonsense and many culpable acts." Three days later, however, she informed her son that "l'affaire est avortée."[55]

What happened in the meantime was that on April 13, after a meeting of the Club de la Révolution, Sand had talked for three hours with Pierre Leroux and Armand Barbès about ways in which the conservative major-ity of the Provisional Government might be forced to resign. The following evening, she met with a larger group including Ledru-Rollin,

[54] *Bulletin de la République*, No. 16. *Collection complète*, 68. For commentary, see Georges Lubin, "George Sand en 1848" in *George Sand Papers: Conference Proceedings, 1976* (New York, 1980), 35–36.
[55] "To Maurice Sand, April 13 and 16, 1848" in *Correspondance*, VIII, 398, 409.

Blanc, Barbès, Flocon and Caussidière to discuss a possible "dix-huit fructidor" – a purge of the Provisional Government. On April 15, however, rumours spread across Paris that allies of Auguste Blanqui were planning to take over Louis Blanc's demonstration and to mount a full-scale coup d'état with the aim of indefinitely postponing elections to the National Assembly and replacing the Provisional Government with a radical Committee of Public Safety.[56] At this point, several radical leaders – including Cabet and Raspail – announced that they wanted nothing to do with the demonstration. And Ledru-Rollin, whose position had been equivocal, decided to oppose any attempt to purge the Provisional Government.

On the morning of April 16, as 30,000 workers gathered on the Champ de Mars and prepared to march on the Hôtel de Ville, Ledru-Rollin called out the National Guard, announcing that they would be needed to protect the Provisional Government should it come under attack. Thus at 2 pm, when the workers' procession reached the Hôtel de Ville, they met 100,000 National Guards, Mobile Guards and government troops with their bayonets drawn and "armed to the teeth." Sand reported that by evening the workers were gone, but the streets were full of "bourgeois, students, shopkeepers, flâneurs of all kinds" who were shouting "A bas les communistes!" and "Mort à Cabet!" as they guzzled their wine. Thus, the peaceful demonstration organized by Louis Blanc turned into a massive show of strength by conservatives.[57]

That evening Sand wrote her son that Paris was behaving like La Châtre. "I am afraid," she wrote, "that today the Republic was killed in its principle and in its future, at least in its near future." She could not tolerate the spectacle of an "armed bourgeoisie" claiming to support the Republic but shouting "Death to the communists" and "Death to Cabet." "And this cry came from 200,000 mouths 19/20ths of which were repeating it without any idea of what communism actually is." To make matters worse, her picture of republican leaders was darkening. "Men are false, ambitious, vain, egotistical," she wrote Maurice. "It is truly sad to see this up close." The people she most admired – she named

---

[56] The principal source for this account is an autobiographical fragment "Souvenirs de mars-avril 1848" dictated by Sand to Victor Borie in George Sand, *Oeuvres autobiographiques*, 2 vols. (Paris, 1971) II, 1187–1189. On Sand's role in the preparation of the *journée* of April 16, 1848, see Henri Guillemin, *La Tragédie de quarante-huit* (Geneva, 1948), 152–205; Bernard Hamon, *George Sand et la politique* (Paris, 2001), 263–268; and Hayat, *Quand la République était révolutionnaire*, 211–247.

[57] "To Maurice Sand, night of April 16–17, 1848" in *Correspondance*, VIII, 411–420. This letter offers a full account of the *journée*.

Barbès, Etienne Arago and Caussidière – were all figures of the second rank. "All on the first level live with this ideal: *Me. Me, me.*"[58]

But Sand's discouragement did not last. A few days later on April 20, she exulted at the enthusiasm and the diversity of the participants in the Fête de la Fraternité, which she watched, with the members of the Provisional Government, from the top of the Arc de Triomphe. For twelve hours as an enormous crowd marched from the Place de la Bastille to the Arc de Triomphe, she marvelled at the spectacle of "all the costumes, all the pomp of the army, all the rags of the *sainte canaille,* with the whole population of all ages and both sexes as witness, singing, shouting, applauding, joining the cortège."[59] Inspired by this spectacle, Sand wrote an exuberant article in her weekly paper, *La Cause du Peuple,* looking forward to a day when, thanks to progressive taxation and the socialization of the instruments of labour, poverty would disappear and "individual wealth would give way to social wealth."[60]

Still, she could not help worrying. "It's a sad thing," she wrote, to be caught between the alternatives of "fraternal fervour" and "hateful suspicion."[61] In her journal she wondered whether she and her friends in the Provisional Government weren't asking too much of the people: "There is as much danger," she wrote, "in trying to move a nation forward too rapidly as there is in trying to halt its progress."[62] The massive victory of the Party of Order in the elections of April 23 reinforced her fears. She wrote a friend that for several days after the election she had been wracked "by doubt and sadness" and had "cried bitterly." To escape her gloom, she had spent time on the street, and there she got some encouragement from what she heard in the clubs. She noted that "the instincts of the crowd" now seemed surer to her than the pronouncements of politicians and journalists."[63]

Sand's final *Bulletin de la République* appeared on April 29. The next day she announced the suspension *La Cause du Peuple,* after just three issues. But she soon found a new venue for her journalism. From May 2 to June 11, she published thirteen articles in Théophile Thoré's daily, *La Vraie République.* On May 4 she called on the Assembly to avoid "modest remedies" and "palliatives" and to confront the social question. "The house is on fire!" she announced, and capital could not continue to

---

[58] Ibid, 411, 418.   [59] "To Maurice Sand, April 21, 1848" in *Correspondance,* VIII, 431.

[60] "L'Application de l'égalité, c'est la fraternité," *La Cause du Peuple,* 3 (April 23, 1848) in *Politique et polémiques,* 326.

[61] "To Maurice Sand, April 23, 1848" in *Correspondance,* VIII, 432.

[62] "Souvenirs de mars-avril 1848 (April 26, 1848)" in *Oeuvres autobiographiques,* II, 1189.

[63] "To Eliza Ashurst, April 29, 1848" in *Correspondance,* VIII, 437.

exploit labour "forever."[64] In subsequent articles she warned against the popular election of the president of the Republic, which she feared would lead to conflict between the president and the Assembly and eventually to "social war"; she condemned the shooting at Rouen of workers protesting the election results; and she urged the Assembly to respect the rights of republicans. Finally, taking account of the predominance of Catholics in "the very Christian Assembly of the Palais Bourbon," she denounced the Church hierarchy and called on Catholics to "Be Christian in the Church of Fraternity, which is called the Republic."[65]

Sand wrote Charles Poncy on May 5 that his day would come. If the election results were disappointing, at least the form of the Republic had been accepted: "It seems to me impossible that one could now contest its fundamental principles." She added hopefully that while conservatives had played on the fears of peasants by evoking "the phantom of communism," this tactic would not work for long. "Everywhere," she insisted, one could witness the beginnings of "a healthy reaction against bourgeois opinion."[66]

This was putting a good face on things. Judging from her long conversation at this time with Alexis de Tocqueville, George Sand's true feelings were much less hopeful. This conversation – the only significant exchange that she and Tocqueville ever had – took place at a dinner party given in Sand's honour by the English Member of Parliament, Richard Monckton Milnes. According to Tocqueville, Sand described "with striking vivacity" the condition of the Parisian workers and her dread concerning the possibility of a terrible explosion. "She herself seemed to fear a popular victory," Tocqueville recalled, "and there was a touch of solemnity in her pity for our anticipated fate."[67] As Tocqueville recognized, Sand was actually divided with regard to the revolution. She called for radical change, but she abhorred the violence that she regarded as necessary if change was to come about.

The conversation between Sand and Tocqueville took place on May 3. The next day the National Assembly met for the first time, and tensions flared between the conservative majority and radicals both within and outside the Assembly. Rumours spread concerning the possibility that the radicals would try to overthrow the elected assembly and establish a revolutionary dictatorship. Such a coup was actually attempted on May

---

[64] "La Question sociale," *La Vraie République*, May 4, 1848 in *Politique et polémiques*, 430–432.
[65] "La religion de la France," *La Vraie République*, May 11, 1848 and "Le Dogme de la France," *La Vraie République*, May 12, 1848 in *Politique et polémiques*, 452, 461.
[66] "To Charles Poncy, May 5, 1848" in *Correspondance*, VIII, 445–446.
[67] Tocqueville, *Souvenirs*, 209–211.

15, when a demonstration in support of Polish independence turned into an abortive effort to dissolve the Assembly. The consequence of the failed coup of May 15 was that many of the leaders of the democratic and socialist left were arrested. Their number included not only Blanqui and Raspail but also Sand's close friends, Barbès and Thoré. To make matters worse, Sand was blamed in some quarters for having encouraged the coup with her threat in the sixteenth *Bulletin de la République* that the election of a conservative Assembly might force "le peuple irrité" to "violate the sanctuary of the national representation." People even claimed to have seen Sand herself egging on the demonstrators. At one point during the *journée* of May 15, while she was caught up in a crowd on the rue de Bourgogne, she saw a woman leaning out of a café window and haranguing the crowd. When she asked who the woman was, someone told her that it was "George Sand."[68]

All of this was devastating to Sand. "I am crushed and broken," she wrote Etienne Arago on May 16:

The spectacle of the bourgeois reaction saddens me to the point of making me sick. Yesterday's events set us back ten years. What deplorable madness! The names of Louis Blanc and Barbès mixed up with those of Blanqui, Raspail, etc.! What will become of Barbès, that poor great soul, disoriented and as it were in love with his own destruction?[69]

The next evening Sand left Paris for Nohant. She told her friends that she only wanted "a few days' rest." In fact, she would not return for eighteen months.

Back in Nohant, Sand continued to follow the course of events in the capital through letters from her friends. In her own letters, she railed against politics – and against Paris. "I won't talk politics with you," she wrote a friend. "I'm sick and tired of it. At this point it's a tissue of fables, accusations, suspicions and recriminations, and the absurd and deplorable affair of May 15 has done nothing to make people disposed to fraternity."[70] If her aim in quitting Paris had been to leave all that behind, she was not successful. For she found at Nohant that she herself was now seen as a dangerous communist by the very peasants whose virtues she had celebrated in her pastoral novels: "Here in Berry, so romantic and sweet, so good, so calm, in this *pays* that I love so tenderly, ... I am regarded as the enemy of the human race, and if the Republic has not

---

[68] Lubin, "George Sand en 1848," 38; Perrot in *Politique et polémiques*, 30; "To Thoré, May 18, 1848" in *Correspondance*, VIII, 462; "To Caussidière, May 20, 1848" in *Correspondance*, VIII, 467.

[69] "To Arago, May 16, 1848" in *Correspondance*, VIII, 457.

[70] "To Jules Boucoiran, May 21, 1848" in *Correspondance*, VIII, 470.

kept its promises, it is evidently my fault."[71] Sand found that she was regarded as having conspired, together with an old man called *le Père Communisme*, to prevent the bourgeoisie from continuing to enrich the lives of the common people. She was going to lay claim to all the fields and vineyards in Nohant, and then she and Old Man Communism were planning to solve the problem of food shortages by killing off young children and the elderly. Those who were left would be forced to work for miserable wages while Madame Sand and *le Père Communisme* caroused in her castle.

There was more. Word spread among the peasants of Nohant that, after May 15, Sand's allies had proclaimed the communist Etienne Cabet King of France and that George Sand herself had personally locked up her political enemies in the dungeon at Vincennes. These were the sorts of stories that were circulating among "the good and gentle peasants" of Berry. "If you didn't know them." wrote Sand, "you might imagine that all of these follies were born in their superstitious brains. But nobody knows better than I their good sense and intelligence. Only they are credulous like all those who live far from the facts, and they believe what they are told."[72] Who was making up these stories and providing the peasants with "all this moral and philosophical instruction"? After just three days back in Nohant Sand knew who they were. But what mattered more was that similar stories were being spread throughout the French provinces by agents of the Party of Order.

In an article of May 27, Sand compared the "red scare" of 1848 to the Great Fear of 1789:

In 1789 there was an incredible terror which spread like a current of electricity from one end of France to the other. Everywhere people claimed to see *brigands*. Towns barricaded themselves, peasants hid in wheat fields ... Well, 1848 will be a second year of fear. People have dreamed of cannibalistic communists. Better yet, they have seen them. Every political candidate put on the index by the reactionaries for belonging to some republican nuance has been transformed into a communist in the eyes of terrified populations.[73]

So Ledru-Rollin was a communist; Lamartine was a communist; the whole Provisional Government was communist. And so were the working-class candidates who had the nerve to run for the Assemblée Nationale. In addition, they were drunkards, thieves, wife beaters, child abusers and drinkers of human blood! All over France, such stories had been circulating since April.

---

[71] "Lettre à Thoré. Le Père Communisme," *La Vraie République*, May 27, 1848 in *Politique et polémiques*, 471.
[72] "Le Père Communisme," *Politique et polémiques*, 472.   [73] Ibid, 469–475.

Sand was deeply troubled by the red scare of 1848. She saw it as a tactic that had helped elect conservative candidates to the National Assembly. But it had another more lasting consequence. Such "imbecilic calumnies" about the immorality of democrats poisoned the minds of the rural population by introducing "fear, suspicion, hatred, insult, menace" into the manners of people who were naturally placid by temperament and who had initially been sympathetic to the revolution. Sand was arguing, in other words, that "the people" were naturally good and well-disposed to democracy but that the intervention of outsiders had turned them against it at the very moment when they were being given the opportunity to make their own choices. The red scare had "corrupted the minds of the people in the provinces, at the moment when their natural intelligence was about to develop and to attain an understanding of its rights. [It had] soiled and blackened the purest and most beautiful thing made by God: the consciousness of the simple man."[74] Here was a *cri de coeur* on the part of a woman who had designated herself the champion of the people who had now turned against her. "We devoted our fortune, our life and our soul to the people who are now being told to treat us as wolves."[75]

In her letters of late May Sand repeatedly expressed her disgust with politics. She still followed events in Paris closely, intervening publicly to support two radicals compromised on May 15: Louis Blanc and Armand Barbès.[76] For Barbès she had boundless admiration: she saw him as a republican saint, a man of unequalled courage and dedication to the republican cause. But for all her admiration for individuals, she was losing hope in the cause. She wrote Thoré that she would have no more to do with "the pedants and theocrats" of the left – men like Raspail, Cabet and Blanqui. They wanted to impose "by stealth (or by force if they could) an idea that the people had not yet accepted." They wanted to establish "the law of fraternity not like Jesus but like Mohammed."[77] On June 12, Sand poured out her discouragement to a close friend:

I have just one passion, the idea of equality. It alone brightens my soul and consoles it for all its suffering. But equality is a beautiful dream which I will not see realized. I believed for a month, six weeks perhaps, after February, that the time was ripe for humanity to understand that its evils come from inequality and that, thanks to instinct, need and the desires of almost everyone, habits and

---

[74] Ibid, 474.   [75] Ibid, 475.

[76] "Barbès, *La Vraie République*, June 9, 1848" in *Politique et polémiques* 499–505; "Louis Blanc au Luxembourg," *La Vraie République*, June 2 and 32, 1848, and "Lettre à Théophile Thoré sur la mise en accusation de Louis Blanc," *La Vraie République*, June 11, 1848 in *Politique et polémiques*, 509–524.

[77] "To Thoré, May 28, 1848" in *Correspondance*, VIII, 477–478.

customs would undergo a progressive change ... Today I am undeceived; men are not yet ready. They are too steeped in rancor, fear, small mindedness.[78]

A few days later, in a long letter to Giuseppe Mazzini, she was no less pessimistic. "The people are not ready to govern themselves," she wrote, adding that Christ's preaching of charity and fraternal love had become "incendiary" and that if Jesus returned to earth, "he would be seized by the National Guard as a seditious anarchist."[79]

As the situation in Paris worsened, Sand became increasingly restive at Nohant. By the second week of June calm had returned to the country-side. But in small towns like nearby La Châtre lingering tensions and "personal hatreds" persisted, and she feared that an explosion was coming in Paris. "I am happy to be in the countryside," she wrote on June 9, "and I would not leave if I did not feel a duty to share in the dangers, the pains, and the turbulence of [the capital]." She might be useless at Paris, but by going there she could at least spare herself the sense of reclining in the shade and listening to the birds sing while Paris was suffering. "I'll go back there as soon as the fighting starts."[80]

In late June, however, when news reached Nohant of the terrible insurrection in Paris – and it's crushing by the army, the National Guard, and the Mobile Guards – Sand was too devastated to return to Paris. "My heart is heavy," she wrote an old friend. "You know ... how I suffer to see our bright dream of a fraternal republic come to such an end." To another friend she described herself as "crushed and appalled, feeling 100 years old." To the publisher Hetzel, she wrote: "What is there to say? There's nothing else to do but cry, and the future looks so dark that I feel a great desire and a great need to blow my brains out." To the prefect Marc Dufraisse she wrote that the June insurrection was not a conflict between "natural enemies" – the bourgeoisie and the working class. It was a conflict between two factions within *le peuple*. There were poor on both sides. Modest peasants from the provinces descended on Paris along with rich landowners to help put down the insurrection, and the Mobile Guards, who differed from the insurgents only by virtue of their youth, fought bravely and effectively against their own class. Thus the "saddest and most frightening" aspect of the crushing of the insur-rection was "the dreadful blindness of poor France, both workers and peasants, who rose up en masse and rushed off to shoot their brothers just as they would go after a pack of wolves." She concluded despairingly: "We were not ready for the Republic ... The people were not with us.

---

[78] "To Hortense Allart de Méritens, June 12, 1848" in *Correspondance*, VIII, 507.
[79] "To Mazzini, June 15, 1848" in *Correspondance*, VIII, 513.
[80] "To Richard Monckton-Milnes, June 9, 1848" in *Correspondance*, XXV, 566–567.

They are generally greedy, brutish and nasty. They still need masters."
Finally, in mid-July, in a letter to Charlotte Marliani, she offered a bitter
and memorable verdict on the Second Republic: "I no longer believe in
the existence of a republic which starts out by killing its proletarians."[81]

In the aftermath of the crushing of the June insurrection, the now-
triumphant Party of Order made a concerted effort to find scapegoats.
The National Assembly appointed a committee to determine the causes
and "responsibilities" for May 15 and the June Days. George Sand could
hardly be blamed for the latter since she had left Paris more than a month
earlier, but there was talk of holding her accountable for May 15 on the
ground that the sixteenth *Bulletin de la République* was a "call to insurrection." In the end, nothing came of this; but Sand was left with a bitter
taste in her mouth when Ledru-Rollin, who as Minister of the Interior
was nominally responsible for everything that appeared in the *Bulletins*,
refused to take any share of responsibility for its publication.

George Sand was never again to recover the political faith that had
inspired her for a few weeks after the February Revolution. In letters to
friends that summer she asserted that she remained confident in the
future of the republic and the eventual triumph of the people. For the
next few years, she kept abreast of disputes within the exile communities
in London, Brussels and Switzerland. But she saw little to hope for in the
near future. She found some solace in her correspondence with
Lamennais, Mazzini and with Charles Poncy. And she energetically
came to the defence of Mikhail Bakunin in July when Karl Marx errone-
ously reported in his *Neue Rheinische Zeitung* that she possessed documents proving that Bakunin was a secret agent of the Russian Tsar.[82] But
none of this engaged her on a deep level, and her strongest desire in the
summer of 1848 was to be done with politics – to write more pastoral
novels, to return, as she put it, to her lambs and her sheepfolds. "I am so
tired," she wrote in the preface to *La Petite Fadette* (September 1848), "of
spinning in a vicious circle in politics, so sick of blaming the minority that
governs and then being forced to recognize that this minority was elected
by the majority, that I want to forget all of that, even if only for an
evening."[83] She was surely overstating the point. Her later pastoral
novels – including *La Petite Fadette* – don't celebrate the peasantry as a

---

[81] "To Augustine de Bertholdi, June 29, 1848"; "To Eugénie Duvernet, July 15, 1848";
"To Pierre-Jules Hetzel, July 4, 1848"; "To Marc Dufraisse, July 4, 1848"; "To
Charlotte Marliani, mid-July 1848": *Correspondance*, VIII, 527, 540, 532, 544; and
XXV, 578–579.

[82] Wladimir Karénine, *George Sand, sa vie et ses oeuvres*, 4 vols. (Paris, 1899) IV, 129–138.

[83] George Sand, *La Petite Fadette* (Paris, 1926), viii–ix.

retreat so much as they focus on its plight, and on the stratification of peasant society.

Sand and Louis-Napoleon

During the 1840s, when she sat at the feet of Pierre Leroux and served as mentor and guide to worker poets like Charles Poncy, George Sand was confident that writers like herself had it in their power to reach and inspire the uneducated masses. The experience of 1848 called this confidence into question. It made Sand aware of the intractability of peasant culture and the limits of her ability to influence "le peuple." At the same time, she came to regard politics as a realm of narrow-mindedness and trickery and to believe that detachment from politics was the best stance that she could adopt. The process by which Sand adopted these views is clear enough from the narrative of her activities in 1848. But further light can be shed on the nature of that process, and its outcome, by considering Sand's relations with Louis-Napoleon Bonaparte, the future Napoleon III, who was both the only elected president of the Second French Republic and its gravedigger.

Although Louis-Napoleon and George Sand had apparently met at a Parisian salon in the 1830s, their first important contact came in 1844 when, while a prisoner in the fortress of Ham, he sent her a copy of his essay "Sur l'extinction du paupérisme." Her reply was thoughtful and sympathetic, though more sympathetic to Louis-Napoleon's social criticism than to his proposed remedies. He responded with a series of letters in which he parried her criticism, showered her with compliments, and eagerly sought her approval. He praised her for possessing "the qualities of a man without the faults," and went on to explain that, while he considered himself a democrat with advanced social views, he was not a republican since he believed a republic to be impossible in a Europe dominated by monarchies.[84]

In early June 1848 Sand described herself as having "personal sympathy" for Louis-Napoleon – adding that this sympathy would not outlast an attempt on his part to stage "an 18th Brumaire" of his own."[85] After September 17, when Louis-Napoleon was elected to the National Assembly by voters in five departments, some of whom apparently believed they were voting for his uncle, Sand's doubts about him

---

[84] "Louis-Napoleon Bonaparte to Sand, April 2, 1845 and January 29, 1845" in Karénine, *George Sand*, IV, 161, 158.
[85] "To Hortense Allart de Méritens, June 12, 1848" in *Correspondance*, VIII, 506.

hardened. She came to believe that a vote for him as president would be a vote for "an ignoble imperial restoration."[86]

Louis-Napoleon's candidacy was well orchestrated. When he was still in England his French supporters published brochures portraying him as a reincarnation of his uncle. In one such document, an *Almanach populaire de la France pour 1849*, Louis-Napoleon's portrait was framed by facsimiles of letters from Louis Blanc, Béranger, Chateaubriand, Odilon Barrot and George Sand. The obvious implication was that all these individuals supported his candidacy. Sand denounced this electoral trick in an open letter published in three radical newspapers shortly before the election. In this letter, she explained that if a republic had not been declared in France, Louis-Napoleon might be considered "the best intentioned" and "least dangerous" of candidates. "But," she continued, "under a republic, Monsieur Louis Bonaparte, who is *an enemy by system and by conviction of the republican form of government*, does not have the right to be a candidate for the presidency of a republic."[87] This provocation went unanswered. But in the presidential election of December 10, Louis-Napoleon won three times as many votes as all his opponents combined.

Two weeks later Sand published an article in *La Réforme* attempting to explain the meaning of Louis-Napoleon's massive victory. This article is fascinating because it shows Sand trying simultaneously to register her deep disappointment at the outcome of the election and her continuing respect for *le peuple* – the peasants and artisans who voted for Louis-Napoleon. At first glance, she writes, one might see the election as proof of the fact that the vast majority of the French are not republican. But the situation, she argues, is not so simple. "The people" – here Sand refers both to peasants and urban workers – voted for Louis-Napoleon not simply because of his name but first and foremost because he was an outsider. He was not part of the existing political establishment and he had nothing to do with the bloodshed in June.

Educated democrats and republicans – including Sand herself – remained bitter about Cavaignac's role in the June Days. But they also recognized that Cavaignac had since demonstrated his commitment to republican institutions. They were willing to "put the somber tragedy of June behind them" and to support Cavaignac, "claiming to see in him, not their ideal but a man necessary in the situation, the savior of the

[86] "To Emile Aucante, November 10, 1848" in *Correspondance*, VIII, 696.
[87] "To the editors of *La Réforme*, *La Démocratie pacifique*, and *Le Peuple*, December 1, 1848" in *Correspondance*, VIII, 718. Italics are Sand's – as is the designation "Monsieur" Louis Bonaparte.

Republic menaced by the Bonapartist party." The people made no such concessions. The "socialist proletarians from the large cities" had voted for Louis Bonaparte out of hatred for Cavaignac; and in the countryside "the great mass of rural proletarians took vengeance on a bourgeois republic which had deceived them with fine promises."[88]

Sand went on to make a virtue out of the gullibility and simple-mindedness of le peuple. Even if the peasants had a blind faith in the power of a name, at least they had a faith. Even if they were loyal to a charlatan, at least they were capable of loyalty. She concluded her article with an odd encomium to "the people." She wrote that she felt no resentment toward the people, even when they took positions contrary to her wishes. For le peuple, this "abstract and collective being," had always meant more to her than individuals and parties. To le peuple alone could she dedicate herself without reserve. And should le peuple make mistakes, she would support them: "I will endorse their follies and accept their errors."[89] As this sad statement makes clear, Sand's faith in politics was gone. So was her confidence in her own ability to influence the course of events. And so were the hopes that she had placed in "the people." Her comments about them in her letters were consistently dark and even demeaning. In 1850 she advised Louis Blanc that his ideas would find no echo in the French provinces:

I don't know anything about Paris at this point, but as for the departments, I can tell you that they are not with you. They don't understand, they don't *want* any kind of ideal. They are ruled uniquely by the idea of personal interest.[90]

On December 2, 1851, when Louis-Napoleon's long-anticipated coup took place, Sand shed no tears for the Republic; and her initial reaction to news of the massive movement of provincial resistance, was relief that the insurrection had failed and that her own region, and her property, had been spared.[91] But then, as a wave of repression swept the country, many of her republican friends were arrested or in hiding. Rumours circulated that she herself might be deported. Asking her cousins, René and Apolline de Villeneuve, to intervene on her behalf with Louis-Napoleon, Sand rehearsed the arguments that might be used to save her:

I can swear before God that for the past three years, without giving up my utopia which as you know is Christian and peaceful, as are my instincts, I have not lifted

---

[88] "A propos de l'élection de Louis Bonaparte à la présidence de la République," *La Réforme*, December 22, 1848 in Perrot (ed.), *Politique et polémiques*, 562–567.

[89] Sand, *Politique et polémiques*, 566–567.

[90] "To Louis Blanc, August 27, 1850" in *Correspondance*, XXV, 745–746.

[91] Peter McPhee, *The Politics of Rural Life: Political Mobilization in the French. Countryside, 1846–1852* (Oxford, 1992), 243; Sand, *Correspondance*, X, 579–664.

a finger against official society. I have devoted all my time to my art and to talking sense, patience, and mildness to the hotheads I happened to meet.[92]

It soon became evident that Sand was not in danger. But many of her friends were. She wrote Louis-Napoleon, requesting an interview to plead their case. He granted her the interview, and on January 30 he listened sympathetically as Sand made her plea for a general amnesty and an end to arrests in the department of the Indre. The next day she reported to her cousins that, although Louis-Napoleon had refused to grant a general amnesty, "he *asked* me to ask him for whatever I wanted for my friends who had suffered from these injustices, and he showed the greatest respect for my character, even though I told him that I am just as republican, as communist as when he first knew me, and that I would never change."[93] Louis-Napoleon granted Sand a second interview on February 6; and for the next two months she remained at Paris, pressing her case in audiences with members of the government from Persigny, the Minister of the Interior, to lowly secretaries in the Ministry of Police. She also visited political prisoners including her friend Marc Dufraisse and her erstwhile antagonist Proudhon.[94]

After her return to Nohant in April, Sand continued for several months to bombard authorities – including Louis-Napoleon – with letters alternately imploring and demanding that justice be done. Thanks to Sand's efforts twenty-six republicans had their sentences reduced and four soldiers awaiting execution were freed.[95] But another result was that the Bonapartist press publicized Sand's visits to the Elysée Palace just as if they had won a convert. This led zealous republicans to conclude that Sand had indeed been won over by Louis-Napoleon. She was accused of dishonouring herself, of fatally compromising her principles, of having become a Bonapartist.[96] Some republicans never forgave her. Edgar Quinet wrote that he was "revolted" by Sand's sycophantic behaviour. He had once admired her and had adored her writings, but he could no longer even read her after learning of her visits to the Elysée "cap in

[92] "To René de Villeneuve, January 13, 1852" in *Correspondance*, X, 643. On Sand's response to December 2, see *Oeuvres autobiographiques*, II, 1198–1222; and Karénine, *George Sand*, IV, 172–238.
[93] "To Apolline and René de Villeneuve, January 31, 1852" in *Correspondance*, X, 682.
[94] Proudhon, who was surprised and touched by Sand's visit, described her in his journal as a plainspoken woman of "great good sense" and "a good heart." He concluded: "George Sand has lived a fast life [*rôti le balai*] more by fantasy, I think, than by sensuality or passion." See Pierre Haubtmann, *Proudhon: Sa vie et sa pensée 1849–1865*, 2 vols. (Paris, 1988), I, 165.
[95] Karénine, *George Sand*, IV, 237, 203.
[96] "To Pierre-Jules Hetzel, February 22, 1852" in *Correspondance*, X, 734–738.

hand."[97] From London, Louis Blanc lectured her: "You do not have the right to ask pardon! By your entreaties you are compromising us."[98] She replied that she was simply acting as a woman whose law was compassion. Blanc was moved by her words. But he continued to maintain that her appeal to Louis-Napoleon was a political mistake. Not surprisingly, Sand was embittered by these attacks. On February 22, she wrote Hetzel that they filled her with "profound scorn and disgust for the partisan spirit." She had had enough of "the reds." She was now ready to give her "political resignation" – to drop out of politics altogether.[99] Thus, well before Louis-Napoleon's proclamation of the Second Empire on December 2, 1852, Sand ceased trying to influence the regime. She made no more appeals to Louis-Napoleon, and in 1857, when she sought to persuade the government to lift its suspension of *La Presse*, she addressed herself to the Empress Eugénie.

If Sand ceased to have significant personal relations with Louis-Napoleon after 1852, she drew close to other members of the family – notably the Emperor's cousin, Princess Mathilde, and her brother, Prince Jérôme Napoleon, familiarly known as Plon-Plon. These were the liberal members of the extended family. Jérôme was a supporter of Italian unification and enough of a free spirit to offer Victor Hugo asylum after December 2. During the Second Empire Sand stayed in touch with the Princess and her brother. When in Paris, she occasionally attended Mathilde's salon; and Jérôme became a friend, an occasional visitor to Nohant and the godfather of Sand's beloved granddaughter Aurore.[100]

Over the years Sand gradually put her adventurous past behind her. She became the calm, composed, and apparently serene woman depicted in the photographs of Nadar (see Figure 3.1). After 1867, she settled in at Nohant with her son Maurice, his wife Lina and their two daughters and a little court consisting of friends from the old days. At Nohant she busied herself writing, managing the household, botanizing, doting on her granddaughters and organizing puppet shows and plays with Maurice. She generally enjoyed company, but when she wanted solitude, she could retreat to a cottage purchased for her in the nearby village of Gargilesse by her last lover, Alexandre Manceau. Her visits to Paris now were brief and often timed to include one of the bi-monthly dinners at

[97] Edgar Quinet, *Lettres d'exile à Michelet et à divers amis*, 2 vols. (Paris, 1886), I, 27.
[98] "Louis Blanc to Sand [c. March, 1852]" in *Correspondance*, X, 795 n 2.
[99] "To Pierre-Jules Hetzel, February 22, 1852" in *Correspondance*, X, 737.
[100] Bernard Hamon (ed.), *George Sand et le prince Napoléon: Histoire d'une amitié 1852–1876* (Vendoeuvres, 2008).

the restaurant Magny where she was the only woman in a distinguished group of writers including Flaubert, Sainte-Beuve, Renan, Gautier, Turgenev and the Goncourt brothers. Her favourites in that group – Flaubert and Turgenev – came to visit her at Nohant, and she in turn made two memorable visits to Flaubert at Croisset. She cultivated an impression of serenity. But when Flaubert complimented her on it, she replied that it was not natural to her, but the result of a sense of duty and an effort of will.[101]

Looking Back on 1848

What was the elderly George Sand's attitude toward the dreams and ideals of 1848? How did she remember the revolution of 1848? She often claimed that she had changed little, that she still looked forward to a democratic republic in which "the people" would exercise their sovereignty wisely and well. But when she got beyond statements of principle and spoke in more specific terms about her vision of the future, it is clear that she had lowered her expectations. As she wrote Flaubert in 1875, speaking of "a very wise and kind letter" that she had just received from Prince Napoleon, "He now sees that a disciplined republic ('une république sage') would be a relatively good solution, and I think it possible. It would be very bourgeois and not very ideal, but we must begin at the beginning."[102] What about the democratic ideas that Sand had found so inspiring in the 1840s? There is not much mention of them in her correspondence; and when they do appear, it is sometimes in a starkly negative light, as in a letter expressing her "contempt" for "the exploitation of poverty by so-called democrats who make it serve their low ambitions."[103]

Sand wrote critically about the conduct of all sides in 1848. In the preface to her play *Cadio* (1868), to illustrate a point about crimes that go unpunished during civil wars, she tells the story of a National Guard unit from an unnamed provincial town (probably LaChâtre). When news of the June insurrection reached the town, the townspeople set off for Paris "to restore order." They were ordinary people – "bourgeois and artisans of all shades and all opinions, most of them decent folk, peaceable husbands and fathers." Reaching Paris during the fighting, they did not know what to do. Finally, in the evening, "ashamed of their idleness," they killed a passer-by who had the misfortune to be wearing the *blouse* of

---

[101] Renée Winegarten, *The Double Life of George Sand: Woman and Writer* (New York, 1978), 316.
[102] "To Gustave Flaubert, January 16, 1875" in *Correspondance*, XXIV, 201.
[103] "To Antoine Scipion du Roure, January 4, 1875" in *Correspondance*, XXIV, 193.

a worker and therefore *"looked like* an insurgent." Sand's informant confessed that "we didn't know how to prevent this."[104]

What is the place of the revolution of 1848 in Sand's fiction? At first glance, it appears to be modest. Of the twenty-eight novels that Sand published during the course of the Second Empire, not a single one deals centrally with the history of the Second Republic. But in many of these novels, 1848 is evoked as part of the recent past. The failure of the revolution and the ultimate collapse of the Second Republic form the backdrop – and in some cases the explanation – for the discouragement or resignation or the sense of hopelessness of the central character. As Eric Bordas has written in an illuminating essay, the heroes of these novels "have nothing to look forward to in life apart from a little love affair to keep them busy."[105] So 1848 is remembered in her novels as a failure and a turning point in the lives of those who lived through it.

An example of the way in which 1848 figures in Sand's later fiction can be found in her 1857 novel *La Daniella.* In this novel, the narrator is a man who has never entirely abandoned the hopes inspired by the February Revolution. A younger man, Jean Valreg, tells the narrator of his own reaction when as an adolescent he witnessed the collapse of the revolutionary hopes:

You belong to a generation open to the inspiration of generous ideas. When you were my age, you breathed the air of the future, you dreamed of immediate and rapid progress that you expected to see realized after the July Revolution. Your ideas were repressed and persecuted, your hopes thwarted by reality; but they were not crushed, and the struggle continued until February 1848 ... when a new explosion allowed you to recover your youth and your faith. Everything that has happened since then has not caused you to lose hope. You and your friends have become used to believing and waiting; you will always be young just as you are now at the age of fifty.

The inner history of Jean Valreg's generation was totally different:

Our spirit spread its wings for the first time in the sun of the Republic; but suddenly we fell, and the sun was blocked out. I was thirteen years old when I was told: "The past no longer exists; a new era is beginning." ... Then came the June Days, which brought panic and rage into the heart of our countryside. Peasants saw bandits and incendiaries in every passer-by ... I understood that hatred had devoured the seeds of fraternity before they had time to germinate. My soul hardened, and my saddened heart lost its illusions?[106]

---

[104] In *Cadio* (Paris, 1868), i. On this incident, which seems to have involved a National Guard unit from La Châtre, see "Sand to Marc Dufraisse, July 4, 1848" in *Correspondance*, XXV, 579.

[105] Eric Bordas, "Les Romans du Second Empire" in Martine Reid and Michèle Riot-Sarcey (eds.), *George Sand: Littérature et politique* (Nantes, 2007), 115.

[106] George Sand, *La Daniella*, 2 vols. (Paris, 1869), I, 10–11.

In this text, the narrator's viewpoint is described with sympathy, but also with a bit of condescension: the sense of hope will never leave him, and he will always be young. Most importantly for us, 1848 is here presented very clearly as an ending and not a beginning – as an irretrievable part of a lost past. A new era is now beginning, and Valreg will have a role to play in it. But not the narrator: he can keep his ideals and regrets, but they will not serve him in the new world.

We can return to Sand's correspondence for another – bleaker – view of what the experience of 1848 came to mean to her and what was left at the end of her life of the ideals that she had brought to the February Revolution. Here the key documents are the extraordinary letters that she exchanged with Flaubert during the final decade of her life.[107] Already in 1868, she was adopting a disabused and even condescending tone with regard to "generous-hearted" 'forty-eighters like Louis Blanc and their dream of a social order based on a purified and idealized Christianity. "I too held that illusion," she told Flaubert, "but as soon as you look back into the past you will see that this dream cannot be revived." She was sure that Louis Blanc himself would now be smiling at his illusions in 1848. Intelligent 'forty-eighters had surely changed their way of thinking in the past twenty years, and it would not be generous to reproach them for beliefs that they no longer held.[108]

Opposites in temperament and personality and in many of their most cherished assumptions about the world, Flaubert and Sand became deeply attached to each other. They felt free to say anything to each other – to vent, hector, lecture or play, as the spirit moved. The Paris Commune, which took them both by surprise, brought out all of these responses except the last. From the beginning, Flaubert and Sand reacted differently to events. She rejoiced in the fall of Napoleon III and the declaration of the Third French Republic; he expected nothing from the Republic. Flaubert, whose home in Normandy was requisitioned by German troops, was incensed by the German occupation and supported French efforts at resistance; Sand wanted immediate peace. During the siege of Paris, the creation of the Paris Commune, and its annihilation by French troops based at Versailles, Flaubert inveighed

---

[107] Both sides of the correspondence can be read together in French or in an excellent English edition. See Alphonse Jacobs (ed.), *Gustave Flaubert–George Sand: Correspondance* (Paris, 1981); and *Flaubert–Sand. The Correspondence*, trans. Francis Steegmuller and Barbara Bray (London, 1993). A recent study of the correspondence, which sees Sand's egalitarian and democratic ideals as relatively untarnished after 1871 is Peter Brooks, *Flaubert in the Ruins of Paris: The Story of a Friendship, a Novel, and a Terrible Year* (New York, 2017).

[108] "To Flaubert, July 31, 1868" in *Correspondance*, XXI, 74.

against zealots on both sides, seeing everything as a confirmation of his low view of human nature. Sand on the other hand, while occasionally distancing herself from the French government at Versailles, was unrelenting in her criticism of the "horrors" of the "ignoble" and "infamous" Paris Commune.

What is striking in Sand's letters to Flaubert is not merely that she inveighs repeatedly against "the vile excesses of the Commune" but also that she sees the Commune as a demonstration of the bankruptcy of her old radical and democratic faith. She confesses to Flaubert that the spectacle of the Commune has awakened her from a naïve, idealistic dream. For so long, she says, she saw everything through rose-coloured glasses. "I imagined that everyone could enlighten and correct and control themselves – that the years which had passed over me and my fellow creatures were bound to show the effects of reason and experience. And now I awake from a dream to find a whole generation divided between idiocy and delirium tremens. Anything is possible now!"[109] During Bloody Week she wrote Charles Poncy that "this chimerical insurrection" was a "calamity" for those, like her, who believed in "the noble instincts of the masses."[110] Three weeks later, in a letter to Juliette Adam, Sand adopted an even more despairing tone with regard to her own hopes in 1848:

Let us shed tears of blood over our illusions and our errors. We believed that the townspeople were good and brave. They are nasty when they are brave, cowardly when they are good. The Empire made them dangerous. A possible Republic can only make them inoffensive, and an ideal republic is far, far in the future[111]

The severity of Sand's criticism of the Commune distressed and astonished her friends. It has also been distressing to many of Sand's scholarly admirers, who are well aware that in terms of sheer numbers the bloodbath that accompanied the destruction of the Commune dwarfed the killing of 69 hostages and the burning of public buildings for which the Communards themselves were responsible. Images of les pétroleuses, the shooting of the Archbishop of Paris, and the destruction of the Napoleonic column in the Place Vendôme were widely disseminated in the aftermath of the Commune; and the building of the Basilica of Sacré Coeur was regarded as a spectacular gesture of public penitence for the sins of the Commune. But thanks to her network of republican and democratic friends, Sand herself was in a position to know a good deal

---

[109] "To Flaubert, June 14, 1871" in *Correspondance*, XXII, 419–420.
[110] "To Charles Poncy, May 25, 1871" in *Correspondance*, XXII, 392.
[111] "To Juliette Adam, June 13, 1871" in *Correspondance*, XXII, 416.

about the ferocity of the repression of the Commune. It didn't seem to matter greatly to her.[112]

What she saw in the Commune was mob violence. The Commune was not inspired by any "social and humanitarian" impulse, she wrote. It was "the saturnalia of the plebians after the saturnalia of the Empire."[113] She condemned the "cowardice" of Parisians who had in her view allowed a mob of "cretins" and "bandits" to drive out of Paris the republican government headed by Adolphe Thiers.[114] And she repeatedly expressed her admiration for Thiers himself, whom she described as "a bridge thrown up between Paris and the provinces, between the Republic and the reaction."[115] Barely a month after the conclusion of "Bloody Week," during the course of which close to twenty thousand Parisians were massacred by troops acting under orders issued by Thiers, Sand wrote an American friend that she believed in "the sincerity, the honour, and the great intelligence of Monsieur Thiers and the 'moderate nucleus' that works with him."[116] And in May 1873, at the time of Thiers' resignation, Sand wrote him personally to express her respect, admiration, and "immense gratitude" for his service as president of France.[117]

---

[112] From 1870 through 1873 Sand kept what amounted to a diary in which she commented on Parisian news, local events, and visitors to Nohant. (Like Marie d'Agoult, she used engagement books or *Agendas* for that purpose.) Although most of the newspapers that she received and read in 1871 were moderate republican or conservative, there are relatively frequent references in her *Agenda* to *Le Rappel* and other pro-Communard papers. She was also in regular contact at this time with the radical republican Edmond Plauchut. The fact that she came to adopt the positions, and the language, of the most extreme critics of the Commune and to accept as fact rumors about Parisian women offering poisoned drinks to French soldiers and enlisting their children to help set fire to public buildings cannot be explained in terms of her ignorance and isolation at Nohant. Her *Agenda* also includes repeated denunciations of the Commune, more shrill than anything in her letters and published writings. (On April 23, she calls the Commune "a riot of madmen and imbeciles mixed up with gangsters." On May 19, learning of the demolition of the Vendôme Column, she writes: "I don't know why the army doesn't put an end to this orgy.") All of this makes it difficult to accept Peter Brooks' claim, in *Flaubert in the Ruins of Paris*, 193, concerning Sand's "continuing adherence to the principles of 1848." For extensive extracts from the *Agendas*, see Annarosa Poli, *George Sand et les Années Terribles* (Bologna-Paris, 1975), 325–466. The originals at the Bibliothèque nationale de France NAF 24832–24835 have been transcribed and annotated by Anne Chevreau in George Sand, *Agendas*, 6 vols. (Paris, 1993), IV. See also Hamon, *George Sand et la politique*, 441–457; and Géraldi Leroy, "Une 'chimérique insurrection': la Commune de Paris dans les Agendas et la Correspondance de George Sand" in Noëlle Dauphin (ed.), *George Sand: Terroir et histoire* (Rennes, 2006), 263–273.

[113] "To Alexandre Dumas *fils*, April 22, 1871" in *Correspondance*, XXII, 367.
[114] "To Flaubert, April 28, 1871" in *Correspondance*, XXII, 371.
[115] "To Edmond Plauchut, March 27, 1871" in *Correspondance*, XXII, 352.
[116] "To Henry Harrisse, July 6, 1871" in *Correspondance*, XXII, 450.
[117] "To Adolphe Thiers, May 30, 1873" in *Correspondance*, XXIII, 528.

When she was criticized by her republican friends for her support of the crushing of the Paris Commune and Thiers' efforts to establish a conservative republic, she had a ready response: "Don't attempt to justify me when I'm accused of not being 'sufficiently republican'. On the contrary, tell them I'm not republican *in their sense*. They have ruined and will continue to ruin the republic, exactly as the priests have ruined Christianity. They are proud, narrow, doctrinaire, and never have the slightest doubt about what they can and cannot do."[118] She often reproached the republicans for this lack of realism. They did not see the limits of the possible. They were too strongly committed to ideal visions. It was as if she were criticizing her former self!

All this caused George Sand to look back on the experience of 1848 with a cold and critical eye. Her early hopes now seemed totally misguided. As she wrote Flaubert in October 1871: "I have lived through revolutions and have had a close view of the major participants. I saw into the depths of their souls, or rather into their depths, pure and simple." What she saw there was "no principles and therefore no genuine intelligence or strength or perseverance." Only Barbès had principles and stuck to them.[119] She wrote derisively of the other 'forty-eighters. Among artists and writers, she found "nothing of substance." Of her former friends in the Provisional Government, only Louis Blanc was worthy of faint praise. As for Ledru-Rollin, her ally in April, she had long ago come to the conclusion that he was "a *woman* in the worst sense of the word."[120]

In her later years, George Sand often asserted that throughout her life she had remained faithful to the ideal of an egalitarian republic. What she detested was violence; and she came to believe that what had gone wrong in 1848 was the refusal of romantic radicals, including herself, to separate themselves from the violent elements in the revolutionary tradition – from 1793 and 1794. As she wrote a young poet: "I hate bloodshed and I'm fed up with those who say: 'Let's do evil to bring about good; let's kill in order to create.' No, no! My old age protests against the tolerance into which I drifted in my youth ... We've got to get rid of the theories of '93; they have ruined us. Terror and Saint Bartholomew's Eve: it's all the same."[121] The problem here, and in much of her later writing, is that in her detestation of revolutionary violence, Sand turned a

---

[118] "To Edmond Plauchut, June 16, 1871" in *Correspondance*, XXII, 424.
[119] "To Flaubert, October 25, 1871" in *Correspondance*, XXII, 595. Sand always admired Barbès. At his death she described him to Flaubert as "one of my religions, one of those beings who reconcile one to humanity": *Correspondance*, XXII, 103.
[120] "To Mazzini, October 5, 1849" in *Correspondance*, IX, 732.
[121] "To Alfred Gabrié, October 21, 1871" in *Correspondance*, XXII, 590.

blind eye to the violence exercised by those in power. When she condemned the violence of "Bloody Week," what she had in mind was the shooting of sixty-nine hostages by the Communards and not the killing of 20,000 Parisians by the National Guard and the army.

Why did Sand write so little about 1848 in retrospect? Clearly, the whole history of the Second Republic was full of painful memories. The Republic, her political allies, and the People on whom she counted so much – they had all disappointed her. And despite her insistence that she had not changed, she came to regard her youthful democratic and republican ideals in 1848 as inadequate. But what could take their place? Flaubert endorsed Renan's view that democracy is dangerous and that the best that could be hoped for was the rule of mandarins. "Free compulsory education will do nothing but swell the number of imbeciles," he wrote. "What we need most of all is a *natural aristocracy* – that is a legitimate one. Nothing can be done without a ruling element; and universal suffrage as it now exists is more stupid than divine right."[122] Sand did not believe in a natural aristocracy. And what, she asked, was government by mandarins? Who would appoint them? How could they be removed? Flaubert had no answer to these questions.

When Sand wrote Flaubert of her bitter unhappiness at the bloodbath of the Paris Commune, he replied coolly that there was nothing to be surprised about. "Why are you so sad? Humanity is displaying nothing new ... I believe that the crowd, the mass, the herd, will always be detestable."[123] Then Flaubert proposed a remedy: "Ah! Dear good Master, if you could only hate! That's what you lack: Hatred." This cavalier response both wounded and infuriated Sand. She sent a ten-page reply not to Flaubert but to the newspaper *Le Temps* to be published in the form of a letter to an unnamed "Friend": "So you want me to stop loving? You want me to say that I've been wrong my whole life, that humanity is contemptible, hateful, has always been so and always will be? And you criticize me for my pain, calling it weakness, childish regret for a lost illusion? You assert that the people have always been vicious, the priest always hypocritical, the bourgeois always cowardly, the soldier always a brigand, the peasant always stupid?"[124] She could never hold such views. For her, there was no possibility of human community without love and mutual respect. And she went on to argue eloquently

[122] Gustave Flaubert, "Flaubert to Sand, October 7, 1871" in *Correspondance*, Jean Bruneau (ed.), 5 vols. (Paris, 1973–2007), IV, 384.
[123] "Flaubert to Sand, September 8, 1871" in *Correspondance de Flaubert*, IV, 375–376.
[124] "To Flaubert, September 14, 1871 – published in *Le Temps*, October 3, 1871" in *Correspondance*, XXII, 545.

against the view that detachment and isolation and hatred of humanity were a foundation on which to build a life.

Sand concluded her letter by calling on the French to love one another, to respect differences, and to avoid politics "because it divides us and arms us against each other." But these fine sentiments did not prevent her from attacking the Communards in fiercely vitriolic and partisan terms: "These men were moved by hatred, thwarted ambition, deluded patriotism, fanaticism without an ideal, sentimental stupidity or natural wickedness."[125] Despite her protestations, it is clear that in the end little was left of her faith in the people – and in egalitarian democracy.

George Sand died in 1876, at a time when the animosities inspired by the Commune and its bitter, bloody end were still very much alive. But it was not for her attack on the Communards and her disavowal of the "illusions" of the 'forty-eighters that she was remembered. What is striking about the outpouring of tributes to Sand at her death is that she was remembered as one of the most eloquent voices of a distant age of hope and idealism. A particularly moving tribute came from a great distance – from Dostoevsky, who wrote in his *Writer's Diary* that "she was entirely one of *our* contemporaries – an idealist of the 1830s and 1840s," who, in a time of "impossible hopes," had helped his generation articulate its own convictions and aspirations.[126] By the mid-1840s, wrote Dostoevsky, "the fame of George Sand and the faith in the force of her genius stood so high" in Russia "that we, her contemporaries, all expected something incomparably greater from her in the future, some new word ... These hopes were not realized ... By the end of the '40s, she had said everything that she was destined to say." But Dostoevsky concluded with a remarkable tribute. He called the anti-clerical Sand "the most Christian of all the French writers." By this he apparently meant that she had an intuitive grasp of the unassuaged "spiritual thirst of humanity" that was his own deepest obsession. For Dostoevsky George Sand gave voice to the noble side of the youthful idealism which had led him to radical activism and penal servitude. [127]

George Sand's death was mourned by writers all over Europe – from Hugo and Turgenev to George Eliot and Henry James. Her greatest literary admirers were her contemporaries – writers who had, like

[125] Ibid, 548.
[126] Fyodor Dostoevsky, *A Writer's Diary*, trans. Kenneth Lantz, 2 vols. (Evanston, 1993–1994), I, 505.
[127] Dostoevsky, *Writer's Diary*, II, 507–514. Renée Winegarten, "The Reputation of George Sand," *Encounter*, XXV(1) (January, 1977), 30–38.

Dostoevsky, begun to read her before 1848. These readers, men as well as women, believed that she was speaking not only to but also for them. "Her books," wrote Ernest Renan, "will always bear witness to what we have wished, thought, felt, suffered."[128] After Sand's death Turgenev recalled "the enthusiasm and amazement" that her work had aroused in him in the 1840s. "I all but worshipped her."[129] More specifically, many of Sand's early readers believed she was articulating their own desire for a better world. As Matthew Arnold put it, "We do not know her unless we feel the spirit which goes through her work as a whole." And that spirit was, in his words, inseparable from "the aspiration towards a purged and renewed human society." Arnold added that while Sand's idealism grew dim in her later writings, those who had been touched by *Lélia* and *Consuelo* could never forget them.[130] Clearly Sand lost confidence after 1848 in her ability to give voice to the "aspiration for a social new-birth." But, for her early readers, she never ceased to personify the hopes of 1848.

---

[128] Ernest Renan, *Feuilles détachées* (Paris, 1892), 294.

[129] "Ivan Turgenev to A. S. Suvorin, June 9, 1876" in A. V. Knowles (ed.), *Turgenev's Letters* (New York, 1983), 223. See also Patrick Waddington, *Turgenev and George Sand: An Improbable Entente* (London, 1981).

[130] Matthew Arnold, "George Sand" in *The Complete Prose Works of Matthew Arnold*, R. H. Super (ed.), 11 vols. (Ann Arbor, 1960–1977) VIII, 216–236.

4   Marie d'Agoult
A Liberal Republican

Marie Catherine Sophie de Flavigny, Countess d'Agoult, was famous in her own time on two counts (see Figure 4.1). In 1835, at the age of thirty, she left her husband and daughter and fled to Switzerland with her lover Franz Liszt. Her relationship with Liszt lasted almost ten years and produced three children, one of whom – Cosima – became the lover and then-wife of Richard Wagner. The Countess d'Agoult was also known as "Daniel Stern," the pen name she adopted as a writer. Although she wrote much, she is best remembered for her *Histoire de la Révolution de 1848* which appeared in three volumes between 1850 and 1853. Based on wide reading, interviews and her own observation, the book was one of Flaubert's principal sources for *L'Education sentimentale*. It remains the most vivid, readable and carefully researched of all the contemporary histories of 1848.

The book and the love affair were two chapters in a life high in drama.[1] Another chapter concerned Marie d'Agoult's intense and short-lived friendship with George Sand. The two women were almost exact contemporaries, and their lives intersected at many points. They were close friends for a few years in the 1830s and rivals for many years thereafter. They were temperamental opposites – Sand warm, spontaneous and resilient, and d'Agoult cool, analytical and depressive – and their falling out in 1839 was bitter. But they had much in common. Both were of noble birth and educated in convent schools. Both left unsatisfying marriages to take younger men as lovers. (In d'Agoult's case there was just one lover; in Sand's case there were many.) Both were professional writers who wrote under pseudonyms and

---

[1] On Marie d'Agoult's biography see Jacques Vier's remarkable, *La Comtesse d'Agoult et son temps*, 6 vols. (Paris, 1955–1963). This work, which represents a lifetime of scholarship, is a rich and not uncritical source of information on d'Agoult and her world. Good one-volume biographies are Charles F. Dupêchez, *Marie d'Agoult* (Paris, 1989) and Phyllis Stock-Morton, *The Life of Marie d'Agoult alias Daniel Stern* (Baltimore, 2000).

Figure 4.1 Portrait of Marie d'Agoult by Chassériau, 1841.

became role models for young women with literary aspirations. Neither had much sympathy for the emerging feminist movement, but both cared deeply about women's issues. Both were idealistic republicans drawn to socialism. But in 1848 they differed in one important respect:

Sand was, at least for a brief period, an activist; and d'Agoult was always an observer.[2]

Liszt and Sand

In an age of rising nationalism, Marie d'Agoult was a true European. Fluent in four languages, she was born in Frankfurt in December 1805. Her father was an émigré French nobleman and her mother from a wealthy German banking family. She grew up reading the Grimms' fairy tales and Schiller's plays, but in 1809 her family returned to France. At the age of twenty-one she married a French count, Charles d'Agoult, a veteran of the Napoleonic Wars who had rallied to the Bourbons in 1814. The wedding contract was signed by Charles X and the entire royal family, and the ceremony was attended by much of the Parisian nobility.

The count was seventeen years older than his bride, a good soldier and a decent man, but narrow-minded and entirely conventional in his opinions. She asks in her memoirs how she could ever have consented to a loveless marriage with a stranger whose tastes and values were utterly foreign to her own. All she can say is that she found the marriage negotiations so repellent that she asked her mother and brother to make the decision for her.[3] Not surprisingly, Marie d'Agoult felt no love – no connection even – with the man she married. She felt only a sense of "complete isolation of heart and mind," and, as a modern biographer puts it, "the intimate aspects of married life were repugnant to her."[4]

For five years Marie d'Agoult attempted to make the best of the situation. Always a voracious reader, she escaped into books, learning English to read Scott and Shakespeare and Byron's *Manfred*. She read *Faust* and *Werther* and Senancour's *Obermann* and plunged into romantic novels which took her out of her unsatisfying life. She devoured George Sand and identified passionately with Sand's unhappily married heroines. She had two daughters and tried to absorb herself in their education. She turned for a time to Christianity, losing herself in the contemplation of Christ's suffering, and wrote a life of the French mystic, Madame Guyon. But she probably derived more satisfaction from entertaining at the family's handsome hôtel on the quai Malaquais and at their château in Brie.

---

[2] For an illuminating comparison of the lives and careers of d'Agoult and Sand, and also Hortense Allart and Delphine Gay, see Whitney Walton, *Eve's Proud Descendants: Four Women Writers and Republican Politics in Nineteenth-Century France* (Stanford, 2000).

[3] *Mémoires, souvenirs et journaux de la comtesse d'Agoult (Daniel Stern)*, Charles F. Dupêchez (ed.), 2 vols. (Paris, 1990), I, 292–296.

[4] Stock-Morton, *Life*, 17.

By the last years of the Restoration the salon of the young Countess d'Agoult was one of the liveliest Legitimist salons of the Faubourg Saint-Germain. After 1830, it welcomed a wider public including bourgeois, *anoblis*, writers and artists. She was a talented pianist, and her guests included celebrated musicians like Rossini and Maria Malibran and the writers Vigny and Sainte-Beuve. In later life she described herself as lacking the temperament of a successful *salonnière*. She was too serious, too candid, too reserved. She was thoughtful but lacked a quick wit. Like Molière's misanthropic Alceste, she knew how to please, but only when it pleased *her* to do so. *Politesse* became second nature for her, but she never learned the art of feigning feelings that she didn't have. As she well understood, these "flaws" – above all her reserve and her candour – made her attractive and a bit mysterious to many people, especially to men.[5]

It was in December 1832 that she met Franz Liszt, then best known as a virtuoso pianist. She was swept off her feet by the young prodigy. She later described her first glimpse of him as an encounter with an apparition. He was "the most extraordinary person I had ever seen. Tall, excessively thin, with a pale face and great sea-green eyes that flashed with sparks of light like breaking waves ... He seemed not to stand on the ground but to glide distractedly like a phantom waiting to be called back into the shadows."[6] In her memoirs she depicted Liszt as a man of wide learning; and indeed, his early letters to her abound in literary references – to Augustine, Petrarch, Montaigne, Chateaubriand, Hugo. Liszt's learning was half-digested compared to hers. But to her he personified an ideal: the ideal of "seeing the world through a pure love for an active, generous, great man." She felt that he was the embodiment of "a divine mystery."[7]

One topic on which Liszt could readily serve as Marie d'Agoult's guide was social thought. Prior to their meeting she had taken little interest in social questions, whereas he knew the Saint-Simonians and had been in the audience in November 1831 when their leader, Prosper Enfantin, announced the coming of the "Female Messiah."[8] Liszt also admired the Christian radical Félicité Lamennais whose long struggle with the papacy culminated in December 1833 with his decision to leave the Church.

[5] *Mémoires, souvenirs et journaux*, I, 259–260, 267–269; Vier, *La Comtesse d'Agoult*, I, 118–127.

[6] *Mémoires, souvenirs et journaux*, I, 299.

[7] Vier, *La Comtesse d'Agoult*, I, 142, citing an unpublished fragment for the *Mémoires* from the Archives Daniel Ollivier.

[8] Stock-Morton, *Life*, 24; Ralph P. Locke, *Music, Musicians, and the Saint-Simonians* (Chicago, 1986), 101; Vier, *La Comtesse d'Agoult*, I, 156.

Shortly after meeting Liszt, d'Agoult could write that she was impressed by "the power, clarity and soundness" of the ideas of the Saint-Simonian Eugène Rodrigues and excited by the views of Lamennais whom Liszt adopted as his spiritual father when his enthusiasm for Saint-Simonism waned. She was never a follower of Lamennais or the Saint-Simonians, but her encounter with their ideas deepened her awareness of social inequalities.[9]

Her relationship with Liszt was never easy. She brought to it expectations that no man could satisfy; and he showed himself at times stunningly insensitive to her desires and needs. She never quite forgot that she belonged to the highest French aristocracy while he was the descendent of a German serf. There were frequent misunderstandings. He wrote her extravagant letters – "You are my country, my heaven, my single love!" – and then went off to enjoy the company of other adoring women.[10] She lived in a state of painful alternation between moments of ecstasy in which she could write that their life together was "one long vow of love" and periods of despair and depression. Both referred repeatedly in their letters to their "suffering." But just four months after their first meeting, she could tell him that whatever her sufferings, he had done her good: "You have managed to break all the lines that still attach me to the world of high society."[11]

By the summer of 1834 Liszt and Marie d'Agoult were talking in coded language about eloping. She worried, understandably, about what it would mean for her to give up everything she possessed: her family, her children, her position in society. Looking to the future, he was untroubled: their lives together would be radiant with purity and dignity.[12] He sometimes argued that if she was worried about her social position, perhaps they should separate. She could not contemplate separation. She also found the secrecy of the affair intolerable. They had begun to meet at Liszt's apartment on the rue de la Sourdière, which they called "the rat-hole" (*Ratzenloch*). But this could not go on. She began to speak of suicide, and he of withdrawing to a monastery. Then she discovered that she was pregnant. From that point on, the question was not whether they should elope, but when.

On June 1, 1835, Marie d'Agoult left Paris for Basel where Franz Liszt was waiting. For six weeks the two lovers travelled through Alpine

[9] "D'Agoult to Liszt, 1833" in *Correspondance de Liszt et de la comtesse d'Agoult, 1833–1846*, Daniel Ollivier (ed.), 2 vols. (Paris, 1933–1934) I, 54; Vier, *La Comtesse d'Agoult*, I, 155.
[10] "Liszt to d'Agoult, April 18–30, 1838" in *Correspondance de Liszt et de la comtesse d'Agoult, 1833–1846*, Daniel Ollivier (ed.), 2 vols. (Paris, 1933–1934), I, 218–224.
[11] "D'Agoult to Liszt [April 1833]" in *Correspondance Liszt-d'Agoult*, I, 55.
[12] "Liszt to d'Agoult, July 1, 1834" in *Correspondance Liszt-d'Agoult*, I, 99.

villages on an idyll that she later described as uninterrupted by a single letter or contact with a single familiar face.[13] Finally, in late July, they settled in Geneva. She looked forward to a future in which they would live together quietly "out of the public view." She would be his muse, and he would compose great works. But from the beginning they lived in separate worlds. Once visibly pregnant, she preferred to stay in their apartment. He led a busy social life, dining out, concertizing, and teaching piano to a dozen young women. And he loved performing. She wrote later that when she attended one of his concerts, she was so troubled by his showmanship that she hardly recognized him. "It was Franz whom I saw and it was not Franz. It was like a character who portrayed him on stage with much skill and truthfulness, but who nonetheless had nothing in common with him."[14]

Left alone more than she would have liked, she succumbed to fits of depression. But she also embarked on a program of reading. She read Montesquieu and Herder and German philosophy, commenting on her readings as had her role model, Madame de Staël. And she gathered around her a group of intellectuals – the historian Sismondi, the orientalist Adolphe Pictet, and the future mayor of Geneva, James Fazy. These gatherings had a warmth and spontaneity that the participants long remembered.[15] She began to write. Liszt often commended art as a means of personal salvation and the artist as "the living expression of God, nature, and beauty." She attempted to elaborate his ideas in articles published in the *Gazette musicale* under Liszt's name. These articles, one of which celebrated "two large and splendid compositions" by Hector Berlioz, *Harold in Italy* and *The Fantastic Symphony*, marked the beginning of her career as a published writer.[16]

In April 1836, shortly after the birth of their daughter Blandine, Liszt left Geneva on a six-week concert tour in France. During his tour he wrote Marie long letters with vehement protestations of love. In these letters he explains that he does not *think* of her because thinking is arid. He *dreams* of her. Every night he reads her letters *religiously*. Her letters are his prayers, his poetry. They purify him – and he concedes that he needs purification.[17] When Liszt returned in early June, after a triumphal concert at the Paris salon of the Princess Belgiojoso and intense conversations with his mentor Lamennais, he announced that he would soon

---

[13] In fact they were accompanied by her maid.
[14] *Mémoires, souvenirs et journaux*, I, 336.
[15] *Mémoires, souvenirs et journaux*, II, 17; Vier, *La Comtesse d'Agoult*, I, 203.
[16] David Cairns, *Berlioz*, 2 vols, (Berkeley, 2000), II, 225.
[17] "Liszt to d'Agoult, April, 1836" in *Correspondance Liszt-d'Agoult*, I, 138, 141.

have to leave for concerts in Lausanne and Dijon. His absences and the obvious pleasure he took in the adulation of women at every concert, were painful for her. She wanted to think of herself as his Beatrice, as his "avenue to a higher life." But it was becoming clear that he didn't really need her.

The relationship with Liszt was to last three more years. There were memorable moments and an extended period of happiness in Italy, with an idyllic two months on Lake Como before the birth of their daughter Cosima in December 1837. But the following spring, while Liszt was performing in Vienna, she got seriously ill, and it took him a month to tear himself away from the wild applause at his concerts, from the receptions given him by noble families, and from the adulation of dozens of adoring women. On his return he confessed that he had been unfaithful, offering the not very satisfactory excuse that "the women of Vienna had thrown themselves at him."[18] A month later, after angry words, and in a mood of resignation, d'Agoult wrote Liszt simply: "My love is drying you up ... It is five years now that this has lasted, and perhaps that is enough. Let me go away. When you call me, I will come back."[19]

It was not until October 1839, after more recrimination, reconciliation and renewed hostilities, that Liszt and Marie d'Agoult decided to separate. They agreed that the separation would be temporary. She would live in Paris with their children and he would travel around Europe concertizing and earning money to support the children. She would open a salon and surround herself with writers who would help launch her literary career. He did not want to end the relationship; he wanted the freedom to take occasional breaks, and then to return, as he chose, to enjoy the warmth of her love.[20]

Her view was decidedly less upbeat. For her separation meant abandoning the dream of being his inspiration. But she could no longer bear a life in which she was constantly worrying about his fidelity. "I don't mind being your mistress," she told him, "I just don't want to be *one* of your mistresses."[21] Still, it took four more years for her to reconcile herself to a final break. Their reunions were sometimes spoiled by her inability to contain her anger at Liszt's multiple infidelities. But in his absence she would write that she could not live without him. From 1841 to 1843, they spent three summers together at a former Benedictine convent on the

---

[18] *Mémoires, souvenirs et journaux*, II, 251.
[19] "D'Agoult to Liszt, June 25, 1838" in *Correspondance Liszt-d'Agoult*, I, 234.
[20] Stock-Morton, *Life*, 64.
[21] D'Agoult quoted in "Liszt to d'Agoult, March 5, 1843" in *Correspondance Liszt-d'Agoult*, II, 217.

Rhine. Here too there were misunderstandings and arguments. As she later wrote, the convent became both "the sanctuary and the tomb of our love."[22]

Finally, in May 1844, after learning of Liszt's well-publicized fling with Lola Montez and getting word that he had dedicated his "Reminiscences of Norma" to Marie Pleyel, Marie d'Agoult had had enough. Writing a friend, she tried to be detached: "In losing Liszt, it was less love that I wept for than the *ideal* I dreamt of finding in his life. I wanted the two of us to make a beautiful and noble protest against prejudice. I wanted us to show ... that free love can be stronger, more faithful, more serious than marriage!"[23] She realized at last that she would have to renounce her dreams and make her own way in the world.

As painful as it proved to be, Marie d'Agoult's relationship with Franz Liszt freed her from a loveless marriage and enabled her to discover in herself unrecognized depths of feeling. It opened her mind and widened her horizons. But d'Agoult's intense friendship with George Sand was hardly less important for her intellectual and emotional life. In fact, the two relationships were closely connected. Liszt helped bring the two women together, and their first significant meeting took place over dinner at his mother's apartment in Paris early in 1835. That fall, after the lovers were settled in Geneva, d'Agoult and Sand began to exchange letters regularly. The two women quickly became attracted to each other. "The first time I saw you," wrote Sand, I found you pretty; but you were cold, and so was I. The second time I told you that I detested the nobility. I didn't realize that you were yourself a noblewoman. Instead of giving me a cuff, which I deserved, you opened your soul to me as if you had known me for ten years."[24] Sand, whom one scholar describes as "the cavalier in this dance of friendship," came quickly to the point: "My beautiful countess with lovely blonde hair, I do not know you personally, but I've heard Franz speak of you and I have seen you. After that, I believe I can without folly and without misplaced familiarity, say that I love you and that you seem to me to be the only beautiful, estimable, and truly noble thing that I have seen shine in the patrician sphere."[25]

[22] "D'Agoult to Marie von Czettritz-Neuhaus, August 27, 1846" in Dupêchez, *Marie d'Agoult*, 160.

[23] "D'Agoult to Marie von Czettritz-Neuhaus, July 11 [1844]" in Dupêchez. *Marie d'Agoult*, 167.

[24] "Sand to d'Agoult, early January, 1836" in *Marie d'Agoult, George Sand, Correspondance*, Charles F. Dupêchez (ed.) (Paris, 1995), I, 29–30.

[25] Jacques Vier, *La Comtesse d'Agoult*, I, 208; "Sand to d'Agoult, late September, 1835" in *Correspondance d'Agoult-Sand*, I, 20.

Sand was drawn to d'Agoult both by her beauty and by her courage in breaking with her aristocratic family to assert her right to love. D'Agoult was attracted by their differences: "From the moment I saw you," she wrote, "I felt that the bizarre contrasts between our two natures could and must be harmonized one day."[26] D'Agoult believed that she could confide in Sand and learn from her – especially about writing. Sand was quick to give her encouragement: "You want to write, well then, write ... Write quickly without thinking too much ... Write while you are inspired, while it is God who speaks through you and not memory."[27]

For a year the relationship between the two women was epistolary. Letters flew back and forth between Nohant and Geneva in which Sand described herself as a "gross and fantastic porcupine" and d'Agoult called herself a "turtle" whose hard shell hid spontaneity and sympathy. They even drew up a playful "contract" to protect their friendship. Finally, in September 1836 d'Agoult and Liszt met Sand and her two children at Chamonix for a week-long excursion in the Alps on mule-back. For the next ten months, Sand and d'Agoult spent most of their time together (sometimes with Liszt, sometimes without him) – first at Geneva, then at Paris and finally at Nohant where d'Agoult made two long visits to Sand in 1837. In Paris for a few months the two women shared a salon.[28]

Looking back from the 1860s, Marie d'Agoult fondly recalled her extended visits to Sand at Nohant:

We rode horseback together along the *traînes* of the Vallée Noire that she has described so well. Her two children were there. Solange wore boys' clothes. Good reading, intelligent conversation, astronomy. Botany, music which she loved passionately. Dissertations on the abolition of the death penalty, on all the ideas that were then called humanitarian, on the Republic. These three months remain a very poetic memory in my life.[29]

But even in this idyllic setting there were problems. Marie suspected that Sand was herself in love with Liszt. She was put off by Sand's impulsiveness, her blunt, unceremonious speech, and the rapidity with which she changed lovers. For her part, Sand was irritated by Marie's fastidiousness and her obsessive cleanliness, and she saw how difficult Marie could be during her spells of depression. Marie and Franz finished by outstaying

[26] "D'Agoult to Sand, January 15, 1836" in *Correspondance d'Agoult-Sand*, I, 36.
[27] "Sand to d'Agoult, late September, 1835" in *Correspondance d'Agoult-Sand*, I, 21.
[28] George Sand, "Histoire de ma vie" in *Oeuvres autobiographiques* Georges Lubin II (ed.) (Paris, 1971), 390–391.
[29] *Mémoires, souvenirs et journaux*, II, 30.

their welcome at Nohant, and Marie's subsequent letters to Sand from Italy went largely unanswered.

There was worse to come. After the couple's departure from Nohant, Marie wrote snide letters to friends about Sand's promiscuity and its effect on her writing. These comments got back to Sand, and she never forgave Marie. Earlier (in February 1838) Sand was visited by Balzac, whom she told of the troubles of Marie and Franz. It would make a wonderful novel, Sand explained, but she could not write it herself because she was Marie's friend. Balzac gratefully noted the facts and wrote the novel, *Béatrix*, which included malicious portraits of both d'Agoult and Liszt. In 1841 Sand published a novel, *Horace*, which included a nasty portrait of d'Agoult as the Vicomtesse de Chailly, a cold, artificial, alarmingly thin society lady with fine hair and bad teeth who "had never been beautiful but very much wished to appear beautiful and managed, by dint of effort, to pass for pretty." Finally, in 1846, d'Agoult returned the compliment by publishing her own *roman à clef*.[30]

So, the warm relationship between Sand and d'Agoult was over by the end of 1839. Each believed she had been treacherously maligned by the other. Sand claimed she did her best to forget d'Agoult; and when friends told her that Marie still loved her she refused to believe it: "She never sincerely loved me. She lived in her imagination. She had infatuations, followed by hatred and disgust."[31] This may be a better description of Sand's part in the relationship than Marie's. For Marie d'Agoult could not "forget" her former friend: she had Sand in mind in 1843 when she dedicated her novella *Julien* "to a broken friendship." In her memoirs, d'Agoult acknowledged the extent of her debt to Sand:

She developed in me a love of nature and a poetic understanding, and by her praise she relieved me of some of the mistrust I had of myself. She introduced me to her republican friends. She made me examine and probe the mysteries of my own heart much more than I had.[32]

D'Agoult's debt to Sand was not only literary but also deeply personal.

If George Sand was a model for d'Agoult, she was also a foil. From the mid-1830s on, Sand was a hugely successful writer, celebrated by the poet Béranger as "the Queen of our new literary generation."[33] So powerful was Sand's presence in the culture that none of the emerging women writers of the period attempted to imitate her. As Whitney Walton has written, they all "set themselves apart from such a dominant

---

[30] George Sand, *Horace* (Paris, 1889), 123–124; Daniel Stern, *Nélida* (Paris, 1846).
[31] "Sand to d'Agoult, c. October 16, 1850" in *Correspondance d'Agoult-Sand*, 276.
[32] *Mémoires*, II, 29–30.   [33] Ibid, 28; Walton, *Eve's Proud Descendants*, 103.

figure by writing in genres other than fiction and by cultivating an unambiguous femininity." D'Agoult's engagement with Sand was uniquely intense. More than the others, d'Agoult came to see Sand as a rival, and it was "in contrast to Sand" that d'Agoult "consciously created herself as a writer."[34]

Femme de lettres

When Marie d'Agoult established herself at Paris in October 1839, she was embarking on a new life. Her first aim was to create a salon to rival those of Delphine Gay and Cristina Belgiojoso as a meeting place for artists and intellectuals. She chose an attractive apartment on the rue Neuve des Mathurins in the heart of the Faubourg Saint-Honoré, and she hired a cook, a groom and a valet as well as an interior decorator to help in the choice of furnishings. She purchased rugs, paintings, marble statuettes, silver lamps, Chinese vases, a Venetian chandelier and a tiger skin for two salons, one in Renaissance style and the other Moorish. And she had David d'Angers create bronze medaillons of Goethe, Byron, André Chénier, Mickiewicz, Chateaubriand and Lamennais for the boudoir, which was also her private study.[35]

Her salon attracted writers and artists and also diplomats, politicians and titled foreigners like Sir Henry Bulwer Lytton and Count Bernard Potocki, and a number of her guests became aspiring suitors. Her status as a countess gave her a social prestige which she described to Liszt as her "bird trap." Her first notable catch was the critic Sainte-Beuve, whose novel *Volupté* had fascinated her. Sainte-Beuve had had an affair with Adèle Hugo a few years earlier, and Marie d'Agoult seemed no less desirable a conquest. Thus Sainte-Beuve, who was not considered a handsome man, began an assiduous courtship punctuated by flattering letters and poems. Marie loved the attention and appreciated Sainte-Beuve's literary advice, but she offered him little more than fine dinners and a place of honour in her salon. When he finally made an explicit declaration of love, she rebuffed him. Later Marie wrote that Sainte-Beuve "could have been very useful to me" if he had reviewed her work, but her rejection had "wounded" him and he never said a word about her in print.[36]

An equally well known, but less insistent, member of Marie's salon was her friend, the poet Alfred de Vigny. Like her, Vigny was an aristocrat

---

[34] Walton, *Eve's Proud Descendants*, 103 and 71–74.
[35] Vier, *La Comtesse d'Agoult*, II, 11–14; Dupêchez, *Marie d'Agoult*, 125–126.
[36] *Mémoires*, II, 36.

who detested the July Monarchy and abhorred bourgeois philistinism. Like her, he had been through a "passionate and painful relationship" with an artist – in his case the actress Marie Dorval. But Vigny was a private person – not a charismatic celebrity who would be the idol of her salon. Marie hoped for a while that this role might be played by Victor Hugo. But Hugo was not interested: after a few dinners, he refused her invitations. Much later, during the Second Empire, their shared hostility to Napoleon III united them. But when she died, Hugo wrote in his journal: "Pas de talent. Petite âme."[37]

Marie had more success with Félicité de Lamennais and Alphonse de Lamartine. Lamennais was no admirer of women with intellectual pretensions, and just when she was recruiting him for her salon, he could write that he had "never met a woman capable of following a line of reasoning for ten minutes."[38] Did he make an exception for Marie d'Agoult? She wanted to think so; and her memoirs note Lamennais' interest in her work: "He responded enthusiastically to my first literary essays. He gave me advice ... He believed he saw strength in my talent."[39]

Like d'Agoult, Lamartine had left behind the conservative royalism of his class; and though he had not yet formally identified himself as a republican, he came to believe that "only the creation of a democratic republic could save France from explosive social forces." On January 27, 1843, in a memorable speech to the Chamber of Deputies, Lamartine asserted that the July Monarchy had lost its way and joined the parliamentary opposition. Marie d'Agoult was thrilled. She wrote him rapturously: "You come to those who suffer, to those crushed by poverty, and you bring them the holy eloquence of your spotless life and your prophetic speech."[40] Lamartine responded to Marie's overtures, and for a time he gladly let her play the role of his *égérie*.[41]

Another adornment of Marie d'Agoult's salon was the publisher, Emile de Girardin, a self-made man known as "the Napoleon of the press." Girardin, who had a wandering eye, was attracted by Marie; and for four years this influential publisher, the husband of the popular writer Delphine Gay, pursued Marie d'Agoult with an ardour almost as intense as Sainte-Beuve's. She kept him at a respectable distance. Nonetheless, he helped launch her career as a professional writer. Between 1841 and

---

[37] Hubert Juin, *Victor Hugo* (Paris, 1986), III, 232.
[38] Lamennais, *Discussions critiques et pensées diverses sur la philosophie* (Paris, 1841), 267 in Vier, *La Comtesse d'Agoult*, II, 37.
[39] *Mémoires*, II, 24.
[40] "Marie d'Agoult to Lamartine, February 20, 1843" in Dupêchez, *Marie d'Agoult*, 197.
[41] Vier, *La Comtesse d'Agoult*, II, 42.

1844 d'Agoult published nineteen articles on German cultural life in Girardin's newspaper, *La Presse*. And with his help she hit upon the pseudonym she was to use for the rest of her life: Daniel Stern.[42]

In her articles d'Agoult described Germany as a "crucible" in which new cultural realities were fermenting. "Germany is embarking upon a new course," she wrote in an essay on Heine and Freiligrath, "and this country which seems to us so calm on the surface is beset by a strange spirit of unrest."[43] Her apartment became a meeting place for German émigrés fleeing from repression east of the Rhine. Their spokesman was the writer Karl Gutzkow, the founder of Young Germany. Another member of the German emigration at this time was Karl Marx. But Marie was not greatly interested in him or in the young Hegelians who surrounded him. "Their works are shot through," she wrote, "with a complete disdain for the teachings of history, a contempt for facts and reality ... They proclaim the unlimited liberty of man, and they do not see that liberty, understood in this way, is only the destruction of all form, the absence of all society."[44]

This criticism of the Young Hegelians appeared in an article on the young German poet, Georg Herwegh, who was to play an important role in d'Agoult's life and, later, in Alexander Herzen's.[45] Herwegh had only recently arrived in Paris. He had won a huge reputation among young Germans for his effusive "Poems of a Living Man." In December 1842, he was banished from Prussia for publishing an open letter to King Frederick William IV calling on Prussians to throw off the yoke of despotism. Marie sent him her articles, and quickly an intense correspondence developed between the unhappy countess and the handsome young poet. At first their exchanges focused on German literature and philosophy. Marie plied him with questions, and he replied with little disquisitions on Bettina von Arnim and Ludwig Feuerbach. He knew and admired Marx whose work, he told Marie, "breathes the whole truth of passion while respecting the most severe logic."[46] In late February 1844, he gave Marie copies of the first (and only) volume of Marx and

---

[42] Review signed "Un inconnu" in *La Presse*, January 9, 1841; Vier, *La Comtesse d'Agoult*, II, 96–101; *Mémoires*, II, 31–32.

[43] "*Revue des deux mondes*, December 1, 1844" in Dupêchez, *Marie d'Agoult*, 188.

[44] "'Georges Herwegh et les Hégéliens politiques,' *La Presse*, November 17, 1843" in Dupêchez, *Marie d'Agoult*, 188.

[45] On Herwegh's poetry and politics, see William J. Brazill, "Georg Herwegh and the Aesthetics of German Unification," *Central European History*, V(2) (June 1972), 99–126.

[46] "Herwegh to d'Agoult, February 25, 1844" in *Au Printemps des dieux*, Marcel Herwegh (ed.) (Paris, 1929), 40. This volume includes all the surviving letters exchanged by Herwegh and Marie d'Agoult, 1843–1861.

Arnold Ruge's *Deutsch Französische Jahrbücher* to which he was a contributor. She replied that she was just "too French" to understand what Marx and his colleagues were getting at. "They are right on some points, but they betray a great lack of knowledge of Christianity and therefore of the Middle Ages."[47]

Herwegh was married and thirteen years younger than Marie. But in her letters she soon moved from literary queries to confessions that revealed the depth of her emotional needs. In recent years, she wrote, she had been trying to fly on two wings called freedom and love. Like Icarus she had fallen into the sea. Herwegh's appearance was like a sail on the horizon of her life. He had rescued her from despair with his fraternal affection. He responded in kind. He wished to provide her soul with "wings more durable than those of Icarus." He wished to "elevate" their friendship, to "sanctify" it by joining with her in the pursuit of a shared ideal.[48]

Marie d'Agoult craved affection and admiration, especially when it came from attractive younger men with artistic pretensions. In addition to Herwegh, her admirers also included the portraitist Henri Lehmann, the shy and devoted young poet, Louis de Ronchaud, and the playwright François Ponsard. These relationships were long-lasting. Until Marie's death Ronchaud remained at her beck and call, and after her death he served as her executor. Marie's relationship with Herwegh was both more intense and more complicated than the others, as she for several years offered him a friendship which looked very much like love.

1847 was a fruitful year in Marie d'Agoult's budding literary career. That year, along with two essays in the *Revue indépendante* on reform and revolution in Prussia and various articles on German literature and philosophy, she published an *Essai sur la liberté considérée comme principe et fin de l'activité humaine*. Abstract in form but intensely personal in inspiration, the *Essai sur la liberté* was an attempt to create a personal belief system. It was a response to the criticism that she continued to receive for her violation of the norms of respectable morality in abandoning husband and daughter to run off with Liszt. Seeking "another reason to live" than the egoistic pursuit of individual happiness or the submissive acceptance of the religious consolation offered to women by traditional moralists, d'Agoult sought to spell out her own views on education, marriage, the family, maternity, and the condition of women.[49] She

---

[47] "D'Agoult to Herwegh [late February, 1844]" in *Au Printemps des dieux*, 42.

[48] "D'Agoult to Herwegh, February 29, 1844"; "Herwegh to d'Agoult, March 1, 1844" in *Au Printemps des dieux*, 48–51.

[49] Daniel Stern, *Essai sur la liberté considerée comme principe et fin de l'activité humaine*, 2nd ed (Paris, 1862), x.

criticized existing authorities, institutions and practices that affected the lives of women. Drawing on her own experience, she attacked the indissolubility of marriage, criticized the primacy of resignation and chastity in the education of women, and challenged the notion that parents have rights over their children rather than ("august and sacred") duties toward them. She called for the equality of the sexes and the rehabilitation of pleasure within marriage.

Hers was not a consistently radical vision: her notion of equality did not call into question the view of the household as the woman's sphere, and she did not argue for women's suffrage. But she did call for the liberty of women within marriage – the right of women to control money and property and to seek divorce. In some respects, such as its assertion that the organization of quality public education for both women and men was the first responsibility of any government, the book was indeed radical. The gist of her argument was to challenge male authority in all spheres of life. "The time has come," she wrote, "to substitute the sole legitimate authority, that of reason, for all the authorities that succeed one another in the life of women and bestow their despotic scepter" on "the father, the husband, the confessor, the lover."[50]

This book was not a popular success. Not surprisingly, it was criticized by many of d'Agoult's male friends including Lamennais and Lamartine. It appeared on a list of dangerous "anarchistical" publications issued in 1847 by the Paris prefect of police, Gabriel Delessert.[51] Nonetheless, it won her recognition among democrats as a serious writer whose views were to be reckoned with. The feminist writer and lecturer Clémence Royer wrote d'Agoult later that the *Essai sur la liberté* would bring her "glory" and that its publication "did honour to women." The romantic nationalist Adam Mickiewicz was lavish in his praise.[52] And admiration came from unexpected quarters: Proudhon confessed that he "was surprised by the power of assimilation that enables you to write so naturally and simply about things that we pretentious theorists can only discuss with the help of more elaborate terminology."[53] Even Liszt, who by this time was doing much to make life miserable for his former mistress, had words of praise: "The book is beautiful and good," he

---

[50] *Essai sur la liberté*, 118–119.
[51] Dupêchez, *Marie d'Agoult*, 193; Vier, *La Comtesse d'Agoult*, II, 207, 296.
[52] "Clémence Royer to d'Agoult, December 29, 1862" in Vier, *La Comtesse d'Agoult*, III, 358. Roman Koropeckyj, *Adam Mickiewicz: The Life of a Romantic* (Ithaca, 2008), 304.
[53] "Proudhon to d'Agoult, February 17, 1847" in Pierre-Joseph Proudhon, *Correspondance* (Paris, 1875), I, 236. Proudhon was here responding to an essay, "Pensées sur les femmes," published in the *Revue indépendante*, which makes arguments similar to those developed in the *Essai sur la liberté*.

wrote her. "It comforts, provokes and improves."[54] Such praise meant much to Marie d'Agoult. On October 4, 1847, she wrote in her diary: "La gloire vient."[55]

By the end of 1847, Marie d'Agoult had established herself as a respected journalist and won a place among the more prominent liberal and republican critics of the July Monarchy. Although she was no socialist, her work was accepted by the circle of democrats and socialists around Pierre Leroux's *Revue indépendante*. And her salon (now on the rue Plumet in the Faubourg Saint-Germain) took on a political character as Sainte-Beuve and Vigny and the musicians were replaced by Herwegh, Lamartine and Littré, and by republican exiles from the east.[56] The anarchist Mikhail Bakunin was an occasional visitor, and so perhaps was Alexander Herzen.[57]

She was forty-two years old now, and her hair had turned prematurely white, but she retained her charm and elegance, and she still enjoyed going to concerts and the theatre in the company of her attentive young men. Her social life did not come to an end in 1848, but the events of that year plunged her into politics

Salonnière and Journalist in 1848

Marie d'Agoult was elated by the proclamation of the Second Republic. Unlike George Sand, she was a moderate Republican who did not participate in street demonstrations or consort with revolutionaries. Sand idealized "le peuple" and sought to touch them; d'Agoult was most comfortable observing the people from a distance. In March and April she herself was apparently one of the *femmes du monde* whom she later described as borrowing clothes from their chambermaids and "furtively" slipping into club meetings, "protected by the dim light of weak oil lamps," to listen to harangues against rich people like herself.[58] But her customary sphere of action was the *salon*, and in the Provisional Government her closest ally was not Ledru-Rollin or Louis Blanc but Lamartine.

---

[54] "Liszt to d'Agoult, July 17, 1847" in *Correspondance Liszt-d'Agoult*, II, 384–385.
[55] *Agenda*, October 4, 1847, BnF Mss. NAF 14324.   [56] Dupêchez, *Marie d'Agoult*, 197.
[57] Bakunin's name appears twice in d'Agoult's *Agenda* for 1847 on a long list of friends and guests. Herzen's name is not on this list, though he is mentioned elsewhere in the *Agenda* and in d'Agoult's correspondence. See also Zimmerman, *Midpassage*, 39, 240; and Vuilleumier, *Autour d'Alexandre Herzen*, 17–18.
[58] *Agenda*, May 5 and 6, 1848, BnF Mss. NAF 14325; Daniel Stern, *Histoire de la Révolution de 1848*, 3 vols. (Paris, 1850–1853), II, 159. Unless otherwise indicated, references to the *Histoire* will be to this first edition.

Like Sand, d'Agoult produced much political journalism in 1848 – notably a series of eighteen "Lettres républicaines" which appeared in the *Courrier français* between May 25 and December 7. But whereas Sand generally addressed herself to peasants and artisans and sometimes assumed the identity of a peasant from Berry, d'Agoult's "Lettres républicaines" were mostly addressed to political leaders (Lamartine, Cavaignac, the Prince de Joinville) or to radical intellectuals (Proudhon, Lamennais, Mickiewicz, Littré). In the one "Lettre républicaine" addressed to Parisian workers, she adopted a patronizing tone: "The electoral success for which you are congratulating your-selves," she tells the workers, "is not, I believe, of a nature to give you real strength."[59] In fact, d'Agoult's audience was pretty much the same no matter whom she claimed to be addressing. She saw herself as an intellectual speaking to an educated elite.[60] And in her *Histoire de la Révolution de 1848*, she focused on individual leaders on the assumption that events were shaped by their choices.

The February Revolution did not take d'Agoult completely by sur-prise. She had followed the Banquet Campaign and praised Lamartine's speech at the Banquet of Macon predicting a "revolution of contempt." On February 22, she was in the visitors' gallery of the Chamber of Deputies to hear Odilon Barrot attack Guizot and his government. Two days later, after Lamartine's decisive speech, she wrote in her diary: "Lamartine très grand," and on February 26 she exulted: "All my friends are going to be in power." That day the Orléanist Louis de Viel-Castel told her that "in the exaltation of [her] language," she "sounded like Madame Roland."[61]

Her most important friend was Lamartine, and on March 7 she was overjoyed to receive a note announcing that he would call on her the next day. "You don't neglect such forces," he wrote deferentially.[62] Lamartine was adept at this kind of flattery; and as it turned out he was guarded in his relations with her. But once he did ask her advice on diplomatic appointments; on March 25 she proudly gave him a list of recommendations. Lamartine's request heightened her sense of her own influence to the point that she could fantasize in her diary about obtaining posts for Lamennais and Louis Tribert. And in April she counted it a personal triumph that she could bring

[59] "Lettres républicaines," XIII, September 23, 1848.
[60] Walton, *Eve's Proud Descendants*, 210.
[61] *Agenda* February 24 and 26, 1848, BnF Mss. NAF 14325; and "Louis de Viel-Castel to d'Agoult, February 26, 1848" in Vier, *La Comtesse d'Agoult*, III, 12.
[62] See *Questions politiques et sociales*, 210, cited in Vier, *La Comtesse d'Agoult*, III, 16. *Agenda*, March 7, 1848, BnF Mss. NAF 14325.

Lamartine and Lamennais together at her salon to discuss the latter's constitutional project.[63]

Insofar as Marie d'Agoult played a role at the outset of the Second Republic, it was through her salon. In addition to Lamartine, Lamennais and Girardin, her guests included the utopian communist Etienne Cabet and republicans from Germany and Central Europe. Karl Gutzkow called her the "muse of the arts," and she clearly liked to think of herself as such.[64] In her diary for this period she carefully records the impression she thinks she is making. On March 16 she notes Cabet's praise: "'You are a political woman. Mme Sand is full of contradictions, doesn't understand anything about politics.' [Cabet] asks me to write for *Le Populaire*. He is enchanted by my ideas. Wants to take me to Icarie." Later she boasts of her skill at keeping Cabet at a respectful distance: "I am simple, curt, almost rude with him. I don't treat him like a beau." [65]

D'Agoult's diary reveals how fiercely competitive she was regarding the other leading women of the Second Republic, Princess Cristina Belgiojoso and George Sand. According to the popular press, there were "three amazons who dispute over the universe," and d'Agoult was pleased to describe herself as "surpassing Belgiojoso by talent and Sand by good sense." In the fall of 1848, when Sand and Belgiojoso had retreated to their country estates, she revelled in her triumph: "Mme Sand has sunk, la B. [Belgiojoso] can't write. She wanted to play a role beyond her abilities."[66]

D'Agoult had mixed feelings about the election results in April. She was pleased that extremists – "terroristes et communistes" – had been defeated. But she was disappointed at the success of many elderly conservatives – "balding heads, greying beards, stooped backs, heavy steps and broken voices."[67] Still, as the votes were being counted, she was excited. The Place de l'Hôtel de Ville was "lit up by a multitude of torches and Bengal lanterns. The mixture in the crowd of uniforms and workers' smocks, the singing, the animation without tumult, all these things were a real pleasure for me."[68] It was, to be sure, from the safe

[63] *Agenda*, March 6, 23 and 25, 1848, BnF Mss. NAF 14325; Vier, *La Comtesse d'Agoult*, III, 17, 301. See also Dupêchez, *Marie d'Agoult*, 199.

[64] Karl Gutzkow, *Briefe aus Paris*, 2 vols. (Leipzig, 1842) II, 38; Stock-Morton, *Life*, 129.

[65] *Agenda*, March 16 and March 24, 1848, BnF Mss. NAF 14325.

[66] Dupêchez, *Marie d'Agoult*, 201; Stock-Morton, *Life*, 144. Marie d'Agoult's coolness toward the Princess Belgiojoso was reciprocated. See Beth Archer Brombert, *Cristina: Portraits of a Princess* (New York, 1977), 340–349.

[67] Daniel Stern, "Physionomie de l'Assemblée nationale," *Courrier français*, June 4, 1848, reprinted in *Esquisses morales et politiques* (Paris, 1849), 21.

[68] To Claire d'Agoult [April 30, 1848] in Dûpechez, *Marie d'Agoult*, 199.

distance of the balcony of the Hôtel de Ville that she enjoyed the spectacle, but her excitement was genuine.

At the opening session of the National Assembly on May 4, she sat with Madame de Lamartine and other "dames provisoires" including the wives of Ledru-Rollin, Flocon and Carnot. For the next few weeks she attended the sessions faithfully, sitting in the President's Box with tickets provided by Lamartine. She saw little of him, and her comments in the "Lettres républicaines" suggest that she was beginning to tire of "the splendid eloquence of the poet" whose "dazzling" waves of oratory seemed to "fall from the heavens and then to melt away before touching ground."[69] In her diary she lamented his failure to provide her friend, Pascal Duprat, with an expected diplomatic appointment. Then, on May 13, she wrote of her "deep sadness" at the emergence of pettiness and egotism in the life of the Republic.[70]

Like so many others, d'Agoult was devastated by the June Days and overwhelmed by the sheer magnitude of the conflict. For 72 hours Paris had been menaced by the uprising, which she described as "the cry of vengeance" of a population suffering from poverty and hunger, and it was crushed in "rivers of blood."[71] Early in the morning of June 25, as Cavaignac was preparing to unleash a massive assault on the insurgents, she wrote a worried letter to her daughter Claire: "General Cavaignac is dictator now and he has taken command. If the Faubourg Saint-Antoine does not surrender, it will be bombarded. The number of dead is frightful. The Mobile Guard is heroic, but the insurgents are desperate. I don't doubt that they will be defeated, but it will be a disastrous victory for the Assembly ... It is not a Bonapartist or Legitimist uprising. It is a social war."[72] In her eye-witness account she marvelled, as did Tocqueville and Marx, at the organization of the insurgents – the rapidity with which barricades went up, the role played by women and children, and by the leaders of the revolt who "remained in the shadows" but coordinated operations "with a firm hand" and with "consummate skill."[73]

In her "Lettres républicaines" she sided with the Assembly and Cavaignac. She praised the "admirable discipline" of the army, the

[69] "Physionomie," *Courrier français*, June 4, 1848.

[70] *Agenda*, May 11, 1848: "Je suis mécontente de Lamartine. Toutes mes espérances Duprat ainsi tombées." May 13, 1848: "Je suis d'une profonde tristesse. Les affaires publiques rentrent dans une sphere mesquine, et il n'y a plus moyens de rester au ton héroïque." See *Agenda*, BnF Mss. NAF 14325.

[71] "Lettres républicaines," V, "Les Quatre fatales journées," *Courrier français*, June 23–28, 1848.

[72] "To Claire d'Agoult, 8:30 am, June 25, 1848" in Dûpechez, *Marie d'Agoult*, 201–202.

[73] "Lettres républicaines," V, "Les Quatre fatales journées," *Courrier français*, June 28, 1848.

"vigilance" of the National Guard, the "prodigious courage" of the Mobile Guard, and the "fraternal zeal" of the provincials who "flew to the aid of Paris."[74] And yet ... she attempted in her journalism and in the *Histoire* to explain what drove the rebels into the streets. Her "Lettre républicaine" of June 28 was an appeal to the victors to act with compassion. She wanted the National Assembly to understand that the rebels were not criminals. Their revolt was in their eyes a just protest against a violation of their rights by a government which had broken its promises to them.

Furthermore, the rebels had been misled by radical leaders. D'Agoult conceded that many of the utopians – Icarians, Fourierists, Pierre Leroux – preached reconciliation. Louis Blanc's theories, and even those of Proudhon, the *bête noir* of the bourgeoisie, were non-violent. There was a moderate socialism. Who then was to blame? Writing in the immediate aftermath of the insurrection, she claimed (as did Proudhon initially) that "foreign money" helped inflame the Parisian proletariat.[75] D'Agoult soon recognized that this was not the case. Then who were the radicals and "demented utopians" who had fanned the flames of revolt? She was vague. She referred to "sectarian socialists" whom she described as "fanatical men" shouting in their "clubs, which they call churches," for "the overthrow of the established order" and sowing hatred, vengeance and bitterness "in the loving heart of the poor."[76] But who were they? Perhaps she had in mind Auguste Blanqui and the radical republican neo-Jacobins.

Before June Marie d'Agoult had never spoken of herself as a socialist. Her political stance in February was liberal and republican. But what emerged clearly from her journalism in 1848 was her sympathy for non-violent socialism. She condemned conservatives who "throw on socialism the blame and even the odium" for the June insurrection. "You seem to take it as a fact," she told them, "that socialism has created a situation which it has simply called attention to." In fact, she says, "socialism sought remedies before it occurred to you to do so, and it has perhaps carried on the search with greater ardour than you."[77]

Throughout the summer d'Agoult regularly attended sessions of the National Assembly (see Figure 4.2). She was in the visitors' gallery as the Assembly voted to shut down the radical clubs, to smother the popular

[74] "Lettres républicaines," VI, "Les Trois socialismes," *Courrier français*, July 8, 1848.
[75] "Lettres républicaines," V, "Les Quatre fatales journées," *Courrier français*, June 28, 1848.
[76] "Lettres républicaines," VI, "Les Trois socialismes," *Courrier français*, July 8, 1848.
[77] "Lettres républicaines," VI, "Les Trois socialismes," *Courrier français*, July 8, 1848.

L'Assemblée en récréation

Figure 4.2 "The Constituent Assembly at Play" by Cham, 1849. In this
depiction of a session of the Assembly, we see the Montagnard Felix
Pyat attacking Proudhon, Adolphe Thiers pulling the hair of Pierre
Leroux, Jules Favre aiming an arrow at Thiers and the President of the
Assembly, Armand Marrast, vainly trying to restore order. Originally
published in *L'Illustration* and reprinted in Auguste Lireux, *L'Assemblée
nationale comique* (1850). Photograph: Alamy

press, and to bring charges against those held responsible for the June
insurrection and the events of May 15. She was also in the audience as
the Assembly declared exile and penal servitude to be the punishment for
all insurgents caught with weapons. About 15,000 men and women had
been thrown into prison; and on July 31, Cavaignac appointed a commission to decide where the prisoners would be deported. On August 17,
she addressed a public letter to Cavaignac imploring him to be generous
toward the arrested insurgents. She did not question the need to crush
the insurrection. But she distinguished between the instigators and the
"simple people" who had naïvely followed them and were now
"crammed into prison cells, thrown together with assassins, looters and
informers." She urged Cavaignac to send those whose main crime was

their naïveté not to distant French colonies like New Caledonia but to French Algeria. They would be "precious colonists," she wrote, and their labour in the fertile fields of Algeria would earn them "both the esteem of their fellow citizens and the restorative well-being that pacifies rebellious instincts and wild desires."[78]

As her "Lettres républicaines" show, d'Agoult admired Cavaignac and supported his policies. In a letter dated July 28 she expressed the hope that Cavaignac's government would "not encounter insurmountable obstacles in constituting a truly democratic state." But this was whistling in the dark. Just a few days earlier she had published a lament on the loss of republican idealism and the rise of conservatism and vulgarity in France. To understand the "absurd tragi-comedy that is playing out before our eyes," she wrote, consider the "striking antithesis" between Lamartine, who represented the generous and idealistic aspirations of the first months, and Thiers, who was in person "the vulgar dénouement" of an abortive revolution. In "the aftermath of a revolution that had shaken society to its foundations," Lamartine had "disarmed the victorious rage of the people," but now Thiers, with his calculating bonhomie, was rekindling the fires of class hatred. It was the grinning face of Thiers that d'Agoult saw behind the "rivers of blood" spilled in June. [79]If Thiers and the Party of Order were taking over the Republic, others were trying to destroy it. Notable among these were the Legitimists, the partisans of the comte de Chambord, the "miracle child" of 1821. On September 2, d'Agoult addressed a "Lettre républicaine" to him. Recalling that she had been raised in a Legitimist household, she shared the Bourbons' loathing of the July Monarchy. But she urged the Bourbon pretender to stay out of politics. Since 1830 too much had changed in France for any king to win widespread support. The task now was to improve the conditions of life of a whole people, and this could only occur peacefully and under a republican government.[80]

In her letter of September 23, d'Agoult warned the Parisian working class that their support of socialist candidates would frighten the bourgeoisie, and two weeks later she urged Lamartine to reconsider his

---

[78] "Lettres républicaines," X, "Les Suppliantes" Au général Cavaignac, *Courrier français*, August 17, 1848. The final decree of October 25 made Algeria the principal site for deportation. But most of the prisoners were released early, and only 459 were actually sent to Algeria. See Maurizio Gribaudi and Michèle Riot-Sarcey, *1848. La Révolution oubliée* (Paris, 2009), 262.

[79] "Lettres républicaines," VIII, "Le Général Cavaignac et les partis politiques," and VII, "M. de Lamartine—M. Thiers," *Courrier français*, July 28, July 17, 1848.

[80] "Lettres républicaines," XI, "A Henri Bourbon, comte de Chambord," *Courrier français*, September 2, 1848.

support for the election of the president by universal suffrage. She no longer trusted the common sense of the uneducated masses: they were too gullible to think independently. She feared the Bonapartists, that "audacious party" supporting "a candidate whose sole qualification is his name." Eight years earlier she had witnessed the passions aroused among ordinary people by the return of Napoleon's ashes to France. Now she feared the rekindling of these energies among "the people who don't analyze or examine things, who never really believed in the death of Bonaparte and who always preferred the glorious calamities of this magical reign to the humiliating prosperity of Bourbon rule."[81]

Finally, a month before the presidential election, in a letter to the voters – *le peuple-électeur* – d'Agoult endorsed Cavaignac.[82] She recognized that many could never forget his brutality in June. Nonetheless, she argued, his republican principles and his spotless reputation made him the best choice for the presidency. As for Louis-Napoleon Bonaparte, she could hardly find words to express her contempt for this "cipher" whose supporters were making a supreme virtue out of his "absence of serious claims to the trust of the public."[83] The Legitimists believed that by manipulating this "blockhead" (*soliveau*), they could set the stage for a Bourbon restoration. But she challenged the assumption that Louis-Napoleon needed their aid. She saw that he had massive support among "country people" and "even among a fraction of the working class of the cities." The peasants were discontent. The 45 centîme tax increase had turned them against the Republic. They wanted "a strong power that would guarantee the use and the inheritance of their property." And they could only conceive of power in a personal form. Having seen two monarchies fall without resistance, the peasantry did not seek the restoration of the monarchy. Nor did they want a president Louis Bonaparte. What they really wanted was an emperor.[84]

Marie d'Agoult's "Lettres républicaines" were intended to shape opinion and influence the course of events. She published the last of them just three days before the election. But she continued to set down her observations in a notebook that has remained unpublished. On election day, Sunday, December 10, she wrote that after voting, she and her daughter Claire took a walk in the Bois de Boulogne. It was a "divine day." The sun and the bright blue sky reminded her of the Florence she had visited

---

[81] "Lettres républicaines," XIV, "Election du président de la République. A M. de Lamartine," *Courrier français*, October 5, 1848.
[82] "Lettres républicaines," XVI, "Au Peuple-électeur," *Courrier français*, November 9, 1848.
[83] Ibid.   [84] Ibid.

with Liszt.[85] Two days later, as Louis-Napoleon's massive victory became known, everything had changed: "Rainy weather. I feel the pain in my bones. I keep myself from bursting into tears. Shame on us, shame on France, on the Republic. Shame on democracy, shame on the people ... I miss the reign of Louis Philippe! Then at least we had hope and illusions about ourselves. As calm and *moderate* as I am, I feel hatred in my heart. I feel that I could become a *terrorist*."[86]

The next three years brought Marie d'Agoult many more disappointments, culminating in Louis-Napoleon's coup d'état on December 2, 1851. Ten days later she sent Emma Herwegh a dark assessment of the political situation:

You are writing to the wrong person if you're looking for hope. *I have no hope.* Here is my *personal* opinion. The representatives are making lots of noise. But it's salon chatter that won't last long. The *shopkeepers, businessmen,* etc. are happy. The army and its leaders are so compromised with the president that they can no longer retreat or hesitate, and they will commit any crime that is asked of them. The peasants (apart from a little *jacquerie* here and there) will *justify* all of this by *making* it legal with their vote. The *workers* didn't resist. They didn't *understand* what was going on. Between a royal assembly and a despot who brought them universal suffrage, they remained uncertain. In any case the Paris population hasn't yet gotten over the great defeat in June. A few brave republicans got themselves killed on the barricades for honor's sake. The police encouraged these barricades to give the troops the opportunity of "saving society from pillage and anarchy."[87]

Disillusioned with politics, Marie d'Agoult now turned back to the history of 1848 on which she had begun to work shortly after the February Revolution.

A Moderate Republican History of 1848

In the preface to the second edition of her *Histoire de la Révolution de 1848* d'Agoult observed that she had written the book "with a nervous pen" and "in the midst of great political agitation." Often, she wrote, "I took up my pen after the stormy debates of a parliamentary session had left me upset. At other times I wrote while an uprising roared in the street; more than once my work was interrupted by the noise of warfare, by anguish,

---

[85] *Journal*, December 10, 1848, BnF Mss. NAF 14326.
[86] *Journal*, December 12, 1848, BnF, Mss. NAF 14326. These observations are from a journal that Marie d'Agoult kept between November 27 and December 21, 1848. The entries in this journal are much fuller than those contained in the small engagement calendars or *agendas* that she normally used to record comments on events and people.
[87] "To Emma Herwegh, December 12, 1851" in *Au Printemps des Dieux*, 157–158.

by the cruel heartbreaks of our civil wars."[88] Still, her book was by far the most carefully researched of all the contemporary histories of 1848. Her bibliography included the records of parliamentary debates and committee meetings, the major newspapers and journals, as well as numerous brochures, reports, proclamations and petitions, published and unpublished. She interviewed or corresponded with revolutionary actors. She travelled to the island of Jersey to interview Louis Blanc; she asked the socialist Ange Guépin to report on the condition of the working class in Lille and Rouen; the young Emile Ollivier was her source for Marseille and the Midi. She even prevailed upon General Lamoricière to draw up a map showing the deployment of government troops during the Paris street fighting in June. Other informants included her friends Viel-Castel, Girardin and Ronchaud, and the writers Auguste Barbet, Pascal Duprat, Emile Littré, and Adolphe Guéroult.[89]

This book, which appeared in three volumes between March 1850 and May 1853, is often described as the most "balanced," "fair-minded" and "objective" account of the revolution of 1848. True enough. Indeed, d'Agoult sometimes goes out of her way to correct errors and even "calumnies" spread by her republican allies.[90] But her history is hardly neutral. She speaks at one point of the "petty and vindictive politics" of the Right, and elsewhere of the "unbelievable cynicism" of the Bonapartists, the frivolity of the dynastic opposition, of "royalist factions blinded by petty rancour," and of the "ignoble calumnies" of the enemies of Lamartine.[91] The book abounds in critical judgments of the main actors. Odilon Barrot is a "buffoon" whose speeches are "sonorous and empty," and he plays the role of the leader of the dynastic opposition with an "imperturbable aplomb" and without the least awareness of its "inanité." Ledru-Rollin is weak-willed, vain and impulsive.[92] Falloux is a stage villain, a kind of Iago, who plays a variety of roles "with a marvellous facility," maintaining, with his sober language and elegant manners, "a sort of modest dignity which hid from all eyes his ambitions and his profound hatreds."[93] Only Lamartine emerges relatively unscathed; and if the book has a hero, it is he. But he is a flawed hero, whose "negligent optimism" contributes to both his rise and his rapid fall.[94]

[88] Marie d'Agoult, *Histoire de la Révolution de 1848*, 2nd ed, 2 vols. (Paris, 1862), I, v.
[89] Vier, *La Comtesse d'Agoult*, III, 71–80.
[90] See for example d'Agoult's statement (*Histoire*, I, 54) that Marshall Bugeaud had no role in the massacres of the rue Transnonain for which he was blamed by virtually the entire left.
[91] *Histoire*, III, 109, 124, 120.   [92] *Histoire*, I, 25–26, 62–63, 65.   [93] *Histoire*, III, 148.
[94] Ibid, 103.

D'Agoult's presence is felt in more significant ways than in her judgments on individuals. The events of 1848–1851 are set within the framework of a progressive view of history growing out of her reflection on the work of Michelet, Louis Blanc and, especially, Augustin Thierry whom she describes in her diary as "the first in France to seek the history of the masses and not that of individuals, races, civilization."[95] D'Agoult draws on Thierry's view of modern French history as the story of the rise of the Third Estate and the enlargement of its freedoms. But unlike Thierry, she argues that at an early point the Third Estate was split and by the eighteenth century two classes within it were vying for recognition: the bourgeoisie and le peuple, or the *classes lettrées* and the *classes laborieuses*.

D'Agoult assigns the eighteenth-century philosophes a central role in radicalizing each of these "classes." "Descending from the palace of the king, the salon of the great, the boudoir of the courtisanes, eighteenth-century philosophy made its way into the garret of the worker and the cottage of the plowman, where its work was slower but also more lasting and more destructive."[96] D'Agoult argues that the philosophes' attack on priestly authority and their demand for liberty and equality had a resonance that outlived the reverses of the Restoration. Thus, she can speak of the February Revolution as "the logical consequence of a double effort of the French who, in the eighteenth century, won freedom of thought for the lettered classes and freedom of action for the labouring classes. It was the culmination of the critical philosophical movement ... which, starting in the heights of society, destroyed little by little all the bases on which the authority of divine right was founded in Catholic and monarchical society. It was at the same time the ... external manifestation of the organic movement which, starting from the popular masses, has since 1789 sought to bring them into social life."[97]

Once this framework is recognized, the main outlines of d'Agoult's argument come into sharp focus. At the outset she writes that the February Revolution was the result of an "involuntary accord" between the bourgeoisie and le peuple. In the third and final volume, she makes a similar point with one significant change in wording: the February Revolution was the result of the common action of the bourgeoisie and the "proletariat."[98] Throughout she insists on the class character of the revolution or, more accurately, of the two revolutionary movements that worked in tandem in 1848. First, there was the bourgeois revolution, which was the logical consequence of the Enlightenment and the demand for free thought by the educated classes. Then there was the social

[95] *Agenda* cited in Vier, *La Comtesse d'Agoult*, III, 91.   [96] *Histoire*, I, vi–vii.
[97] Ibid, ii–iii.   [98] *Histoire*, I, ii; III, 263.

revolution sought by the proletariat, which was an indirect consequence of Enlightenment ideas. For the abolition of the guild system in 1791, which was inspired by the Encyclopedists' demand for the liberty of commerce and industry, left the working class vulnerable to "all the caprices of a blind destiny."[99]

The July Monarchy had antagonized both the bourgeoisie and the working class. Limiting political rights to a tiny minority of the population, the king and his ministers had created a system ruled by egotism and self-interest. The king himself was the personification of "the egoistic indifference of the bourgeoisie."[100] And the "classes laborieuses" were seen only as "a menacing force that had to be contained, repressed, and kept at a distance from political life."[101] Although the bourgeoisie and the proletariat worked together to bring down the July Monarchy, d'Agoult argues that after the revolution the bourgeoisie found itself confronted by "a whole people ... demanding to live a human life and no longer the life of brutes." Their response to this "just" and "simple," yet unforeseen demand from a forgotten class was "stupor" and "immense surprise."[102]

In discussing the first three months of the revolution, d'Agoult speaks of both the illusions of the proletariat and the shortcomings of the Provisional Government. She sees the proletariat – notably the workers at Paris and Lyon – as having been awakened intellectually by the socialists after 1830. They had come to believe that their lives could be bettered by peaceful means – that "without violence and without disrupting the social order, the state could provide them with education, work, and leisure if it really wished to do so." Their "error" was to believe that such a reform could be accomplished "by decree and by the sole action of the government."[103] Here d'Agoult refers specifically to Louis Blanc's plan for the organization of work as a source of error; and her critical perspective resembles that of Proudhon who repeatedly criticized the socialists for their belief that social change could be imposed from above by legislative fiat.

If d'Agoult regards the Parisian workers as naïve and easily misled, her strongest criticism is aimed at the Provisional Government. Its members could have assumed the role of guiding and educating the people – of helping them acquire "the moral force which establishes and enriches the right of sovereignty." But seventeen years of opposition had not prepared republicans and democrats to exercise power.[104] The effectiveness of the Provisional Government was further undermined by the "hidden

---

[99] *Histoire*, I, vii.   [100] Ibid, I, xlv.   [101] Ibid, I, xvi.   [102] Ibid, I, lix.
[103] *Histoire*, II, 36–37.   [104] *Histoire*, I, 273–274.

struggle" within its ranks, pitting radicals like Louis Blanc, Ledru-Rollin and Flocon, against the moderate majority. In d'Agoult's view, Lamartine was the one man of quality in the Provisional Government – a brave and admirable man, but an inept and irresponsible politician. The others were "political orators, lawyers, or journalists" and not statesmen. "Divided against themselves, they could be seen colliding and stumbling at every step."[105]

D'Agoult attributes the failure of the Second Republic primarily to "the ignorance of the rich and educated classes with regard to the people" and their misunderstanding of the demands of the proletariat. The rich believed they were up against a "pitiless" enemy endowed with "insatiable appetites." They were terrified by "the ghosts of '93," and behind uprisings in the name of justice they saw only "the turbulence of a few trouble makers."

Because they were not sufficiently close to the people, they confused the sectarian spirit with the progress of civilization, terrorism with social-ism, the convulsions of a dying Babouvism and a dying Jacobinism with the legitimate efforts of the proletariat to become part of society.[106]

In the face of this, the Provisional Government, "divided from the very start, ... was reduced to practicing a politics of expedients, without grandeur and strength."[107] They could do nothing to lessen the mutual suspicion that only increased with the election of a Constituent Assembly hostile to the very idea of democracy.

Like most historians of 1848, d'Agoult regards the June Days as marking the collapse of the dream of a democratic republic. But in characterizing the action of the government in June, she appears to be of two minds. In her first volume (1850) she describes the recourse to armed repression as a repetition of the tactics of the July Monarchy. "Frightened by their inability to find quick solutions to problems accu-mulated during a long reign, the Republic of 1848 resorted to arms, as had the July Monarchy, to repulse with canons and bayonets a movement born of popular despair. Thus the political revolution waged war against the social revolution."[108] In the third volume (1853) d'Agoult defends the insurgency as a principled act:

The insurgent proletarians in June did not form ... the dregs of the human race. What accounts for the strength of the June insurrection and its incredible length, even though it was not planned and had no leader, is that from the beginning to the end it had in the minds of many of its participants the character of a just protest against the violation of a right.

---

[105] Ibid, I, 151, 274.   [106] *Histoire*, II, 13.   [107] Ibid.   [108] *Histoire*, I, lix.

Despite the violence, she argues, the insurgency grew out of "a moral principle, a principle misapplied but inspiring enthusiasm, dedication, and heroism" (see Figure 4.3).[109]Having said this, d'Agoult goes on to emphasize the "moral force" that also animated the repression, and she gives a deeply sympathetic account of the arguments by which long-standing republicans justified their support of Cavaignac and the crushing of the June insurrection. She speaks of the "incredible surge of courage and dedication" that inspired the Mobile Guards, the Republicain Guards and the army as they defended the Constituent Assembly against the rebellion. and she argues that it was "moral force that made the repression successful":

> The most committed republicans, men who throughout their lives had fought for the progress of democratic ideas, men like Guinard, Bixio, Dornès, Clémont Thomas, Edmond Adam, Carras, Charbonnel, Arago, were persuaded this time that the people, in rebelling against the national representatives, would bring down, along with law and right, the Republic and perhaps the State in their disastrous triumph. Thus broken-hearted but firm, they went to battle against this strange enemy whose emancipation had been, for twenty years, the goal of all their efforts.[110]

This passage is written with such strong feeling that it is hard to believe that d'Agoult herself did not share the position she describes – the "broken-hearted" acceptance of the need to defend the Second Republic, the Constituent Assembly, and the "political revolution" against the "strange enemy" whose emancipation had long been the goal of democrats and republicans.

In d'Agoult's analysis the crushing of the June insurrection marked the end of the alliance between the bourgeoisie and the proletariat which had been formed in February. The proletariat now "left the stage" and the social revolution was dead. But the political revolution was also in trouble. For the bourgeoisie did more than crush the social revolution. It also "joined the reaction against the political revolution," casting out the moderate republicans "after they had helped exclude the socialists and the radicals."[111] In this period of reaction, the leader of the Republic was Eugène Cavaignac, and d'Agoult describes his ascendency as a lost opportunity.

For d'Agoult Cavaignac was "a man whose name and whose sword were at once a symbol and a pledge of the republican order." He had saved France from the menace of anarchy and placed the Republic on a relatively firm footing. Socialism with its "excessive demands" was no

---

[109] *Histoire*, III, 155.   [110] Ibid, III, 186.   [111] Ibid, III, 263–264.

Figure 4.3 On June 23, 1848, before the heavy fighting had started, members of the Executive Committee went out to the barricades and attempted to persuade the insurgents to lay down their arms. Here we see Odilon Barrot addressing the insurgents at the Porte Saint-Denis. Bettmann Archive via Getty

longer to be feared; the republican majority in the Assembly was secure, confident, and loyal to Cavaignac; the royalist factions were still danger-ous, but they had been reduced to "feigning acquiescence to the repub-lic"; the army was loyal; the moderate French republic was respected abroad. France now asked for republican leadership, and Cavaignac might have provided it.[112] Unfortunately he was not up to the job. Unlike Lamartine, who had "too vast an ideal of revolution" and "neg-lected to provide for the establishment of republican government," Cavaignac got bogged down in "a scrupulous, mistrustful and timid application of republican government" and "closed his mind to the bold inspirations of the revolution." These two men, different in so many ways, were both failures as political leaders. "Lamartine, who dreamed of glory, lost his authority; Cavaignac, who sought to defend his authority and preserve his honour, had no understanding of those surges toward glory which move men." Confronted by an assembly which wished to be guided, neither was able to lead.[113]

What about the book's *conclusion*? In 1853, when d'Agoult published the third and final volume, it was impossible to harbour illusions about the exercise of universal male suffrage. With the coup of December 2, 1851, the Republic had been buried by its first democratically elected president. The third volume concludes with a long chapter on "The Reaction" of the summer and fall of 1848, culminating in an assessment of Louis-Napoleon's massive victory in the presidential election of December 10, 1848. D'Agoult tries to take a positive view of the election. What matters, she argues, is that there *was* an election and that it engaged the huge peasant population of France in the political life of the nation. If French peasants voted for Louis-Napoleon Bonaparte, it was because they believed that he represented them in a way that Cavaignac and Ledru-Rollin did not. Just as Marx describes December 10, 1848, as "the day of the Peasant insurrection," d'Agoult writes that for "le peuple des campagnes" the election of Louis Bonaparte meant "the victory of equality over privilege, the victory of democracy over kings and nobles, the victory of the French Revolution over the European dynasties."[114]

Finally, d'Agoult is hopeful about the future of democracy in France. In conclusion she asks if the French are destined to repeat the Roman experience, offering the masses no more than bread and circuses and an ultimate barbarian invasion. She concedes that the victory of Louis-Napoleon and of the peasants might appear to represent a "return to a sort of relative barbarism." But she insists that at a deeper level

---

[112] Ibid, III, 266–269.   [113] Ibid, III, 269–270.   [114] Ibid, III, 342.

something encouraging is going on: the people are now playing a role in national politics. "With the awareness of their strength, they have acquired the consciousness of their rights," and the struggle between "the social instinct of the people" and "the political science of the educated classes" is moving towards resolution. She looks forward to the day when the people and the bourgeoisie "will institute together the laws of a new society."[115]

It would seem that Marie d'Agoult only half-believed these fine words. She struck a much less optimistic note in her private correspondence. "I'm writing the third volume of my history," she wrote Emma Herwegh on Christmas day 1851. "I expected too much of the people, and I put too much faith in the power of principles alone. We all got drunk on our own enthusiasm. We failed to understand the customs of our time ... What we took for *heroism* was *bluster*, and what we took for *the spirit of liberty* was just *sloppy thinking*."[116]

The Shaping of the Narrative

Marie d'Agoult's *Histoire de la Révolution de 1848* is impressive for the quality of its research, the clarity of the argument, and its considered and carefully nuanced judgments. In these (and other) respects it puts all the other contemporary histories in the shade. No less interesting for us is the care the author has taken to give dramatic form to the book and to endow the whole story with the feel of high drama. The shape of the book is striking in itself. The first volume is entirely devoted to the February Revolution, and the June insurrection stands at the centre of volume III, preceded by the abortive coup of May 15 and followed by the reaction of the summer and fall, culminating with Louis-Napoleon's massive victory in the presidential election of December 10. The second volume, covering the period from February to May, is organized topically and thematically, focusing not only on the *journées* of March 17 and April 16 but also on the clubs and the working class, and each of the major ministries. In addition there is a long and original discussion of the situation in the provinces prior to the parliamentary elections of April 23.

D'Agoult was an admirer of the Roman historians, especially Livy and Tacitus, and she shared with them the belief that the principal task of the historian is to put engaging pictures of the past before readers – not only to represent the past but also to recreate it, to make it alive. To this end, she deployed a whole set of rhetorical devices and dramatic techniques

---

[115] Ibid, III, 346.
[116] "To Emma Herwegh, Christmas 1851" in *Au Printemps des Dieux*, 159–160.

perfected by the Romans and adapted by the great French writers of the classical age. In telling her story she creates a mood for each episode, providing atmospheric details and foreshadowings. Thus, the storm that broke out at the Macon banquet in Lamartine's honour – with thunder and lightning, broken dishes and a flapping tent – is described as "striking" and "prophetic." The fear of revolution among the propertied classes in January 1848 is accompanied by the recurrence of "sinister" memories and the presence of an "importunate shadow" at the dinner tables of the rich. The "stormy sky" during the night of March 17 offers "the image of the indefinable agitation of people's minds." And the discussion of Quentin-Bauchart's report, indicting Louis Blanc and Caussidière for their role on May 15 and in the June Days, is preceded by "the pale light of dawn which, entering through the windows and mixing with the dying light of the chandeliers, created a lugubrious effect in the hall."[117]

Often the atmospheric details reinforce the effort to capture confused or fearful states of mind through rhetorical questions. Thus, the narrative of February 22 begins with dark, lowering clouds and the contrast between the apparent security of the royal family and the fears and hopes and the mutual suspicions of the Parisians. Early in the morning large crowds gather in the Paris streets. "Has the banquet really been cancelled?" they ask. "Why are the streets full of troops?" "What are we doing wrong?" "Is it illegal to talk in public?"[118]

The *mise en scène* is vivid and dramatic. Having created a mood, d'Agoult then takes the reader inside the minds of the actors. For example, in her account of the reaction to the news that Barrot and the dynastic opposition had called off the banquet scheduled for February 21, she first shows us the uncertain response of the republicans in the offices of the journal, *La Réforme*. This is followed by a delicious account, rich in dramatic irony, of the joyous reaction at the Tuileries Palace:

The courtiers were swooning with delight. The Queen was beside herself. The King couldn't control his emotions. He shook hands effusively with his ministers. He kept complimenting Monsieur Duchâtel in particular. For a long time he hadn't shown such wit, such joviality, such verve. He included himself in all the praise he addressed to his government. He had always thought, always said, that this conceited opposition was composed only of glib talkers and cowards. His loquaciousness on this point was inexhaustible.[119]

Here d'Agoult manages both to capture the viewpoint of the king's entourage and to mock them.

[117] *Histoire*, I, 15, 70; II, 231; III, 284–285. [118] *Histoire*, I, 105–107.
[119] Ibid, I, 101.

To heighten the drama d'Agoult often presents contrasting pairs of images. In Volume I, for example, two dinners are described. First, the "sumptuous dinner" offered by the interior minister Duchâtel to his conservative colleagues on the evening of February 23, shortly after the dismissal of Guizot. "Stimulated by the fine wines," the guests comment "with a mocking eloquence" on Guizot's misfortune and speculate on his possible successor. Epigrams are polished and predictions made. But then the group gets word that the Municipal Guard is defecting and a crowd is marching on the interior and foreign ministries. The hostess, Madame Duchâtel, discretely retires to remove her jewels and change into clothes suitable for flight.[120] In contrast to this is a second dinner, the modest meal shared the next evening by the members of the newly formed Provisional Government. They had not eaten since morning, and all they could scare up was some bread, a little Gruyère cheese left behind by soldiers, a bottle of wine and a bucket of water brought by a man of the people. Flotard provides a pocketknife and they all drink out of a single cracked glass. "Here's a feast that augurs well for a government of the people," says Lamartine gaily. "Then, the meal finished, they went back to work."[121]

The most powerfully dramatic use of this device of contrasting images comes near the end of the first volume, with descriptions of two women. First, the account (borrowed by Flaubert for *L'Education sentimentale*)[122] of a prostitute posing motionless with a pike in her hand and a red cap on her head in the courtyard of the Tuileries Palace just as the crowd bursts in on February 24. Her lips are pursed, her gaze is steady, and the crowd approaches her respectfully. "A sad image of the capricious justice of fate," comments d'Agoult. "The prostitute is the living symbol of the degradation of the poor and the corruption of the rich. Insulted by the rich in supposedly normal times, she has her moment of triumph in all our revolutionary saturnalias."[123] Just a few pages later d'Agoult offers a poignant account of the vain attempt of the frightened but dignified duchesse d'Orléans to win the support of the Chamber of Deputies for a regency. Here the roles are reversed as the woman representing power and wealth is depicted as vulnerable: she stands helpless before the crowd as pleas on her behalf are ignored.[124]

If d'Agoult makes frequent use of the device of contrasting images, the images she chooses are often portraits of individuals. Here a word should

---

[120] Ibid, I, 131–132.   [121] Ibid, I, 258.
[122] Gustave Flaubert, *L'Education sentimentale* (Paris, 1963), 291.
[123] *Histoire*, I, 204–205.   [124] Ibid, I, 210–224, 232–234.

be said about the importance of portraiture in the *Histoire de la Révolution de 1848*. D'Agoult was working self-consciously within a venerable tradition for which the art of portraiture was central. The French masters of that tradition – La Bruyère and La Rochefoucauld – sought to present clear, vivid, nuanced, and arresting images of complex individuals; and in doing so, they often began with physical description and moved on to moral traits, finally concluding with the subtle analysis of paradoxes and contradictions. D'Agoult does this in her *Histoire*. A good example is the portrait of Guizot early in the first volume. She begins with his physical appearance – his "huge head, too heavy for the puny shoulders it rested on," his "pale and austere face," his "great lined forehead," his proud, tight lips, his "thin temples," and finally his eyes burning with "a contained fire." All of this suggests an inner struggle in which disorderly passions have been overcome. But when one hears his voice and "the inveterate skepticism hiding behind his obligatory formulas," the picture becomes more complicated. "Angular and contradictory lines" appear, and we are left with the image of a "noble mind tied to low ambitions," of "magisterial eloquence defending ignominies," and of the contrast between "simplicity, integrity, even grandeur in private life" and "the corrupting spirit of the statesman."[125]

On the other side of the political spectrum the most searching portrait is that of Auguste Blanqui whom d'Agoult treats as a "strange" and mysterious figure – a kind of puzzle. Here too she begins with a physical description. After evoking the "febrile" energy that enables Blanqui to attract and dominate followers, she describes him as a small man, "pale, sickly, his eyes shining with a concentrated fire," already subject to "a heart condition that sleeplessness, destitution and prison would render incurable." He appears to be struggling to restore "the weak breath of an existence which threatens to come to an end before satisfying its ambitions." But what are his ambitions? D'Agoult characterizes them in one long sentence: To breathe new life into the old Jacobin traditions, to raise high the banner of equality, "to personify in himself the pain, the complaint, and the menace of the proletarian so often deceived by abortive revolutions; thus to lay claim to the dictatorship of revenge, to give vent in a day of triumph to what he called 'the thundering of the Marseillaise,' to hold, if only for an hour, society ... in its iron grip – such seems to have been the dream of this taciturn heart."[126]

How did Blanqui communicate his dream? To what did he owe his power? Here d'Agoult stresses Blanqui's personal magnetism, the power

---

[125] Ibid, I, xviii–xix.   [126] *Histoire*, II, 24–30.

of his example, and his sheer intelligence. His dream and his asceticism gave him "a prodigious ascendency" over young people:

> He was endowed with rare faculties. Along with audacity and initiative, he possessed a profound sensitivity to shifting opinions and to the influence of circumstances on people's views. Never hindered by a need for rest, patient, skillful at underground conspiratorial activity, at *pretence* and *concealment*, as Sallust says, quick at arousing a crowd, he was practiced in the art of stirring up, and containing, the fire of the passions. By his life of poverty and concealment, by his humble appearance, by the suffering imprinted on all his features, by the sarcastic smile on his tight, cool lips, by the vigorous curses which would suddenly break through his lofty reserve, he inspired compassion and fear at one and the same time, and he played as he wished on these two great impulses of the human soul.[127]

D'Agoult goes on to discuss the role played by Blanqui during the February Revolution, insisting above all on his realism and his "political finesse." By her account, Blanqui understood "his inability to revive the spirit of '93 in the masses" and "the inanity of plotting in the midst of so profound a revolution." Thus having initiated his own conspiratorial movement in February, he called it off and "withdrew into the shadows," letting his subalternates "interpret the mystery of his conduct in the light of their own limited views."[128]

This portrait stands in stark contrast to the memorable portrait of Blanqui in Tocqueville's *Souvenirs*. Tocqueville's picture of this man who seemed to have just emerged from the sewers – a man with the "sickly, malign [and] dirty look" of a "mouldy corpse" – conveys powerfully the image of Blanqui that existed in the minds and imaginations of the propertied classes and among all those who feared him.[129] But Tocqueville's portrait is one-dimensional. D'Agoult goes farther. She attempts to convey some sense of what he meant to his followers and she also seeks to understand him on his own terms through sympathetic imagination. Tocqueville did not, and probably could not, do that.

For d'Agoult, Guizot and Blanqui are the two deepest and most intelligent figures respectively of the July establishment and the extreme left. But neither epitomizes his group. For that purpose simpler, less complex figures are needed. In the case of the July Monarchy conservatives it is the Minister of the Interior Duchâtel; for the radicals it is Ledru-Rollin. She makes this explicit: "Endowed with an intelligence infinitely less broad and less elevated than Monsieur Guizot, but much more suited to business and to the handling of men, Monsieur Duchâtel, though belonging by his antecedents to the doctrinaire party, was by

---

[127] Ibid, II, 25–26.   [128] Ibid, II, 29–30.   [129] Tocqueville, *Souvenirs*, OC XII, 135.

temperament, by taste, and by his style of life, the veritable representative of the conservative party which put up with Monsieur Guizot but felt no sympathy for him."[130]

As for Ledru-Rollin, d'Agoult describes him as epitomizing the limitations of Jacobin democracy in 1848. She writes that "nature seemed to have prepared him for the role of a popular leader." His imposing physical presence and his youthful appearance "which contrasted with the tired bearing of the veterans of radicalism," inspired sympathy. But Ledru-Rollin lacked one essential quality: authority. "Neither his disorderly private life, nor his sincere but blustering patriotism, nor his open and generous but unsteady character, nor his superficial learning, nor even a natural rectitude that was too often debased by a desire for popularity, fitted him for leadership." He was aware of these shortcomings, and to compensate for them "he spoke bombastically, adopted an overblown language and an overbearing style." Fearing himself unable to impose respect naturally, he tried to force respect. "There lay the secret of all his contradictions and inconsistencies ... The more his language outran his thought ... the more his words betrayed his intentions, the more he thought himself a profound politician." He thought naïvely that the best way to avert the furies of 1793 was to threaten their return. So, he surrounded himself with "theatrical claptrap" and encouraged his followers to wear Montagnard caps and Robespierrist waistcoats. "He didn't understand that this would only fool the vulgar. He believed himself to be a great democratic leader, whereas in reality he was only the echo of Jacobinism."[131]

There are two more symbolic figures whose opposition towers over the whole book: Lamartine and Thiers. These two epitomize the movement of the revolution from idealism to calculation, from mystique to politique. This contrast was the theme of a "Lettre républicaine" in which Lamartine personifies the idealism of the revolution and Thiers the "vulgar outcome."[132] But the contrast also stands at the centre of the *Histoire de la Révolution de 1848*.

Lamartine is the flawed hero of the *Histoire*, capable of seducing public opinion but not of satisfying it. He is an eloquent orator but an inept politician. "He who knew how to anticipate everything proved incapable of executing anything." In her third volume, d'Agoult illustrates her critique of Lamartine with the grand extended metaphor quoted in Chapter 2: "As his star shone in the sky with an incomparable brightness,

[130] *Histoire*, I, 2.   [131] *Histoire*, I, 27–28; II, 65–66.
[132] "Lettres républicaines", VII, July 17, 1848; Vier, *La Comtesse d'Agoult*, III, 30–32.

as he seemed to command the winds that filled his sails and the furious waves that died at his feet, his distracted hand rested on the tiller without guiding it."[133]

Against this image of the negligent, distracted dreamer, d'Agoult juxtaposes the burlesque figure of Adolphe Thiers whom she depicts as a consummate politician who enjoys intrigue as "an exercise useful to the elasticity of his mind" – as a supple-minded, alert and cynical man whose mobile physiognomy inspires not respect but watchfulness. "As a public speaker, and in meetings, M. Thiers is not imposing; he is insinuating. There is a strong will but no authority in the square lines of his face." Thiers disappears from the narrative on the morning of February 24, waving his arms and crying that assassins are about to enter the Chamber of Deputies. But he returns triumphantly after the crushing of the June insurrection as the defender of property against the dangerous socialist, Proudhon. His importance, in the long run, is to undermine the idealism of February, to reinforce "the narrow egoism that became the political creed of the influential class," and thus to "prepare and consummate little by little the ruin of the Republic."[134]

Second Edition: Trying to Reach a New Generation

With the publication in March 1850 of the first volume of the *Histoire de la Révolution de 1848* Marie d'Agoult established herself as writer, historian and intellectual. Twelve years later, d'Agoult recalled the "violence" of the attacks on her and the "coolness" of some of her defenders.[135] Indeed, in leading conservative journals such as the *Journal des débats* and the *Revue des deux mondes* the praise was grudging and mixed with personal attacks describing her as a "femme déclassée" bent on keeping alive old quarrels and dredging up "sad stories about rioters, schemers and orators."[136] Nonetheless praise for the book's "clarity," its "impartiality," and the "elegance" of its style came from readers and reviewers of all persuasions. Louis Blanc, who was upset by his portrayal, could nonetheless congratulate d'Agoult for "un bon et beau livre."[137] Varnhagen von Ense praised her "impartial judgment' and her "evident love of liberty" and asserted that in writing history she had found a

[133] *Histoire*, III, 102–103. See Chapter 2 above.
[134] *Histoire*, I, xxiii–xxv, 209; III, 286–294.   [135] *Histoire* (1862), vii.
[136] Cuvillier-Fleury, *Journal des Débats*, April 14, 1850; Pontmartin, *Revue des deux mondes*, April 1, 1850; both in Vier, *La Comtesse d'Agoult*, IV, 80–81.
[137] "Louis Blanc to Marie d'Agoult, December 3, 1851" in Jacques Vier, *Daniel Stern: Lettres républicaines du Second Empire. Documents inédits* (Paris, 1951), 69.

domain in which her own voice coulld emerge.[138] Finally, d'Agoult was told
that Adolphe Thiers, whose portrait was anything but flattering, was
impressed by the book and its author, supposedly telling a friend: "She's not
benevolent, but she's impartial. That bitch of a woman has a good mind."[139]
Democrats and republicans loved the book. Republican newspapers like
Le Siècle and *Le National* published excerpts, and the former Saint-
Simonian Adolphe Guéroult published a compendium of positive reviews
in *La République*. The reviewer for *L'Artiste* found d'Agoult's portraits a bit
harsh but praised almost everything else, notably her "fraternal sympathy"
for the poor who were defeated in June.[140] Another reviewer enjoyed the
"picquant" contrast between the archaic elegance of the writing and "the
strongly democratic inspiration" of the argument.[141] The publication of the
second volume brought another round of praise – from women in particular. Jeanne Deroin, to whom d'Agoult gave a copy, praised the "noble
impartiality" of her judgments and the "feminine delicacy" evident in her
critical portraits. And Hortense Allart celebrated the book: "I don't know
another woman who could have written a volume so well researched, argued
and organized." To her the book gave the impression of having been written
by a man! Allart's response to the third volume was even more enthusiastic.
This was "the first free and bold voice" heard in Paris under the Empire."[142]

By 1862, when a second edition of the *Histoire* appeared, Louis-
Napoleon Bonaparte had ruled France as Emperor Napoleon III for a
decade, and the Second Republic was a distant memory. Learning that
d'Agoult was preparing a new edition, her old friend Viel-Castel asked
her how she could still celebrate the overthrow of the July Monarchy. "It
seems to me," he wrote, "that February 24 could be a pleasant memory
today only for the partisans of the Empire."[143] D'Agoult attempted to
answer this question in the preface to the new edition. Here she evoked
the vast distance between 1862 and 1848 and described her book as a

[138] Varnhagen von Ense to Marie d'Agoult, April 18, 1850, and Marie d'Agoult, *Journal inédit*, April 21, 1850, BnF Mss. NAF 14327, both cited in Vier, *La Comtesse d'Agoult*, III, 291, 361, and IV, 79.
[139] *Agenda*, May 10, 1851 in Vier, *La Comtesse d'Agoult*, IV, 78. For a comprehensive overview of the reviews see Vier, *La Comtesse d'Agoult*, IV, 77–99.
[140] *L'Artiste*, July 1, 1850 in Vier, *La Comtesse d'Agoult*, IV, 82.
[141] *L'Opinion publique*, August 1850 in Vier, *La Comtesse d'Agoult*, IV, 285. The one negative voice from the left was that of Alexander Herzen. In her diary for April 12, 1850, d'Agoult notes that Herzen "says of my book that it does not have a *political color* and has no *raison d'être*": *Journal*, April 12, 1859, BnF Mss NAF 14327.
[142] Jeanne Deroin to Marie d'Agoult, September 15, 1851; Hortense Allart to Marie d'Agoult, November 26, 1851; Hortense Allart to Marie d'Agoult, March 27, 1853; all in Vier, *La Comtesse d'Agoult*, IV, 83–84.
[143] Undated letter Viel-Castel to d'Agoult in Vier, *La Comtesse d'Agoult*, IV, 94. "Impérialistes" here means Bonapartists, supporters of the Second Empire.

relic of a remote past. "The living echo of a bygone time, this book retains the passionate accents of that time. In leafing through it, I can still feel some of the electricity with which the atmosphere was charged and which touched the coldest people. I find in it words that have lost their meaning for us. Love of country and love of liberty spoke a language that we no longer understand."[144]

Why then did Marie d'Agoult republish this history of "a failed revolution"? One reason was simply to enlarge the audience for what she considered a true and unprejudiced account of a revolution that had inspired so many partisan apologies. She mentions no names, but clearly she had in mind the histories of the revolution by Lamartine, Louis Blanc, Proudhon, and Garnier-Pagès. All these histories were exercises in self-justification. This was most obviously true of the eleven-volume *Histoire de la Révolution de 1848* published by Louis-Antoine Garnier-Pagès, the Finance Minister under the Provisional Government. This history, which began to appear in 1861, was a justification of the work of the Provisional Government and, above all, of its author's role in the promulgation of the 45 centîmes tax increase, which did much to turn the peasantry against the revolution. One of Marie d'Agoult's motives in publishing a second edition in 1862 was to set the record straight.

But she had another motive. This was to reach a new audience. "It is not," she wrote, "at people who made or endured the Republic that my book is aimed." She wanted to be heard by a new generation – a generation of young people born around 1830, attached to science, industry and practical politics, and no longer captivated by romantic myths. She admired their skepticism, their realism, their freedom from religious illusions. And she recognized that for the new generation revolution had a new meaning. Revolution had abandoned the underground world of conspiracies and secret societies. It no longer spoke through the voice of sybils and prophets. Revolution now found its strength in palpable realities, in science, in industry, in the mathematical rigour of positive truths. "In the nineteenth century," she concluded, "science is profoundly revolutionary," and she wanted to be read by a generation that understood this.[145]

To reach this audience d'Agoult made several changes in the second edition. For one thing, she downplayed partisan politics. She was less harshly critical of the Orleanists. (She had always been partial to the Bourbons whom she associated with her own childhood.) She was gentler with regard to Thiers and the Orleanist leadership under the July

---

[144] *Histoire*, I (1862), vi.   [145] Ibid, xii-xiii.

Monarchy. Victor de Broglie's intelligence, which was "sterile" in the first edition, became "hautaine" in the second. But the most striking change was the suppression of the religious language that had permeated the first edition. She removed most of her own references to divine purposes and the workings of Providence. "A vulgar wisdom that never takes account of the ways of Providence, of the unexpected and unlikely twists of morality and right that God plans for humans when and if it suits him" became simply "the small surmises of a vulgar wisdom."[146] In the first edition she wrote that in 1848 "Providence" took the right of sovereignty from the Orleanist dynasty and the bourgeoisie. In the second edition Providence is replaced by a passive: "Sovereignty was taken from them."[147] Likewise, a reference to "the finger of God" in the first edition simply disappeared in the second.[148] At the same time d'Agoult took pains to remove from her second edition passages evoking elements of communitarianism and "primitive communism" (her term) that had survived in Catholic doctrine down to the nineteenth century.[149] The effect of her revisions was to put distance between socialism and Christianity, to minimize the importance of the Christian radicalism that had been so prominent a feature of the language of the 'forty-eighters.

On one final point d'Agoult made no changes: the role of women. In both editions she argued that the feminists who demanded women's suffrage in 1848 were premature, that the struggle of women for equality within marriage was more important than the vote. The questions that mattered, she insisted, concerned the education, careers and wages of women, the dignity of wives, the authority of mothers in the family.[150] Thus she spoke disparagingly about Jeanne Deroin's proposed candidacy for the National Assembly in May 1849, and she reviled the "vulgar eccentricities" of the women warriors who called themselves "Vésuviennes." "All this bizarre behaviour, this superficial noise," she insisted, could only serve to scare off good people and reinforce prejudice. While she saw little value in women's clubs and "journals that no one reads," she could not entirely ignore the efforts of working-class feminists like Deroin, Pauline Roland, and Désirée Gay (née Véret) to obtain government support for cooperative workshops, restaurants, laundries and lodging for needy women. At the conclusion of her discussion of the role of women in 1848 d'Agoult reprinted such a petition sent to the Provisional Government by Désirée Gay on March 3. But it may be

---

[146] *Histoire*, I (1850), 105; (1862), I, 166.   [147] *Histoire*, I (1850), 273; (1862), I, 339.
[148] *Histoire*, I (1850), 272. "The finger of God" is invoked in the first edition to explain the rapid collapse of the July Monarchy and the *ralliement* of Orleanists to the Republic.
[149] *Histoire*, I (1850), xli–xlii; (1862), I, 39.   [150] *Histoire*, II (1851), 190; (1862), II, 35.

indicative of her desire to maintain distance from the feminists that their names are never mentioned.[151]

After 1851 Marie d'Agoult reigned as a hostess and *salonnière* in a series of elegant townhouses and apartments, all of them located in fashionable quarters near the Etoile or the Parc Monceau. During the Empire her salon became a centre of moderate republican opposition to Napoleon III. She took pleasure in surrounding herself with what she called republicans of goodwill and "sincere convictions," having weeded out "the posers and phrase makers."[152] Liberal journalists and newspaper editors gravitated to her, as did influential politicians and intellectuals including Hippolyte Carnot, Jules Grévy and Ernest Renan. She also gathered around her an entourage of young men – notably the ever-faithful poet Louis de Ronchaud and the future senator Louis Tribert, both of whom provided moral (and at times material) support in her later years. She wrote and published prolifically during the Empire – historical dramas on Mary Stuart, Joan of Arc and Jacques Coeur, an ambitious set of dialogues on Dante and Goethe, and a well-received history of the origins of the Dutch Republic. She wrote over 100 journal articles, collaborated on newspapers such as *Le Temps* and *La Revue de Paris*, saw new editions of her earlier works through the press, and began to write her memoirs.

By the early years of the Empire Marie d'Agoult had become one of the most prominent *femmes de lettres* in France, and the success of her *Histoire de la Révolution de 1848* did much to establish that reputation. Still, she was never really satisfied by her literary accomplishments and, for that matter, never entirely at ease in her role as *salonnière*. During the 1860s she was beset by periods of depression – "spleen" as she called it – and twice had to be hospitalized. Even in good times she was fragile, insecure, easily wounded. She kept noting compliments and criticism in her diary, adding bitter and sometimes nasty reflections on the achievements of others. In 1862 she complained that George Sand's success remained "indisputable" despite her literary failures, despite her equivocal role on May 15, and despite her "increasing obesity." "It is unbelievable," she lamented, that "with my growing talent, my enduring beauty [and] my noble and elegant manners, I do not achieve greater results. I sense that the least fault will do me in."[153] D'Agoult's diaries and journals are full of

---

[151] *Histoire*, II (1851), 190–192; (1862), II, 37. Michèle Riot-Sarcey, *La Démocratie à l'épreuve des femmes: Trois figures critiques du pouvoir 1830–1848* (Paris, 1994), 170–261.

[152] "To Charles Dolfuss, August 15, 1857" in *Lettres Républicaines*, 122.

[153] *Journal*, May 15, 1862, BN NAF 14330 in Dupêchez, *Marie d'Agoult*, 274.

such complaints about the literary and social successes of others – men as well as women. She terminated her passionate and quasi-maternal relationship with her protégé, the beautiful and ambitious Juliette Lamber, when the younger woman set up a very successful salon of her own. Even Flaubert, whom d'Agoult had never met, was a target for her jealous pique. "Everyone wants to talk about *Salammbô*," she confided to her journal on Dec 19, 1862, "and everyone ignores me."[154]

D'Agoult began to acquire real political influence toward the end of the Empire when her son-in-law Emile Ollivier (the widower of her daughter Blandine, who died in childbirth) helped establish the Liberal Empire. This created problems for d'Agoult: she had to hold separate receptions for her adamantly republican admirers and the Bonapartists. Finally, it was the republicans who prevailed; and a fascinating study has been written on five *habitués* of d'Agoult's salon – Emile Littré, Charles Dupont-White, Etienne Vacherot, Eugène Pelletan and Jules Barni – who became "central actors in the political and intellectual process which led to the establishment of the Third Republic."[155]

During these years d'Agoult spent much of her time looking back. She made plans to publish her correspondence, and in 1865 she began to write her memoirs. The following year she wrote her daughter Claire that she had already completed a volume on her childhood and on the world of the salons during the Restoration.[156] Only after her death were these chapters published along with fragments on her later life. It is clear, however, that she wanted most to be remembered for her love affair with Liszt. As she wrote Ronchaud in 1858: "I would like that great love ... to be respected and honoured after my death by those who have misunderstood or slandered it in my lifetime."[157]

She never reached 1848 in her memoirs. But there is no mystery about her attitude. In 1856 she wrote Emma Herwegh: "If I ... sustain with some liveliness the equality of women, ... it is not, believe me, that I want to see reborn from their cinders those sad phoenixes of the revolution of 1848, women's clubs, women candidates, women's periodicals, etc., etc. No, I hate *le tapage révolutionnaire* (revolutionary noise) more than ever. I simply return to the thought of Condorcet: equality of education. After which, let us see what women are capable of."[158]

---

[154] *Journal*, December 19, 1862 in Dupêchez, *Marie d'Agoult*, 270.
[155] Sudhir Hazareesingh, *Intellectual Founders of the Republic: Five Studies in Nineteenth-Century French Republican Political Thought* (Oxford, 2001), 16.
[156] "To Claire de Charnacé, September 1, 1866" in Dupêchez, *Marie d'Agoult*, 287.
[157] "To Louis de Ronchaud, December 26, 1858" in Dupêchez, *Marie d'Agoult*, 220.
[158] "To Emma Herwegh, December 18, 1856" in *Au Printemps des Dieux*, 171.

In the end, like George Sand, she came around to Thiers. She wrote no admiring letter to Thiers; and she did not, like Sand, fulminate against the Communards. But she believed that Thiers' canny politics had made possible the establishment of lasting republican institutions after the war, the Commune, and the German occupation. She was grateful for this, paying tribute publicly "to the skillful and highly patriotic leader."[159] She would have appreciated a little more Lamartinian idealism. But finally, she was willing to settle for a conservative republic not unlike that imagined by Lamartine and briefly led by Cavaignac. As for her personal life, she was at the end disappointed. Looking back, she wrote that she had had five great passions: God, Liszt, the Republic, maternity, and Italy. "Only the passion for Italy has not deceived me."[160]

[159] "Open letter to Littré in *Le Temps*, November 14, 1872" in Vier, *La Comtesse d'Agoult*, VI, 47.
[160] *Mémoires inédits* in Vier, *La Comtese d'Agoult*, V, 135.

5   Victor Hugo
The Republic as a Learning Experience

Unlike so many of his contemporaries who turned away from radical politics after June 1848, Victor Hugo was both energized and radicalized by his experience of politics during the Second Republic. At the end of 1847, he had been in the public eye for more than two decades. Celebrated as playwright, poet and novelist, he was elected to the Académie française in 1841. He was a peer of France, Chevalier of the Légion d'honneur, a confidant of Louis Philippe, an intimate of the Crown Prince and an adornment of the salon of the Duchesse Hélène d' Orléans. The ultimate *notable*, Hugo also enjoyed a moral authority that gave weight to his views on questions ranging from capital punishment and child labour to Polish independence.

Just four years later, Hugo was a political refugee with two sons in prison. On the evening of December 11, 1851, he took a train from the Gare du Nord to Brussels, wearing a workman's cap and black coat and holding a passport that identified him as Jacques-Firmin Lanvin, a compositor. The next morning, he arrived in Brussels to begin a career as the self-appointed conscience of France, hurling verbal bombs at the Emperor during an exile that was to last nineteen years.

Hugo's political vision had evolved over time. A royalist and a catholic in his youth, he wrote poems celebrating the martyrdom of the Virgins of Verdun and other victims of the Terror, and in 1825 he wrote the official ode for the coronation of the last Bourbon king, Charles X. By 1830 he had become a humanitarian liberal preoccupied with the welfare – and the dignity – of the poor. In poems and in his short story *Claude Gueux* he dramatized the responsibility of the rich for the hunger of the impoverished artisan and the desperation of the prostitute. And he came to have a lofty vision of the poet's mission: to criticize power, to calm civil conflict, to read the future in the Book of Nature. Throughout the July Monarchy he repeatedly urged his wealthy contemporaries to look beyond the petty political debates that preoccupied the Chamber of Deputies and to

consider "the substitution of social questions for political questions."[1]
But still, prior to 1848 he never went far beyond the respectable views of
the liberal and philanthropic bourgeoisie.

Hugo wrote voluminously about the Revolution of 1848, the rise and
fall of the Second Republic, and Louis-Napoleon's seizure of power.
I will, of course, consider these writings. But the central thread of this
chapter concerns Hugo himself and the process by which he was radicalized. How and why did this consummate Establishment figure become
the incarnation of implacable republicanism? And why was his experience of the Second Republic so different from that of his contemporaries? Why did he take heart from the failures of the Republic whereas most
of them ultimately retreated from politics?

Peer to Representative of the People

Despite his intimacy with the royal family, Hugo had no illusions about
the July Monarchy. "In my opinion," he wrote in 1847, "the great fault of
our government for the past seventeen years is to have governed France
without glory, as one would govern a Hohenzollern principality or the
kingdom of Yvetot." The July Monarchy was in his view "the narrow and
mean government of interests, expedients, and profit." He believed
France wanted something better. "I will not say to our government that
it is vile; I will say that it is feeble. I will not say that it is time to cease
being base; I will say that it is time to cease being petty."[2] Hugo was well
informed about the scandals that beset the regime because, as a member
of the Chamber of Peers, he sat in judgment on several spectacular cases.
In July 1847, after hearing testimony concerning the sale of peerages and
medals, he summed things up in an epigram: "Monsieur Guizot is
personally incorruptible and he governs by corruption. He gives me the
impression of an honest woman who runs a bordel."[3]

The most talked-about instance of corruption at this time was the so-
called Teste-Cubières scandal in which two former ministers were
accused of taking bribes in return for a mining concession. Hugo did
not want to believe in the corruption of former ministers. He was particularly attached to Cubières who had fought bravely at Waterloo and
had been gracious to him at the time of his appointment to the Peerage.

[1] Victor Hugo, "Introduction" in *Littérature et philosophie mêlées* [1834], 2 vols. (Paris, 1976), I, 19, cited in Paul Bénichou, *Les Mages romantiques* (Paris, 1988), 280.
[2] *Choses vues*, 1847 in Victor Hugo, *Oeuvres completes [OC] Histoire* (Paris: Robert Laffont, 1987), 991.
[3] *Choses vues*, June 20, 1847, *OC Histoire*, Laffont, 637.

But as the evidence mounted, Teste attempted (unsuccessfully) to commit suicide; and Hugo wrote that during the course of the trial General Cubières became Monsieur de Cubières, then simply Cubières, and finally "the convict Cubières."[4] Both men and several accomplices were sentenced to civil degradation and fines, and Teste also received three years in a prison which, Hugo observed wryly, had been built during his tenure as Minister of Public Works. Shortly after the sentencing of Teste and Cubières, Parisians learned of a spectacular crime of passion involving the Duke de Choiseul-Praslin. This man had brutally killed his wife, the daughter of a former Minister of War, stabbing her thirty times and finishing her off with blows from a candelabra. By this time, public opinion had turned against the July Monarchy to the point that moderate newspapers like *Le Constitutionnel* attributed this domestic crime to Guizot's policies.[5]

Hugo was fascinated by the Praslin affair and wrote about it at length in his journals. But he was more deeply engaged by another issue brought to the Chamber of Peers in June, 1847 – the petition of Napoleon's only surviving brother, Jérôme Bonaparte, who sought the repeal of the law exiling members of the Bonaparte family. "I declare without hesitation," Hugo told the peers. "I am on the side of exiles and proscrits."[6] He obviously could not know that he himself was to spend almost two decades in exile. But one exile who mattered to Hugo in 1847 was the first Napoleon. In his speech to the Chamber of Peers Hugo contrasted the pettiness and corruption of the July Monarchy with the grandeur of Napoleon's Empire:

As for me, in witnessing the collapse of conscience, the reign of money, the spread of corruption, the taking of the highest places by people with the lowest passions, (*Prolonged reaction*) in witnessing the woes of the present time, I dream of the great deeds of the past, and I am now and then tempted to say to the Chamber, to the press, to all of France: "Wait, let us talk a little of the Emperor. That will do us good!" (*Intense and profound agreement*).[7]

After this speech, the elderly Jérôme Bonaparte personally thanked Hugo; and his daughter, the Princess Mathilde, invited him to dinner. Hugo was now regarded in some quarters as a Bonapartist.

---

[4] *Choses vues*, July 16, 1847, *OC Histoire*, Laffont, 741.
[5] H. A. C. Collingham, *The July Monarchy: A Political History of France, 1830–1848* (London, 1988), 394–395.
[6] "La Famille Bonaparte," June 14, 1847, *Actes et paroles* I in Victor Hugo, *Oeuvres complètes Politique* (Paris: Robert Laffont, 1985), 137.
[7] "La Famille Bonaparte," *OC Politique*, Laffont, 138–139.

Hugo argued in this speech that France had nothing to fear from the Bonapartes. He believed that Napoleon's nephew, Louis-Napoleon Bonaparte, had irretrievably compromised himself with his two pathetic attempts to foment unrest in military garrisons in 1836 and 1840. The real threat to public order now, Hugo asserted, was posed by the poverty and hunger of the rural population: whereas "all the intrigues of all the pretenders" would do nothing to inspire a movement of rebellion in the army, a peasant revolt like that at Buzançais in January 1847 risked opening up "an abyss" of violence in France.[8] In that instance a traditional grain riot or *jacquerie* escalated into three days of violence, culminating in the killing by pitchfork of a farmer who had shot one of the protesters.[9]

By 1847 Hugo had lost confidence in the government, but he had no sympathy for the various opposition movements. His Bonapartism was nostalgic and familial (his father had been a Napoleonic general) and not revolutionary. He detested the socialists, those "new doctrinaires of pillage and theft."[10] He distanced himself from the republicans: his attitude toward republican revolution had changed little since 1832 when he denounced the rioting at the funeral of the republican General Lamarque as "folly drowned in blood." "We shall have a republic one day," he wrote, "and when it comes of its own accord, it will be good. But let us not harvest in May fruit that will only ripen in July. Let us learn to wait." A republic, he added, "will be a crown for our white hair."[11]

Hugo spoke eloquently for the reform of child labour and of prison conditions, but he had no interest in the movement for the widening of the suffrage led by the opposition to the Guizot ministry. He was a political lone wolf who enjoyed the fruits of status within the July Monarchy. Indeed, Henri Guillemin has argued plausibly that if Hugo had died in January 1848, he would be remembered as "a distinguished poet, a bit of a rebel in 1830, but one who quickly managed to make a fine career for himself as a juste-milieu bourgeois."[12] In 1850, Karl Marx's assessment of Hugo was similar if more brutal: "an old notability

[8] On 'the pitchforks of Buzançais' see Chapter 1, p. 45 and note 94.
[9] See Chapter 1, p. 43.
[10] Hugo to Ulric Güttinger, July 10, 1848, *Oeuvres complètes*, 18 vols., Club français du livre [OC CFL] (Paris, 1967–1970), VII, 750. Cited in Marieke Stein, "Victor Hugo et les partis politiques sous la Seconde République" in Jean-Claude Caron and Annie Stora-Lamarre (eds.), *Hugo politique* (Besançon, 2004), 30.
[11] *Choses vues*, June 6–7, 1832 in Hubert Juin (ed.), *Choses vues: souvenirs, journaux, cahiers, 1830–1885* (Paris, 2002), 76.
[12] Henri Guillemin, *Victor Hugo par lui-même* (Paris, 1962), 16.

from the time of Louis Philippe."[13] Nevertheless, Hugo's commitment to the regime was shallow, and on February 24, 1848, when Louis Philippe fled to England and the Chamber of Peers ceased to exist, Hugo was not about to go into mourning.

Victor Hugo's experience of the February Revolution is described in fascinating detail in the notes, drafts, journal entries and occasional writings that make up the posthumously published *Choses vues*. This work, first published in 1887 and stitched together by his admirer Paul Meurice, has since appeared in a variety of editions, each of them different. This obviously creates a problem for the historian, a problem compounded by the fact that the arrangement of the texts and in some cases the texts themselves are the work of Meurice. This is notably the case of a detailed narrative of Hugo's activities during the two crucial *journées* of February 24 and 25 which, although based on fragments by Hugo, is at least partly fictional.[14]

Still, if used critically, *Choses vues* is a wonderfully rich source for Hugo's experience of the February Revolution. It leaves one with the sense that, whatever doubts he had about the Republic, Hugo was eager to see what was happening. On February 22 he witnessed the building of the first barricades near the Place de la Concorde. At the Chamber of Deputies, he heard stories about bands of workers ready to descend on Paris. The next day he watched barricades multiply around the Hôtel de Ville and noted that the new barricades were made not only of paving stones but also of chairs, tables, trees and carriages. The streets were crowded; the National Guard was fraternizing with the crowd; there was singing in the streets – the Marseillaise, the Chant des Girondins, the Chant du Départ. At the Chamber of Deputies Hugo joined a group of worried politicians and journalists. He told them that the government was to blame for allowing the protest over the banned banquet to escalate. Now a revolt was underway and the authorities didn't know what to do about it. That evening, returning home along the quays, Hugo met crowds of people who reminded him of "an aroused anthill." At the Place du Châtelet he heard a man tell a group, "It's 1830 all over again!" "No,"

---

[13] Karl Marx, *Class Struggles in France, 1848 to 1850* (New York, 1964), 139. On this issue see Guy Rosa, "Victor Hugo, Louis–Philippard?," *Cahiers de l'Association internationale des etudes françaises*, 38 (1986), 267–282.

[14] On the problems posed by *Choses vues* see especially Jean-Marc Hovasse, *Victor Hugo, I: Avant l'exil, 1802–1851* (Paris, 2001), 1015–1018, and the *mise au point* of Franck Laurent, "*Choses vues?*" Communication au Groupe Hugo du 22 Septembre 2012. See also Guy Rosa *et al.*, "Notice générale" to *Choses vues*, *OC Histoire*, Laffont, 1415–1422; Guy Rosa, "Génétique et obstétrique: l'édition de Choses vues" in Béatrice Didier and J. Neefs (eds.), *Hugo de l'écrit au livre* (Paris, 1987), 133–148; and Guy Rosa, "Hugo en 1848: de quel côté de la barricade?," *48/14 La Revue du Musée d'Orsay*, 8 (1999), 59–69.

he thought, "in 1830 behind Charles X there was the Duc d'Orléans. In 1848 behind Louis Philippe there's nothing."[15] He went to bed that night unaware of the shooting on the Boulevard des Capucines that left fifty killed and marked the beginning of the end for the July Monarchy.

When Hugo awoke on the 24th, Paris was covered with barricades. His house on the Place Royale (soon to be rebaptized the Place des Vôsges) was next to the Mairie (city hall) of the eighth arrondissement (now the fourth), and from his balcony he watched a little drama unfold below him. Thirty municipal guards were protecting the Mairie, and a large crowd, including some National Guards, was taunting them, demanding their rifles. The policemen refused, and the situation grew tense. Then two National Guards intervened: "What's the point of more bloodshed?" they said. "Resistance would be useless." The policemen gave up their arms and their ammunition and withdrew without incident.[16]

Shortly after this episode the mayor of the eighth arrondissement summoned Hugo to the Mairie. He told Hugo of the massacre on the Boulevard des Capucines; and while they talked, reports arrived that all over Paris National Guard units had joined the insurgents. The army, unnerved by the shooting of the night before, was refusing to fire on the insurgents. The mayor then went off to the Hôtel de Ville to see if there was still a municipal government, and Hugo reconnoitred the Place Royale, finding "agitation, anxiety, feverish waiting." The mayor returned with the news that the King had dismissed Guizot and called on Thiers and Odilon Barrot to form a new government. He had been asked to announce the news to the people of the eighth arrondissement. As he did so, it became evident to him – and to Victor Hugo – that the change in ministry had come too late. The insurrection continued to progress, and when the two men walked the short distance to the Hôtel de Ville, they discovered that it was now in the hands of the insurgents. They went on to the Chamber of Deputies, traversing with difficulty "the human ocean" that covered the Place de l'Hôtel de Ville and talking their way past a huge barricade on the rue de la Mégisserie. When they finally reached the Palais Bourbon, they were greeted by "the shrill voice of Monsieur Thiers" who told them that Louis Philippe had abdicated in favour of his grandson, the ten-year-old Comte de Paris, with the understanding that the count's mother, Duchesse Hélène d'Orléans would serve as Regent.[17]

---

[15] *Choses vues*, February 22, 1848, *OC Histoire*, Laffont, 1009–1010.
[16] *Choses vues*, February 24, 1848, *OC Voyages* (Paris: Robert Laffont, 1987), 1217.
[17] *Choses vues*, February 24, 1848, *OC Voyages*, Laffont, 1217–1220.

A Regency was just what Hugo wanted, and he was more than willing to announce the news to the people of his quartier. Thus after meeting with Odilon Barrot and trying unsuccessfully to contact the Duchesse d'Orléans (who was then on her way to the Chamber of Deputies), Hugo returned to the Place Royale where, standing on the balcony of the Mairie, he announced the abdication of the king and the proclamation of the Regency. Cheers greeted the report of the king's abdication, but news of the Regency evoked only "grumbling." Discouraged, the mayor told Hugo that the Regency would never be accepted by the Parisians. But Hugo would not give up. Determined to inform and persuade working-class Paris, he had himself escorted by two officers of the National Guard to the Place de la Bastille where, at two o'clock in the afternoon, he went to the base of the column commemorating the revolution of July 1830 to proclaim the abdication and the Regency.[18]

The Place de la Bastille was just a ten-minute walk from the Place Royale, but socially it was a world away. The Place Royale, once the setting for royal fêtes, was the heart of the old aristocratic quarter of the Marais,[19] whereas the Place de la Bastille was the centre of working-class Paris and a place where workers often came to demonstrate. On this occasion the crowd that gathered to hear Hugo consisted largely of workers, many carrying rifles seized from army barracks or from individual soldiers. Their response to Hugo's announcement of the Regency was not encouraging: "No! No! No Regency! Down with the Bourbons! No King, no queen! No masters!" Hugo tried to spar with the crowd: "I don't want a master any more than you do. I've defended liberty all my life!" "Then why do you proclaim the Regency?" came the retort.[20]

Just then a worker aimed his rifle at Hugo and cried: "Down with the peer of France!" By his own account Hugo looked straight at the man and raised his voice: "Yes, I am a peer of France, and I speak as a peer of France. I have sworn fidelity not to the person of the king but to the constitutional monarchy. Until another government is established, it is my duty to be faithful to this one. And I have always thought that the people do not like it when, for whatever reason, one fails to do one's duty." According to Hugo, this reply earned "a murmur of approval and even a few bravos." But when he returned to the subject of the Regency, the protests recommenced. A worker shouted: "We won't be governed by a woman." Hugo replied that he did not wish to be governed by either

[18] Ibid, 1221; Delclou to Hugo, March 3, 1848, *OC* CFL, VII, 746.
[19] The Place Royale was so identified with the monarchy that in 1848 its name was changed to the Place des Vôsges, which is the name it still bears.
[20] *Choses vues*, February 24, 1848, *OC Voyages*, Laffont, 1222.

a woman or a man. A voice in the crowd shouted "Vive la République!" But there was no echo. Then the noise of the crowd – the shouts and threats – became so loud that Hugo gave up trying to make himself heard. As he left, the crowd gave way before him, curious and inoffensive. Not far from the column, the man who had threatened him earlier reappeared and took aim at him again, this time shouting "Death to the peer of France!" By Hugo's account, a young worker then disarmed the man, and cried out: "No, we respect the great man!" Hugo clasped his hand in thanks and left.[21]

That afternoon, at the Palais Bourbon, the fate of the Regency was decided. Hélène d'Orléans had come to the Chamber of Deputies, and Odilon Barrot and others spoke on her behalf. But Lamartine's speech in support of the Republic carried the day. By nightfall on the 24th, a Provisional Government had established. itself at the Hôtel de Ville.

On the morning of February 25 Hugo and his nineteen-year-old son, François-Victor, set out from the Place Royale to take a look at Paris in the aftermath of the revolution. The sky was overcast but the previous day's rain had stopped. Workers continued to fortify existing barricades and to construct new ones "with an unbelievable ardour." Bands of people circulated waving flags, beating drums, and shouting "Vive la République!" or singing the Marseillaise and "Mourir pour la patrie!" The cafés were packed and stores closed. "It was like a holiday."[22]

According to the narrative pieced together by Paul Meurice, Hugo and his son spent much of the morning of February 25 at the Hôtel de Ville where Hugo met with Lamartine, who offered him a position as Minister of Public Instruction in the Provisional Government. This cannot be true. The position had already been given to Hippolyte Carnot, and it is unlikely that Hugo and Lamartine even met on that day.[23] Hugo was in fact offered a temporary position as mayor of the 8th arrondissement. Although his tenure as mayor was brief, he apparently enjoyed it. Later he boasted that he "reigned for a week in the 8th arrondissement. The people adored me. I addressed them from the balcony of the Mairie. Workers blew me kisses when I passed them in the street. I organized the

---

[21] Ibid, 1222–1223. The details in this account, which puts Hugo in such a good light, are suspect. But we do know that on February 24 Hugo spoke in favour of a Regency before hostile and well-armed crowds at both the Place Royale and the Place de la Bastille. See "Réplique à Montalembert," May 23, 1850, *Actes et paroles* I, *OC Politique*, 253; and Delclou to Hugo, March 3, 1848, *OC CFL*, VII, 746.

[22] *Choses vues*, February 25, 1848, *OC Voyages*, Laffont, 1224–1225.

[23] This is the clear implication of a letter written by Hugo to Lamartine two days later. See Hovasse, *Victor Hugo*, I, 1016.

mail service; I had the barricades removed and the cobblestones put back in the street. I had the prisons guarded, the streets lit up at night."[24]

One reason for the brevity of Hugo's tenure as mayor of his arrondissement was that he was actually not universally adored. Many workers of the quarter regarded him as hopelessly aristocratic and conservative. Take for example, a letter from the Société du peuple du VIIIe arrondissement: "We have no confidence at all in your dedication to the democratic institutions of the French Republic ...We have known for a long time about your disdainful, haughty and aristocratic ways."[25] Nonetheless, Hugo's tenure as temporary mayor lasted long enough for him to officiate at the planting of a Tree of Liberty in the newly renamed Place des Vosges on March 2. He gave a little speech, apparently concluding with a celebration of "la République universelle."[26] Still, during the next few months he went out of his way to avoid associating himself with republicans and republicanism. On May 29, while running for election to the National Assembly, he wrote, "Do you know why I don't loudly proclaim myself a republican? It's because too many people shout that. Do you know why I feel a sort of modesty and have scruples about flaunting republicanism in this way? I see too many people who are not republican at all making more noise than you who are convinced republicans."[27]

If Hugo's commitment to a republican government remained hesitant, he fully supported Lamartine and the measures taken by the Provisional Government – notably the abolition of slavery, the adoption of the tricolor flag, and the decree abolishing the death penalty for political crimes. On February 27 he wrote Lamartine that the abolition of capital punishment was "a sublime deed." During the next few weeks he was delighted by the energy and good humour of the crowds that gathered every day around the Place Royale. "I don't understand how one could fear the sovereign people," he wrote in mid-March. "The people are all of us. To fear them is to fear one's self." He went on to describe the view from his balcony: "For the past three weeks I have observed [the people] every day from my balcony ... I see them calm, joyful, good, witty when I join their groups, imposing when they march in columns with flags

---

[24] *Choses vues, OC Histoire,* Laffont, 1025–1026.
[25] Auguste Maurin to Hugo, March 1, 1848, *CFL* VII, 746 in Hovasse, *Victor Hugo,* I, 1017.
[26] "Plantation de l'arbre de la liberté," *Actes et paroles,* I, *OC Politique,* 148.
[27] "Séance des cinq associations d'art et d'industrie," May 29, 1848, *Actes et paroles,* I, *OC Politique,* 162. See also Hovasse, *Victor Hugo,* I, 1018 and 1243, n.369.

flying and drums beating. I see them, and I swear to you that I have no fear of them."[28]

In April when elections were held for the National Assembly Hugo did not formally present himself as a candidate. But on March 29 he published a *Lettre aux électeurs* indicating his willingness to serve if elected. Two weeks later, just ten days before the election, he was elected president of the Society of Dramatic Authors and Composers and designated as its official candidate. At the Society's meeting, Alexandre Dumas spoke warmly of him as a "friend of the people" and a "man of humanity."[29] But his half-hearted candidacy was not publicized in the daily press, and it was too late for endorsements to make a difference. Hugo was not elected, though he received close to 60,000 votes, a sufficiently respectable total to convince him to declare his candidacy in the complementary elections of June 4.

Hugo later claimed that he only decided to stand for election after May 15. In fact, his campaign began earlier when, with the help of the literary entrepreneur, Baron Isidore Taylor, he managed to enroll several artistic societies behind his candidacy. He then got the support of the moderate right-wing papers, *Le Constitutionnel* and *Le Siècle.* On May 26 he issued a profession of faith, *Victor Hugo à ses concitoyens*, which was widely reprinted. In this document he argued that the task at hand was to establish order – to "crush the insolence" of the dictatorial democrats who had tried to overthrow the National Assembly on May 15 and to create a climate in which shops and factories could reopen and France could get back to work. For the long term, Hugo outlined an ambitious program including free education, penal reform, railway building, and the democratization of property. All this he framed within a vision of two possible republics: the red republic and the tricolor republic. The red republic would declare bankruptcy and ruin the rich without enriching the poor; it would abolish property and the family and stifle the arts; it would threaten dissidents with death. The tricolor republic, Hugo's republic, would unite people in a democratic "holy communion." It would found "a liberty without usurpation and without violence, an equality which will give free play to each individual's natural bent, a fraternity not of monks in a monastery but of free men; it will give everyone education gratuitously, just as the sun gives light; it will introduce clemency into penal law and conciliation into civil law."[30]

This was sufficiently vague to appeal to a wide public. But Hugo's principal backing came from the conservative Comité de la rue de

---

[28] *Choses vues, OC Histoire*, Laffont, 1030.   [29] Hovasse, *Victor Hugo*, I, 1019–1020.
[30] "Victor Hugo à ses concitoyens," *Actes et paroles*, I, *OC Politique*, 152–153.

Poitiers, and his name appeared on the electoral list of *Le Constitutionnel* along with those of General Changarnier and Adolphe Thiers, both despised by the Left. Hugo received some support from centrist liberals and a few socialist newspapers. But most democrats and socialists opposed him. Particularly pointed was the portrait of Hugo in a paper published by followers of Louis Blanc: "A favourite of Guizot, a regular visitor to the Tuileries Palace, a practiced courtier, running after all honours, all celebrities, displaying his bored grandeur for all to see, posing on a clay pedestal moulded by his own hands."[31]

In the end, Hugo was easily elected along with Thiers and Changarnier, and the socialists Proudhon and Pierre Leroux. On June 10, he took his place on the right in the National Assembly (see Figure 5.1). He was not impressed by the hall, which had been rapidly constructed in the Cour d'honneur of the Palais Bourbon to accommodate an assembly of 900 members. With its wooden beams instead of columns and painted surfaces instead of marble, it reminded him of a huge music hall.[32] Once settled in the Assembly, Hugo was immediately confronted by the question of the National Workshops. Like many on both the right and the left, he believed the Workshops were a disaster. They produced nothing and were "an enormous waste of resources."[33] In his maiden speech on June 20, he urged that they be closed, asserting that unemployed workers were being tricked by radicals who were intoxicating the people with promises that could never be kept. He apparently believed that by voting to dissolve the National Workshops, he was not voting to shelve the question of unemployment. He was wrong.

On June 21 the Executive Commission issued a proclamation dissolving the National Workshops. Workers under the age of twenty-five were to be drafted into the army. All others were ordered to go to work in the provinces. This was understood in Paris as a declaration of war on the poor and the hungry. The next morning protesters gathered around the Pantheon, the Hôtel de Ville, and the Faubourg Saint-Antoine. A delegation of workers led by the eloquent Blanquist, Louis Pujol, failed in a last-minute confrontation with the minister Pierre Marie to secure any concession from the Executive Commission. Then both sides prepared for armed conflict.[34]

[31] *L'Organisation du travail*, 1 (June 3, 1848); Edmond Biré, *Victor Hugo après 1830* (Paris, 1891), II, 120.
[32] *Choses vues*, OC Histoire, Laffont, 1048.
[33] *Choses vues*, "Ateliers nationaux," OC Histoire, Laffont, 1050.
[34] Daniel Stern, *Histoire de la Révolution de 1848*, 3 vols. (Paris, 1853), III, 149–155; Donald McKay, *The National Workshops* (Cambridge, 1933), 136–142.

Figure 5.1 Portrait of Victor Hugo in 1848 while a member of the Constituent Assembly. Hulton Archive via Getty

Victor Hugo's June Days

Victor Hugo never forgot what he saw and did between June 22–26. Unlike our other writers, he participated in the fighting, and he did so on the side of the government. Reminiscences of those five days abound in

his later writings – notably in *Les Misérables* where an account of the
barricade fighting on June 5 and 6, 1832 and of Gavroche's "frightful
game of hide-and-seek with death" is suffused with echoes of 1848.[35]
There is also a separate chapter devoted to "the fatal insurrection of June
1848, the greatest war of street fighting in history." In this chapter, as
elsewhere in *Les Misérables*, Hugo seeks to give symbolic form to the
chaos of the insurrection.

This chapter, "The Charybdis of the Faubourg Saint-Antoine and the
Scylla of the Faubourg du Temple," is built around the description of
two huge barricades, one blocking the entrance to the Faubourg Saint-
Antoine and the other at the approach to the Faubourg du Temple. The
Saint-Antoine barricade is jagged, makeshift and irregular, composed of
doors, grilles, screens, bedroom furniture and kitchen stoves well as
paving stones and buttressed by pillars consisting of piles of rubble.
The Faubourg du Temple barricade is different. Built largely of paving
stones, it is a perpendicular wall: "immaculate in design, flawless in
alignment, symmetrical, rectilinear and funereal, a thing of craftsman-
ship and darkness." In describing these two barricades, Hugo moves
rapidly to their symbolic dimensions. The Saint-Antoine barricade is "a
place of thunderous defiance' and spontaneous fury," while the
Faubourg du Temple barricade is "a place of silence." "The one was a
roaring open mouth, the other a mask." Hugo loved allegory, and here he
believed he had found a way to grasp the dual nature of the June
insurrection which was "at once an outburst of fury and an enigma." In
what sense an enigma? The answer that Hugo gives in *Les Misérables* is
that June 1848 was "a revolt of the people against itself." By attacking the
democratic republic, the insurgents were, Hugo argues, attempting to
destroy the instrument of their own liberation.[36]

Les Misérables was published in 1862, fourteen years after the June
insurrection. In the mid-1870s, writing prefaces to the collected edition
of his speeches and political articles, Hugo was still attempting to grasp
the meaning of the June Days and to give a satisfactory answer to the
question of the legitimacy of the insurrection.[37] But he was trying to
make sense of the June Days from the very beginning. Like an artist with
his sketchbook, he filled his notebooks with stories and vivid images of
the building of barricades, the street fighting, and the atmosphere of

---

[35] Victor Hugo, *Les Misérables*, Marius-François Guyard (ed.), 2 vols. (Paris, 1963), II,
407–504, esp. 458–461.
[36] Hugo, *Les Misérables*, II, 407–412.
[37] "Paris et Rome," *Actes et paroles* III, *OC Politique*, Laffont, 702.

Paris. Sometimes he simply records "things seen" without comment. In other passages he starts from a scene witnessed or read about, and attempts to find in it clues as to the significance of the insurrection. Take, for example, this description of the beginning of the insurrection:

> From the outset the June revolt displayed strange features. It took on monstrous and unknown forms in the eyes of a terrified society. The first barricade was built on Friday morning the 23rd at the Porte Saint-Denis; it was attacked the same day ... When the attackers were within range, a tremendous volley came from the barricade and left the cobblestones strewn with the bodies of National Guards. The National Guard, more irritated than intimidated, rushed toward the barricade at break-neck speed. At this moment a woman appeared on the top of the barricade, a young, beautiful, disheveled, dreadful woman. This woman, who was a streetwalker, raised her dress up to the waist and shouted at the National Guards in horrible brothel-language that has to be translated: "Cowards. Fire, if you dare, at the belly of a woman!" Here the story gets ghastly. The National Guard did not hesitate. A barrage of bullets from the peloton flattened the poor woman. She fell with a great shriek. There was a horrified silence behind the barricade and among the attackers. Suddenly a second woman appeared. She was younger and even more beautiful. She was almost a child, barely seventeen years old ... It was another streetwalker. She raised her dress, showed her belly and cried: "Fire away, brigands!" They fired. She fell, riddled with bullets, on the body of the first woman. That is how this war began.[38]

Did Hugo actually witness this episode? Not at all. It appears in other contemporary narratives of the June days, and it was first reported on June 24 in *La Réforme* where Hugo's "streetwalker" is a "shop girl."[39] But what is interesting here is the way he uses the episode to dramatize a point about the heroism of the "abject" insurgents. He does this by adding a few lines that frame the events and give them a broader meaning: "The heroism of the abject is a hideous thing which reveals all the strength contained in weakness [and] shows this civilization, attacked by cynicism, defending itself with barbarism. On the one side the despair of the people, on the other the despair of society."[40]

By mid-morning on June 24 the insurgents controlled half of Paris – the eastern half which included Hugo's house on the Place des Vosges. Early that morning Hugo, who had participated in an all-night session at

---

[38] *Choses vues, OC Histoire*, Laffont, 1052–1053.
[39] *La Réforme*, June 24, 1848 in Maurizio Gribaudi and Michèle Riot-Sarcey, *1848, la révolution oubliée* (Paris, 2009), 210–211. The first woman in *La Réforme* is a "fille de magasin." She becomes a "fille publique" in Hugo. See also Stern, *Révolution de 1848*, III, 172–173, and Louis Ménard, *Prologue d'une revolution* (Paris, 1904), 151.
[40] *Choses vues, OC Histoire*, Laffont, 1052–1053.

the National Assembly, left for the Place des Vosges, hoping to reassure himself about his wife's safety. But as he approached the Faubourg Saint-Antoine, officers warned him not to proceed. The danger was too great. By eight o'clock he was back at the Assembly in time to participate in the vote to declare a state of siege and to confer full executive powers on General Cavaignac. Until then Cavaignac, who was already Minister of War, had allowed the insurrection to spread, refusing to order an attack until the insurgents had fully revealed themselves – and until he himself had been given absolute power. Hugo was divided about the state of siege; and in his extensive notes on June 24 he later altered the chronology of his day, claiming that when he returned to the Assembly, the vote had already been taken.[41]

June 24 was the turning point of the insurrection. Once given full powers, Cavaignac swiftly organized a massive attack on the insurgents' strongholds. By the end of the day the tide of battle had turned. Shortly before the declaration of the state of siege Hugo went to see Lamartine in the office of the Executive Committee. He found Lamartine exhausted and reduced to a state of total passivity – deathly pale, haggard, unshaven, his clothes rumpled and dirty. The other members of the Executive Committee were not much better off. Their meeting room was "like a cell where accused criminals were waiting to learn their sentence."[42] Around noon Hugo was appointed to a group of sixty representatives whose mission was "to stop the spilling of blood" by fanning out in the capital to inform the insurgents that, with the state of siege declared and Cavaignac given full powers, resistance was futile.

Just because he was divided about the state of siege, Hugo seems to have convinced himself that the best way to limit bloodshed was to defeat the insurrection rapidly. For the next three days he became a tiger, "haranguing insurgents, storming barricades, taking prisoners, and somehow remaining alive" (see Figure 5.2).[43] On this point we have more than Hugo's selective memory; we also have the testimony of someone who fought with him. On June 27 a member of the National Guard sent Sénard, the President of the National Assembly, a detailed account of Hugo's role in the taking of barricades on the rue Turenne:

On Saturday the 24th, about 2:00 in the afternoon, a man wearing a grey coat and without any kind of badge, cried out in our midst: "Let's get it over, boys! This war of snipers is lethal. We'll lose fewer men if we march bravely toward the

---

[41] Ibid, 1053; Graham Robb, *Victor Hugo* (London, 1997), 269.
[42] *Choses vues*, June 24, 1848, *OC Histoire*, Laffont, 1054. See also Hovasse, *Victor Hugo*, I, 1026–1027.
[43] Robb, *Victor Hugo*, 275.

Figure 5.2 Storming a barricade during the June Days. Bettmann Archive via Getty

danger. Forward!" This man, Monsieur le Président, was M. Victor Hugo, a representative for Paris. He was unarmed and nonetheless he led us; and while we took cover behind houses, he alone kept to the middle of the street. Twice I tugged at his sleeve, telling him: "You'll get yourself killed!" "That is why I am here," he answered, and he continued to shout: "Forward! Forward!" With such a man to lead us, we reached the barricades and took them, one after another.[44]

There seems to have been something suicidal about Hugo's behaviour over the next three days. He claimed afterwards that he knew he had God's protection.[45] But as Hugo himself recognized, divine protection didn't help the Archbishop of Paris, Monseigneur Affre, who was shot in the back as he approached the Faubourg Saint-Antoine "with a sublime smile" and "raising his crucifix above the civil war."[46]

[44] Cahagne de Cey to Antoine Sénard, June 27, 1848, *OC* CFL, VII, 750. For other testimony, see Bernard Leuilliot, "Les Barricades mystérieuses," *Europe* (March 1985), 127–136 and Robb, *Victor Hugo*, 274–275.
[45] Hugo to Ulric Guttinguer, July 10, 1848, CFL VII, 750: "J'avais une ferme foi, pas une balle ne m'a atteint."
[46] "La Liberté de l'enseignement," *Actes et paroles* I, January 15, 1850, *OC Politique*, Laffont, 222; Hovasse, *Victor Hugo*, I, 1028, 1244 n.406.

Two more images of the fighting appear in passages from *Les Misérables*. In one passage Hugo intervenes, speaking in the first person singular, to describe his own experiences. Here he writes of a moment on June 25 when he was looking down from a rooftop on the Boulevard du Temple:

From time to time if someone, a soldier, an officer, a *représentant du peuple* ventured to cross that deserted stretch of road, you would hear a faint, shrill whistle and the person would fall, either wounded or dead. If he escaped, you would see a bullet bury itself in a shutter or a housefront ... There were corpses here and there and pools of blood on the cobblestones. I remember seeing a white butterfly flutter up and down the street. Summer does not take a vacation in wartime.[47]

Here Hugo's butterfly is an image of normalcy in a world at war. In the second passage, evoking his sense of exhaustion, confusion and emptiness in the aftermath of the fighting, there is no reminder of another reality:

Leaving a barricade, you don't remember what you have seen. You have done terrible things, and you don't remember them. You have been caught up in a struggle of ideas bearing human faces, your head plunged into the light of the future. There were corpses on the ground and phantoms standing up. The hours lasted forever, like the hours of eternity. You lived in death.[48]

Throughout these three days Hugo was cut off from both his wife and his mistress. The Place des Vôsges was at the heart of the insurgency. The Mairie had been taken over by the rebels and turned into a kind of insurrectionary headquarters. On the 24th, Hugo was told that while his wife and children were safe, the insurgents had set fire to their house. This was not true. When he finally got back to the Place des Vôsges, he found fourteen bullet holes around carriage entrance, but everything in the house was intact: rugs, furniture, silverware, wall hangings, ancient swords and muskets, and above all his manuscripts. A leader of the insurgents, a school teacher and a reader of Hugo, had even led tours of the house for other insurgents.

It was only on June 26 that Hugo found time to write his wife and his mistress. He told his wife Adèle that he had been worried sick about her and the children but that it had been impossible for him to return home. He was more forthcoming to his mistress, Juliette Drouet:

I've spent three days and three nights on my feet in the midst of things, without a bed to sleep on, sitting down on the stones briefly, without eating and almost

---

[47] *Les Misérables*, II, 413.   [48] *Les Misérables*, II, 473–474.

without drinking. Good people gave me a slice of bread and a glass of water; someone else gave me clothing. At last this terrible war of brothers is over! As for me, I am safe and sound, but what disasters! I will never forget the terrible things I've seen during the past forty hours.[49]

That same day, June 26, the last pockets of resistance in the Faubourg Saint-Antoine were taken by Cavaignac's troops. Then the reprisals began.

During the following week there were over 15,000 arrests. The cellars under the terrace between the Tuileries Palace and the Seine were turned into a temporary prison, a kind of holding tank that became rank with excrement, vomit and dried blood. Suspected insurgents were herded into it and bayoneted or shot if they made trouble. Hugo knew about the terrible conditions in this prison, and one of the odder texts in *Choses vues* is the beginning of an essay on the history of these cellars, contrasting their use in 1848 with their origin as a walkway for the pregnant Duchesse de Berry after the assassination of her husband in 1820.[50] Hugo made no public statement about the abuse of these prisoners, which Flaubert was to describe vividly in *L'Education sentimentale*. But he did intervene with the authorities on behalf of individual insurgents; and early in the morning of June 26, on hearing rumours that Cavaignac was considering setting fire to the Faubourg Saint-Antoine by way of reprisal, Hugo went directly to Cavaignac to beg him not to do it. Cavaignac of course did not burn down the whole quarter. But in late November, when Cavaignac was running for president against Louis-Napoleon, Hugo noted, as a bit of useful information, that in the four days of fighting "to preserve civilization" Cavaignac's troops had fired 2,100,000 cartridges.[51]

As the years passed, Hugo became increasingly sympathetic to the *misérables* who became insurgents in June of 1848 and whom he had helped hunt down as enemies of the Republic. There are passages in *Les Misérables* in which this sympathy, together with Hugo's doubts about his own role in the crushing of the insurrection, is very near the surface:

It sometimes happens that in defiance of principles ... an outcast element of the populace. the rabble, rises up in its anguish and frustration, its privation and its fever, its distress, its stench and its darkness, to protest and do battle with the rest of society. The wretched [*les gueux*] attack the common law; the mob rebels against the people.

---

[49] Hugo to Juliette, June 26, 1848, Juliette Drouet, *Lettres à Victor Hugo*, Evelyn Blewer et al. (eds.), 111; Hovasse, *Victor Hugo*, I, 1030.
[50] *Choses vues*, June 30, 1848, *OC Histoire*, Laffont, 1057.
[51] *Choses vues*, November 25, 1848, *OC Histoire*, Laffont, 1116.

He describes these as "dismal moments" because there is "always a certain amount of right in this madness." And he concludes with a blunt observation: "Words that are meant as terms of abuse – wretched, rabble, mob, mobocracy – point, alas! to the fault of those who rule rather than that of those who suffer, rather to the fault of the privileged than to the fault of the disinherited."[52]

Hugo did not express such doubts in the summer of 1848. But neither did he lend his voice to the well-orchestrated chorus of attacks on the socialists, the communists and the poor that followed the crushing of the June insurrection. On the contrary, he immediately went on the attack against Cavaignac's prolongation of the state of siege, against the government's shutting down of newspapers, and against the decision of the National Assembly to bring charges against Louis Blanc and Marc Caussidière for their alleged role in the *journée* of May 15.

In due course Hugo's view of the June Days crystallized. The insurrection was, he maintained, an attack on civilization and it had to be opposed. But he could not bring himself to hold the insurgents solely responsible for actions that were so clearly a response to their suffering and their sense of betrayal. As he asked an insurgent nine months later, "Who inspired you all, in this sad month of June, to attack society, civilization, France! You were generous-hearted people! Who could have blinded you to this point? You should have defended what you were attacking. That was the cause of all the trouble."[53] In *Les Misérables* he writes simply that the June insurrection "had to be put down because it was an attack on the Republic." But then he adds that "the man of probity" could understand its roots and "venerate it even while attacking it."[54]

Break with the Party of Order and with Louis-Napoleon

With the voting of a constitution on November 4, 1848, the state of siege finally came to an end. Hugo, who along with Proudhon was one of just thirty representatives to oppose the final text of the constitution, strongly opposed the creation of a single legislative assembly. This reminded him, he said, of the Convention of 1793; and it seemed "so threatening to the tranquility and prosperity of the country" that he could not bring himself to vote for the Constitution.[55] He was still nominally a member of the

[52] *Les Misérables*, II, 407–408.
[53] Hugo to G. Hugelmann, March 27, 1849 in Bénichou, *Mages romantiques*, 333.
[54] *Les Misérables*, II, 408–409.
[55] Letter to *Le Moniteur*, November 5, 1848, *OC* CFL VII, 1345.

conservative Comité de la rue de Poitiers and did not support the inclusion of the right to work in the new constitution. But on many other issues, such as the death penalty, censorship, and the assertion of the rights of man in the preamble to the constitution, Hugo voted with the Left. And as he observed the contrast between the importance of the issues discussed and the triviality of the interventions of the conservative majority, his heart sank. After a session in which Charles Lagrange, "the Don Quixote of the Mountain," had been overwhelmed by "witty" hecklers from the Party of Order, he wrote that the amusement of the speakers made his heart bleed, because he "heard the sobs of the people behind the bursts of laughter."[56]

In the month prior to the presidential election, two leading candidates emerged, Cavaignac and Louis-Napoleon Bonaparte. Hugo detested Cavaignac whom he held responsible for the magnitude of the killing in June; and on November 25, when the Assembly voted by a margin of 503 to 34 that Cavaignac had "served the country well," Hugo was one of the dissenting 34. His initial sympathies went to Lamartine. But when it became evident that Lamartine's candidacy was going nowhere, he looked elsewhere. On November 19 he had a chance to talk with Louis-Napoleon at a reception given by Odilon Barrot and was not unimpressed. "Louis Bonaparte," he wrote, "is distingué, cold, calm, intelligent with a certain quality of deference and dignity."[57]

We can follow the rise and fall of Hugo's interest in Louis-Napoleon Bonaparte through the newspaper L'Evénement, which had been created by a consortium including Hugo's two sons. Hugo disclaimed responsibility for its articles, but its endorsement of Louis-Napoleon on October 28 clearly reflected his position. Hugo did not endorse an article by his son Charles, comparing Cavaignac to two would-be assassins of Louis Philippe. But he had no complaint when, on the eve of the election, L'Evénement published a one-page supplement containing nothing but the name Louis-Napoleon Bonaparte, repeated a hundred times.

Shortly after his massive victory in the presidential election, Louis-Napoleon held his first state dinner. Hugo was invited, and he seized the opportunity to urge the new president to create a government that would be remembered not for its military victories but for its intellectual and cultural conquests – a government that would "adorn peace ... with all the glory of the arts, letters and sciences [and] with the conquests of industry and progress."[58] A few days later L'Evénement ran an article by

---

[56] Choses vues, November 25, 1848, OC Histoire Laffont, 1118.
[57] Choses vues, November 1848, OC Histoire Laffont, 1114.
[58] Choses vues, December 20, 1848, OC Histoire Laffont, 1133.

August Vacquerie urging the new president to create "a ministry of peace."[59] Hugo would surely have accepted such a position. But Louis-Napoleon had his own agenda and no offer was made. For the next six months, Hugo continued to support Louis-Napoleon and generally to vote with the Party of Order, but there was no more talk in his entourage about a special relationship with the President (see Figure 5.3).With the drafting of a constitution and the election of a president, the Constituent Assembly had completed its work; and the date for new legislative elections was set at May 13, 1849. Hugo was once again a candidate, and once again he had the support of the Party of Order. In public statements he presented himself as a consistent defender of order against anarchy and liberty against arbitrary rule.[60] But in his private writings he distanced himself from conservative leaders such as Thiers and Molé, Berryer and de Broglie. "Deep down I don't see eye to eye with those people," he wrote in March 1849. "I don't share their religion, their political colouring. But when a ship is sinking, every passenger becomes a sailor and runs for the pumps."[61] Parisian voters were not aware of Hugo's reservations, and he was easily reelected as one of 450 representatives identified with the Party of Order. At the same time the democrats and socialists made significant gains (180 seats). The big losers, the moderate republicans, were reduced to a mere seventy-five seats, and Lamartine, their leader, was defeated. Hugo regretted Lamartine's defeat. As he wrote a friend, "Lamartine has made big mistakes ... but he rejected the red flag and abolished the death penalty. For two weeks he was the luminous man of a sombre revolution. Today we are passing from luminous men to flamboyant men, from Lamartine to Ledru-Rollin. Next, we will go from Ledru-Rollin to Blanqui."[62]

During the summer and fall of 1849, Hugo finally broke with the Party of Order. Two speeches marked the break, each eliciting howls of protest from conservatives. The first was his speech of July 9 on poverty, "Sur la misère." At issue was the creation of a commission to prepare "laws relative to welfare and public assistance." Not citing names, Hugo denounced those who believed that there was "nothing to do" about poverty. And he went on: "I am not, messieurs, one of those who believes we can eliminate suffering in this world. Suffering is a divine law. But I am with those who think and affirm that we can destroy poverty." This

---

[59] Auguste Vacquerie in *L'Evénement*, December 25, 1848 in Bénichou, *Mages romantiques*, 334]
[60] "Après le mandate accompli," May 6, 1849, *Actes et paroles*, I, *OC Politique*, Laffont, 164.
[61] *Choses vues*, March 1849, *OC Histoire*, Laffont, 1204.
[62] Hugo to Charles de Lacretelle, May 24, 1849, *OC CFL VII*, 756.

ACTUALITÉS.

Nº 171.

M.M. Victor Hugo et Emile Girardin cherchent a élever le prince Louis sur un pavois, ça n'est pas très solide !

Figure 5.3 Victor Hugo and Emile Girardin trying to support Louis-Napoleon. Lithograph by Daumier in *Le Charivari*, December 11, 1848. Hugo's brief period of support for Louis-Napoleon Bonaparte ended shortly after the latter's massive victory in the presidential election of December 10. Lithograph by Daumier in *Le Charivari*, December 11, 1848. Photograph: Getty

prompted "violent disapproval" from the Right. Then Hugo raised the issue of socialism. Noting that he himself had warned against "chimerical socialism," he asked whether there wasn't something to be learned from socialism rightly understood. Had not the socialists grasped "a part of the sad realities of our time"? He asked his colleagues to reflect on the fact that "it is anarchy that opens up chasms between people, but it is poverty that digs them." Then he concluded: "You have made laws against anarchy. Now make laws against poverty."[63]

The second speech marking Hugo's break with the Party of Order took place on October 19, 1849. It concerned "the Roman Question" – specifically the liquidation by French troops of the short-lived Roman Republic and the restoration of papal rule in Rome. Earlier in the summer, on June 13, left-wing members of the newly elected Legislative Assembly had organized a demonstration protesting the military action taken by French troops against the Roman Republic. The government declared the demonstration an insurrection, arresting its leaders, shutting down democratic and socialist newspapers, and proclaiming a state of siege. Hugo initially supported the actions of the government and wrote mockingly that the Mountain had produced a mousetrap. But when Changarnier's troops sacked the offices of left-wing newspapers, Hugo rose in the Assembly to ask why the government was ignoring "these veritable attacks on legality, liberty and property."[64]

Four months later, after the Pope had been reestablished in the Vatican by the French army and then refused to accept constitutional limits on his power, Hugo exploded, arguing that with French support the Pope was attempting to "plunge his people back into the night" of superstition and intolerance. The result of the French intervention, he said, was to subject Rome to the "fanatical and violent authority" of a clerical government led by three cardinals. This unleashed a flood of shouted denials, objections and "violent interruptions" on the right and (according to the transcript) "thunderous applause" and "explosions of bravos" on the left. In conclusion, Hugo strung together a whole series of sentences beginning: "What is not possible ..." "What is not possible,"

[63] "La Misère," July 9, 1849, *Actes et paroles*, I, *OC Politique* Laffont, 199–206. On this speech and on the problems posed by Hugo's rewriting of his speeches, and of the response to them, in *Actes et paroles*, see Guy Rosa, "'Lord Clown' ou comment Victor Hugo devint un orateur républicain" in *La France démocratique, combats, mentalités, symbols, mélanges offerts à Maurice Agulhon* (Paris, 1998), 335–342; and Thomas Bouchet, "Figures libres: "'Orateur Hugo en République (1848–1851)" in Jean-Claude Caron and Annie Stora Lamarre (eds.), *Hugo politique* (Besançon, 2004), 189–196.
[64] Assemblée législative, June 15, 1849, *Actes et paroles* I, *OC Politique*, Laffont, 374.

he intoned, is that a military "expedition undertaken in a spirit of humanity and liberty should culminate in the reestablishment of the Holy Office." That the "generous liberal ideas that France carries everywhere in the folds of its flag" should not have had any influence in Rome. That France should have shed the glorious blood of its soldiers and engaged its sacred flag and its moral responsibility before all nations without attaining significant results. In descending from the speaker's rostrum, the transcript tells us, Hugo received the congratulations of a crowd of representatives, including his enemy, General Cavaignac, and the monarchists Charles Dupin and La Rochejaquelein, while an "explosion of bravos and applause" rained down on him.[65]

Three months later, on January 15, 1850, Hugo made another dramatic intervention in support of a secular state. At issue this time was the proposal by the Minister of Education, Count Alfred de Falloux, to reorganize the French educational system, placing primary schools under church control and allowing priests to teach in secondary schools without the university degree required of lay teachers. Hugo opposed the measure, while insisting that he did not oppose religious education. He believed in God and in an afterlife, and he venerated many Christian saints from Saint Francis down to Vincent de Paul. But, he reminded his Catholic colleagues, there was a darker side to the history of the Church. To make sure that there was no misunderstanding, he referred specifically to Torquemada, the Inquisition and the Index. In a series of rhetorical flourishes, he conjured up images of books burned, liberty betrayed, intelligence bound and gagged, and sermons replacing the press in a world darkened by the shadow of the cassock and in which the sacristy was sovereign. He insisted that he was all for liberty of education, but in a secular state and not one controlled by "the clerical party."[66]

By March, when the Legislative Assembly approved the Falloux Law by a vote of 399 to 237, Hugo had become a leader of the parliamentary opposition to the Party of Order and "the clerical party." He had not yet completely burned his bridges with Louis-Napoleon, but he led the resistance to a series of measures proposed by the President's ministers including laws on deportation, on the death penalty, on freedom of the press, and on the right to vote. In the most significant of these debates, Hugo defended universal suffrage against an attempt by the government

[65] "Affaire de Rome," Octobre 19, 1849, *Actes et paroles*, I, *OC Politique* Laffont, 207–215.
[66] "La Liberté d'enseignement," January 15, 1850, *Actes et paroles*, I, *OC Politique* Laffont, 217–227. The violence of Hugo's language is particularly striking given the fact that when the Falloux law was first considered, Hugo supported it.

to disenfranchise almost a third of the electorate. What prompted this was the success of left-wing candidates in by-elections, culminating with the victory in Paris of Eugene Sue, the celebrated author of *Les Mystères de Paris* and a recent convert to socialism. Conservatives were disturbed by the fact that Sue, and other victorious socialists and democrats, clearly owed their election to working-class votes. The stock market plunged, and there was talk of moving the Assembly to Bourges or Tours. At this point, Adolphe Thiers proposed limiting the right to vote to males who had been domiciled for three years in the same electoral district. This would disenfranchise many members of the working class, who were obliged, by the nature of the labour market, to move frequently.

Hugo's speech of May 20 was an eloquent defence of universal (male) suffrage, which he described as a means of educating and bringing hope to the poorest and most vulnerable members of society. He made a political argument as well as a moral one. By giving the poor a role to play in the life of the nation, a non-violent alternative to blind revolt, universal suffrage would "take the gun out of their hands." The right to vote would render the right of insurrection meaningless. Hugo's eloquence made no difference, and Thiers' proposal, which was adopted on May 31, 1850, by a margin of almost two to one, resulted in a reduction of the electorate from 9.6 million to 6.8 million voters.[67]

Hugo's last major speech before the Legislative Assembly came on July 17, 1851. The issue was the revision of the constitution to enable Louis-Napoleon to serve as president for another four-year term. Hugo now found himself opposed to both the conservative monarchists and the clique of opportunists, adventurers, and admirers of the first Napoleon, who had gathered around his nephew. This speech, during which Hugo was interrupted a hundred times according to the transcript, lasted three and a half hours. Far from limiting himself to the topic at hand, Hugo described vividly just what had become of the Second Republic under the presidency of Louis-Napoleon:

All our liberties ambushed, bound and gagged, one after another: universal suffrage betrayed, falsified, mutilated … All reforms put off or flouted, onerous and unfair taxes maintained or restored, a state of siege imposed on five departments. Paris and Lyon placed under surveillance … the press hounded, juries rigged, not enough justice and too many police.[68]

[67] "Le Suffrage universel," May 20, 1850, *Actes et paroles*, I, *OC Politique*, Laffont, 240–250.
[68] "Révision de la constitution," July 17, 1851, *Actes et paroles*, I, *OC Politique*, Laffont, 288.

Hugo ranged across French history from the monarchical restorations of 1814 to the imperial restoration that he (rightly) believed the Bonapartists were contemplating:

After the ruin of Napoleon, after the exile of Charles X, after the fall of Louis Philippe, after the French Revolution in a word, that is to say, after the complete, absolute, prodigious renewal of principles, of beliefs, opinions, situations, influences and facts, it is the republic which is on solid ground and the monarchy which is at risk.[69]

But the greatest risk would be the reestablishment of the Empire, which was what the Bonapartists really had in mind when they called for the revision of the Constitution. Hugo addressed Louis-Napoleon directly:

What! Because there was once a man who won the Battle of Marengo and who reigned, you want to reign ... You wish to take in your small hands the scepter of the Titans and the sword of the giants! To do what? After Augustus, Augustulus! What! Because we have had Napoleon the Great, must we now have Napoleon the Little![70]

Such language was new. No other member of the Legislative Assembly would have dared address Louis-Napoleon in such terms. It was no longer a case of burning bridges. It was war. Hugo, who enjoyed parliamentary immunity, could not be prosecuted. But by mid-September both his sons were in the Conciergerie, convicted of press crimes, and their newspaper, L'Evénement, was silenced.

Having failed to secure the ¾ vote majority needed to revise the Constitution, Louis-Napoleon prepared to overthrow the republic. The date he chose was December 2, the anniversary of his uncle's coronation as Emperor and of his victory at Austerlitz. That morning Hugo awoke to learn that during the night the principal adversaries of Louis-Napoleon, including Cavaignac, Charras, Thiers and the generals Lamoricière, Changarnier and Bedeau had been arrested. Posters were glued to walls all over Paris announcing the dissolution of the Legislative Assembly, the restoration of universal suffrage, and a plebiscite to sanction the new regime.

Victor Hugo's first impulse was to organize resistance to this *coup d'état*. He quickly took charge of the small group of representatives who were determined to defend the Republic. For three days he tried and failed to stoke the fires of popular protest, writing appeals to the people, meeting with leftwing representatives, and haranguing anyone who would listen. He then moved into an apartment on the rue Richelieu

[69] "Révision," *OC Politique*. Laffont, 284.
[70] "Révision," *OC Politique*, Laffont, 289–290.

where for several nights he was fed and watched over by his mistress Juliette Drouet. Later he moved to another apartment, the home of a friend who conveniently ran a Bonapartist newspaper. The Prefect of Police subsequently claimed that Hugo's whereabouts were known and "we might have arrested him ten times over" but did not wish to make a martyr of him.[71] Many historians have accepted this claim. But the police were looking for him, and he believed he would be shot if captured. On December 11 he took the night train for Brussels.

"Napoleon the Little"

During his two decades of exile – first briefly at Brussels, then on the Channel Islands of Jersey and Guernsey, British but just off the French coast – Hugo played out his self-appointed role as the republican conscience of France. He wrote and published voluminously. *Les Misérables* (1862) was only the biggest and best of the many works that he completed during the Second Empire. But his first order of business was to settle accounts with Louis-Napoleon Bonaparte.

For five months after his arrival in Belgium Hugo worked unstintingly on a history of the *coup d'état*. This book was both a narrative and an indictment. He initially called it *Le Crime du deux décembre*. Beginning with a detailed account of the surprise attack on the sleeping city by troops loyal to Louis-Napoleon, he went on to describe the closing of the National Assembly and the arrest of representatives, the organization of resistance, two days of sporadic street fighting, the massacre on December 4 of several hundred bystanders on the boulevards, and the subsequent collapse of resistance. In a draft preface to this book, Hugo commented, "There is something priestly about my function: I replace the magistracy and the clergy. I judge, which the judges have failed to do. I excommunicate, which is what the priests have failed to do."[72]

By May 1852 Hugo's manuscript ran to 600 pages. It was almost done. But he decided not to publish it. He kept accumulating material that raised questions about aspects of the story he wished to tell. This in itself would not have stopped him. But he also found it difficult to get such a long work published. He had a tacit understanding with the Belgian government that, while he remained in Belgium, he would publish nothing that might compromise relations between the Belgian monarchy and Louis-Napoleon's France. An alternate plan to publish in England

---

[71] Charlemagne-Emile Maupas, *Mémoires sur le Seconde Empire*, 2 vols. (Paris, 1884–1885), cited in Robb, *Victor Hugo*, 303.
[72] *Histoire d'un crime*, projets de préface, *OC Histoire*, Laffont, 1399

proved problematic. In May Hugo stopped trying to tinker with *Le Crime
du deux décembre*. (It was only twenty-five years later, at a time
when another anti-republican *coup d'état* seemed imminent, that he
published the book under the title *Histoire d'un crime: Déposition
d'un témoin*.) Instead in just one month, between June 14 and July 12,
he wrote a much shorter book – a bitter satirical pamphlet entitled
Napoléon le petit. It was published in Brussels on August 8, a week after
Hugo's departure from Belgium. It appeared in two editions, one of
normal size and the other small enough to be easily smuggled into
France.

Hugo once said of *Napoléon le petit* that it was not a book but a cry of
pain.[73] Such statements (and there are others) have inspired some commentators to refer to it as one long vituperation or, in the words of an
American biographer, "simply a diatribe or philippic against the dictator."[74] Hugo is indeed a remarkably resourceful and imaginative satirist.
He has a rich command of the language of invective, and his portrait of
Louis-Napoleon as a "vulgar, puerile, theatrical individual" who loves
spangles and feathers and whose "great talent is silence" is a small
masterpiece.[75] There is truth in André Maurois' characterization: "This
was a piece of vivid improvisation, an indictment in the great Roman
tradition: Cicero's sweep, the vigour of Tacitus, the poetry of Juvenal. Its
prose was the prose of a poet, rhythmical, broken, with something in it of
that controlled madness in which the beauty of poetry lies. The tone was
marked, now by the invective of the Prophets, now by the terrible
humour of Swift."[76]

But the book is more than that. It has an argument that Hugo works
out with the enthusiasm, the hyperbole, and the rhetorical flourishes of a
zealous prosecutor. It is also elegantly shaped, as it moves from the man
to his government, to his crimes, to his fraudulent attempts to legitimize
his rule, and finally to the contrast between the initial grief and abjection
of his opponents and the prophecy of their ultimate triumph. It begins
with a carefully worked out antithesis between the solemn oath sworn by
Louis Napoleon before the National Assembly on December 20, 1848 to
respect the constitution and safeguard the Republic, and the violation of
that oath on December 2, 1851. Having established the antithesis, Hugo
moves on to other matters only to return to the question of oaths later,

[73] Notice to *Histoire d'un crime, OC Histoire*, Laffont, 1374.
[74] Matthew Josephson, *Victor Hugo: A Realistic Biography of the Great Romantic* (New York, 1942), 361.
[75] *Napoléon le petit, OC Histoire*, Laffont, 14–15.
[76] André Maurois, *Olympio: The Life of Victor Hugo* (New York, 1956), 305.

when he describes the process by which the oath-breaker imposes *his own* oath on all state functionaries who duly "swear fidelity to his treason."[77]

Hugo's language is so richly metaphorical that his main points are often delivered in poetic form as striking images or ornate fantasies. The book begins and ends with elaborately extended metaphors. "We are in Russia, The Neva is frozen. Houses are built on the ice ... ." Thus Hugo introduces his initial prophesy that "the brand new empire of Louis Bonaparte" will prove no more able to resist the warm rays of liberty than the ice to resist the summer sun.[78] Finally, in conclusion, Hugo creates an even more elaborate fantasy to illustrate the point that the trappings of power surrounding Louis-Napoleon will soon melt away.[79]

Napoléon le petit is, first and foremost, an attempt to awaken the French public from what Hugo describes as "the monstrous sleep of conscience" that permitted Louis-Napoleon to overthrow the Republic and seize power with relatively little resistance – and to kill hundreds of people in the process. Hugo says little about the provincial resistance to the *coup d'état*.[80] And in the section entitled "The Crime" he does not offer a narrative of the events of December 2. Instead, under the title "The Coup d'Etat in Trouble," he provides a detailed account of the events of December 4, when a clean-up operation turned violent as soldiers patrolling the *grands boulevards* fired on crowds of unarmed curiosity-seekers, killing several hundred Parisian men, women and children.[81] This section, described as "a chapter from an unpublished work," is based largely on eye-witness accounts of the killing and of the appearance of central Paris in the immediate aftermath. Here Hugo seeks both to show that the massacre of December 4 was *intended* to provoke fear and obedience and to describe the carnage in such graphic detail that no reader could fail to be revolted.

All this is interspersed with passages of gothic horror and dark humour. "The second of December," he says, "is a crime shrouded in night, in a closed and silent coffin from the slits of which flow streams of blood. We are going to open this coffin."[82] Opening the coffin means exposing to the light of day the names of the victims, the circumstances under which they were killed, and the premeditation of the crime by a

[77] *Napoléon le petit*, OC Histoire, Laffont, 114.   [78] Ibid, 11.   [79] Ibid, 152.
[80] Hugo's brief chapter "La Jacquerie" has as much to say about the orchestration of the "red scare" as about actual movements of protest in the provinces. See *Napoléon le petit*, OC Histoire, Laffont, 83–86.
[81] According to Roger Price, *People and Politics in France, 1848–1870* (Cambridge, 2004), 391, about 200 Parisians were killed on December 4, 1851. Hugo's numbers are inflated.
[82] *Napoléon le petit*, OC Histoire, Laffont, 50.

usurper who was bent, Hugo believes, on terrifying Parisians into blindly accepting his rule. Throughout the text Hugo repeatedly contrasts darkness and light, describing Louis-Napoleon as "a man of darkness" who normally "kills in the night, in obscurity, in solitude, the shadows" but who chose to kill openly on December 4 in order to intimidate the whole nation.[83] A related contrast for Hugo is that between speech and silence. If Louis-Napoleon is a "man of darkness," he is also a "man of silence." Silence is his weapon and his "great talent." Calling on his fertile poetic and painterly imagination, Hugo develops these themes and extends these metaphors, creating a vivid image of the Little Napoleon as a "man of silence and night" whose crime is "a mixture of audacity and shadow."[84]

Along with the argument, the imagery and the vitriol, there is an affirmative vision – a vision which could be described as a kind of prologue or overture to the depiction of a future French republic. Here three elements are particularly striking. First, there is Hugo's idealization of "la tribune française," by which he means the French tradition of parliamentary debate. Secondly, there is the sketch of a democratic republic included in his chapter on "Progress Associated with the Coup d'Etat." Finally, there is the rhapsodic celebration of intellectual and material progress with which Hugo concludes the book.

The term "parlementarisme" had been coined by Louis-Napoleon to characterize the republican parliamentary system that he did away with. For him it was a term of denigration. For Hugo, it is a term of commendation. He defines it broadly and in extravagantly positive terms.[85] But in his chapter on "parlementarisme" he focuses specifically on the tradition of parliamentary debate and oratory that developed in France starting with Mirabeau and the French Revolution. What is striking about his evocation of this tradition is its inclusiveness. He begins by reeling off the names of the great revolutionary orators: Mirabeau, Vergniaud, Camille Desmoulins, Saint-Just, Danton, Robespierre. He then goes on to pay tribute to the Legitimist Chateaubriand, the Orleanist Guizot, the doctrinaire liberal Royer-Collard, and the moderate republican Lamartine. His point is that progress occurs when diverse voices are heard, in a climate of free discussion among opposing political parties. Thus, his celebration of French political oratory, of what he calls "la tribune française," is a celebration of political liberalism and of parliamentary government, denigrated as sterile by the Napoleons. It is also a tribute to the renewal of spirited parliamentary debate during the Bourbon

---

[83] Ibid, 78.   [84] Ibid, 70.   [85] Ibid, 95.

Restoration. He commends the "ardent, fecund, tumultuous" character of the contentious parliamentary debates following the fall of the first Napoleon.[86]

Hugo sees the tradition of parliamentary oratory as a source of strength and virtue. He celebrates the "varied aptitudes" and the "services rendered" by orators of opposing views, both revolutionary and conservative. Like Condorcet celebrating the role of the printing press in banishing superstition, Hugo extravagantly praises political oratory as "the terror of all tyrannies and all fanaticisms" and "the hope of all who are oppressed." The orator, he says, is "a sower" who "casts his instincts, his passions, his beliefs, his sufferings, his dreams, his ideas in handfuls among men. Every brain is a furrow for him."[87] This French tradition of political oratory, which Hugo describes as a "prodigious turbine of ideas," spreading enlightenment through the world, was, he says, silenced by the first Napoleon and silenced again by Louis Bonaparte on December 2. But it cannot be permanently repressed. For speech itself is divine in origin and ultimately irrepressible.

In his chapter on the possible outcomes of the *coup d'état* Hugo paints in broad strokes the picture of a future republic. Here the emphasis is on decentralization, local liberties, and a rich communal and associative life. The central institution would be an autonomous or "sovereign" commune run not by a central administration but by an elected mayor. Elected judges would replace a permanent irremovable magistrature, and elections would be held by universal (male) suffrage. Priests would play no political role; war would be limited to the defence of national territory; and the army would have the status of a national guard.[88] In an earlier chapter, Hugo also emphasizes the importance of an informed public and hence of a free press in a democratic republic. "The liberty of the press," he writes, "is the essential condition of universal suffrage."[89]

The final affirmative element in *Napoléon le petit* is the celebration of intellectual and material progress with which Hugo concludes the book. Here he argues that the forces for enlightenment and modernization that have emerged in the west since the sixteenth century are irrepressible. Hugo's language is again richly metaphorical – laden with striking images and ornate fantasies. It is sometimes said, he writes, that the revolutions of 1848 opened an abyss between past and future. This is wrong: the cadaver of the past remains present in Europe. 1848 opened a trench into which the cadaver should have been thrown. But this did not happen. Instead, everything that belonged to the past survives – kings, cardinals,

---

[86] Ibid, 87–96: Book V: "Le Parlementarisme."
[87] *Napoléon le petit, OC Histoire*, Laffont, 93.   [88] Ibid, 125–126.   [89] Ibid, 100.

judges, captains and, along with them, the "social fictions" that justify
their power. The traditional elites are now attempting to fill up the trench
and cover it over, crushing throughout Europe "the immense vegetation
of free thought" inspired by the work of Luther, Descartes and Voltaire.
Their goal is to bring back the Inquisition and the Index, to suppress
journals, books, prints, free speech. They want to "extinguish individual
initiative, local life, national élan." They want "to destroy the sense of
national identity among people who have been separated and divided up,
to destroy constitutions in constitutional states, to destroy the republic in
France, to destroy liberty everywhere."[90]

Hugo notes that among the oppressed nations, there is one which has
long assumed a leading role in the resistance against the forces of tradition. This is France, a nation which has spoken in behalf of the fraternity
of all nations "with the voice of its writers, its poets, its philosophers, its
orators." Hugo then adopts Biblical imagery to describe the experience
of France during the Second Republic:

For over three years men of the past, scribes, pharisees, publicans ... crucified the
Christ of the people, the French people. Some provided the cross, some the nails,
others the hammer. Falloux placed the crown of thorns on the head of this Christ.
Montalembert pressed to his mouth the sponge soaked in vinegar and gall. Louis
Bonaparte is the miserable soldier who struck Jesus and made him cry out: "My
God, why hast thou forsaken me?"[91]

Identifying France with Jesus Christ and December 2 with the crucifix-
ion, Hugo then asks his readers to look forward to the resurrection.

The last half-dozen pages of *Napoléon le petit* are the verbal equivalent
of the final movement of a Bruckner symphony. Hugo ends on a soaring,
lyrical, hugely hopeful note, piling climax on climax, anticipating the
resurrection not just of France but of the whole human race. "Let us look
to the future," he begins. We don't know what storms await us, but we
can already catch a glimpse of our destination. "The future is the republic for all." Hugo then enumerates the achievements of the nineteenth
century – "this century, directly born of the French Revolution." He
celebrates the accomplishments of the artists, poets, philosophers and
musicians of the century and the "miracles" achieved by science, technology and medicine: the railroad, balloon flight, anaesthesia, photography, the Voltaic battery, the electric telegraph. These innovations have
broken down traditional barriers and altered man's relationship to time,
space, and suffering. Lithography and the rotary printing press have
made possible the dissemination of knowledge around the world. Now

---

[90] Ibid, 144.   [91] Ibid, 146.

"despite censorship, despite the Index, books and journals rain down everywhere. Voltaire, Diderot, Rousseau fall like hail on Rome, Naples, Vienna, Petersburg." A new life is about to begin, a life which will bring peace and harmony to the world. Nothing that the modern followers of Torquemada and Philip II can do will hold back the tide of progress, which will sweep them away along with Louis-Napoleon and his attempt to reconstitute an empire.[92]

Hugo concludes by evoking the situation of French exiles, *proscrits* like himself, scattered about Europe "like a handful of ashes," some in Belgium, Piedmont and Switzerland "where they are not free," others in London "without a roof over their heads." Their careers destroyed, their family ties broken, they cope with adversity as best they can. Louis-Napoleon has apparently triumphed. But he will not last. The forces for change will sweep him and his followers away, and the trappings of power that now surround this little man will prove to be illusory:

Don't you see that December 2 is just an immense illusion, a pause, a momentary stop, a sort of curtain behind which God, the marvelous scene changer, is preparing the final act, the supreme and triumphal act of the French Revolution.[93]

Using the ghostly imagery that also appealed to Marx, Hugo tells his fellow *proscrits* that they should not be taken in by the "mixture of caricatures and ghosts" that now confront them. They imagine a lackey called Rouher, a valet named Troplong, a eunuch by the name of Baroche, and a pasha who calls himself Louis Bonaparte. They do not see that these are all "chimeras" that will soon disappear. "You do not hear, on the other side of the curtain, in the shadows, a muffled sound! You do not hear someone who is moving about! You do not see the curtain trembling from the breath of someone standing behind it."[94]

Napoléon le petit was an instant success. 8,500 copies were bought up in the first two weeks, and almost 40,000 were sold by the end of 1852. English, German, Italian and Spanish translations quickly appeared. In London, where the book was a bestseller, a squadron of twenty "sandwich-men" walked around the city advertising the "People's Shilling Edition," and several thousand tricolor posters were plastered on walls and the sides of railway carriages. According to Hugo, who kept close track of such matters, extracts appeared in newspapers "from London to Calcutta, from Lima to Quebec."[95]

---

[92] Ibid, 147–148.   [93] Ibid, 152.   [94] Ibid.
[95] "Note of V. H., April 1853," *OC CFL*, VIII, 1118.

The small-sized French edition, which was intended to be smuggled, made its way into France not only through Belgium and the Channel ports but also by way of Switzerland, Savoy and Nice. Graham Robb's biography of Hugo includes a vivid evocation of the ingenuity of the smugglers:

Hugo's work reached its [French] public like exotic produce, smelling of distant adventures. It came in bales of hay, packets of contraband tobacco, carriage clocks, lead-lined boxes which were lashed to fishing boats below the waterline and unloaded at night on deserted beaches, hollowed-out blocks of wood were thrown overboard just out of range of the coastguard's telescope. Sandwiched between two sheets of metal, it slipped into France as a tin of sardines. French tourists arrived in St Helier wearing baggy trousers and left with bundles of pages strapped to their legs. Hugo's visitors proudly revealed their tricks: trunks with false bottoms, shoes with false heels, hollow walking-sticks and cigars rolled with sheets of *Napoléon le petit*, specially printed on onion paper. Hugo was delighted to learn that women were sewing his publications into their clothes and securing them under their garters: the ultimate compliment.[96]

Hugo would have been equally delighted to learn that a friend of Alexandre Dumas had managed to smuggle two dozen copies of the compact edition into France by hiding them inside a bust of Louis-Napoleon![97] Victor Hugo was not yet done with Louis-Napoleon. If *Histoire d'un crime* had to wait until 1876 to see the light of day, Hugo did publish in 1853 an extraordinary volume of poems, *Les Châtiments*, which he described as a "natural and necessary sequel to *Napoléon le petit*."[98] He sometimes referred facetiously to the relation between the two works: "Louis Bonaparte has only been cooked on one side," he wrote his publisher, "It's time to turn him over on the grille."[99] In fact, Hugo struck a deeper note in these poems than in *Napoléon le petit*. In the earlier work Hugo plays the role of History's *juge d' instruction* (examining magistrate). In *Les Châtiments* he speaks from on high with the voice of an Old Testament prophet, scourging a disloyal sovereign in the name of Jehovah and a humiliated people.[100]

---

[96] Robb, *Victor Hugo*, 321–322.
[97] Alexandre Dumas, letter of November 17, 1852 in Michel Winock, *Victor Hugo dans l'arène politique* (Paris, 2005), 58.
[98] Winock, *Victor Hugo dans l'arène politique*, 60.
[99] Hugo to Hetzel, November 18, 1852 in Sheila Gaudon (ed.), *Victor Hugo, Pierre-Jules Hetzel, Correspondance. Tome I (1852–1853)*, (Paris, 1979), 173.
[100] Paul Bénichou, *Mages romantiques*, 348–349.

Karl Marx's response to *Les Châtiments* is not known. But his verdict on *Napoléon le petit* is famous:

Victor Hugo confines himself to biting and witty invective against the author of the *coup d'état*. The event itself appears in his work like a bolt from the blue. He sees in it only the violent act of a single individual. He does not notice that he makes this individual great instead of little by ascribing to him a personal power of initiative that would be without parallel in world history.[101]

Was Marx correct? Certainly. But more interesting than the question of Hugo's limitations as a political thinker is the question we posed at the outset: How do we explain the fact that, unlike virtually all his intellectual contemporaries, Victor Hugo was not disheartened but energized by the failures of 1848? Most of the others fell silent and eventually rallied to the Second Empire (if only by accepting the terms of the amnesty proposed by Napoleon III in 1859) or retreated into a rancorous exile, their remaining energies too often claimed by factional disputes.

Hugo on the other hand made the most of exile. Installing himself and his family (and an entourage which included his mistress Juliette Drouet and various admirers) on the Channel Islands, first Jersey then Guernsey, he resisted opportunities to return to France prior to the fall of Napoleon III. Taking pride in the title of "le banni" as if it were not simply a circumstance of his life but an *identity*, he came to symbolize in his own person the republican opposition to imperial rule.[102] At the same time, he embarked on a period of literary creativity that culminated with the publication of *Les Misérables* in 1862.

How do we explain this transformation? The short answer, and probably the best, is that unlike most of the other subjects of this book, Victor Hugo did not at the outset expect much of anything from the Republic. In February he would have preferred the declaration of a regency, and during the first year of the Second Republic he gave his support, somewhat grudgingly to be sure, to the Party of Order most of whose leading members were monarchists. Eventually, he joined the republicans and became a leading voice among supporters of "the democratic and social republic." But the huge disappointments felt by George Sand and Lamartine and so many others didn't touch him because his initial expectations had been so low. And whereas they eventually made their

---

[101] Karl Marx, Author's Preface to the 2nd edition of *The Eighteenth Brumaire of Louis Bonaparte* (New York, n.d.), 8.
[102] Bénichou, *Mages romantiques*, 337; Franck Laurent, *Victor Hugo: Espace et politique* (Rennes, 2008), 246–257.

peace with the Empire, Hugo turned himself into a living symbol of fidelity to the republican ideal, to France, and to the universal republic of the future. "It is not I, monsieur, who have been outlawed, but liberty," he wrote in January 1852. "It is not I who have been exiled, but France."[103]

---

[103] Letter to André van Hasselt, January 6, 1852, cited in Guy Rosa, *"Ce que c'est que l'exil" de Victor Hugo*, communication au Groupe Hugo du 20 octobre 2001: http://groupugo.div.jussieu.fr/Groupugo/01-10-20rosa.htm

6   Tocqueville
"A Vile Tragedy Performed by Provincial Actors"

There is a fascinating passage in Alexis de Tocqueville's *Souvenirs* of 1848 in which he describes his only meeting with George Sand. It was at a luncheon given in Paris by Richard Monckton Milnes, an eccentric English MP and patron of the arts. The other guests at this remarkable luncheon included the writers Prosper Mérimée and Alfred de Vigny, the historian François Mignet, and the socialist Victor Considerant. The date was May 3, the day before the first meeting of the National Assembly, to which both Tocqueville and Considerant had been elected.

Tocqueville observes that while some of the guests did not know each other, "others knew one another too well." This was the case of Sand and Mérimée. Tocqueville had learned from gossip something that Milnes, the host, did not know: some time earlier Sand and Mérimée had had "a very tender but very ephemeral relationship" – a relationship so ephemeral, he comments archly, that it had followed Aristotle's rule for classical tragedy by beginning and ending in a single day. Tocqueville appears to have been much amused by the situation. To make a good story better he omits the fact that the brief liaison had taken place fifteen years earlier.

Tocqueville writes that Milnes had seated him beside George Sand and observes that while he knew of her work, he had never met her since he "had not lived much in the world of literary adventurers that she inhabited." He adds that "I had a strong prejudice against Madame Sand, for I detest women who write, especially those who systematically disguise the weaknesses of their sex, instead of interesting us by displaying them in their true colours. Despite this, she charmed me." Tocqueville goes on to comment brusquely on George Sand's "rather massive" features, her "wonderful" expression ("all her intelligence seemed to have retreated into her eyes"), and her "simplicity of manner and language which was, perhaps, mingled with a certain affectation of simplicity in her clothes." All this is very much within the seventeenth-century tradition of literary portraiture which Tocqueville had made his own. But what is most interesting about this passage is Tocqueville's account of George Sand's political views.

For about an hour they talked politics. Sand was already disillusioned with the revolution, and she would shortly retreat to Berry, only to discover that there she was regarded as a dangerous communist. But her conversation fascinated Tocqueville because this was "the first time I had found myself having a direct and easy conversation with someone who could and would tell me what was going on in the enemy camp."

> Madame Sand painted for me, in great detail and with striking vivacity, the condition of the Paris workers, their organization, their numbers, their arms, their preparations, their opinions, their passions, their terrible intentions. I thought the picture exaggerated; it was not, as subsequent events clearly proved. She herself seemed frightened of a popular victory, and there was a touch of solemnity in her pity for our anticipated fate. "Monsieur, try to persuade your friends," she said to me, "not to drive the people into the streets by alarming or irritating them. On my side, I would like to persuade my people to be patient; for, if the battle is joined, you must understand that you will all perish.[1]

George Sand did not understand – nor did Tocqueville – that the balance of power in Paris had already shifted and that the Paris workers were no longer in a position to win even a short-lived victory. Nonetheless, this exchange is important. For it was the fear of popular violence that lay behind much of what Tocqueville did and said during the first four months of the Republic. And this fear served to justify in his mind the fierce repression of the June insurrection. Unlike George Sand, Alexis de Tocqueville had no trouble believing in a republic that began by killing its citizens.

"We Are Sleeping on a Volcano"

At the time of the February revolution Tocqueville was forty-two years old. *Democracy in America* was well behind him. It had made him famous at the age of thirty and had gotten him elected to the Académie française. It had also launched him on a political career as a member of the Chamber of Deputies representing the arrondissement of Valognes in Normandy. For the nine years prior to 1848 he had been absorbed in national politics. Regularly reelected by his 600 constituents, he had played an active role in the life of the Chamber, giving speeches (some of which remain celebrated), serving on numerous committees, and participating in the meetings of the liberal opposition. Especially important was his role as a leader of the committee investigating conditions in the new French colony of Algeria. In that capacity he travelled to Algeria

---

[1] Alexis de Tocqueville, *Souvenirs* (Paris, 1978), 209–211 [hereinafter *Souvenirs*].

with fact-finding groups, wrote reports, proposed new laws.[2] A consistent if not entirely uncritical supporter of what he called the "necessary barbarism" of the French colonial enterprise, he was able to justify "burning harvests, emptying silos, capturing unarmed men, women and children" as "unfortunate necessities" of colonial war.[3]

Tocqueville's political career gave him little satisfaction. For he did not have the success in the Chamber that he had had as a writer. He was not a compelling speaker: he had a weak voice and an unimposing physical presence. He tired quickly in front of an audience. And he found the political life of the July Monarchy trivial and enervating. He voted with the dynastic opposition led by Odilon Barrot but found its members hopelessly mediocre. Later he wrote that he preferred working with aristocratic royalists with whom he disagreed rather than with his bourgeois political allies. Trying to characterize "the parliamentary world of the July Monarchy" in his *Souvenirs*, he claimed that he could not provide anything like a clear narrative. "I lose the thread of my recollections in the labyrinth of petty incidents, petty ideas, petty passions, personal viewpoints and contradictory projects in which the life of public men at that time was frittered away."[4].

In retrospect Tocqueville wrote that the whole history of France from 1789 to 1830 could be seen as "forty-one years of bitter struggle" between the Old Regime, with its traditions, memories, hopes, and aristocracy, and the new France led by the middle class. In 1830 that struggle had culminated with the decisive triumph of the bourgeoisie. So complete was that triumph, Tocqueville believed, that after 1830 "all political powers, all franchises, all prerogatives, indeed the whole government, was confined and stuffed within the narrow limits of the bourgeoisie."[5] Tocqueville had never expected much from the political leadership of the July Monarchy. But during the summer of 1847 he began to fear for the future of the regime. For seventeen years, he

---

[2] Tocqueville's principal writings on Algeria are reprinted in Alexis de Tocqueville, *Ecrits et discours politiques*, André Jardin (ed.), 3 vols. (Paris, 1962, 1985, 1990). These three volumes constitute Tome III of Tocqueville, *Oeuvres complètes* which began publication in 1952 and now runs to 18 Tomes, some of which include several volumes. Volumes will be cited as OC III i, OC III ii and OC III iii.

[3] *Travail sur l'Algérie (octobre 1841)* in Tocqueville, *Ecrits et discours politiques*, I, OC III i, 226–228. Tocqueville was hardly unique. During the July Monarchy the French conquest of Algeria was supported by intellectuals of all political persuasions from Guizot to Louis Blanc. On the arguments used by Tocqueville in his colonial writings see Cheryl B. Welch, "Colonial Violence and the Rhetoric of Evasion: Tocqueville on Algeria," *Political Theory*, XXXI(2) (April 2003), 235–264.

[4] *Souvenirs*, 38.   [5] Ibid, 39.

Figure 6.1 Portrait of Tocqueville in 1848 by Léon Noël. Bettmann
Archives via Getty

reflected, the government had been corrupting the *pays légal*, turning it
into "a petty, corrupt, vulgar aristocracy," and it was now despised even
by the people who benefitted most from its favours. "I don't know if your
pays resembles mine," he wrote François de Corcelle in September 1847:

Here, people's minds are calm, even apathetic, not much concerned with politics, with no marked liking for any idea or any man, but surprisingly full of a deep and steadfast contempt for all ministers and administrators, a contempt informed by the unshakeable conviction that everything is up for sale or may be gotten by favour and that political immorality is the widespread, habitual atmosphere in which the political world moves.

Tocqueville did not see how a government with so little support could continue to function. "For the first time since the July Revolution," he added, "I fear that we may have still more revolutionary trials to live through (Figure 6.1)."[6] The scandals of the summer of 1847 – the trial and conviction of two former Orléanist ministers for bribe-taking, the murder of the Duchesse de Choiseul-Praslin by her husband – had only served to heighten Tocqueville's fears. He wrote a friend that "this succession of criminal, shameful deeds erupting among the upper classes" demonstrated "a profound sickness in the moral state of the country" and threatened to discredit the *notables* who dominated French political life.[7] In light of these fears, Tocqueville began for the first time to study socialism. He wrote the former Saint-Simonian, Prosper Enfantin, praising Enfantin's "lively awareness of the suffering of the poor," and adding that he too believed that the movement of history was "towards a greater development of equality on the Earth and a more and more equal sharing of the goods that it produces." But with regard to the socialist attack on property, which had been made most explicitly by Proudhon, Tocqueville was implacable. The right of private property was, he argued, the last guarantee of a civilized social order, and it had to be protected at all costs.[8]

At the same time, Tocqueville claimed that he now saw clearly that the July Monarchy had become identified with the propertied class and that it would be challenged on this ground. "It is between those who have possessions and those who don't that the political struggle will now be waged. The great battlefield will now be property, and political questions will turn chiefly on the modification of property rights." If the current political parties continued to ignore the question of property, Tocqueville believed, there would eventually be a grave crisis.[9]

---

[6] Tocqueville to Francisque de Corcelle, September 29, 1847, *Correspondance Tocqueville-Corcelle*, 2 vols. (Paris, 1983), OC XV i, 239.
[7] Tocqueville to Gustave de Beaumont, 23 August 1847, *Correspondance Tocqueville-Beaumont*, 3 vols. (Paris, 1967), OC VIII i, 608.
[8] Tocqueville to Enfantin, 10 November 1847 in Tocqueville, *Lettres choisies*, Françoise Mélonio and Laurence Guellec (eds.) (Paris, 2003), 591–592; Hugh Brogan, *Alexis de Tocqueville. A Biography* (New Haven, 2006), 413–415.
[9] "De la classe moyenne et du peuple," OC III ii, 740; Brogan, *Tocqueville*, 416.

Tocqueville's awareness of the plight of the propertyless and the need to confront the problem of poverty was not shared by his allies in the Chamber of Deputies. For these people – Odilon Barrot was their leader and his followers included Tocqueville's friend Gustave de Beaumont – the central issue was electoral reform, specifically a widening of the suffrage and the denial of the right of prefects and other government officials to stand for election to the Chamber of Deputies. This issue was at the heart of the banquet campaign launched by Barrot and the opposition in the summer of 1847. Tocqueville refused to participate in the campaign, arguing that if it succeeded in rousing the people, it might unleash uncontrollable forces.

By the end of the year, it seemed that the banquet campaign had failed. The final banquet, which was planned for Paris after the opening of the Chamber of Deputies, was in doubt; and the main result of the campaign had been to demonstrate the division of the opposition. At this point the prime minister, Guizot, decided to take a hard line. In response, on January 27 Tocqueville gave a speech which proved to be the most memorable of his whole career:

> People say that there is no danger because there are no riots; they say that since there is no significant disorder on the surface of society, revolution is far from us. Gentlemen, permit me to tell you that I think you are deceiving yourselves ... Look at what is going on among the working classes who today, I admit, are peaceable ... Are you not listening to what they say every day among themselves? Don't you hear them repeating incessantly that all those above them are incapable and unworthy of governing? That the present distribution of goods in society is unjust? That the foundations of property are not equitable?[10]

Tocqueville asserted that if such ideas were allowed to spread, there would be a revolution. The government had to propose reforms that dealt with the real problem. And Tocqueville asked the Chamber to consider the fate of Louis XVI and the old Bourbon monarchy. Why had the monarchy fallen? The cause was not the deficit, the tennis court oath, or the actions of Lafayette and Mirabeau. And it was most definitely not an accident. "No gentlemen; there was a deeper, truer cause, and that cause was that the ruling class had become, by its indifference, its egoism, its vices, incapable and unworthy of governing." Tocqueville warned the deputies that "we are sleeping on a volcano."[11]

Representative of the People

In the end, events took the course that Tocqueville had feared. When the final Parisian banquet was banned by the government, the leaders of the

---

[10] *Discours prononcé à la Chambre des* Députés, January 27, 1848, OC III ii, 750.
[11] *Discours*, January 27, 1848, OC III ii, 756–757, 751.

opposition were relieved. But Parisians took to the streets. Three days of demonstrations and missteps by the king led to a confrontation on the night of February 23 that left fifty demonstrators dead. The next morning barricades rose over much of Paris. After several hours on the streets, Tocqueville, arrived at the Chamber of Deputies just in time to watch Odilon Barrot's vain effort to save the July Monarchy by persuading the Chamber to recognize the Duchesse d'Orléans as regent and her young son, the Comte de Paris, as heir apparent. Two years later he wrote that "the only thing that really touched me during that whole day was the sight of the woman and child on whom had fallen the weight of faults they did not commit."[12]

That evening Tocqueville returned to his apartment on the rue de la Madeleine, and he was still telling his wife the story of the day when a visitor arrived. It was his friend, Jean-Jacques Ampère, whom he expected to share his regret at the fall of the monarchy. On the contrary, Ampère was ebullient. Tocqueville then let loose a torrent of repressed anger directed against "the people" who had made the revolution and their upper-class apologists. He accused Ampère of judging politics "like some Parisian idler, or a poet"

I tell you that these people whom you so naïvely admire have just finished proving that they are incapable and unworthy of living in freedom. Show me what they experience has taught them. What new virtues have they acquired, and what old vices have they discarded? No, I tell you, they are always the same; just as impatient, careless, and contemptuous of the law as ever.[13]

This outburst, which Tocqueville soon regretted, is revealing. For he was now speaking of lower-class Parisians and their naïve bourgeois admirers with the fierce hostility of a wealthy provincial landowner.

Despite his harsh words to Ampère, Tocqueville shed no tears for the July Monarchy. He had come to disdain its leaders; and on reflection he realized that its fall opened up new possibilities. He quickly decided to stand for election to the new National Assembly, and in mid-March he returned to Normandy to present himself to the voters. But he was unprepared for what he found there. He wrote his wife that in Normandy he felt that he was "in a different country from the France of Paris."

People minding their own business, artisans, labourers all peaceable – the tranquillity of the countryside, unworried peasant faces – it all formed such a contrast with what I had left behind that I began to wonder if it was I, not the placid people I was meeting, who had the wrong ideas. The truth is that

---

[12] *Souvenirs*, 100–101.   [13] Ibid, 120.

revolution has as yet shown itself only in Paris. Everywhere else it is known only by hearsay.[14]

The election campaign of April 1848 proved to be immensely satisfying for Tocqueville.

In organizing the elections by universal male suffrage, the Provisional Government had replaced the old system of *scrutin d'arrondissement* with the system of *scrutin de liste* in which each voter would vote for representatives for the whole department. This favoured candidates like Tocqueville who were widely known. But Tocqueville himself thought that his greatest strength as a candidate was that he was not troubled by the possibility that he might lose. This made his mind "calm and limpid" and gave him self-respect and "a contempt for the follies of the time" that he could not have felt had he been moved "only by the passion to succeed." Thus, he attended few political meetings and spoke rarely, refusing to answer the "insolent" questions posed by republican electoral committees. "Such refusals might have seemed disdainful," he wrote later, but in fact "they were seen as showing dignity and independence toward the new sovereign authority." When he was asked to explain his refusal to support the banquet campaign, he could say bluntly that he had not wanted a revolution, adding that "hardly any of those who sat down at those banquets would have done so if they had known, as I did, what the result would be." He was now prepared to support the Republic; but unlike other liberals, he had understood where the banquet campaign was likely to lead.[15]

On election day, Easter Sunday, April 23, Tocqueville joined the large crowd gathered in front of the village church at Tocqueville. Voting was to take place in the *chef lieu* of the canton of St. Pierre which was five kilometres away. It was assumed that the entire male population would walk together – double file and in alphabetical order – to the polling place. Tocqueville's description of the scene in his *Souvenirs* is a masterpiece which shows, among other things, the degree to which he continued to enjoy a patriarchal relationship with the villagers:

The local people had always been kindly disposed to me, but this time I found them positively affectionate ... I took the place [near the end of the line] that my name warranted, for I knew that in democratic times and countries, one must allow oneself to be put at the head of the people, but must not put oneself there. The crippled and sick who wished to follow us came on pack horses or in carts at the end of this procession. Only the women and children were left behind. We

---

[14] Tocqueville to Marie de Tocqueville, March 14, 1848, *Correspondance familiale* (Paris, 1998), OC XIV, 507.
[15] *Souvenirs*, 148–152.

were in all a hundred seventy persons. When we got to the top of the hill overlooking Tocqueville, we paused. I realized that they wanted me to speak. I climbed to a high point. A circle formed around me, and I said a few words appropriate to the occasion.[16]

The procession arrived in good time at St. Pierre, and all the villagers voted together. Tocqueville concludes by observing: "I have reason to think that almost all voted for the same candidate." He was right about that. Of 120,000 votes cast in the département de la Manche, he received 110,704 votes; and it appears that he got support not only from the rural *notables* – prosperous farmers, functionaries and professional men – who had supported him during the July Monarchy but also from many legitimists, from peasant landowners and even from some of the newly enfranchised workers at Cherbourg.[17]

In his *Souvenirs*, Tocqueville offers an oddly ambivalent account of his impressions during his first days as a *représentant du peuple* in the National Assembly. He speaks with amused condescension about the new representatives – "complete novices" who "scarcely knew what an assembly was, or how one should behave and talk in it" and who could think of nothing better to do than to fill the cavernous hall with fifteen cries of "Vive la République!" during the first session. And he describes the Montagnards as half-educated savages who spoke a strange jargon which mixed coarse jokes and sententious comments. Obviously, these were people who belonged "neither in a cabaret nor a salon" and who must have "fed their minds not on literature but on the newspapers." But he adds that these plebians were outnumbered by large landowners and aristocrats and prosperous city dwellers who shared his desire to defend the rights of property and to "protect the ancient laws of society against the innovators" by making sure that the new republic was conservative. Thus he claims that despite the gravity of the situation, he felt a sense of well-being that he had never known before. He enjoyed speaking in this huge Assembly. Although its members were inexperienced and coarse, he found them "more impressionable and more sincerely concerned with the larger interests of the country" than were his colleagues in the old Chamber of Deputies where the parties were constantly "fighting petty wars, ambushing each other and quarrelling about nuances of meaning." Furthermore, in supporting a conservative republic, he felt that for the first time since he had entered public life, he was on the side of a majority, "moving in the only direction that my taste, my reason, and

---

[16] Ibid, 158   [17] Ibid, 159–160; Brogan, *Tocqueville*, 437–438.

my conscience could approve, and this was a new and delightful sensation for me."[18]

What Tocqueville wanted from the Republic in April 1848 was in fact quite similar to what Lamartine wanted. The big difference between the two was that Tocqueville had no desire to play a leading role. Furthermore, Tocqueville believed that Lamartine was actually in a ticklish position. In Tocqueville's view, Lamartine "had done more than anyone else for the success of the February revolution," Many conservatives distrusted him for just this reason. It was likely that once the radical movement had been brought under control, "a contrary current would carry the nation in the opposite direction faster and farther than Lamartine might wish to go. The Montagnards' success would bring about his immediate ruin, but their defeat would render him useless, and sooner or later power would slip from his hands."[19]

Tocqueville believed that Lamartine was actually playing a double game. He was "striving to dominate the Montagnards without overthrowing them and to damp down the revolutionary fire without putting it out." He wanted the country to "bless him for providing security" but not to feel "safe enough to forget about him." What made Tocqueville so suspicious of Lamartine? One thing was Lamartine's behaviour toward him during the first meetings of the National Assembly. Lamartine avoided Tocqueville but then sent word to him not to take offence, since his position forced him to behave coolly toward members of the old Chamber of Deputies. Once things had settled down, Lamartine promised, Tocqueville could take the place that awaited him "among the future leaders of the Republic."[20]

Tocqueville's principal activity in May and June was his participation in the committee elected by the National Assembly to draft a constitution. It was a large committee – eighteen members whom Tocqueville described with typical acerbity as a group of mediocrities of whom "nothing remarkable was to be expected." There were just two democrats on the committee – the former priest Lamennais and the Fourierist Victor Considerant – and Tocqueville dismissed them both as "no more than fantastic dreamers."[21] But he was equally disdainful of the majority, which was composed of moderate republicans like Armand Marrast and old-line politicians from the July Monarchy like Odilon Barrot. Still, Tocqueville's role on the committee was curiously ineffectual. He wrote a draft of the preamble, and in September he helped make sure that the constitution was not soiled by any reference to the right to work. But his

[18] *Souvenirs*, 163–172.   [19] Ibid, 174–175.   [20] Ibid, 177–178.   [21] Ibid, 255.

proposal for a bicameral legislature was easily defeated; he could not prevent the elaboration of a highly centralized system of local government; and his initial opposition to the popular election of the president was futile. One issue on which Tocqueville was successful was his proposal to limit the president to a single term of four years. But the consequence was to create a situation in which a popular president, like Louis-Napoleon Bonaparte, would have a strong incentive to overthrow the constitution. Already, early in 1851, Tocqueville could write that "this vote, and the great influence that I had on it, is my most bitter memory of that time."[22]

The June Days

The preliminary draft of the constitution was delivered to the Assembly on June 9. It was then sent out for examination to various legislative committees. But before they had time to report on it, the June days intervened, and Tocqueville was caught up in the crisis. One might expect him to have frequented the National Assembly during the June Days. He did spend a part of every day there, and his *Souvenirs* include vivid descriptions of the debates and of the atmosphere in the Assembly as rumours made their rounds. But during the three crucial *journées* – June 23, 24 and 25 – he spent much of his time on the street, trying to find out for himself what was actually going on in the city. On the morning of June 23, before the shooting had begun, Tocqueville and Corcelle walked through the labyrinth of small, dark streets around the Hôtel de Ville, marvelling at the concentration and sobriety of the workers as they built their barricades:

The people carried on this work with the skill and precision of engineers, only digging up as many cobblestones as they needed to create ... a thick, very solid, and even fairly neat wall in which they were careful to leave a little opening next to the houses so that people could move about.

That evening the Assembly met for what Tocqueville described as a "tumultuous" session in which the pleas of Victor Considerant for a gesture of peace toward the insurgents were shouted down "with a sort of fury." But that night, as Tocqueville walked home from the Palais Bourbon, crossing the Seine at the Pont Royal, he could see the city of

---

[22] Ibid, 271 and *Ecrits et discours politiques*, OC III iii, 13–21. For detailed accounts of Tocqueville's work on the constitution committee, see Edward T. Gargan, *Alexis de Tocqueville: The Critical Years 1848–1851* (Washington, DC, 1955), 90–121 and Sharon B. Watkins, *Alexis de Tocqueville and the Second Republic: 1848–1852* (Lanham, 2003), 81–140, 189–256.

Paris, "enveloped in shadows" and silent and "calm as a sleeping city." He had trouble persuading himself that everything he had seen and done that day wasn't a figment of his imagination.[23]

The next morning Tocqueville woke up to the sound of cannon-fire. On his way to the Assembly he encountered armed National Guardsmen and grim-faced workers, both seemingly ready for civil war. It seemed evident to him that "the whole working class" – including those who had not taken up arms – supported the uprising, and that "our homes, the very places where we thought we were masters," were now "swarming with domestic enemies." At the National Assembly he found "a thousand sinister rumours" circulating: ammunition was running out, the insurrection was gaining ground, government troops were refusing to obey orders. Adolphe Thiers told Tocqueville that, to avoid being massacred, the whole National Assembly should quit Paris and then put the city to siege.[24]

Inspired by such fears, the representatives voted to declare a state of siege and to give dictatorial powers to General Cavaignac. The Assembly then voted a second bill calling for sixty representatives to go out through the city to explain their decisions to the National Guards. Although Tocqueville himself had voted against the state of siege, he accepted this assignment. Walking for several hours through the narrow streets of central Paris, he and three colleagues were greeted with enthusiasm by National Guard units throughout the city. Tocqueville returned to the Assembly with "confidence that we would win out in the end."[25]

On the third day, June 25, the tide of battle turned. After waiting for the insurgents to deploy all their forces, Cavaignac struck with massive force on the centres of resistance, pounding them with cannon-fire. Tocqueville writes that he spent much of the day not at the Assembly ("where I did not think there were important decisions to make") but in those parts of Paris which "were still disputed" and where he could hear the sounds of cannon-fire. "I wished to judge for myself the state of affairs because, in my complete ignorance of warfare, I couldn't understand why the combat was lasting so long." Thus he walked north past the porte Saint-Denis to the place du Château d'Eau, where he first encountered "débris left by the insurrection in its retreat: broken windows, doors pushed in, houses pitted by cannonballs or bullets, trees knocked down, paving-stones heaped up, straw mixed with blood and mud, such were these sad remains."[26]

---

[23] *Souvenirs*, 215–220.   [24] Ibid, 220–226.   [25] Ibid, 235.   [26] Ibid, 242.

At the Château d'Eau Tocqueville found a large concentration of government troops and a cannon firing down an empty street. He soon realized that the street was not empty at all. Beyond a bend, the street "bristled with barricades all the way to the Bastille." Troops were seeking to get control of the street and to wipe out pockets of snipers before attacking the barricades. This was not easily done; and Tocqueville devoted a long passage in the *Souvenirs* to an account of his own experience of the dangers of sniper-fire. Suddenly, he writes, insurgents appeared on a roof nearby and began to fire on the troops below:

As the sound of their guns echoed loudly off the buildings on the other side of the street, it seemed that an attack was coming from that side as well. Immediately our column fell into utter confusion. In an instant artillery, infantry and cavalry got all mixed up; the soldiers fired in every direction without knowing what they were doing and fell back sixty paces in a tumult. The retreat was so disorderly and so sudden that I was thrown against the wall of the of the houses facing the rue du Faubourg-du-Temple, where I was knocked down by the cavalry and trampled so that I lost my hat and came close to losing my life. That was certainly the greatest danger that I was in during the June Days.[27]

What Tocqueville was witnessing was actually a clean-up operation. Like much else that he saw during the June Days, it made him reflect on the fact that, during periods of civil war, life is cheap and a taste for violence spreads rapidly.

Two conclusions can be drawn from the long account of the June Days in the *Souvenirs*. First, there was never the slightest doubt in Tocqueville's mind that the insurrection would have to be wiped out. He repeatedly speaks of the fear felt by his friends and colleagues that all of Paris would fall into the hands of the rebels and of his conviction that no compromise could or should be reached with the insurgents who, in his view, were bent on destroying civilized society. "The insurrection was of such a nature," he wrote, "that any compromise with it appeared to be absolutely impossible, and it left us from the start with no other alternative than to conquer or perish." Thus, for Tocqueville the June Days were both "necessary and dreadful."[28]

What is also striking in Tocqueville's account of the June Days is his almost total inability to enter into the minds of the insurgents. One of Tocqueville's great gifts as a historian of Old Regime France and as a sociologically minded observer of Jacksonian America was his capacity for empathy. In both *Démocratie en Amérique* and *L'Ancien Régime et la Révolution française* he repeatedly attempts to characterize the hopes,

[27] Ibid, 245–246.   [28] Ibid, 223, 252.

fears and motives of people with whom he has little in common. In his correspondence in the summer of 1848 one occasionally finds him trying to reach a sympathetic understanding of the motives of the insurgents – most notably in a letter to Eugène Stoffels of July 21 in which he takes pains to refute the claim that the insurgents were "the dregs of humanity" motivated solely by "the gross passion of pillage":

> Many of these men who strove to overthrow the most sacred rights were inspired by a kind of erroneous notion of right. They sincerely believed that society was founded on injustice, and they sought to give it another foundation. It is this sort of revolutionary religion that our bayonets and our canons cannot destroy.[29]

Such an effort of understanding is nowhere to be found in the *Souvenirs* where Tocqueville generally describes the insurgents as motivated by "false theories" and "greedy, blind and gross passions."[30] There is only one point in the *Souvenirs* when an individual close to the insurgents enters his narrative. Returning to the Assembly one afternoon, he finds his way barred by an old woman pushing a vegetable cart. They exchange words, and then the woman angrily attacks Tocqueville. "Her hideous and terrible expression horrified me," he tells us, "so clearly did it express the fury of demagogical passions and the rage of civil war." All we learn about the woman is that her expression is "hideuse et terrible."[31]

Foreign Minister: The Roman Republic and the Pope

Throughout the first fifteen months of the Second Republic Tocqueville was an observer rather than a shaper of events. In February he looked on at Lamartine's feats of oratory; on May 15 he sat impassively as the crowd pushed into the National Assembly; and in June he walked around Paris observing the rise and fall of the insurgency. He played a limited role in the drafting of the constitution, and in the presidential election he quietly supported Cavaignac. Quite appropriately then the stance that he assumed in the *Souvenirs* was that of a critical bystander.

At one period in the history of the Second Republic, however, Tocqueville was in a position to lead. This was the five-month period from June 3 to October 31, 1849, when he served as Minister of Foreign

---

[29] Tocqueville to Eugène Stoffels, July 21, 1848, *Correspondance et oeuvres posthumes d'Alexis de Tocqueville* (Paris, 1866), 458–459.
[30] *Souvenirs*, 224: "les passions cupides, aveugles et grossières." See also *Souvenirs*, 213: "ce mélange de désirs cupides et de théories fausses"; and *Souvenirs*, 252: "passions cupides et envieuses."
[31] *Souvenirs*, 225.

Affairs in the second cabinet of Odilon Barrot.[32] This was a government
of expediency designed to restrain the Montagnard faction, which had
won 150 seats in the elections of May 1849. Tocqueville wrote in the
Souvenirs that the idea of taking a post that many feared to take "flattered
both my integrity and my pride." He took over the role that Lamartine
had hoped to play – that of saving the Republic by keeping it "regular,
moderate and conservative." He saw this as difficult because those who
believed in the republic "were incapable or unworthy of leading it" while
those who could have "established and led it, hated it."[33]

The *Souvenirs* has much to say about Tocqueville's role in successfully
brokering peace between Austria and Piedmont and about his resistance
to the demands of the Russian Tsar Nicholas I for the surrender of Polish
and Hungarian refugees who had sought sanctuary in Turkey. But
Tocqueville skates lightly over the much more difficult situation he
walked into on becoming Foreign Minister. This was the Roman problem – the problem of France's role in determining the fate of the Roman
Republic and the Papal States. In November 1848, rioting had driven
Pope Pius IX out of the Vatican and into exile. From Gaeta in January
1849 the Pope had appealed to Catholic Europe for help in restoring his
temporal power. Meanwhile at Rome, a constituent assembly had been
elected and on February 9, 1849, the Roman Republic was proclaimed.
Even before the arrival of Mazzini on March 5, major reforms were
undertaken. Church property was nationalized and old church buildings
converted into housing for the poor. Censorship was abolished, the
Inquisition suppressed, and clerical control of the university terminated.
Soon Mazzini was expounding to the Roman Assembly his doctrine of a
Third Rome, the Rome not of the emperors nor of the Pope but of
the People.

The Roman Republic never had more than a precarious existence. By
the end of March 1849, Austria, Naples and Spain were all preparing to
use force to restore papal rule in Rome. The French government also
began to discuss intervention to keep the Austrians out of Rome and to
ensure that the Pope, once returned to the capital, would maintain the
secular institutions introduced in the spring of 1848. On April 16, the
Constituent Assembly voted by a large majority (including Tocqueville)
to send a French expeditionary force to Rome. Odilon Barrot presented

---

[32] On Tocqueville's tenure as Minister of Foreign Affairs and his handling of the Roman
question, see André Jardin, *Alexis de Tocqueville, 1805–1859* (Paris, 1984), 405–425;
Gargan, *Tocqueville: The Critical Years*, 122–179; Watkins, *Tocqueville and the Second
Republic*, 323–431.
[33] *Souvenirs*, 287–288.

this intervention as an attempt at mediation between the Pope and his rebellious subjects, whom the French would "protect" against Austrian designs. From the beginning, though, it was clear that the French troops could be used *against* the Roman Republic.

On April 24 the French force of 10,000 men under General Oudinot landed at Civita Vecchia, the Roman port. Meeting no initial resistance, they set out for Rome expecting (in the words of a British agent) "a glorious reception." In fact, the Romans had determined to defend their city against all invaders. Although their military position looked hopeless, it improved on April 27 with the arrival of 1200 of Garibaldi's followers. Then, on April 30, as Oudinot attempted to force his way into the city, he was suddenly attacked on the flank by Garibaldi's troops and forced to retreat to Civita Vecchia.

Oudinot's unexpected and humiliating defeat created what amounted to a constitutional crisis in France. On May 7, just a week before the legislative elections, the Constituent Assembly passed a resolution effectively forbidding the French expeditionary force to attack Rome. The following day, however, the pro-government journal *La Patrie* published a bellicose letter from Louis-Napoleon to Oudinot: "Our soldiers have been received as enemies; our military honour is at stake. I shall not allow it to be stained. You will not lack reinforcements." And reinforcements were sent. In May, while a young French diplomat, the future canal-builder Ferdinand de Lesseps, attempted to reach a negotiated settlement with the Romans, the French tripled their garrison and supplied it with enough food and artillery to mount a prolonged siege.

The crisis reached a head at the end of May when the government secretly sent Oudinot orders to attack Rome. Tocqueville learned of this order just three days before taking office as Foreign Minister, and he told Barrot that he did not approve of the idea of an attack on Rome – though apparently his main reason was that he believed an attack to be premature rather than inherently wrong. But then on June 3, the same day that Tocqueville's appointment took effect, the attack began. Once it was underway, Tocqueville gave it his full support – presumably because it was too late to do anything else. On June 12, when Ledru-Rollin proposed to censure the ministry for violating the Constitution, Tocqueville refused to turn over copies of his diplomatic correspondence to the Assembly. And on June 13 he unhesitatingly supported the crushing of the left-wing protest demonstration in Paris, the imposition of a state of siege, the suspension of political clubs and the freedom of the press, and the subsequent trial and punishment of thirty-one democratic and republican representatives. At the same time, Tocqueville sent reinforcements to Oudinot. But in his private correspondence he described the attack on Rome as a huge error:

I don't hide from myself [he wrote his envoy Corcelle] that from now on the real responsibility for the Roman business weighs on us. I will bear this responsibility bravely, as a duty, but with great anxiety and deep sadness. If Rome is sacked and half-destroyed as a result of this dubious and useless expedition, we will have no excuse in the eyes of history.[34]

In the *Souvenirs*, Tocqueville describes the order to attack Rome unambiguously as an act of "flagrant disobedience to a sovereign assembly's injunctions … and in defiance of the terms of the Constitution."[35] Indeed it was. The Constitution, for which Tocqueville had voted, forbade the use of French armed forces against the liberty of any other people (article 5 of the preamble).

Tocqueville may have justified the attack in his own mind by arguing that, by taking Rome, France could put pressure on the Pope to liberalize his government. This was wishful thinking. The Romans capitulated on July 2, and Oudinot immediately dissolved the Roman assembly, shut down the radical clubs, disarmed the populace, and turned over the government of the city to a triumvirate of cardinals who arrived in Rome on July 31. Within two weeks the Inquisition was reestablished and political arrests multiplied.

Tocqueville's response was divided. In his private correspondence with Corcelle he threatened to "resign a hundred times" rather than take responsibility for the return of the "detestable institutions" which had "debased the population of Rome for centuries."[36] But in his official dispatches, Tocqueville praised the good intentions of the pope, and for public purposes he adopted the Vatican's position. On August 7 he assured the National Assembly that the Roman Republic had been "a regime of terror" and that Mazzini was a "modern Nero" whose removal "merited the gratitude not only of humanity but of liberty itself." And he repeated that France would not allow its Italian intervention to culminate in "a blind and implacable restoration."[37] Writing Monckton Milnes shortly thereafter, he claimed that he still hoped to see liberal political reforms in Rome and that it was for this reason alone that he had supported the French intervention.[38] But the Pope did what he pleased,

---

[34] Tocqueville to Corcelle, July 1, 1849, OC XV i, 293.   [35] *Souvenirs*, 305.
[36] Tocqueville to Corcelle, July 11, 1849, OC XV i, 305–306.
[37] *Le Moniteur*, August 7, 1849, OC III iii, 332.
[38] Tocqueville to Monckton Milnes, August 18, 1849, *Correspondance anglaise*, 3 vols. (Paris, 1954, 1991, 2003), OC VI iii, 123.

finally issuing a proclamation (or *motu proprio*) in September in which he refused to make political reforms and offered the Roman republicans an amnesty so limited as to be meaningless. Tocqueville continued publicly to praise "the great spirit of moderation" exhibited by the Vatican, but in his private correspondence with Corcelle he gave vent to his "indignation and profound irritation," characterizing the pope's declaration as "a perfect model of political trickery" in which "not a single concession was made without including the means to retract it."[39]

In October Adolphe Thiers won a large majority in the National Assembly for a motion, opposed by both Tocqueville and Louis-Napoleon, stipulating that the restoration of Pius IX should be effected without requiring any guarantees whatever from the pope concerning the form of his restored government.[40] Thus thanks largely to the intervention of the French, the Roman Republic was crushed, and the restoration of papal power in Rome was complete six months before the actual return of Pius IX in April 1850.

Tocqueville, who had become increasingly frustrated by the intransigence of the Vatican, eventually found himself at odds with almost everyone – with the French defenders of the Pope, with republicans, with Louis-Napoleon, and even with his old friend Francisque de Corcelle, whom he had sent to Rome as the French government's official envoy. In October when Tocqueville attempted to justify his Roman policy before the Assembly, the heckling from the left was so intense that he could hardly get through his speech. Meanwhile, relations between the president and the Barrot ministry were worsening; and finally, on October 31 Louis-Napoleon dismissed the entire ministry, including Tocqueville. He then sent a message to the Assembly, criticizing the Barrot government for failing "to maintain order within France" or to "defend the dignity of France abroad," and declaring that he wanted ministers who would do as they were told.[41]

Tocqueville, who described this message as "insolent," had already written a brief epitaph to his ministerial career in a letter to Beaumont: "What a pain it is to direct the foreign affairs of a people who, retaining

[39] Tocqueville to Corcelle, October 1, 1849, OC XV i, 434–436. On the diplomatic imbroglio in which Tocqueville was entangled, see Françoise Mélonio, "Tocqueville et la restauration du pouvoir temporel du pape (juin-octobre 1849)," *Revue historique*, 549 (January–March 1984), 109–123. See also Laurent Reverso, "Tocqueville et la République Romaine de 1849: Les Apories du Libéralisme," *Revue française d'histoire des idées politiques*, XXX(2) (2009), 299–325.

[40] Adolphe Thiers, "Discours sur le projet de loi relatif à des crédits extraordinaires pour l'expédition de Rome, présenté le 12 octobre [1849] à l'Assemblée nationale" in *Discours parlementaires de M. Thiers*, Marc-Antoine Calmon (ed.) (Paris, 1879), VIII, 307–326.

[41] Brogan, *Tocqueville*, 482–483.

the memory of great strength and living the reality of limited power, aspire to everything while neither wishing nor daring to do anything."[42] He was now convinced that Louis-Napoleon intended to resurrect the Empire. On November 4 he wrote Beaumont that "The President is a monomaniac who will only give up the imperial dream with his last breath." He went on to describe Louis-Napoleon as "audacious to the point of imprudence and insanity," but "at the same time lymphatic and apathetic":

He never makes two moves in succession. He has just given his vanity great satisfaction; he thinks he has humiliated the Assembly and all the party leaders, and that he has much improved his standing in the eyes of France. That is enough for him for the moment. He will live off it for a while, until a new prod rouses him to jump the last ditch.[43]

Tocqueville was right both about the matter of timing and about Louis-Napoleon's ultimate aim.

Tocqueville's dismissal left him exhausted and depressed, and over the winter he and his wife were often sick. In March, he coughed up blood: this was an early symptom of the tuberculosis that would kill him at the age of 53. He then took a leave of absence from the Assembly. A quiet summer in Normandy brought his health back, and in July he began to work on his *Souvenirs*. He wrote fast. By the end of the month he had virtually completed the first part, which concludes with the proclamation of the Republic. In late August he felt well enough to attend the meeting of the *conseil général* of the department of the Manche at Saint-Lô to argue for the repeal of the law of May 31 by which the now strongly antidemocratic Assembly had disenfranchised three million French citizens. Then, as *président du conseil*, he had to give a speech of welcome when Louis-Napoleon came to Cherbourg for a naval review. When he returned home, he was again exhausted and sick. On October 31, just one year after his dismissal as foreign minister, Tocqueville and his wife set out for Italy where, on doctor's orders, they planned to spend the winter. After a few weeks in Naples, which Tocqueville found "inconceivably" dirty, noisy and poor, they found a villa for rent in Sorrento, overlooking the Bay of Naples. There, between December 1850 and March 1851, Tocqueville wrote the long second part of his *Souvenirs*, which covers the period from February through the June Days with an additional chapter on the drafting of the constitution.

[42] Tocqueville to Beaumont, 12 October 1849, OC VIII ii, 201.
[43] Tocqueville to Beaumont, 4 November 1849, OC VIII ii, 233. See also *Souvenirs*, 301–304.

After his return to France at the end of April 1851, Tocqueville's time and energy were claimed by politics, and he could not resume work on his memoirs until September. He then jumped over the period between the June Days and the legislative elections of May 1849 in order to discuss his five month's tenure as foreign minister while his memories were still fresh. This section, which constitutes Part III, is less polished and more self-serving than the rest of the book. Tocqueville clearly intended to revise and enlarge the whole manuscript. But he never had the opportunity. For throughout the summer and fall of 1851 he was caught up in the debate over the revision of the constitution to permit Louis-Napoleon Bonaparte to serve a second term as president.

Much as he distrusted Louis-Napoleon and feared and detested Bonapartism, Tocqueville was even more disturbed by the manoeuvres of Adolphe Thiers and the resurgent Orleanists in the National Assembly, who were cynically using professions of republican loyalty as a veil to cover their own plotting for a royalist restoration. After the dismissal of the Barrot ministry therefore, Tocqueville continued to work with Louis-Napoleon. Regarding the president's desire for a second term as legitimate, Tocqueville joined with other conservatives including the Duc de Broglie, Montalembert and Berryer in seeking a constitutional amendment that would permit his reelection. The problem was that the constitution that Tocqueville had helped draft made amendment just about impossible: for an amendment to become law the Assembly had to vote for it three times at monthly intervals, passing it each time by a three-quarters majority. [44] In the end, the effort to revise the constitution failed; and in the summer of 1851 Louis-Napoleon and his entourage began to make plans for the forcible seizure of power.

Before dawn on December 2 troops loyal to Louis-Napoleon were deployed throughout Paris; every ministry was occupied; and the Palais Bourbon was surrounded, making the National Assembly inaccessible. Seventy-eight leading representatives, generals and journalists were arrested, and posters appeared all over Paris proclaiming the dissolution of the National Assembly and the restoration of universal suffrage and announcing new legislative elections and a plebiscite to confirm Louis-Napoleon's seizure of power. Tocqueville was not among those initially arrested, but he was part of a group of over 200 representatives who gathered in the *mairie* of the tenth *arrondissement* (now the sixth) to pass motions deposing Louis-Napoleon and declaring themselves an emergency government. The building was quickly surrounded; and after a

---

[44] Brogan, *Tocqueville*, 506–511.

brief standoff, they were all herded down the narrow streets of the quartier Saint-Germain to the military barracks at the Quai d'Orsay, where they were held overnight. The next day Tocqueville was transferred to the military prison at Vincennes. On December 4 they were all released. Thus, Tocqueville's symbolic gesture of opposition to Louis-Napoleon's *coup d'état* cost him two days of not very onerous captivity.[45]

Tocqueville was never to forgive what he always referred to thereafter as Louis-Napoleon's "crime." He may on some level have recognized that he himself had done more than a little to make it possible. But there is no hint in his writings that he could ever bring himself to acknowledge the full extent of his own complicity in the destruction of republican institutions in both France and Rome. He now saw himself as "a foreigner in my own country," and he inveighed against "the French" for acquiescing so readily in the destruction of free institutions and for being so eager to sacrifice their country's "liberty, dignity and honour" in exchange for material well-being.[46] His national political career was now over.

From this point on Tocqueville's great intellectual concern was the writing of *L'Ancien Régime et la Révolution*. At the centre of this book stood the question: Why in the space of sixty years had a democratic revolution in France twice culminated in the dictatorship of a Napoleon? Not surprisingly, he found it hard to shake off the experience of 1848–1851 as he worked on the book. One issue that he found particularly hard to disentangle from his memories of 1848 was his discussion of what he called the "abstract literary politics" of the philosophes. A key aspect of his argument in the *Ancien Régime* was the claim that because the eighteenth-century philosophes had no experience of practical politics, their ideas were hopelessly abstract and radical, taking no account of the specific problems confronting would-be reformers. This claim may have some truth with regard to Rousseau (especially if one ignores Rousseau's preoccupation with local conditions in his projected constitutions for Poland and Corsica). But it makes little sense with regard to the political ideas of Voltaire and Turgot (an abstract thinker but a controller-general and former intendant) and in fact the majority of the French philosophes. The whole concept of "abstract literary politics" actually seems to fit 'forty-eighters such as Lamartine, George Sand and Hugo, much better than the eighteenth-century French philosophes. And Tocqueville's use of the concept in his great study of the origins of the Revolution would seem to reflect his inability to detach himself from

[45] Ibid, 518, 523.
[46] Tocqueville to Edouard de Tocqueville, December 7, 1851, OC XIV, 272.

his experience during the Second Republic. Learned disquisitions have been written on the literary sources of Tocqueville's *Ancien Régime*. No less important, I think, are the experiential sources.

Souvenirs: Portraits, Tableaux, Antitheses

When the *Souvenirs* were finally published in 1893, the book came as a surprise to most of Tocqueville's admirers because it was so different from the two great works which had made him famous. It was a memoir, not a history. And it had none of the abstraction and the cool, detached analysis characteristic of *Démocratie en Amérique* and the *Ancien Régime et la Révolution française*. Instead what Tocqueville offered was an account of events as he saw and experienced them, along with a series of vivid portraits and vignettes and at times extraordinarily blunt judgments on his contemporaries. He wrote at the outset that he regarded his memoir as "a form of relaxation for my mind and not at all a literary work." He was writing "in solitude" and for himself alone during a period of momentary withdrawal from "the theatre of public life." He wanted his pages to be "a mirror in which I will take pleasure in looking at my contemporaries and myself" and not a picture for public view. He would not even discuss the manuscript with his friends because he wished to "remain free to describe myself and them without flattery."[47] His goal was to uncover "the secret motives which make us act," and to that end he announced that he would speak only of events that he himself had witnessed during the period running from the February Revolution down until October 30, 1849, the last day of his tenure as Foreign Minister.[48]

Although Tocqueville wrote fast, his prose is deliberate and it is marked by a somewhat archaic elegance. It has the clarity, the suppleness and the assurance characteristic of the writing of the seventeenth-century French *moralistes*. It is rich in character sketches in the manner of La Rochefoucauld, La Bruyère and the Cardinal de Retz. It spins antitheses and abounds in aphorisms, anecdotes, and commentary delivered in the voice of an observer skilled at unmasking pretentions (especially those of his political allies) and calling attention to the disparity between pro-claimed beliefs and real motives at a time when people made every effort to avoid talking about what really mattered to them.[49] One remarkable feature of the *Souvenirs* is the brutal clarity of Tocqueville's judgments.

---

[47] This statement is not literally true. In addition to discussing the book regularly with his wife, Tocqueville also sent bits of the manuscript to friends, notably Nassau William Senior. See Tocqueville to Senior (December 1848), OC VI ii, 112–114.
[48] *Souvenirs*, 37–38.   [49] Ibid, 206.

He takes a dark view of both the leaders of the July Monarchy and the republicans and socialists who brought it down. He argues that by limiting participation in politics to a narrow stratum, the July Monarchy had fatally impoverished the notion of public interest; at the same time he maintains that the radicals who had a chance at power in 1848 were so lacking in political experience that they could only play at revolution, mimicking the roles and gestures of the revolutionaries of 1789–1794.

The *Souvenirs* does not offer a continuous narrative but rather a series of *tableaux*. A contemporary rhetorician, Pierre Fontanier, defined the tableau as "a scene described in such vivid detail and sense of mood that readers would 'see' it as if they were looking at a picture."[50] This is a pretty good description of what Tocqueville offers. In the first two parts of the book Tocqueville presents four great tableaux: the fall of the July Monarchy on February 24; the parliamentary elections of April 23; the invasion of the Assembly and the abortive putsch of May 15; and the insurrection of June 24–26. There are several lesser tableaux (the Banquet Campaign, the first sessions of the National Assembly, the *fête de la Concorde* of May 21) and an account of his relations with Lamartine. In the rest of the first two parts Tocqueville puts the tableaux in context. The third part is largely devoted to an account of Tocqueville's tenure as Minister of Foreign Affairs.

This mode of organization means that much is left out of Tocqueville's account. There is nothing, first of all, on the fierce reprisals taken against the insurgents after the suppression of the June insurrection. In his account of the June Days Tocqueville deplores "the frightening rapidity ... with which the taste for violence and the disdain for human life spread in these miserable times."[51] But there is no indication, even in his notes, that he gave any thought to depicting the real massacre that followed the triumph of the Party of Order. There is also nothing on the Cavaignac government and the reaction of the summer of 1848, nor on the presidential campaign; nothing on the revival of the Left in 1849, nor on the political struggle for the allegiance of the peasantry that was going on in 1850 as he worked on his *Souvenirs*; nothing on his contacts with Louis-Napoleon before entering the Barrot ministry. Even considering the events on which he focuses, Tocqueville's range of vision is limited. The presence of the working classes – both peasants and urban

---

[50] This is Larry Shiner's paraphrase of Pierre Fontanier's conception of the *tableau* in *Les Figures du discours* (1830). See L. E. Shiner, *The Secret Mirror. Literary Form and History in Tocqueville's Recollections* (Ithaca, 1988), 17–18.

[51] *Souvenirs*, 248.

workers – is only indicated in general terms and often via politically loaded commentary.

The tableaux that Tocqueville does offer are intensely visual – we see settings and vivid (often unflattering) descriptions of individuals – and the perspective is always personal. Tocqueville describes for us what he saw on his walks around Paris during the June days, from his seat in the National Assembly on May 15, and on his visit to Louis Philippe at the Elysée Palace shortly before the February Revolution. His tableaux gain density and texture from the portraits of individuals. Often these portraits come in contrasting pairs: the prolix and petty but intelligent Louis Philippe and the engaging image of the brave Duchess of Orleans vainly pleading in the National Assembly to be appointed regent; the contrast between Tocqueville's flattering self-portrait and the opportunism of his colleague, Havin, during the election campaign; the contrasting portraits of Tocqueville's drunken porter and his loyal valet during the June Days. The latter are particularly striking. Tocqueville first describes his nocturnal encounter with the porter – "a drunkard and a good-for-nothing" and "a socialist by temperament" – who had been boasting in a tavern of his intention to kill Tocqueville. Then he introduces the loyal valet who, after polishing Tocqueville's boots and brushing his clothes, asks for permission to put on his National Guard uniform (paid for by Tocqueville) and go out to fight the insurgents.[52]

Just as there are grand tableaux and smaller ones, there are also grand portraits and more modest sketches of individuals in a few lines. The grand portraits often have symbolic or allegorical weight, as does the portrait of Louis Philippe whose qualities and defects are shown to mirror those of the bourgeoisie in the July Monarchy. Other portraits identify individuals with particular moments or *journées*. Anyone who has read Tocqueville's account of May 15, for example, will find it hard to forget the portrait of Auguste Blanqui who appears like an apparition as if he had only just "emerged from a sewer" with the "sunken, withered cheeks," the white lips, and the "sickly, malign, dirty look" of "a mouldy corpse."[53]

There are also quick and incisive sketches in which physical features are likened or contrasted to moral qualities. At times one senses that in drawing these sketches Tocqueville is creating a bestiary in the manner of a Grandville or a Daumier. Thus Hébert, the last minister of justice under the July Monarchy, has "a narrow, shrunken weasel face"; the

---

[52] Ibid, 238–241. Such stories became anecdotes that Tocqueville used in society. See Gargan, *Tocqueville: Critical Years*, 82–83.

[53] *Souvenirs*, 189. For an extended discussion of this portrait, see Chapter 11 below, pp. 426–428.

deputies on February 23 are like "a pack of hounds" deprived of their prey; and on May 15 Lacordaire looks like "a vulture" while Louis Blanc, trying to wriggle out of the grasp of his admirers, reminds Tocqueville of "a snake with its tail pinched." Finally, André Dupin, Tocqueville's colleague on the Constitutional Committee, is described as "half ape and half jackal, constantly biting, grimacing, gambolling, and always ready to fall upon the wretch who slipped." As these examples suggest, Tocqueville chooses his targets from all parties.[54]

One of Tocqueville's key devices as a portraitist is antithesis. Duchâtel has a "heavy body" but a "supple mind"; Sauzet has "handsome but undistinguished" features with "the dignity of a cathedral verger" and waggling arms; Goudchaud is vain, irascible and valiant, and in him a "veneer of reasonable ideas" conceals "mad theories"; and Tocqueville's sister-in-law, who thinks only of her family on February 24, is "the most respectable woman and the worst citizen one could find."[55] Often antithesis is combined with what Joseph Epstein describes as Tocqueville's "penchant for sentences with trapdoor endings." An example, which includes several trapdoors, is Tocqueville's appreciation of Lamartine's wife: "I often reproached myself for not having cultivated Madame de Lamartine's acquaintance more, for I have always appreciated her genuine virtue." But then he adds that "she had just about every defect that can be associated with virtue and, without altering its character, makes it less agreeable. She had an imperious temper, great pride, and a mind that, although upright, was inflexible and sometimes harsh, so that it was impossible not to respect her but equally impossible to like her."[56]

These devices and strategies give an extraordinary vividness to Tocqueville's tableaux, which helps explain why selections from the *Souvenirs* are so often used to illustrate historical accounts of the revolution of 1848. But more important in shaping Tocqueville's judgments are a few recurring dichotomies which serve to frame his representations of 1848–1851. The most frequently invoked of these dichotomies recurs throughout Tocqueville's writing and not only in the *Souvenirs*: this is the distinction between a higher and a lower self. Repeatedly in Tocqueville one finds a contrast drawn between the generosity and unselfishness of the citizen and the craving for material well-being of the individual, the virtues of heroism and the comforts of peace, the exercise of rights and the gratification of desires. Usually, Tocqueville identifies the lower self with the sphere of private interests and the higher self with the

---

[54] *Souvenirs*, 62, 72, 188, 193, 265.   [55] Ibid, 59, 90, 229–230.
[56] Ibid, 182; Joseph Epstein, *Alexis de Tocqueville. Democracy's Guide* (New York, 2006), 133.

228 Tocqueville: "A Vile Tragedy Performed by Provincial Actors"

recognition of collective ties. Thus, in *L'Ancien Régime et la Révolution française* he could celebrate freedom as "alone capable of lifting men's minds above mere money worship" and of making them aware of their shared devotion to their country.[57]

In the *Souvenirs* the opposed terms are most often the high-minded and the petty, or grandeur and greed (*élévation* and *petitesse*, or *grandeur* and *cupidité*).[58] Often Tocqueville associates *petitesse* with the pursuit of material well-being and creature comforts, while *grandeur* and *élévation* imply high intellectual and moral aims and the willingness to sacrifice one's private interests for the public good. Each of these traits has many nuances, but what is interesting is the regularity with which particular associations recur. We are told repeatedly in reading the *Souvenirs* that the great exemplar of both pettiness and greed is the bourgeoisie. And toward the end of the *Souvenirs* Tocqueville boasts that now that Thiers (that quintessential bourgeois) and his allies have returned to politics with their *petite passion* for offices, they can easily be manipulated by appeals to "their ambition or their greed."

But in Tocqueville's moral universe the working class is also moved by greed – or by a combination of greed and envy. The difference between the greed (*cupidité*) of the bourgeoisie and that of the workers is that whereas bourgeois greed is associated with pettiness and with political complacency, the greed of the workers is associated with extreme political passions. Repeatedly Tocqueville tells us that it was "greedy and envious passions" that drove the workers to revolt in June. He does, it is true, pay tribute in a famous passage to "the resolution" of the June insurgents – their "wonderful powers of coordination" and their astonishing "military expertise." But then he goes on in the next paragraph to explain that "it was the mixture of greedy ideas and false [socialist] theories that engendered the insurrection and made it so formidable."[59]

Where are *grandeur* and *élévation* in the *Souvenirs*? There is a great deal of pettiness, vanity, myopia, selfishness, stupidity and greed. But nobler impulses are conspicuous by their absence. One is tempted to suggest that Tocqueville has cast himself in the role of the embodiment of *grandeur* when he informs us that he had "too much integrity" to adapt himself to the "petty practices necessary for quick success" and that he has rarely seen in his contemporaries that "disinterested concern for the good of mankind that I think I do find in myself."[60]

---

[57] OC II i, 75.
[58] For a carefully worked out and richly suggestive analysis of the pictorial and thematic "code" of the *Souvenirs* see Shiner, *The Secret Mirror*, 78–111.
[59] *Souvenirs*, 212–213.   [60] Ibid, 139–141.

But there is in the *Souvenirs* one moment of collective behaviour that Tocqueville regards as marked by *grandeur*. This is the arrival at Paris, in the last days of June insurrection, of trainloads of provincials – peasants as well as great landowners and bourgeois National Guard units – to join the army in crushing the revolt. Or to mimic Tocqueville's more elevated language: the coming together of rural France to "deliver the nation from oppression by the workers of Paris."[61] This collective movement, made possible by the construction in the 1840s of railroad lines connecting Paris and the provinces, was to be treated by Flaubert as an act of revenge marked more by sadism than heroism. But Tocqueville sees it as a heroic movement of national unity worthy of celebration in lyric language:

> By every route that the insurgents did not control thousands of men entered the city, rushing to our aid from all parts of France ... These men belonged without distinction to all classes of society. Among them were many peasants, many bourgeois, many great landowners and nobles, all mixed together in the same ranks.[62]

On the morning of the last day of the fighting, 1,500 volunteers from Tocqueville's department of La Manche reached Paris, having travelled over 80 leagues on foot. Among them Tocqueville recognized "land-owners, lawyers, doctors, farmers, my friends and my neighbours," and he was impressed by the fact that almost all the old nobility of Lower Normandy was there:

> It was the same in almost all of France. From the impoverished squire in the depths of his province to the elegant and idle heirs of great families, they all recalled at this moment that they had once belonged to a warlike ruling caste. Everywhere they displayed exemplary resolution and vigour, so great is the vitality of these old aristocratic corps.[63]

Here, Tocqueville asserts, was a moment when French people of all classes regained for an instant a sense of common purpose, common roots, and common identity. This moment, as we shall see, is described in very different terms by Proudhon, Marx and Marie d'Agoult, as well as Flaubert.

The other major antithesis in the *Souvenirs* is that between literature and truth. Tocqueville signals the importance of this opposition at the outset when he announces that he does not intend to write a work of "literature" but rather to express himself "honestly" which he can only do when writing for himself alone. He develops the point in a long introspective passage in Part II in which he contrasts the difficulties he

[61] Ibid, 252.   [62] Ibid, 235.   [63] Ibid, 251.

faces in trying to write honestly about himself with the tricks of memoir-writers for whom candour takes second place to the desire to impress their readers. Thus, the Cardinal de Retz is not credible even when he "confesses" his hypocritical devotions and charities and his plot to assassinate Richelieu. In such cases "it is not the love of truth" that moves him but the desire to be thought a "good conspirator" and a "clever fellow." But even when one *wishes* to be sincere, the main problem is that one can never see oneself clearly. One "easily loses sight of oneself among all the views, interests, ideas, tastes and instincts that make one act."[64]

It is in Tocqueville's devastating portrait of Lamartine that the opposition between literature and truth is most fully developed. He writes of Lamartine that he has never met " a mind more devoid than his of any thought of public good."

> I have never known a less sincere mind, or one that more completely despised truth. When I say that he despised truth I am wrong: he never honoured it enough to be concerned with it in any way at all. Talking or writing, he departed from the truth and returned to it without taking any notice, being solely concerned with the particular effect he wanted to produce at a given moment.[65]

The problem with Lamartine (and to some degree with all writers) is that he is only concerned with the effect his words will have on an audience and not at all with the degree to which they will promote an understanding of the truth.

This scorn for truth is a central feature of what Tocqueville calls the "literary spirit" which thrived in the salons of the eighteenth century and which Lamartine, among many others, has imported into politics. What this refers to in its simplest form is the preference for what is interesting over what is true:

> What I call the literary spirit in politics consists of looking for what is ingenious and new rather than what is true, liking what makes an interesting picture rather than what serves a purpose, appreciating good acting and fine speaking without reference to the play's meaning, and finally judging by impressions rather than by reasons.[66]

For Tocqueville, the key to an understanding of what went wrong in 1848 was to recognize the corrosive influence of the intrusion of the literary spirit in politics.

Another dimension of the opposition between literature and truth that fascinates Tocqueville is the contrast of theatre and truth, or theatre and reality. Looking back on the revolutionary events of February 24,

---

[64] Ibid, 137–138.   [65] Ibid, 176.   [66] Ibid, 119.

Tocqueville writes that the scenes he observed lacked grandeur because they "lacked truth." They were gestures of imitation consistent with the French habit of mixing literary and theatrical reminiscences with historical memory. Unfortunately in this case "the imitation was so obvious that the terrible originality of the facts remained hidden." This was a moment when the imagination of the French had been "smeared by the crude colours" of Lamartine's *Les Girondins*. The first French Revolution was alive in everyone's mind, and everything Tocqueville saw that day was "stamped with the visible imprint of such memories." "The whole time it seemed to me that people were staging a play about the French Revolution, rather than continuing it."[67]

> They tried without success to warm themselves at the hearth of their fathers' passions. They imitated their gestures and poses as they had seen them on stage without being able to imitate their enthusiasm or feel their fury. A tradition of violent action was being followed, without real understanding, by cold-hearted people. Although I saw that the denouement of the play would be terrible, I could not take the actors very seriously. It all seemed like a vile tragedy performed by a provincial troupe.[68]

Once established, this theatrical metaphor – with its implicit contrast to reality – recurs again and again in Tocqueville's narrative.

The metaphor of revolution as theatre is especially prominent in Tocqueville's account of the February Revolution. The July Monarchy had been a "long parliamentary comedy" in which every politician contracted the habit of "colouring the expression of his feelings outrageously" and exaggerating the danger posed by the policies of his opponents, thus being "unable to appreciate the real and the true." On February 24 the National Guard officers are described as marching "theatrically up to the tribune, waving their flags, prancing about, gesticulating melodramatically and bawling some revolutionary gibberish." That afternoon as the names of possible members of the Provisional Government are read out to the crowd that had invaded the Chamber of Deputies, tragedy gives way to comedy. "Cheers greeted most of the names, some were rejected with groans and others were the target of jokes. For as in Shakespeare, when the people play a part, burlesque and terror jostle together, and jokes are intermingled with revolutionary fervour." The next day in the few shops still open for business, the "frightened and, still more, astonished bourgeois" looked like "an audience at a theatre who, after the play is over, still wonder what it was about."[69]

---

[67] Ibid, 100.   [68] Ibid.   [69] *Souvenirs*, 53, 97, 102, 122.

Since the description of the revolution of 1848 as cheap theatre –
"a vile tragedy played out by a provincial troupe" – is echoed by many
contemporaries, it is worth asking exactly what Tocqueville means by it.
What does he see as the significance of the preoccupation of the 'forty-
eighters with models drawn from the first French Revolution, and what is
the function of theatrical metaphors within the rhetorical framework of
Tocqueville's analysis? In thinking about these questions, one cannot fail
to be struck by the parallel between Tocqueville's and Marx's views of
1848 as a theatrical parody of 1789. In *The 18ᵗʰ Brumaire of Louis
Bonaparte* Marx contrasted 1789 and 1848 by arguing that the first
French revolutionaries invoked Roman precedents and traditions in
order to "glorify new struggles" whereas the imitation of 1789 by the
'forty-eighters was an attempt to mask the modesty of their real aims.[70]
For Tocqueville, the "new struggles" are not defined as those of a single
class, but otherwise his point is similar. He depicts the 'forty-eighters as
frozen in fantasies about the past. Unable to understand their situation or
to formulate realistic goals, they seek models in half-understood revolutionary traditions. They substitute posturing and declamation for the
search for constitutional safeguards to secure liberty. Dissatisfied with
the democratically elected Assembly, all the radicals could think of doing
on May 15 was to dissolve the Assembly and march to the Hôtel de Ville
to proclaim a new provisional government – all of which was simply "a
parody of February 24, just as February 24 was a parody of other
revolutionary scenes."[71] For Tocqueville theatricality was the moving
force in the events of both May 15 and February 24, and this theatricality
was, in his view, a central feature of the "semi-madness" of democratic
revolution.

A Moment of Grandeur and a World of Fools

There is a powerful passage in the *Souvenirs* in which Tocqueville sums
up his reactions to the two revolutions of 1830 and 1848 and explains
why it was that, despite his family's longstanding attachment to the
Bourbons, he was more upset by the overthrow of Louis Philippe in
1848 than by that of Charles X in 1830:

At daybreak on July 30, 1830 I saw Charles X's carriages pass along the outer
boulevards of Versailles. Their escutcheons had already been scratched out, and
they moved slowly, one after the other, as if at a funeral. I could not hold back my
tears at the sight. This time [in 1848] my feelings were different, but stronger ...

---

[70] Marx, *Eighteenth Brumaire* (New York, 1962), 13–15.   [71] *Souvenirs*, 195.

Both of these revolutions had pained me, but how much more bitter were the impressions left by the second. Up until the end I had felt some remnants of hereditary affection for Charles X. But that king fell because he had violated rights that were dear to me, and I was hoping that his fall would revive rather than extinguish my country's freedom. Today that freedom seemed dead to me. The princes who were fleeing meant nothing to me, but I felt that my own cause was lost.[72]

Tocqueville goes on to describe himself as having "spent the best years of my youth in a society that seemed to regain prosperity and greatness as it regained freedom."

I had conceived the idea of a freedom moderated, regulated and contained by beliefs, customs and laws; the beauties of that freedom had moved me; it had become the passion of my whole life. I felt that I could never be consoled for its loss; and now I saw that I must give it up forever.[73]

Tocqueville believed that, for all its shortcomings, the July Monarchy was based on representative institutions within which the political and personal freedoms that really mattered to him could flourish. He also believed that revolutions, whatever their professed goals and ideals, were inimical to the preservation of liberty.

In discussing the causes of the February Revolution, Tocqueville relied on a distinction that he used in all his writings on revolution: the distinction between "general" and particular or "accidental" causes. The principal general cause was the rapid growth of the working-class population over the previous thirty years. This growth, which was stimulated by work on the fortifications of Paris begun in 1841, had made Paris the leading manufacturing city in France and had brought to the capital a volatile, discontent population often subject to prolonged periods of unemployment. In the best of times this population was restless: their attitudes were shaped by "the democratic disease of envy" that was "silently at work" throughout the society as a whole, and by the "passion for material possessions" that pervaded the culture of the July Monarchy. But with the unemployment and the general economic downturn of 1846 and 1847, this new Parisian working class became particularly vulnerable to the blandishments of the socialists who were beginning to attract notice with their theories attributing human misery to unjust laws and not to the workings of divine providence. In Tocqueville's opinion the working class had been "inflamed" by the view that poverty could be eliminated by challenging the legitimacy of private property and changing the social system.[74]

---

[72] Ibid, 116, 452.   [73] Ibid, 116–117.   [74] Ibid, 113.

Tocqueville enumerated other general causes without which the revolution of 1848 would have been impossible. These included the contempt felt by the rest of society for the ruling class; the centralization of the whole French political and administrative system; and finally "the mobility of everything – institutions, ideas, mores and men – in a society on the move, which had been stirred up by seven great revolutions in less than sixty years." But the principal cause of the February revolution – the thing that gave it its specific character – was the spread of socialist ideas, and notably the belief that the great obstacle to the establishment of a just and egalitarian society, was the institution of private property. Thus, in noting the variety of socialist theories, Tocqueville argued that their common denominator was the attack on property and that this lay at the heart of the February Revolution. "Socialism will remain the essential feature and the most frightening memory of the February Revolution," he wrote. "Seen from a distance, the Republic will appear only as a means and not an end."[75]

The "accidents" or secondary causes that led to the overthrow of the July Monarchy were, according to Tocqueville, the tactical errors or "clumsy passions" of the dynastic opposition which "prepared the way for a riot when it wanted reform"; the "excessive" attempts to suppress disorder in Paris, culminating in the massacre of the Boulevard des Capucines and the subsequent unwillingness of the government to employ force of any kind; the "mistakes and mental disorientation" of Thiers and Molé, the ministers appointed to succeed Guizot; and finally "the senile imbecility of Louis Philippe." In fact, this list of "accidents" provides a neat summary of the "selfishness, ineptitude, stupidity and weakness catalogued in the portraits and tableaux" of the first part of the book.[76]

In reading the *Souvenirs* it is hard to avoid the impression that Tocqueville saw himself as living in a world of fools. No one – least of all his friends and relatives – is spared. But no group comes in for more withering criticism than the longstanding republicans – the *républicains de la veille* – who made up the Provisional Government which for two or three months appeared to control the fortunes of France. Like Marx on this point, Tocqueville believed that the members of the Provisional Government had exceeded the tolerable bounds of stupidity.[77] In the period prior to the April elections, the Provisional Government had great

---

[75] Ibid, 114, 129.   [76] Ibid, 114–115; Shiner, *The Secret Mirror*, 57.

[77] The phrase is Raymond Aron's, *Main Currents in Sociological Thought*, 2 vols. (New York, 1968) I, 316.

influence. What they did with this influence was enough to terrify the bourgeoisie and a good part of the peasantry, but not enough to make themselves respected. Their first mistake was their failure to organize national elections immediately after the February Revolution. But this was followed by many other mistakes:

There have been more wicked revolutionaries than those of 1848, but I don't think there were ever any stupider. They did not know how to make use of universal suffrage or how to manage without it. If they had held elections right after February 24, when the upper classes were stunned by the blow that they had just received and when the common people were more astonished than discontent, they might perhaps have obtained an assembly to their liking. If they had boldly seized dictatorship, they might have retained it for some time. But they handed themselves over to the nation while doing everything possible to alienate it.[78]

What Tocqueville has in mind here is the 45 *centimes* tax, the clumsy attempts of the Provisional Government to influence the elections, and the hastily thrown together National Workshops program. Tocqueville also ridicules the Provisional Government's nonsensical mixture of strident rhetoric and weak policies, writing that they "threatened" the nation while "putting themselves at its mercy." In retrospect, Tocqueville would add: "In establishing universal suffrage they thought they were arming people to support the revolution." In fact, "they were only arming them against it."[79]

There was nothing particularly original about Tocqueville's criticism of the Provisional Government. It was echoed, with slight variations, by contemporary observers of all political persuasions. But along with this critique Tocqueville also offers in the *Souvenirs* a highly personal analysis – one is tempted to call it a celebration – of the origins and triumph of the Party of Order. This is fascinating and unlike anything in the contemporary literature because it does not focus, as one might expect, on Parisian politics and on the process by which Orleanists and Legitimists discovered that it was in their mutual interest to pay temporary lip service to the Republic. Instead, Tocqueville characterizes the social roots of the Party of Order by taking us out into the countryside during the election campaign of April 1848. There, in his ancestral *pays* of Normandy, Tocqueville finds himself "in a different country from the France of Paris." He finds widespread fear of Paris – fear of new taxes, fear of an attack on property, disgust with "Parisian demagoguery." But what is most striking in Tocqueville's account is his insistence on the

[78] *Souvenirs*, 160.   [79] Ibid, 161.

absence of class divisions in the countryside. In reporting on this, his tone becomes hushed:

In the countryside all landowners, whatever their origin, antecedents, education, and wealth, had come together and seemed to form a whole: all the old political hatreds and rivalries of caste and wealth had vanished. Neither jealousy nor pride separated the peasant from the rich, or the gentlemen from the bourgeois; instead there was mutual confidence, respect and good will. Ownership constituted a sort of fraternity, linking all who had anything.[80]

Surely there is a good deal of exaggeration in this picture of totally harmonious class relations in Lower Normandy. Writing in *Les Paysans* about a different area, Burgundy, a few years earlier, Balzac could describe a snake-pit of longstanding class and intra-class hatred. And Tocqueville himself conceded in 1851 that "experience has proved that this union itself was not as close as it seemed to be."[81] In any case, in Tocqueville's account an alliance was formed in June 1848 uniting peasants and their aristocratic landlords against Parisian workers and their demagogical socialist leaders. And this alliance bore fruit in a "moment of grandeur" when, as we have seen, provincials of all classes came to Paris to save the Republic and their property from the Parisian workers and the socialists.

One of the most distinctive features of Tocqueville's whole account is his treatment of the June Days. In other contemporary writers, the confrontation between the insurgents and the very mixed bag of defenders of the Republic is often described as "tragic." But for Tocqueville the June uprising was a battle between haves and have-nots which was "necessary," "inevitable," and even "desirable." "I had always believed," Tocqueville wrote later, "that the February Revolution would not be stopped except all at once by a great battle fought in Paris ... that this battle was not only inevitable but imminent and that it would be desirable to seize the first opportunity to start it."[82] If the June Days did not permanently "quench the fire of revolution in France," they did at least temporarily put it out.

But the most important feature of the June insurrection for Tocqueville was that it provided the occasion for a rescue operation which constituted the last hurrah of the rural aristocracy. In participating in the crushing of the June insurrection "the impoverished squire from a provincial backwater and the elegant and idle sons of the great houses all remembered that they had once formed part of a warlike ruling class."[83] In celebrating the unexpected "vigour" to be found in the old aristocracy,

---

[80] Ibid, 146.   [81] Ibid, 147.   [82] Ibid, 163.   [83] Ibid, 251.

Tocqueville rises to heights of lyric mysticism worthy of Michelet: Even when these old aristocratic corps seem reduced to dust, "they retain some trace of their former selves: and they rise briefly from the shadow of death before sinking back into eternal rest."[84]

Most contemporary histories of the revolution of 1848 culminated with the crushing of the June insurrection. If Tocqueville's narrative had ended at this point, his *Souvenirs* could be read as a celebration of the triumph of order, property, and *grandeur* over "the combination of greedy desires and false theories that engendered the insurrection and made it so formidable."[85] He himself says as much: "The June Days delivered the nation from oppression by Paris workers and restored to it the control of its own fate." This was a victory that, by Tocqueville's account, at least momentarily drew social classes together, distracted the bourgeoisie from its materialistic preoccupations, and gave a new life to the old aristocracy.[86]

But this celebration of the victory of order and property over anarchy and greed is short-lived. "I realized at once" writes Tocqueville "that the fight in June was a necessary crisis, but that afterward the temper of the nation would be in some way changed." Socialist theories would continue to spread among the people, "sowing the seeds of future revolutions," but the "socialist party" was now beaten and impotent. The Montagnards "soon felt that they had been struck down beyond recall by the same blow." Even the moderate republicans were quick to recognize that the defeat of this insurrection challenging the authority of the republican government did not bode well for the future of the Republic. As for Tocqueville himself, "detesting the Montagnards and not attached to the Republic but adoring liberty," what he felt after the June Days was above all "fear for the Republic."[87]

Tocqueville feared that in the "inevitable" reaction of the propertied classes to the insurgents' abuse of freedom, "the old love of independence would be replaced by a dread of, and perhaps a distaste for, free institutions." Looking back from Sorrento, Tocqueville asked how far the retreat from liberty might go:

The movement of retreat began in effect after June 27; at first it was very slow and almost invisible to the naked eye, then more rapid, then impetuous and irresistible. Where will it end? I don't know. I think we shall find it difficult not to go back far beyond the point we had reached in February, and I foresee that all of us – socialists, Montagnards, liberal republicans, will fall into the same discredit.[88]

[84] Ibid.   [85] *Souvenirs*, 213; Shiner, *The Secret Mirror*, 60.
[86] *Souvenirs*, 252; Shiner, *The Secret Mirror*, 61.   [87] *Souvenirs*, 252–253.
[88] Ibid, 253

This dark prophecy concludes Tocqueville's account of the June Days and forms a coda to the narrative of Part II.

By March 1851 Tocqueville could hardly escape the conclusion that the victory for order and property that he had celebrated in June 1848 had led to the defeat of liberty. But in the *Souvenirs* he tells us virtually nothing about the course of the reaction against liberty during the following year. Instead, he jumps ahead to describe his tenure as Minister of Foreign Affairs "while my memories are still fresh." The consequence of Tocqueville's silence is, first of all, that he does not have to comment on the massacre of unarmed prisoners and suspected insurgents at the end of the June Days. Nor does he need to mention his support for legislation shutting down political clubs and limiting free speech. Since we know Tocqueville to have been a longstanding critic of political and administrative centralization in France, it is also significant that he does not concern himself with the fact that the full force of the centralized bureaucracy was applied from the beginning in an effort to crush the socialists and other "reds."

What Tocqueville does consider, on the other hand, is the repression of radicals following the abortive insurrection of June 13, 1849, at a time when he was himself a member of the government. He writes that after putting down the "insurrection" (which was actually a non-violent demonstration), his government put Paris, Lyon and several departments under a state of siege, suspended six radical newspapers, cashiered three legions of the Paris National Guard, and arrested or brought charges against thirty-one democratic and socialist representatives in the National Assembly. Here, far from being evasive, Tocqueville writes bluntly, and apparently with some pride, about his role in organizing the repression:

For my part, I believed that it was wise and necessary to make great concessions to the terror and legitimate resentment of the nation, and that after such a violent revolution [sic], the only way to save freedom was to restrict it. My colleagues agreed with me. Accordingly we introduced the following measures: a law to suspend the clubs, another to suppress the vagaries of the press even more forcefully than had the Monarchy; and a third to regularize the state of siege.[89]

When a member of the democratic opposition shouted, "Your law establishes a military dictatorship," Tocqueville's ally Jules Dufaure replied: "Yes, it is a dictatorship, but a parliamentary one. No individual rights can prevail over the inalienable right of society to save itself."[90]

---

[89] Ibid, 324.   [90] Ibid.

There does, in the end, seem to be something disingenuous about Tocqueville's "adoration" of liberty and his anxious reflections on its "retreat." For the text of the *Souvenirs* makes plain not only that the June Days resulted in a reaction against liberty but also that Tocqueville himself was during his tenure as Foreign Minister a willing instrument of that reaction. Thus, to call Tocqueville a "willing instrument of the reaction" may help us make sense of his role as a political actor in 1848–1849. But it does not do anything like full justice to the complexity of his thought or to the uncertainties that emerge in the text of the *Souvenirs*. For his strongest condemnation of socialism in Part II, Chapter 2 is directly followed by a question that a hide-bound reactionary would never ask: "Will socialism remain buried in the contempt that so justly covers the socialists of 1848?" Tocqueville's hesitant and deeply relativistic answer is worthy of a Montesquieu or a Montaigne:

The more I study the former state of the world, and the more clearly I see the contemporary world, I am struck by the prodigious diversity found, not only in the laws but in the principles of the laws and the different forms that the right of property has taken ... on this earth, I am tempted to believe that what we call necessary institutions are often just the institutions to which we are accustomed, and that in matters of social constitution the realm of the possible is much wider than people living in particular societies imagine.[91]

Like the rest of us, Tocqueville had the prejudices of his period, culture and class. Like few of us, he had the ability to rise above these prejudices at times and the imagination to see himself and his world as if from a very great distance.

[91] *Souvenirs*, 131.

7   Proudhon
"A Revolution without an Idea"

Four of the individuals considered thus far had been important public figures before 1848. Lamartine and Tocqueville had served as legislators under the July Monarchy; Hugo was both a peer and an internationally celebrated writer; and George Sand's novels had won her enormous influence as a spiritual guide to the young, and especially to women. While our fifth writer, Marie d'Agoult, was only beginning to acquire influence as a writer in the late 1840s, she was already well known as a *salonnière* and for her "scandalous" relation with Liszt. The situation of Proudhon was different (see Figure 7.1). He was an outsider. This is not to say that he was unknown. The publication of *Qu'est-ce que la propriété?* in 1840, with its provocative "Property is theft!" had won him notoriety. He had also become a presence in the culture of the Left, crossing swords with Victor Considerant and the young Marx. But in 1847 he was not close to enjoying the fame of our other writers.

Thus, the revolution of 1848 was in a personal sense hugely important for Proudhon. It drew him into a new life. It made him a representative of the people and an influential journalist. It made him the butt of attacks, but also gave him a much wider audience than he had previously enjoyed. He became the scapegoat of the Right, the target of mockery by Thiers and by cartoonists of all persuasions. But in the course of 1848, and especially after the June Days, he also became the spokesman for "the people" betrayed by the revolution.

A bitter – though not consistent – critic of Louis-Napoleon after his election as president, Proudhon was eventually convicted of crimes against the government. He then fled to Belgium but returned to Paris only to be arrested on June 5, 1849. He spent most of the ensuing three years in prison. But thanks to prison reforms that, ironically, had been introduced by Adolphe Thiers, he continued in prison to keep busy, editing two newspapers and writing his "confessions" as well as two other important works. In these books, Proudhon developed a powerful critique of the revolutionary government and the radical "Jacobin" Left, and he began to situate himself with regard to the revolutionary tradition.

Figure 7.1 Photograph of Proudhon by Nadar, 1862.

Making His Way: Roots, Marx, Journalism

Of all the leading French radicals of the 1830s and 1840s, only Proudhon had deep roots in the rural working class. He was the son of a cooper from Franche-Comté – a maker of wine casks and beer barrels who later worked as a brewer and tavern keeper. As a boy, Proudhon worked by turns as a cow-herd and a cellar boy in a tavern run by his father, before being apprenticed at the age of eighteen to a printer in Besançon. Although he attended the Collège de Besançon, an excellent secondary school by the standards of the time, Proudhon did not complete his studies there; and he was in some respects self-taught. He learned Latin and some Greek and Hebrew while working as a compositor and proofreader, and his knowledge of theology seems to have come largely from his work as a proofreader of ecclesiastical works. His great break-through as a provincial intellectual came at the age of twenty-nine when he was awarded the Pension Suard, a three-year fellowship offered by the Académie de Besançon to promising young men of modest background. In his application for the pension, Proudhon described himself in terms that convey a sense of the pride he took in his origins:

Born and raised in the bosom of the working class, belonging to it still by heart and feeling, above all by shared suffering and shared desires, my greatest joy if I am chosen by the Academy, would be to work tirelessly in philosophy and science with all the energy of my will and all the power of my mind, for the physical, moral and intellectual betterment of those whom it pleases me to call my brothers and my comrades.[1]

He was always to remain proud of his working-class roots and to cherish an ideal image of the rural life that he had known as a boy. Much in his mature thought can be seen as an effort to recapture that ideal.

Proudhon was the first French intellectual to call himself an "anarch-ist," but more often he spoke of his "socialist" ideas, relishing the fact that his socialism had "received the baptism" of a conservative learned society. The Fourierist Victor Considerant had been his schoolmate at the Collège de Besançon, yet he never felt close to Considerant or to any of the romantic socialists of his generation. He proudly announced in 1849 that in his initial attempts to deepen his grasp of political economy and the problem of poverty, he had "never sought enlightenment from the socialist écoles."[2] Thus in working out his own ideas, he rejected both

---

[1] Proudhon to MM. de l'Académie de Besançon, May 31, 1837, *Correspondance de P.-J. Proudhon*, 14 vols. (Paris, 1875), I, 24ff.

[2] P.-J. Proudhon, *Les Confessions d'un révolutionnaire*, Daniel Halévy (ed.) (Paris, 1929), 173.

the state socialism of a Louis Blanc and the communitarian socialism of the Fourierists. He believed that all attempts to impose social change from above were doomed to failure. It was essential, he maintained, to return control of the production process to the workers themselves and to create conditions in which individuals, acting freely on their own initiative, could organize their own collective life.

By 1840 Proudhon had worked out a sweeping indictment of the social order. This was an order ruled and exploited, he believed, by a new "mercantile and landed aristocracy, a thousand times more rapacious than the old aristocracy of the nobility." At this time Proudhon worked as a partner in a small printing shop in Besançon. The business never flourished, and in 1843 he sold it, moving to Lyon to work as an agent for a shipping firm. At Lyon, he established ties with the *canuts*, the silk weavers who had been at the forefront of the French workers' movement since the early 1830s. But Proudhon's work also took him to Paris; and it was there in the mid-1840s that he made contact with a group of foreign exiles including several young German Left-Hegelians and "four or five Russian boyars." One of the Russians was Mikhail Bakunin, and among the Germans was an unknown radical exile, the twenty-six-year-old Karl Marx.

Long afterwards Marx recalled all-night conversations during which he "infected" Proudhon with Hegel's philosophy. After their initial meetings, Marx effusively praised Proudhon as a trenchant critic of private property whose work "makes a real science of political economy possible."[3] So impressed was Marx that he invited Proudhon to serve as the Paris correspondent of an international Correspondence Committee designed to spread communist theory and practice throughout Europe. Proudhon's cautious response shows that he already suspected that Marx would not share his undogmatic libertarian views:

Let us work together, if you like, to discover the laws of society, the ways in which these laws are realized, and the process by which we can discover them. But for God's sake, when we have demolished all the *à priori* dogmas, let us not think of indoctrinating the people in our turn ... Let's give the world an example of wise and farsighted tolerance, but simply because we are leaders of a movement let us not instigate a new intolerance. Let us not set ourselves up as the apostles of a new religion, even if it be the religion of logic and reason.[4]

---

[3] Karl Marx and Friedrich Engels, *The Holy Family or Critique of Critical Critique* (Moscow, 1956), 46.

[4] Proudhon to Marx, May 17, 1846, *Correspondance*, II, 198–199.

Proudhon also challenged the notion that significant social change could be brought about by a revolutionary seizure of power:

Perhaps you still believe that no reform is now possible without a political takeover, without what used to be called a revolution ... I confess to you that my recent studies have made me completely reject this position. I believe that ... we should not specify *revolutionary* action as a means of social reform because actually this so-called means is simply an appeal to arbitrary force ... I prefer to get rid of property little by little rather than giving it a new life by calling for a Saint Bartholomew's eve massacre of proprietors.[5]

Proudhon was to remain hostile to violent revolution until the end of his days, and this was just one of the points on which his friendship with Marx foundered.

Proudhon's first foray into political journalism came in 1847 when a group of radicals – including Théophile Thoré, Félix Pyat and Victor Pilhès – asked him to collaborate on the founding of a newspaper to be called *Le Peuple*. Proudhon was so enthusiastic about the project that, even before sufficient capital had been raised, he moved to Paris. On October 24, 1847, he wrote a friend, describing what he hoped would come of this project:

In becoming a journalist, I'm not going to carry on the way others do and compete verbally with my future colleagues in the Parisian press. They can write as they see fit. Let them sell editorials, installment novels, harsh reviews, anecdotes and advertisements: that does not concern me. When we get that far, we'll see. The journal *Le Peuple* will be the first act of the economic revolution, the battle plan of labour against capital, the central organ of the campaign that I am going to initiate against the property system. From criticism I move to action; and the action begins with a journal.[6]

In the end, nothing came of this journal. But this letter stands as a succinct statement of what Proudhon hoped to achieve through journalism.

Proudhon remained apart from the protest movements leading up to the February Revolution. He had no interest in the Banquet Campaign or in the reforms proposed by the Dynastic Opposition. He was not greatly disturbed by the venality of the July Monarchy's elites, and he ridiculed the reformers' claims that the right to vote should be extended to include the educated bourgeoisie as well as the very rich. In his view, the educated classes – the "intellectual capacities" – were "the most corruptible, and generally the most cowardly, the most perfidious of all

[5] Proudhon to Marx, May 17, 1846, *Correspondance*, II, 199–200.
[6] Proudhon to Bergmann, October 24, 1847, *Correspondance*, II, 272.

the capacities."[7] He believed that the widening of the suffrage and the other political reforms envisaged by the opposition could only serve to distract attention from the need for radical economic and social reforms that would confront the real problems of the emerging industrial society. He derided Barrot, Thiers and Tocqueville; and he wrote a friend in January 1848 that "The greatest happiness that the French people could attain would be to see one hundred opposition deputies thrown into the Seine with chains around their necks."[8] As for Lamartine, Proudhon called him a clown and wrote in his journal that Lamartine's speech at Macon warning of a coming revolution was a "blague superbe" – a huge joke worthy of Daumier's con man Robert Macaire – and that projects of electoral reform were no more than "a new mystification." In his view, the widening of the suffrage would do nothing to create jobs or to feed the hungry, and political reform could only be "the effect and not the means" of more fundamental social reform.[9]

In the Revolution

In an article published on the first anniversary of the February Revolution Proudhon wrote that "the fusillade of the rue des Capucines changed everything for me in an instant."[10] In fact, and even though he never believed significant change could be imposed from above by legislative fiat, Proudhon was quick to identify himself with the insurgents of February. On the morning of the 24th, the day after the killing of unarmed demonstrators on the rue des Capucines, he wrote in his journal that the opposition had been crushed "and here we are back at the status quo for the next six months."[11] Toward noon of that day, however, Proudhon walked across the Seine from his tiny apartment on the rue Mazarine to the offices of the democratic journal *La Réforme*, near the Palais Royal. On the way he watched insurgents exchanging gunfire with government troops stationed at the entrance to the Louvre. When Ferdinand Flocon, the director of *La Réforme*, saw Proudhon, he shouted: "You, Proudhon, you're a printer. I've just written a proclamation. Print it up for us." Flocon read from his proclamation: "Citizens! Louis Philippe had you shot at just as Charles X did. Let him go the way

---

[7] *Carnets de P.-J. Proudhon*, Pierre Haubtmann (ed.), 4 vols. (Paris, 1960–1974), II, 71 (April 1847).
[8] Proudhon to Maurice, January 22, 1848, *Correspondance*, II, 277.
[9] *Carnets*, II, 157 (July 1847) and 229 (October 1847).
[10] *Le Peuple*, article of February 25–26, 1849 in P.-J. Proudhon, *Mélanges. Articles de journaux 1848–1852*, 3 vols. (Paris, 1868–1870), II, 7.
[11] *Carnets*, II, 369 (February 24, 1848).

of Charles X!" Without hesitating, Proudhon began to set the proclamation in type. "You are holding a revolutionary post," said Flocon. "We are counting on your patriotism!" "You can be sure," answered Proudhon, "that I won't quit until I've finished the job." He finished in five minutes. Thus by his own account, Proudhon joined the ranks of the insurgents.[12]

Later that day Proudhon made other gestures of sympathy with the insurgents. He broke through a barrier on the Boulevard Bonne-Nouvelle, and at the Place de la Bourse he uprooted a tree, carried paving stones to a barricade and recruited others to do the same. But from the beginning, he had doubts that he set down in his journal. The revolution was a "mess" made by "a horde of lawyers and writers, each more ignorant than the others. And they are going to contend for power ... The Lamartines, the Quinets, Michelet, Considerant, the Montagnards, etc., etc. Mysticism, Robespierrism, Chauvinism are in power. They've made a revolution without an idea ... There's no place for me in all that." Proudhon later wrote that he participated in the February Revolution without any great hope or deeply held conviction, but because he did not "want to abandon [his] comrades."[13]

During the first three months in the life of the Republic – the whole period of Lamartine's ascendancy – Proudhon remained on the sidelines, an observer and not an actor. He fulminated in his corner about the "sham" and the "humbuggery" of it all – about a "revolution fabricated from memories," about France as a "nation of play-actors,"[14] about his exclusion by "the chatterers of democracy and socialism,"[15] and about the "detestable politics" of the Provisional Government which he accused of having compromised not only the tranquillity of the country but also "the future of the revolution."[16] From the beginning, Proudhon was particularly critical of the National Workshops which he described as "an experiment in so-called organization" in which nobody believed and which was tolerated by members of the Provisional Government either as a stop-gap measure or as a means of compromising the very idea of social reform.[17] Nor did he share the enthusiasm of democrats for universal (male) suffrage. He believed (correctly as it turned out) that illiterate and uneducated peasants would vote, for the most part, to return traditional elites. Thus his response to the decree of March 5

---

[12] Proudhon to Maurice, February 25, 1848, *Correspondance*, II, 281.
[13] *Carnets* II, 369, and *Carnets*, III, 10 (February 24, 1848).
[14] *Carnets*, III, 12 (February 24, 1848).   [15] *Carnets*, III, 39 (late March).
[16] *Lettre aux électeurs du Doubs* in *Correspondance*, II, 303.   [17] Ibid.

establishing universal suffrage was to write prophetically that "universal suffrage is counter-revolution."[18]

Proudhon did participate in the club movement. On March 21, he was inducted into the Club central révolutionnaire along with Barbès, Pilhès, Arago, Thoré and Sobrier. The next evening he dined with several club members, commenting wryly in his diary: "We agreed that Louis Blanc doesn't know what he is doing, but then we conceded that we don't know any more than he does."[19] Proudhon also attended meetings of the Club de la Révolution and the Club des Clubs. But he was depressed by the shallowness and the zealotry of what passed for discussion. On April 8, after an evening at the Club des Clubs, he inveighed in his *carnets* against the "idiocy" of the meeting. "It's laughable, it's pathetic, it's frightening ... They ranted, raved and floundered with an earnestness, a vivacity and an enthusiasm that makes one worry about the sanity of the public mind."[20] Two days later he wrote a friend, "Right now fanaticism exceeds all limits. I have witnessed a meeting of 500 people decide in five minutes and with thunderous applause the most difficult questions of political economy ... I have heard the craziest motions adopted with enthusiasm, and childish, ridiculous propositions given unanimous support." And he stressed the revolutionary orators' total lack of understanding of the challenge that confronted them. "The February Revolution is an economic revolution, that is to say the most commonplace, the most bourgeois of revolutions. To organize credit and circulation and to increase production does not require the temperament of '92."[21]

Proudhon's two major preoccupations between February and June were his collaboration on a daily newspaper and the writing of a long article criticizing the leaders of the new republic and indicating the means by which they might come seriously to grips with the social question. The newspaper, which began to appear regularly on April 1, was called *Le Représentant du Peuple. Journal des travailleurs*, and the first page was adorned with mottoes recalling abbé Sieyès' pamphlet, *What is the Third Estate?*:

> What is the producer? Nothing. What should he be? Everything.
> What is the capitalist? Everything. What should he be? Nothing.

The paper's founder was the writer Jules Viard, and the other collaborators were modest individuals: the printer Louis Vasbenter and the

---

[18] "La Réaction," *Le Représentant du Peuple*, 29 April 1848 in *Mélanges*, I, 1.
[19] *Carnets*, III, 36 (March 22).   [20] *Carnets*, III, 47–48 (April 8, evening).
[21] Proudhon to Gaudon, April 10, 1848, *Correspondance*, VI, 370–372.

retired *bonnetier* Charles Fauvéty. Proudhon's first articles focused on the ineptitude of the Provisional Government – its failure to honour its promise to guarantee the right to work and the "bad faith" and "absence of principles" evident in the attempt to postpone the date of the elections for the National Assembly once it became evident that the big winners were likely to be royalists.

The article, "Solution du problème social," appeared in *Le Représentant du peuple* in three installments between March 22 and April 7.[22] In the first two installments Proudhon attempted to explain the rapid, and largely unforeseen, collapse of the July Monarchy, offered criticism of the social and economic policies of the Provisional Government, and attacked political democracy as "exclusive and doctrinaire," "retrograde and contradictory," and "impotent to resolve the social question."[23] In particular, he criticized the National Workshops and argued against the state socialism of Louis Blanc, lumping together Jacobins and state socialists as perpetuating the regime of authority inherited from the past. He concluded his second article with a sketch of an ideal republic:

In the Republic every citizen, doing what he wants and only what he wants, participates directly in legislation and government, just as he participates in the production and circulation of wealth. There every citizen is king because he has the plenitude of power: he reigns and governs. The Republic is a positive anarchy.[24]

In his third installment, Proudhon attempted to write a program for the Second Republic. Confronted by a revolution which didn't know where it was going, he sought to give it direction, first by outlining in broad terms what a genuine republic might look like, and then by describing the major reform that he hoped to introduce: a system of free credit which would liberate workers and small property owners from dependence on existing authorities.

For traditional republicans the creation of a new political order was the key to social and economic change, but Proudhon insisted on the primacy of the economic sphere. "Social reform will never come out of political reform," he wrote. "It is political reform which on the contrary

[22] The first two installments were also published separately as a brochure: *Solution du problème social par P.-J. Proudhon* (Paris, 1848). The third part, entitled *Organisation du crédit et de la circulation*, appears with the first two parts in other contemporary brochures also entitled *Solution du problème social*.

[23] P.-J. Proudhon, *Solution du problème social* (Paris, 1868), 50, 64, 68. This edition, which will be cited, includes all three parts of the work and constitutes Volume VI of *Oeuvres complètes de P.-J. Proudhon*, 26 vols. (Paris, 1868–1876).

[24] *Solution du problème social*, 87.

must come out of social reform."[25] The social problem, as Proudhon understood it, was the problem of the material and mental impoverishment of the working class, and the root cause of this impoverishment was an economic system that made the vast majority of producers dependent on a small class of possessors of capital. What was needed was to free the producers from the grip of the traditional financial elites. The way to do this was to give the producers access to capital through the creation of a People's Bank or Bank of Exchange that would provide credit and loans for a very small charge, thus liberating workers and small property owners and enabling them to enjoy the whole product of their labour without part of it being taken by the capitalist.[26] The bank would issue "exchange notes" that would circulate as money. These notes would represent commodities already produced and delivered (or promised for delivery) by members of the bank. The notes would eventually be circulated universally and exchanged like cash in commercial transactions.[27]

Control of the Bank of Exchange would be exercised by a General Assembly composed of delegates elected by workers in all branches of production and public service. Proudhon, who had no faith in representative government as traditionally understood, insisted that, unlike representatives, his delegates would be subject to an "imperative mandate" and "permanent revocability." The General Assembly in turn would elect a Board of Directors to run the bank and a Council of Surveillance to oversee the directors. As the Bank grew and attracted more members, it would become "the true representative of the people." This was because the Bank of Exchange represented the real economic interests of its individual members whereas a representative assembly only represented a fictitious "general interest" which disguised the special interests of particular groups. The first version of this proposal appeared in print on April 7. The next day Proudhon sent a copy to Louis Blanc with a long letter urging the Provisional Government to put its resources behind the creation of a Bank of Exchange.[28] In the absence of a reply, Proudhon eventually decided to create his Bank through a direct appeal to the public. But his immediate concern in April 1848 was with the approaching elections.

[25] Ibid, 48.
[26] Proudhon's supporters and his critics often spoke of him as promising interest-free loans to workers. In fact his scheme called for a small charge by the bank (in the form of a discount on the notes issued) to cover administrative costs.
[27] Hoffman, *Revolutionary Justice* (Urbana, 1972), 125. For an excellent full study see Olivier Chaïbi, *Proudhon et la banque du peuple (1848–1849)* (Paris, 2010).
[28] Proudhon to Louis Blanc, April 8, 1848, *Correspondance*, II, 305–308.

General elections for the Constituent Assembly were held on April 23, and despite his oft-expressed skepticism concerning parliamentary democracy and universal suffrage, Proudhon presented himself as a candidate. The new election law permitted candidates to stand in several circumscriptions, and Proudhon allowed his candidacy to go forward not only in Paris but also in Besançon, Lyon and Lille. He made a particular effort in Besançon, his birthplace, and tried to reassure voters there that his positions on property and religion were more moderate than the press claimed. In a letter to a political ally in Franche-Comté, he recalled that his family was "known for its piety, its civic-mindedness, its respect for Franc-Comtoise traditions." Then he made a candid admission: "It is in my nature always to contradict authority. I have in general great respect for clergymen and public functionaries; but I have always been rebellious toward the Church and toward government."[29] On April 3 he sent an open letter to the electors of the Doubs deploring the "street comedy" in Paris and arguing that the country could only be saved by an "integral reform of our economic institutions" in which the "classe travailleuse" and the "classe bourgeoise" would have to collaborate.[30]

This was a good try. But Proudhon was not yet well known. Furthermore, he noted in his *carnets*, the curés determined the outcome of elections in Franche-Comté, and in Paris everything depended on "rivalries and jealousies" among the radical leaders. In the end, he was not surprised to lose badly in the provinces. But after the election he commented bitterly about the silence of the Parisian press and the members of the Provisional Government concerning his candidacy.[31]

During the next few weeks, Proudhon became much better known. On election day, he published a powerful article entitled "How Revolutions are Lost" criticizing the Provisional Government and predicting an imminent catastrophe. On April 29, the day election results were published, he asserted that "the social question has been postponed" and that the bourgeoisie would "determine," as it had in the past, the condition of workers. He laid the blame for this on "the men of February" and especially on Louis Blanc and Ledru-Rollin. The following day he denounced "the mystification of universal suffrage." And on May 4 he observed that France was no longer on the verge of civil war but that civil war had already begun. It was no longer feared as a great evil; it was accepted as a necessity. "In the countryside as in town people are making gunpowder and bullets; they are readying arms. The leaders are giving

---

[29] Proudhon to Abram, March 31 (not May 31), 1848, *Correspondance*, II, 333.
[30] "Aux électeurs du Doubs," April 3, 1848, *Correspondance*, II, 299–304.
[31] *Carnets*, III, 50, 54 (April 17 and April 29, 1848).

instructions and issuing their manifestos. You hear people everywhere uttering these fatal words: 'Il faut en finir!'" What was the cause of this discord? It was the elections which had inspired, and deceived, great hopes. "Universal suffrage," concluded Proudhon, "has lied to the People."[32]

These articles were widely read – especially in the working-class quarters of Paris. Louis Blanc later wrote that copies of the *Représentant du peuple* were "snatched up" by workers in the faubourgs, and Alfred Darimon described each of Proudhon's articles as a "trumpet call" capable of "awakening the dullest mind."[33] In just a few weeks Proudhon acquired a following that he had never previously possessed. Proof of this came during the *journée* of May 15. This was an abortive insurrection that Proudhon had opposed. But when the insurgents began to draw up lists of members of a new revolutionary government, Proudhon's name regularly appeared alongside those of Barbès, Louis Blanc, Ledru-Rollin and Pierre Leroux. Three weeks later, when by-elections were held to fill eleven still-vacant seats in the Constituent Assembly, there was widespread support for Proudhon in Paris.

The list of candidates for the by-elections of June 4 was strong – it included Victor Hugo, Adolphe Thiers, Louis-Napoleon Bonaparte, General Charngarnier, as well as radicals like Pierre Leroux and Marc Caussidière – and Proudhon's campaign, such as it was, was inept. His "program," spelled out in three numbers of *Le Représentant du peuple*, consisted largely of a series of proposed decrees, not all of them consistent with each other. Nonetheless, he was elected, receiving 77,000 votes (just 9,000 fewer than Hugo). Why? Clearly his journalism had struck a chord. On June 10, Proudhon entered the National Assembly and took his place at the rear of the hall among the representatives of the Left. Barely two weeks later civil war broke out on the streets of Paris.

Given Proudhon's repeated denunciations of "the mystification of universal suffrage," one wonders why he was willing to stand for election. Surely one aim was to win support for the People's Bank. Perhaps

---

[32] "Comment les Révolutions se perdent," *Représentant du peuple*, 22, April 23, 1848; "La Réaction," *Représentant du peuple*, 28, April 29, 1848; "La Mystification du suffrage universel," *Représentant du peuple*, 29, April 30, 1848; "Aux patriotes," 33, *Représentant du peuple*, May 4, 1848: all in *Mélanges*, I, 7–22; Pierre Haubtmann, *Pierre-Joseph Proudhon. Sa Vie et sa pensée (1809–1849)* (Paris, 1982), 864–867.
[33] Alfred Darimon, *A Travers une révolution (1847–1855)*, (Paris, 1884), 38; Haubtmann, *Proudhon (1809–1849)*, 871–872. The press run of the *Représentant du peuple*, which was between 4,000–5000 copies at the end of April rose to 8,000 by mid-May. See Proudhon to Victor Gauthier, April 30 and May 13, 1848, *Correspondance inédite de P.-J. Proudhon*, III (Tokyo, 1997) in Edward Castleton, unpublished paper, "Révolutionnaire de la veille, Révolution du lendemain: Proudhon et les ironies du futur passé de 1848," 99.

Proudhon believed his influence as a journalist would be increased if he could sign himself "Représentant du Peuple." It's also likely that his success as a journalist inspired him to stand for election. As he wrote later, "Journalism made me a representative."[34] At any rate, from the start, his experience as a legislator disappointed him. He conscientiously carried out his duties, attending meetings of the Finance Committee to which he was assigned. But he found the work isolating. "As soon as I set foot in the parliamentary Sinaï," he wrote in the *Confessions*, "I ceased to be in touch with the masses."[35] By his own account, he was so absorbed in the work of the Assembly that the June insurrection took him by surprise.

In the National Assembly, the first response to the news that barricades were rising was confusion and, in some cases, panic. Rumours of all sorts circulated. Some believed that the revolt had been fomented by foreign money; others saw in it the machinations of the agents of Louis-Napoleon Bonaparte; still others believed that Paris had been taken over by a secret organization of bandits seeking to pillage the wealthy quarters of the capital. In his *cahiers* Proudhon acknowledged the power of such myths over his own thinking; and he later told Darimon that he initially believed that "the movement was directed by political factions and financed by foreigners."[36] So absorbed was he in the work of the Assembly that he had "ceased to see things clearly." In his *Confessions*, Proudhon was blunter. Noting that the President of the Assembly, Antoine Sénard had accused him of cowardice during the June Days, Proudhon replied: "No, Monsieur Sénard, I did not behave like a coward. I've just been an imbecile like you."[37]

For three days, as Paris exploded, Proudhon walked all over the city, observing the struggle in the streets, trying to talk with combatants on both sides. More than once he was asked to identify himself to government troops and members of the National Guard. When he did so, he found that the mere mention of his name was enough to shock people. Yet he spent as much time fraternizing with the forces of order as with the insurgents. He later recalled that when General Négrier was shot, he rushed to the general's aid and helped carry the dying man to a makeshift hospital at the Hôtel de Ville. Overwhelmed by emotion, he threw himself into the arms of a young aide de camp and both burst into tears.[38]

---

[34] Proudhon to Bergmann, March 5, 1854, *Correspondance*, VI, 6.   [35] *Confessions*, 169.
[36] Darimon, *A Travers une révolution*, 53.   [37] *Confessions*, 169.
[38] Ibid, 205 and Darimon, *A Travers une revolution*, 54. See also Haubtmann, *Proudhon (1809-1849)*, 901–902; and Edouard Dolléans and Jules L. Puech, *Proudhon et la Révolution de 1848* (Paris, 1948), 55.

Proudhon spent the morning of June 26 in the Faubourg Saint-
Antoine between the Place de la Bastille and the Hôtel de Ville:

At ten o'clock in the morning I was on the Place de la Bastille and the cannonade
started again. I witnessed the terrible and sublime spectacle. Soon a man
appeared holding a sign of peace. The barricade was taken. I traversed the rue
Saint-Antoine at eleven o'clock, asking questions of the bourgeois. They told me
that no more than four or five hundred insurgents remained behind the
barricades.[39]

It was all over by noon. Two days later the National Assembly voted on a
resolution thanking all who had helped crush the insurrection. The text
included a denunciation of "savage doctrines in which family is just a
word and property is theft." At these words, recalled a witness, "the
whole auditorium turned to look at Proudhon."[40] When the whole
Assembly rose to express its approval, Proudhon alone remained seated.

That day Proudhon wrote in his diary that mass arrests and summary
executions were still going on at the Conciergerie and the Hôtel de Ville.
"They are shooting wounded and disarmed prisoners. They are spreading the most atrocious lies about the insurgents in order to provoke
vengeance against them. Citizens are arrested in their homes. Then they
are taken to the Pont d'Arcole and shot and thrown into the river."[41] The
same day, writing an old friend, Proudhon observed that the rebels had
given up but were not defeated. "I walked wherever the fighting took
place," he went on, "thanks to my insignia as a representative." Several
times he encountered members of the National Guard; and when he
identified himself they were shocked and even frightened. There had
been "thousands" of arrests:

A decree voted by the National Assembly this evening turns [suspected
insurgents] over to a Military Commission and threatens them with deportation
across the ocean. The triumphant bourgeois are as fierce as tigers. The provinces
rush in, imagining that a flood of convicts poses a real threat to family and
property. The newspapers lie about the situation, spreading calumny and
deceiving the country.[42]

Tocqueville was to celebrate this movement in his *Souvenirs* of 1848: men
of all classes had buried their differences and hastened to Paris "to deliver

[39] Déposition de Proudhon devant la Commission d'Enquête, reprinted in *Journal des
débats*, August 19, 1846, 6 in Haubtmann, *Proudhon (1809–1849)*, 899.
[40] *Ere nouvelle* (June 29, 1848) in Haubtmann, *Proudhon (1809–1849)*, 897. In fact, there
was no more fervent left-wing supporter of the family than Proudhon.
[41] *Carnets*, III, 66–67 (June 28).
[42] Proudhon to Dr. Maguet, June 28, 1848, *Correspondance*, II, 337–338.

the nation from oppression by the workers."[43] Proudhon saw something different: the descent on Paris of trainloads of "ferocious" provincials egged on by the mendacious reports of right-wing journalists.

Speaking for the Paris Artisans

Proudhon had long been opposed to violent revolution, and he did not support the June insurrection. He had also been outspoken in his criticism of Louis Blanc, the Luxembourg Commission, and the Provisional Government, which may explain why the *Représentant du peuple* was not shut down following the June Days, as were virtually all the other radical dailies. In any case, Proudhon seized the opportunity to become a spokesman for the insurgents and for all the poor of Paris, whom he regarded as having been betrayed by the National Assembly. In a letter to Charles Fauvéty, the political director of the *Représentant du Peuple*, he called for pity: "Please, Monsieur, don't pour salt and vinegar on open wounds. Don't drive to despair confused people who have been deplorably deluded but who after all are not criminal." In the same letter, he defended the insurgents against the "calumnies of the reaction" and repeated the view that the workers were not to be blamed. "There are no culprits," he wrote, "there are only victims." But quickly his tone became more aggressive. The cause of the June insurrection, he wrote, was the poverty to which 100,000 households had been reduced in Paris alone, by unemployment. "When the French worker asks for work and you offer him charity instead, he rebels and shoots at you." English, German and Spanish workers might accept charity, he added, "but I prefer the French worker, and I take pride in belonging to a proud race which refuses to accept dishonour."[44]

Proudhon then made a specific proposal. On July 8, a week before the day on which Parisian renters were required to clear all outstanding debts to their landlords, he wrote a long article in the *Représentant du peuple*. calling for a moratorium on the payment of renters' debts.[45] This attack on a practice deemed almost sacred was seen as another Proudhonian attack on property. It got the publication of the journal suspended. Proudhon then reformulated his proposal as a legislative bill and submitted it to the National Assembly's Finance Committee. The proposal was clumsily written and actually more a statement of principles than a *projet*

[43] Tocqueville, *Souvenirs*, *OC*, XII, 178.
[44] Letter to the editor, *Représentant du peuple*, 94, July 6, 1848 in *Mélanges*, I, 90–92
[45] "Le 15 juillet," *Représentant du peuple*, 96, July 8, 1848.

de loi. It might have died a natural death in committee had not Adolphe Thiers seen in it a way of reviving his own flagging political fortunes. By calling for a full discussion of Proudhon's proposal, Thiers, who had been marginalized after February, believed he could play the role of the defender of society against the menace of "socialism" as personified by Proudhon (see Figure 7.2). He could indeed. In the course of two full days' discussion within the committee (July 15 and 17), Thiers eviscerated Proudhon. On July 26, in presenting a derisive report on Proudhon's bill to the whole National Assembly, Thiers seized upon the opportunity to discredit not merely Proudhon and "the socialists" but the very concept of a right to work. The sole right that counts, he asserted, is the right to the ownership of property, and the right to work should never be allowed to call it into question.[46]

Proudhon had the right to reply, and he did so five days later. His speech of July 31 was at once a defence of his proposal, a somewhat muddled dissertation on taxes and credit, a cogent critique of universal suffrage and representative government, and a forceful attack on the Provisional Government for its failure to make good on its commitment to guarantee the right to work. Proudhon was a halting speaker with a strong franc-comtois accent, and the initial response to his speech – especially to his economic dissertation – was laughter and ironic comment. When Proudhon tried to explain what he had really meant by the statement "Property is theft," he only left his audience confused. And when he "gave notice" to property owners concerning their obligation to support the work of the revolution, a representative paraphrased him ironically: "That's very clear: 'Your money or your life.'" But when Proudhon began to employ the language of class war, the laughter changed into anger and indignation:

Citizen Proudhon: When I used the pronouns "you" and "us," it is evident that I was then identifying myself with the "proletariat," and identifying you with the "bourgeois *class.*" *[New exclamations.]*
Citizen Saint-Priest: It's social war!
A member: It's June 23 at the rostrum!

When, near the end of his speech, Proudhon was accused of sedition, he replied to an audience that was no longer laughing: "Don't speak here of

---

[46] Thomas Bouchet, *Un Jeudi à l'Assemblée. Politiques du discours et droit au travail dans la France de 1848* (Montréal, 2007), 135; and Adolphe Thiers, "Rapport ... sur la proposition du citoyen Proudhon relative à la reorganization de l'impôt et du crédit," July 26, 1848 in Proudhon, *Deuxième Mémoire sur la Propriété*, Michel Augé-Laribé (ed.) (Paris, 1938), 347–358.

ACTUALITÉS.

Le Père Molé apportant des étrennes au Petit Thiers.

Figure 7.2 Proudhon as a scapegoat for the Party of Order: "Father Molé bringing a New Year's present to Little Thiers." Lithograph by Daumier in *Le Charivari*, January 15, 1850. Author's collection. Photograph: Mark Traugott

sedition. The seditious are those who, having no other right than force, refuse to recognize the rights of others."[47]

"Noisy and prolonged agitation" was, according to *Le Moniteur*, the response of the Assembly to Proudhon's speech. This is not hard to believe. He had offended everyone – the right with his attacks on property, and the left by blaming radicals for having made promises they could not keep. After an hour of noisy debate, the Assembly voted to condemn Proudhon for "an odious attack on the principles of public morality" and for having "slandered" the February Revolution. [48] The resolution passed by a vote of 691:2. The two were Proudhon himself, and the Lyonnais *canut* Louis Greppo.

Proudhon's speech of July 31 was widely regarded as a disaster. For the bourgeoisie, it confirmed Proudhon's reputation as a menace to society. *L'Illustration* denounced the speech as a "disgusting appeal to the lowest and most brutal" appetites.[49] A popular print depicted Thiers as St. Michael defeating the dragon, and even the majority of socialists and democrats regarded the speech as at best an embarrassment. When the constitution of the Second Republic failed to include a specific endorsement of the right to work, Ferdinand Flocon, the same journalist whose proclamation Proudhon had set in type on February 24, told Proudhon bluntly: "It is you who have killed the right to work." And in her *Histoire de la Révolution de 1848* Marie d'Agoult could write that Thiers' attack on Proudhon "was judged by public opinion as a final and definitive victory of the Party of Order over the revolution."[50]

Still, Proudhon was not universally regarded as the loser in his duel with Thiers. The conservative Catholic Montalembert wrote in his diary that Proudhon exposed "with unlimited audacity and pitiless logic, and even with remarkable aptness of expression, the theory of the destruction of property."[51] Several weeks later when news of the speech reached Russia, the radical Nikolai Speshnev (later to serve Dostoevsky as a model for Stavrogin in *Demons*) wrote excitedly: "This shakes the foundation of the social order."[52] Other Russian radicals found Proudhon's

[47] Daniel Halévy, Introduction to his edition of Proudhon, *Confessions*, 32–35. For the whole speech see Pierre-Joseph Proudhon, "Discours prononcé à l'Assemblée nationale le 31 juillet 1848" in Proudhon, *Deuxième mémoire sur la propriété*, 359–406.
[48] Bouchet, *Un Jeudi à l'Assemblée*, 35. See also Dolléans and Puech, *Proudhon et 1848*, 58n.
[49] *L'Illustration*, August 5, 1849.
[50] Flocon quoted in Proudhon, *Confessions*, 200 and Daniel Stern, *Histoire de la Révolution de 1848*, 3 vols. (Paris, 1850–1853), III, 292.
[51] Charles de Montalembert, *Journal intime inédit*, Louis LeGuillou and Nicole Roger-Taillade (eds.) (Paris, 2004), IV, 565.
[52] Speshnev, letters to his mother, August 5 and 9, 1848 old style, in J. H. Seddon, *The Petrashevtsy: A Study of the Russian Revolutionaries of 1848* (Manchester, 1985), 129.

speech inspiring. Bakunin wrote him later that "the speeches you gave at that time [after the June Days] were more than speeches, they were acts."[53] Long afterwards Alexander Herzen recalled admiringly the stolid, earnest Proudhon's challenge to the cynical roué Thiers:

Thiers, in rejecting Proudhon's financial scheme, made an insinuation about the moral depravity of the men who disseminated such doctrines. Proudhon mounted the tribune, and with his stooping figure and his menacing air of a stocky field-worker said to the smiling old creature: "Speak about finance, but not about morals ... If you persist, I shall not challenge you to a duel [but] to another sort of contest. Here from this tribune I shall tell the whole story of my life, fact by fact, and anyone may remind me if I forget or omit something. Then let my adversary tell the story of *his* life!"[54]

Herzen observed that the smile was wiped from "the old creature's" face, and he sat silent and scowling as every eye in the Assembly was turned on him.

Workers in the faubourgs Saint-Antoine and Saint-Jacques also admired Proudhon's courage in standing up to Thiers and the bourgeoisie. The day after his condemnation by the National Assembly Proudhon received a grateful letter from the Club de la Révolution thanking him for his "courageous and excellent" speech. "The pygmies who are howling around you," they wrote, will not prevent you from reaping the honours owed you by posterity.[55] The printed version of Proudhon's speech sold over 100,000 copies.[56] A month later, when *Le Peuple* replaced the *Représentant du peuple*, its circulation soared to 40,000. Even Karl Marx, who had become Proudhon's enemy, later described the speech as "an act of lofty manliness." In his conflict with Thiers, Marx wrote, "Proudhon took on the proportions of an antediluvian colossus." But Marx could not resist adding that the speech also displayed how little Proudhon understood about economics.[57]

---

[53] Bakunin to Proudhon, December 12, 1848, *La Gazette Druot*, vente du 21 février, 2013: available online at www.auction.fr/fr/lot/Mikhail-bakounine-1814-1876-3961999 (Accessed May 17, 2020).

[54] Alexander Herzen, *My Past and Thoughts. The Memoirs of Alexander Herzen*, 4 vols. (New York, 1968), II, 810. Translation revised.

[55] Members of the bureau of the Club de la Révolution to Proudhon, August 1, 1849, Anne-Sophie Chambost, *Proudhon, l'enfant terrible du socialism* (Paris, 2009), 107. On the visual campaign against Proudhon see Thierry Menuelle, *Le Charivari contre Proudhon* (Paris, 2006).

[56] Edward Castleton, "The Many Revolutions of Proudhon," in Douglas Moggach and Gareth Stedman Jones (eds.), *The 1848 Revolutions and European Political Thought* (Cambridge, 2018), 53.

[57] Marx, cited in Herzen, *Past and Thoughts*, II, 1017. Full citation in Russian edition: Alexander Herzen, *Sobranie sochinenii* (Moscow, 1956), X, 482. Marx, 1865 article in *Sozial-Demokrat*, in Haubtmann, 922 and 1051. See also the unsigned article (probably

This speech gave Proudhon a notoriety that no one on the Left had previously possessed. For some, he was a figure of fun, ridiculed in cartoons, in the press and on stage. For others, he was "l'homme terreur" – a man whose ideas threatened the very foundations of society. As such, he received anonymous letters threatening him with the wrath of God; pious women sent him relics and holy medals; prostitutes and convicts (or people claiming to be such) sent him obscene letters of congratulation. Petitions arrived at the National Assembly calling for his expulsion. The Spanish diplomat Donoso Cortés published an essay announcing gravely that Proudhon was possessed by a devil.[58] Not surprisingly, ladies came to the visitors' gallery of the National Assembly for the express purpose of catching a glimpse of this monster; and Proudhon commented that they sometimes seemed disappointed that he didn't actually have horns and claws.Proudhon rather enjoyed his new-found notoriety. He preferred bad publicity to none at all. And he was actually amused when, in November, a play opened in Paris poking fun at him. Called "Property is Theft, a socialist folly in three acts and seven tableaux," it portrayed Proudhon as a bespectacled serpent who tempted Adam and Eve and incited them to envy, revolt and evil.[59] He was less happy about death threats and about articles attributing to him views that he did not hold. But his general reaction to attacks was simply to persevere. He put it this way in a letter to a friend:

I live in the fire like a salamander, and from day to day I keep expecting to be burned. If I persist, it is because I believe that an important philosophical and social issue is at stake here and that audacity and brilliance are necessary to make the world aware of the question of labour and [the need for] the total revision of our institutions. The calumnies, the insults, the perfidy and persecution of our adversaries, are the soil out of which the new seed will germinate and grow ... For this reason, you will excuse my sad celebrity.[60]

Eighteen months after the June Days and Proudhon's duel with Adolphe Thiers, Louis Blanc wrote an article from exile warning French democrats against "the dangerous doctrines of Citizen Proudhon." But before embarking on his critique, Blanc paid tribute to Proudhon's conduct in the aftermath of the June Days:

After June Proudhon was admirable. Decent people were appalled; calumny strode with its head high and its feet in blood; truth kept quiet and hid itself. The Republic seemed only to have enough strength to put on its mourning

by Marx) in the *Neue Rheinische Zeitung*, 66, August 5, 1848; "Proudhon's Speech against Thiers," MECW 7:321–324.
[58] Proudhon, *Confessions*, 203n.   [59] Darimon, *A Travers une révolution*, 123–127.
[60] To M. Tourneux, 1848 (n.d.), *Correspondance*, II, 355–356.

clothes. Proudhon, with a talent only equalled by his courage, relit the flame of generous sentiments ...He put imposture to shame, he made his journal a barrier to reaction ... He was, I repeat, admirable.[61]

There was no love lost between Blanc and Proudhon, and Proudhon had often voiced his distaste for Blanc's Jacobin socialism. But Blanc was still generous enough to give public recognition to Proudhon's courage and to the fact that Proudhon had found an audience in the artisans and skilled workers of the faubourgs who "snatched up" the "intrepid articles that he issued each morning ... with an ardour mixed with gratitude." Proudhon may have been isolated in the National Assembly, but he was the hero of the faubourgs Saint-Antoine and Saint-Jacques.

The high point of Proudhon's identification with the Paris artisans came in mid-August when he published a series of attacks on the government. On August 7 Cavaignac allowed Proudhon's paper to renew publication. Three days later he published an article denouncing measures taken against the liberty of clubs and of the press – notably the requirement that the publishers of all daily papers post caution money of 24,000 francs. Lamennais, who was forced by this requirement to shut down his paper *Le Peuple constituent*, responded with a famous article: "Today you need gold, a lot of gold, to have the right to speak. We are not rich enough. *Silence au pauvre!*"[62] Proudhon's response was to insist on the hypocrisy of government policy. "Deceit, bad faith, farce in the law! That's what democracy was waiting to teach us ... 24,000 francs! That is our criterion of genius, virtue and patriotism!"[63] The next day Proudhon published a long article entitled "Les Malthusiens." "The unpardonable crime of the French Revolution," he wrote, "was to have protested against the Malthusian principles of the government, according to which mass poverty was a necessary consequence of economic development. Proudhon was proud of this essay, which he described as a "thunderbolt" that had "great impact." In fact, the 20,000 published copies of that issue quickly sold out, as did a much larger number of copies of a separate printing.[64]

On August 14 and 16, Proudhon published two more articles attacking the moderate republicans of the daily newspaper *Le National.* The real

---

[61] Louis Blanc, *Le Nouveau monde*, 6 (December 15, 1849) in Chambost, *Proudhon, l'enfant terrible*, 103 and Haubtmann, *Proudhon (1809–1849)*, 1051.

[62] Lamennais, *Le Peuple constituent*, 134, July 11, 1848.

[63] Proudhon, *Représentant du peuple*, August 10, 1848 in *Mélanges* I, 103–104. See Haubtmann, *Proudhon (1809–1849)*, 43.

[64] Proudhon, "Les Malthusiens," *Représentant du peuple*, 98, August 11, 1848 in *Mélanges*, I, 105–110; Haubtmann, *Proudhon (1809–1849)*, 945 gives the figure of 300,000 copies for the press-run of the offprint.

"enemies of society and of the Republic," he wrote, were not the socialists but rather the "gens du *National*" who refused to recognize the
importance of the social question and were now selling out to the
monarchists. In the next few days, Proudhon published three more
slashing attacks on the government in the *Représentant du peuple*, only to
see the paper seized each time, first for attacking property, then for
stirring up class hatred, and finally for an article denouncing the "idiocy"
of the official government report on the June insurrection. On August 21,
Proudhon wrote prophetically of the threats to the continued existence of
republican government in France: "We are no longer living in a republic;
we are in a period of transition. FRANCE WANTS A KING. It doesn't
matter if it is Henri V, Bonaparte, or Joinville, provided the chosen
individual swears on the Bible to exterminate the socialists, the last
Christians."[65] That day the government shut down the *Représentant du
peuple* for good.

Within two weeks Proudhon managed to scrape together enough
money to issue the prospectus of a second journal called simply *Le
Peuple*. Many of the staff members of this "Journal de la République
démocratique et sociale" were hold-overs from its predecessor, but now
Proudhon was entirely in control. Due to the difficulty of raising caution-
money, *Le Peuple* was not published until November 1, and it only began
to appear as a daily paper on November 23.[66] But with a press run of
40,000 copies, it quickly took its place as the leading radical journal.
Prominent socialists – notably Cabet and Thoré – and several
Montagnards initially tried to form a united front with Proudhon; and
in his prospectus Proudhon himself referred to the new journal as "the
collective organ of the extreme left of the National Assembly."[67] But his
good relations with other radicals did not last long. There were personal
conflicts and even a duel between Proudhon and the Montagnard Félix
Pyat. And there were arguments about the right to work, which
Proudhon identified with the organization of interest-free credit; about
Proudhon's refusal to follow the Montagnard line in the National
Assembly; and, above all, about the presidential elections in which the
Montagnards supported Ledru-Rollin, whom Proudhon detested, while
he wavered between the socialist Raspail and Cavaignac, whom the
Montagnards never ceased calling "the butcher of June."

---

[65] *Représentant du peuple*, 106, August 21, 1848 in *Mélanges* I, 127.
[66] The prospectus or "Manifeste du Peuple" appeared on September 2, 1848, but it was
only on November 23 that *Le Peuple* became a daily paper. The reason for the delay was
that caution money had to be raised – 12,000 francs for a weekly and 24,000 francs for a
daily paper. Haubtmann, *Proudhon (1809–1849)*, 950–951.
[67] Proudhon to Abram, September 23, 1848, *Correspondance*, II, 347.

Although Proudhon was one of only thirty representatives voting against the constitution, he had much to say about the presidential election in *Le Peuple*. From the start, he was hostile both to the candidacy of Louis-Napoleon Bonaparte and to the institution of the presidency. On November 8 he published a long article arguing that in practice there was little difference in France between a king and a president, especially a popularly elected president. France was "monarchical to the core," and the popular election of a president would only serve to excite the French "craving for monarchy." And Louis-Napoleon, who possessed a name recognized in all of France, was well-positioned to take advantage of this craving. So Proudhon called on him ironically to "take control of this race of Tartuffes" and sycophants. "They say that you are only a moron, an adventurer, a madman ... Well, I tell you, you're just the man we need ... Come on, renegades of every reign are waiting for you, ready to deliver their consciences and their wives to you ... The Bonapartes' name needed a bit more glory. Come bring an end to our discord by taking our liberties!"[68]

Despite these sardonic expressions of contempt for the French, Proudhon was surprised by the magnitude of Louis Napoleon's victory. Until the end, he believed that Cavaignac had a chance; and in endorsing Raspail, who had no chance of winning, he was tacitly supporting Cavaignac.[69] Reflecting on the results, he conceded that Louis-Napoleon owed his victory not only to the peasantry but also to the detestation of Cavaignac by urban workers all over France. After the election, Proudhon tried to put a good face on things by asserting that in order to hold power Louis-Napoleon would eventually have to move to the left: "Bonaparte will be a republican, a democratic republican and socialist, or else, like Louis Philippe, Lamartine and Cavaignac, he will fall under ridicule and scorn ... A socialist or a traitor, there's no middle way for him."[70] After December 2, 1851, Proudhon would work out this argument in detail in *La Révolution sociale démontrée par le coup d'état*. But, for the time being, he had to live with the fact that Louis-Napoleon was "the president of the reaction."[71]

Louis-Napoleon's first act as President of the Republic was to form a ministry which did not include a single republican. Its leader was the Orleanist Odilon Barrot, and its most prominent figure was the legitimist

---

[68] "La Présidence," *Le Peuple*, 3, November 8, 1848. Reprinted in *Idées Revolutionnaires*, 159–182.

[69] Haubtmann, *Proudhon (1809–1849)*, 1028.

[70] *Le Peuple*, December 15, 1848 in Haubtmann, *Proudhon (1809–1849)*, 1029.

[71] "Louis-Napoleon Bonaparte," *Le Peuple*, 31, December 18, 1848 in Haubtmann, *Proudhon (1809–1849)*, 1029.

Count Alfred de Falloux. Proudhon recognized immediately that a struggle was bound to develop between Louis-Napoleon, whose imperial ambitions were never far below the surface, and the National Assembly, which had drafted the constitution and "founded the democratic republic." Although Proudhon himself had voted against the constitution, he now saw it as the only real barrier to counter-revolution and to the eventual restoration of either monarchical or imperial rule. Thus at the end of January in three issues of the *Le Peuple* – each of which was seized by the government – he accused Louis-Napoleon of conspiring with the Jesuits, the absolutists, and "with all the monarchical coteries," to overthrow the Republic. His argument in a nutshell was that "all the forces, all the ideas, all the hopes of the Revolution are focused on the National Assembly" while "all the forces, ideas and hopes of the Counter-Revolution rest on the head of Louis Bonaparte."[72]

The first two of these articles served as the basis for the bringing of criminal charges against Proudhon, who was accused of inciting hatred of the government, the constitution, the citizens, and the President of the Republic. On February 14, the National Assembly voted to lift Proudhon's parliamentary immunity from prosecution. Six weeks later, on March 28, appearing before the Cour d'assises de la Seine, he was found guilty on all counts and sentenced to three years in prison and a fine of 3,000 francs. He had expected a guilty sentence, but he was stunned by its severity. In February, while the charges against Proudhon were working their way through the French legal system, he wrote a friend that he would willingly go to prison for six months, but if the sentence was much longer he would prefer to go into exile. This is what he initially did. On March 30, having appealed to his sentence, Proudhon, who remained free until his appeal was heard, got on a train for Belgium. Travelling under a false name, and changing trains twice, he entered Belgium on April 1. A week later, however, he was back in France, where he remained in hiding until June 5.

Why did Proudhon return to France? He later claimed that he needed to oversee the liquidation of his People's Bank, which had begun to fail even before charges were brought against him. But his own explanations were neither clear nor convincing. Clearly, another reason was that he

---

[72] "Le Président de la République est responsable," *Le Peuple*, 70, January 27, 1849. The other articles were "La Guerre," *Le Peuple*, 69, January 26, 1849, and "Première campagne de Louis Bonaparte," *Le Peuple*, 74, January 31, 1848. All three of these issues were seized, and the first two formed the basis of the criminal charges brought against Proudhon. Actually the first article, "La Guerre," was written in large part by one of Proudhon's colleagues, probably Alfred Darimon, but when charges were brought, Proudhon took full responsibility for it. See Darimon, *A Travers une révolution*, 130.

had decided to get married and arrangements had to be made. Be that as it may, Proudhon was recognized by a police agent and arrested on the evening of June 5, 1849. He was to spend the next three years in prison, during which period he was to marry, father a child, edit two more newspapers, and write three books. The most important of these books for our purposes is *Les Confessions d'un révolutionnaire*, which he began to write at the Conciergerie in July 1849, shortly after his imprisonment.

Confessions: Writing "With the Vehemence of an Oracle"

Proudhon wrote *Les Confessions d'un révolutionnaire* in a white heat. The book is over 300 pages long, and he wrote it in barely three months, finishing at Sainte-Pélagie in mid-October.[73] The writing is vigorous, argumentative, colloquial. He sometimes speaks with what he later described as "the vehemence of an oracle."[74] But there were enough lyric passages for Sainte-Beuve to call it the "plus beau" of Proudhon's works.[75] There are also picturesque images, burlesque passages, and flights of fancy worthy of Marx in *The Eighteenth Brumaire*. The book is full of pithy one-liners, many of them directed against democrats and socialists such as Louis Blanc (whom he derisively calls "Robespierre's monkey"). Like Tocqueville, Proudhon is hardest on his putative allies; and like Tocqueville, he mocks phrase-makers and their literary pretensions. But while Proudhon insists that "the stylist must give way to the man of action,"[76] he himself is always on the lookout for incisive formulas and well-turned phrases.

What was the public for which Proudhon was writing? The work is easy to read and Proudhon avoids philosophical language. He told Herzen that he would not find in the *Confessions* "the barbarian verve that German philosophy taught you," adding that he was "writing for the French."[77] Judging from the text, it is clear that no single audience is targeted. Sometimes Proudhon addresses the reader as an adversary to be cajoled or browbeaten into agreement. Sometimes he addresses his allies in the working class, warning the June insurgents about the traps set

---

[73] Proudhon spent most of his three years in prison in the relative comfort of the Sainte-Pélagie prison just outside the Jardin des Plantes in Paris. After the abortive uprising of June 13, 1849, he was transferred for three months to much less inviting quarters in the Conciergerie and at Doullens.

[74] Proudhon to Charles Edmond, July 9, 1854, *Correspondance*, VI, 39.

[75] C.-A. Sainte-Beuve, *Premiers lundis* (Paris, 1891), III, 218.

[76] "Ce que la Révolution doit à la littérature," *Le Représentant du Peuple*, 57 (May 28, 1848) in *Mélanges*, I 37–42.

[77] Herzen, *Past and Thoughts* II, 814; Raoul Labry, *Herzen et Proudhon* (Paris, 1928), 96.

for them.[78] At other moments his audience is clearly bourgeois; and at one point he speaks directly to Adolphe Thiers, mocking him for his failure "to finish off" socialism. Hyperbole and exaggeration are constants in Proudhon's writing, but for all the extravagance, and at times the verbal violence, of his language, his message is almost always moderate. He is, according to Daniel Halévy's pertinent expression, "a moderate who speaks in a loud voice" and whose "verbal vehemence is deployed on the surface of his thought."[79]

The *Confessions* is in some respects an enigmatic work, and the uncertainty starts with its title. It is not at all obvious what Proudhon is confessing and to whom. The book begins with an epigraph, a verse from *Deuteronomy* (32:40), that is more a proud affirmation than a confession of sin or error. "I lift up my hand to heaven, and say: 'I live forever,'" the Latin passage reads in the King James English translation. But Proudhon mysteriously translates it as: "I will lift up my hand to heaven, and I will say: "My IDEA is immortal." The book does include a chapter on "the idea" by which Proudhon was obsessed throughout the Second Republic: the idea that the solution of the social question lies in the creation of a People's Bank which would provide credit without interest to artisans, peasants, and small landowners. But apart from that, and a brief political "profession of faith," the book consists largely of a history of the first sixteen months of the Republic – a personal history during the course of which, Proudhon tells us, "I describe my dreams." But the history of his dreams – which Proudhon also calls his "socialist meditations" – is accompanied by the narration of his "political acts," and together they add up to "the history of a thinker caught up in spite of himself in the somnambulism of his nation." What does Proudhon mean by "the somnambulism of the nation"? This is probably a reference to what he calls "the governmental illusion" – the illusion that the introduction of a democratic government elected by universal (male) suffrage could possibly lead to radical social change. Proudhon who after all was elected to the National Assembly, seems to be confessing here that he himself was for a time caught up in the illusion that political change – the replacement of the July Monarchy by a democratic republic – could lead to significant social change.

Proudhon's history begins in a provocative manner with an ironic celebration of the July Monarchy in which he announces that his aim is to "avenge" Louis Philippe for all the abuse inflicted on him and to show

<hr />

[78] *Confessions*, 167.
[79] Halévy, Introduction to Proudhon, *Confessions*, 5; Daniel Halévy, *Le Mariage de Proudhon* (Paris, 1955), 270.

him to have been "the most active and intelligent instrument of the Revolution."[80] As Edward Castleton has shown in his fascinating study of Proudhon's unpublished manuscripts, this chapter is actually a reworking – with minimal changes – of a text written in the spring of 1847. In the earlier text, Proudhon's praise for the corruption of the July Monarchy was part of a broad critique of the movement for electoral reform that culminated with the banquet campaign and the February Revolution. In that manuscript, Proudhon pays tribute to Louis Philippe as "the hero of corruption" and "the Napoleon of our decadence" whose achievement was to discredit political and religious ideals and to confirm Boileau's dictum that "virtue without money is just a useless piece of furniture."[81]

But what does Proudhon's celebration of Louis Philippe and the July Monarchy mean in the post-revolutionary context? Its meaning is actually not all that different. Proudhon argues in the *Confessions* that the July Monarchy had "accomplished *the work of dissolution*" initiated by the French Revolution. "To the monarchical faith and the authority of the Church, the cult of interests and the religion of property were substituted."[82] Thus the mission of Louis Philippe – the mission that had been given him in 1830 – "was to make the bourgeois idea predominate" – to "spread the morality of interest, to inoculate all classes with political and religious indifference," and thus – "by the ruin of parties and by the depravation of consciences" – to "lay the foundations of a new society."[83]

For Proudhon the revolution of 1848 was "the workers' revolution"; the Provisional Government was "the workers' government"; and "the birth certificate of the Republic" was the decree guaranteeing the right to work.[84] But this leads Proudhon to pose a series of questions. "What is a workers' *government*? Can labour govern or be governed? What do labour and power have in common?" Proudhon claims that these are new questions and that they have no easy answer. The reality is that "the people" could not conceive of exercising power on their own. Thus, when power "fell into their laborious hands," they immediately returned it to a certain number of respectable individuals who were charged by them to found a Republic and to resolve, along with the political problem, the social problem, the problem of the proletariat." "We will give you three months," said the people. "We will put three months of poverty

---

[80] *Confessions*, 97.
[81] Edward Castleton, "Révolutionnaire de la veille, Révolution du lendemain: Proudhon et les ironies du futur passé de 1848," unpublished paper, esp. pp. 6–7, 23–24. See also Castleton's earlier unpublished paper "Aux origines de l'ontologie sociale proudhonienne: L'apport des manuscrits inédits."
[82] *Confessions*, 96.   [83] Ibid, 99.   [84] Ibid, 108.

in the service of the Republic." For Proudhon, this cry was "sublime in its naïveté." "Antiquity and the Revolution of '92 offered nothing to compare with this cry wrenched from the guts of the people of February."[85]

In fact, the Provisional Government, according to Proudhon, was a "government without an idea" or a common goal. "It was a mixture of conservatives, doctrinaires, Jacobins and socialists, each speaking his own language,"[86] and it did nothing during its three months in power. Why? For Proudhon the answer is simple. The reason for the inaction of the Provisional Government is that they *were* a government. In times of revolution, the first and last concern of governments is to maintain their own power. Initiative is repugnant to them. For eighteen years democrats and socialists had been repeating the same mantra: "Social revolution is the goal; political revolution is the means." But after February, writes Proudhon, they should have realized a truth that even Adolphe Thiers could understand: "government is not made to give work to the worker."[87]

Proudhon's narration of the period from February to June is organized, like most histories of the period, around accounts of the principal *journées* – March 17, April 16 and May 15. In the course of his narrative Proudhon insists on two themes: (1) the preoccupation of the Provisional Government with maintaining its own power, and (2) the incapacity of the government to face up to the question of the right to work. Thus, in discussing the *journée* of March 17 – which led to the postponement of the elections – Proudhon notes Louis Blanc's call for the Provisional Government to assume dictatorial power. "Once they acquire power," he writes, "all men are alike. It's always the same zeal for authority, the same distrust of the people, the same fanaticism of order."[88] Thus also, in his discussion of the *journée* of April 16, Proudhon insists on the propensity of the democratic leaders to assume that social change would necessarily follow from change in political institutions. "All the errors, all the miscalculations of democracy," writes Proudhon, "derive from the fact that the people, or rather the leaders of the insurrectionary bands, after having gotten rid of the king and the dynasty, believed that they had transformed society because they had transformed the personnel of the monarchy."[89]

Proudhon's narrative is cut in two by the June Days. Addressing the insurgents directly, he tells them that—although the "victims of an odious bad faith" – they were wrong to "give way to indignation and rage." "Your mistake was to demand those in power to fulfill a promise that

---

[85] Ibid, 110.   [86] Ibid, 114.   [87] Ibid, 111.   [88] Ibid, 122.   [89] Ibid, 135.

they could never keep; your fault was to rebel against the representatives of the nation and the government of the Republic." And for the first time, he makes his own confession: "For me, the memory of the June Days will weigh on my heart as an eternal source of remorse." He explains that he was completely unprepared for the insurrection, having been absorbed in the work of the National Assembly. He confesses that his isolation in "the parliamentary Sinaï" had cut him off from any kind of understanding of the real situation of the common people and the roots of their rebellion. It is this personal experience that leads Proudhon to reject the idea that popular sovereignty could ever be adequately expressed through elected representatives in any sort of parliament. "You have to have lived in the cocoon that is called a National Assembly," he writes, "to understand that the men most thoroughly ignorant of the state of a country are almost always those who represent it."[90]

In a fascinating autobiographical chapter entitled simply "Who am I?" Proudhon describes the transformation that he underwent after June. During the first four months of the Republic, he tells us, he was a spectator. Once the revolt had started, as he walked all over Paris for three days, his role continued to be that of a *spectateur*, almost a *badaud* in the Baudelairean sense. But using the irresistible theatrical metaphor, he explains that after the crushing of the June insurrection, he knew he had to leave his place in the audience and to "entrer en scène." "I had to get established in the opposition, to put those in power on the defensive, to enlarge the field of battle, to simplify the social question by generalizing it, to astonish the enemy by the audacity of my propositions, to act henceforth on the people rather than on its representatives." This could not be done by a party. The tactic "required a determined and even an eccentric individual, a person practiced in protest and negation. Pride or intoxication," he writes, "I believed my turn had come ... And from my bench in the spectators' gallery I jumped onto the stage, a new actor."[91]

What this meant was to carry on the struggle against the Party of Order singlehandedly – taunting, provoking, attacking the government, playing the fool when necessary, and never letting those in power lose sight of the fact that they had not "finished with" the poor and the hungry. Again Proudhon uses theatrical imagery to create a context for his new role: "The democrats, seduced by memories of our glorious revolution,

[90] Ibid, 168–169. On this point see the astute commentary in Anne-Sophie Chambost, "Entre mémoire altérée et traumatisme du souvenir: le poids de 1848 dans l'oeuvre de Proudhon," *Revue des études proudhoniennes*, I (2015), 23–26.
[91] *Confessions*, 171.

wanted to replay the drama of 1789 in 1848. While they are acting, let's try to make history."[92]

The theatrical metaphor – the image of the revolution as a staged play – is central to much of the writing on 1848. In Tocqueville's *Souvenirs*, the February Revolution is repeatedly represented as bad theatre – as "a bad tragedy played by mediocre provincial actors."[93] And in Marx' *18th Brumaire of Louis Bonaparte* 1848 is depicted as a farcical replay of the great revolution of 1789 in which each class plays its role. But none of these other writers invokes the metaphor of the theatre in order to speak of himself and his own role. In Proudhon's *Confessions*, however, the story of the revolution in the end becomes *his* story, as his account of the unmaking of the revolution becomes the story of his own making as a revolutionary.

Thus, the second half of Proudhon's narrative focuses on his efforts to "raise the spirits of the workers, to avenge the June insurrection for the calumnies of the reaction" and "with redoubled energy and with a sort of terrorism, to pose the social question." Here he describes his oratorical duel with Thiers, his efforts at launching his credit bank, and his role in the building of a democratic-socialist alliance. He boasts that by the end of July he had acquired a reputation as *"l'homme terreur"*:

I have been sermonized, mocked, satirized, placarded, biographed, caricatured, blamed, derided, cursed. I have been held up to scorn and hatred, handed over to justice by my colleagues, accused, condemned by those who elected me, suspected by my political allies, spied on by my collaborators, denounced by my adherents, contradicted by members of my own community.[94]

Proudhon continues in this vein for several pages, comparing himself explicitly to Job and implicitly to Jesus Christ. Having chosen his role, he plays it with gusto.

The two great political events of the last months of 1848 were the adoption of the constitution of November 4 and the election of Louis-Napoleon Bonaparte as president of the Second Republic. In the *Confessions*, Proudhon explains his position on each event. He says that he voted against the constitution because it *was* a constitution. "To vote for the constitution of 1848 in which social guarantees are considered as an emanation of authority "would have been to "recant" his socialist beliefs.[95] As for Louis-Napoleon Bonaparte, Proudhon did not support his candidacy. After some initial uncertainty and an inconclusive face-to-

---

[92] Ibid, 170.   [93] *Souvenirs de Alexis de Tocqueville*, Luc Monnier (ed.) (Paris, 1942), 64.
[94] *Confessions*, 202.   [95] Ibid, 228.

face meeting with the future president on September 26, Proudhon gave his support to Raspail.

But the important question for Proudhon was the question of the *meaning* of Louis-Napoleon's massive victory. In the end, Proudhon came to believe that "France elected Louis Bonaparte President of the Republic because France is tired of parties, because all the parties are dead [and] because with the parties power itself is dead." Proudhon believed that Louis-Napoleon would soon be forced to make a choice between the party of order and the revolution and that he would embrace the revolution, adopting policies favourable to the working class. But this optimistic take on Louis-Napoleon's election did not prevent Proudhon from attacking the president regularly in his journals. As we know, one of these attacks led to his arrest and imprisonment for three years.

Proudhon's narrative concludes with a chapter on the *journée* of June 13, 1849. This *journée* began with a demonstration protesting the French military intervention against the Roman Republic. Although the demonstration was peaceful, Ledru-Rollin had threatened armed resistance to the government, which gave Louis-Napoleon a pretext to crush the demonstration and send its leaders into exile. In his chapter Proudhon insists on the need for democrats and socialists to present themselves to the nation as a party of order respectful of the constitution.[96] But Ledru-Rollin's conduct had been equivocal. Proudhon concedes that, had he not been arrested five days earlier, he would have joined the protest of his "co-religionnaires politiques" on June 13. But as things worked out, the demonstration was "ill-timed, impolitic [and] badly organized."[97]

According to Proudhon, the protest of June 13 was the last gasp of the Jacobin tradition. Resuscitated in 1830, Jacobinism was "ambitious without intelligence, violent without heroism," and it "perished from consumption and inanity."[98] And its decease was part of a more comprehensive collapse. "At one blow, mystical, theological and transcendental socialism vanished like a ghost." In other words, the failures of the Left in 1848 and 1849 demonstrated the collapse not only of the "governmental utopia" of Louis Blanc but also of the communitarian tradition, which Proudhon describes as "the Phalansterian, Icarian and Saint-Simonian utopia."[99]

What remained? For Proudhon what remained after the collapse of the other ideologies of the Left was a libertarian socialist tradition in which the initiative came from the people and not from the government. In his conclusion, Proudhon sketches rapidly the main elements of this

[96] Ibid, 319.   [97] Ibid, 330.   [98] Ibid, 333.   [99] Ibid, 334.

libertarian socialist tradition for which liberty is both a principle of creation and a principle of criticism, an enemy of all dogmatism, and a force that "produces everything in the world, even what it has just destroyed: religion, government, nobility, property." [100] And in a final lyric peroration Proudhon ends his book with an extraordinary celebration of irony as "true liberty." Here Proudhon represents himself as a worshipper and irony as a woman – a goddess: "Sweet irony! You alone are pure, chaste and discrete ... Your smile calms dissension and civil war: you make peace among brothers, you cure fanatics and sectarians. You are the mistress of Truth."[101]

Many of Proudhon's readers, including some of his greatest admirers, have been mystified by the conclusion of his *Confessions* with its paean to irony. What, they have asked, is such a passage doing among Proudhon's "socialist meditations"? No one doubts its eloquence. But what does it *mean?* How does it relate to the rest of the book?[102] I would say that it relates in two ways. First, Proudhon sees the ironic – and for him Voltairean – spirit as a necessary antidote to the flood of sentimental idealism that came to suffuse socialist thought in the run-up to 1848. Here, it is not by accident that he links Fourierists, Icarians and Saint-Simonians as devotees of a single utopia. For him, they are *all* infected by the romantic and idealist malady. No less important than this is the fact that the ironic and critical spirit is a central element in Proudhon's vision of a free society: "Ironie, vraie liberté."

In the end, all the emphasis in Proudhon's *Confessions* is on criticism. He criticizes the Provisional Government, the Party of Order, the *républicains de la veille* and the *républicains du lendemain*, the "Jacobin" socialists (Louis Blanc) and the "metaphysical" socialists (Pierre Leroux), representative government and universal suffrage (that "stepping-stone to despotism") and "the blatherers" of all shapes and sizes. Even in his most unambiguously celebratory mode, Proudhon is celebrating the critical spirit.

On some specific points there is a remarkable parallel between Proudhon's *Confessions* and the better-known writings of Marx and Tocqueville on 1848. All three were at one in their contempt for the revolutionary leaders – both the members of the Provisional Government and the more radical democrats and socialists. All three write that a great weakness of the radicalism of the 'forty-eighters was their fixation on the

---

[100] Ibid, 341.   [101] Ibid, 342.
[102] For a thoughtful exploration of Proudhon's (and Herzen's) concept of irony, see Aileen Kelly, "Herzen and Proudhon: Two Radical Ironists," *Views from the Other Shore* (New Haven, 1999), 82–113.

first French Revolution and their inability to think their way beyond the traditions, practices and ideologies of 1789–1794. All three make a vital distinction between the facile eloquence of the democrats and socialists and the desperate strivings of the working class. But one distinguishing feature of Proudhon's account of the revolution of 1848 is that it is explicitly autobiographical. The *Confessions* is an account of the process by which Proudhon became the spokesman for the people betrayed by the revolution. It is an account of both the making of a revolutionary and the unmaking of a revolution.

In framing his analysis, Proudhon adopts and makes his own the metaphor of the theatre. As we have seen, his account is very close to Marx's depiction of 1848 as a farcical replay of 1789 and to Tocqueville's representation of the February Revolution as a "bad tragedy performed by inept provincials." But the difference is that, as the play goes poorly, Proudhon himself is finally induced to leap on stage and to become an actor in the play. Thus the central thread in the second half of Proudhon's narrative is his description of his own efforts to lift the spirits of the workers, to defend the June insurgents from the calumnies of the reaction, and to pose "with a sort of terrorism" the social question.

At the outset, Proudhon had announced that the February Revolution was a revolution "without an idea." What he meant by this was that while democrats and republicans had been repeating ad nauseam: "Social revolution is the goal; political revolution is the means," they had not a clue about how to attain their goal once the political revolution had taken place. Proudhon had attempted in his *Solution du problème social* to describe the course of action that should be followed by the revolutionary leaders. But they had not listened. Thus he took it upon himself to demonstrate by his actions as well as his words what needed to be done. And in moving from history to autobiography – in linking his analysis of the collapse of the revolution to a discussion of his own growth as a revolutionary – he was inviting his readers to take heart and to recognize that while revolutions could not be made by fiat, they could begin with skepticism and ironic distance with regard to authority.

Arguments and Restatements

Les Confessions d'un révolutionnaire sold well. Three weeks after its publication on October 30, 1849, in a printing of 3,000 copies, Proudhon was already preparing a cheap popular edition, and a third edition appeared in October 1852. The reviews were mixed, some marked by perplexity as to Proudhon's tone and his assault on democrats and socialists. The *Times* of London rejoiced in the spectacle of the "terrible" Proudhon attacking socialists, and the conservative *Patrie* invited the "eminent dialectician" Proudhon "to return to the fold of the moderate party."[103] Writing for the respectable *Journal des débats* the academician Alfred-Auguste Cuvillier-Fleury praised Proudhon's concluding peroration on irony as "a classic page, a lightning-flash in the night." But he seems to have been both mystified and repelled by the "perfume of funereal metaphors" that the book exuded "like the smoke of mourning candles around a bier."

The most unambiguously positive review was an extravagant celebration of Proudhon's "eloquence" and his "metaphysical laughter" by the young liberal Eugène Pelletan in Emile de Girardin's *La Presse*. (Pelletan went on, however, to concede that he didn't really understand the book!) The Russian socialist Alexander Herzen admired the *Confessions*. But most French democrats and socialists were shocked and angered by the book. The usually gentle Constantin Pecqueur erupted in a long and vituperative review in his short-lived monthly *Le Salut du Peuple*, charging Proudhon with striking poses and shamelessly seeking celebrity: "Be satisfied, you have plenty of celebrity. But do you also have truth? Are you right? What I deplore, and what ought to pain you, is that, in order to obtain the favour of a false renown ... you have had to collude with error, to [indulge yourself] in paradox, and to pass yourself off as a sophist and an intellectual boxer."[104] On November 11, 1849, in another long review Pierre Leroux criticized Proudhon's "monstrous" atheism, and accused him of undermining the socialist movement by preaching a doctrine that resembled the celebration of individualism and selfishness in the work of the liberal economist Charles Dupin.[105] Four days later Louis Blanc weighed in with a twelve-page review in his own monthly journal *Le Nouveau monde*. Criticizing Proudhon's "crazy assertions" and "frightful confusions," he described the *Confessions* as "the most audacious negation of socialism ever written." He conceded that Proudhon had performed great services to the cause of revolution, but regretted that his "immeasurable pride" and his "boundless and unprecedented love of paradox" had "ruined" him. Proudhon believed himself a socialist, but in reality he carried individualism "to a frenetic extreme."[106]

[103] Both reviews cited in Pierre Haubtmann, *Pierre-Joseph Proudhon. Sa Vie et sa pensée (1849–1865)*, 2 vols. (Paris, 1988), I, 73.
[104] Constantin Pecqueur, "Première lettre au citoyen Proudhon," *Salut du Peuple*, 1 (December 10, 1849), 28–38.
[105] Pierre Leroux in *La République*, November 11, 1849; Haubtmann, *Proudhon (1849–1865)*, I, 43.
[106] Louis Blanc in *Le Nouveau monde*, November 15, 1849; Haubtmann, {*Proudhon (1849–1865)*, I, 43.

Never one to let criticism go unanswered, Proudhon responded vigorously to Leroux and Louis Blanc in three successive numbers of *La Voix du Peuple*. Leroux in turn announced his intention of producing a book-length critique of "Monsieur P-J Proudhon's manifesto against God and socialism," as he now called the *Confessions*[107]. The exchanges between Proudhon and Pierre Leroux – which went on for several months – eventually moved to higher ground. But this was not true of Louis Blanc's polemic with Proudhon. In January 1850 Blanc was continuing to express "disgust" at Proudhon's "gibes," which were only adding to "the martyrdom of the workers."[108] Proudhon finally lost interest in the argument. He was obsessed by the need to understand the February revolution and to explain to his own satisfaction what had gone wrong in its aftermath. He spent much of the year 1850 reading and thinking about this problem in his prison-cell; and he came to believe that 1848 had to be understood in historical context and as part of a revolutionary tradition going back to 1789 and beyond.

The outcome of Proudhon's reflections was *L'Idée générale de la révolution au XIXe siècle*, a work that George Woodcock once described as coming "nearer than anything else Proudhon wrote to presenting his view of the ideal libertarian society, based on contract instead of laws, with authority decentralized in communes and industrial associations, with frontiers abolished and flexible federation replacing the centralized national state."[109] For our purposes it suffices to say that in this work Proudhon built on the argument of the *Confessions* that the great error of the 'forty-eighters was to believe that one could bring about a social revolution by seizing political power. Revolution is not insurrection, Proudhon insists. It is social change. All the revolutionary *journées* of 1848 were romantic imitations of 1792 and 1793. The revolution of the nineteenth century does not lie in these retrospective fantasies. And it most certainly does not lie in calls for class war, pitting bourgeois against proletarian. On the contrary, writes Proudhon, the revolution of the nineteenth century will become possible only when the bourgeoisie and the proletariat join forces to build together "a new edifice of industrial institutions" in place of the traditional system of feudal and military rule.[110]

Indeed, Proudhon opens *L'Idée générale* with a dedication "to the bourgeoisie" in which he calls upon this class to finish the work begun by the

---

[107] Pierre Leroux in *La République*, November 18, 1849; Haubtmann, *Proudhon (1849–1865)*, I, 43.

[108] Louis Blanc in *Le Nouveau monde*, January 15, 1850; Haubtmann, *Proudhon (1849–1865)*, I, 46.

[109] George Woodcock in *Encyclopedia of Philosophy*, Paul Edwards (ed.) (New York, 1967), VI, 508.

[110] Proudhon, *Idée générale de la revolution au XIXe siècle* (Paris, 1923), 95, 153–154.

revolutionary bourgeoisie of the past. In language reminiscent of Marx's encomium to the bourgeoisie in the *Communist Manifesto*, Proudhon asserts that throughout history the bourgeoisie have been "the most intrepid, the most skillful of revolutionaries." It is they who, "opposing the commune to the castle, the king to the great vassals, vanquished feudalism." Proudhon reminds his bourgeois contemporaries that starting in the Enlightenment, the bourgeoisie had proclaimed all the modern revolutionary ideals – freedom of religion, freedom of the press, freedom of association. "It is you, you alone, yes you," he tells them, "who defined the principles and laid the foundations of revolution in the nineteenth century."[111] But to finish the job, the bourgeoisie must not try to make revolution from the top down through the seizure of political power.

Proudhon insists in *L'Idée générale* that up to now political revolutions have always led to tyranny. Why should this be so? he asks. His answer is that revolutionaries have lacked the good sense and imagination to get rid of the apparatus of government. Government has always appeared to be the giver of justice, the protector of the weak, and the guardian of peace. But "experience shows that government, no matter how popular at its origin, has always supported the wealthiest, most cultivated class against the poorest and most numerous ... The history of governments is the martyrology of the proletariat."[112] The task confronting future revolutionaries is to replace the existing institutions of government with a society organized around real economic forces.[113] Proudhon believed that history was moving toward the dissolution of government and that economic forces would eventually be so organized that governmental institutions could be absorbed into the economy. The task was to "melt, immerse and dissolve the political or governmental system into the economic system by reducing, simplifying, decentralizing, suppressing one after the other all the cogs in the great machine that is called Government or the State."[114]

Proudhon's aim in the *Idée générale de la Révolution au XIXe siècle* was to explain to those who had made "a revolution without an idea" what a revolution *with* an idea might look like. What he had to offer was not "harangues" or governmental theories" but "plans of economic renovation" in which the state would be "dissolved in industrial organization." But even in this work, where he claimed to move beyond criticism to an account of the "industrial institutions" of the future, his language is vague. It is only on the attack that he achieves eloquence – as in his epilogue, when he reminds his readers what it means to be governed:

---

[111] Proudhon, *Idée générale*, 93.   [112] Ibid, 183–184.   [113] Ibid, 237.
[114] Ibid, 240.

To be GOVERNED is to be locked up, inspected, spied upon, directed, legislated, regulated, cooped up, indoctrinated, preached at, controlled, evaluated, appraised, censored, ordered around by people who have neither rank, nor knowledge, nor virtue ... To be GOVERNED is to be [constantly] graded, registered, counted, taxed, stamped, measured, numbered, assessed, patented, dismissed, authorized, certified, admonished, forbidden, reformed, corrected. It is under the pretext of public utility and in the name of the general interest, to be deployed, exercised, ransomed, exploited, monopolized, extorted, pressured, mystified, robbed; then at the least resistance, at the first word of complaint, to be repressed, fined, vilified, harassed, hunted, scolded, judged, condemned, deported, sacrificed, sold, betrayed, and on top of all that, tricked, fooled, outraged, dishonoured. That is government, that is its justice, that is its morality![115]

Here, wrung out of him by his own experience of the consequences of the February Revolution, is the anarchist core of Proudhon's mature thought.

[115] Ibid, 344.

8 Alexander Herzen
A Tragedy Both Collective and Personal

In his *Writer's Diary* Dostoevsky described Alexander Herzen (in French) as a "gentilhomme russe et citoyen du monde."[1] Dostoevsky, who preferred Russians to world citizens, did not mean this as a compliment. But it gets at two important facets of Herzen's identity. He was, first of all, a gentleman. Even though he was legally an illegitimate child, he was raised as an aristocrat, he inherited his father's large fortune and – while never ceasing to hold radical ideas – he lived the life of a *grand seigneur*. Secondly, Herzen was a European in the fullest sense of the word – fluent in five languages, at home in each of the major European cultures and an important figure in the long tradition of Russian Europeans running from Alexander Radishchev to Boris Pasternak and beyond (Figure 8.1).

The great drama in the lives of educated Russians of Herzen's class and generation lay in the contrast between their western education and Russian realities. They were expected to make careers in the army or the state bureaucracy, but the more sensitive had no stomach for either of these professions. Many lapsed into an uneasy existence as "superfluous men." Some became more deeply detached from their society and tried to make sense of their lives, and of Russia's future, by immersing themselves in the study of German philosophical idealism (Schelling and Hegel). Herzen was one of the latter. But whereas his contemporaries found German idealism attractive largely because it afforded an escape from an unpleasant reality, Herzen was the first Russian to find in Hegel what he later called the "algebra of revolution." He was the first Russian, in other words, to interpret Hegel's account of the march of reason in history as a demonstration of the necessity of the collapse of existing social institutions. Thus the reading of Hegel led Herzen to the reading

This chapter is based on previously unpublished material in "Alexandre Herzen et la Révolution de 1848" in Edward Castleton and Hervé Touboul (eds.), *Regards sur 1848* (Besançon: Presses Universitaires de Franche-Comté, 2015), 217–259.
[1] Fyodor Dostoevsky, *A Writer's Diary*, Kenneth Lantz (trans. and ed.), 2 vols. (Evanston, IL, 1993), I, 126.

of French radicals and utopian socialists. Ultimately, given the dim prospects for radical political change in Russia, it led him into exile.

During the 1840s, Herzen emerged as a leading figure in the debate within the intelligentsia between Westernizers and Slavophils, and he did much to formulate the issues that were central to that argument. He consistently identified himself as a Westernizer. But his views were actually more nuanced than the positions he took in debates. His doubts about the achievements of the West, and more generally his latent skepticism about the powers of human reason, came to the surface after 1847, when he emigrated to Western Europe. Dismayed by what he regarded as the narrowness, uniformity and corrosive philistinism of western bourgeois culture, Herzen turned eventually to a faith in the basic goodness of the Russian people and to the belief that the Russian peasant commune, with its unique traditions of land redistribution, might serve as the basis for an authentically Russian socialism in which the quest for individual freedom might be reconciled with the need for collective responsibility.

Herzen's conception of Russian socialism owed something to his reflections on the ideas of his former antagonists, the Slavophils. But it was the failure of the European revolutions of 1848, which he observed first-hand, that moved him decisively away from what he came to regard as the naïve Westernism of his youth. In two series of essays, Herzen set down his angry response to the crushing of the revolutionary movement, lamenting the broken dreams of 1848, pouring scorn on the forces of reaction, but also criticizing the dogmatic and illiberal character of European radicalism. The republicans and socialists of Europe, Herzen believed, were unable to formulate a vision of the good society that was not itself coercive and limiting – some new form of oppressive "secular monasticism."

Throughout his years of exile, Herzen wrote indefatigably, attempting both to dispel Western ignorance of Russia and to influence events inside Russia. In a series of essays published in the early 1850s – notably *The Russian People and Socialism* (1851) – he outlined for Western readers his conception of Russian socialism. His essay *On the Development of Revolutionary Ideas in Russia* (1850) helped constitute a Russian revolutionary tradition. Through his Free Russian Press and his Russian-language journals, Herzen succeeded in reaching a wide audience in Russia, especially during the years just prior to the emancipation of the serfs in 1861. Although living and writing in London, he became an inspiration to young radicals and a powerful influence on moderate reformers. His following in both groups declined sharply after 1863, however, when his support of the Polish insurrection against Russian rule antagonized many Russian nationalists. But he had already established a reputation as an enormously gifted journalist, possessing (in Isaiah Berlin's words) "a singular combination of fiery imagination, capacity for meticulous observation, moral passion, and intellectual gaiety, with a talent for writing in a manner at once pungent and distinguished, ironical and incandescent, brilliantly entertaining and at times rising to a great nobility of feeling and expression."[2]

For all the practical importance of Herzen's essays and articles, his greatest achievement in exile was the writing of the memoirs he entitled *My Past and Thoughts*. This work, written in fits and starts after 1852, is at once a literary masterpiece, built around the great romantic theme of lost illusions, and a vast historical fresco illuminating the experience of a whole generation of radical intellectuals. At its centre stands the revolution of 1848.

Paris and Revolution: Broken Hopes

On January 19, 1847, Alexander Herzen and his wife Natalie left Moscow, accompanied by their three children, his mother, two servants, and two women friends brought along to help care for the children. Herzen's passport, which was good for six months, showed that they were travelling for his wife's health to Germany and Italy. In fact, their destination was Paris, and for Herzen there were other reasons for the trip. For many years he had lived vicariously in the West, reading the latest books and articles and keeping up with debates over German philosophy and French socialism. It was time, he believed, to see the West for himself. But getting out of Russia was difficult. Herzen's status as a former political exile had made it impossible for him to acquire a passport, and furthermore, his father opposed his departure. By the end of 1846, these obstacles had been removed. His father died that year, and he finally received his passport. Arriving in Paris in late March 1847, Herzen rented a comfortable apartment on the Avenue Marigny, just off the Champs Elysées. His first publications from Europe were a series of "Letters from Avenue Marigny" addressed to his Moscow friends and published in the Russian literary journal, *The Contemporary*.

Looking back a year later on his first days in Paris, Herzen wrote that the French capital was so closely linked in his imagination with the French Revolution and "the colossal struggle for thought, for rights, for human dignity" that he arrived "with my heart beating timidly, as once

---

[2] *Russian Thinkers*, 2nd ed. (London, 2008), 94.

people arrived in Jerusalem and Rome."[3] In his memoirs, he evoked the excitement he had felt on his arrival:

And so I was really in Paris, not in a dream but in reality. Here was the Vendôme column and the rue de la Paix ... I had been dreaming of this moment since my childhood. If I might only see the Hôtel de Ville, the Café Foy in the Palais Royal, where Camille Desmoulins picked a green leaf, stuck it on his hat as a cockade, and shouted: 'A la Bastille!'[4]

The impression Herzen clearly seeks to convey is that his illusions with regard to the western revolutionary tradition were alive and well until his arrival in France. By his own account, it was his contact with the West, and above all his experience of the revolution of 1848, that led him to despair of the possibility that a viable revolutionary movement could come from France.

Martin Malia has argued convincingly that Herzen's disillusionment with the West, and with western radical thought, was well underway before he left Russia.[5] Still, the encounter with Paris did serve to shatter some of Herzen's remaining dreams about the city and its culture. He and Natalie dined out often and attended the theatre regularly, and his letters to Moscow were full of gibes about the philistinism and vulgarity of French middle-class culture. He was especially put off by the theatre, and he devoted the second of his "Letters from Avenue Marigny" to a little tract on the decline of the French bourgeoisie as seen through the history of the Paris theatre. An organizing element here was the contrast between the Figaro of Beaumarchais – "the cunning, evasive barber and butler who sparkled like champagne" – and the bourgeois characters of the nineteenth-century playwright Eugène Scribe, "the courtier, the flatterer, the preacher, the buffoon, the teacher, the fool and the poet of the bourgeoisie." Beaumarchais' Figaro was an upwardly mobile free spirit, but his counterparts in the plays of Scribe had "thickened up" – they hated the hungry and did "not believe in poverty, calling it laziness and vagrancy."[6]

What particularly disturbed Herzen was the influence of bourgeois culture throughout French society. In Russia, where the bourgeoisie was weak, standards were set by the aristocracy. In French society, as

---

[3] Alexander Herzen, Letters from France and Italy, 1847–1851, trans. Judith E. Zimmerman (Pittsburgh, 1996), 128.
[4] Alexander Herzen, My Past and Thoughts, trans. Constance Garnett, revised by Humphrey Higgins, 4 vols. (New York, 1968), II, 646.
[5] Martin Malia, Alexander Herzen and the Birth of Russian Socialism, 1812–1855 (Cambridge, MA, 1961), 336, 341.
[6] France and Italy, 27–29.

Herzen saw it, the same narrow and mercenary culture was predominant everywhere. Only in the Parisian working class could he detect hints of an independent class consciousness.[7] There were also personal roots to Herzen's discontent with Paris in 1847. In Moscow, the centre of his social and intellectual life had been a tight-knit circle of friends: westernized intellectuals, mostly of aristocratic origin, who discussed philosophical and personal questions with a passionate intensity that did not exist in Paris. Herzen's Moscow circle had begun to break up prior to his departure. But still for him, as for other members of the emerging Russian intelligentsia, the memory of the circle provided a "model of what life in a humanely organized society" might be like, and he suffered from its absence in Paris.[8]

Another difficulty of life in Paris was simply that Herzen was unknown. In Russia, he had been a respected intellectual. But in France, there was little interest in a writer who wrote in a language that no one knew. Herzen was an unimportant outsider; and this was hard for a proud man. He thought it demeaning to seek introductions to literary and political celebrities or to regard a café conversation with Louis Blanc as "something like a promotion, an honour." And he disliked "the tone of condescending superiority which Frenchmen assume with Russians."[9] Thus his closest ties at the outset were with German expatriates like the musician Adolf Reichel, and the poet Georg Herwegh.[10]

Two Russians whom Herzen saw frequently in Paris were the peripatetic man of letters Pavel Annenkov and the young Ivan Turgenev. Not yet the great novelist whom we know, Turgenev had already begun his lifelong pursuit of the married Spanish singer and composer, Pauline Viardot, and this kept bringing him back to Paris. Herzen's closest Russian friends at the outset were Mikhail Bakunin and Nikolai Sazonov, both of whom he had known as students in Moscow. Bakunin, who had left Russia in 1840, had lived in Germany and Switzerland before settling in Paris in 1844. By this time, more because of the company he kept than because of any overt revolutionary activities, Bakunin had won a reputation as a dangerous revolutionary; and in

---

[7] Ibid, 40–41.
[8] Judith E. Zimmerman, *Midpassage. Alexander Herzen and European Revolution, 1847–1852* (Pittsburgh, 1989), 4.
[9] *Past and Thoughts* II, 664, 961–962.
[10] On Herzen's extensive links with the European revolutionary community in exile see Marc Vuilleumier, *Révolutionnaires et exilés du XIXe siècle: Autour d' Alexandre Herzen*, (Genève, 1973), 9–66; Zimmerman, *Midpassage*, 15–134 and 194–228; and S. A. Makashin and L. R. Lanskii (eds.), *Gertsen i zapad, Literaturnoe nasledstvo*, 96 (Moscow, 1985).

December 1844 Tsar Nicholas I issued a decree stripping Bakunin of his aristocratic privileges, confiscating his property in Russia, and condemning him in absentia to Siberian exile. In Paris Bakunin made contact with both Marx and Proudhon and formed a close personal bond with the latter whom he introduced to Herzen. Nikolai Sazonov had lived in Paris even longer than Bakunin and had established an elaborate network of contacts with French democrats and radical émigrés. Thanks to these two Russians, Herzen began to form ties with both French and émigré radicals.[11]

In getting to know French radical intellectuals, Herzen was disappointed to find that they had little interest in Russian affairs. The French had made the Polish cause their own. But Russia was Poland's oppressor, and Russia had no discernable revolutionary movement of its own. Thus, when Herzen tried to speak to French democrats of the struggle against autocracy and serfdom, they ignored him. Conversely, when he tried to tell his compatriots Bakunin and Sazonov that European-style conspiratorial revolutionary action was "hopelessly premature" in Russia, they did not listen either.

After six months Paris began to lose its charm for Herzen. He had had enough of French bourgeois culture; and the repeated revelations in the press of scandals and corruption left him feeling that France was undergoing a "grotesque moral collapse." On October 21, he and his family left Paris for Italy, where they hoped to find sun, sea breezes, and a "people not as exhausted, as afflicted with moral senility" as the French.[12] Italy responded, as it has so often, by giving these northern travellers exactly what they wanted.

The Herzens arrived in Rome in late November, and they took an apartment on the Via del Corso, planning to stay through the winter. In December Herzen wrote his friends in Moscow an exuberant account of his change of heart. "I left France, seeking calm, the sun, works of art ... As soon as I set foot on Italian soil, I was embraced by another milieu, vital, energetic, and flowing in strength and health."[13] Herzen's buoyancy was due not only to a change in the weather but also to a change in the political climate. He had arrived in Rome at an exciting moment. On January 2, 1848, he looked on as 20,000 people cheered the Pope for taking what appeared to be a step toward constitutional government by entrusting the Vatican's administration to an advisory council. The

---

[11] Zimmerman, *Midpassage*, 34–37; Malia, *Alexander Herzen*, 347–348; Franco Venturi, *Studies in Free Russia* (Chicago, 1982), 187–215.
[12] *France and Italy*, 61–62.   [13] Ibid, 69.

crowd shouted other demands too – "Long live a free press!" and "Down with the Jesuits!" [14]

Two weeks later reports reached Rome of an uprising in Palermo against the King of the Two Sicilies. Herzen thought of going to Palermo. But when revolt broke out at Naples, he went there, and witnessed, first, an amnesty of political prisoners, then wild celebrations as King Ferdinand prepared to issue a Neapolitan constitution. Within the next few days Pius IX, Leopold of Tuscany and Charles Albert of Piedmont had all proclaimed constitutional governments for their territories. Watching events at Naples, Herzen marvelled at the political resilience of Italy – "a country that, three centuries earlier, lost its political existence, was subjected to every possible humiliation, was conquered and divided up by foreigners." How, Herzen wondered, did it happen that such a country should "suddenly appear with energy and force, with claims to political independence and civil rights, and to new participation in European life?"[15]

On March 4, 1848, word reached Rome that the July Monarchy had fallen and that a Republic had been declared in France. Herzen's first reaction was ecstatic. "Is this a dream or waking?" he asked. "The pulse of history is beating feverishly; and personal views and feelings get lost in the grandeur of what is taking place."[16] Still, even though this was news that he had long been waiting for, he did not hurry back to Paris. Events in Italy engaged him. And while he was disappointed by the "mean and deformed" constitution finally granted by Pius IX, he had hopes that republican government might emerge all over Italy. His family was also happier and healthier in Rome than they had been in Paris; and it was not until the end of April that the Herzens finally left Rome.

Arriving in Paris on May 5, the day after the first meeting of the National Assembly, Herzen missed the euphoria of the February Revolution. Reading his letters from Italy on events in France, one is struck by their flat joylessness. Later he described himself as having "rapturously flown" to Paris, only to be "cured" of his "hopes and delusions" on his arrival. Actually, he was prepared for the worst before he got to Paris. While still in Rome, he was "seized by fear" on learning the composition of the Provisional Government: "Lamartine's name boded nothing good"; Marrast was known as "a great intriguer"; and most of the others were unknown lawyers. "Only Ledru-Rollin seemed to represent something," while "Louis Blanc and Albert stood apart." In Marseille, Herzen read of the killing of workers at Rouen protesting the

[14] Ibid, 84.   [15] Ibid, 88.   [16] Ibid, 111–112.

election results. "This was the first blood after February 24, it was an ill omen."[17]

Once in Paris, Herzen began a new series of "letters" describing his impressions of life in the Second French Republic for his friends in Moscow. He wrote disdainfully of the "remarkable insipidity" of debates in the National Assembly, the conservatism of the representatives, and the "bombastic" speeches in which Lamartine "humbled himself before the Assembly, flattered it and called it sovereign." A week after the opening of the National Assembly, Herzen commented, "it was hated by all Paris, except the party of the *National* and the innately stupid liberals."[18]

The first revolutionary *journée* that Herzen witnessed was that of May 15. On that day he was "on the street from morning to night":

I saw the first column of people arriving at the Chamber. I saw how the triumphant crowd set out from the Assembly to the Hôtel de Ville. I saw Barbès at the window of the Hôtel de Ville. I saw the National Guard's eagerness to begin the slaughter and the triumphant procession of the victorious Lamartine and the victorious Ledru-Rollin from the Hôtel de Ville to the Assembly ... Barbès and his companions set out at the same time, covered with curses, to prison ... I got home at nine in the evening. I felt wretched.[19]

Most observers on the left regarded the insurrection of May 15 as a terrible mistake. It served the purposes of the emerging Party of Order so well that some believed it to be the work of *agents provocateurs*. Aloysius Hubert, who proclaimed the dissolution of the Assembly, was widely thought to have been an informer; and even Auguste Blanqui, who had had a long interview with Lamartine a few days earlier, was suspected in some quarters of having reached an "understanding" with Lamartine concerning the insurrection. In the end, many club members, including Barbès and Thoré, decided on the night of May 14 to oppose any attempt to seize power, on the ground that this could only play into the hands of conservatives.

Alexander Herzen had no such doubts. He shared the view of some radical club members that the goal of any popular action on May 15 should be the establishment of a revolutionary dictatorship. He briefly exulted in the dissolution of the National Assembly, and he wrote his friends in Moscow later that "the people" were initially "enchanted."[20] Of course, the "enchantment" was short-lived; and the same letter includes Herzen's own eye-witness account of the manhandling by the

[17] Ibid, 121.   [18] Ibid, 123, 125.   [19] Ibid, 120–121.
[20] Herzen to his Moscow friends, August 2–8, 1848, Alexander Herzen, *Sobranie sochinenii v tridstati tomakh*, 30 vols. (Moscow, 1954–1965), XXIII, 86.

National Guard of Louis Blanc and General Courtais, the moderate
commander of the National Guard:

These janissaries tore Louis Blanc's coat, one of them seized him by the hair, and
pulled so hard that a tuft of hair remained in his hand. Others grabbed old
Courtais, tore off his epaulettes, beat him in the face, spat on him – these are
the methods of the bourgeoisie. I saw myself the cannibalistic joy of these
pretorians, when they took the Hôtel de Ville.[21]

Herzen's hopes for the Republic were shattered. "May 15 removed the
blindfold from my eyes," he wrote on June 10. "There remained no room
even for doubt – the revolution has been defeated, and next the republic
will be defeated as well."[22]

Herzen's own revolutionary activities in May and June amounted to
little – a few visits to radical clubs and "three or four banquets" where he
"ate cold mutton and drank sour wine, listened to Pierre Leroux and old
Cabet and joined in singing the Marseillaise."[23] He and Natalie felt in a
strange and ominous state of limbo. "There is ferment, even movement,"
she wrote a Russian friend on June 8, "and sometimes it seems as if
something is going to come of it – but so far all this is like a struggle of
elemental forces, stifling, heavy, a strange agitation in the blood – clouds
gather and there is a burst of thunder and lightning – but the air is not
cleansed, the sun does not appear."[24]

This language – metaphorical in Natalie's letter – is echoed by Herzen
in a richly orchestrated *mise en scène* for his own account of the beginnings
of the June insurrection. It was 4 pm on the afternoon of June 23, he
writes in *From the Other Shore*. He was walking along the Seine toward the
city's rebellious eastern quarters. Rain was falling, shops were closing
and barricades were rising. As he stopped on the Pont Neuf to take in the
scene, he saw a sudden flash of lightning. Then peals of thunder, the
sound of tocsin calling the proletariat to arms, and "a few rays of sunlight
gleaming brightly from underneath a cloud."[25] An hour later Herzen had
reached Place Maubert. As he stood in the rain and watched the completion of a huge barricade, someone offered him a rifle. After a moment's
hesitation, he refused. Long afterwards he was to replay the scene in his
mind, questioning his choice.[26]

[21] Herzen to his Moscow friends, August 2–8, 1848, *Sobranie sochinenii*, XXIII, 86–87.
[22] *France and Italy*, 120.   [23] *Past and Thoughts*, II, 670.
[24] Natalie Herzen to Tatiana Astrakova, June 8, 1848, *Sobranie Sochinenii*, XXIII, 75.
[25] Alexander Herzen, *From the Other Shore*, trans. Moura Budberg (Oxford, 1956), 45–46;
Past and Thoughts II, 842.
[26] *France and Italy*, 181; *Past and Thoughts*, II, 850–851.

Herzen's published memories of the June Days are a series of disconnected vignettes: a brief confrontation with a drunken Bonapartist at a
café on the quai d'Orsay; the confiscation of his papers by a police agent;
the moment on June 26 when he and Natalie sat speechless in their
apartment listening to the volleys of firing squads. Herzen also writes of
the morning of June 24, when he and Annenkov decided to make a tour
of the elegant quarter in which they lived. The previous night's cannonade had ceased; the Champs-Elysées were empty except for the occasional National Guardsman; the only sound was the distant crackle of
rifle fire. On the Place de la Concorde they met a detachment of Mobile
Guards – very young boys, half-drunk, exhausted, their eyes bloodshot
from lack of sleep and their faces blackened with gunpowder. One of the
boys, "a lad of seventeen", boasted to them of having stuck his bayonet
up to the hilt in the bellies of five or six insurgents. "They'll remember
us," he gloated, "trying to assume the air of a hardened malefactor."[27]

Silent and saddened, Herzen and Annenkov walked on to the
Madeleine. They were stopped several times by National Guard units,
questioned, and finally detained by a Guardsman – "a shopkeeper in
uniform" by Herzen's derisive description. The man claimed to have
seen Herzen at a political meeting. The two Russians were marched off to
a police commissariat. On the way, they encountered a member of the
National Assembly whom Herzen recognized as Alexis de Tocqueville.
But Tocqueville was not the least interested in getting them released, and
he enraged Herzen by insisting pedantically as he bowed himself off that
the legislative authority had no right to interfere with the executive. At
the police station, their captors identified them as "foreign rioters." They
were then sent under escort to another police bureau at the Hôtel des
Capucines, where they were at last rescued from the "armed bourgeois"
by an elderly police officer who advised them to stay indoors for the rest
of the day.[28]

Herzen remained a spectator, but he was to remember the June Days
as a crisis that destroyed what was left of his faith in the democratic ideals
that had inspired the revolutionaries of February 1848. The June Days
"drew a line across my life," he wrote later.[29] That summer he sank into a
state of depression deeper than the distress he had felt a year earlier on
discovering that Paris was not the city of his dreams. He wished he had
died, rifle in hand, on the barricades. If only he had accepted the gun that

---

[27] *Past and Thoughts*, II, 657.
[28] Ibid, II, 658–659; Herzen to his Moscow friends, August 2–8, 1848, *Sobranie Sochinenii*,
XXIII, 81.
[29] *Past and Thoughts*, II, 841.

had been offered him on the Place Maubert, he might at least "have borne two or three beliefs with me to the grave."[30] Now he no longer believed even in the ideals for which the revolutionaries had been fighting. To his mind the failure of the revolution had tarnished everything, starting with the assumption that there was some kind of sense to history. "We have marvelled enough at the abstract wisdom of nature and of historical development," he wrote. "It is time for us to perceive that in nature as in history there is much that is fortuitous, stupid, unsuccessful and confused."[31]

These reflections on the meaninglessness of history, to which Herzen gave memorable expression in *From the Other Shore*, mingled in his mind with fantasies of escape to a world in which the conflicts that had riven old Europe would no longer be meaningful. Eventually, he would discover the possibilities inherent in Russia's "backwardness." But in the first flush of his rejection of the ideals and traditions of Western Europe, Herzen fantasized about a new life in the United States. "Anyone who can put off the old European Adam and be born again a new Jonathan had better take the first steamer to some place in Wisconsin or Kansas. There he will certainly be better off than in decaying Europe."[32]

Exile Communities

Looking back on the autumn of 1848, Herzen described himself as surrounded increasingly by strangers. One by one, the Herzens' Russian friends began to leave. "Until the autumn we were surrounded by our own friends, and gave vent to our anger and grief in our own language," he wrote later. "But after the blood-bath [of June] Paris had no more hold on them."[33] This is not to say that the Herzens' house was empty. They had lots of foreign visitors, and in October they moved from the apartment on the avenue Marigny to a large house with a garden on the Champs Elysées, which quickly became a second home for dozens of German refugees. One of these Germans later spoke of the Herzens' generosity with regard to their guests: extra places were set for every meal; the Herzens often gave money to help tide over new arrivals; two Hungarian women were invited to deliver their babies in the Herzen home.[34] Herzen himself commented later that the moments of intimacy

---

[30] Ibid, II, 850–851.   [31] Ibid, II, 744.   [32] Ibid, II, 745.

[33] Ibid, II, 848. Herzen describes Annenkov and Turgenev as regular visitors through the summer of 1848 while Maria Fëdorovna Korsh and the Tuchkovs (Natalie and Elena and their parents) lived in the same house. All of them returned to Moscow in the fall.

[34] Zimmerman, *Midpassage*, 95.

288	Alexander Herzen: A Tragedy Both Collective and Personal

that he and Natalie had enjoyed initially in Paris and Rome were rare by the fall of 1848. "The number of visitors kept increasing about us, and by evening our little drawing-room in the Champs Elysées was full of strangers. For the most part, these were newly arrived *émigrés*, good, unfortunate people, but I was intimate with only one man."[35] That one man, Herzen's closest friend throughout 1848 and 1849, was Georg Herwegh, who would become the lover of Natalie Herzen.

Given Herzen's close ties with the various émigré communities in Paris, it's not surprising that his first effort to enter the world of Parisian journalism focused on a newspaper that sought its readers among Parisian political refugees. The paper was *La Tribune des peuples.* Its director was Adam Mickiewicz, the Polish émigré poet who had won a large following lecturing at the Collège de France. The paper was funded by one of Mickiewicz's Polish admirers, and its principal collaborators were liberal and nationalist activists. Its lifespan was brief. Founded in March 1849, suspended for much of the summer, it was permanently shut down in November. Early in 1849, Herzen was approached by a young friend of Mickiewicz, Charles-Edmond Chojecki, who attempted to enlist him as a correspondent for the paper. The offer appealed to Herzen because, in addition to being genuinely internationalist, *La Tribune des peuples* was willing to publicize the views of Russian opponents of the Tsarist regime. In the end, nothing came of this proposal. Herzen was put off by the obsequiousness of Mickiewicz's followers and by the strange mixture of Polish nationalism, romantic messianism, and Bonapartism that lay at the centre of Mickiewicz's thought. But this episode shows that Herzen was beginning to think of journalism as the means by which he might make a mark in Western Europe. It also suggests that he saw himself not only as a spokesman of Russia to the West but also as someone who might "speak to Russians of Russian liberty."[36]

Until the spring of 1849 Herzen's radicalism had been manifest almost entirely through the written word. He had not accepted the offer of a rifle in June 1848, and he had kept his distance from activist political groups. For this reason, we need to ask why Herzen became involved in the "stupid" demonstration of June 13, 1849, protesting the attack by French troops on the Roman Republic. He was of two minds about the demonstration, which in the end gave the government a pretext to arrest dozens of French democrats and socialists, many of them members of the National Assembly. He later wrote that the day before, when his friend

---

[35] *Past and Thoughts*, II, 735.
[36] Zimmerman, *Midpassage*, 102–104. See also *Past and Thoughts*, II, 665–670.

Nikolai Sazonov urged him to participate, his initial reaction was to laugh. He told Sazonov that it would be "stupid" for him to march in the demonstration. Sazonov replied that it was certainly "quieter and safer to stay at home and write skeptical articles while others were championing the liberty of the world and the solidarity of peoples." Herzen could not resist this challenge. Inspired by what he later described as "a vile emotion ... that has led and will lead many men into great errors," Herzen asked, "What makes you imagine I am not going?" And he added: "I said it was stupid, but I didn't say that I never do anything stupid."[37]

At nine o'clock that evening Herzen met Sazonov at the Café Lemblin in the Palais Royal, where several dozen German refugees were discussing plans for the next day's demonstration. Seven years later, describing this evening in *My Past and Thoughts*, Herzen painted a vivid portrait of the café agitators and rhetorical revolutionaries – the lovers of "banquets, demonstrations, protests, gatherings, toasts and banners" – whom he called "the choristers of the revolution":

In the café various *habitués* of the revolution were sitting with dignity at a dozen little tables, looking darkly and consequentially about them from under wide-brimmed felt hats and caps with tiny peaks. These were the perpetual suitors of the revolutionary Penelope, those inescapable actors who take part in every popular demonstration and form its *tableau*, its background, and who are as menacing from afar as the paper dragons with which the Chinese wished to intimidate the English.[38]

After two hours of "empty chatter" in which nothing was decided, Herzen and Sazonov moved on to the editorial offices of the journal, *La Vraie République*, whose editor, Théophile Thoré, was an organizer of the demonstration. About twenty people, mostly Poles and Germans, were there; a statement was drawn up protesting the French military action; and talk went on until daybreak.

The next morning a procession formed at the Château d'Eau. A crowd of twenty or thirty thousand formed rows of twenty abreast and began marching down the boulevards toward the Madeleine. At the head of the procession were Etienne Arago, the former foreign minister Jules Bastide and other prominent democrats. Immediately behind them was a contingent of radical exiles including Herzen and possibly also Karl Marx. Then came five thousand members of the National Guard, in uniform but unarmed, and many workers and students. A large crowd of spectators lined the boulevards. Although few joined the line of march, they

---

[37] *Past and Thoughts*, II, 672.   [38] Ibid, II, 673.

waved and cheered as the demonstrators began to sing the Marseillaise. "At that moment," recalled Herzen, "there was really something grand about the demonstration."[39]

All went well until the marchers reached the rue de la Paix, near the spot where Garnier's Paris Opera was to rise two decades later. There they were met by three columns of troops under General Changarnier. Without even ordering the crowd to disperse, Changarnier commanded his cavalry to charge. They did so, cutting the procession in two, isolating the leaders, and pushing the followers back down the boulevard toward the working-class quarters from which they had come. Some demonstrators tried to argue or plead with the soldiers, but they were pushed aside or knocked to the ground. "The dragoons in a frenzy fell to riding down people," Herzen wrote, "striking them with the flat of their swords and using the edge at the slightest resistance." Shouts of "Aux armes!" were heard as the demonstrators dispersed, but the only response was the slamming of doors and the closing of shutters. Likewise, a few feeble attempts were made to form barricades with the chairs and tables of nearby cafés. But these were quickly destroyed by Changarnier's troops. This was the end of the peaceful demonstration.[40]

That afternoon a state of siege was declared; National Guard units sacked the offices of *La Vraie République* and half a dozen other radical journals; and orders were issued for the arrest of thirty-one representatives. The leadership of the French left was decimated, and those not captured were forced into an exile that, in some cases, would last for two decades. Like Marx and Proudhon, Herzen was subsequently caustic in his criticism of the leaders of the June 13 demonstration. As he summed up their strategy: "Inspiration was to descend upon them as the Holy Ghost once descended upon the heads of the apostles. There was only one point on which all were agreed – *to come to the meeting-place unarmed.*"[41]

Herzen prudently left the scene of the action in time to avoid arrest. Later the French police came to his house in search of demonstrators. He had briefly sheltered two of them – Karl Blind, who was eventually arrested and Arnold Ruge, who managed to escape.[42] As for Herzen himself, the French government may not even have known of his participation in the demonstration. But he believed they knew. A few days later

---

[39] Ibid, II, 678–679.
[40] Ibid, II, 679. See also Bernard H. Moss, "June 13, 1849: The Abortive Uprising of the French Radicals," *French Historical Studies*, XIII (1984), 406.
[41] *Past and Thoughts*, II, 676.
[42] Herzen to his Moscow friends, September 27, 1849, *Sobranie Sochinenii*, XXIII, 186.

to avoid arrest he procured a false passport and left abruptly for Geneva, leaving Natalie to follow with the children as soon as possible. His plan was to find a permanent residence there for the family. On July 10, Natalie and the children arrived, accompanied by their friend Georg Herwegh.

If Herzen chose Geneva – rather than England or Belgium – as his family's next place of exile, it was because the previous winter at Paris he had gotten to know James Fazy, the founder of the Geneva Radical party and the author of the Geneva Constitution of 1847 which upheld democracy and the separation of powers. The president of the canton of Geneva in 1849, Fazy was a political liberal and an admirer of Adam Smith and Jean-Baptiste Say. He was sympathetic to refugees seeking asylum in Switzerland, as he had been to Marie d'Agoult. And he attempted whenever possible to downplay the threat they might pose to the established order. When the conservative *Journal de Genève* attacked Fazy for welcoming Herzen and Herwegh, Fazy replied in his *Revue de Genève*: "And why shouldn't these gentlemen be here? M. Hertzen, a distinguished Russian writer, a man of independent wealth, a property owner in France and still owning property in Russia, travels in Switzerland for pleasure, and for this, he is here accused of being a propagandist."[43]

In the summer of 1849, as the political climate in France became increasingly conservative, Geneva replaced Paris as the chief continental rallying point for failed European revolutionaries. With the collapse of revolutionary movements in Baden and the Palatinate and the dissolution of the Frankfurt Parliament in May 1849, German exiles such as Arnold Ruge, August von Willich and Julius Froebel gravitated to Geneva, and they were joined by Mazzini and Aurelio Saffi. By the summer of 1849, the cafés of Geneva were crowded with political refugees from all over Europe. Herzen got to know many of them; and despite his growing skepticism about their hopes, he attended their meetings and participated in their discussions.[44]

One exile to whom Herzen was particularly attracted was Mazzini, whom he found "wise, gay, accustomed to misfortune and success" and "without a doubt the greatest political figure of the present time":

In his little room, with the everlasting cigar in his mouth, Mazzini at Geneva, like the Pope in the old days at Avignon, held in his hands the threads that like a spiritual telegraph system brought him into living communication with the whole

---

[43] *Revue de Genève*, July 14, 1849 in Vuilleumier, *Autour de Herzen*, 21–22.
[44] Vuilleumier, *Autour de Herzen*, 30–31.

peninsula ... A fanatic and at the same time an organizer, he covered Italy with a network of secret societies connected together and devoted to one object.[45]

Although Herzen and Mazzini differed on many issues – religion and private property to name just two – they were to remain friends for the rest of their lives.

The one activity to which almost all the refugees were drawn was journalism. With few real responsibilities, radicals in exile devoted themselves to planning and publishing a long succession of newspapers. "The publication of newspapers was an epidemic disease then," Herzen observed drily. "Every two or three weeks projects arose, specimen issues appeared, prospectuses were circulated, then two or three issues – and it all disappeared without a trace."[46] Gustav Struve, a radical republican who dabbled in phrenology and vegetarianism, enlisted Herzen's aid in publishing a trilingual journal which, in the end, never got off the ground. Nor did three other proposed Genevan journals. Herzen was invited to collaborate on all of them; and in each case, he declined. But then in July 1849, he received an offer he could not refuse. This was an invitation from his hero, Pierre-Joseph Proudhon – relayed to Herzen by Nikolai Sazonov – to collaborate financially and editorially on the publication of a journal to be called *La Voix du peuple*.

When Herzen and Proudhon first met in the summer of 1847, Herzen was already an admirer of Proudhon's writing.[47] He appreciated Proudhon's rejection of authority, his passion for individual liberty, and his willingness to stand alone in defence of his ideas. His admiration only increased after the June Days when Proudhon became the sole member of the National Assembly to speak out forcefully on behalf of the insurgents. On March 28, 1849, Herzen was in the audience as Proudhon was sentenced to three years in prison and a heavy fine for publishing "seditious" articles. At that time Herzen had already concluded that Proudhon was the most significant radical in France. He wrote his friends in Moscow that "if they don't kill him in prison (as they hope to do), if he does not die of cholera, ... you will hear of him yet."[48] Herzen

---

[45] *Past and Thoughts*, II, 694, and Herzen to his Moscow friends, September 27, 1849, *Sobranie sochinenii*, XXIII, 188.

[46] *Past and Thoughts*, II, 691–692. Translation slightly modified.

[47] On Herzen and Proudhon see Michel Mervaud, "Herzen et Proudhon," *Cahiers du monde russe et soviétique*, XII, 1–2 (January–June 1971), 110–189; Aileen Kelly, "'A Glowing Footprint': Herzen, Proudhon, and the Role of the Intellectual Revolutionary," *Modern Intellectual History*, II(2) (2005), 179–204; and Zimmerman, *Midpassage*, 114–134; Raoul Labry, *Herzen et Proudhon* (Paris, 1928) remains valuable.

[48] Herzen to his Moscow friends, September 27, 1849, *Sobranie Sochinenii*, XXIII, 189. See also *Past and Thoughts* II, 806, 812–814.

volunteered to pay Proudhon's fine and to post the bond of 24,000 francs required by law as security against future fines. In return, he requested the right to insert his own articles in *La Voix du peuple* and to control the foreign section of the journal – to recommend editors and correspondents and to require payment for articles published.[49]

Herzen asserts in his memoirs that Proudhon accepted these conditions, and he gives a glowing account of the "success" of *La Voix du peuple*, adding that "Proudhon from his prison cell conducted his orchestra in masterly fashion."[50] But Michel Mervaud and Judith Zimmerman have shown that while Proudhon gladly took on Herzen as a member of the newspaper's editorial board, he was unwilling to cede control over any part of the paper. The newspaper, which lasted just eight months (September 1849–May 1850), disappointed Herzen. He did publish one important essay, "La Russie," in *La Voix du peuple* as well as six other pieces including a letter to Mazzini and a critique of the views of the Spanish royalist, Donoso Cortés, later reprinted in *From the Other Shore*.[51] But there was little sustained coverage of the international revolutionary movement. And it disturbed Herzen that Proudhon seemed increasingly eager to win over the bourgeoisie. He began to suspect that Proudhon regarded him simply as a financial backer and not as a collaborator.[52]

The relationship between Herzen and Proudhon eventually warmed up – with sympathy and respect on both sides. Herzen's disillusion with the journal did not prevent him from praising Proudhon's *Confessions d'un révolutionnaire* as "admirable" and singling out the concluding celebration of irony as "the highest poetry" and expressive of "the deepest understanding of the reality of life."[53] On his side, Proudhon was impressed by Herzen's brochure "The Russian People and Socialism" which he found "better, clearer and more categorical than anything he has done up to now," adding: "One almost knows the Slavic people, one

[49] For an exhaustive account of Herzen's collaboration on *La Voix du people*, see Zimmerman, *Midpassage*, 122–134.
[50] *Past and Thoughts* II, 815. In fact Herzen's initial negotiations with Proudhon were conducted by Charles Edmond Chojecki and Nikolai Sazonov, both of whom knew Proudhon better than Herzen.
[51] For Herzen's seven contributions to *La Voix du people*, see Michel Mervaud, "Herzen et Proudhon," *Cahiers du monde russe et soviétique*, XII(1–2) (January–June 1971), 120. According to Mervaud the daily *tirage* of the journal ran from 35,000 to 60,000 copies.
[52] Herzen to Emma Herwegh, October 10, 1849; *Sobranie Sochinenii*, XXIII, 197. See also Mervaud, "Herzen et Proudhon," 121–122.
[53] Herzen to Emma Herwegh, November 7, 1849; *Sobranie Sochinenii*, XXIII, 207.

feels them, divines them, after reading these few pages."[54] Then after the deaths of Herzen's son and mother in November 1851, Proudhon sent Herzen a heartfelt letter of sympathy. Six months later, after Natalie's death, Proudhon gave Herzen complete and unwavering support at a time when he needed it badly.[55]

Herzen could offer financial support to Proudhon because he was unique among radical Russian expatriates in having managed to transfer most of his wealth to the West. This was possible because, even after deciding not to return to Russia, Herzen concealed his decision from the Russian government. Late in 1849 when his mother's property and investments were sequestered by the Tsarist regime, he enlisted the aid of James de Rothschild in recovering his mother's funds. Months of negotiations ensued, but in the end, a very simple strategy was adopted: Herzen's mother transferred her property to Baron Rothschild, and the banker (who for his own reasons was happy to score a small victory over Nicholas I) then collected compensation for the property from the Russian Tsar. Thus, by the middle of 1850, Herzen had managed to transfer to the West virtually all of his mother's assets in Russia as well as his own inheritance. Subsequently, the money was invested for him by Rothschild, and he was able for the rest of his life not only to keep himself and his family in comfort but also to support other radical expatriates and eventually to create his Free Russian Press and to publish his Russian-language journals.[56]

Herzen's negotiations with Rothschild kept him in Paris from January to June 1850. This was long enough to attract the attention of the French police, and in April 1850 he was informed that his presence in France was "subversive of order and dangerous to public tranquillity." He managed to delay his expulsion for two months. But he no longer wished to return to Geneva, which – like the rest of Switzerland – had by 1850 become inhospitable to radical émigrés. Obliged to find another place of residence, he decided to settle with his family at Nice, which was then part of the Kingdom of Sardinia-Piedmont. Shortly after his arrival at Nice, Herzen received an order from the Russian consul to return immediately to Russia or lose his Russian nationality. He refused, and then applied to James Fazy at Geneva for naturalization as a citizen of Geneva. Under pressure to adopt stricter policies on the naturalization of

[54] Proudhon to Charles Edmond [Chojecki], November 25, 1851 in Labry, *Herzen et Proudhon*, 122.
[55] Michel Mervaud, "A propos du conflit Herzen-Herwegh: Un inédit de Proudhon," *Cahiers du monde russe et soviétique*, XIV(3) (July–September, 1973), 333–348.
[56] *Past and Thoughts*, II, 757–765; Zimmerman, *Midpassage*, 101, 168–169. See also Vuilleumier, *Autour de Herzen*, 43, 46.

political refugees. Fazy prevaricated, and Herzen looked elsewhere. Finally, with the help of the German naturalist (and future antagonist of Karl Marx) Karl Vogt, Herzen and his family were granted citizenship by the Swiss canton of Freiburg on May 6, 1851, Thereafter, his status as a Swiss citizen enabled him to travel freely in much of Western Europe.[57]

At Nice, Herzen was once again in a milieu of political exiles. Thanks to its location between France and Italy and its relative freedom, Nice was a natural gathering place for French and Italian radicals, and Herzen soon found himself at the centre of a community of émigrés which also included Poles and Germans. He was especially close at this time to Vogt and to Felice Orsini, who was to be executed in 1858 for attempting to assassinate Napoleon III.[58] But Herzen's most fateful relationship at Nice was with the poet Georg Herwegh. It was at Nice late in 1850, that the Herzen family drama reached its *dénouement*.[59]

Broken Marriage

Almost from the beginning of his stay in France Herzen had regarded Georg Herwegh as his closest friend in Europe. In April 1848, Herwegh had led a legion of 800 German democrats into Baden, hoping to join republican rebels there. This military expedition was a fiasco. The legion was routed in its first battle; fifty of the volunteers were killed, and Herwegh himself was lucky to escape capture. But this did nothing to lessen the warmth and sympathy with which both Alexander and Natalie regarded the German poet. The man was handsome and talented, and he had what E. H. Carr describes as a vulnerable, "almost feminine" side that both the Herzens found appealing.[60] Rapidly a passionate friendship developed among the three of them – with Herwegh's wife Emma a marginal member of the group.[61] They saw themselves as forming an island of warmth and mutual affection in a cold and impersonal world.

---

[57] *Past and Thoughts*, II, 779–783, 797–804; Zimmerman, *Midpassage*, 173–174.
[58] *Past and Thoughts* II, 701–704, 787–797; Zimmerman, *Midpassage*, 172–177; Venturi, *Studies in Free Russia*, 140–186; Vuilleumier, *Autour de Herzen*, 40–64.
[59] On the Herzen family drama E. H. Carr, *Romantic Exiles* (Harmondsworth, 1933), 53–139 remains the most complete narrative. For new perspectives see Irina Paperno (ed.), "Intimacy and History: The Herzen Family Drama Reconsidered," *Russian Literature*, LXI(1–2) (special issue, 2007). Irina Paperno's introduction to this volume (1–65) offers both a critical retelling of the story and a fresh discussion of the composition and publication of Herzen's memoirs.
[60] E. H. Carr, *Romantic Exiles*, 62.
[61] This was Herzen's view. For a more sympathetic portrait of Emma Herwegh, see the charming chapter in Gordon A. Craig, *The Triumph of Liberalism: Zurich in the Golden Age, 1830–1869* (New York, 1988), 211–233.

The men, both disappointed in their political hopes, regarded themselves as comrades in arms and as spiritual "twins," and they gave each other names (as did Natalie and Herwegh) borrowed from George Sand's latest novel, *La Petite Fadette*. Later Herzen claimed that his relationship with Herwegh was one-sided – that Herwegh "forced himself" on him. Herzen's warm and affectionate letters to his "brother" Herwegh show a different picture.[62]

After June 13, 1849, when the Herzens moved from Paris to Geneva, they were joined by Herwegh, whose wife was left behind in Paris to take care of their children. It was at Geneva, during the summer of 1849, that Herwegh became Natalie Herzen's lover. Herzen suspected nothing, and when Natalie had a miscarriage in the fall each man assumed that the child was his own. Natalie adored Herwegh, but still she apparently never contemplated leaving her husband. She loved them both in different ways. She dreamt of a communal life in which she and Alexander and the Herweghs might live together harmoniously with all parties recognizing the beauty, and even the sanctity, of her love for Herwegh.[63]

Early in 1850, while Herzen was in Paris negotiating with Baron Rothschild, Emma Herwegh, who knew pretty well the real state of affairs, warned Herzen that his wife might be having an affair with her husband. He refused to listen. He could not believe that his best friend was betraying him or that his wife might have found with another man satisfaction that she could not find in their marriage. But Herzen recognized that Herwegh and his wife were estranged; and when he attempted to act as an intermediary between them, he became suspicious. Instead of suffering in silence, Herzen then wrote Natalie and asked her to tell him the truth. If she was in love with Herwegh and wished to live with him, she had but to tell him and he would disappear from her life. This was not at all what Natalie had in mind. She broke off her affair with Herwegh and abruptly left Geneva with her children to join Herzen in Paris. This was all he needed to restore his confidence in Natalie – and in Herwegh. For Herzen the matter was closed, and in writing Herwegh he returned to a tone of warm friendship.

In August 1850 at Nice, the two families formed a single household (with Herzen paying the expenses). For five months they lived together in a rented villa on the Promenade des Anglais with a verandah overlooking

---

[62] Herzen apparently destroyed Herwegh's letters, but Herwegh saved Herzen's. Written in French with a few passages in German and occasional affectionate outbursts in Italian ("caro mio..."), Herzen's several hundred letters to Herwegh may be found in *Sobranie sochinenii*, vols. XXIII and XXIV. For Herzen's later view of Herwegh, see *Past and Thoughts*, II, 937–938.

[63] Zimmerman, *Midpassage*, 168.

the Mediterranean. Prior to Herwegh's arrival Herzen wrote him that by living communally, they might "give an example of individual liberty to others by emancipating ourselves from the interests of a world which is heading for its own death."[64] When he wrote these words Herzen was unaware that Natalie and Herwegh were again exchanging passionate letters. After Herwegh's arrival, which Herzen had encouraged, the two lovers renewed their physical relationship; and it was not long before the situation exploded.

At the beginning of January, after a series of misunderstandings and confrontations, Natalie confessed to her husband that her affair with Herwegh was not over. Herzen's reaction was fierce. He insisted that she tell him everything, and he demanded again that she choose. She repeated that she could never leave him. But when she asked him to be gentle with Herwegh because he might commit suicide, Herzen roared with bitter laughter. He now saw Herwegh as a vile seducer who had been abusing his trust and his friendship for eighteen months, and he ordered Herwegh and his wife to leave immediately.

The Herweghs left for Genoa the next morning. He and Natalie continued to correspond for several months. But his letters became wild: he told her to choose between joining him or committing suicide. Finally, she cut off the correspondence. Herwegh took revenge on Herzen by spreading word of the affair throughout the exile community. He claimed that Natalie still loved him and that she had promised to join him in Switzerland when her husband was "calmer," and he described Herzen as a fraud who posed as an upholder of the rights of women but used his authority as a husband to prevent her from joining the man she really loved. In June 1851, while visiting Nikolai Sazonov, in Geneva, Herzen heard this story (much of which Sazonov believed) and learned that affair had become "a European scandal."[65] This, on top of everything else, was a great blow to Herzen's pride; but Natalie, who cared nothing about émigré gossip in Geneva, could only think of restoring her husband's trust. She wrote him that she was determined "to live or die for you." And she sent another letter to Herwegh, telling him that "after untold struggles, I saw that I was destroying Alexander's peace of mind without ever being able to satisfy you. I saw that you were incapable of the smallest sacrifice, that you lived only for yourself."[66] Natalie then set out to meet her husband at Turin on his return from Switzerland.

---

[64] Herzen to Herwegh, July 10, 1850. *Sobranie sochinenii*, XXIV, 107. Herzen is actually quoting here from the text of the first (German) edition of the "Epilogue 1849" to *From the Other Shore.* See *Sobranie sochinenii*, XXIV, 470.
[65] *Past and Thoughts*, II, 888, 902, 941, 944.   [66] Quotes in Carr, *Romantic Exiles*, 115.

Their three days together in Turin and the next few months in Nice seemed to Herzen a second honeymoon. The couple was apparently reconciled, and throughout the fall of 1851 they enjoyed what E. H. Carr has described as "the Indian summer of their love."[67] But in November disaster struck. Herzen's mother and his deaf-mute son Kolya drowned in the shipwreck of a steamer that was bringing them back to Nice from Marseille after a visit to the Reichels in Paris. The horror of this tragedy stunned them all. Natalie, who was now expecting another child, never recovered. Herzen, consumed with grief, hardly noticed Louis Bonaparte's coup d'état of December 2. Natalie's health collapsed – she was diagnosed with pleurisy – and for a time Herzen was ready to give up. On New Year's Day 1852 he wrote Maria Reichel: "The last year has been so bad that I honestly have in no desire to see January 1, 1853. It's all the same to me whether I am alive or dead, whether in America or Nice, or in [the prison of] Schlüsselburg."[68]

In January 1852 Herwegh, who had been brooding in Zürich for nine months, wrote Herzen, challenging him to a duel. Herwegh could no longer hope to win back Natalie. But he wanted to make Herzen suffer as he had suffered. "*I shall shrink from no scandal*," he wrote, bragging that Natalie had told him that she "never belonged" to Herzen and that she had "remained virgin" in his embraces. He claimed that Herzen "knew only how to *insult* women" and to drive away their lovers "by every kind of falsehood, hypocrisy and manoeuvre," and he mocked Herzen's pretensions to liberality and "greatness of soul," boasting that "Fate has decided between you and me, by drowning your progeny and your family in the sea."[69]

Herzen later described himself as springing up from the reading of this letter "like a wounded beast" in fury. His first impulse was to go to Zürich and kill Herwegh "like a dog." His considered response was to ask a friend to write Herwegh denying his right to issue a challenge.[70] Herzen then proposed the constitution of a "court of honour" composed of members of the international revolutionary community to judge between him and Herwegh. He apparently convinced himself that the formal censure of Herwegh by "democratic opinion" would be an important example for all democrats. At the same time, Natalie wrote a

---

[67] Carr, *Romantic Exiles*, 117.

[68] Herzen to Maria Reichel, January 1, 1852. *Sobranie sochinenii*, XXIV, 223.

[69] Carr, *Romantic Exiles*, 124–126. Herwegh's letter is vile, but Natalie did make the statements he attributes to her.

[70] Carr, *Romantic Exiles*, 127; *Past and Thoughts*, II, 903.

letter to Herwegh, inspired (and edited) by Herzen himself, defending her "noble husband" and denouncing Herwegh's "base calumnies."[71]

In this conflict of male egos, Natalie had become little more than a pawn. And while she seemed to be on the mend in February, she suffered a relapse in March. She ran a dangerously high fever; and the advanced state of her pregnancy only complicated the situation. By the middle of April, she knew she was dying, and she sent for her friend Maria Reichel in Paris, asking her to take care of the children. On April 26, Natalie wrote a last letter to Georg Herwegh assuring him that she would never say anything to harm him. "Have you hurt me?" she asked. "You ought to know that better than I – I only know that my blessings will follow you everywhere, always." Herzen was never told of this letter.[72]

On April 29, Maria Reichel arrived from Paris. Later that day a boy was born almost two months prematurely. The baby died a few days later, but Natalie, exhausted by childbirth and only semi-conscious, never knew it. On May 2, she herself died. Maria Reichel took the Herzens' two surviving daughters back to Paris, and their thirteen-year-old son Sasha stayed with his father in Nice. "I am surrounded by tombstones." Herzen wrote Adolf Reichel after the departure of his daughters. "I am not alive anymore, but I endure." To Maria Reichel three days later he added: "There is no limit to my moral weariness and to my insignificance."[73] The sense of loss left by Natalie's death remained with him for the rest of his life.

After having Natalie buried at Nice, Herzen could not bear to remain in a place that had been the scene of so much pain. In early June he left Nice and spent the next two months wandering with Sasha from town to town in northern Italy and Switzerland – from Genoa, to Lugano, to Lucerne, to Geneva. He thought of emigrating to America. Friedrich Kapp had written from New York that his ideas were attracting attention there thanks to the publicity given to them by another German émigré, Julius Froebel.[74] But learning that Herzen might quit Europe, Mazzini wrote him warmly: "Do not go! Stay here in Europe with us old campaigners. What will you find in America? Freedom? But don't you carry that within you?"[75]

Herzen could not bring himself to quit Europe. One reason was that he remained obsessed with the desire to punish Herwegh whom he now held

[71] Carr, *Romantic Exiles*, 128–129.   [72] Ibid, 132–133.
[73] Herzen to Adolf Reichel, May 21, 1852, and to Maria Reichel, May 24, 1852, *Sobranie sochinenii* XXIV, 274–275.
[74] Herzen to Herwegh, May 30, 1850, *Sobranie sochinenii*, XXIV, 68.
[75] Mazzini to Herzen, May 27, 1852 in Jan Meijer (ed.), "Lettres de Mazzini à Herzen," *Bulletin of the International Institute of Social History*, 8 (1953), 19.

responsible for Natalie's death. And he needed to justify, once again, his refusal to accept Herwegh's challenge to a duel. He wrote an appeal to his "brother democrats" asking that "justice be done without prosecutor or gendarmes, in the name of the solidarity of peoples and the autonomy of the individual."[76] In time his friends responded appropriately, issuing the "verdict" that Herwegh had "forfeited his honour" and that a duel between Herzen and such a man was "impossible."

Eventually, the quarrel between Herzen and Herwegh became common knowledge among political émigrés throughout Europe. Updates on the quarrel appear in Marie d'Agoult's diary, and finally, even Karl Marx got wind of it. In September 1852 he reported gleefully to Engels that Herzen was "sending round memoirs against Herwegh, who has not only cuckolded him but has extorted 80,000 francs from him."[77] Herwegh did his part to keep the controversy alive; and his claim that the whole affair had been mounted with "Russian subsidies" gave Herzen the opportunity to note that nobody had ever been "subsidized" by him except his domestic servants and *"Georg Herwegh himself."*[78] Ironically, it was largely due to Herzen's efforts that the affair became so widely known. During the summer of 1852, Herzen sent long explanations of his conduct, supplemented by fierce attacks on Herwegh, to political allies such as Mazzini, Michelet and Proudhon and to Richard Wagner (who was a friend of Herwegh and wanted no part in Herzen's campaign).[79]

Herzen also attempted to contact George Sand through the good offices of the German scholar Hermann Müller-Strübing, who had once been Sand's lover. Describing Sand as "the highest authority in all that pertains to woman," Herzen wrote that *"She* ought to know this story, she who resumes in her person the revolutionary conception of woman." Herzen's timing was less than perfect, since the German's tenure as Sand's principal lover had been brief, and he had left Nohant more than two years earlier. Nonetheless, Müller-Strübing forwarded Herzen's letter promptly. Sand's response, if any, is unknown, but this episode

[76] "Je vous prends pour juges," Herzen to his brother democrats (1852), *Sobranie sochinenii*, VII, 386–387.
[77] Marie d'Agoult, *Agenda* for 1851, entries for May 3 and June 1, BnF NAF 14328. D'Agoult's source was the German writer Karl Solger and his French wife Adèle; Marx to Engels, September 28, 1852, Karl Marx and Frederick Engels, *Collected Works*, 50 vols. (London, 1975–2004) XXXIX, 199.
[78] Carr, *Romantic Exiles*, 137–138; *Past and Thoughts*, II, 926.
[79] For the letters to Michelet (July 25, 1852), Proudhon (September 6, 1852) and Wagner (July 1852), see *Sobranie sochinenii*, XXIV, 307–310, 324–330 and 295–297. Herzen wrote first to Mazzini, February 6, 1852, but this letter is lost.

underlines the importance of George Sand in the lives of both Alexander and Natalie Herzen.[80]

From the early years of their marriage, Alexander and Natalie Herzen lived in an emotional world shaped, in significant ways, by the novels of George Sand. Like many of their Moscow friends, the Herzens were, as Kate Holland has written, "swept away by [Sand's] novelistic representations of the contradictions and pitfalls of the emotional relations between men and women, and in particular, her figuration of the love triangle in novels such as *Jacques* (1834), *Horace* (1842), and *Consuelo* (1842–1843)."[81] In each of these novels love is celebrated as the noblest of emotions and the highest of virtues. "Why should it be a weakness to abandon oneself to one's own heart?" asks the hero of *Jacques*. "It is when one can love no more that one should weep for oneself and blush to have let the sacred fire go out."[82] In each of these novels also, a tension is set up between a woman's obligations to a conventionally bourgeois partner and the sanctity and irresistibility of love.

This vision of love as a "sacred fire" was Natalie's essential article of faith; Alexander, who had initially been moved by Sand's appeal to the sanctity of love, had long ceased to be guided by that vision. But it was precisely because he remained an admirer of George Sand and because he continued to believe in principle in the right of a woman to follow her desires outside of marriage that Herzen was so deeply wounded by Herwegh's charge that he had used his authority as a husband to prevent his wife from following the dictates of her heart. He kept insisting that Natalie did not really love Herwegh and that he had "seduced" her. Her letters indicate that she was not at all the passive victim that Herzen made her out to be. But the desire to tell his story in his way would inspire him to write what became one of the great European autobiographies.

Herzen's overture to George Sand was his last attempt to get a hearing for his case against Georg Herwegh. When he finally abandoned the effort, he had already settled in London. He had no great fondness for the English, but his options were limited. In any case, he believed his life was over, and what he mainly wanted was peace and quiet. Among the

[80] Herzen to Müller-Strübing, October 18, 1852, *Sobranie sochinenii*, XXIV, 350–351, 516–517. See also Wladimir Karénine, *George Sand. Sa vie et ses oeuvres*, 4 vols. (Paris, 1926), IV, 141–144, which includes the text of Müller-Strübing's letter to Sand.
[81] Kate Holland, "Literary Contexts of Triangular Desire: Natal'ja and Aleksandr Gercen as Readers of George Sand," *Russian Literature*, LXI(I/II) (2007), 175–205.
[82] George Sand, *Jacques* (Paris, 1854), 50. This text appears in Carr, *Romantic Exiles*, 72–73, where it is wrongly attributed to the heroine of Sand's novel. It is spoken by the hero, Jacques, not the heroine, Fernande, and the reference is not to sin (*péché*) but to weakness (*faiblesse*).

302   Alexander Herzen: A Tragedy Both Collective and Personal

old acquaintances Herzen contacted after his arrival in England was Arnold Ruge whom he had last seen following the demonstration of June 13, 1849. "Since that time," Herzen wrote Ruge, "everything has collapsed." France had become "a cave of brigands and a people of lackeys." Of himself, Herzen wrote: "I have lost everything. I have lost my mother and one of my sons in a shipwreck. I have lost my wife. Struck down even in my own home, after terrible, bitter experiences, I wander without occupation or goal from one country to another. Now here I am in London." Herzen said he planned to stay on in London "for about ten days."[83] In fact, he was to remain in the English capital for twelve years and to begin a new life.

The Testimony of a Witness

Herzen never stopped writing about 1848 and its aftermath. His two volumes of essays appeared contemporaneously. Then came his memoirs, the central section of which (Part V) was a three hundred-page account of his personal and political experience of the years 1847–1852. This was written during the ensuing five years, but for the rest of his life he kept on returning to people and events associated with 1848. In the essays he reflects on the meaning of events as he lives through them. In the memoirs he does something different. He attempts to show the link between his own personal tragedy in those years and the failure of the revolutionary movement in 1848 to make good on its promise.

Taken as a whole, Herzen's writings on 1848 and its aftermath occupy a unique place among all the first-hand accounts of these years. What is unique is Herzen's presence in the texts. His tone is not detached and ironic like Tocqueville's and not at all celebratory and narcissistic like that of Lamartine. In his memoirs Herzen is closer to Flaubert, and his *Past and Thoughts* can be read as an ironic and disabused account of his own "sentimental education."[84] But in the essays written in 1848 and 1849 he is first and foremost a witness. A witness who records what he sees and hears and reflects on its meaning, but cannot do anything. A witness who has little to say about the motives of individuals, but who leaves us with vivid images of the face of Paris "after the storm" and of his own reactions: his despair, his sense of hopelessness, his

---

[83] Herzen to Arnold Ruge, September 20, 1852. *Sobranie sochinenii*, XXIV, 342.
[84] See Dolf Oehler, *Le Spleen contre l'oubli. Baudelaire, Flaubert, Heine, Herzen* (Paris, 1996), 225–237.

Figure 8.1 Alexander Herzen late in life. Photograph by Sergei Lvovich Levitsky, Paris 1861. A cousin of Herzen, Levitsky was a pioneer of Russian photography. Photograph: Getty

frustration, and his anguish during the June Days as he sits "with hands folded," listening to the sounds of the killing going on outside.[85] What Herzen has to offer is less analysis than testimony. His writings focus as much on his own responses and his own predicament as on the revolution itself. In the words of the great Russian literary critic Lydia Ginzburg, what Herzen does in his writings on 1848 is to give a "personal and passionate voice to the historical drama of the Russian revolutionary, shaken by the revolution's collapse in Europe."[86] The great question, posed explicitly by Russian intellectuals from Chernyshevsky to Tolstoy and Lenin – What is to be done? – hangs over Herzen's two cycles of essays: What is the radical Russian intellectual to do in the light of the failure of revolution in Europe? Herzen does not answer this question directly. He says at the outset of *From the Other Shore* that he has no answers. Rather, he takes as his main task the destruction of old illusions that have made it impossible for radicals of his generation to act effectively in the world. "We do not produce a new revelation," he writes, "we eliminate the old lie."[87]

Herzen's *Letters from France and Italy* begins in a modest key as a series of conventional travel sketches in a genre popular in Russia ever since the time of Catherine the Great. At the outset, Herzen acknowledges his forerunners in this tradition, paying tribute to "the light hand" of Denis Fonvizin, whose travel letters were published in 1777–1778, and to the popular and influential *Letters of a Russian Traveller* by Nikolai Karamzin, whose letters from a trip to Western Europe in 1789–1790 became a Russian classic. The first four letters (published in Moscow as "Letters from Avenue Marigny") constitute a kind of breezy travelogue recording Herzen's first impressions of Europe. There is comment on theatres, cafés, newspapers, cooks, servants and popular balls; there are frequent comparisons to Russian or "Slavonic" types, institutions and people. But Herzen also tries to generalize, to touch on large issues like Russia's relation to the West, and to offer his own derisive assessment of French bourgeois culture. The next four letters are all from Italy. They discuss with breathless enthusiasm Herzen's discovery of the warmth and energy of the Italians; his delight in the vigour and independence of municipal life in Italy; his identification with the revolutionary movement that swept across the Italian peninsula in the winter of 1847–1848; and, finally, his return to Paris after the February Revolution.

---

[85] *From the Other Shore*, 45.
[86] Lydia Ginzburg, *On Psychological Prose* (Princeton, 1991), 195.
[87] *From the Other Shore*, 3.

What is immediately striking about Herzen's six letters from France is the sheer vividness of the writing. Here, for example, is Herzen's picture of Paris immediately after his return:

Paris had changed greatly since October. There was less magnificence, less foppish cleanliness, fewer rich carriages – and more people moving on the streets. Something sharp and invigorating was borne on the air, ... there was a feeling that revolution had just rushed by on these streets. Crowds of workers surrounded speakers in the shade of the chestnuts of the Tuileries Garden, there were trees of liberty at all the intersections, and sentries in workmen's blouses and overcoats; Caussidière's *montagnards* with large red lapels and with strongly republican, theatrically militant faces, swaggered along the streets. The walls were covered with political notices, the wounded heroes of the barricades, in hospital coats and with pipes in their teeth, looked out from the windows of the Tuileries. On the boulevards and the great streets crowds of boys and girls sold proclamations with a cry and with various tricks. The well-known cry: "Demandez la grrrande colère du Père Duchêne, – un sou! Il est bigrrr-ement en colère le père Duchêne, – un sou cinq centimes!" resounded among a hundred new ones.[88]

No less striking are the portraits of individuals: Lamartine with his unctuous and empty speeches; the earnest Louis Blanc preaching the socialist gospel at the Palais de Luxembourg; Adolphe Thiers, "the wit, the gray gamin, the joker, the windbag, the liberal covered with the blood of Lyon."[89] Significantly, there is little direct discussion of Herzen's initial response to the February Revolution. When his early hopes are evoked, it is almost always retrospectively, In his first letter from Paris, dated June 10, 1848, he already speaks of the failure of the revolution: May 15 had removed the blindfold from his eyes and shown him that the revolution had been defeated.[90]

Why did the Second French Republic so rapidly disappoint the hopes placed on it by democrats? Herzen writes that the revolutionary democrats were betrayed by a Provisional Government divided between radicals and moderates. But he insists that the main reason for the failure of the revolution was that the revolutionaries had not been able to emancipate themselves from traditional ideas and authorities – whether Christian, monarchical or republican. The Provisional Government "lacked faith in its own cause," he writes. "It was afraid to break with the previous order, and it had no new idea of state organization."[91] The monarchy was overthrown and a republic proclaimed, but the centralized apparatus of the state wasn't touched: the police, the army, the courts and the hierarchy of functionaries continued to operate as before. Here

---

[88] *France and Italy*, 122.   [89] Ibid, 123, 151, 178.   [90] Ibid, 120.   [91] Ibid, 147.

Herzen's view came close to that of Proudhon, who described the Provisional Government as "devoid of ideas and goals"[92] and as having attempted to impose from above political solutions to social problems. Ironically, this was something that Herzen himself urged for a brief period. After the June Days he wrote that democrats within the Provisional Government – notably Ledru-Rollin – should have seized dictatorial power to "save the revolution." But by the end of 1848, and possibly under the influence of Proudhon, Herzen had abandoned his faith in force as an instrument of liberation.[93]

The essays collectively entitled *From the Other Shore* are at once more reflective than the *Letters from France and Italy* and more thoroughly infused by passionate feeling. Gone is the artifice of the travelogue. Gone too is the attempt to narrate the course of political events to his Russian readers. Now Herzen is writing for all of democratic Europe. Now he is attempting to come to terms with the past and with his own experience. He is attempting to locate and criticize the assumptions underlying European radicalism – notably the faith in historical progress and the belief in the value of self-sacrifice in the name of a future good – and he is looking for a perspective from which the collapse of his (and Europe's) pre-revolutionary ideals and dreams might make sense. To this end, he adopts two literary genres: the dialogue and the lament or jeremiad.

There are three dialogues in *From the Other Shore*. The protagonists are an elderly skeptic and a young idealist. The idealist wants to believe that history has a sense and a direction. He wants to find something to believe in, something worth fighting for. "What is this mission of ours?" he asks in the first dialogue. "Where is our banner? What *do* we, and what do we not, believe in?" The older man, the skeptic, insists that there is nothing in history, or in our experience, to which we can or should cling. "You are looking for a banner," he says. "I am trying to lose one."[94] The task confronting us today, he insists, is to learn to live in a world without goals – a world in which there is nothing beyond the present. History, he insists, is one long improvisation. "There are no frontiers, no itineraries," and "no libretto."[95]

But this view can only be held by someone who is totally detached, replies the young man. "Your detachment seems suspect to me. It is too much like dead despair." For the living, there must be some goal. "It is painful for man that he cannot see even in the future the harbour towards which he is moving." The skeptic replies that he prefers to think of life,

[92] Pierre-Joseph Proudhon, *Confessions d'un révolutionnaire* (Paris, 1929), 110.
[93] *France and Italy*, 155. Aileen Kelly, "Glowing Footprint", 189.
[94] *From the Other Shore*, 27–28.   [95] Ibid, 39.

and therefore of history, "as an end attained than as a means to something else." He then introduces a powerful metaphor: "And what, pray, is the end of the song that the singer sings? ... The sounds that burst from her throat, the melody that dies as soon as it has resounded? If you look beyond your pleasure in them for something else, for some other end, you will find that the singer has stopped singing, and then you will have only memories, and regrets, and remorse because, instead of listening, you were waiting for something else. You are misled by categories not fitted to catch the flow of life"[96]

The debate continues in various registers through two more dialogues. The second is set on a wet November day marking the proclamation of the Constitution of the Second Republic. On this occasion, which is actually grim and joyless, the young idealist and the middle-aged skeptic meet in the crowd. A year has passed since their first encounter, but for the idealist it feels like a hundred years: "To see all one's finest hopes, all one's innermost aspirations being realized, to see the possibility of their fulfillment and then to fall so low, so far! To lose everything, and not in battle, not in a struggle with the enemy, but by one's own impotence and ineptitude, that's what's terrible." The skeptic observes that his colleague hasn't changed. "You would rather suffer than understand ... You're afraid of facts that don't fit your theories. You believe there is no salvation for the world except along the paths that you have found." You want the world to "dance to your tune," says the skeptic. "You haven't enough curiosity to watch it dance its own dance."[97]

This opens up a broader discussion of the constraints imposed on human freedom by nature and history. We understand the limitations placed on us by nature, says the skeptic, but we haven't grasped those imposed by history. We exaggerate our ability to shape our world. And, what's more, we have an utterly unjustifiable faith in the saving power of political ideals. We believed in February 1848 that the proclamation of a republic was the dawn of a new age. We failed to understand that the old institutions of centralized, monarchical government lived on and that the republic was simply a buttress for a crumbling political order. Now we can no longer delude ourselves. With the emergence of the Party of Order behind a republican façade, and with the crushing of the June insurrection by a republican government, the "religion of the republic," which was "colossal" in 1793, has lost its power to move people. And that is a good thing, for "it is time to stop believing in one sole, saving Church." The task of the present age is not yet to create a new world, but to destroy the vestiges of the old one: "to execute institutions, destroy

---

[96] Ibid, 35.   [97] Ibid, 73–74.

beliefs, break prejudices, shatter hopes of any return to the past, holding nothing sacred, making no concessions, showing no mercy."[98]

The third dialogue is set in Montmorency, the village outside of Paris, where for five years Jean-Jacques Rousseau took refuge from "the noise, the mud and the smoke" of the capital, communed with nature, and wrote three of his greatest works. Here the younger interlocutor is a young woman, an admirer of Rousseau. She shares Rousseau's disappointment with the world, while the older man expects nothing of his fellow humans and is never disappointed. They argue about human nature, about the sympathies and aptitudes of "the masses," and about the process by which the "liberating spirit" of early Christianity turned into "tyrannical catholicism." What particularly disturbs the skeptic is the influence that Christian habits of mind continue to exercise in a secular age. "Having discarded positive religion," he asserts, "we have retained all the habits of religion, and having lost paradise in heaven we believe in the coming paradise on earth and boast about it." The question he addresses to the idealist – and to those committed to any kind of secular utopia – is this: "Could you please explain to me why belief in God is ridiculous and belief in humanity is not; why belief in the kingdom of heaven is silly, but belief in utopias on earth is clever?"[99]

It has been suggested that in these dialogues Herzen was contrasting his own views with others that he held to be erroneous.[100] A more illuminating perspective is that of Lydia Ginzburg who argues that the clash of opposing views "constitutes the very substance of the book [and] defines its intellectual and artistic structure."[101] Herzen was giving expression to conflicts and tensions that he could not finally resolve. He respects the skeptical wisdom of the older man. The individual with low expectations is less likely to be disappointed. And the skeptic certainly gets the best of the argument. But there is more than an argument at stake. Herzen understood that without frustrated idealism, nothing is accomplished. Both views are necessary. And Dostoevsky recognized this, telling Herzen so on his visit to London in 1862. Recalling this visit in his *Writer's Diary*, Dostoevsky went on to make a shrewd remark about Herzen, which helps

[98] Ibid, 84, 98.   [99] Ibid, 120.

[100] Aileen Kelly and Evgeny Lampert, for example, refer to the skeptic as "Herzen" or "Herzen's alter ego" and argue that the views of the young idealist are rejected by Herzen. See Kelly, "Herzen and Proudhon: Two Radical Ironists," in *Views from the Other Shore*, 109 and "Glowing Footprint," 194; and E. Lampert, *Studies in Rebellion* (New York, 1957), 205, 218, 230. See also Ya. El'sberg, *Gertsen, zhizn' i tvorchestvo* (Moscow, 1963), 280–282.

[101] L. Ya. Ginzburg, "'S togo berega' Gertsena (Problematika i postroeniie)," *Izvestiia Akademii nauk SSSR. Otdelenie literatury i iazyka*, 21(2) (1962), 112–124.

us understand the importance that he attached to dialogue as a process involving the constant testing and criticism of one's own views: "Self-reflection – the ability to make of his own deepest feelings an object which he could set before him, pay it tribute, and in the next breath perhaps, ridicule it – was a thing [Herzen] had developed to the highest degree."[102]

If the dialogues in *From the Other Shore* are organized around questions, the laments or jeremiads are written in a very different tone – a tone that combines anger and the sustained expression of grief. The first of these laments, entitled "After the Storm," is the most succinct and the most powerful. It is a lament written shortly after "those painful, ghastly, degrading June Days." It begins with Herzen offering tears and a vivid image to an unnamed reader who has lived through the June Days with him. The image is that of the great dramatic actress Rachel (Elisa Félix) chanting the "Marseillaise" in a desperate broken voice in May after a performance of Racine at the Théâtre français. Herzen, who actually heard Rachel's Marseillaise at least once, describes her voice as "a reproach, a dread premonition, a moan of despair amidst hope."[103] This was no longer the bright, joyous Marseillaise of February (see Figure 8.2). "She was calling men to battle without the faith that they would follow her." Herzen addresses the reader: "The article that I am giving you," he says, "is *my* Marseillaise."

He offers it "not in order to describe or explain the blood-stained events, but simply to talk about them, to give vent to words, tears, thoughts, gall." Seeking to release stored-up impressions and feelings, he evokes sights and sounds but makes no effort to synthesize or generalize:

How can we at this moment describe, collect information, assess what has happened? Our ears are still ringing with the sound of shot, the clatter of galloping cavalry, and the heavy muffled sound of the gun carriages rattling through the dead streets; isolated moments still flicker in the mind's eye, a wounded man on a stretcher pressing his hand to his side and a few drops of blood running down it, omnibuses filled with corpses, prisoners with their hands bound, cannons on the Place de la Bastille, a camp at the Porte Saint-Denis and another on the Champs-Elysées, and the grim nocturnal cry: "Sentinelle, prenez garde à vous!"[104]

During the heaviest fighting, Herzen was confined to his apartment, listening to gunfire and screams, with no possibility of going out. It was

---

[102] Dostoevsky, *Writer's Diary*, I, 127.
[103] *From the Other Shore*, 43. Rachel sang the Marseillaise at the Théâtre Français ten times between May 5 and May 25. Herzen heard her "probably more than once." See B. F. Egorov et al., *Letopis' zhizni i tvorchestva A.I. Gertsena*, 5 vols. (Moscow, 1974), I, 452; and *Sobranie sochinenii*, VI, 40–41.
[104] *From the Other Shore*, 45.

Figure 8.2 "Mademoiselle Rachel reciting the Marseillaise," 1848. While Herzen was mesmerized by Rachel's "despairing" recitation of the Marseillaise, Marie d'Agoult grasped the anger in her voice: "You felt that a curse was the one thing living in her. Her gutteral voice seemed stained with blood. Her fixed stare stalked its prey." Lithograph by Marie-Alexandre Alophe, dit Menut Alophe, on the cover of sheet music published by Lefébure-Wély. Courtesy of Marvin Duchow Music Library, McGill University

enough, he says, "to drive one insane." But at the outset, on the afternoon of June 23, as the barricades were going up in streets and alleys, he
walked along the Seine toward the Hôtel de Ville, and he describes the
scene in a manner worthy of Flaubert:

Shops were closing, detachments of the National Guard, looking menacing, were
marching in various directions, the sky was covered with clouds, it was raining.
I stopped on the Pont-Neuf ... There was a sudden flash of lightning from behind
a cloud, peals of thunder came one after another and in the middle of this the
measured lingering sound of the tocsin rang out from the tower of St. Sulpice ...
A few rays of sunlight gleaming brightly from underneath a cloud cast an unusual
radiance over [Notre-Dame] and all the buildings along the river. One could hear
the drums from all sides; the artillery was moving slowly from the Place
du Carrousel.

Herzen then inserts himself. "I listened to the thunder and the tocsin and
gazed avidly at this panorama of Paris. It was as though I was taking leave
of it. At that moment I loved Paris passionately. It was my last tribute to
the great city; after the June Days it grew hateful to me."[105]

The next *tableau* comes three days later, on the evening of June 26, as
Herzen and his wife sit in their apartment listening to the sound of
gunfire outside. "'The firing squads,' we all said with one voice, and
turned away from each other." Then comes a reflection startlingly similar
to one made in similar circumstances by the narrator of Flaubert's
Education sentimentale: "Moments like these make one hate for a whole
decade, seek revenge all one's life."[106] Herzen continues:

After the slaughter, which lasted four days, silence descended, the calm of a siege;
the streets were still cordoned off and only very occasionally would you see a
carriage. The arrogant National Guard, with an expression of savage, dull cruelty,
protected its shops, threatening passers-by with butt and bayonet; the exultant
crowds of the drunken Garde Mobile marched along the boulevards, singing:
"*Mourir pour la patrie.*" Boys of sixteen, seventeen, boasted of the blood of their
brothers which had dried on their hands; they were thrown flowers by shopgirls
who ran out from behind their counters to greet the victors. Cavaignac carted
about with him in his carriage some monster or other who had killed dozens of
Frenchmen. The bourgeoisie was triumphant. And the houses of the Faubourg
Saint-Antoine were still smouldering the walls broken by shells were falling in,
the interiors of rooms laid bare gaped like stone wounds ... broken furniture was
lying in rotting heaps, pieces of broken mirrors glistened amongst the litter.[107]

[105] Ibid, 45–46.
[106] Ibid, 47. See Gustave Flaubert, *L'Education sentimentale*, Edouard Maynial (ed.) (Paris,
    1961), 338: "The public's reason was deranged as if by some great natural upheaval.
    Intelligent people lost their sanity for the rest of their lives."
[107] *From the Other Shore*, 47–48.

A final *tableau*, reminiscent this time not of Flaubert but of Rimbaud's extraordinary poem on the aftermath of the Paris Commune, "Paris se repeuple," describes the return of elegant ladies and idle strollers and the resumption of normal life with only the passing of patrols and gangs of prisoners to remind one of "the dreadful days." As the dawn illuminates the devastation of a night battle, "such a dawn was now breaking in the soul ...Half our hopes, half our convictions had been killed, ideas of negation and despair stirred in our mind and took root ... After such convulsions the human being cannot remain what he was."[108]

In the rest of the chapter Herzen reflects on the June Days as a potential catalyst for change. He argues that there are two possible responses to a devastating experience which calls into question ideals, convictions and inherited beliefs. Either "the soul clings with desperate stubbornness to its convictions," or else one submits one's most cherished beliefs to the "rough justice" of reason, logic, and skepticism. The metaphor that Herzen calls upon to illustrate the power of logic and the rational criticism of traditional beliefs is that of the guillotine. "Within every man," he writes, "there is a permanent revolutionary tribunal, there is a merciless Fouquier-Tinville and, above all, there is a guillotine. Sometimes the judge may nod, the guillotines grow rusty, and then all that is false, obsolete, romantic, weak raises its head, until suddenly some wild shock rouses the dormant court, the slumbering hangman. Then rough justice begins."[109]

We like to think of ourselves as bold and unflinching inquirers. But it is not easy to part with thoughts that we have grown up with. For the mind is inherently conservative. It wants to hold on to traditional ways of thinking; and when people reject one religion, they often find its attributes in another. Now it is a political religion, the religion of the democratic republic, that needs to be subjected to "rough justice." The lesson of 1848, Herzen asserts, is that, after doing nothing for three months, a democratically elected assembly could rise to its full height and crush the protest of its poorest, most vulnerable citizens. "It is time for man to put the republic on trial, along with its legislation, its system of representation, all our notions about the citizen and his relation to other citizens and to the State."[110]

The second of Herzen's laments is entitled "Year LVII of the Republic, One and Indivisible" and dated October 1, 1848. It begins as a eulogy for the republicans – the true believers in the republican tradition of 1792. The archaic, backward-looking quality of their belief is

---

[108] Ibid, 48.   [109] Ibid, 49.   [110] Ibid, 51–52.

suggested by the title itself, which refers to the anniversary of the first day of the first month in the revolutionary calendar. Herzen describes a speech delivered on this occasion by Ledru-Rollin – a "brilliant" speech "full of red roses for the Republic and prickly thorns for the government." Herzen, who was there, found the occasion moving and celebrates the "energy, courage [and] nobility" displayed by French republicans "when they have torn themselves out of the mean and squalid bourgeois atmosphere which covers the whole of France like a green scum."[111]

But Herzen also writes that he is "sorry for this handful of men, noble, devoted, intelligent, gifted, the finest flower, perhaps, of the new generation." He is sorry for them because of "the sincerity of their delusions, their honest belief in what could never be, their ardent faith, as pure and unreal as the chivalry of Don Quixote." What inspires Herzen's pity is his belief that "the Republic, as *they* imagine it, is an unrealizable abstraction, the fruit of theoretical reflections, the apotheosis of the existing state organization, the transfiguration of *what already exists.*" The republicans are "men of the past who, for all their revolutionary temper, remain tied to the old world, body and soul." Their "fatal error," was that "they threw themselves into the task of liberating others before they had liberated themselves." They said they were "prepared for terrible sacrifices." But, Herzen asks, are they prepared for "those that the new life demands of them? Are they ready to sacrifice contemporary civilization, their way of life, religion, accepted conventional morality?"[112]

After February 24, Herzen argues, liberal republicans became frightened. They wanted freedom and a republic, provided it was confined to their own cultivated circle. Beyond the limits of their circle they became conservatives. "They called for the destruction of "the monarchic and feudal order" in the name of equality and the suffering of the oppressed and the hunger of the poor. But when confronted by the object of their pity, when "the proletarian ... finally asked what was to be his share in all these blessings, what were *his* freedom, *his* equality, *his* fraternity," the liberals were aghast at the ingratitude of the worker. "They took the streets of Paris by assault, they littered them with corpses, and then they hid from their *brother* behind the bayonets of martial law in their effort to save *civilization* and *order!*"[113] Finally, Herzen asserts, *this* civilization and *this* social order cannot be saved. "You cannot save your world," he tells the republicans, "either by martial law or by a republic, or by executions, or by charities, or even by a redistribution of land." A new

---

[111] Ibid, 55–56.   [112] Ibid, 56–58.   [113] Ibid, 59–60.

world is in the making, and "it is no surprise that the world of the bourgeoisie has exhausted itself so soon and has no capacity for self-renewal."[114]

The collapse of the old world is the theme of Herzen's third jeremiad, entitled "*Omnia mea mecum porto*" and dated April 3, 1850. In this essay, Herzen considers the position of the individual at a time when traditional guides are gone, when there is nothing external to rely upon. At such times we are thrown back on our own resources. "We shall find no haven but in ourselves," he asserts, "in the consciousness of our unlimited freedom, of our autocratic independence." Herzen claims that self-emancipation can be the instrument of collective emancipation. "If only people wanted to save themselves instead of saving the world, to liberate themselves instead of liberating humanity, how much they would do for the salvation of the world and the liberation of humanity."[115]

Considered as a whole, *From the Other Shore* vibrates with a sense of horror at the violence and brutality of the repression of the June insurrection. But Herzen's central preoccupation is not the criticism of Cavaignac or the National Assembly or the Party of Order. Rather, it is the critique of the republicans, democrats and socialists who first supported and then betrayed the insurgent Paris workers. At the heart of his argument is the conviction that the great lesson to be learned from 1848 is the inadequacy of the ideas and ideals of the European radicals. They are men of the past, Herzen writes, and their republic is "an unrealizable abstraction ... the last dream, the poetic delusion of the old world."[116] For all their revolutionary temper, they remain tied to the old world, and they cannot abandon old forms like the belief in progress, the belief that history has a goal, and the belief that the beautiful future predicted by radicals can and should justify the sacrifice of a present generation. All of this Herzen sees as a replay of the Christian faith in a glorious afterlife that will justify all earthly pain – or of the ancient religions whose gods had to be placated with human sacrifice.

What gives poignancy to Herzen's argument is the fact that he too looks forward to a future – though not one that can be mapped or charted. He insists that instead of seeking meaning and purpose in the future (or in an idealized past), we need to learn how to live in the present. But Herzen's very title looks forward to "the other shore" that lies beyond the tides of 1848. In his 1855 introduction he urges his son Alexander not to remain on *this shore* but to join the effort to build a bridge to the future.[117] And the text itself abounds in references both to a

[114] Ibid, 66, 68.   [115] Ibid, 128.   [116] Ibid, 57.   [117] Ibid, 3.

future "socialism" and to the possibility of "a new barbarian invasion" in the course of which "Russia will pour into Europe."[118] Thus there are hints in *From the Other Shore* that Herzen's indictment of European radicalism might open the way to a new order.

1848 in Herzen's Memoirs

During the year after his wife's death Herzen referred several times in his correspondence to a "detailed memorandum" in which he planned to refute exhaustively the calumnies spread about by Georg Herwegh, to lay bare the true story of Herwegh's seduction of Natalie, and to vindicate his own reputation and hers. He never wrote this *mémoire* – which he hoped to send to George Sand and to his "brother democrats." But it grew into something much bigger. It became the multi-volume autobiography that told the story of Herzen's life and at the same time offered a picture of Russian and European history running from Napoleon's occupation of Moscow to the café conspiracies of the 1850s and the emergence of Bismarck's Prussia as the dominant European power. Herzen began work on his autobiography in 1852. The writing was to occupy him for the rest of his life. Until his death in 1870 he tinkered with the text, adding chapters, inserting introductions, appendices, and retrospective commentaries. The first five sections (through 1852) had a relatively clear shape, but the last half of the book, which focuses on the London years, is plotless – a collection of fragments.

In an introduction written in 1866, Herzen insisted that the apparently disordered organization of the book was no accident and that he wished the fragmentary structure of his narrative to echo the fragmentary, discontinuous character of his experience. "*My Past and Thoughts*" is not a historical monograph," he wrote, "but a reflection of historical events on a man who has accidentally found himself in their path." Herzen says that he chose to "string together" his disconnected chapters "like the mosaic pictures in Italian bracelets – all of which refer to one subject but are only held together by the setting and the chain."[119] From the beginning, Herzen's plan was to treat his family drama in detail and to establish a close connection between the public and private dimensions of his life during the years 1847–1852. He was convinced that the tragic outcome of his family drama was inextricably linked to the tragic outcome of the revolutions of 1848. As he wrote Karl Vogt in November 1852. "The sad history which took place around my home represents exactly ... the

---

[118] Ibid, 34, 66.   [119] *Past and Thoughts*, II, 639.

February 24 of all the nations." A year later, as he began to work on *My Past and Thoughts*, he wrote that between 1848 and 1852 "everything was shattered – public and private: the European revolution and my home, the freedom of the world and my personal happiness."[120]

The autobiography does indeed turn on 1848 and its aftermath, and in the text Herzen creates an image of himself as speaking from a mountain top reached only after a bitter struggle that has cost him all his illusions. He describes himself as isolated, impotent, crushed by events, "broken and morally mutilated," no longer capable of joy or wonder. "Almost everything has become a matter of indifference to me," he writes, "and I desire as little to die tomorrow as to live long." He has attained some recognition, but along with it he has lost all his beliefs, all that matters to him. "From the middle of the year 1848 I have nothing to tell but agonizing experience, unavenged offences, undeserved blows. My memory holds nothing but melancholy images, my own mistakes and other people's: mistakes of individuals, mistakes of whole peoples. When there was a possibility of salvation, death crossed the path."[121]

Along with his dark and often despairing self-portrait, Herzen also insists on the fundamental inability of historical actors (including himself) to change the world according to a plan – the powerlessness of human beings in the face of facts and movements greater than the will of any individual. This is shown in Herzen's frequent use of the passive voice. He has been moved by events; he is not their mover. He has been thrust about by revolution. He has been caught up in the "pitiless whirlwind of events, lives, peoples, revolutions." But Herzen himself remains immobile. He describes himself as "utterly alone," sitting "in London where chance has flung me."[122]

The almost unrelieved gloom of Herzen's self-presentation in the latter sections of his autobiography underlines his sense of loss in the wake of the multiple tragedies of 1848–1852. But there was another, more optimistic note in Herzen's writing in the aftermath of the June Days. In a series of pamphlets published between 1850 and 1852 Herzen went beyond the indictment of Europe as the reincarnation of Rome in its decline and the critique of Western European radicalism that had been at the heart of *From the Other Shore*. He began to look to Russia and to the Slavic peoples as the bearers of a new socialist ideology that would sweep away the market system and the political economy that were the main achievements of the European bourgeoisie. Herzen came to believe that

---

[120] Herzen to Karl Vogt, November 21, 1852; *Sobranie sochinenii*, XXIV, 361; *Past and Thoughts*, II, 654.
[121] *Past and Thoughts*, II, 654.   [122] Ibid, II, 655.

the Russian peasant commune, with its unique traditions of self-management, might serve as the basis for an authentically Russian socialism. Thus a few years later, as he settled into London and established the Free Russian Press (1853) and then *The Polar Star* (1855) and the enormously influential newspaper *The Bell* (1857), Herzen created for himself the foundations of a rich and productive second life. But his most lasting achievement in that life was neither the journalism nor the founding of the press but rather the writing of *My Past and Thoughts*.

There are, however, two ironies connected with the writing and publication of Herzen's memoirs. The first is that even though he claimed to have written *My Past and Thoughts* in order to tell the story of his family drama, Herzen did not in the end feel that he could publish that section. Not until 1919, a half-century after his death, did the book appear in its intended shape with the long section on Herzen's family drama. This was in part simply because he could not bring himself to rehash in public the intimate details of the family drama.[123] But more specifically, by the later 1850s Herzen once again found himself in a situation – an amorous triangle – not unlike that in which he, Natalie and Herwegh had been involved – only now he was himself playing the role of Herwegh! This is the second irony connected with the writing and publication of *My Past and Thoughts*. As he was attempting to bring the book to its completion, he was living with the wife of his best friend, Nicholas Ogarëv. Herzen and Natalie Tuchkova-Ogarëva had three children together. But all three were given Ogarëv's name, and not a word was said in the memoirs about any of this.[124] The problem was that any discussion of the facts of his life in the 1850s would have weakened the thematic structure and the coherence of *My Past and Thoughts* in which the innocence of Natalie and the perfidy of Herwegh echo and reinforce the contrast between a young and virile Russia and the corrupt and dying European world. Thus, Herzen never stopped seeking to make his own sense of the shattering events of the five years that followed the revolution of February 1848.

[123] On the history of the composition and publication of Herzen's memoirs, see Paperno, "Intimacy and History," 20–51.
[124] There was nothing secret about Herzen's relationship with Natalie Tuchkova. As Evgeny Lampert writes (*Studies in Rebellion*, 188): "The arrangement turned into a *mariage à trois*, to be more precise, a *mariage à trois à la russe*, involving none of the twists, mystifications, sublimations and betrayals of which the Herwegh affair provides such abundant evidence. Besides, Herzen undoubtedly loved Ogarev more than his mistress, and Ogarev, in turn, loved Herzen more than his wife."

9   Marx

The Meaning of a Farce

More has surely been written about Karl Marx than about all our other writers put together (see Figure 9.1). In recent years special attention has been given to *Class Struggles in France* and *The Eighteenth Brumaire of Louis Bonaparte*. But there is no consensus on how these works should be read. For Frederick Engels Marx was the inventor of the "science" of historical materialism; and Engels asserts that they constitute the first application of Marx's method to the study of a problem in contemporary history.[1] Others approach these texts biographically as the work of a political journalist and activist attempting to explain to the German working class the lessons to be drawn from the defeat of the proletariat in 1848–1849. Still, others argue that *Class Struggles* and *The Eighteenth Brumaire* should be considered and criticized as historical writings. Thus Mark Traugott has published an important historical critique of Marx's concept of the *lumpenproletariat;* and Roger Price has written a history of 1848 in France the express aim of which is to question the adequacy of Marx's key concepts to an understanding of 1848.[2] Gareth Stedman Jones has taken the critique a step farther, arguing that the bourgeoisie was not a real social and political actor at all but "a rhetorical creation," a force deployed for political ends by both governments and oppositions.[3] Finally, a number of contemporary critics have been drawn to these texts above all by the power of Marx's language – by what Dominick LaCapra describes as the "powerfully carnivalized style" of the *Eighteenth*

[1] Frederick Engels, "Preface to the Third Edition" [1885] of Karl Marx, *The Eighteenth Brumaire of Louis Bonaparte* (New York, 1963), 14.
[2] Mark Traugott, *Armies of the Poor: Determinants of Working Class Participation in the Parisian Insurrection of June 1848* (Princeton, 1985); Roger Price, *The French Second Republic: A Social History* (Ithaca, 1972); Maurice Agulhon, *1848 ou l'Apprentissage de la République: 1848–1852* (Paris, 2002).
[3] Gareth Stedman Jones, "Elusive Signifiers: 1848 and the Language of Class Struggle" in Douglas Moggach and Gareth Stedman Jones (eds.), *The 1848 Revolutions and European Political Thought* (Cambridge, 2018), 430.

Figure 9.1 Karl Marx in London, 1861. Hulton Archive via Getty

Brumaire, a style "that exceeds any narrowly productive or didactic project or goal."[4]

My approach in this chapter is initially biographical and contextual, though, like LaCapra and many others, I too have been drawn to Marx by the sheer rhetorical power of his writing. And since one of my aims in the whole book is to look closely at the language of each writer and to consider the relations between style and substance, much of what I have to say about Marx will focus on questions of metaphor, imagery and rhetoric. But first, something must be said about the Hegelian background to Marx's thought and the intellectual journey that took Marx from Hegel to Feuerbach to communism.

Hegel and History: Paris and Brussels

Marx famously claimed that his theory of history was Hegelian idealism "turned upside down." He put it this way in the Afterword to the second German edition of *Capital*:

My dialectic method is not only different from the Hegelian, but its direct opposite. To Hegel the life process of the human brain, i.e. the process of thinking, which, under the name of "the Idea," he even transforms into an independent subject, is the demiurgos of the real world, and the real world is only the external, phenomenal form of "the Idea." With me, on the contrary, the ideal is nothing else than the material world reflected by the human mind, and translated into forms of thought.[5]

Writing in 1873, Marx took pride in the fact that much earlier, as the "peevish, arrogant, mediocre epigones" of German philosophy were treating Hegel as a "dead dog," he had openly identified himself as "the pupil of that mighty thinker." In its "mystified form" the dialectic had been fashionable for a time because it seemed to glorify the existing state and society. But the mystification that the dialectic suffered in Hegel's hands did not prevent him from being "the first to present its general form of working in a comprehensive and conscious manner." With Hegel, the dialectic was "standing on its head." It had to be "turned right side up ... to discover the rational kernel within the mystical shell."[6]

---

[4] Dominick LaCapra, "Reading Marx: The Case of 'The Eighteenth Brumaire" in *Rethinking Intellectual History: Texts, Contexts, Language* (Ithaca, 1983), 288. See also Donald Reid, "Inciting Readings and Reading Cites: Visits to Marx's *The Eighteenth. Brumaire of Louis Bonaparte,*" *Modern Intellectual History*, IV(3) (2007), 545–570.

[5] Karl Marx, *Capital: A Critical Analysis of Capitalist Production*, 3 vols. (Moscow, 1961), I, 19. "Afterword to the Second German Edition."

[6] Marx, *Capital*, I, 19–20.

In the 1870s, Hegel seemed part of a lost world. But in the early 1840s Marx, like many of his "Young Hegelian" contemporaries, simultaneously argued with Hegel and looked to him for guidance as to Germany's way forward. In his lectures on the *Philosophy of History* (given in the 1820s but only published in 1837) Hegel had charted two paths in the modern history of freedom. As Stedman Jones has succinctly characterized them, the first, the philosophical path, began with the German Reformation. By freeing religion from external authority, Luther had encouraged the development of the German virtues of inwardness and reflective thought. This path culminated with Kant and the liberation of the individual from received beliefs. The second or political path led to the French Revolution. Despite the Terror, the French Revolution had created conditions in which the individual's internal freedom could be expressed in external and institutional form. In his later years, Hegel came to believe that in Prussia a program of rational reforms was accomplishing peacefully what the French Revolution had tried to impose by force.[7]

Hegel's hopes were already being called into question in the 1820s. Nothing came of Frederick William III's promise in 1815 to call a representative assembly in Prussia. The Carlsbad Decrees of 1819 limited freedom of the press, speech, and assembly, and inaugurated a decade of police persecution in Prussia and most of the other German states. The revolutions of 1830, which brought independence to Belgium and widened the suffrage in France, only served to put German rulers on the defensive. In 1832 the German Confederation tightened censorship and political repression. Hopes that Prussia might become a constitutional monarchy receded; and they were not improved in 1840 with the succession to the Prussian throne of the romantic conservative Frederick William IV.

During his student years at the universities of Bonn and Berlin (1836–1841), Marx got caught up in the "grotesque craggy melody" of Hegelian philosophy and was enthralled by the effort of the Young Hegelians to work out the critical implications of Hegel's philosophy of religion. He came to believe with Feuerbach that Christianity was humanity's unrecognized projection of its own powers and faculties on the alienated and abstract form of a domineering God. In 1841, he produced a dissertation on the materialist philosophies of Democritus and Epicurus which was – in its methods if not its conclusions – inspired by Hegel. With the completion of this dissertation, Marx appeared to be

---

[7] Gareth Stedman Jones, *Karl Marx: Greatness and Illusion* (Cambridge, MA, 2016), 69.

on his way to a career as a professor of philosophy. But in the spring of 1842, after the dismissal of his mentor Bruno Bauer from his teaching post at Bonn, it became evident that there was no future in the German academic world for the atheist and materialist that Marx had become.

In the fall of 1842, Marx accepted a position as editor of the *Rheinische Zeitung*, a newspaper founded a year earlier by a group of wealthy liberals in Cologne. During his tenure as editor Marx argued for a free press, religious freedom and the rights of poor peasants, making what was in fact the last major attempt to chart a progressive path for Prussia in Hegelian terms. He reached a wide audience. But nothing came of his appeal for reforms that would bring Prussia closer to the Hegelian ideal of a rational state. Indeed, the Prussian authorities shut down the *Rheinische Zeitung* as of April 1843. Six months later, convinced that there could be no political solution to Germany's problems, Marx moved to Paris with his new bride, Jenny von Westphalen. His plan was to collaborate with Arnold Ruge on the publication of an annual journal, to be called the *Deutsch-Französische Jahrbücher*, which would bring German philosophy and French socialism to bear on the critical analysis of the contemporary world and Germany's place in it.[8]

During his sixteen months in Paris (October 1843–February 1845) Marx discovered socialism and the proletariat, inaugurated his life-long partnership with Engels and became possessed by an image of the French Revolution as the prototype of a future German revolution. Preoccupied, like many German intellectuals, with a sense of German backwardness, he imagined a German revolution which would go beyond and complete the French Revolution.[9] He embarked on an intense study of French history, French socialism and British political economy. He thought about the nature of revolution, the limits of political reform, and the importance of economic forces as keys to historical change. He read and criticized Smith, Ricardo and Say in the light of French socialism and German historical theory. He studied the French materialist philosophers and found in them weapons to turn on Hegelian idealism. At the same time, he used Hegelian categories (alienation, dialectics) to understand labour and material life.

In the Introduction to his "Contribution to the Critique of Hegel's *Philosophy of Right*" which appeared in February 1844 in the first (and

[8] See Lucien Calvié, "Ruge and Marx: Democracy, Nationalism, and Revolution in Left Hegelian Debates" in Douglas Moggach (ed.), *Politics, Religion, and Art: Hegelian Debates* (Evanston, IL, 2011), 301–320.

[9] François Furet, *Marx and the French Revolution*, trans. Deborah Kan Furet (Chicago, IL, 1988), 3.

only) issue of the *Deutsch-Französische Jahrbücher*, Marx declared that the critique of religion (which he memorably described as "the sigh of the oppressed creature, the heart of a heartless world ... the *opium* of the people") was now complete. Feuerbach had shown that religions were human creations, forms of alienated consciousness in which human beings projected their own powers onto an imaginary God. Now that human self-alienation had been "unmasked in its *holy form*," the task was "to unmask [it] in its *unholy forms.*" [10] This meant turning from the criticism of theology to the criticism of politics. It also meant the rejection of the pursuit of the Hegelian ideal of a rational state and the adoption of a new language of politics. In his "Critique of Hegel's *Philosophy of Right*," we find Marx for the first time speaking of "civil society" and "popular revolution" and the "total redemption of humanity." Here "emancipation" is understood not in Hegelian terms as the product of the progress of Spirit but as the result of a "human" transformation of the "relations between man and man." In conclusion, Marx for the first time identified "the proletariat" as the instrument whereby *political* self-alienation could be overcome. [11]

In Marx's subsequent writings his language was to undergo further transformations as he made his own the concepts of political economy. This is already evident in the "Economic and Philosophical Manuscripts" of 1844 where the concept of alienation is applied not to religious belief or to political forms, but to material life and specifically to the labour process. Here history is seen as the story of man's alienation in his life as a producer; and communism, the goal of the historical process, is presented as the final transcendence of alienation through the abolition of private property.

Marx spent most of his sixteen months in Paris reading and writing. He plunged into that "endless sea of books" which, as Arnold Ruge observed, was his real element. [12] But his writing at this time also grew out of his contact with the life of the city. He found Paris exciting. In fact, he thrilled at "the boldness, the frankness, the graceful petulance" of the dancers at Le Bal de la Chaumière, and in *The Holy Family* he mocked a poor German critic whose Kantian categories did not permit him to

[10] Karl Marx, "Contribution to the Critique of Hegel's Philosophy of Right. Introduction" in Karl Marx (ed.), *Early Writings*, trans. Rodney Livingstone and Gregor Benton (New York, 1975), 244. Also in Karl Marx and Frederick Engels, *Collected Works*, 50 vols. (London, 1975–2005), III, 175–176. (Henceforth: MECW.)
[11] Marx, "Contribution" in *Early Writings*, 255–257; MECW, III, 186–187.
[12] Arnold Ruge quoted in David McLellan (ed.), *Karl Marx: Interviews and Recollections* (Totowa NJ, 1981), 8.

appreciate the "frank human sensuality" of the dancers.[13] But more important than Marx's occasional forays into dance halls was his discovery of the Paris of workers and artisans. It was in Paris that for the first time Marx met real workers. Many of these workers were members of the large German community of journeyman artisans who had come to France in search of work.[14] Marx was close to the émigré artisans who made up the radical secret society, the League of the Just. But his most memorable encounters seem to have been with French workers. He said as much in a famous passage in the 1844 manuscripts:

> When communist *workmen* gather together, their immediate aim is instruction, propaganda, etc. But at the same time they acquire a new need – the need for society – and what appears as a means has become an end. This practical development can be most strikingly observed in the gatherings of French socialist workers. Smoking, eating, and drinking, etc., are no longer means of creating links between people. Company, association, conversation, which in its turn has society as its goal, is enough for them. The brotherhood of man is not a hollow phrase, it is a reality, and the nobility of man shines forth upon us from their work-worn faces.[15]

The ordinarily unsentimental Marx must have been deeply moved by his visits to these "gatherings of French socialist workers." For he used identical language in describing them to Ludwig Feuerbach: "You would have to attend one of the meetings of the French workers to appreciate the pure freshness, the nobility which burst forth from these toil-worn men." In *The Holy Family*, he returned once again to "the studiousness, the craving for knowledge, the moral energy, and the unceasing urge for development" of the French workers, which he saw as evidence of the "nobility" of their movement.[16] These encounters surely stimulated Marx's analytic efforts as much as his readings in economics and history.

Marx was not much interested in salon life or in making friends in Parisian literary circles. But he was part of the large community of radical German expatriates living in Paris at the time. Briefly, after his arrival in Paris, he and Jenny shared a house with Ruge and his wife – and also with Alexander Herzen's future nemesis, Georg Herwegh and his wife. Marx

---

[13] Marx and Engels, *The Holy Family or Critique of Critical Critique* (Moscow, 1956), 91; MECW, IV, 68.

[14] See B. Nicolaievski and O. Maenchen-Helfin, *Karl Marx*, trans. Marcel Stora (Paris, 1937), 73: "According to the reports of secret Prussian agents, who festered at Paris, Marx was, during the summer of 1844, a regular visitor at the gatherings of artisans at the Barrière du Trône on the rue de Vincennes."

[15] Marx, "Economic and Philosophical Manuscripts" in *Early Writings*, 365; MECW, III, 313.

[16] Marx to Feuerbach, August 11, 1844 in MECW, III, 355; Marx and Engels, *Holy Family*, 113.

sometimes participated in the meetings of the writers and staff of the biweekly radical newspaper *Vorwärts!* for which he wrote occasional articles; and his relations with the best-known German expatriate in Paris, Heinrich Heine, were warm. When he left Paris early in 1845, Marx wrote Heine that "of all the people I am leaving behind here, those I leave with the most regret are the Heines. I would gladly include you in my luggage!" [17] But the most important event for Marx during the Paris period was the visit of Frederick Engels. On August 28, 1844, Engels met with Marx at the Café de la Régence near the Palais Royal. They had met once before – in the office of the *Rheinische Zeitung* two years earlier – and had had an unmemorable conversation. This time they understood and appreciated each other. The conversation, which soon moved to Marx's apartment on the rue Vaneau, went on for ten days, during the course of which they established a partnership that was to last until Marx's death. Forty years later, Engels could write: "When I visited Marx in Paris in the summer of 1844, it was clear that we were in complete agreement on all theoretical questions; our joint work dated from that time."[18]

Marx's relations with French socialists were less satisfactory. He later wrote that toward the end of his stay in Paris he and Louis Blanc concluded "a sort of alliance, but an alliance that was not particularly cordial."[19] Otherwise, Marx had little to do with the French socialists except for Proudhon. He and Ruge had no success in convincing any of them to write for the *Jahrbücher*. Thus, the project of Franco-German collaboration got nowhere.

Marx's two most significant non-German relationships in Paris were with his future adversaries Bakunin and Proudhon. The extroverted Bakunin had entered enthusiastically into the expatriate community in Paris, and he and Marx saw each other often. Although Marx was four years younger than Bakunin, he was the dominant partner; and much later Bakunin paid tribute to the intelligence of this young man who was "already an atheist, an informed materialist, and a conscious socialist" at the age of twenty-six. Despite their intellectual and temperamental

[17] Marx to Heine, end January-February 1, 1845 in MECW, XXXVIII, 21. On Marx and *Vorwärts*, see Stedman Jones, *Karl Marx*, 158–165, and Jacques Grandjonc, *Marx et les communistes allemands à Paris* (Paris, 1974), 58–84, 142–163.
[18] Frederick Engels, "On the History of the Communist League" in Karl Marx and Frederick Engels, *Selected Works*, 2 vols. (Moscow, 1962), II, 344. (Subsequently: MESW). Also in MECW, XXVI, 318. The partnership was lasting, but the "complete agreement" was a retrospective fantasy on Engels' part.
[19] Nicolaevski and Maenchen-Helfen, *Karl Marx*, 74. Marx's first contact with French radicals seems to have occurred only in March 1844, when he attended a banquet organized by the republican socialist journal *La Réforme*.

differences, Bakunin claimed that during the summer and fall of 1845 he learned much from Marx:

We met fairly often because I very much admired him for his knowledge and for his passionate and earnest devotion to the cause of the proletariat, although it always had in it an admixture of personal vanity; and I eagerly sought his conversation, which was instructive and witty so long as it was not inspired by petty spite – which, unfortunately, happened very often.[20]

Despite Bakunin's barbs, it was only much later, at the time of the founding of the First International, that the great falling out between the two occurred.

Marx's period of close personal contact with Proudhon was brief. But the relationship was intense on both sides. Marx was later to claim that he "taught" Hegel to Proudhon. But he also celebrated Proudhon as an authentic proletarian, and in *The Holy Family* he paid tribute to Proudhon for having offered "the first resolute, pitiless, and at the same time scientific investigation of the foundation of political economy, *private property.*" Proudhon had, wrote Marx, made "a real science of political economy possible."[21] But after Proudhon's publication in 1846 of *La Philosophie de la misère*, Marx turned on Proudhon. Accusing Proudhon of misunderstanding the dialectic and describing historically changing economic relationships as if they were "pre-existing eternal ideas," Marx denounced his work as "petty-bourgeois sophistry."[22]

Marx was expelled from France in January 1845, and for the next three years he lived in Brussels. His goal in Brussels was to carve out for himself a leading position in the German emigration, to rally German-speaking radicals throughout Europe, and through his writings to bond German theory and the French revolutionary tradition. In the process, he repeatedly became embroiled in arguments with other radicals – notably Weitling, Hess, Grün and Stirner – and his attempts to reach a German audience were often fruitless.[23] But he was nothing if not persistent, and he had some success not only in Brussels but also in London.

In Brussels Marx was in regular contact with the members of various German communist workers organizations. He gave lectures, printed

[20] E. H. Carr, *Michael Bakunin* (New York, 1961), 135.
[21] Marx and Engels, *The Holy Family*, 46; MECW, IV, 32.
[22] Marx, *La Misère de la philosophie* (Paris, 1847); McLellan, *Karl Marx*, 104, 159–166; Werner Blumenberg, *Karl Marx: An Illustrated Biography* (London, 2000), 66–67. For Proudhon's perspective, see above, Chapter 7, pp. 243–244.
[23] Jonathan Sperber, *Karl Marx: A Nineteenth-Century Life* (New York, 2013), 177–185, 188–190.

circulars and wrote articles in the radical newspaper, the *Deutsche Brüsseler Zeitung*. He also established a German Workers' Circle which soon had a hundred members and featured musical entertainments and poetry readings as well as weekly political discussions.[24] His most ambitious venture at Brussels was the creation of a Communist Correspondence Committee, intended, as he told Proudhon, "to put German socialists in touch with English and French socialists."[25] This committee was almost entirely German, and its ranks were occasionally reduced by purges. But it was, in David McLellan's words, "the embryo of all the subsequent Communist Internationals."[26]

London, where Marx was to take up permanent residence in 1849, was already important to him during these years. In the summer of 1845 on a visit to London, Marx was introduced by Engels to a group of German radicals who were members of a revolutionary secret society called the League of the Just. Although some of these men were educated intellectuals, the majority were working class; and their first intellectual guide was the journeyman tailor and Christian communist, Wilhelm Weitling, whom Marx initially praised as a persecuted proletarian prophet but soon came to dismiss as a utopian dreamer.[27] To recruit new members, the leaders of the League of the Just had created a non-secret society, the German Workers' Educational Association, which at its height had 700 members to whom it offered adult education and a mutual benefits fund. Its leaders were the shoemaker Heinrich Bauer, the watchmaker Joseph Moll and the former typesetter Karl Schapper. Marx met these three in London and was impressed by their energy and determination. They were a bit suspicious of him as an ambitious intellectual with his own agenda. But in the short run they were useful to each other.[28]

In 1846, Marx replaced Weitling as the ideological mentor of the League of the Just; and in June 1847 the League (then headed by Schapper) merged with Marx's Communist Correspondence Committee to form a new organization called the Communist League. At a London Congress in November 1847 Marx and Engels were

---

[24] Stedman Jones, *Karl Marx*, 237–238.
[25] Marx to Proudhon, May 5, 1846, MECW, XXXVIII, 39.
[26] McLellan, *Karl Marx*, 154.
[27] Sperber, *Karl Marx*, 179–181; Francis Wheen, *Karl Marx: A Life* (New York, 2000), 99–105; Alan Gilbert, *Marx's Politics. Communists and Citizens* (New Brunswick, NJ, 1981), 74–79.
[28] Sperber, *Karl Marx*, 155–158; McLellan, *Karl Marx*, 167–170. On the German Workers' Educational Association, see Christine Lattek, *Revolutionary Refugees: German Socialism in Britain, 1840–1860* (London, 2006), 22–47.

commissioned to prepare a new program for the Communist League. Engels wrote two drafts, both in the form of a catechism. But the two agreed that it would be better to adopt a more forceful tone and to call the document a "manifesto."[29]

The Communist Manifesto, which in the end was almost entirely written by Marx, included little that the authors had not already said. What was new was the way it was said – the depiction of the limitless power and global reach of modern capitalism, the production by the bourgeoisie of "wonders far surpassing Egyptian pyramids, Roman aqueducts and Gothic cathedrals," the evocation of the bourgeois present as a time of constant upheaval in which all fixed relations are swept away and "all that is solid melts into air," the cascade of images from the "spectre haunting Europe" at the outset to the "chains" of the conclusion.[30] The rhetorical power of the text, the relentless logic of the argument, and the clarity and forcefulness of the language, now virtually devoid of Hegelianisms, were to make the work unforgettable to subsequent generations. At the time, however, it was scarcely noticed. Just a few days after its appearance revolution broke out in France: barricades rose all over Paris, the July Monarchy fell, and a Provisional Government took power with the mandate of organizing elections for a National Assembly that would draw up a republican constitution.

"The Beautiful Revolution" and Its Aftermath

In retrospect, Marx derided the February Revolution as the "beautiful revolution" – a pale, ghostly imitation of 1789, in which real issues and conflicts were hidden in clouds of rhetoric about fraternity and class harmony. At the time, however, Marx and Engels were jubilant. On the night of February 25–26, Engels wrote from Brussels that the revolution in France was a triumph for democracy in all of Europe. "The flames of the Tuileries and the Palais Royal are the dawn of the proletariat ... If the Germans have any energy, any pride or any courage, then in a month's time we too shall be able to shout, 'Long live the German Republic!'"[31] On February 27, Marx received word that the Central Committee of the Communist League in London was transferring its powers to Brussels and to him. The next day, as vice-president of the Brussels Democratic

---

[29] On the background to the writing of the *Communist Manifesto*, see Gareth Stedman Jones, "Introduction" to his edition of *The Communist Manifesto* (London, 2002), 39–73.
[30] Marx and Engels, *Communist Manifesto*, Stedman Jones (ed.), 222–223.
[31] Engels, "Revolution in Paris," *Deutsche-Brüsselet-Zeitung*, 17, February 27, 1848; MECW, VI, 558; Oscar J. Hammen, *Red '48ers. Karl Marx and Friedrich Engels* (New York, 1969), 196.

Association, Marx co-signed a letter to the Provisional Government in Paris, expressing confidence that Belgium would soon overthrow its monarchy and establish a republic of its own.[32]

Meanwhile, after an initial moment of panic, the Belgian King Leopold I took steps to deal vigorously with any popular demonstration. Having informed his cabinet that he was ready to abdicate if the people wished it, he mobilized the Civic Guard and placed the army on alert. Brussels was quiet on February 26. The following day the Brussels Democratic Association held a large but peaceful meeting. That evening a big crowd gathered on Brussels' Grand Place in front of the Hôtel de Ville, but after a brief demonstration it was dispersed by mounted soldiers. The apparent ringleaders were arrested and a few bystanders were detained. That was the end of the Belgian Revolution.

Marx was not involved in the demonstration of February 27. But as a politically active foreigner, he was an easy target for the Belgian authorities who blamed the unrest on "exalted Germans." On March 3 he was ordered to leave Belgium. A few days earlier, the "brave and loyal Marx" had been formally invited by Ferdinand Flocon, a member of the Provisional Government, to return to the French Republic, the "asylum for all friends of liberty." He was happy to accept the invitation.[33]

Marx arrived in Paris on March 5. Eight days later demonstrations in Vienna forced the resignation of Metternich and the appointment of a liberal ministry. On March 18 the revolution reached Berlin, and King Frederick William IV was compelled to grant an elected Prussian parliament, a free press, and an assembly which would meet at Frankfurt to draw up a constitution for all of Germany. It now became possible for exiled German radicals to return home. In Paris, a group of German exiles, led by Georg Herwegh and Adalbert von Bornstedt, were proposing to enroll German artisan émigrés in a German Democratic Legion. The idea was to march them into South Germany and establish a German republic. Marx rightly regarded this scheme as hair-brained and convinced the Communist League (and the initially enthusiastic Engels) to oppose it. Nonetheless, Herwegh and Bornstedt went ahead with the plan, which turned out to be the disaster that Marx had anticipated. The Legion was badly defeated in its first encounter with the Prussian army; and Herwegh only managed to get away from the field of battle by disguising himself as a woman.[34]

---

[32] Hammen, *Red '48ers*, 196–197.
[33] Hammen, *Red '48ers*, 196–200; Sperber, *Karl Marx*, 214–216.
[34] Sperber, *Karl Marx*, 216–217.

While in Paris, Marx was totally absorbed in German affairs.[35] Seeking to build a social-democratic coalition in support of bourgeois revolution, he formed a new Central Committee of the Communist League and got its approval for a political program that he drew up with Engels in late March. This was a set of seventeen specific "Demands of the Communist Party in Germany" intended to be circulated as a leaflet for emigré artisans to distribute on their return to Germany. To attract bourgeois support these demands were limited: a single, indivisible German republic, universal male suffrage, salaries for representatives, abolition of feudal obligations, a state bank, free schooling, nationalized transportation, separation of church and state, inheritance rights curtailed (but not abolished), etc.[36] Marx had written in the *Manifesto* that since "the bourgeois revolution in Germany" would be "the prelude to an immediately following proletarian revolution," it was important "to instill in the working class the clearest possible recognition of the antagonism between bourgeois and proletariat."[37] But in the short run he urged German Communists to join the struggle of bourgeois democrats against the "feudal" monarchy of Frederick William IV and for the establishment of representative institutions like those won by the French in 1789.

Early in April, after just a month in Paris, Marx moved to Cologne along with Engels and other members of the Communist League. Now that political censorship had ended in Prussia, Marx hoped to reclaim the influential role that he had played six years earlier as the editor of the *Rheinische Zeitung*. After difficult negotiations with potential financial backers, the *Neue Rheinische Zeitung*, began to appear on June 1. The paper would survive for almost a year; and despite recurrent financial problems, it flourished. Its press run reached 6,000 copies an issue; it became the most influential radical newspaper in the Rhineland; and Marx was in total control, serving as chief editor with a three-year contract that guaranteed him editorial autonomy and a handsome salary. In accordance with its subtitle, "Organ of Democracy," the *Neue Rheinische Zeitung* gave its support to Cologne's democratic clubs and exhorted the liberal bourgeoisie throughout Germany to separate itself boldly from the monarchy and its agents. Attacking the Prussian monarchy, the bureaucracy and the army, the paper ridiculed the Prussian Constituent Assembly and the Frankfurt Parliament for failing to act in a

---

[35] Contrary to claims sometimes made, Marx did not participate in French club meetings during his month in Paris. See Hammen, *Red '48ers*, 200–201.

[36] Marx and Engels, "Demands of the Communist Party in Germany" in MECW, VII, 3–7.

[37] Marx and Engels, *The Communist Manifesto*, 258. See also Introduction by Stedman Jones, 15–16.

manner becoming to a revolutionary bourgeoisie by abolishing all vestiges of feudalism as the French had in 1789. In place of their pitiful
political moderation, wrote Marx, evoking the slogan of French revolutionaries in 1792, the goal of democrats should be "the German
Republic, One and Indivisible."[38] To unite Germany's democrats and
republicans, Marx urged a revolutionary war against Russia. Here again,
he was inspired by the example of 1792: revolutionary war had made
radical revolution possible then, and Marx saw a new revolutionary war
as leading to the same goal in 1848.[39] From the beginning, however,
Marx and Engels ran up against the fact that what most liberals wanted
was not a republic but a constitutional monarchy.[40]

During its first six months, the *Neue Rheinische Zeitung* had little to say
about working-class politics. At this point, Marx believed that the main
task of the workers should be to support the bourgeoisie in its struggle
against the monarchy and feudalism. Thus, he distanced himself from
the workers' movement at Cologne and its most articulate and influential
leader, Andreas Gottschalk. Marx opposed Gottschalk's proposal to
stand a separate slate of workers' candidates in parliamentary elections;
he resisted Gottschalk's agitation for the establishment of a workers'
republic in Germany; and in July 1848, while Gottschalk was in prison
on trumped-up charges, Marx and his followers moved to take over
Gottschalk's hugely successful Cologne Workers' Association, turning
it into the educational arm of the democratic movement. The problem
with this strategy was that the workers themselves were not interested in
bourgeois revolution; and membership in the Cologne Workers'
Association dropped precipitously after the takeover.[41]

The one exception to the downplaying of proletarian revolution in the
Neue Rheinische Zeitung was its coverage of the June Days in France.
Engels wrote half a dozen daily reports on the fighting in Paris. But more
interesting to us is a single article published by Marx on June 29. This
article is striking in two respects. First, it is really a celebration of the June
insurrection. This distinguishes it from almost all the commentary produced by left-wing writers throughout Europe. The June insurrection
was an attempt to overthrow a democratically elected assembly, and most
German republicans and democrats were appalled by it. The organ of the
Cologne Democratic Society, *Der Wächter am Rhein*, saluted the French

---

[38] Sperber, *Karl Marx*, 225.
[39] Ibid., 226; Hammen, *Red '48ers*, 276; Franz Mehring, *Karl Marx, The Story of his Life*,
trans. Edward Fitzgerald (London, 1951), 169.
[40] Hammen, *Red '48ers*, 229–234.
[41] Sperber, *Karl Marx*, 219–221, 228–229; Hammen, *Red '48ers*, 257–263.

government's victory over the "anarchy" that would have led to a "Red Republic."[42] Marx's article, on the other hand, is an encomium. He describes the rebels as "plebians tormented by hunger, reviled by the press, ... abused by honest folk as thieves, incendiaries and galley-slaves," and concludes: "It is the *right* and the *privilege of the democratic press* to place laurels on their dark, threatening brows."[43]

The second striking feature of this article is that it anticipates the rhetorical fireworks of the *Class Struggles in France* and *The Eighteenth Brumaire*. The main theme is stated at the outset: the workers of Paris have been "*overwhelmed* by superior strength" but "not *subdued.*" The "triumph of brute force" is only "momentary," Marx writes, and it has been purchased at a high cost – "the destruction of all the delusions and illusions of the February revolution" and the division of France into "two nations, the nation of owners and the nation of workers." Then comes a plethora of literary devices that Marx was to use to great effect in the *Class Struggles* and the *Eighteenth Brumaire:* ghostly metaphors ("the Executive Committee, the last official vestige of the February revolution, vanished like a ghost in the face of these grave events"); explosive metaphors ("Lamartine's fireworks turned into the incendiary rockets of Cavaignac"); the ironic use of metaphors of colour ("the tricolor republic now displays only *one color*, the color of the defeated, the *color of blood.* It has become a red republic.") Here the irony lies in the fact that, as Marx's readers would recognize, radicals had fought unsuccessfully for the adoption of a red flag. Now they were getting the colour they wanted, but with a totally different meaning.[44]

Marx draws more ironic contrasts between the hopes of February and the realities of June. The *fraternité* that was "proclaimed and inscribed in large letters on the façades of Paris" in February now finds "its true, unadulterated and prosaic expression in *civil war.* " The false friends of the people who had helped lull "the proletarian lion" to sleep now reveal themselves. Cavaignac returns now as "the brutal echo" of the bourgeois republicans elected to the National Assembly. And all of this culminates with the basic distinction between "the *nice* revolution" of February and "the *ugly* revolution" of June.[45]

What was the response to this article? Some support for Marx's position came from the journal of the Cologne Workers' Association and

[42] Hammen, *Red '48ers*, 250.
[43] Marx, "The June Revolution," written on June 28 and published in the *Neue Rheinische Zeitung*, 29 (June 29, 1848), MECW, VII, 144–149. Translation slightly altered. On the NRZ's overall treatment of the June days, see Hammen, *Red '48ers*, 243–251.
[44] Marx, "June Revolution" in MECW, VII, 144.   [45] Ibid, 147.

from Stefan Born's *Das Volk*, the journal of the Berlin Workers' Brotherhood. But liberals and democrats in Cologne (including most of the shareholders of Marx's newspaper) were fierce in their criticism. The liberal *Kölnische Zeitung* simply reprinted an article from a Bonn newspaper: "The *Neue Rheinische Zeitung* calls itself an 'Organ of Democracy.' We call it an organ of the Red Republic. No one who preaches riot and anarchy is a supporter of democracy."[46]

By fall the tide of revolution was ebbing everywhere. After June the French National Assembly clamped down on both the insurgents and the socialists whose "savage doctrines" had inspired these "new barbarians."[47] In Austria periods of repression had been followed by episodes of popular protest, and the feeble-minded Emperor Ferdinand I was twice obliged to flee Vienna. After a siege of four days in late October, he was reinstalled in Schönbrunn Palace by troops under Prince Windischgrätz who had already subjected the rebellious city of Prague to an artillery barrage in June. Reviewing the situation in his article "The Victory of the Counter-Revolution in Vienna," Marx asserted that the June Days in Paris had been the first act of the counter-revolutionary "drama"; the second act was performed in Vienna in October; and the third would follow soon in Berlin. Bad as the situation looked, Marx still had high hopes for the future; and he concluded by asserting that "the crushing counter-blow [to] the June insurrection will be struck in Paris."[48] He could already detect "the first subterranean rumbles" announcing from Paris "the earthquake that will bury the respectable republic under its own ruins. *The outlook brightens.*"[49]

In Prussia, the summer had been marked by the replacement of one impotent liberal ministry by another slightly less liberal and equally impotent. But in September Germans in the northern duchies of Schleswig and Holstein rebelled against Danish rule, seeking inclusion in a united German state. Prussia initially supported the insurrection, but then under pressure from Tsar Nicholas I and ignoring the protests of the Frankfurt Parliament, it signed an armistice with the Danes and abandoned the insurgents. As Jonathan Sperber observes, "This was an issue tailor-made for Germany's leftists, combining nationalist sentiments, opposition to the Tsar, and hostility to a return of the conservatives to

[46] Hammen, *Red '48ers*, 250; Gilbert, *Marx's Politics*, 143–144.
[47] Frederick de Luna, *The French Republic under Cavaignac* (Princeton, 1969), 152.
[48] Marx, "The Victory of the Counter-Revolution in Vienna," *Neue Rheinische Zeitung*, November 7, 1848; MECW, VII, 504–505.
[49] Marx, "The Latest News from Vienna, Berlin and Paris," *Neue Rheinische Zeitung*, November 5, 1848; MECW, VII, 499.

power in Prussia."[50] What made the situation at Cologne explosive was that it coincided with the outbreak of violent conflict between civilians and Prussian soldiers stationed at Cologne. Marx and his colleagues in the city's Democratic Society created a Committee of Public Safety and organized a huge protest meeting at Worringen just outside Cologne. A few days later barricades went up at Frankfurt and two conservative deputies were lynched. On September 25 the Prussian government responded by declaring martial law, disbanding the Civil Guard, and shutting down the *Neue Rheinische Zeitung*. Marx managed to restart the paper after three weeks. But he now lost most of the paper's wealthy shareholders and had to pawn his wife's jewels.

Encouraged by the defeat of the revolutionaries in Vienna, Frederick William announced in November that the Prussian Assembly would be moved from Berlin to Brandenburg. Then, on December 5, he dissolved the Assembly, imposed a constitution of his own devising, and called for new elections. The only resistance that the deputies could muster was to appeal to the people not to pay taxes until constitutional government was restored. Marx took up their cause, and for a while the *Neue Rheinische Zeitung* appeared with the words "No More Taxes!" on its masthead. The Prussian authorities countered by bringing Marx and several colleagues to trial for sedition. Marx was ready for them. Arguing that it was hypocritical for the Prussian authorities to invoke laws that they themselves had flouted by dissolving the Assembly, he convinced two juries to acquit him and the other defendants.[51] Despite this personal triumph, he knew that the German revolution was a lost cause. He now believed that with its supine bourgeoisie and weak working class, Germany would never initiate an enduring revolutionary movement on its own. The initiative would have to come from outside. That is, from France. As he wrote in November in an article on the "Counter-Revolution in Berlin": "The crowing of the Gallic cock in Paris will once again rouse Europe."[52]

By the end of 1848, the liberals and democrats assembled in the Frankfurt Parliament understood that the Germany for which they were writing a constitution would have to be attached either to Prussia or to Austria. They chose Prussia; and on March 28, 1849, after long debate, they elected Frederick William ruler of their newly constituted empire. Predictably, Frederick William refused to accept a constitution from

---

[50] Sperber, *Karl Marx*, 229. This whole paragraph is based largely on Sperber.
[51] "The Trial of the Rhenish District Committee of Democrats" in MECW, VIII, 323–339.
[52] Marx, "Counter-Revolution in Berlin," *Neue Rheinische Zeitung*, November 12, 1848; MECW, VIII, 17.

their hands. Initially, this did not greatly disturb Marx who had finally abandoned his strategy of cooperating with democratic and republican revolutionaries. In April he formally cut his ties with his bourgeois democratic associates to focus exclusively on the organization of the working class.[53] But no sooner had he broken with the democratic Left than it began to show signs of life. By May, it was clear that the King's rejection of the Assembly's constitution had touched a nerve. Violent protest movements broke out in western and southern Germany. There were barricades in Dresden, insurrections in the Palatinate, and a major democratic insurgency in Baden. Engels could not resist joining the insurgents in his native Wupper valley. Marx was more cautious, and in the *Neue Rheinische Zeitung* he warned the working class against involving themselves in this "bourgeois" political movement and thereby giving the authorities cover for their own acts of violence. Engels quickly came round to Marx's viewpoint, arguing that if the workers were "provoked into disorders," they would "only be pulling chestnuts out of the fire for the bourgeoisie and at the same time for the government."[54] In the final issue of the *Neue Rheinische Zeitung*, Marx and Engels issued a formal warning to the workers of Cologne: "We warn you against any revolt in Cologne. In the present military situation you would be irretrievably lost."[55]

Ironically, given Marx's reluctance to involve himself or his followers in the protest movement at Cologne, the crisis gave the Prussian authorities the pretext they needed to shut down the newspaper and expel Marx from Prussia. On May 19, he left Cologne with Jenny and their children. After a few days in Frankfurt and a week in Baden, where he vainly urged the insurgents to march on Frankfurt, Marx went on to Paris.[56] On his arrival, he found Paris in the midst of a cholera epidemic with royalists ebullient after a massive victory in parliamentary elections. "For all that," he wrote Engels on June 7, "never has a colossal eruption of the revolutionary volcano been more imminent than it is in Paris today ... I consort with the whole revolutionary party, and in a few days time I shall have all the revolutionary journals at my disposal."[57]

[53] Sperber, *Karl Marx*, 234; McLellan, *Karl Marx*, 209–212; Stedman Jones, *Karl Marx*, 292–294.
[54] Engels, "Longing for a State of Siege," *Neue Rheinische Zeitung*, May 6, 1849; MECW, IX, 403.
[55] Collective statement, "To the Workers of Cologne," *Neue Rheinische Zeitung*, May 19, 1848; MECW, IX, 467.
[56] McLellan, *Karl Marx*, 221–223.
[57] Marx to Engels, June 7, 1849 in MECW, XXXVIII, 199.

Marx's repeated expressions of optimism in the face of the advance of the counter-revolution are hard to understand. The fifteen months between his arrival in Paris in March 1848 and his return to the French capital in June 1849 were for him a period of almost unmitigated disaster. The European working class had been defeated again and again – in Paris, Vienna and Berlin, in Prague and Budapest, and even in London where a mass demonstration at Kennington Common on April 10, 1848, marked the effective end of the Chartist movement. Repeatedly in his articles in the *Neue Rheinische Zeitung* Marx describes a defeat but then concludes by evoking the imminent eruption of the "revolutionary vol-cano" or the "Gallic cock" that will rouse Europe. Even an article including a memorable evocation of England as "the rock against which the revolutionary waves break," concludes optimistically: "The table of contents for 1849 reads: '*Revolutionary rising of the French working class, world war.*'"[58] How could the normally realistic Marx sustain his opti-mism in the face of repeated defeat? Is it really enough to speak, as does Francis Wheen, of the "talent for paradox and perversity" with which "Marx could discern potential triumph in every disaster, silver linings behind every cloud"?[59] Or to observe, with Jonathan Sperber, that "apocalyptic dreams of a revolutionary future were one way for exiles to bear the wretched conditions of their daily lives"?[60] Beyond this, Marx had his reasons, and the hopes he placed in France were not unfounded.

Marx was a close reader of the French left-wing press, and he was well aware of the regrouping of the Left that had taken place in France after the debacle of the June days. The period from July 1848 to May 1849 was marked by the formation of a *démoc-soc* movement which was largely bourgeois but had working-class elements. This was a movement in which socialists and neo-Jacobin democrats came together. They consti-tuted a distinct minority in the National Assembly. But the same elec-tions of May 1849 that had given 3.3 million votes to the royalist and conservatives in the Party of Order also gave almost two million votes to the *démoc-socs*. (The great losers were the moderate republicans.) Through their journals and clubs, the *démoc-socs* had become a force in French political life. This was hardly a proletarian movement: its leaders were lawyers like the utopian communist Etienne Cabet and the neo-Jacobin orator Ledru-Rollin, or Polytechniciens with scientific training like the Fourierist Victor Considerant and several former Saint-Simonians. But many of Cabet's followers were workers, as were the Lyon silk weavers or *canuts* who had created their own newspaper, *L'Echo*

---

[58] Marx, "The Revolutionary Movement," January 1, 1849 in MECW, VIII, 214.
[59] Wheen, *Karl Marx: A Life*, 142.   [60] Sperber, *Karl Marx*, 253.

de la fabrique, in the early 1830s and who devoured the writings of the Fourierists and the Saint-Simonians. So were the artisans in the Faubourg Saint-Antoine who vied with each other in the summer and fall of 1848 to obtain copies of Proudhon's journals. These were the people whom Marx seems to have had in mind when he talked about the Gallic cock and the coming earthquake.[61]

Marx's arrival in Paris in early June came at a key moment in the history of the French Left. The big issue now was France's relation to the Roman Republic that had come into being in February 1849 after Pope Pius IX had fled the Vatican. In a few months major reforms were undertaken at Rome: Church property was nationalized, censorship and the Inquisition abolished. But as we have seen, the Roman Republic had only a precarious existence.[62] In April Louis-Napoleon ordered French troops to Rome, nominally to protect the city against Austrian intervention. From the beginning, it was clear that the troops could be used against the Republic. They were.

The democrats and socialists in France's Legislative Assembly denounced the French military intervention as a violation of the constitution, which expressly forbade the use of military force "against the liberty of any people." The *démoc-socs* then introduced a bill of impeachment against Louis-Napoleon. The bill was voted down by the large conservative majority. But in presenting it, the leader of the Left, Ledru–Rollin, made the mistake of threatening armed resistance: "We shall defend the Constitution by all possible means, even by force of arms."[63] When an unarmed protest demonstration was held on June 13, the government treated it as an insurrection and crushed it, decimating the leadership of the French Left.

Did Marx participate in the demonstration of June 13? He later wrote derisively of the *journée*, observing that if June 1848 had been a revolt of masses without leaders, June 1849 was a revolt of leaders without masses. Still, he may have participated. His subsequent account of June 13 includes details that could only have come from an eyewitness.[64] The French authorities clearly regarded him as suspect. On July 19, he was banished to the Department of the Morbihan in Brittany. After

---

[61] On the *democ-soc* movement, see Edward Berenson, *Populist Religion and Left-Wing Politics in France, 1830–1852* (Princeton, 1984), 74–168. On working class support for early socialist ideologies, see Christopher H. Johnson, *Utopian Communism in France. Cabet and the Icarians, 1839–1851* (Ithaca, 1974) and Ludovic Frobert (ed.), *L'Echo de la Fabrique. Naissance de la presse ouvrière à Lyon* (Lyon, 2010), esp. 111–139 and 327–343.
[62] See above, Chapter 6, pp. 217–220.   [63] Beecher, *Victor Considerant*, 250.
[64] Marx, "The 13th of June," *Der Volksfreund*, 26, June 29, 1849 in MECW, IX, 478; Sperber, *Karl Marx*, 242.

vainly protesting his exile to the "Pontine Marshes" of France, Marx left
for England on August 24. A week earlier he wrote Engels that he was
still anticipating "an early revolutionary resurrection" in France and that
the resistance of the Hungarians to the Russians was "splendid."[65] He
had not yet learned that Kossuth had fled across the Ottoman frontier
and that all Hungarian resistance had collapsed on August 13.

Marx's first years in London were hard for him and his growing family.
He did not expect his stay to last long. In fact, he was to remain a
Londoner until his death; and for him the move to London marked the
beginning of a new life. It was, for the first six years, a life of desperate
poverty. In May 1850, after being evicted from an expensive apartment
in Chelsea, the Marx family settled on Dean Street in Soho. Noisy,
bustling, picturesque, full of beggars, immigrants and prostitutes, with
street vendors on every corner, Soho was also dirty and disease-ridden.
After renting two "miserable" rooms for six months, the Marx family
moved farther down Dean Street to slightly more commodious lodgings
that they shared with two Italian families and an Irish language teacher.
In 1856 Jenny came into an inheritance that made it possible to get the
family out of what she called the "evil, frightful rooms" on Dean Street
and into a small house on the outskirts of London near Hampstead
Heath "where we slept in our own beds for the first time, sat on our
own chairs, and even had a parlour with second-hand furniture."[66] Their
life improved after 1856. But during their six years in Soho the family
lived from hand to mouth, tormented by sickness and domestic worries,
and lost three children. When their infant daughter Franziska died in
April 1852, Marx spent the day of the funeral raising money to buy a
coffin.[67]

In June 1850 Marx obtained a reader's card at the British Museum.
During his first weeks he went methodically through back-issues of the
London *Economist*, and for decades thereafter he frequented the reading
room of this magnificent library, which became for him a second home,
and "a favourable vantage point for the observation of bourgeois society."[68] Throughout the 1850s his only source of income, apart from
occasional support from Frederick Engels, came from weekly articles
that he wrote with Engels for the *New York Tribune* on subjects ranging
from European diplomacy to British rule in Ireland and India. The

---

[65] Marx to Engels, August 17, 1849 in MECW, XXXVIII, 211; MECW, IX, 478.
[66] Asa Briggs and John Callow, *Marx in London* (London, 2007), 52; Jenny Marx to Bertha
Markheim, January 28, 1863 in Jerrold Seigel, *Marx's Fate: The Shape of a Life*
(Princeton, 1978), 254.
[67] Mary Gabriel, *Love and Capital* (New York, 2011), 222; Sperber, *Karl Marx*, 261.
[68] Marx, Preface to *Critique of Political Economy* in MESW, I, 365.

family sometimes went hungry until the arrival of a postal money order from Engels improved the situation. Jenny's family silver and her jewelry were often in pawn; and in September 1852 Marx wrote Engels that for a week he had been feeding the family solely on bread and potatoes and that the butcher, baker, milkman, grocer and tea merchant were all demanding to be paid.[69]

During his years in Cologne as editor of the *Neue Rheinische Zeitung* Marx had been a leader of the German revolutionary movement. Now the movement was moribund and Marx had joined the flood of failed revolutionaries who converged on London after 1848. Some of these refugees were international celebrities and were made much of in the British press. But Marx had neither the charisma nor the gift for self-promotion of a Mazzini, a Garibaldi or a Kossuth. Nor was he independently wealthy like Alexander Herzen. He carried on his work with limited means and in obscurity. And just as Herzen a few years later managed to reach and give voice to compatriots in Russia through the publication in London of a Russian-language journal, Marx hoped to influence – and to speak for – the revolutionary movement in Germany through the publication of a German-language monthly edited in London, published in Hamburg and distributed in Germany.[70] Marx baptized this journal *Neue Rheinische Zeitung, Politisch-ökonomische Revue*. The first number appeared in March 1850 and included the first instalment of *Class Struggles in France* along with articles by Engels and Karl Blind.

Marx's aim in founding the *Revue* was to breathe new life into the revolutionary movement. Down until the summer of 1850, he continued to believe that a working-class uprising in France would serve as the catalyst for a revolutionary upheaval that would engulf Europe. This belief survived the fiasco of June 13, 1849. It also informed his efforts during his first year in London to revitalize the Communist League and to establish ties with the followers of Auguste Blanqui. Writing to Joseph Wedemeyer in December 1849, Marx asserted that a "mighty industrial, agricultural and commercial crisis" was "looming up" in England, though it was "as yet imperceptible on the continent."[71] He had "little doubt" that by the time the second or third monthly issue of the *Revue* had appeared, "a world conflagration will intervene." In the first issue of the *Revue*, Marx looked to the French peasantry as a possible source of

---

[69] Marx to Engels, September 8, 1852 in MECW, XXXIX, 181–182.
[70] In 1850, Hamburg was an independent municipal republic "where liberal ideas were stronger and the pressure of the Prussian government weaker than in most of central Europe." See Sperber, *Karl Marx*, 249.
[71] Marx to Weydemeyer, December 19, 1849 in MECW, XXXVIII, 220.

revolt.[72] And in his "Address to the Communist League" of March 1850 Marx called for the creation of an independent workers' party free of the influence of bourgeois democrats.[73]

In March 1850, Marx's hopes for the French working class peaked with the victory in Parisian by-elections of three radical candidates: the June deportee Paul de Flotte, the socialist theorist François Vidal, and the bourgeois democrat Hippolyte Carnot. At last, Marx asserted, a revolutionary coalition had emerged to challenge the bourgeoisie and the government; and this time "the proletariat was at the head of the revolutionary league." Marx exulted at this electoral victory and described its significance in extravagant terms. The election of March 10, 1850, was "the revocation of June 1848." With this election, he wrote, "the moral influence of capital is broken" and the bourgeois republic had "entered the phase of its dissolution." It had shown itself to be "the hot-house of the revolution."[74]

This moment of euphoria was short-lived. By fall Marx had ceased to believe in the imminence of revolution in France, announcing cavalierly in the final issue of the *Revue* that the electoral victory of March 10 had lost its revolutionary meaning because François Vidal, who had been elected in two circumscriptions, was replaced in Paris by the novelist Eugène Sue, a "sentimental petty-bourgeois social-fantast" whose candidacy "the proletariat could best accept as a joke to please the *grisettes.*"[75] As for the French peasantry, Marx wrote that their position – "in debt, sucked dry by usury and crushed by taxes" – was "anything but splendid" and that recent history had shown that the French peasants were "absolutely incapable of any revolutionary initiative."[76]

---

[72] Marx, "Review" (January–February 1850), *Neue Rheinische Zeitung. Politisch-ökonomische Revue* (1850) in MECW, X, 262. This article was written in January, though the first issue of the *Revue* did not actually appear until March.
[73] Marx and Engels, "Address of the Central Committee to the Communist League" (March 1850) in MESW, I, 110 and MECW, X, 281. For fuller accounts of Marx's political activity in the Communist League and his ties with radicals such as August von Willich and the French followers of Auguste Blanqui in 1849–1850, see Stedman Jones, *Karl Marx*, 297–301 and Lattek, *Revolutionary Refugees*, 48–82.
[74] Marx, *Class Struggles*, 128; MECW, X, 128–129. The text cited here, from Pt III of *Class Struggles*, was originally published in April 1850 in the third issue of the *Revue*.
[75] Marx, "Review" (May–October 1850), *Neue Rheinische Zeitung. Politisch-ökonomische Revue* (1850) in MECW, X, 516. This article was written in September or October 1850, largely by Marx but with some help from Engels. It was published in the final double issue of the *Revue*. In preparing a separate edition of *Class Struggles in France* in 1895, Engels included parts of this article as a fourth chapter to *Class Struggles*. Thus these passages also appear in MECW, X, 135.
[76] Marx, "Review" (May–October 1850), *Neue Rheinische Zeitung. Politisch-ökonomische Revue* (1850), MECW, X, 509. Also in *Class Struggles*, MECW, X, 134.

How do we account for Marx's rapid loss of a revolutionary faith that had previously withstood so many disappointments? The answer lies in the intensive study of recent economic history that he had begun at the British Museum in June 1850. This study convinced Marx that England and the United States were entering a period of industrial prosperity that would soon spread to the continent, and that while the boom lasted, there could be no European revolution. "A new revolution is only possible in the wake of a new crisis," he wrote in the final number of the *Revue*. He then went on to write almost lyrically about the expansion of the railway system and the cotton industry in Britain and about the economic consequences of the discovery of gold in California. "With this general prosperity," he concluded, "there can be no talk of real revolution."[77] Marx continued to believe that revolution would follow in the wake of economic crisis. But he no longer expected a proletarian revolution to succeed in France or Germany in the foreseeable future. Many more years of industrial growth were necessary; and the development of a powerful revolutionary movement in Germany, which had once seemed imminent, was now a dream deferred.

What remained unresolved at the end of 1850 was the political situation in France. This had evolved into a struggle between President Louis-Napoleon Bonaparte and a National Assembly controlled by the Party of Order. Marx followed this struggle closely, and with wry amusement, from the vantage point of London. For the moment all the factions of the Party of Order were proclaiming their allegiance to the Republic. But behind "the unedifying comedy of the so-called republicans" and the posturing of the petty-bourgeois democrats was the commercial and industrial prosperity which "prevented any attempt at revolution on the part of the proletariat."[78]

On May 31, 1850, reacting to the electoral success of the Left in the March by-elections, the National Assembly passed a new electoral law disenfranchising voters who were not registered taxpayers with a fixed address for three years. This law, which was followed by the passage of a newly repressive press law, cut the number of registered voters by almost three million. Recognizing its unpopularity, Louis-Napoleon ostentatiously distanced himself, thereby presenting himself as a progressive reformer. At the same time, he repeatedly attacked "the monarchist

[77] Marx, "Review" (May–October 1850), *Neue Rheinische Zeitung. Politisch-ökonomische Revue* (1850), MECW, X, 510. Also in *Class Struggles*, MECW, X, 135. Translation slightly modified.
[78] Marx, "Review" (May–October 1850), *Neue Rheinische Zeitung. Politisch-ökonomische Revue* (1850), MECW, X, 517. Also in *Class Struggles*, MECW, X, 137.

hallucinations" of the leaders of the Assembly and presented himself as a partisan of tranquillity and industrial growth.

The struggle between Louis-Napoleon and the Assembly reached a climax in the fall of 1851 with the debate over the revision of the Constitution which stipulated that the President of the Republic would serve a term of four years and was not eligible for reelection. Louis-Napoleon tried and failed to persuade the Assembly to revise the Constitution to permit him to serve another term. But he did succeed through skilful political manoeuvring in finally discrediting both the Assembly and the Constitution itself. Thus there was relatively little resistance in Paris when on December 2, 1851, Louis-Napoleon Bonaparte staged a carefully planned coup d'état, suspended the republican constitution, and announced a plebiscite to be held by universal male suffrage on the extension of his mandate. "The immediate and palpable result," wrote Marx, "was the victory of Bonaparte over parliament, of the executive power over the legislative power, of force without phrases over the force of phrases."[79]

News of the coup d'état travelled instantly across the English Channel thanks to the underwater telegraph cable laid by the British from Dover to Calais a year earlier. The very next day Engels sent Marx a long, bemused commentary on the event. "The history of France has entered the stage of the most perfect comedy," wrote Engels:

Can one imagine anything funnier than this travesty of the 18th Brumaire, effected in peacetime with the help of discontented soldiers by the most insignificant man in the world without, so far as it has hitherto been possible to judge, any opposition whatsoever? And how beautifully have all the old jackasses been caught! The slyest fox in the whole of France, old Thiers, the astute advocate of the *barreau*, M. Dupin, caught in the trap set for them by the most notorious blockhead of the century.[80]

Engels went on to put the comedy in a historical perspective suggested by Hegel:

It really seems as though old Hegel, in the guise of the World Spirit, were directing history from the grave and, with the greatest conscientiousness, causing everything to be re-enacted twice over, once as grand tragedy and the second time as rotten farce. Caussidière for Danton, Louis Blanc for Robespierre, Barthélemy for Saint-Just, Flocon for Carnot, and the moon-calf [Louis Bonaparte] together with the first available dozen debt-encumbered lieutenants for the little corporal and his band of marshals. Thus the 18th Brumaire would already be upon us.[81]

There are times when Marx and Engels were totally of one mind, and this was one of them. Within a month Marx had hastily written a hundred-page pamphlet in which the image of Louis-Napoleon's coup acquired immortality as a farcical repetition of his uncle's seizure of power fifty-two years earlier on the 18th Brumaire of the Revolutionary Year VIII.

Ghosts, Shadows and Nightmares

Both *Class Struggles in France* and *The Eighteenth Brumaire of Louis Bonaparte* were written immediately after the events they described, and both were published in obscure German journals with modest circulations. *Class Struggles* originally appeared as a series of articles in the short-lived *Politisch-ökonomische Revue* in which Marx attempted to revive his successful daily *Neue Rheinische Zeitung*.[82] *The Eighteenth Brumaire* first appeared in the United States. It was written in January and February 1852 for a German-language political weekly proposed by Marx's friend, Joseph Weydemeyer. The weekly never appeared, and Marx's text was finally published in April 1852 in New York as the first number of Weydemeyer's monthly, *Die Revolution*. Marx later observed that "a few hundred copies found their way into Germany at that time, without, however, getting into the actual book trade."[83] The response to the second (1869) edition was muted. It was not until Engels republished both works in 1885 that they were widely read and effectively entered the Marxist canon.

Both works were written hastily, allowing no time for sustained reflection. Both were aimed at a working-class audience. Yet, both are difficult works, full of buried quotations and allusions to world literature – to the *Iliad*, the *Bible*, Shakespeare, Schiller, Heine, and Goethe's *Faust*.[84] Much of this could hardly have been recognized by Marx's readers,

---

[82] The first three of these articles were written in January and February 1850 and published in the first three numbers of the *Neue Rheinische Zeitung. Politisch-ökonomische Revue*. These numbers were dated January, February and March, 1850, though they were only published in March and April. What is now the fourth section of the *Class Struggles* is part of a much longer article largely devoted to the economic recovery in Great Britain and America and published in the final double issue of the journal, which was dated May–October 1850. These four papers were first published together under the title *Die Klassenkämpf in Frankreich* with an introduction by Engels in 1895. There is a striking difference in form and perspective between the first three articles in which Marx is still hopeful about the possibility of a European revolution starting in France, and the fourth article on the economic boom in which Marx abandons hope of revolution.

[83] Karl Marx, Preface to the Second (1869) Edition of *The Eighteenth Brumaire of Louis Bonaparte*, MESW, I, 243.

[84] For a rich general account of Marx's reading and the place of literature in his thought, see S. S. Prawer, *Karl Marx and World Literature* (Oxford, 1976).

and even the title of *The Eighteenth Brumaire*, comparing Louis-Napoleon Bonaparte's coup d'état to that of the first Napoleon on November 9, 1799 (18 Brumaire Year VIII on the revolutionary calendar) was probably mysterious to many. Why did Marx write in an idiom that must have been obscure to his readers? This is a question to which I shall return.

To begin, a few general remarks. First, if one looks closely at *Class Struggles in France*, it becomes evident that during the first months of the 1848 revolution, Marx never doubted that the Second French Republic was going to be the last French bourgeois social formation. He really believed, in other words, that in February 1848 a process had been set in motion that would culminate in a proletarian revolution. So, the blood-bath of June 1848 was a great shock to Marx. And the coup of December 2 was an even greater shock. Much of what Marx wrote thereafter was an attempt to explain what had gone wrong, and to draw lessons for German workers from the defeats of the French proletariat between 1848 and 1851. He did this by systematically contrasting the world of historical reality – the class struggle – and the realm of shadow and illusion in which historical actors fancy that their speeches, posturing and parliamentary manoeuvres make a difference.

For someone who comes to these essays today after reading the *Communist Manifesto* there are many surprises. First, a crucial role is assigned to peasants, about whom we hear little in the *Manifesto* apart from an occasional remark on "the idiocy of rural life." Secondly, various social formations are considered in these essays, whereas in his other works Marx focuses on classes and conflicts essential to his argument. Third, there are fascinating discussions of key concepts like "class," "ideology" and "state power" in which the definitions seem more open and problematic than one would expect from a reading of the *Communist Manifesto*. In the *Manifesto* the state is described as "a committee for managing the common affairs of the whole bourgeoisie." But the discussion of the state in the *Eighteenth Brumaire* is complex and nuanced. The interests of the propertied classes find expression in four distinct and often-warring groups: Legitimists, Orleanists, Bonapartists and bourgeois republicans. The state is presented as relatively autonomous with respect to class interests. And Marx insists on the uniqueness of the French state which, with its half-million civil servants, "enmeshes, controls, regulates, superintends and tutors civil society" while the "material interests of the French bourgeoisie are interwoven in the closest fashion with the maintenance of the bureaucracy."[85] Finally, one cannot read

[85] Karl Marx, *The Communist Manifesto*, MESW, 1, 36; *Eighteenth Brumaire*, MESW, I, 284; MECW, XI, 139.

these essays without marvelling at their sheer rhetorical power – the literary skill with which Marx evokes the ghosts and shadows, the dreams and riddles and masquerades, that constitute the realm of ideology and illusion, blinding historical actors to the real meaning of their action. Marx's essays on 1848–1851 give substance to his theories of ideology and false consciousness, and they do so in a way that fuses the spell-binding power of the imagery and the spell-banishing power of the historian.

The task that Marx set himself in *Class Struggles in France* was to show how a series of apparently crushing defeats could provide the stimulus for the development of a revolutionary movement. Only by a series of defeats, he argues, could the proletariat free itself from the traditional attitudes, illusions, conceptions and projects that blinded it to the neces-sity of revolutionary struggle. The revolution made headway "not by its immediate tragi-comic achievements, but on the contrary by the creation of a powerful, united counter-revolution" – an opponent against which the proletariat could ripen into a real revolutionary party.[86]

This reference to the "tragi-comic achievements" of the revolution is not casual. With it, we are introduced to the controlling metaphor of the whole work: the metaphor of the theatre. This becomes clear when we are told that the proclamation in February 1848 of a republic based on universal manhood suffrage thrust onto the "revolutionary stage" classes that had never previously played a role in politics. "Instead of a few small fractions of the bourgeoisie, whole classes of French society were sud-denly hurled into the circle of political power, forced to leave the boxes, the stalls and the gallery and to act in person upon the revolutionary stage!"[87]

The metaphor of the revolution as theatre – as a staged play – which appears in much of the contemporary writing on 1848, is given elaborate extension in *Class Struggles*. With the proclamation of the Republic, writes Marx, the old elites exchanged their monarchist titles and cos-tumes for new republican ones. For the bourgeois republicans of the *National* "the republic was only a new ball dress for the old bourgeois society." The two major street demonstrations of March and April 1848 are described by Marx as a "melodramatic scene" and a "clumsily constructed comedy."[88] In the elections of April radicals discovered that universal suffrage was not the "miraculous magic wand" they expected it to be. They were not prepared for the election of a Constituent Assembly dominated by royalists and conservatives. But the merit of the elections

[86] Karl Marx, *Class Struggles in France (1848–1850)* (New York, 1964), 33; MECW, X, 47.
[87] *Class Struggles*, 40; MECW, X, 54.   [88] *Class Struggles*, 53; MECW, X, 64–65.

from Marx's standpoint is that they dispelled a great illusion – the belief that universal suffrage would bring to power a united and harmonious people. Bourgeois democrats had regarded France as a nation made up of "*citoyens* with the same interests, the same understanding, etc. This was their cult of the people."[89] But the elections brought to light the real people with their diverse and contradictory desires and interests, and the reality of class conflict. Thus, the elections set the stage for a confrontation – for the civil war of the June Days in which the elites, still wearing their republican masks, run the proletarian "lion" right off the stage.

What is striking about Marx's discussion of the June insurrection is his insistence on its ultimately positive character. It was a defeat for the proletariat, to be sure, but a defeat which "tore to pieces the veil that shrouded the republic," revealing its class character and freeing the proletariat from crippling and deferential attitudes and assumptions.[90] After the June Days, Marx asserts, the "February republic," the republic of class collaboration, was dead, and the "bourgeois republic," the republic run by and for the bourgeoisie, had come into being. Henceforth the proletariat was on the side-lines and could only watch as the "parliamentary comedy played itself out." And while the bourgeois republicans "played the principal and state role on the proscenium, an unbroken sacrificial feast went on in the background – the continual sentencing by courts-martial of the imprisoned June insurgents and their deportation without trial."[91]

With the presidential election of December 10, 1848, in which the nephew of the great Napoleon was elected President of the Republic, a new character comes on stage. Marx introduces him with a fanfare of oxymorons:

Clumsily cunning, knavishly naïve, doltishly sublime, a calculated superstition, a pathetic burlesque, a cleverly staged anachronism, a world historical piece of buffoonery ... Napoleon was the only man who had exhaustively represented the interests and the imagination of the peasant class.[92]

So Marx believed that the emergence of Louis-Napoleon and his election as President could be explained by his appeal to the French peasantry; and he calls December 10 "the coup d'état of the peasants." But still when he wrote *Class Struggles* Marx could not imagine that Louis-Napoleon would turn out to be anything other than a tool of the ruling bourgeoisie. He observes that the new president allowed "the chiefs of the royalist bourgeois factions" to persuade him to appoint as his first

---

[89] *Class Struggles*, 54; MECW, X, 65.   [90] *Class Struggles*, 56–59; MECW, X, 67–70.
[91] *Class Struggles*, 62; MECW, X, 73.   [92] *Class Struggles*, 71; MECW, X, 80.

minister Odilon Barrot, the last minister of Louis Philippe. Other key posts were given to former "creatures" of the bourgeois monarchy. Thus Marx writes that "the first act" of the Barrot ministry was the restoration of the administration of the old bourgeois monarchy. "The official scene was transformed in a trice – scenery, costumes, speech, actors, supers, dummies, prompters, the position of the parties, the theme of the drama, the content of the conflict, the whole situation."[93]

Then, on December 27, Louis-Napoleon proposed the restoration of the salt tax, which had been abolished by the Provisional Government. This tax was detested by the peasants who saw it, along with the wine tax, as a main source of their poverty. Marx concludes that Louis-Napoleon's identification with the peasantry was over. "With the salt tax, Bonaparte lost his revolutionary salt – the Napoleon of the peasant insurrection dissolved like an apparition, and nothing remained but the great unknown of royalist bourgeois intrigue."[94] Henceforth, Marx argues, Louis-Napoleon could only rule in partnership with the royalist bourgeoisie.

During the year following his election as president, Louis-Napoleon sometimes clashed with the Party of Order, but basically, according to Marx, he and the "royalist bourgeois faction" (Legitimists and Orleanists) presented a united front against all efforts to alter the existing political order. In January 1849 an alliance was formed between the socialists and the petty-bourgeois democrats in the Constituent Assembly. The following May, when elections were held for a new Legislative Assembly, the number of "democ-soc" representatives increased. But so did the number of royalists, and on several occasions the petty-bourgeois radicals were "tricked" by the Party of Order. Finally, on June 13, 1849, they were lured out into the streets to protest the government's military intervention against the Roman Republic. This demonstration gave the Assembly and Louis-Napoleon a pretext to crush the resurgent Mountain and the socialists. Thus, Marx writes that while June 1848 marked the defeat of the proletariat, June 1849 brought an end to the attempt of the petty-bourgeois democrats to assume the leadership of the revolutionary movement. In June 1849, it was not the workers who were vanquished but the petty bourgeoisie.[95]

The consequence of June 13, 1849, was to free the proletariat from their last republican illusions and to convince them that their emancipation must be their own work. Marx remained hopeful that the proletariat would be called back on stage. Indeed, he noted the rise of peasant

[93] *Class Struggles*, 75; MECW, X, 83.   [94] *Class Struggles*, 76; MECW, X, 84.
[95] *Class Struggles*, 94; MECW, X, 100.

protest in the south and east of France and the radicalization of the working class in the larger cities. He describes France as split into two hostile camps.[96] Together, the President and the two dominant groups within the Party of Order, the Legitimists and the Orleanists, represented the bourgeoisie; and they stood in opposition to a proletariat consisting not only of urban workers and artisans but also a growing number of radicalized peasants.

How had the peasants been radicalized? Marx's answer is unambiguous. It was the restoration of the wine tax proposed by Montalembert that drove the peasants away from religion and from Louis-Napoleon Bonaparte:

> The French peasant, when he paints the devil on the wall, paints him in the guise of the tax collector. From the moment when Montalembert elevated taxation to a god, the peasant became godless, atheistic, and threw himself into the arms of the devil, socialism. The religion of order had lost him; the Jesuits had lost him: Bonaparte had lost him.[97]

The radicalization of the peasants was one facet of a broader movement of revolt against the Party of Order and the "dictatorship" of the bourgeoisie – a movement which, in Marx's view, also involved peasants and the petty bourgeoisie. For Marx, the culmination of this broader movement came on March 10, 1850, with the victory in Parisian by-elections of the radicals de Flotte, Vidal and Carnot (see Figure 9.2). He concludes somewhat hastily that the moral influence of capital is broken and that revolution is imminent.[98]

The upbeat conclusion of *Class Struggles* was no longer possible when Marx wrote *The Eighteenth Brumaire*. In this work, written after Louis-Napoleon's coup d'état, Marx's task was to explain what had gone wrong – what had enabled a "mediocrity" to play a hero's role. The theme of the theatre continues to be explored. And Marx lets us know from the first line where he tells us that great events occur twice – first as tragedy and then as farce. In this account 1848 appears as a farcical replay of the first French Revolution, and Louis-Napoleon is cast in the role of a comic imitator of his uncle. But how could such a cheap parody succeed? How could it propel the ordinary Louis-Napoleon to power? That is Marx's main question. But for us, a prior question is posed by Marx's language and imagery.

---

[96] *Class Struggles*, 123; MECW, X, 125.
[97] *Class Struggles*, 115–116; MECW, X, 118–118.
[98] *Class Struggles*, 127–131; MECW, X, 128–131.

ACTUALITÉS.

LE FESTIN DE BALTAZAR - VÉRON.

Figure 9.2 "The Banquet of Baltasar-Véron." Lithograph by Daumier
in *Le Charivari*, March 27, 1850. Louis Véron was the owner and
director of the Bonapartist newspaper, *Le Constitutionnel*. Daumier's
print shows Véron's dinner guests hiding behind the newspaper as the
bright light of revolution approaches. Photograph: Getty

If the theatrical metaphor remains important in the *Eighteenth
Brumaire*, one is also struck by the profusion of images, metaphors and
buried quotations that point as much to magic and sorcery and witchcraft
as to the theatre. *The Eighteenth Brumaire* is a work in which ghosts walk
and shadows dissolve and spectres are conjured up – a work in which
cardsharps do tricks and objects change shape before one's very eyes.
And Marx keeps emphasizing the contradictions and anomalies and
illusions and confusions of the period.

What is Marx up to here? How does one make sense of all the ghostly
imagery? And what relation does this imagery have to Marx's interpretation of 1848? The best way to begin, perhaps, is to look closely at a
passage in which Marx characterizes a whole period, a phase in the
history of the Second Republic, but does so in a way that emphasizes

the confusion, the contradictions, the apparent chaos of events when they are considered from a purely political and ideological standpoint:

> The period that we have before us comprises the most motley mixture of crying contradictions: constitutionalists who conspire openly against the Constitution; revolutionists who are confessedly constitutional; a National Assembly that wants to be omnipotent and always remains parliamentary; a *Montagne* that finds its vocation in patience and counters its present defeats by prophesying future victories; royalists who form the *patres conscripti* of the republic and are forced by the situation to keep the hostile royal houses to which they adhere, abroad, and the republic, which they hate, in France; an executive power that finds its strength in its very weakness and its respectability in the contempt that it calls forth; a republic that is nothing but the combined infamy of two monarchies, the Restoration and the July Monarchy, with an imperial label – alliances whose first proviso is separation; struggles whose first law is indecision; wild, inane agitation in the name of tranquility, most solemn preaching of tranquility in the name of revolution; passions without truth, truths without passion; heroes without heroic deeds, history without events; development, whose sole driving force seems to be the calendar.[99]

What is Marx doing here? He is, for one thing, telling us that there is no making sense of the events of 1848–1851 if we look only at what people say and do – if we look only at the level of overt and explicit political discussion and behaviour. All we can see in this case is contradictions or sheer nonsense, which is pretty much what Flaubert saw.

These contradictions can be resolved and history can make sense. But only, Marx argues, if we get below the superficial level of appearances to the deeper level of class – only if we get below politics and ideology to discover the real interests of the groups involved. This is what Marx tries to do. He insists, for example, on the paradox that after the June Days, the strongest defenders of the Republic were the two royalist factions, the Legitimists and the Orleanists. Why? Because the republic offers the Legitimists and the Orleanists the possibility of ruling jointly without confronting their differences and having to choose between their pretenders. The point that emerges from Marx's analysis is that politics and ideology are realms of false consciousness and illusion. And a striking feature of the *Eighteenth Brumaire* is the skill with which Marx uses metaphor and simile to heighten the contrast between the world of reality and the class struggle, on the one hand, and the realm of shadow and illusion on the other.

Of all the rhetorical devices that Marx uses to dramatize the contrast between illusion and reality, four are particularly important. First, there

---

[99] *Eighteenth Brumaire*, 37; MECW, XI, 124–125.

is the use of mock-heroic diction that contrasts Louis Napoleon's solemnity in acting out his high imperial role with the vulgarity of his actual methods: "As a fatalist [Bonaparte] lives in the conviction that there are certain higher powers which man, and the soldier in particular, cannot withstand. Among these powers he counts, first and foremost, cigars and champagne, cold poultry and garlic sausage."[100] The second of Marx's devices is oxymoron, the linking of opposites. This is illustrated above by the "clumsily cunning" and "doltishly sublime" Louis Bonaparte. Then there is the rhetorical device of chiasmus to which Marx returns repeatedly to contrast pretensions and realities, images and facts. The term "chiasmus" refers to a passage made up of two balanced parts which have their elements reversed: Louis Bonaparte is "the serious buffoon who no longer takes world history for a comedy but his comedy for world history." "Rather an end to terror, cries the bourgeois, than terror without end."[101] The reversals that take place here contrast appearance and reality, illusion and truth. The point is that politics and ideology are indeed realms of mystery and illusion which can only be dispelled by class analysis.

Finally, there is personification, which Marx uses to give substance and vivid definition to the forces at work within society. Here it is the verbs that do the work: the bourgeoisie moans, poses, blurts, snorts and greets its deliverer. The radical petty bourgeoisie is alternately "stupefied" by the June Days, dumbfounded by Louis-Napoleon's election as president, and tricked by the Party of Order on June 13, 1849. The bourgeois republicans of Le National "amuse themselves" by putting on a new ball dress in February. Then there is the proletariat, which "dictates the republic" to the Provisional Government, "steps into the foreground" as an independent force, "displays its giant body" in February, "joins battle" with the bourgeoisie in June and then, defeated, retires to lick its wounds.

The Collapse of the Bourgeoisie and the Triumph of the Pseudo-Bonaparte

Turning from imagery to argument, we should recall that the main protagonist of The Eighteenth Brumaire is not the proletariat – it is relegated to the audience after the June Days – but the bourgeoisie. Marx is ambivalent about the bourgeoisie. In the Communist Manifesto he celebrates the achievement of the bourgeoisie in destroying feudal ties and

---

[100] Eighteenth Brumaire, 67; MECW, XI, 150–151.
[101] Eighteenth Brumaire, 66, 96; MECW, XI, 150, 176.

creating new instruments and relations of production.[102] In *The Eighteenth Brumaire*, however, the bourgeoisie plays an inglorious role, and Marx's aim is to explain why. How could the bourgeoisie, just two generations after its assumption of the leading role in 1789, have done everything possible to contain the revolutionary energies unleashed in 1848? Seeking to answer this question, Marx identifies three main groups within the French bourgeoisie – the great landlords, the industrialists, and the finance capitalists – and two more groups on its margins: the petty bourgeoisie and the "pure" or republican bourgeoisie. He associates each marginal group with a newspaper. The republican bourgeoisie is "a coterie of writers, lawyers, officers and officials" gathered around the newspaper *Le National*. This group is united by shared enemies, by "memories of the old republic," and by French nationalism.[103] The petty bourgeoisie consists of skilled artisans and small tradesmen and the lawyers and journalists who represent them, and they are the democratic republicans associated with the journal *La Réforme*.

Each of these marginal groups would have its moment, but the two groups that Marx regards as central to the history of the Second Republic are the landlords and the merchants and industrialists. These groups form the two opposed wings of the Party of Order. Both groups are dominated by monarchists: the landlords support a return to the Bourbon dynasty of Louis XVI, and the merchants and industrialists favour the Orleanist dynasty of Louis Philippe. Landed property and capital are at odds, and the great advantage of the democratic republic for them is, as we've seen, that it enables them to put off settling their differences.[104]

In *The Eighteenth Brumaire*, the period running from the June Days to the presidential election of December 10 is defined as a time of "exclusive rule" by the bourgeois republicans. This is a period of red scare and repression during which the state of siege imposed in June serves as the "midwife" to the drafting of a conservative republican constitution. After Louis-Napoleon's election as president, the dominant role in the Assembly is taken over by the two monarchist factions, the Legitimists and the Orleanists, whose leaders have discovered that the Republic is "the form of state in which they could rule conjointly." In this period, which runs from December 1848 to the dissolution of the Constituent Assembly in May 1849, the Assembly has to share power with the newly elected president. Here Marx revises his earlier assessment of the role

---

[102] Marx, *Communist Manifesto*, 222.
[103] *Eighteenth Brumaire*, 23; MECW, XI, 112–113.
[104] *Eighteenth Brumaire*, 42; MECW, XI, 129.

played by Louis-Napoleon. In *Class Struggles* he argued that the royalist bourgeoisie, who controlled the Assembly, had the upper hand in relations with the President. Now he treats Louis-Napoleon as a masterful tactician who feigns weakness and passivity while conspiring "behind the back of the National Assembly."[105]

The final period in the life of the Republic runs from the election of the Legislative Assembly in May 1849 to its overthrow. Marx describes this period as a time of "the most motley mixture of crying contradictions" in which royalists are the strongest defenders of the Republic and the executive power "finds its strength in its very weakness." The pure republicans take a big loss in the parliamentary elections of May 1849 and the monarchist factions continue to control the Assembly. But a strong opposition party emerges in the new Legislative Assembly. This is the social democratic party, *les démoc*-soc, who constitute the "Mountain" in the Assembly and get considerable support from the army. They command 180 votes (out of 705) in the Assembly. But their moment of influence is brief. Just two weeks after the convening of the Legislative Assembly, the crushing of the demonstration of June 13, 1849, serves to break "the influence of the *Montagne* in parliament and the power of the petty bourgeoisie in Paris."[106]

On November 1, 1849, Louis-Napoleon announced the dismissal of the Barrot ministry. "No one," Marx comments acerbically, "has ever sacked lackeys with less ceremony than Bonaparte his ministers."[107] Behind this ministry he initially effaced himself, donning the mask of a follower. But now the mask comes off and Louis-Napoleon appoints a "ministry of office boys." Marx sees the dismissal of the Barrot ministry as a turning point in Louis-Napoleon's relations with the Party of Order. With the dismissal, he writes, "the Party of Order lost, never to reconquer it, an indispensable post for the maintenance of the parliamentary regime, the lever of executive power." Marx argues that the centralization of the body politic in France was such that to lose control of the ministry was to "forfeit all real influence" in the country at large.[108] During the winter of 1849–1850, Louis-Napoleon continued to jockey with the Legislative Assembly while growing unrest in the countryside made the conservative majority in the Assembly increasingly nervous. In March 1850, they voted a new education law which strengthened the influence of the Catholic Church in both primary and secondary education. Then

[105] *Eighteenth Brumaire*, 31–35; MECW, XI, 119–123.
[106] *Eighteenth Brumaire*, 45. MECW, XI, 132.
[107] *Eighteenth Brumaire*, 52; MECW, XI, 137.
[108] *Eighteenth Brumaire*, 53–54; MECW, XI, 139.

ACTUALITÉS.

RATAPOIL FESANT DE LA PROPAGANDE.
— Si vous aimez votre femme, votre maison, votre champ, votre génisse et votre
veau, signez, vous n'avez pas une minute à perdre!........

Figure 9.3 Ratapoil doing propaganda. Lithograph by Daumier in *Le Charivari*, June 19, 1851: "If you love your wife, your house, your field, your heifer and your calf, sign up. You don't have a minute to lose." Photograph: Alamy

in May, following radical victories in Parisian by-elections, they passed an electoral law cutting the number of registered voters by almost three million,[109] This law, which Marx describes as "the coup d'état of the bourgeoisie," set the stage for "a life-and-death struggle" between the President and the National Assembly.[110]

In 1850, in *Class Struggles* and in his *Revue*, Marx had written derisively of the "ridiculous," "commonplace" and self-deceived "pseudo-Bonaparte" who believed he owed his importance to the magic of his name and the brilliance of his impersonation of the First Napoleon. His followers, according to Marx, knew better. They had in fact "so little faith in the magic effect of his personality that they surrounded him with *claqueurs*" from the Society of December 10, who cheered him on as he travelled around France (see Figures 9.3 and 9.4). In *Class Struggles*, Marx had described Louis-Napoleon as the "marionette" of "the

---

[109] *Eighteenth Brumaire*, 62; MECW, XI, 148.
[110] *Eighteenth Brumaire*, 64; MESW, 294.

Figure 9.4 Ratapoil and his Staff: "Long Live the Emperor!"
Lithograph by Daumier in *Le Charivari*, January 1, 1851. Daumier's
Ratapoil was not only a shady con-man and electoral agent for Louis-
Napoleon, but also the principal cheerleader for the would-be emperor.
Hulton Archive via Getty

Bonapartists" who "put speeches into his mouth," criticizing the electoral law and presenting himself as the protector of universal male suffrage. Despite all the efforts of his followers, Marx wrote in the fall of
1850, "these journeys were anything but triumphal processions."[111]

In *The Eighteenth Brumaire* Marx takes Louis-Napoleon – or
"Bonaparte," as he always calls him – more seriously. Far from being a
marionette manipulated by his advisers, Marx's Bonaparte now controls
them. He is a "crafty *roué*" who appoints himself "chief of the
lumpenproletariat," who conceives of politics and political ceremonial
"as comedy in the most vulgar sense, as a masquerade where the grand
costumes, words and postures merely serve to mask" his own knavish
designs. In his struggle with the National Assembly, he is detached from
the role he plays. Whereas the bourgeoisie plays comedy in a serious
manner and is "half convinced of the solemnity of its own performance of
state," Bonaparte, the adventurer, wins by playing comedy as comedy.
"Only when he has eliminated his solemn opponent, when he himself
takes his imperial role seriously and under the Napoleonic mask imagines
that he is the real Napoleon, does he become the victim of his conception

---

[111] *Class Struggles*, 144; MECW, X, 523–525.

of the world, the serious buffoon who no longer takes world history for a comedy but his own comedy for world history."[112]

Along with its depiction of Bonaparte as crafty *roué*, the *Eighteenth Brumaire* also portrays the "Society of December 10" as a kind of Praetorian Guard for the would-be emperor. Created in 1849 in the guise of a "benevolent society," the Society of December 10 constituted both a fighting force and a support group for Louis Bonaparte on his tours through the provinces. Its task was "to improvise a public for him, to create the impression of public enthusiasm," and "to howl 'Vive l'Empereur!'"[113] Its members came from a social group which Marx described as one of two key supports of Louis Bonaparte: the *lumpenproletariat*.[114] Marx's description of this "class" is both strange and unforgettable:

Alongside decayed *roués* with dubious means of subsistence and of dubious origin, alongside ruined and adventurous offshoots of the bourgeoisie, were vagabonds, discharged soldiers, discharged jailbirds, escaped galley slaves, swindlers, mountebanks, *lazzaroni*. pickpockets, tricksters, gamblers, *maquereaux* brothel keepers, porters, *literati*, organ-grinders, rag-pickers, knife grinders, tinkers, beggars – in short, the whole indefinite disintegrated mass, thrown hither and thither, which the French term *la bohème*. From this kindred element Bonaparte formed the core of the Society of December 10.[115]

This is strange because in painting this vivid picture of an urban under-class – a "bad" proletariat as it were – Marx was buying into an urban myth widespread in the 1840s. This was the myth, popularized in the novels of Dickens, Balzac and Eugène Sue, that the poor in great cities such as Paris and London constituted a criminal class.[116] It is strange also because Marx's other example of a lumpenproletarian group, the Mobile Guard that helped crush the June insurrection, had little in common with the Society of December 10 apart from the fact that both were incapable of representing themselves politically.[117]

In contrast to his depiction of the craftiness of Bonaparte and his entourage, Marx describes the Party of Order as caught up in an equivo-cal game, dissipating its energies in "petty jurisdictional squabbles,

---

[112] *Eighteenth Brumaire*, 65–66; MECW, XI, 149–150.
[113] *Eighteenth Brumaire*, 66; MECW, XI, 150.
[114] The role played by the second support group for Louis Bonaparte, the small-holding peasantry, is described below.
[115] *Eighteenth Brumaire*, 65; MECW, XI, 149. Mark Traugott cogently describes the *lumpenproletariat* as "a 'nonclass' defined in terms of the *absence* of bonds of solidarity grounded in the constraints of material life-conditions." See *Armies of the Poor*, xiii.
[116] See Louis Chevalier, *Classes laborieuses et classes dangereuses à Paris pendant la première moitié du XIXe siècle* (Paris, 1958).
[117] On this issue, see Stedman Jones, *Karl Marx*, 339–340.

pettifoggery [and] legalistic hair-splitting."[118] Indeed, the whole period
from the passage of the electoral law of May 31, 1850, to the *coup* of
December 2, 1851, is characterized by Marx as marked by the political
collapse of the bourgeoisie. During these eighteen months the Party of
Order loses its parliamentary majority, loses control of the army, fails in
its efforts to regain administrative power, and finally disintegrates. In
conclusion, Marx sums up the "accomplishments" of the bourgeoisie in
a brilliant series of chiastic propositions:

The bourgeoisie ... apotheosized the sword; the sword rules it. It destroyed the
revolutionary press; its own press has been destroyed. It placed popular meetings
under police supervision; its own salons are under the supervision of the police. It
disbanded the democratic National Guard; its own National Guard is disbanded.
It imposed a state of siege; a state of siege is imposed upon it. It supplanted the
juries by military commissions; its juries are supplanted by military commissions.
It subjected public education to the sway of priests; the priests subject it to their
own education. It transported people without trial; it is being transported without
trial. It repressed every stirring in society by means of the state power; every
stirring in its society is suppressed by means of the state power.[119]

Here in a series of repeated antitheses, each embedded in a parallel
construction, Marx contrasts action and result, intention and consequence, pretension and reality, and finally paints a picture of the bourgeois republic twisted "into a monstrous shape" not by means of the
black magic of a Circe but by the conniving of the bourgeoisie itself.

A New Drama in a New Language?

In introducing a new edition of Marx's *Eighteenth Brumaire* in 1885,
Frederick Engels called it a "work of genius" which "laid bare the whole
course of French history since the February days." Marx, he said, "had
first discovered the great law of motion of history, the law according to
which all historical struggles ... are in fact only the more or less clear
expression of struggles of social classes." In writing about the history of
the Second French Republic, wrote Engels, Marx "put his law to the
test ... and even after thirty-three years we must still say that it has stood
the test brilliantly."[120]

Engels had his own reasons for wrapping Marx in the mantle of
science. In the 1880s, he was addressing a generation of radicals whose

[118] *Eighteenth Brumaire*, 72; MECW, XI, 155.
[119] *Eighteenth Brumaire*, 103; MECW, XI, 182.
[120] Engels, Preface to Third German Edition, *Eighteenth Brumaire*, 10; MECW,
XXVI, 303.

views had been shaped not by Hegel and utopian socialism but by the scientific ideas of Darwin, Spencer and Comte. In their wake several generations of Marxists continued to regard Marxism as a science based on the assumption that historical events can best be understood in terms of the conflict of economically defined classes.[121] But Engels' description now seems curiously antiseptic with regard to a work which abounds in invective, denunciation, sarcasm, parody and extravagant imagery, and which has in recent years been plausibly described as a "*danse macabre*" and as a study in "self-deception, delusion, hysteria and hallucination."[122]

Considering the *Eighteenth Brumaire* as a whole, one of its most startling features is the attention given to the power of myth and the ubiquity of illusion in political life. At the heart of the book lies Marx's attempt to unpack the illusions that made Louis-Napoleon Bonaparte so appealing to the impoverished small peasantry. But reflections on myth and illusion run throughout the text. Much of it is devoted to an exploration of the fantasy worlds of the two royalist parties, the various bourgeois factions, and the socialists. One of Marx's key concepts is "parliamentary cretinism" which "holds those infected by it fast in an imaginary world and robs them of all sense, all memory, all understanding of the rude external world."[123] And of course, the famous opening passage directly raises the question of myth and its relation to revolution: "Men make their own history, but they do not make it just as they please; they do not make it under circumstances chosen by themselves, but under circumstances directly encountered, given and transmitted from the past." Significant here is the fact that the "circumstances ... transmitted from the past" that shape and constrain the way in which people can make their own history are not economic conditions or relations of production but rather traditions, memories, and historical references. It is not material life but cultural memory – "the tradition of all the dead generations" – that weighs "like a nightmare on the brain of the living":

And just when they seem engaged in revolutionizing themselves and things, in creating something that has never yet existed, precisely in such periods of

---

[121] For an illuminating critical genealogy of "scientific socialism," see Paul Thomas, *Marxism and Scientific Socialism: From Engels to Althusser* (London, 2008).

[122] Claude Lefort, *The Political Forms of Modern Society: Bureaucracy, Democracy, Totalitarianism* (Cambridge, MA, 1986), 167–180; Massimiliano Tomba, "Marx as the Historical Materialist: Rereading *The Eighteenth Brumaire*," *Historical Materialism: Research in Critical Marxist Theory*, XXI(2) (2013), 33; Terrell Carver, "Marx's Eighteenth Brumaire of Louis Bonaparte: Eliding 150 Years," *Strategies: Journal of Theory, Culture and Politics*, XVI(1) (2003), 10.

[123] *Eighteenth Brumaire*, 80; MECW, XI, 161.

revolutionary crisis, they anxiously conjure up the spirits of the past to their service and borrow from them names, battle cries and costumes in order to present the new scene of world history in this time-honoured disguise and this borrowed language.[124]

The French revolutionaries of 1789 dressed themselves up in Roman clothing in order to accomplish a great task: the destruction of feudalism. But the revolutionaries of 1848 were not trying to overthrow capitalism; they only wanted to extend the suffrage and introduce republican institutions. They invoked 1789 in order to hide from themselves and others the modesty of their aims.

Marx goes on to insist that the future proletarian revolution will be different. It will "let the dead bury their dead." It will not seek to draw its inspiration – "its poetry" – from the past, but from the future. The proletarian revolution cannot begin until it has stripped off all superstition with regard to the past. It must nourish itself on constant self-criticism and a realistic understanding of its tasks. It will require a total rejection of the traditions, memories and rhetoric of past revolutions. But this is presented in richly figurative terms. And that is one of the most arresting features of *The Eighteenth Brumaire*. Even in insisting on the realistic, self-critical and austere character of the proletarian perspective, Marx employs a language rich in metaphor and allusion.[125] The theatrical imagery, the ghosts, the conjuror's tricks are not decorative additions; they are essential to his analysis; they are the terms in which his analysis is worked out.

This is not to say that Marx abandons class analysis. Political factions are generally defined in terms of social class, and class itself is (usually) economically defined. Marx postulates a correlation between material existence, class and politics; and in both essays he is explicit about the relation between political factions and social class. If the Bourbon Restoration was "the political expression of the hereditary rule of the lords of the soil," the July Monarchy was dominated by the bourgeois *parvenus* who made up the finance aristocracy.[126]

So, Marx seems to be clear and explicit about the social determination of politics. The problem is that he is not consistent in his attribution of thought and action to class interest, and it is not at all clear that economic reductionism stands at the centre of his analytical vision. Of course, class

---

[124] *Eighteenth Brumaire*, 13; MECW, XI, 103–104.
[125] On this point see James Martin's excellent article, "Performing Politics: Class, Ideology and Discourse in Marx's *Eighteenth Brumaire*" in Mark Cowling and James Martin (eds.), *Marx's "Eighteenth Brumaire": (Post)modern Interpretations* (London, 2002), esp. 130–131.
[126] *Eighteenth Brumaire*, 40; MECW, XI, 127.

interests are often presented as the motives for decisions. But, as Claude Lefort writes, "Ultimately it is not the logic of interest which underlies the sequence of events" in *The Eighteenth Brumaire*, "but rather the logic of their misrecognition."[127] The emphasis in the text is less on the "real interests" obscured by day-to-day events than on what has been described as "the imaginary terrain of political conflict in which alliances shift, paradoxes arise, events are mishandled."[128] On that terrain the course of events is shaped not only by material forces but also by the motives and self-perceptions of the actors, however deluded they may be. Illusion, prejudice and opportunism come into play as often as the interests of social classes.

Sometimes Marx simply concedes that class analysis doesn't work in particular cases. In *The Eighteenth Brumaire*, we are told that the bourgeois republicans of *Le National* are "not a faction of the bourgeoisie held together by great common interests and marked off by specific conditions of production" but rather a disparate "clique" of "writers, lawyers, officers and officials."[129] As for the government bureaucracy, the parasitical institution which "enmeshes the body of French society like a net and chokes all its pores," it was "the instrument of the ruling class" under the Restoration and July Monarchy, but under Louis Bonaparte it seems "to have made itself completely independent."[130]

What is striking here is Marx's overriding interest in the symbolic and "imaginary" aspects of social life. He repeatedly poses questions concerning the language and symbols through which class interests come to be represented or, more commonly, misrepresented. As Bob Jessop has written, *The Eighteenth Brumaire* "is more concerned with the discursive limitations on the representation of class interests" than with "the organizational forms in and through which [these interests] might be advanced."[131] This explains the weight that Marx's analysis gives to "superstitions inherited from the past" and to "the traditions of all the dead generations." Marx's fascination with language, symbols and superstructure stems in part from the fact that one of his great concerns is to

---

[127] Claude Lefort, *Political Forms of Modern Society*, 170.
[128] James Martin, "Performing Politics," 131. See also Terrell Carver, *The Postmodern Marx* (Manchester, 1998).
[129] *Eighteenth Brumaire*, 23; MECW, XI, 112–113. See also *Class Struggles*, 88: "The bourgeois republicans of *Le National* did not represent any large faction of their class resting on economic foundations."
[130] *Eighteenth Brumaire*, 108; MECW, XI, 186.
[131] Bob Jessop, "The Political Scene and the Politics of Representation: Periodising Class Struggle and the State in the *Eighteenth Brumaire*" in Cowling and Martin, "Marx's *Eighteenth Brumaire*: (Post)modern Interpretations," 182.

understand why people hold ideas apparently contradictory to their class interests.

The most obvious example of Marx's approach to this problem is his concluding analysis of the process by which Louis-Napoleon Bonaparte came to "represent the interests and the imagination of the peasants. "Bonaparte represents a class," he writes, "and the most numerous class of French society at that, the *small peasants.*"[132] In what sense does Louis-Napoleon "represent" the peasants? On one level, the answer to this question is obvious. Louis-Napoleon represents the small peasants in the sense that they voted for him massively in the presidential elections that were held all over France on December 10, 1848. On that day 5.5 million French citizens – most of them newly enfranchised peasants – cast their votes for Louis-Napoleon, while less than two million voted for all the other presidential candidates put together. In *Class Struggles* Marx explains the election results by asserting that "Napoleon was the only man who exhaustively represented the interests and the imagination of the peasant class."[133]

But again, how did Louis-Napoleon represent the "interests and imagination" of the peasant class? In the concluding section of *The Eighteenth Brumaire* Marx addresses this question in a way that is fascinating but also problematic. Considering Louis-Napoleon now as the representative of the small peasants, he begins by arguing that to the degree that they live in similar conditions, these small peasants constitute a class, but to the degree that they are not aware of their identity of interests with other peasants in similar conditions, they do not constitute a class. "They are consequently incapable of enforcing their class interest in their own name," he writes, "They cannot represent themselves, they must be represented. Their representation must at the same time appear as their master, as an authority over them, as an unlimited governmental power that protects them against the other classes and sends them the rain and the sunshine from above."[134]

"Historical tradition," writes Marx, "gave rise to the faith of the French peasants in the miracle that a man named Napoleon would bring all the glory back to them. And an individual was found who gives himself out as that man because he bears the name of Napoleon."[135] Now what does the younger Napoleon offer to the smaller French peasants? What makes him so attractive to them? Marx argues (and here he offers a

[132] *Eighteenth Brumaire*, 108; MECW, XI, 186–187.
[133] *Class Struggles*, 71; MECW, X, 80.
[134] *Eighteenth Brumaire*, 109; MECW, XI, 187–188.
[135] *Eighteenth Brumaire*, 109–110; MECW, XI, 188.

parody of the title of a work published by the young Louis-Napoleon in 1839.) that there are in fact five "Napoleonic ideas": small property, strong government, big bureaucracy, influence of priests and a strong army. To the peasant, the most important of these Napoleonic ideas is small property. Louis-Napoleon is attractive to the peasants because they see him as a defender of small property.

Marx explains that after the French revolutionaries had abolished all the claims of the traditional aristocracy to seigneurial holdings, and after the French revolutionaries had distributed the land formerly owned by the Church, it was Napoleon who, with the proclamation of the Civil Code, guaranteed to the peasants full rights of ownership over all their land – both the land they had traditionally owned and land that they had acquired since the Revolution. "Napoleon confirmed and regulated the conditions on which [the peasants] could exploit undisturbed the soil of France which had only just come into their possession."[136] What the Napoleonic Code also did – and Marx simply takes this for granted without making it explicit – was to modify and standardize inheritance laws so as to ensure the relatively equal division of a peasant's land among his heirs. In so doing, Napoleon gratified the desire of every peasant to be a landowner.

Marx's point is that the guaranteeing of every peasants' right to the ownership of property, which seemed to liberate the peasantry in 1810, had become by 1850, with the increase in the number of rural proprietors and the increasing subdivision of peasant holdings, a principal but unacknowledged source of the misery of the French peasantry:

What is now causing the ruin of the French peasant is his smallholding itself, the division of the land, the form of property which Napoleon consolidated in France. It is precisely the material conditions which made the feudal peasant a small-holding peasant and Napoleon an emperor ... The "Napoleonic" form of property, which at the beginning of the nineteenth century was the condition for the liberation and enrichment of the French country folk has developed in the course of this century into the law of their enslavement and pauperization.[137]

The peasants were still clinging to an image of the first Napoleon as a saviour who had given them unfettered property rights, and an image of the second Napoleon as a second saviour who would help them realize all the good things they expected to come from the ownership of property. But this could not happen, given the huge indebtedness of peasant

---

[136] *Eighteenth Brumaire*, 111; MECW, XI, 189.
[137] *Eighteenth Brumaire*, 111–112; MECW, XI, 189.

proprietors, the small size of their holdings, and the need of the state to continue to tax them heavily.

The argument that Marx is making here is, in a word, that if Louis-Napoleon Bonaparte's regime actually establishes itself – if he is given the opportunity to act on his "Napoleonic ideas" – their bankruptcy will soon be revealed and the illusions that constitute the Napoleonic myth will be dispelled. This is the point that Marx makes in metaphorical form in the final sentence of *The Eighteenth Brumaire*: "If the imperial mantle finally falls on the shoulders of Louis Bonaparte, the bronze statue of Napoleon will crash from the top of the Vendôme column."[138] Nothing will do more to dispel the Napoleonic myth than the exercise of power by Louis-Napoleon himself.

In both *The Eighteenth Brumaire* and *Class Struggles* Marx insists that there is something to be gained from the victory of the reaction in 1848. His point in *Class Struggles* is that the crushing defeat of the proletariat in the June insurrection has freed the proletariat from the illusion that they could count on the help of bourgeois republicans in their own struggle for emancipation. The defeat of the proletariat has dispelled the illusion of class collaboration. Marx's point in *The Eighteenth Brumaire* is that the parody of empire will free the French peasants from the weight of the Napoleonic myth. Once this has happened, he argues, they can face the future without illusions.

Marx saw himself as a destroyer of illusions. And his attempt to expose the illusions of 1848 was initially rooted in the assumption that one day a class without illusions would emerge – that in a society so polarized that almost everyone had been thrust into the proletariat there would be no need for the representatives of the working class to concoct ideological myths and fictions to justify their claims. In a society where almost everyone was exploited and victimized, the pursuit of self-interest by the underclass would have a universal character. And the proletariat itself would come to see the world without illusions. Unlike earlier social movements, Marx's revolutionary proletariat would have a true understanding of the world and of its own condition.

Between 1848 and 1852 Marx came to question this optimistic view of proletarian revolution. He began to see the social world as a symbolic order and to argue that our sense of what is possible is crucially limited by myths and symbols of our own creation. He had previously regarded the French Revolution as the model for the future proletarian revolution. But now he saw the task confronting the proletariat as vastly harder. And he

---

[138] *Eighteenth Brumaire*, 120; MECW, XI, 197.

drew a new kind of distinction between bourgeois and proletarian revolutions:

Bourgeois revolutions, like those of the eighteenth century, storm swiftly from success to success; their dramatic effects outdo each other; men and things seem set in sparkling brilliants; ecstasy is the everyday spirit; but they are short-lived ... Proletarian revolutions, on the other hand, like those of the nineteenth century, criticize themselves constantly, interrupt themselves continually in their own course, come back to the apparently accomplished in order to recommence it afresh.

The proletarian revolution of the nineteenth century would have to leave all past models behind and "create for itself the revolutionary point of departure."[139]

One question remains: Why, in a work intended not for intellectuals but to raise the consciousness of German workers, should Marx indulge himself with so many literary references and rhetorical flourishes? Why does he fill his text with extended metaphors, buried quotations, metonymy, chiasmus, synecdoche, all sorts of ironies? What is gained? I would answer that Marx's use of language illustrates a component of his argument: language has power. He exposes the emptiness of the old language and the old symbols. But he also insists that the social revolution must find a new language and new symbols in order to prepare itself for the struggles to come. Marx writes that "the social revolution of the nineteenth century cannot draw its poetry from the past but only from the future." *The Eighteenth Brumaire* and *Class Struggles* are attempts to explode "the poetry of the past" and to set the stage, verbally as well as analytically, for a new drama in a new language.

---

[139] *Eighteenth Brumaire*, 16–17; MECW, XI, 106. On this point see Jerrold Seigel, "Politics, Memory, Illusion: Marx and the French Revolution" in François Furet and Mona Ozouf (eds.), *The French Revolution and Modern Political Culture*, Vol: 3, *The Transformation of Political Culture* (Oxford, 1989), 625–637.

10 Flaubert
Lost Hopes and Empty Words

If Karl Marx was a passionately involved observer of French politics during the Second Republic, Gustave Flaubert was detached (see Figure 10.1). So detached was Flaubert that he spent most of the Second Republic working on a novel set in third-century Egypt and then touring the Middle East with his friend Maxime Du Camp. Thus while in France Louis-Napoleon Bonaparte was digging the grave of the Republic and while the Left and Right were waging a war of songs and prints and almanacs for control of the countryside, Flaubert travelled – first vicariously and then actually – throughout North Africa and the Middle East, taking in the sights, sounds and odours of a new and seductive world. He wrote his mother that Egypt had given him his "first bellyful of colours," and his travel notes are full of vivid descriptions of mosques, dervishes and street life, courtesans and camel caravans. Some images from this trip took permanent possession of his mind. Eight years later, recalling a night spent by the pyramids, he could "still hear the jackals howling and the gusts of wind that shook my tent." And in 1880, shortly before his death, he wrote his niece that for two weeks he had been "gripped by the longing to see a palm-tree standing out against the blue sky, and to hear a stork clacking its beak at the top of a minaret."[1]

Flaubert did get to Paris at the beginning and the end of the Second Republic. In February 1848 he witnessed the uprising that brought down Louis-Philippe, and in early December 1851 he was back in Paris, staying at a hotel within earshot of the fusillade that left 200 Parisians dead on the Boulevard des Italiens two days after Louis-Napoleon's coup d'état. But that was all: throughout the life of the Second Republic Flaubert's imagination was never engaged by politics. Still, almost two decades later he made a remarkable effort to grasp 1848 retrospectively as he studied

---

[1] Flaubert to his mother, November 17, 1849, Gustave Flaubert, *Correspondance*, 5 vols. (Paris, 1973–2007), I, 528; Flaubert to Mlle Leroyer de Chantepie, December 12, 1857, *Correspondance*, II, 784; Flaubert to his niece Caroline, February 15, 1880, *Correspondance*, V, 831.

Figure 10.1 Photograph of Flaubert by Nadar, 1880.

the events, personalities and writings of the period in preparing
L'Education sentimentale. This novel offers a vast satirical fresco of
Parisian life under the July Monarchy and culminates with a long section
on 1848 and the Second Republic. It focuses on the experience and the
imaginative life of a particular generation – the generation of young

people who came to maturity around 1840 and whose lives were either broken or redirected by the revolution of 1848. Here Flaubert subsumes an unsparing critique of the sentimental humanitarian radicalism of the 'forty-eighters within a broader dissection of the mentality of the whole generation of romantic idealists of which the revolutionaries were a part.

The Emergence of the Writer

Flaubert was twenty-six years of age at the time of the February Revolution. Six years earlier he had gone to Paris to study law, which he hated. Apparently, his career as a young law student was not unlike that of Frederick Moreau, the central figure of L'Education sentimentale. Like Frederick, he became involved with several women, notably an older married woman named Elise Schlésinger who may have been the model for the novel's heroine, Marie Arnoux. Then, in January 1844, Flaubert had a seizure, probably an attack of epilepsy, which led him to give up his studies and to return to his home in Normandy. Thus at the age of twenty-two he took up residence at his family's country estate at Croisset, near Rouen. For the next dozen years he lived as a self-described hermit, cared for by, and caring for, his mother and living comfortably on the income from family landholdings.

The publication of Madame Bovary in 1856, and his subsequent trial and acquittal on charges of "outrage to public morals," made Flaubert famous. That year he rented an apartment in Paris, where he began to spend winters. He won the friendship of a circle of writers including George Sand, Ivan Turgenev, Henry James, Sainte-Beuve and the Goncourt brothers. He frequented the salon of the Emperor's cultivated cousin, Princess Mathilde. He had mistresses, notably the writer Louise Colet with whom he carried on a passionate correspondence for eight years. But he kept her and the other women in his life, except for his mother and his adored niece Caroline, at a distance. He had a long-standing, intimate, and carefully concealed relationship with his niece's English governess. But he rarely saw her, and his most satisfying sexual relations may have been with prostitutes. He never married and had no desire to do so. The one thing he really cared about was his writing.

As a writer, Flaubert was a slow and painstaking craftsman who made impossible demands on himself. He once wrote that he sought a style that would be "rhythmic like verse, precise like the language of science, with undulations, the deep voice of the cello, and plumes of fire."[2] He could

---

[2] Flaubert to Louise Colet, April 24, 1852, Correspondance, II, 79.

spend a week on a single page, tormenting himself to find the best turn of phrase, the correct adjective, the right verb. He often complained that writing was a torture for him. But there was little else that held much interest for him. "I cannot imagine," he wrote, "how people unconcerned with art can spend their time. How they live is a mystery to me."[3]

Flaubert is often described as the first modern novelist, and Marcel Proust was serious when he wrote that Flaubert's "entirely new and personal" use of tenses, participles, pronouns and prepositions constituted a Kantian Revolution in French prose writing. According to Proust, Flaubert taught a whole generation of French writers to use the imperfect tense, which emphasizes continuity and repetition, rather than the *passé simple* which treats the past as over and done with.[4] The seamless, dreamy past that pervades *Combray* owed much to Flaubert's demonstration of the power of the "eternal imperfect" to blend together unique events and unchanging backdrops to create a resonant and unfinished past. But the most noteworthy of Flaubert's narrative devices was his use of free indirect style, the *style indirect libre*. This is a mode of writing about a character's perceptions, thoughts, or speech in which the views of the character are not quoted but summarized by the narrator in such a way that the reader senses that the voice is that of the character. Often, this involves the use of snatches of conversation that give the impression of direct speech. At the same time, the narrator's presence is felt, fluctuating between empathy and irony.[5]

In Flaubert's correspondence there is an intriguing statement that provides a key to his achievement as a writer:

There are in literary terms two distinct persons in me: One is infatuated with bombast, lyricism, eagle flights, with sonorities of phrasing and lofty ideas. The other person digs and burrows into the truth as deeply as he can, and likes to treat the little facts as respectfully as the big ones. He would like to make you feel almost *physically* the things he reproduces.[6]

---

[3] Flaubert to Louise Colet, September 22, 1846, *Correspondance*, I, 360.

[4] Marcel Proust, "A propos du 'style' de Flaubert" and "A ajouter à Flaubert" in *Contre Sainte-Beuve* (Paris, 1971), 586–600, 299.

[5] On the free indirect style, see William Paulson, *Sentimental Education: The Complexity of Disenchantment* (New York, 1992), 66–83; and Peter Brooks, *Reading for the Plot: Design and Intention in Narrative* (New York, 1984), 174–175, 193–200, 346–347. An example from the very outset of *L'Education sentimentale* is a sentence which introduces Frederick Moreau: "He found that the happiness merited by the excellence of his soul was slow in coming." ("Il trouvait que le Bonheur mérité par l'excellence de son âme tardait à venir.") See *L'Education sentimentale: Histoire d'un jeune homme*, Edouard Maynial (ed.) (Paris, 1961), 2.

[6] Flaubert to Louise Colet, January 16, 1852, *Correspondance*, II, 30.

These two impulses – the lyric and the burrowing – can be seen at work in all Flaubert's writing. Often he chose exotic subjects and wrote about dreams and fantasies. But he generally did so with ironic detachment and in such a way that the lyric flights and exaltation were put in critical perspective.

This comes out clearly in Flaubert's first major work, *Madame Bovary*, which created a furor when it was published in 1856. It did so partly because of its subject matter – the adulterous affairs of the wife of a country doctor. The novel was shocking also because of its aggressive realism – and especially Flaubert's lengthy description of Emma Bovary's suicide by arsenic poisoning. But the book's originality lay elsewhere. Adultery was hardly a novel literary theme in Flaubert's time. And other writers before Flaubert had offered meticulously realistic descriptions of the material world. What *was* new was Flaubert's attempt to convey a sense of what the world looked like from inside to a woman of great imagination and limited experience, whose discontents and fantasies had been nurtured by the reading of exotic novels and gothic romances which developed in her so strong a capacity for vicarious pleasure that everything in her actual life seemed trivial.

Madame Bovary is often regarded as a cruel and pitiless work. There is certainly something unsparing about Flaubert's dissection of the mental processes of a woman whom he shows to be both colossally self-absorbed and inarticulate. Still there is an element of sympathy for Emma Bovary in the novel. It is contained in Flaubert's ability to convey an understanding of the gap between her feelings, impulses, fantasies and desires and her very limited ability to gratify them or even to articulate them. Flaubert makes this explicit in the course of a fascinating exchange between Emma and her lover Rodolphe. She tells him of her undying love, but this jaded aristocrat has heard it all before. For him "Emma was like every other mistress," and the narrator tells us that "this man, of such broad experience, could not distinguish the variety or the depth of feeling beneath the similarity of expression." Rodolphe had failed to understand that "the soul's fulness" can "sometimes overflow through the emptiest metaphors." Then the narrator steps out of his narrative to offer the reader his own spectacular metaphor: "Human speech is like a broken drum on which we beat out tunes to make bears dance, when we would like to move the stars to tears."[7] This focus on the tension between feelings and desires and the ability to articulate them is one of Flaubert's preoccupations in *Madame Bovary*. It is also a major theme

---

[7] Gustave Flaubert, *Madame Bovary* (Paris, 1961), 178–179.

in *Education sentimentale*. Before turning to the novel, however, we need to consider Flaubert's brief personal experience of the February Revolution.

The February Revolution "from an Artist's Perspective"

From the beginning, Flaubert was no friend of the democrats and republicans who made the February Revolution. He particularly disliked their inflated language – the bombast and "mealy platitudes" that nauseated him when he attended a reformist banquet at Rouen in December 1847.[8] Nevertheless, he was curious enough about revolution that when, on February 23, word reached Rouen of demonstrations in the capital, he and his friend Louis Bouilhet took the train to Paris to observe events "from an artist's perspective."[9] That evening they met Maxime Du Camp and set out for a grand dinner at Les Trois Frères Provençaux in the Palais Royal. On the way, they learned that the Guizot ministry had fallen, and they watched Parisians setting out candles and hanging paper lanterns from their windows as the crowd below shouted, "Illuminez! Illuminez!"[10] After dinner, as the three returned to Du Camp's apartment behind the Church of the Madeleine, they found the boulevard des Capucines blocked off. Just as they got to the Place de la Madeleine, they heard a loud noise behind them. Du Camp thought it was fireworks, but to Flaubert it sounded like the crackle of musket shots. The next morning, while breakfasting at Tortoni's, they learned that fifty demonstrators had been killed in what was already being described as the "massacre" of the boulevard des Capucines.[11]

On February 24, Flaubert and his friends were on the street early. The boulevard des Capucines was empty and "lugubrious" until they reached the boulevard des Italiens and Tortoni's. There, crowds had gathered and tradesmen were excitedly discussing the events of the previous day, the falling prices on the Stock Exchange, and the surprising behaviour of the government troops, many of whom were refusing to fight. The three friends watched a barricade go up at the corner of the rue de Helder. Then they saw Odilon Barrot and the official painter Horace Vernet ride by on horseback, gesturing broadly and evidently seeking to pacify the crowd – only to be greeted with laughter and insults.[12]

Soldiers and members of the National Guard were now fraternizing with the insurgents. Bouilhet got lost in the crowd, and Flaubert and Du

---

[8] Flaubert to Louise Colet, late December 1847, *Correspondance*, I, 491.
[9] Maxime Du Camp, *Souvenirs de l'année 1848* (Geneva, 1979), 51.
[10] Du Camp, *Souvenirs*, 51–54.   [11] Ibid, 54–56.   [12] Ibid, 79–81.

Camp were swept up in a band of sailors, insurgents and National Guards marching toward the Tuileries Palace. The marchers met resistance from soldiers charged with defending the Palace. This was the very regiment responsible for the previous night's shooting. These troops were quickly overpowered by a huge crowd of armed insurgents. For a moment it seemed as though the crowd would start a fire and burn the soldiers alive. But suddenly the gates to the Palace swung open and the crowd poured inside.[13] Flaubert and Du Camp were among the first to enter the principal courtyard of the Tuileries Palace. Encountering only a few dazed members of the King's household staff, they entered the royal dining room where they found the table set for breakfast. Du Camp recorded the scene:

On the great white tablecloth there were bowls of fresh milk, silver coffee pots with the king's insignia, baskets full of bread. Some men sat down and ate. One of them cried out: "This is our reform banquet!" The joke was appreciated and people laughed a lot.[14]

At this point, there were no more than 200 people in the royal apartments, and they behaved respectfully. Du Camp believed that they were moved not by anger but by curiosity. Those with bayonets put them back in the scabbard to avoid damaging the tapestries and chandeliers. In the throne room, a well-dressed man sat on the throne and gave a little speech to an appreciative audience.

But the moment of calm was brief. Flaubert and Du Camp watched as a new band of insurgents rushed through the gates below them. "A great din of shouts and rattling weapons rose up to us. We ran to the head of the staircase to be confronted by a mass of men running up the stairs and shouting 'death!' and 'victory!' The stampede almost caused the bannisters to give way." Shots rang out. Insurgents were using the mirrors for target practice (see Figure 10.2).[15]

Finally, the two went on to the Palais Royal, the principal residence of the Ducs of Orléans. There they witnessed behaviour motivated not by curiosity but by resentment and sheer destructiveness. Fires were set in the courtyard of the Palais Royal; the crowd took everything they could carry from the upstairs apartments – furniture, mirrors, porcelain, curtains, tapestries, paintings – and threw it out the windows and onto the fire below.[16]

That evening Flaubert and Du Camp went to the Hôtel de Ville where, they had been told, the Republic was to be declared. They arrived too late. The important decisions had been taken hours earlier at the National Assembly, and now the new Provisional Government was at work behind

---

[13] Ibid, 83–92.   [14] Ibid, 94.   [15] Ibid, 96.   [16] Ibid, 101–104.

Figure 10.2 "Mob in the Throne Room," Tuileries Palace, February 24, 1848. Anonymous lithograph. Photograph: Getty

locked gates. Outside, barely two hundred people milled in the square. Lights were shining behind the tightly shut windows of the Hôtel de Ville. "We had a confused sense that behind those dark walls and shining windows something important was going on." But outside on the square, all was quiet.[17]

Two days later Flaubert was back in Croisset. He remained there through the spring, going into Rouen on rare occasions to perform National Guard duty. On April 11, he did sentry duty, and two days earlier he helped plant a Tree of Liberty. He detested such ceremonies with their bombastic speeches and fulsome appeals to "Jesus the first socialist."[18] And he apparently took no interest in the conflict between workers and National Guards at Rouen, which culminated on April 27 in an insurrection that left thirty-nine dead.[19] In any case, he had no heart for politics. What really mattered to him was the death in early April of his best friend, Alfred Le Poittevin. And during the June Days, while Paris exploded, and while Maxime Du Camp was engaged in the struggle to "save French civilization", Flaubert and his mother were at Forges-les-Eaux dealing with family matters.[20]

[17] Ibid, 107.   [18] Flaubert to Ernest Chevalier, April 10, 1848, *Correspondance*, I, 496.
[19] John M. Merriman, *The Agony of the Republic: The Repression of the Left in France, 1848–1851* (New Haven, 1978), 13–18.
[20] Du Camp, *Souvenirs*, 295; Frederick Brown, *Flaubert: A Biography* (New York, 2006), 216–218.

Limited though it was, Flaubert's experience of 1848 served to fix in his memory a succession of images. Two decades later, describing the February Revolution in *L'Education sentimentale*, Flaubert drew on these images and also on Maxime Du Camp's account of their shared experiences.[21] But, for the time being, he could think about the February Revolution with serene detachment. "It's all very funny," he wrote Louise Colet in March. "It's a real treat to see how upset people are. I'm delighted to observe so many collapsed ambitions. I don't know if the new form of government and society will be favourable to Art. That's a question. But it cannot be more bourgeois or more worthless than the old."[22] In December Flaubert was so disengaged that he didn't bother to vote in the presidential election. Three years later, when describing the "charming" events of December 2, 1851, to his uncle, he adopted a bemused tone: "As you know, I was at Paris at the time of the coup d'état. I was almost beaten up several times ... But I saw everything ... Providence, which knows that I'm an amateur of the picturesque, has always taken pains to send me to opening nights when they are worth it."[23]

In later life Flaubert tirelessly railed against politics. "I have no sympathy for any political party," he wrote in 1857, "or rather I despise them all, because they all seem to me equally limited, false, puerile, focused on the ephemeral without any sense of the whole." Calling himself "an angry liberal," he spoke with particular scorn about socialism, which he called "a pedantic horror that would be the death of all art and all morality." A dozen years later, as political discussion in France became heated, Flaubert remained adamant. As he wrote George Sand: "The citizens who talk fervently for or against the Empire or the Republic seem to me as useful as those who used to argue about efficacious and efficient grace. Now, thank God, Politics is as dead as Theology!"[24] Flaubert's correspondence throughout the Second Empire is full of such outbursts.

Writing *L'Education sentimentale*

In March 1857, after the publication and trial of *Madame Bovary*, Flaubert wrote that he needed "to get out of the modern world. My

---

[21] Some details that appear in the *Education sentimentale* – for instance, Frederick's reference to the bowls of fresh milk left untouched by the royal family on February 24 – are identical to those recorded by Du Camp. Although Du Camp's *Souvenirs* only appeared in 1876, Flaubert read Du Camp's notes in order to refresh his own memory of the February Revolution.

[22] Flaubert to Louise Colet, March 1848, *Correspondance*, I, 492–493.

[23] Flaubert to François Parain, January 15, 1852, *Correspondance*, II, 28–29.

[24] Flaubert to Mlle Leroyer de Chantepie, March 30, 1857, *Correspondance*, II, 698; Flaubert to George Sand, June 24, 1869, *Correspondance*, IV, 60.

pen has been dipped in it too long, and besides I am as weary of portraying it as I am disgusted by the sight of it." He was now planning, he said, "to write a novel in which the action takes place three centuries before Jesus Christ."[25] This was *Salammbô*, a novel set in Carthage after the First Punic War and describing the conflict between the Carthaginian authorities and their mercenary army. At the centre of the novel was the love affair of a mercenary leader, Mâtho, and Salammbô, the daughter of General Hamilcar and a priestess in the Temple of the Goddess Tanit. This novel engrossed him for five years. "I no longer think of anything but *Carthage*," he wrote in 1858, "and that is as it should be. A book has never been anything for me but a *way of living* in a particular milieu. That explains my hesitations, my anxieties, my slowness."[26]

In 1862, after five years of absorption in the exotic world of *Salammbô*, Flaubert was ready to return to modern times. He began to think about a "Parisian novel." It was not clear at first that politics would be central. In its earliest iterations this new novel was titled *Madame Moreau*, and Flaubert conceived of it as a novel of adultery – a Parisian counterpart to the provincial *Madame Bovary* – centring exclusively on a wife, a husband and a lover. Only gradually did he realize that what he wanted to portray was not adultery but rather the malady of a whole generation. He wanted to explain how and why so many of his contemporaries had become caught up in a debilitating romanticism which involved "a radical defect of imagination, a taste for excess, too much sensuality, a lack of coherent thinking, too much dreaming."[27] He called this malady "sentimentalism," and he came to believe that politics – specifically the collapse of the hopes of romantic intellectuals in 1848 – could explain and illuminate its influence on individuals. As he wrote cryptically in a notebook: "Show that sentimentalism (its development since 1830) follows politics and reproduces its phases."[28]

---

[25] Flaubert to Mlle. Leroyer de Chantepie, March 18, 1857, *Correspondance*, II, 691.
[26] Flaubert to Mlle Leroyer de Chantepie, December 26, 1858, *Correspondance*, II, 846. Flaubert's Carthage actually shows a striking resemblance to Paris in the eve of the revolution of 1848. See Anne Green, *Flaubert and the Historical Novel: Salammbô Reassessed* (Cambridge, 1982), 73–93.
[27] *Carnets de travail* for *L'Education sentimentale*, carnet 19, folio 39 in Tony Williams (ed.), *Flaubert, l'Education sentimentale, les Scénarios* (Paris, 1992), 332: "un défaut radical d'imagination, un goût excessif, trop de sensualité, pas de suite dans les idées, trop de reveries."
[28] *Carnets de travail*, carnet 19, folio 38 verso in Williams (ed.), *Scénarios*, 332: "Montrer que le sentimentalisme (son développement depuis 1830) suit la politique et en reproduit les phases." This notation appears to date from the fall of 1862 as Flaubert was just beginning to think about his "Parisian" novel. See Pierre-Marc de Biasi, *Gustave Flaubert: Une manière spéciale de vivre* (Paris, 2009), 294.

For over a year after the appearance of his "Carthaginian novel," Flaubert read around his new topic, took notes, and drew up outlines and "scenarios" as he had with his earlier novels.[29] Finally, on September 1, 1864, he began to write *L'Education sentimentale.* He described the book to a friend as "a novel of modern manners that will take place in Paris," famously adding these words:

I want to write a moral history of the men of my generation; "sentimental" would be more accurate. It's about love, about passion, but passion as it can exist today, which is to say, inactive passion. The subject, as I've conceived of it, is, I believe, profoundly true, but for that very reason probably not very entertaining. Facts, drama, are a bit lacking, and the action is spread over too long a period. In short, I'm having a lot of trouble and I am full of anxieties.[30]

For the next four and a half years, as he wrestled with his subject and sought to wring out the right words, Flaubert repeatedly expressed discouragement about the progress of the novel. The main character was a nonentity; the love affair at the centre of the novel was unrealized; he was fed up with his secondary characters; his mind was deadened by the reading of too many socialist and republican pamphlets; and he was "disheartened' by his long "moral cohabitation" with bourgeois mediocrity. His greatest worry was that the historical background would overwhelm his invented characters and the story he wanted to tell about their inner lives. He explained to a friend that his aim in writing the novel was "to portray a psychological state hitherto ignored," but the milieu in which his characters lived and moved was "so teeming and copious that at every page they risk being swallowed up by it." He had "to make background material of the very things I find most interesting" and to "skim subjects that I would like to treat at length."[31]

Flaubert could not do without extensive historical research. This was the only way he knew to get inside a time and a place. "I need to know everything," he told Sainte-Beuve, "and before I start writing I have to enter into the atmosphere of the time."[32] Thus he showered acquaintances with questions concerning the lunch menu at the Café Anglais in 1847, the workings of the stock market, public transportation between Paris and Fontainebeau, club meetings and troop movements in 1848. He asked George Sand, Armand Barbès, Maurice Schlésinger and Jules

[29] On the genesis and preparation of *L'Education sentimentale*, in addition to Williams (ed.), *Scénarios*, see also de Biasi, *Flaubert. Une manière spéciale de vivre*, 267–361; and Maurice Bardèche, *L'Oeuvre de Flaubert* (Paris, 1974), 282–304.

[30] Flaubert to Mlle Leroyer de Chantepie, October 6, 1864, *Correspondance*, III, 409.

[31] Flaubert to Alfred Maury, August 20, 1866, *Correspondance*, III, 518.

[32] Flaubert to Sainte-Beuve, March 12, 1866, *Correspondance*, III, 484.

Duplan for their reminiscences of 1848. He read Orléanist newspapers from the July Monarchy and "mind-numbing" socialist brochures from 1848. To write a page on the pottery business of Jacques Arnoux, the husband of his heroine, he stood in the rain for two hours at Creil, taking notes as he watched artisans glazing cheap earthenware. To write a few lines on a case of croup, he spent several days at a Parisian hospital observing the symptoms of a sick child. Before writing a key passage on the Château de Fontainebeau (closed to the public during the Second Empire) he arranged for a personal visit. Other visits took him to the Jockey Club, to an auction house on the rue Druot, to a birthing clinic for unwed mothers, to the Père Lachaise cemetery, and to a *bal public*. Flaubert's aim in all of this was not simply to attain some kind of documentary accuracy but rather to "enter into the atmosphere of the time" in such a way that he could invent a complex, richly textured, and plausible world for his imaginary characters.[33]

The problem of striking a balance between the historical background and the depiction of the inner lives of his characters was most acute in the final part of his novel, which dealt with the revolution of 1848. Flaubert wrote in March 1868: "I'm having a lot of trouble fitting my characters into the political events of '48!" He went on to say: "Historical figures are more interesting than fictional ones, especially when the latter's passions are not very intense. Will people be less interested in Frederick than in Lamartine? And also, which of the real facts should I choose?"[34] In the end, Flaubert managed to keep his historical figures in the background. But the question of what to include and what to omit was difficult for him. His solution was to treat big historical events such as May 15 and the June Days obliquely – as they were seen by the characters and impinged on their lives. Nonetheless, he read widely, drawing extensively on Marie d'Agoult's *Histoire de la Révolution de 1848* and Maxime Du Camp's notes for his account of the February Revolution, on contemporary accounts by Louis Ménard, Marc Caussidière and Louis Blanc, and on the formal histories by Hippolyte Castille and Louis-Antoine Garnier-Pagès.[35] Finally, at 4:56 am on May 16, 1869, he could write that his book was "FINISHED!" It appeared in print on November 17.

[33] On Flaubert's documentation see Gustave Flaubert, *Oeuvres completes,* 16 vols. (Paris: Club de l'Honnête Homme, 1971–1976), III, 427–468: "Documentation de Flaubert pour *L'Education sentimentale*"; P.G. Castex, *Flaubert, L'Education sentimentale* (Paris, 1980), 43–50; and especially Fausto Proietti, "Histoire des idées politiques et sources littéraires: *L'Education sentimentale* dans le context des jugements historiques sur juin 1848," *Flaubert. Revue critique et génétique* [En ligne], mis en ligne le 18 mai 2013, consulted January 19, 2018

[34] Flaubert to Jules Duplan, March 14, 1868, *Correspondance,* III, 734.

[35] For examples of passages on the February Revolution in which Flaubert borrows factual details, turns of phrase, and even metaphors from Marie d'Agoult, *Histoire de la*

Overview of the Novel

L'Education sentimentale is first of all a novel about an individual –
Frederick Moreau – and his unconsummated love affair with a married
woman, Marie Arnoux. She is the most elusive figure in the novel. We
are rarely told what she is thinking, and we hardly ever see her directly.
Instead, we see her through Frederick's eyes, as she is transfigured by his
imagination. At the outset, as Madame Arnoux first appears on the deck
of the riverboat taking Frederick home from Paris, she is described as a
vision. Frederick embellishes this vision with his own romantic fantasies.
She is dark, exotic and possibly of Andalusian origin. She looks like the
women in all the romantic novels he has read. She enlarges his sense of
the possible.

From then until the end of the novel, the real subject is Frederick's
attempt to possess an ideal of his own creation. Just as in *Madame
Bovary*, Flaubert's main preoccupation in *L'Education sentimentale* is with
the workings and the limitations of a romantic imagination. The novel
repeatedly illustrates the solipsistic character of Frederick's mental life.
He projects so many of his own fantasies on Madame Arnoux that he
winds up loving a myth of his own making. But Flaubert does more than
this. What is fascinating about the novel is not his analysis of the limitations of the romantic imagination but rather his account of its workings –
of the process whereby the ideal of Madame Arnoux takes possession of
Frederick's mind. Here there are two movements. On the one hand,
Frederick becomes bewitched by particular parts of her body. He is
entranced by the sight of her foot and by the contemplation her fingers.
"For him," we are told, "each of her fingers was something more than a
thing, almost a person."[36] He becomes absorbed in the particulars and
fetishizes them. On the other hand, the image of Madame Arnoux keeps
dissolving in Frederick's mind into its setting. He cannot separate her
from the silk dresses she wears and the rooms she sees her in. Her comb,
her gloves and her rings become objects of special significance to him.
And he keeps finding her image in everything and everyone he meets.
She is the focal point of his universe. She organizes it and renders it
coherent.[37]

Révolution de 1848 see Gilbert Guisan, "Flaubert et la Révolution de 1848," *Revue
d'Histoire littéraire de la France*, 58(2) (April–June 1958), 183–204.
[36] *L'Education sentimentale*, 271.
[37] For a wonderful example of this second movement of Frederick's imagination see
L'Education sentimentale, 68 for the passage concluding: "Paris depended on her
person, and the great city, with all its voices, thundered like an immense orchestra,
around her."

While Frederick Moreau stands at the centre, the novel also concerns his childhood friend, Charles Deslauriers, whose life is shaped by his unrealized political ambitions. Just as Frederick's view of society is coloured by his ideal of Madame Arnoux, Deslauriers is described as "never having seen society except through the fever of his ambition."[38] At the conclusion of the novel, we find Frederick and Deslauriers looking back on their lives and agreeing that their happiest time together was the day, thirty years earlier, when they made an unsuccessful attempt to do business with the prostitutes of Nogent. What was so memorable about that adventure? Apparently, the fact that their ideals were still untarnished by contact with reality.

In addition to Frederick and Deslauriers, there is a host of lesser characters who belong to the same generation and whose careers as writers, artists and political activists end either in failure or the betrayal of their ideals. There is Sénécal, the radical, who combines the reason of a geometrician and the faith of an Inquisitor, and whose dogmatic commitment to socialist ideology is shown to mask an ugly authoritarianism. Then there is the worker Dussardier whose naïve faith in the Republic gets him duped in June 1848 and shot (by Sénécal!) in December 1851. There is also Hussonet, who dabbles in journalism and gets ahead by selling his services to the highest bidder. There is Regimbart, the monomaniacal republican who spends his days declaiming in cafés about the need for France to recover her natural frontiers. He is the one character who is absolutely unaffected by the passage of time. His opposite is Pellerin, the painter, who is constantly reinventing himself and whose artistic evolution takes him from classicism to realism to photography. He is a curious figure – a forger but also a theorist with views on art that Flaubert himself might have espoused. (For example: "the cult of external truth reveals the vulgarity of our time."[39])

The cast of characters also includes Delmar the actor, a consummate fool who is duped into delusions of grandeur by the roles he plays and whose very name changes as his image changes. He is last seen as a high priest of revolution reciting a humanitarian poem about prostitution. Then there is the feminist socialist, Mademoiselle Vatnaz, Flaubert's caricature of an emancipated woman, who argues plausibly that proletarian emancipation requires women's emancipation, but who also dreams of taking power by unleashing "ten thousand citizenesses, armed with good muskets" on the Hôtel de Ville. What the members of this

[38] *L'Education sentimentale*, 79.   [39] Ibid, 47.

generation share is the fact that their careers end in failure or the betrayal of their ideals, or both.

Like everything Flaubert wrote, *L'Education sentimentale* is nothing if not carefully contrived. Flaubert takes great care to relate the public and the private by establishing a counterpoint between the collapse of political ideals in 1848 and the collapse of the hopes and plans of the main characters. The outset of the revolution coincides precisely with the failure of Madame Arnoux to appear at a rendezvous with Frederick. Instead, Frederick takes up with Rosanette, a *lorette* of working-class origin; and the rise and fall of their relationship pretty well parallels the rise and fall of the attempt to establish a republic on the basis of an alliance between the bourgeoisie and the working class. But the most explicit coincidence of public and private spheres comes on December 2, 1851, when Frederick is forced by his new mistress, Madame Dambreuse, to witness the auctioning off of Madame Arnoux's property. For Frederick every object on the auction block has intimate associations with Madame Arnoux. To witness this event, which occurs on the day before Louis Napoleon's coup, is literally to witness the disintegration of his ideal.[40]

What explanation does the novel offer for the personal failures and betrayals of the members of Frederick Moreau's generation? One explanation, clearly, is the solipsistic character of their understanding of the world. Frederick and Deslauriers and many of the lesser characters fail because they cannot see the world as it is. They constantly confuse reality with their own wishes. But the novel offers more than that: it analyzes a mentality but it also shows the relation of that mentality to a larger world, the world of July Monarchy Paris.

As Flaubert describes it, this world includes three distinct realms, each with its own physical centre. The centre of the realm of art is Jacques Arnoux's store on the Boulevard Montmartre, *L'Art Industriel*. The centre of the realm of love is the dance hall on the Champs-Elysées called the Alhambra; and the centre of the political realm is the lavish *hôtel* on the rue d'Anjou of the banker, Monsieur Dambreuse, who is the prototype of the commercial aristocracy that runs the July Monarchy. In every realm, Paris is a world in which money counts, a world in which there is just about nothing that can't be bought. This is most obviously true in the realm of love, where prostitution is the rule. But the theme of prostitution recurs in Flaubert's treatment of art and politics. His Paris is full of artists and journalists who prostitute their talent, and individuals who prostitute

---

[40] Ibid, 413–414.

themselves before power. The super-prostitute is Dambreuse, a man who had truckled to four governments and who "worshipped power so fervently that he would have paid for the privilege of selling himself."[41] Paris is also a world marked by the collapse of taste and by a rampant eclecticism epitomized by the cluttered window displays of Arnoux's shop and by buildings like the Alhambra, the palace of love, with its Moorish arcades and Chinese roof and Venetian lanterns, all of which dominate a courtyard designed to look like a Gothic cloister.

Finally, July Monarchy Paris is a world in which everything that represents the ideal or the transcendent is base or degrading or simply false. Everything, that is, from the cheap religious art produced by Arnoux and the romantic novels that helped Frederick form his image of Madame Arnoux – to the chipped and peeling cupids and the plaster statues of Venus that turn up repeatedly in the course of the novel. It is a world, finally, that shares the desire of Jacques Arnoux to increase profit while maintaining artistic pretensions, a world that shares his motto: "the sublime at a popular price."

In such a world, it might seem, the only way to find meaning is through the pursuit of ideals. The problem is that everything that represents the ideal is base or trite. Even Frederick's efforts to articulate his image of Madame Arnoux are debased by the books he has read and the dreams he has had and the very language he uses. In his efforts to imagine the here kind of life they might lead together he never gets beyond easy exoticism. The point is that there is no escape. The romantic attempt to flee the familiar world for some "higher" realm is not merely a form of evasion. Ultimately it doesn't work. For the imagination that formulates romantic ideals is limited by the horizons of the society in which it finds itself. The imagination itself is ultimately no richer than the society in which it arises. Thus, in a world where the sublime is offered at a popular price and love has become a commodity, the romantic who yearns for a transcendent ideal will find it difficult to do anything else but reproduce the tawdriness of the surrounding society.

Writing the Revolution

L'Education sentimentale begins and ends with a date. "On September 15, 1840, around six o'clock in the morning" the steamer taking Frederick home to Nogent debarks from Paris. "Toward the end of March, 1867, at nightfall" Madame Arnoux comes to see Frederick for one last time.

---

[41] Ibid, 378.

Neither of these dates has any particular historical significance. They simply mark the beginning and the end of the story that Flaubert has to tell. One other date, which is given with great specificity, also marks a key moment in Frederick's personal life: "On December 12, 1845, around nine o'clock in the morning" Frederick receives a letter informing him that he has inherited his uncle's fortune.[42]

What is worth noting here is that the important political events of the period are not dated – and in some cases not even named. The February Revolution, the June Days, the abortive insurrection of May 15 and the formal inauguration of the Republic on April 20 are all referred to in the "scenarios" or outlines drawn up by Flaubert as he was plotting his novel. The scenarios tell us that Frederick wakes up in the arms of Rosanette on February 24, that he makes a vain effort to be heard at a revolutionary club in late March, that Frederick and Rosanette leave Paris for Fontainebleau on June 20, and that Dussardier is killed by Sénécal on Thursday, December 4, 1851, at 5 pm.[43] But none of these dates appears in the final text. One of the last big scenes in the novel takes place on December 1, 1851, but the coup d'état of the following day is described in just three lines: "The next morning his servant brought him the news. A state of siege had been declared, the Assembly dissolved, and some Representatives of the People were imprisoned. Public affairs left him indifferent, so preoccupied was he with his own affairs."[44]

Flaubert was not interested in establishing a chronology of historically significant events in 1848, and his novel does not offer anything like a continuous narrative of events. Indeed, the narrative is conspicuous for what Georg Lukacs called its apparent lack of orderly composition – its juxtaposition of "separate fragments of reality" that lie before the reader "in all their hardness, brokenness and isolation."[45] The events of 1848 are often described to us as they are seen by Frederick. But he is repeatedly portrayed as unable to grasp and make sense of what he is

---

[42] Ibid, 97. Flaubert writes 1845 when the date should be 1846. See de Biasi, *Flaubert. Une manière spéciale de vivre*, 348. Flaubert was scrupulous about most details but oddly casual about dates. In fact, several years just drop out of the novel, and Rosanette's pregnancy lasts three years. See the wonderful send-up by Claire Addison, *Where Flaubert Lies: Chronology, Mythology and History* (Cambridge, 2006).
[43] Tony Williams (ed.), *Flaubert. L'Education sentimentale: Les Scénarios* (Paris, 1992), 178–180; For Dussardier: Maria Amalia Cajueiro-Roggero, "Dîner chez les Dambreuse, 'La réaction commerçante'" in Agulhon *et al.*, *Histoire et langage dans L'Education sentimentale* (Paris, 1981), 66; Gisèle Séginger, *Flaubert, une poétique de l'histoire* (Strasbourg, 2000), 87, 66. In the final version Frédéric and Rosanette leave Paris for Fontainebleau on June 22, and Dussardier is killed on December 5.
[44] *L'Education sentimentale*, 416.
[45] Georg Lukacs, *The Theory of the Novel*, tr. Anna Bostock (London, 1988), 124.

seeing. He is unable to give shape and meaning either to the course of the revolution or to what is going on around him. When his mistress Rosanette tells him her life story, it is as confusing to him as is the flux of events in Paris: "It all came out without transitions, and he couldn't manage to reconstruct the whole picture."[46]

Nor are we told much about important historical actors. We know, for example, from Flaubert's correspondence that he detested both Lamartine and Thiers. He held Lamartine responsible for the collapse of the Second Republic, and described him to Louise Colet as "a eunuch" who "lacks balls" and "pisses clear water."[47] About Thiers Flaubert was even more inventively vituperative: "Can you imagine a more triumphant imbecile, a more abject old fart, a more turd-like bourgeois!" he wrote George Sand.[48] In the novel, however, the names of Lamartine and Thiers come up rarely and usually in the conversations of Flaubert's characters. Thus, while Louis Blanc is mentioned half-a-dozen times, it is as an author read by Sénécal, dismissed as "utopian" by Regimbart, or vilified by a friend of Dambreuse.[49] As for Louis-Napoleon Bonaparte, his name never appears.

How then does Flaubert write about the history of the revolution of 1848? The one-sentence answer is that Flaubert writes history *through* fiction. There is no omniscient narrator providing us with a clear sense of what is happening and why it matters. Historical events and actors are not as a rule described directly. We learn about them indirectly as they are seen and discussed by Flaubert's invented characters. Thus, the first bloodshed of the revolution, the fusillade of the Boulevard des Capucines, is presented obliquely as it is heard, by Frederick. As he and Rosanette wander around Paris, they hear a crackling sound "like the tearing of a huge piece of silk." The next morning Frederick is caught up in the revolutionary crowd, and events are once again described from his perspective as an entertaining spectacle: "The wounded falling to the ground, and the dead lying stretched out, did not look as if they were really wounded or dead. He felt as if he were watching a play."[50] This statement comes near the beginning of a long account of the February Revolution as seen through Frederick's eyes. For half-a-dozen pages we follow Frederick and his friend Hussonnet as they traverse the Tuileries

---

[46] *L'Education sentimentale*, 329. On this point see Anne Green, "History and its Representation in Flaubert's Work" in *Cambridge Companion to Flaubert*, 100.

[47] Flaubert to Louise Colet, April 6, 1853, *Correspondance*, II, 299. In the same letter Flaubert writes: "C'est à Lamartine que nous devons tous les embêtements bleuâtres du lyrisme poitrinaire, et lui que nous devons remercier de l'Empire."

[48] Flaubert to George Sand, December 18, 1867, *Correspondance*, III, 711.

[49] *L'Education sentimentale*, 51, 137, 178, 296, 343.   [50] Ibid, 288.

Palace and the Palais Royal, observing the gaiety – and the destructiveness – of the crowd. What is remarkable in this account, which is the only
extended description of a revolutionary *journée* in the entire novel, is the
multitude of precise details (many of them based on Flaubert's memory
or Maxime DuCamp's memoirs) that bring Frederick's observations to
life and give them a ring of authenticity.[51]

From the first page, when Frederick stands on the deck of the steam-
boat taking him home from Paris and watches the world go by, he is a
passive observer. But his friends are active, and they all get caught up in
the revolution. The ambitious Deslauriers gets himself appointed
Commissaire de la République at Troyes, but later he comes to detest
workers and socialists and finds he can get ahead by inveighing against
Ledru-Rollin. Sénécal the radical becomes the despotic leader of a
socialist political club; he is arrested and imprisoned during the June
Days; but by 1851 his yearning for order has made him a Bonapartist.
The naïve and generous worker Dussardier joins his National Guard unit
to "save the Republic" during the June Days but comes to regret his
decision. He is the first character in the novel to welcome the Republic in
February and the last to defend it in December 1851. Jacques Arnoux is
also a sincere republican – a moderate, law-abiding, bourgeois republican. Regimbart, on the other hand, is the quintessential rhetorical
republican for whom chauvinism is the beginning and end of republican
virtue. Mlle Vatnaz is a lonely spinster who "greeted the revolution as the
harbinger of revenge for everything she had missed."[52] Pellerin joins with
other artists briefly at the outset of the revolution to agitate for government sponsorship of great republican art projects. His major contribution
to the revolution is a painting depicting Christ driving a locomotive
through a virgin forest. Finally, the actor Delmar, who boasts that he
can quell a riot simply by showing his face, is himself a living embodiment of the theatrical and imitative character of the revolution of 1848.

The Party of Order is also well represented among the minor characters. At its centre is the banker Dambreuse who typifies the commercial
elite during the July Monarchy. By birth a nobleman, he gave up the title
of Count d'Ambreuse in 1825. Adapting easily to changes of regime, he
embraces the Republic for a few months. But after the June days, the
Dambreuse salon on the rue d'Anjou becomes a rallying point for conservative landowners, industrialists and businessmen who have, like
Dambreuse himself, "served at least four governments and would have

---

[51] Ibid, 287–294. See also Alexis François, "Flaubert, Maxime Du Camp et la Révolution
    de 1848," *Revue d'Histoire littéraire de la France*, 53(1) (January–March 1953), 44–56.
[52] *L'Education sentimentale*, 323.

sold France, or the human race, in order to safeguard their wealth, or spare themselves discomfort."[53] Other supporters of the Party of Order include Dambreuse's agent, Monsieur Roque, himself a wealthy rural landowner, the Legitimist Cisy, the Orleanist social climber Martinon, and the opportunistic bohemian Hussonnet, The latter two attach themselves to Dambreuse, Martinon by marrying Dambreuse's illegitimate daughter, and Hussonnet as a reactionary journalist. By the end of the novel Martinon and Hussonnet have risen to positions of power and respectability under Napoleon III; Roque is thriving; and the wealthy Marquis de Cisy retires to his ancestral estate, fathers eight children and discovers religion.

Some of these characters are one-dimensional; they are almost cartoon characters. But altogether they constitute a relatively comprehensive panorama of types and characters. Each of them represents a particular milieu and mentality. Each acts in terms of values and codes specific to his class. Each represents a tendency at work in French society in the 1840s. Altogether we are left with a rich portrait of a generation that has come to grief in 1848. Flaubert's invented characters recreate for us the mood of the time – what Flaubert calls "l'état d'esprit." Few specific references to historical events or people are made. But a powerful sense of atmosphere is created.

Two remarks are in order here. First, Flaubert's method is not as far from conventional history as one might think. It is actually very close to the method adopted by the respected French historian Georges Duveau in his history of the revolution of 1848. For Duveau there are two main groups of actors – the people of Paris and the politicians and journalists who ran the clubs, voted in the Assembly, and edited newspapers. To represent divisions within the people of Paris Duveau invents three fictitious characters: a hosier from the Faubourg Saint-Denis, a cabinet-maker from the rue Saint-Antoine, and a mechanic from the new industrial suburb of La Chapelle. As the political history of 1848 unfolds, Duveau regularly alerts us to the shifting attitudes and responses of his artisans. What is gained is a more nuanced account of the role of the Parisian working class than the sparse sources would normally permit. Thus, Duveau's fictitious artisans and Flaubert's imagined characters are not so far apart methodologically: each enables its author to create a richer and more plausible world than would otherwise be possible.[54] Of course, Flaubert's invented characters are almost all from the

---

[53] Ibid, 239.
[54] Georges Duveau, *1848* (Paris, 1965). See also the introduction by George Rudé to the English translation: *1848: The Making of a Revolution*, tr. Anne Carter (New York, 1968), xiii–xv.

bourgeoisie. In Flaubert's novel, only Dussardier speaks and acts as a worker, and he is not a manual labourer but a clerk in a shipping company. In Duveau's history the only invented characters are workers. But the method is similar. Each makes use of invention in order to create a rich and plausible world.

This leads to a second point. One thing missing in Flaubert's world is the working class. Apart from Dussardier, there are only the worn faces of workers seen by Frederick at the Club de l'Intelligence. The absence of artisan-workers is also a feature of Balzac's fiction. His Human Comedy includes many small functionaries but few urban workers. What Flaubert gives us instead of a variety of workers is *"le peuple."* But Flaubert's *peuple* have little in common with *le peuple* celebrated by contemporaries like Michelet, Lamartine and George Sand. For Michelet *le peuple* is a hero who acts, struggles, and makes history. In his *Histoire de la Révolution française* Michelet describes the birth of a collective will when the Third Estate transforms the Estates General into a National Assembly. For Lamartine and George Sand *le peuple* are well-meaning and generous but easily misguided children. For Flaubert, on the other hand, *le peuple* are a force, an often destructive force, which is incapable of acting in its own name, possessing neither will nor self-consciousness.

The difference between Flaubert's characterization of *le peuple* and the image of *le peuple* in the work of contemporaries like Michelet and Lamartine is evident if one considers the imagery used by both parties. While Michelet and Lamartine use imagery that humanizes *le peuple*, Flaubert turns *le peuple* into an inhuman force of nature. In speaking of the street fighting during February, Flaubert writes of waves and torrents and billows of human beings. And in describing the mood of the crowd prior to the outbreak of the June insurrection, he associates it with the gathering of storm clouds. 'The stormy sky electrified the crowd," he writes. "It swirled about, irresolutely surging backwards and forwards. In its depths one could sense an incalculable strength and an elemental force."[55] At the end of the insurrection a similar image is used to characterize the reprisals of the National Guard. "The public's reason was deranged as if by some great natural upheaval. Intelligent men lost their sanity for the rest of their lives."[56] In *L'Education sentimentale* the revolution of 1848 is a kind of natural upheaval, and its main consequence is to unleash wild elemental forces that no one is sure of controlling.

---

[55] *L'Education sentimentale*, 320.   [56] Ibid, 338.

At times the "dehumanization" of *le peuple* is carried to an extreme, as in the passage where, during the February Revolution, Frederick and Hussonnet look on as the crowd bursts into the Tuileries Palace:

> Hussonnet and Frederick leaned over the bannisters. It was the people. They swept up the staircase in a bewildering flood of bare heads, helmets, red caps, bayonets, and shoulders, surging forward so impetuously that some disappeared in the swarming mass as they went up and up, like a spring tide pushing back a river, with a continuous roar and driven by an irresistible impulse.[57]

Here *le peuple* is simply a confused mass of heads, shoulders, and weapons driven forward by a process as blind and unthinking as the flowing of a river.

There is another way in which the novel describes and comments on the events and actors in the history of the Second French Republic. I've already noted the close correspondence between the political and the personal throughout the third part of the novel. This correspondence is so carefully worked out and so important to the structure of the novel that Flaubert's scenes and images of private life sometimes take on the quality of *allegories* of historical events. Thus, the rise and fall of Frederick's relationship with Rosanette evokes the rise and fall of the attempt to build a democratic republic through an alliance between the bourgeoisie and the working class. The pathetic short-lived child of their union symbolizes the ill-fated experiment in republican government that emerged from the February Revolution. The auctioning off of Madame Arnoux's property on December 1, 1851 echoes the disintegration of Frederick's romantic ideal; and the shooting four days later of the worker Dussardier by Sénécal, the socialist-turned-Bonapartist thug, is a metaphor for the collapse of the republican political ideal.

There are several episodes in the lives of Flaubert's invented characters that can be interpreted as allegories but have such density that they deserve closer scrutiny. One of these is Flaubert's account of the trip taken by Frederick and Rosanette to Fontainebleau on the eve of the June insurrection in Paris. In his scenarios Flaubert refers to this trip as a "honeymoon."[58] It is also an escape: Frederick distances himself from Paris at the very moment when the city is about to explode. But it is more than this. It gives the reader a glimpse of Frederick's dreams and his confused sense of the impermanence of his world.

Fontainebleau was the site of a great royal forest and a palace that kings of France had used as a royal retreat ever since the time of François I. The palace had been a favourite of Napoleon. It was there in 1814 that

---

[57] Ibid, 289–290.   [58] Williams (ed.), *Scénarios*, 275, 278, 281.

he said farewell to his troops before his exile to Elbe. What we see, as we watch Frederick and Rosanette visit Fontainebleau, is that the landscape and the palace add their resonance to Frederick's idyll with Rosanette but that they soon become mirrors onto which he projects his hopes and fears. On their first full day at Fontainebleau Frederick and Rosanette visit the palace, which is "rust-coloured like an old suit of armour" and conveys an "impression of royal dignity, of sombre military splendour." For Frederick this visit becomes a retrospective journey into the history of France. The tapestries and paintings depicting the gods of Olympus and the rooms once used by François I and Henri IV evoke in Frederick's mind images of uncorrupted nobility:

The sunshine made the paintings gleam; the blue sky extended to infinity the ultramarine of the arches; and from the depths of the forest, whose misty treetops filled the horizon, there seemed to come an echo of the morts sounded on ivory hunting horns, an echo of the mythological ballets which had brought together under the trees princesses and noblemen disguised as nymphs and satyrs, an echo of an age of primitive science, violent passions and sumptuous art, when the ideal was to transform the world into a dream of the Hesperides, and when the mistresses of kings vied with the constellations.[59]

Frederick fixes on a portrait of Diane de Poitiers, the mistress of Henri II, dressed as Diana the huntress. He feels that "something of her presence still remained there, a faint voice, a lingering splendour," and he is seized by "an indescribable nostalgic lust." He asks Rosanette if she would like to be Diane de Poitiers. Rosanette is totally uncomprehending. After all, it's not her history. She is the daughter of Lyon silk weavers and was sold into prostitution by her mother at the age of fifteen. So, while Frederick savours nostalgic fantasies and feels the presence of the royal and aristocratic dead crowding around him, Rosanette distracts herself by throwing bread into the carp pond to watch the fish jump.

As they walk down into the park behind the palace, Frederick is overcome by an overpowering sense of the weight of the past and the insignificance of all human endeavour in the face of eternal change and death:

Royal residences have a melancholy all their own, which is no doubt due to the disproportion between their vast size and their few inhabitants, to their silence, which is surprising after so many fanfares have been sounded there, and to their unchanging luxury, which proves by its antiquity the transience of dynasties and the eternal impermanence of all things.[60]

---

[59] *L'Education sentimentale*, 321–322.   [60] Ibid, 323.

Frederick's vivid encounter with the past seems to point in two directions. The past presents itself to him in alluring images of beauty and sombre military splendour. These images inspire in him desire and a "nostalgic lust" more intense than any sexual desire he had previously felt.[61] At the same time he is reminded that his present, like the past at Fontainebleau, will soon pass away.

After lunch a carriage takes Frederick and Rosanette on a drive through the Forest of Fontainebleau. The coachman points out the sights – the Siamese Twins, the King's Bouquet, the Wolf's Gorge and the Fairies' Pool – trees and rocks given names to amuse the tourists. But the pathetic fallacy works on many different levels. After the travellers report that "a terrible and bloody battle" is raging in Paris, the landscape becomes a mirror on which Frederick projects his moods. To him the tallest trees look "like patriarchs and emperors" and their long trunks form "triumphal arches." But then they encounter "huge gnarled oaks" that "rose convulsively out of the ground, embraced one another, and ... threw out their bare arms [bras nus] in desperate appeals and furious threats, like a group of Titans frozen in their rage." Farther on the carriage passes through a landscape strewn with great boulders that conjures up thoughts of "volcanoes, floods and great unknown cataclysms."[62] Thus Frederick endows the forest with traits expressing his own half-formed fears regarding the bloody conflict taking place in Paris, and these traits vie in his imagination with the images of nobility and grandeur inspired by the couple's initial tour of the palace.

During their three days at Fontainebleau there are moments at which Frederick and Rosanette give themselves completely to each other. At these times they allow "the solemnity of the forest" to take hold of them and spend hours lying quietly next to each other or driving through the forest, "caught up in a calm intoxication." At other times they chatter away "about nothing in particular, about things they both knew perfectly well, about people they didn't like, about a thousand silly things." Once they hear the sound of drums beating in a neighbouring village. It is the call to arms, summoning villagers to arm themselves and go to Paris to

---

[61] We have been told that Frederick has not been able to imagine consummating his relationship with Mme Arnoux. Only on the next to last page of the book is the word "lust" used to characterize Frederick's feeling for Mme Arnoux. But he chooses not to act on it.

[62] L'Education sentimentale, 326. The sense that the landscape mirrors the terrible social conflict going on in Paris is reinforced by the fact that the French term bras nus was often used to designate members of the working class.

defend the city against "the barbarians." "'Oh listen, the insurrection!'
said Frederick with a disdainful pity. All that agitation seemed trivial
compared to their love and eternal nature."[63]

But then – on Sunday morning, June 25 – while reading a newspaper,
Frederick finds Dussardier's name on a list of the wounded in Paris.
He abruptly decides to return to Paris, leaving Rosanette behind.
With difficulty and at some risk to himself, he finds Dussardier, who
was only lightly wounded and is now being celebrated as a hero by the
Party of Order. At this point Flaubert's narrator shifts from Dussardier's
story to that of Sénécal who had joined the insurgents and was now
imprisoned in a fetid improvised prison underneath the terrace of the
Tuileries.

Scenes and Vignettes

Although there is no direct account in *L'Education sentimentale* of the
street fighting during the June Days, the aftermath of the insurrection is
vividly evoked in two powerful vignettes. The setting for the first vignette
is the underground prison where Sénécal is incarcerated, with 900 other
insurgents, scarcely able to breathe and packed together in the filth of
their own excrement and coagulated blood. Flaubert's narrator tells us
that one of the National Guards posted at the prison was the rich farmer
from Nogent, Monsieur Roque. The narrator adds that "by and large,
the National Guards were merciless. Those who had missed the fighting
wanted to distinguish themselves. In an explosion of panic, they took
their revenge simultaneously for the newspapers, the clubs, the demonstrations, the doctrines, for everything that had been infuriating them
over the past three months."[64] Then Roque is introduced. He is one of
the wealthy provincials who on learning of the June insurrection, rushed
to Paris to save the capital from the revolutionary workers. Tocqueville
had celebrated these provincials, and he saw their descent on Paris as a
heroic moment of national unity.[65] Flaubert's account is darker:

Old Roque had grown very brave, almost reckless. He had arrived in Paris on the
26th with the contingent from Nogent, but instead of going back with them he
had joined the National Guards camping at the Tuileries; and to his delight he
was put on sentry duty at the waterside terrace. There at least he had the outlaws
under his thumb. He took pleasure in their defeat, in their debasement, and he
could not stop himself from railing at them.

[63] *L'Education sentimentale*, 327–328.   [64] Ibid, 337–338.
[65] Tocqueville, *Souvenirs, Oeuvres completes* (Paris, 1964), XII, 178.

What follows must be quoted in its entirety:

One of [the prisoners], an adolescent with long blonde hair, pressed his face to the bars and asked for bread. Monsieur Roque ordered him to be silent. But the young man kept repeating in a pitiful voice: "Bread!"
"Do you think I've got any?"
Other prisoners appeared at the cellar entrance with bristling beards and blazing eyes, all of them pushing and howling. "Bread!" Old Roque was furious at seeing his authority flouted. To frighten them, he aimed his musket at them; and the young man, lifted up to the ceiling by the tide that engulfed him, threw his head back and cried once again: "Bread!"
"Alright! Take that!" said Old Roque, firing his gun. There was a tremendous howl, then nothing. Something white remained on the rim of the bucket.

The bucket to which the narrator refers was a slop-bucket [*baquet*] used to give water to the prisoners. The "something white" that remained on its rim was a bit of the young man's brain.[66]

The extraordinary power of this passage owes much to Flaubert's discretion: the plainness – one might say the austerity – of his language which obliges the reader to figure out, and even to visualize, exactly what has happened. Roque has shot the young man in the face at point-blank range, exploding his skull and scattering fragments of skull and brain. This passage differs from accounts of the repression of the June insurrection left by other writers who, even when fiercely critical of Cavaignac and the army, offer overviews of the repression. Flaubert epitomizes the June Days in a single killing.

Flaubert did not invent this story. He found it in a radical journal, *La Commune de Paris*, in an article describing the shooting of an "innocent provincial property owner" in the underground prison at the Tuileries by a member of the National Guard: "His brain remained stuck to the slop-bucket and his body was left on the ground for more than twelve hours."[67] In incorporating this story into his own narrative, Flaubert made one significant change: the "innocent provincial property owner" became "an adolescent with long blonde hair." Why the change? No doubt it was because Flaubert wanted the story to have symbolic weight – to stand in for the massacre of the propertyless during the June Days. [68]

[66] *L'Education sentimentale*, 338. On *le baquet* (mistranslated in the widely read Penguin Classics edition as "grill"): see de Biasi, 349–352.
[67] *Carnets de travail de Flaubert*, Pierre-Marc de Biasi (ed.) (Paris, 1988), carnet 14, folio 14 verso, p. 392.
[68] The fullest analysis of this episode is Tony Williams, "From Document to Text: The 'terrasse du bord de l'eau' episode in *L'Education sentimentale*," *French Studies* 47 (1993), 156–171. This article includes both a fascinating discussion of the liberties taken by Flaubert in his use of documentary material, and substantial extracts from Flaubert's principal source, a "Notice historique" entitled "Sur le caveau des Tuileries" in *La Commune de Paris*, March 1849. See also Castex, *Flaubert, L'Education sentimentale*, 94–95; and Guisan, "Flaubert et la Révolution de 1848," 199–204.

Flaubert said as much in a bitterly sarcastic letter to George Sand: "I'm now writing three pages on the abominations of the National Guard in June '48, which will make the bourgeoisie love me! I'm rubbing their noses in their turpitude as much as I can."[69] This is exactly what Flaubert was doing. After the description of the shooting, we learn that a source of Roque's anger against the revolutionaries was that his house in Paris had suffered minor damage during the insurrection. Roque still falls ill that evening and has to be put to bed by his daughter and his faithful housekeeper. The daughter assumes that he has "made himself ill, worrying about her." In a line that it must have given Flaubert great pleasure to write, Roque replies: "Yes, you're right. But I can't help it. I'm just too sensitive."[70]

The second vignette focuses on the sumptuous dinner party given by the banker Dambreuse and his wife on July 2, shortly after the crushing of the June insurrection.[71] This party brings together many of the novel's main characters and also various friends of the Dambreuse couple, all of whom are overjoyed by the defeat of the insurrection and consider themselves to have been "saved" by Cavaignac. The party has two functions in Flaubert's narrative. It is the setting for new developments in Frederick's sentimental life. In the course of just a few hours Frederick tries, and fails, to rekindle his relationship with Madame Arnoux, rejects the advances of Louise Roque whom he now sees as an "ugly duckling," and initiates an affair with Madame Dambreuse. But the dinner party is also the occasion for Flaubert's fullest account of the state of mind of the Party of Order after the defeat of the insurrection. This is the moment at which Dambreuse and his friends, who have been paying lip service to the Republic, take off their masks. It is also the moment at which the fears of the wealthy become fully articulate.

The guests at the party represent a cross-section of the conservative elite. They include the diplomat Paul de Grémonville, a wildly reactionary industrialist named Fumichon, the aged Duchesse de Montreuil-Nantua, Monsieur de Nonancourt, an old dandy who "looked as if he had been mummified in cold cream," and Madame de Larsillois, the wife of an Orléanist prefect. As she enters, Madame de Larsillois is trembling violently, for she has just heard a barrel-organ playing a polka that had been described to her as a signal used by the rebels. The guests remind her that there is no longer anything to fear. "Cavaignac has saved us!" they repeat. As they describe atrocities committed during the insurrection, they exaggerate their number and listen eagerly to each other's

[69] Flaubert to George Sand, September 19, 1868, *Correspondance*, III, 805.
[70] *L'Education sentimentale*, 338–339.   [71] Ibid, 341–347.

stories about the 23,000 convicts who had joined the insurgents and about rebel placards calling for pillage, arson and rape.

Monsieur Dambreuse joins the general conversation from time to time. But throughout the evening he also talks privately with the younger guests. Dambreuse listens encouragingly to Martinon's proposal of marriage to his "niece" Cécile (who is actually his illegitimate child). He informs Pellerin the painter that, times having changed, he can no longer display the revolutionary painting he had commissioned from Pellerin. And he has a brief discussion with Hussonnet, who has become the spokesman for a reactionary club and whose pamphlet *L'Hydra* was apparently published at Dambreuse's expense.

Finally, the butler arrives to announce that dinner is served, and the guests file into the dining room. They are greeted by an extraordinary spectacle:

Under the green leaves of a pineapple, in the middle of the tablecloth, a dolphin lay with its head pointing to a side of venison and its tail touching a stack of crayfish. Figs, huge cherries, pears and grapes, all grown in Parisian hothouses, were piled in pyramids in baskets of old Dresden china; here and there bunches of flowers were interspersed with the gleaming silver; the white silk blinds, lowered over the windows, filled the apartment with a soft light; the air was cooled by two fountains containing pieces of ice; and tall servants in knee-breeches waited on the guests.[72]

The waiters' knee-breeches are a throwback to the Old Regime. But what is most striking about this meal is its sheer extravagance. Flaubert's narrator underlines the opulence of the dinner table and the sense of entitlement of the guests: "All this seemed better after the excitement of the past few days. The guests were enjoying once more things that they had been afraid of losing."

The conversation at dinner turns at first to gossip about the members of the Provisional Government. According to Fumichon, Louis Blanc owned a mansion on the rue Saint-Dominique and refused to rent it to workers. He and his colleagues were also known to gorge themselves on pineapple purée at the Luxembourg Palace. Nonancourt is greatly amused by the idea of the portly Ledru-Rollin hunting on the royal estates. Frederick and Jacques Arnoux argue about the role of newspapers. Nonancourt regrets the abolition of the death penalty for political crimes, and Fumichon derides the rebels as cowards because they hide behind barricades. The Vicomte de Cissy, unable even to repeat a rumour coherently, tries to impress Cécile by talking about his tailor,

[72] Ibid, 342.

his shirt-maker and his horses. "Everybody," we are told, "was talking so loud that nothing could be heard." But Roque cuts through the babble to demand "an iron hand" to rule France.[73]

When fine clarets are served, the talk becomes even livelier. Pellerin fulminates about the rebels' destruction of the Spanish museum. He wins the approval of Monsieur Roque by declaring that, from the artist's point of view, a well-run monarchy is the best form of government. In another group Arnoux argues that there are two kinds of socialism, good and bad. This infuriates the industrialist Fumichon who asserts that there is no difference between the two and argues that the ownership of property is a natural right. Everyone agrees on that, he says, even animals. If a lion could speak, he would declare himself a proprietor. And Fumichon boasts that if Proudhon, the great enemy of property owners, were present, he would personally strangle him. "After the liqueurs especially," we are told, "there was no holding back Fumichon."[74]

Hussonnet's arrival changes the tone of the conversation. Hussonnet tries to amuse the guests by ridiculing the orators of the Left, the principles of 1789, and the abolition of slavery. Then he launches into a skit depicting Henry Monnier's pudgy, self-satisfied Joseph Prudhomme fighting at a barricade. But Hussonnet has misjudged his audience. Nonancourt observes gravely that this is no time for levity, and he recalls the killing of General Bréa and the Archbishop of Paris during the June Days. These deaths, the narrator comments, "were always being brought up; they were used as arguments." A discussion ensues as to the relative sublimity of the deaths of the general and the archbishop. This is followed by an argument over the merits of generals Lamoricière and Cavaignac. Frederick declines to participate, confessing that he did not take part in the fighting. This wins him the approval of Dambreuse and Grémonville, both of whom recognize that those who combated the insurrection were still fighting to save the Republic. As the evening comes to an end, Frederick and Madame Dambreuse have initiated what will soon turn into an affair.

In all of this Flaubert presents a searing picture of the conservative elite – the aristocrats, industrialists and functionaries who give their support to the Party of Order. What they all have in common is their wealth and their inanity. Their conversation is a farrago of empty words, and it is clear, as they trade stories about the crimes of the insurgents and the greed of members of the Provisional Government, that there are no limits to what they will believe about the defeated rebels. But the

---

[73] Ibid, 344.   [74] Ibid, 346.

important point is that this scene does not stand by itself. It is the mirror image of another scene in which Flaubert portrays the radicals in 1848 in equally derisive terms. This scene describes Frederick's visit to a radical club, the ironically misnamed Club de l'Intelligence.[75]

To describe this club meeting Flaubert drew on contemporary sources such as *Les Clubs et les Clubistes* by Alphonse Lucas, gathering tiny details but arranging them to suit his own needs. Thus his initial description of the setting is both precise and tendentious. The meeting is held in a hall on the rue Saint-Jacques that was normally used as a carpenter's workshop. Its new walls "smelled of plaster," and four oil-lamps shed a dim light:

The audience sitting on benches consisted of elderly painters, school proctors, and unpublished writers. Among the rows of dirty overcoats and greasy collars could be seen an occasional woman's hat or workman's overall. Indeed, the back of the hall was full of workmen, who had probably come for want of anything better to do, or had been brought along by some of the speakers to applaud.[76]

On entering the hall, Frederick, who is accompanied by his friends Dussardier, Regimbart, Pellerin and Delmar, is startled to see that the chairman of the club is their old comrade, the authoritarian socialist Sénécal. Now a stylish revolutionary with dark glasses and close-cropped hair, Sénécal had distinguished himself among radicals by calling for an attack on the Hôtel de Ville on February 26. The narrator adds that it was customary for "every person in the public eye to model himself on some famous figure, one copying Saint-Just, another Danton, and yet another Marat," and that Sénécal "tried to resemble Blanqui, who in his turn imitated Robespierre."[77]

The meeting begins with the discussion of specific proposals – the erection of a monument to the memory of Robespierre, the adoption of Latin as a common language for European democracy, the ceremonial burning of reactionary newspapers in front of the Pantheon. Then the floor is open to candidates for the National Assembly seeking the club's endorsement. A priest named Ducretot, the author of a treatise on manure, is rejected. "A patriot in a smock" rises to announce that Jesus Christ was the founder of socialism, that "the Gospel led straight to 1789," and that "the age of love was about to begin."[78] An atheistic wine salesman objects and proposes the suppression of churches, sacred vessels, and all forms of worship. A fight breaks out between atheists and neo-Christian radicals. Pellerin presents himself as a candidate for art, but he is interrupted by "a thin man with red spots on his

[75] Ibid, 302–309.   [76] Ibid, 303.   [77] Ibid.   [78] *L'Education sentimentale*, 305.

cheekbones" who demands that the government issue a decree abolishing prostitution and poverty. The actor Delmar then "inflames" the audience with an attack on privileged theatre companies and theatre managers. Finally, Sénécal intervenes to call for the seizure of the wealth of the rich, whom he depicts hyperbolically as "wallowing in crime under their gilded ceilings while the poor, writhing in hunger in their garrets, practice all the virtues." At this point the applause becomes so loud that Sénécal has to stop. The narrator tells us that "he stood for a few minutes with his eyes shut and his head thrown back, as if he were rocking himself to sleep on the wave of anger he had aroused."[79]

Sénécal then calls for "men who are new to politics" to introduce themselves. Frederick, who has a speech prepared, stands up. But Sénécal questions him about his antecedents, life and morals, informing the audience that Frederick broke his promise to fund the creation of a democratic newspaper. Before Frederick can respond, a "patriot from Barcelona" is introduced and begins to deliver a speech in Spanish. When Frederick protests that nobody can understand a word of the speech, the audience becomes infuriated and Frederick is expelled from the hall.

Thus, Frederick's attempt to get a hearing is a failure, and the club meeting is represented as a perfect cacophony. People talk past each other. Nobody listens, and a serious exchange of ideas is impossible. The Spanish patriot's speech, which no one understands (and which Flaubert actually took directly from Lucas' *Les Clubs et les Clubistes*, simply translating it into Spanish!), is a perfect representation of the vehement nonsense that pervades the whole meeting. What is said is absurd; the meeting as a whole is an exercise in futility; and in the course of the meeting Sénécal is revealed as a tyrant whose socialism is a mask for radical authoritarianism.

Finally, we are left with two overlapping images: the fears and fantasies of the Dambreuse salon, and the cacophony of the Club de l'Intelligence. The narrator's insistence on the essential similarity between zealots of the Right and the Left would seem to reinforce his conclusion concerning the significance of the June insurrection. In the wake of the June Days, we are told:

[E]quality ... asserted itself triumphantly: an equality of brute beasts, a common level of bloody atrocities. For the fanaticism of the rich counterbalanced the frenzy of the poor. The aristocracy matched the fury of the rabble, and the cotton nightcap was just as savage as the red bonnet. The public's reason was

[79] Ibid, 308.

deranged as if by some great natural upheaval. Intelligent men lost their sanity for the rest of their lives.[80]

This might seem to be the narrator's last word. Indeed, in much of the scholarship on the politics of *L'Education sentimentale* it is assumed that Flaubert saw "the atrocities of the insurgents" as counterbalancing those of the Party of Order.[81] Yet there is reason to call into question the view of Flaubert as a kind of Solomon dispensing justice even-handedly. The account of Roque's shooting of a defenceless prisoner is one of the most powerful scenes in the entire novel, but there is no corresponding account of an atrocity committed by the insurgents. Indeed, the only references in the novel to such atrocities are the wild and patently false fabrications circulating at the Dambreuse dinner party. Furthermore in his letters to George Sand and to other friends Flaubert was far from neutral. As he wrote Sand on August 10, 1869: "The reactionaries will be treated worse than the others because they seem more criminal to me." [82]

Most of the main characters in *L'Education sentimentale* are absorbed in personal affairs and only episodically involved in the great events of 1848. But there are two individuals – the worker Dussardier and the socialist Sénécal – who stand apart. These two are repeatedly caught up in the stream of events, and their stories are essential for an understanding of what the novel has to say about 1848. In many respects Sénécal and Dussardier are opposites. Sénécal claims to speak for the working class but is not of it. Dussardier, who is close to the working class in education and sympathy, participates in the repression of the workers' insurrection in June. Dussardier was converted to republicanism by witnessing government brutality in 1834. Sénécal's doctrinaire and authoritarian socialism is more the outcome of his reading than of his personal experience. Sénécal yearns to impose his egalitarian and puritanical ideals on the rich and powerful; Dussardier seeks an ideal republic welcoming people of all backgrounds and persuasions. While Dussardier clings to his republican faith throughout the history of the Second Republic, Sénécal's authoritarianism takes him from insurgency and prison in the June Days to the ranks of the Bonapartist police in December 1851. [83]

Finally, on December 5, 1851, three days after the *coup d'état* that brought Louis-Napoleon Bonaparte to power, the two former comrades

---

[80] Ibid, 338.
[81] See, for example, the commentary of Peter Michael Wetherill to his edition of *L'Education sentimentale* (Paris, 1984), 493 n672.
[82] Flaubert to George Sand, August 10, 1868, *Correspondance*, III, 786.
[83] For a rich exploration of the historical resonance of the figure of Sénécal, see Thomas Bouchet, "Flaubert, Sénécal et l'histoire," *Littératures*, 6 (1991), 107–126.

meet. Dussardier has joined a hastily organized protest against the *coup*, while Sénécal is leading a detachment of police charged with clearing the main streets and boulevards of protestors. Flaubert's account describes the scene through Frederick's eyes:

It was five o'clock, and a thin rain was falling. There were bourgeois on the sidewalk in front of the Opera. The houses opposite were shuttered. There was no one at the windows. Taking up the whole width of the boulevard, some dragoons rode by at full speed, bent over their horses, their swords drawn; and the plumes of their helmets and their great white capes spread out behind them, silhouetted against the light of the gas lamps, which swung to and fro in the wind and mist. The crowd looked on, mute, terrified.

Between the cavalry charges, squads of policemen came up to drive the crowds back into the side streets.

But on the steps of Tortoni's stood a man, conspicuous from afar on account of his tall stature, and as motionless as a caryatid. It was Dussardier,

One of the policemen, who was leading the squad, with his three-cornered hat pulled down over his eyes, threatened him with his sword.

Then Dussardier took a step forward and started shouting: "Long live the Republic!"

He fell on his back, with his arms spread wide forming a cross.

A cry of horror rose from the crowd. The policeman looked all around, and Frederick, stupefied, recognized Sénécal.[84]

This scene, which concludes the main body of the novel, irresistibly evokes an earlier scene from the June Days. Like the narration of Roque's shooting of an unarmed and unnamed boy held in the improvised prison below the Tuileries Palace, this account is brief and understated. The thrust of the sword is not even mentioned. We hear Dussardier's shout; we see his body; then "Frédéric, béant, reconnut Sénécal." This is followed by a blank – a silence that Proust called the most beautiful thing in the novel.[85] The next sixteen years are then covered in seven sentences; and suddenly in two final epilogues, without the hint of a transition, we find ourselves in 1867.

Sénécal's killing of Dussardier completes the cycle of betrayals and broken dreams that make up the moral history of Frederick's – and Flaubert's – generation. This scene is not only a grim coda to the story of the disintegration of a group of friends. It also marks the liquidation of the political hopes and ideals of the republicans, democrats and socialists of 1848. And that may be where we must look to find the novel's last word on 1848. However foolish and misguided Flaubert judged the

---

[84] *L'Education sentimentale*, 418.   [85] Proust, "A propos du 'style' de Flaubert," 595.

republicans to be, he gives one of them a claim on our sympathy unmatched by any member of the Party of Order.

Bouvard et Pécuchet: 1848 as Dark Comedy

L'Education sentimentale was not Flaubert's last word on 1848. During his final decade he devoted himself to work on a book in which, he told Turgenev, "I will spit out my bile" at the "swinishness" of modern society and the "wave of relentless Barbarism ... rising up from underground."[86] This unfinished novel, which he described as "a kind of encyclopedia made into a farce," is at once more amusing in its detail and darker in its overall picture of the human condition than anything else Flaubert wrote. Entitled *Bouvard et Pécuchet*, it includes a substantial chapter on the revolution of 1848 as it affected a village in Normandy. It is worth looking closely at that chapter. Though written in an overtly comic vein, it reinforces the picture offered by *Education sentimentale* of history as ruled by elemental forces that overwhelm the plans of individuals.

Bouvard et Pécuchet tells the story of two bachelor copyists who meet by chance while sitting on a bench near the Canal Saint-Martin in Paris. It's a hot day, and they have taken off their hats. Each notices that the other has written his name inside his hat. This discovery initiates a life-long friendship. In due course Bouvard comes into an inheritance. Since both are bored with copying, they decide to quit Paris and purchase a farm in the village of Chavignolles in Lower Normandy where they can live the life of gentlemen farmers. But once they have established themselves in Normandy, they realize that they know nothing about farming. So they begin to study works on agronomy and soil chemistry. These works raise questions that they believe they can answer only by studying biology. But biology raises further questions in their minds. Unable to find satisfactory answers to the most fundamental questions concerning the origin and even the definition of life, they turn to astronomy, geology, archaeology, and then to history, literature, grammar and aesthetics.

At each stage Bouvard and Pécuchet encounter obstacles. In studying history, for example, they are disturbed by the fact that the sources contradict each other, and they cannot establish to their own satisfaction an adequate definition of a historical fact. They narrow their focus to the life of a single individual, the Duc d'Angoulême. But they find that the more information they gather, the less well they know him. In the end, they return to Paris and take up copying again, this time compiling a "dictionary of commonplace ideas." But along the way, something

---

[86] Flaubert to Turgenev, November 13, 1872, *Correspondance*, IV, 604–605.

important has happened. In the course of their search, Bouvard and Pécuchet have raised questions about the sciences of their time that contemporaries were not smart enough to ask. Thus, the novel is at once a parody and a critique of the unexamined assumptions lying behind the faith in progress that was characteristic of the whole French liberal tradition running from the Enlightenment to the materialism and positivism of the late nineteenth century.

Bouvard et Pécuchet offers an even more withering vision of the events of 1848 than does *L'Education sentimentale*. Here the "springtime of the People" is portrayed as a kind of masquerade, a show in which the *notables* of Chavignolles feign loyalty to the Republic. Their first reaction to the news of the overthrow of the July Monarchy is stupefaction. But when they learn that the Parisian Tribunal of Commerce, the courts, the army and the Council of State all support the Provisional Government, the villagers breathe easily. Since Liberty Trees are being planted at Paris, Chavignolles decides to plant its own. Bouvard and Pécuchet, who are political innocents genuinely enthused at the prospect of a republic, offer a tree and help organize a ceremony. On the appointed day the whole village turns out, from the mayor, the notary and the justice of the peace down to the game warden. The village priest, whom we know to detest republican government, gives a totally disingenuous speech, inveighing against kings and asking God's blessing on the Provisional Government. The *notables*, led by the Count de Faverges and the doctor Vaucorbeil, claim to be "charmed" by the revolution. "Everything for the people from now on!" is their motto.

The masquerade lasts two months. During that time the Count de Faverges is often seen at the marketplace respectfully listening to his fellow citizens and buying them drinks. The National Guard is revived, and wealthy villagers compete to purchase new uniforms for their poorer comrades. As the elections approach, several better-off villagers are overcome by "le vertige de la députation." Even the priest briefly entertains the idea of becoming a candidate. But once the votes are counted, the republican charade is over. A monarchist newspaper editor from Caen is elected deputy, and the property owners of Chavignolles listen credulously to the same fantastic fables that had entertained the Dambreuse circle in *L'Education sentimentale*:

People believed in the stories about Louis Blanc's pineapple purées, Flocon's golden bed, the royal orgies of Ledru-Rollin; and as the provinces claim to know everything that happens at Paris, the bourgeois of Chavignolles don't doubt these inventions and swallow the most absurd rumours.[87]

---

[87] *Bouvard et Pécuchet* (Paris, 1954), 195–196.

Other rumours concern conspiratorial activity. The Count de Faverges learns that the Legitimist pretender, the Count de Chambord, has been seen in Normandy; Foureau the mayor has it on good authority that plans are being made to eliminate the socialists; Heurtaux, a captain in the Napoleonic wars, asserts that Louis Bonaparte is about to be named First Consul. But there are also real conspiracies afoot. When local textile production ceases, bands of unemployed workers begin to gather around the countryside.

One Sunday in June such a group of unemployed workers descends on Chavignolles. Arriving by the road from Caen, "dusty, sweaty, their clothes in tatters," they fill up the town square and demand to speak with the city fathers. A discussion ensues concerning measures to provide work for the poor. The extraction of rocks is proposed. But who will pay for this? And how will the rocks be used? The crowd becomes restive. At this point Pécuchet appears at an open window of the city hall. Trying to imitate Lamartine, he begins to harangue the people: "Citizens! ..." But this skinny little tight-lipped man lacks charisma. "Are you a worker?" someone shouts. Before the conversation can proceed, Pécuchet is brushed aside by the quick-witted notary Marescot who announces that the Conseil Municipal has decided to pay workers to use the rocks to pave the road leading to the château of the Count de Faverges. This is "a sacrifice," he explains, "that the commune is undertaking in the interest of the workers." This transparently disingenuous story is enough to disperse the crowd. Thus, this pathetic provincial parody of a revolutionary *journée* comes to a non-violent end.[88]

For several weeks in June anarchy reigns at Chavignolles. Discipline collapses in the ranks of the National Guard. Drills turn into nocturnal expeditions in which doorbells are rung, married couples awakened, and loud drinking parties held in the courtyards of sober citizens. News of the uprising in Paris puts an end to such pranks. For a few days there is talk about organizing a legion to "fly to the aid of Paris" just as Monsieur Roque had done in *L'Education sentimentale* and as thousands of provincials had done in real life. But the leading citizens of Chavignolles find reasons to stay home. Foureau the mayor cannot think of abandoning his functions. Marescot the notary just can't walk away from his office, nor Doctor Vaucorbeil from his patients, nor the fire chief Girbal from his firemen. Pécuchet is eager to go to Paris, but Bouvard is wise enough to stop him.

The summer of 1848 is a time of strange and irrational fears at Chavignolles. One moonlit night a whole detachment of National

---

[88] *Bouvard et Pécuchet*, 199.

Guards is put to flight by the sight of an armed man in an apple tree. Another night a patrol of National Guards sets upon a suspicious-looking individual and beats him up, only to discover that it is Gorju, a former employee of Bouvard and Pécuchet. Although innocent of any crime, Gorju is nonetheless condemned to three months in jail for "subversive speech." He then writes Bouvard and Pécuchet requesting a certificate of good conduct. While getting the certificate notarized by Marescot, Pécuchet protests the harsh treatment of suspected insurgents by the authorities. Marescot invokes the need to defend society. "Public safety," he says, is "the supreme law." Pécuchet replies that individual rights are just as important as the rights of society. Marescot does not deign to reply. "As long as he could continue to draw up his documents," comments the narrator, "and to live ... in his comfortable little home, injustices of every kind could take place without moving him at all."[89]

This is only the beginning of the quarrels of Bouvard and Pécuchet with the *notables* of Chavignolles. Their confidence in the local authorities takes a further blow in April 1849 when the Count, who has just been elected to the Legislative Assembly, justifies the French intervention against the Roman Republic in terms that Pécuchet finds utterly specious. Then Bouvard and Pécuchet witness a confrontation between the republican *instituteur* and the village priest. At issue is the enforcement of the Falloux law of March 15, 1850, which entrusted the clergy with the supervision of primary education. The *instituteur* is a poor man who needs his job in order to support his wife and children. Knowing this, the priest threatens to have him dismissed unless he consents to take communion on Easter Sunday and to extend his hours of teaching catechism and sacred history. Bouvard and Pécuchet quit this confrontation congratulating themselves on their independence of clerical power, but to the reader these pages demonstrate the cruelty and calculation with which that power is exercised.[90]

By 1850, with the passage of the Falloux law and an electoral law excluding three million poor voters, the reaction is in full force. All over France the Party of Order has triumphed. In Chavignolles its leaders are the Count, the mayor, the notary and the curé. These four individuals meet regularly to coordinate the distribution of anti-republican brochures with titles like "God Wishes It" and "Let's Get Out of the Mess." The best of these brochures, we are told, "were dialogues in rustic style written in bad French with profanities, and intended to improve the minds of the peasants."[91] The local Party of Order oversees

---

[89] Ibid, 204.   [90] Ibid, 206–210.   [91] Ibid, 206.

the destruction of the Tree of Liberty, and Bouvard looks on angrily as his contribution to the celebration of the February Revolution is carted off as firewood for the residence of the curé, the very man who had previously blessed the tree.

The great social event of 1850 at Chavignolles is an elegant lunch given by Count de Faverges for the town's richest citizens. Bouvard and Pécuchet are impressed by the sumptuous setting which echoes that of the dinner party given by Dambreuse on July 2, 1848, in *L'Education sentimentale*. It is described in cinematic style with rapid cuts between food and conversation:

A joint of roast beef appeared, and for a few minutes all you could hear was the sound of forks and moving jaws ... And while one dish followed another – chicken in sauce, crayfish, mushrooms, green salad, roast larks – many subjects were discussed: the best system of taxes, the advantages of large-scale farming, the abolition of the death penalty.[92]

Bouvard is surprised at the contrast between the elegance of the surroundings and the triviality of the talk. He and Pécuchet try to intervene. But no one is listening. By the end of the meal the mayor is asserting, like Roque in *L'Education sentimentale*, that what France needs is "a strong-armed ruler (*un bras de fer*)," and the Count confides to the priest: "We must reestablish obedience. Authority perishes if it becomes a matter for discussion. Divine Right is the only thing that matters."[93]

Once out the door, Bouvard and Pécuchet "breathe like people set free." Everything they couldn't say in the Count's dining room now bursts out of them. "What idiots! What meanness! How could people be so pig-headed! And what in the world is Divine Right?"[94] This last question restarts them on the intellectual quest that has occupied them since their arrival in Normandy. They write to an authority who refers them to texts by Filmer and Bossuet, which they do not find helpful. They are more interested in the refutation of divine right theory and the concept of popular sovereignty. This leads them on from Rousseau to socialism; and the concluding pages of Flaubert's chapter on 1848 are devoted to a discussion of the utopian theories – the ideas of Saint-Simon and Fourier and Louis Blanc and Etienne Cabet – that prepared the way for the revolution.

Bouvard is briefly excited by Fourier's sexual fantasies and the opportunities that Fourier's utopia offers to bachelors like himself. But he

---

[92] Ibid, 212.
[93] Ibid, 214. In calling for a *bras de fer*, the mayor is echoing Roque who used the same expression to make the same point in *L'Education sentimentale*, 344.
[94] *Bouvard et Pécuchet*, 214.

complains about the constraints that permeate socialist thinking. "Your socialists," Bouvard declares, "always call for tyranny." Pécuchet objects: "I agree that there are ridiculous things in the thought of the socialists; but still they deserve our love. The hideousness of the world distressed them, and they suffered so much in trying to make it better."[95] Bouvard laughs so loud and so long at Pécuchet's sentimental defence of the utopians that Pécuchet rushes out of the room, slamming the door. But the storm passes, and they move on to their next field of study: political economy.

The studies of Bouvard and Pécuchet are interrupted on December 3, 1851, when they learn of Louis-Napoleon's *coup d'état*. That day they go into the village "to vent their indignation." They are shocked to find that their fellow citizens are not at all disturbed by the news. Marescot the notary is delighted that the bavardage of the Assembly is now silenced. Foureau the mayor is thrilled that the democrats have been "smashed." The curé gives thanks to God, and Captain Heurtaux shouts "Vive l'Empéreur!" Even Petit, the republican schoolmaster, rejoices in the news that Thiers is now in prison. Despairing of the Republic, he takes pleasure in revenge. No more than the others can he keep a higher good in focus. A few days later, when Chavignolles learns that several hundred innocent Parisians have been killed by government troops, there is not a critical voice in the village. Flaubert's narrator summarizes its attitude: "The fusillade on the boulevards had the approval of Chavignolles. No mercy for the defeated, no pity for the victims. Once people revolt, they are criminals."[96]

Alone in their revulsion at the coup d'état, Bouvard and Pécuchet give up on politics. Pécuchet announces that he doesn't care what Louis-Napoleon does: "Since the bourgeois are ferocious, the workers jealous, the priests servile, and since the people will accept any tyrant, provided he lets them keep their snouts in the trough, Napoleon has done well! Let him muzzle the people, trample them, and exterminate them!"[97] Bouvard, as usual, is blunter, cruder: "So what a joke progress is!" and he adds: "And politics is a fine piece of crap!"

The conclusion of the chapter on 1848 mirrors the conclusion of the whole book: the faith in progress – the belief that knowledge is cumulative and that human beings have the capacity to learn from their mistakes and to better their lives as a species – is a myth. And *Bouvard et Pécuchet* reinforces, in darker tones, the picture of revolution offered by *L'Education sentimentale*: an irrational upswelling of passion on the part

---

[95] Ibid, 217–218.   [96] Ibid, 221.   [97] Ibid, 221–222.

of a mindless people – passion in the face of which the words of politicians and the intentions of individuals are absurd, meaningless. According to this view, history is shaped by elemental forces – volcanic eruptions, rivers of energy – that simply overwhelm the plans and intentions of individuals. All we can do is try to make the best sense we can of the world immediately around us. But this world is barely intelligible. Like Frederick Moreau, we grasp it in fragments which we only put together after the fact in the form of stories. And these stories, like those Frederick and his friend Charles Deslauriers tell each other on their final meeting, give our lives as much meaning as they are ever likely to have.

11 Aftermath

Themes and Conclusion

Most modern historians follow Maurice Agulhon in arguing that, for all its shortcomings, the Second French Republic was a period of "apprenticeship" in which the ground was laid for the long-lived republic founded in 1870.[1] The turnout in the first parliamentary election of April 23 was huge: 84 percent of eligible voters cast ballots. Participation remained high in the presidential election of December 10 when 75 percent voted.[2] Between 1849 and 1851 something approaching a modern party system began to emerge as the *démoc-socs* battled the Party of Order, and a significant part of rural France became reliably republican.[3] At the same time, the proclamation of the right to work and the labours of the Luxembourg Commission made 1848, more than 1789, a key moment in the history of the French working class. For Georges Renard, writing in 1906 in Jean Jaurès' *Histoire socialiste*, 1848 was "the Mother Revolution of the working class," and the *démoc-soc* movement marked the beginning of the "practical" democratic socialism of the twentieth century.[4] William Sewell's authoritative study of the origins of the French labour movement reinforces this point: "It was between 1848 and 1851," concludes Sewell, "that socialism took shape as a mass movement, and the French labour and socialist

---

[1] Maurice Agulhon, *1848 ou l'Apprentissage de la République* (Paris, 1973). See also Sudhir Hazareesingh, *From Subject to Citizen: The Second Empire and the Emergence of Modern French Democracy* (Princeton, 1998); and Thomas C. Jones, "French Republicanism after 1848" in Douglas Moggach and Gareth Stedman Jones (eds.), *The 1848 Revolutions and European Political Thought* (Cambridge, 2018), 70–93.

[2] Roger Price, *People and Politics in France, 1848–1870* (Cambridge, 2004), 4.

[3] On the role played by *démoc-soc* organizations in blanketing the provinces with socialist propaganda and in political organizing between November 1848 and December 2, 1851, see Edward Berenson, *Populist Religion and Left-Wing Politics in France, 1830–1852* (Princeton, 1984).

[4] See Georges Renard, *La République de 1848 (1848–1852)* (Paris, 1906), 137; and Julian Wright, *Socialism and the Experience of Time. Idealism and the Present in Modern France* (Oxford, 2017), 63–65.

movements of subsequent years continued to bear the mark of their origins."[5]

Nevertheless, for those who lived through it and participated in it – especially for democrats and socialists who believed they had a stake in the outcome – the revolution was a failure. Indeed, the aftermath of the February Revolution was in their view one long series of disappointments and disasters. The great panacea of republicans in 1848 had been universal male suffrage. But the result of the first national election was a National Assembly dominated by conservatives. Just eleven days after the first meeting of the new assembly, radicals attempted to overthrow it. But the main result of the failed coup of May 15 was the arrest and imprisonment of Blanqui, Barbès and Raspail. As we have seen, George Sand and Alexander Herzen gave up on the Republic after May 15. It now seemed evident to many radicals that when universal suffrage was adopted within the framework of the old state and the old social order and among a semi-literate population, the result was to return traditional elites and perpetuate the existing order.

The definitive collapse of the hopes of February came with the repression of the June insurrection: several thousand insurgents were killed in the fighting and hundreds more shot while held in captivity in makeshift prisons or on the streets. Of the insurgents who faced trial, some 11,000 were condemned to prison or deported to Algeria; and the post-June Red Scare led to the shutting down of newspapers and clubs and the prosecution of individuals involved in the *journée* of May 15 and the June Days. In August Louis Blanc and Marc Caussidière were stripped of their parliamentary immunity. To avoid prosecution and imprisonment, they took the road to exile. The following year, on June 13, 1849, the demonstration protesting the French military action against the Roman Republic led to the arrest or exile of thirty-one members of the National Assembly including the neo-Jacobins Ledru-Rollin and Martin Bernard and the socialist Victor Considerant. Finally, after Louis-Napoleon's coup d'état on December 2, 1851, thousands of democrats and republicans were imprisoned or driven into exile.

In Paris resistance to the coup lasted only a few days. On December 3 barricades rose in the working-class quarters of Paris. Of the roughly 1,200 people who took up arms, about 200 were killed, and the next day several hundred unarmed civilians were shot on the streets when

---

[5] William H. Sewell, Jr., *Work and Revolution in France: The Language of Labor from the Old Regime to 1848* (Cambridge, 1980), 275. See also Samuel Hyat, "Working-Class Socialism in 1848 in France" in Moggach and Stedman Jones, *The 1848 Revolutions*, 120–139.

government troops panicked during cleanup operations.[6] That was the sum total of the resistance in Paris. But in the provinces, scattered protests turned into an insurrection that mobilized 70,000 people. "The insurrection of December 1851 was the most serious provincial uprising in nineteenth-century France," writes Ted Margadant, "and it provoked the largest political purge outside Paris between the Terror and Counter-Terror of the 1790s and the Resistance movement of the Second World War."[7] Thirty-two departments in the south and east of France were placed under a state of siege, and the number of arrests was officially given as 26,884. This number included not only insurgents but also those who "by their speech" had "inculcated in the population a desire for disorder and rendered authority contemptible."[8] In 1852, "mixed commissions" (each consisting of a general, a prefect and a prosecutor) set punishments for individuals who had opposed the coup. In the end, these commissions sentenced 9,581 deportees to Algeria, 239 to the "dry guillotine" of Cayenne in French Guyana, 1,620 to simple expulsion and 5,450 to surveillance in France. About half the deportees to Algeria were able to choose their own place of residence; the other half were placed in death-traps like the prison of Lambessa in the casbah of Bône. Many more made their own way into exile.

Proscription and Internal Exile

England, Belgium and Switzerland were the principal destinations of the French political refugees. The least hospitable to the French was Belgium where *proscrits* were placed under constant surveillance, obliged to report to the police regularly, and often to live outside of Brussels in Flemish-speaking areas. In Switzerland *proscrits* sometimes benefitted from the relative autonomy of each canton. Thanks to the republican sympathies of the Genevan president James Fazy, French exiles flocked to Geneva which became a major centre of the French democratic diaspora. In England, French republicans were not subject to surveillance and free to live where they wanted. Still, their lives were

---

[6] Price, *People and Politics*, 391. Victor Hugo's account in *Napoléon le petit* of the killings on December 4 gives vastly inflated casualty figures.

[7] Ted W. Margadant, *French Peasants in Revolt: The Insurrection of 1851* (Princeton, 1979), xvii. See also Peter McPhee, *The Politics of Rural Life: Political Mobilization in the French Countryside 1846–1852* (Oxford, 1992), 227–259.

[8] Sylvie Aprile, *Le Siècle des exilés: Bannis et proscrits de 1789 à la Commune* (Paris, 2010), 103–104. See also Vincent Wright, "The Coup d'état of December 1851: Repression and the Limits to Repression" in Roger Price (ed.), *Revolution and Reaction: 1848 and the Second French Republic* (London, 1975), 303–333.

often grim. Work was hard to come by; the culture was alien to them, and few spoke English.[9]

London was the single largest centre of the French *proscription*, and from the start its French community was riven by factions. A group led by the Montagnard Félix Pyat outdid the others in verbal violence. But the two principal groups were led by former members of the Provisional Government, Ledru-Rollin and Louis Blanc. Ledru-Rollin sought to establish himself as the French leader of the international democratic movement, but the positions he took in England were an odd mixture of facile French chauvinism and lofty internationalist phrase-making. While in London he wrote a book entitled *On the Decadence of England* in which he prophesied the imminent collapse of the British ruling class, celebrated Joan of Arc as a symbol of "proletarian France," and announced that world revolution must begin with France. He quarrelled with other émigrés and wrote grandiloquent proclamations in the name of a European Democratic Committee that he headed along with Mazzini and Kossuth. As Herzen wrote sardonically, whereas "Mazzini was dreaming of freeing humanity by means of Italy, Ledru-Rollin wanted to free mankind in Paris and then sternly dictate freedom to the whole world."[10]

Louis Blanc, on the other hand, quietly established warm relations with British intellectuals including Mill, Carlyle and George Eliot. Criticizing Ledru, Mazzini and Kossuth for their emphasis on political revolution at the expense of social questions, Blanc managed while at London to finish his history of the French Revolution, to edit his own newspaper, to refute Lord Normanby's attacks on "the men of 1848," and to publish letters on English life in the French newspaper *Le Temps*. A visitor described him as "English from head to foot," living on Montagu Square in rooms furnished with English curtains, an English rug and an English end table, with English engravings on the walls.[11] Still, for all Louis Blanc's industriousness and practicality, and his embrace of England, one has the sense that he, like Ledru-Rollin, was living in the past. Much of his voluminous literary output in the 1850s

---

[9] Fabrice Bensimon, "The French Exiles and the British" in Sabine Freitag (ed.), *Exiles from European Revolutions: Refugees in Mid-Victorian England* (New York, 2003), 88–102; Aprile, *Le Siècle des exilés*, 117–126; Georges Weill, *Histoire du Parti républicain en France (1814–1870)* (Paris, 1928), 268–304.

[10] Alexander Herzen, *My Past and Thoughts*, 4 vols. (New York, 1968), III, 1041; Alvin R. Calman, *Ledru-Rollin après 1848 et les proscrits français en Angleterre* (Paris, 1921).

[11] The visitor was Victor Hugo's son. See Charles Hugo, *Les Hommes de l'exil, précédés de 'Mes Fils' de Victor Hugo* (Paris, 1875), 330; and Fabrice Bensimon, "Louis Blanc en Angleterre" in Francis Démier (ed.), *Louis Blanc: un socialiste en république* (Paris, 2005), 151–157.

and 1860s consisted of efforts to explain and justify his own activities in 1848. It is hard, once again, to disagree with the comments of Alexander Herzen who recalls in his memoirs an evening spent with Louis Blanc and Armand Barbès in London in 1856. As he listened to the two old 'forty-eighters recalling "the past days of glory and misfortune," Herzen realized that he had heard it all before, that Blanc and Barbès, like all the other émigrés, were no longer engaged with the world around them. "I saw with unhappy clarity that they, too, belonged to the history of *another decade*, which was finished to the last page, to the cover. Finished, not for them personally but for all the émigrés and for all the political parties of the day."[12]

There were, of course, many 'forty-eighters who did not go into exile or prison. Some put the struggles of 1848–1851 behind them and came to terms with the regime of Napoleon III. But many could not do this and were broken by the struggle. As a contemporary wrote later, "These men, Lamennais, François Arago, Michel de Bourges, Emile Souvestre, were destroyed by December 2nd. The bitterness that they could not contain made that clear to me."[13] Others attempted to keep the faith, defending the republic verbally in salons and through guarded contributions to obscure periodicals. To suggest the range of 'forty-eighters' responses to the collapse of the Republic, we can cite three individuals: Hippolyte Carnot, Leconte de Lisle and Constantin Pecqueur.

Hippolyte Carnot, the Second Republic's first minister of education, came from a distinguished family. His father, Lazare Carnot, "le Grand Carnot," was an important mathematician, the Revolution's best general, and a member of the Committee of Public Safety. His older brother, Sadi Carnot, helped invent thermodynamics, and his son, also named Sadi Carnot, became the fourth president of the Third Republic. He grew up in exile with his father, returning to France in 1823. Later he joined the Saint-Simonians; and under the July Monarchy he was elected to the Chamber of Deputies. In 1848 as Minister of Public Instruction, he drafted a broad reform proposal, guaranteeing free, secular and compulsory education for both sexes, improving conditions for teachers, and calling on them "to teach children the virtues of the democratic republic."[14] His forced resignation on July 5, 1848, marked the beginning of the post-June reaction. Unlike many moderate republicans, Carnot refused to swear allegiance to Louis-Napoleon. Elected to the Senate

[12] Herzen, *Past and Thoughts*, 3:1063.
[13] Hermione Quinet, *Edgar Quinet depuis l'exil* (Paris, 1889), 83.
[14] Georges Duveau, *La Pensée ouvrière sur l'éducation pendant la Seconde République et le Second Empire* (Paris, 1947), 30–32.

three times under Napoleon III, he could not take his seat. He took pride in his fidelity to the republican cause. Nonetheless, like Marie d'Agoult, he eventually made peace with the Empire, serving as a member of the Corps Législatif after 1864. In the elections of 1869, he was defeated by the younger Gambetta and Henri Rochefort, and during the campaign he was denounced for supporting the repression of the June Insurrection in 1848. His time had passed.[15]

Leconte de Lisle was a poet, born in 1818 on the French island of Réunion, who settled in France as a young man. Drawn to the Fourierist movement, he published dozens of poems in Fourierist periodicals. In 1847, irritated by the immorality of Fourier's doctrine and by the "ineptness" of the Fourierists in the discussion of artistic questions, Leconte de Lisle left the movement.[16] He rejoiced in the February Revolution and threw himself into the effort to transform French society. But his experience as a democratic missionary in Brittany, campaigning for republican candidates, was a disaster. Writing Louis Ménard, he inveighed against "the brutishness, the ignorance and the natural stupidity" of the Bretons, adding that he had been thrown back on poetry and "the serene contemplation of divine forms."[17] This was the direction that his career would take. While remaining republican and fiercely anti-clerical, he accepted honours and pensions from Napoleon III and made his reputation during the 1850s and 1860s as a Parnassian poet creating ideal images of beauty in a realm removed from the struggles of the ephemeral present.[18]

If Leconte de Lisle moved beyond "le rêve sacré" that had inspired him in the 1840s, Constantin Pecqueur did not. Pecqueur was a central figure in both the flowering of socialist theories and the attempt to give substance to these theories in 1848.[19] After passing through both Saint-Simonism and Fourierism, he emerged in the 1840s as the only early socialist who was entirely at home in political economy and who had original things to say about industrial technology. In 1848 he served alongside Louis Blanc and François Vidal on the Luxembourg Commission, the "parliament of labour" which had been given the

[15] Price, *People and Politics*, 113–114, 165, 417.

[16] Christophe Carrère, *Leconte de Lisle ou la passion du beau* (Paris, 2009), 127.

[17] Leconte de Lisle to Louis Ménard, April 30, 1848, in Carrère, *Leconte de Lisle*, 142.

[18] In Jean-Paul Sartre's gargantuan study of Flaubert's development as a writer, Leconte de Lisle figures as a "knight of nothingness" whose retreat from politics after 1848 exemplifies the movement of French bourgeois literary culture. See Sartre, *L'Idiot de la famille*, 3 vols. (Paris, 1971–1972) III, 192–202 and *passim*.

[19] On Pecqueur, see Clément Coste, Ludovic Frobert and Marie Lauricella (eds.), *De la République de Constantin Pecqueur* (Besançon, 2017).

mandate of drafting legislation concerning the organization of work. Pecqueur published his own journal, *Le Salut du people*, in 1849 and served as an informal advisor to three "red" working-class deputies from Lyon. Shocked by the coup d'état of December 2, 1851, he joined the brief effort at armed resistance, helping to build the last barricades.[20]

Pecqueur never lost his republican faith. After the coup he, like Carnot, refused to pledge allegiance to Louis-Napoleon. He kept his job as an assistant librarian at the National Assembly only by agreeing to a subterfuge whereby he was repeatedly rehired as a temporary worker at a reduced wage.[21] For years thereafter he corresponded with exiled democrats and socialists like Louis Blanc and Martin Nadaud, and repeatedly commented in his letters on the duty of the "true democrat" to work for a future he might not live to see. In fact, he lived until 1887, writing thousands of pages in an attempt to synthesize his views on "all the problems of the moral, social, religious, economic and political order."[22] Finally, he concluded that the sources of "social evil" were deeper than he had initially imagined. In his later writings he denounced the "homicidal" character of work in modern industrial society and questioned his Saint-Simonian faith in technological progress. He called for "a new kind of history: the history of the barbarity of civilization in the nineteenth century."[23] Although a lifelong enemy of organized religion, he kept returning to questions of God, Providence, and theodicy. He was evidently trying to explain to himself how his dreams of an ideal republic could have come to nought.

The Second Empire and Beyond

What about our nine writers? How did they fare after Louis-Napoleon's coup d'état? What was their attitude toward the Second Empire? How did the events of 1848–1851 shape their lives and attitudes? Two of them, Tocqueville and Lamartine, remained in France but ceased to involve themselves in public life. Alexis de Tocqueville gave up his positions as deputy and as president of the *conseil général* of the Department of La Manche. For eight years – he died of tuberculosis in 1859 – he worked on a book that would explain why since 1789 democratic revolution in France had twice culminated in the dictatorship of a Napoleon. In this

[20] Ludovic Frobert, "Pecqueur après Pecqueur. Quelques remarques sur les travaux postérieurs à 1851" in *De la République de Constantin Pecqueur*, 293.
[21] Jacques Thbaut, *Constantin Pecqueur (1801–1887): Un collectivisme à visage humain. Esssai de biographie critique* (mimeographed, n.d.), 186–190. Pecqueur's biography remains to be written, but this work of 231 pages is a good start.
[22] Frobert, "Pecqueur après Pecqueur," 295.   [23] Ibid, 312–316.

book he showed how centralized institutions emerged under the Old Regime, destroying local autonomy, local traditions and local institutions that might have provided the basis for resistance to dictatorship. In Tocqueville's view both Napoleonic empires were built on foundations laid by Richelieu, Louis XIV and the rise of a centralized and bureaucratic monarchy in the seventeenth and eighteenth centuries. The result of the Revolution and Napoleonic rule was only to reinforce centralization and to strengthen the hold of the bureaucracy over the whole of society. Neither the restored Bourbon monarchy nor the July Monarchy made a serious attempt to decentralize the structures of authority. The foundations had become so solid by mid-century that those who opposed authoritarian rule could do no more than "graft the head of Liberty onto a servile body."[24] Tocqueville only finished the first of two volumes of *L'Ancien Régime et la Révolution en France*. But that volume was to make him the *maître à penser* of liberal critics of the Second Empire including Marie d'Agoult.[25] It stands as one of the greatest studies ever written on the origins and significance of the French Revolution.

Lamartine's period of "internal exile" was a decade longer than Tocqueville's but vastly less fruitful. His first reaction to the coup d'état was rage: "The people accept it! The people are nothing but sand!" A month later he was lecturing himself on the need for self-control, vowing to "be moderate in my defeat just as I tried to be moderate in victory."[26] In January Guizot described him as "having aged prodigiously and displaying an air of both sadness and bravado." His parliamentary career was over, as was his tenure as president of the *conseil général* of Saône-et-Loire. His main occupation after 1851 was writing. Seeking to pay off his enormous debts, he produced a series of superficial histories and an interminable *Cours familier de littérature*. These added nothing to his reputation and did not begin to pay his debts. In 1860 he sold his estate at Mâcon and his childhood home in Milly. He reduced the number of his servants to three and kept just one candle burning in the candelabra in his Parisian residence. For several years prior to his death in 1869, visitors described him as withdrawn and bitter, a shadow of his former self.[27]

---

[24] Tocqueville, *L'Ancien Régime et la Révolution française*, OC, II, 248.
[25] Françoise Mélonio, *Tocqueville et les français* (Paris, 1993), 163–213.
[26] Letters of Lamartine December 3, 1851, and January 7, 1852; Fernand L'Huillier, *Lamartine en politique* (Strasbourg, 1993), 247, 251.
[27] William Fortescue, *Alphonse de Lamartine: A Political Biography* (London, 1983), 260–271.

Three other writers – Sand, d'Agoult and Flaubert – remained in France and participated to varying degrees in the intellectual life of the Second Empire. Of these three only Marie d'Agoult remained intensely interested in politics. After the coup d'état, she wrote her daughter that, as a known republican, she might be forced "to cross mountains and seas in order to continue writing and speaking freely."[28] She was exaggerating the danger she faced. Throughout the Second Empire she continued to publish freely. While her residence became a centre of liberal opposition to Napoleon III, the moderate republicans who gathered regularly at her salon – notably Hippolyte Carnot, Emile Littré, Jules Grévy and Charles Dupont-White – were never harassed. After 1859, when the French victories over the Austrians at Magenta and Solferino helped pave the way for Italian independence, she drew closer to the regime. She never abandoned her republican views. But a decade later, when her son-in-law Emile Ollivier helped create the Liberal Empire, she relished the opportunity to play a role in politics.[29]

George Sand's links with the regime were initially closer than d'Agoult's. She was criticized by many republicans for her interviews with Louis-Napoleon and Persigny after the coup d'état. Throughout the Second Empire she had warm relations with the "liberal" Bonapartists, the Emperor's cousin Princess Mathilde and her brother Prince Jérôme Napoleon. Sand always claimed that she had remained faithful to the ideal of the republic, and she admired no one in public life more unreservedly than the romantic revolutionary Armand Barbès. But by the spring of 1871, as we have seen, there was little left of the social radicalism that had informed her republicanism and her sympathy for the workers' movement in 1848. The important thing, she believed, was to stabilize the existing republic and to win over the conservative masses through moderate leadership and education.[30] The "chimerical" Paris Commune drove her to vituperation. It was "the saturnalia of the poor" and the work of a sectarian minority led by rabid Blanquists.[31]

As to the horrors of the Commune [she wrote a friend], you are mistaken in believing that it is the work of the same men and the same ideas as in '48. Oh, no! No! You don't see things correctly. Barbès would have disavowed the assassins,

[28] Marie d'Agoult to Claire de Charnacé, December 8, 1851, in Charles Dupêchez, *Marie d'Agoult, 1805–1876* (Paris, 1989), 218.
[29] Jacques Vier, *La Comtesse d'Agoult et son temps*, 6 vols. (Paris, 1955–1963) V, 13–32, 93–132.
[30] Sand to Edmond Plauchut, March 24, 1871, *Correspondance*, XXII (Paris, 1987), 350.
[31] For the *"cauchemar insensé"* see Sand to Charles Poncy, April 16, 1871, and for *"les saturnales de la plèbe"* see Sand to Alexandre Dumas fils, April 22, 1871, *Correspondance*, XXII, 366 and 368.

414   Aftermath: Themes and Conclusion

the incendiaries, the thieves and the traitors. He disavowed Blanqui. He *abhorred* him, and the insurrection made Blanqui its idol.[32]

Finally Sand found a way to pay tribute retrospectively to the revolution of 1848 and to her hero Armand Barbès by contrasting them to the Paris Commune and Auguste Blanqui.

Flaubert was initially divided about Louis-Napoleon. But in May 1852 he could write Louise Colet that he was beginning to admire the Prince-President for having crushed "noble France" under his feet, adding that he would gladly stand in line "to kiss his ass, to thank him personally" if the line weren't already too long![33] Finally, he gave Napoleon III a kind of ironic support: "I thank Badinguet. Bless him! He has brought me back to scorning the masses and to hating everything popular."[34] Throughout the Second Empire Flaubert continued to rail against politics and politicians. But as time passed, he came to feel at home in Imperial France. What changed his mind – and his life – was the success of *Madame Bovary* and his acquittal in the much-publicized trial of the novel for attacking "good morals and religion." The trial made Flaubert a celebrity. Starting in 1857, he kept a rented apartment in Paris, hired a domestic and began to entertain and eat out regularly at elegant restaurants. His circle of friends widened to include George Sand, Turgenev, Gautier, Renan and the Goncourt brothers. He became a participant, when in Paris, at the *dîners chez Magny*, the bi-monthly dinners at which these writers and others (including Sainte-Beuve and Herzen's Polish friend Charles-Edmond Chojecki) gathered to argue about literature and life.[35]

The next step for Flaubert was entering the world of the Bonapartes, and that came quickly. In January 1863, the Goncourts introduced him to Princess Mathilde. Soon he became a regular at her salon on the rue de Courcelles. Then came invitations from her brother, Prince Napoleon, and finally from the Empress Eugénie. Flaubert was happy to spend weekends at Mathilde's country house at Saint Gratien, to sit in

---

[32] Sand to Marie-Sophie Leroyer de Chantepie, March 6, 1872, *Correspondance*, XXII, 756. Armand Barbès died on June 26, 1870. It is not at all clear that he would have opposed the Paris Commune. On Sand and the Commune see Michelle Perrot, "George Sand: une républicaine contre la Commune" in Claude Latta (ed.), *La Commune de 1871: L'évènement, les hommes et la mémoire* (Saint-Etienne, 2004), 145–156.

[33] Flaubert to Louis Colet, May 29, 1852, *Correspondance*, II, 100.

[34] Flaubert to Louise Colet, March 2, 1854, *Correspondance*, II, 529. See Michel Winock, *Flaubert* (Paris, 2013), 148–149 on Flaubert's *ralliement passif*.

[35] On Flaubert's assimilation into the literary world of Paris see Winock, *Flaubert*, 183–205, 241–256. On the *diners Magny*, see Jonathan Dewald, "A la Table de Magny,'*Lost Worlds: The Emergence of French Social History, 1815–1870* (University Park, PA, 2001), 17–53.

the Imperial box at the opera, and to visit the Empress at Compiègne. He was happy also to accept the rosette of the *Légion d'honneur* obtained for him by Mathilde. Critics called this odd behaviour on the part of a writer well known for his dictum (in a letter to Maupassant) that "honours are dishonouring," and well-known also for the last line of *Madame Bovary* in which the statement that the pharmacist Homais "has just received the cross of honour" marks the triumph of deceit and perfidy.[36] But for all the pleasure that Flaubert took in winning support at the highest level of Imperial society, he did not give up his independence.

The most convincing proof that Flaubert was not "bought off" by the Bonapartists during the Second Empire is his novel, *L'Education sentimentale*. But the point can also be made with a wonderful story from the memoirs of Maxime Du Camp. One evening at the Château de Compiègne in the circle of the Empress Eugénie, a courtier was criticizing Victor Hugo. Flaubert interrupted: "Stop! [Hugo] is the master to all of us, and he should only be spoken of respectfully." The courtier continued, "But surely you will agree, Monsieur, that the man who wrote *Les Châtiments* ... "Flaubert cut him off and replied with his eyes on fire: "*Les Châtiments!* There are magnificent verses in it. I will recite them for you if you like!" At this point, according to Du Camp, someone managed to change the subject.[37]

The four remaining writers in our study spent most of the 1850s and '60s in exile – Herzen and Marx in London, Hugo on the Channel Islands. As for Proudhon, he began the period serving a three-year prison sentence that ended only in June 1852 and later spent four years (1858–1862) in exile in Belgium. Each of these four made extraordinarily productive use of the possibilities of exile. Each started a new life. This is most obviously true of Victor Hugo who arrived in Brussels in disguise early on the morning of December 12, 1851. For Hugo exile became an identity.

Hugo's exile lasted nineteen years. Refusing to accept the amnesty offered by Napoleon III in 1859, he only returned to France after the fall of the Second Empire. During these years he lived just off the coast of France on the islands of Jersey and Guernsey, surrounded by an entourage including both his wife and his mistress, three children, various cooks, maids and servants, and an assortment of disciples and hangers-on-in-exile. In the early years he hosted weekly political meetings,

[36] Flaubert to Guy de Maupassant, January 15, 1879, *Correspondance*, V, 501: "Les honneurs déshonorent; le titre dégrade; la function abrutit." See also *Madame Bovary* (Paris, 1961), 324: "Il vient de recevoir la croix d'honneur."
[37] Maxime Du Camp, *Souvenirs littéraires*, 2 vols. (Geneva, 1993), II, 269.

delivered funeral orations for deceased *proscrits*, and published statements supporting victims of oppression from John Brown to the Polish people. Needing peace and quiet in order to write, he eventually distanced himself from the exile community and its factionalism. After 1855, when he moved to Guernsey, the political meetings were replaced by weekly dinners, organized by his wife, for the poor children of the island.

Hugo often described his exile as a period of solitude. "I live on the shore, at the edge of the sea," he wrote in 1853. "Every day I plunge more deeply into isolation, into solitude, into the depths of nature, into oblivion."[38] This was far from true in any literal sense. Hugo's exile increased his fame, and throughout this period he was surrounded by people whose greatest happiness was to do his bidding. He also corresponded actively with republican friends in France, thanks to a distribution network in which Flaubert participated.[39] What is so impressive about Hugo's life in exile is the sheer volume of brilliant writing he produced. Between 1852 and 1870, in addition to his trilogy on Louis-Napoleon's coup d'état, he published three major collections of verse and three novels, including *Les Misérables*. This novel, begun in the 1840s, put aside in 1848, and completed on Guernsey under Napoleon III, is among many other things a meditation on the relations of law and morality, on the history of France, the geography of Paris, and the effect of poverty on human nature. All this is accompanied by magnificent digressions on slang, sewers, and barricades. As the initial exchange between Bishop Myriel and an old *Conventionnel* makes clear, the novel is also an effort to reconcile revolutionary France and Catholic France and thus to heal the wound deepened in June 1848.

In his first letter to Alexander Herzen, Victor Hugo greeted him as "cher concitoyen," observing that "until we have a Universal Republic, exile is our common homeland."[40] It was indeed as political exiles, citizens of the future Universal Republic, that Hugo and Herzen became acquainted in the 1850s. They were never close friends. Herzen formed deeper relationships with Proudhon and Michelet. But these two ebullient narcissists respected each other, and they had much in common. Each had suffered painful losses, and each made a new life in exile. For

---

[38] Victor Hugo, "Choses vues, December 1853" in *Choses vues: souvenirs, journaux, cahiers, 1830–1885*, Hubert Juin (ed.) (Paris, 2002), 840.

[39] Peter Brooks, *Flaubert in the Ruins of Paris* (New York, 2017), 15.

[40] Victor Hugo to Alexander Herzen, July 25, 1855 in Victor Hugo, *Oeuvres completes*, Jean Massin (ed.), 18 vols. (Paris, 1969–1972), IX, 1096. See also Jonathan Beecher, "Victor Hugo et Alexandre Herzen: deux frères d'exil" in Jean-Claude Caron and Annie Stora-Lamarre (eds.), *Hugo Politique* (Besançon, 2004), 189–196.

Herzen, as we have seen, the years 1848–1852 were marked by both political and personal tragedy in the course of which he lost his mother, his younger son, and finally his wife. In August 1852 when he moved to London, he regarded his life as finished at the age of forty. But he set to work on two projects that were to absorb him for the rest of his life. One was the writing of his memoirs which began as an attempt to explain his own personal tragedy both to others and to himself. Herzen's other project was his attempt to make contact with the Russia that he had left in 1847 – to make his voice heard in Russia and, most importantly, to give Russians an uncensored voice in the west.

By 1850 Herzen had already published in French two substantial essays on the emergence of revolutionary and socialist ideas in Russia. These essays were translated into Russian. But Herzen wanted to reach Russian readers directly. Once settled in London, he purchased a printing press with Cyrillic type. He then published portions of his memoirs in Russian, some addressed specifically "To My Brothers in Russia." He also published brochures intended to be smuggled into Russia. In 1855 he issued the first in a series of yearly almanacs called *The Polar Star* in memory of the eponymous publication edited by martyred Decembrist rebels from 1823 to 1825. Finally, in 1857, during the "thaw" that followed the death of Nicholas I, Herzen and his close friend Nicholas Ogarëv began to publish a monthly journal called *Kolokol* or *The Bell* which became the first revolutionary periodical to be widely distributed in Russia. During its decade of existence, *Kolokol* reached a peak circulation of 2,500 and became an influential voice for criticism of serfdom and autocracy, a clearing house for anonymous reports on conditions in Russia, and, since it was actually read by government officials, a significant influence on the negotiations leading to the abolition of serfdom in 1861.[41]

The aftermath of 1848 was also important for Herzen's intellectual development. Convinced that 1848 had revealed the bankruptcy of French radical thought, he published, between 1849 and 1853, a series of essays setting forth his theory of a native Russian socialism based on the peasant commune.[42] There were two key elements in Herzen's Russian socialism. The first was a critique of capitalism that focused more on the culture and consumption patterns of late capitalism than on the economic hardships of the period of primitive accumulation.

---

[41] See Kathleen Parthé (ed.), *A Herzen Reader* (Evanston, 2012) for a rich selection of articles from *Kolokol*.

[42] See especially Alexander Herzen, "The Russian People and Socialism: An Open Letter to Jules Michelet" in *From the Other Shore* (Oxford, 1979), 163–208.

Herzen criticized capitalism not only because it produced poverty and exploitation but also because he believed it degraded people with its crass material values and its mass culture. Much of his social criticism was an attempt to characterize the culture of capitalism and the links between the mores of bourgeois society and the market economy. Herzen also stressed the hegemonic character of the new bourgeois culture – the way its values and virtues of moderation, punctuality, thrift and decorum were internalized by workers who wished to rise within bourgeois society, a society in which, as he remarked sarcastically, "the bright image of the shopkeeper hovers as the ideal before the eyes of the casual labourer."[43]
The second central element in Herzen's Russian socialism was the idea that the Russian peasant commune contained in itself the basis of a new and higher social form. Here Herzen called attention to the traditions of self-government associated with the periodic redistribution of land within the commune. Land belonged to the whole community, and each member had an equal right to its use, but never to absolute ownership of it in the western sense.

In his later years, Herzen came under attack by younger Russian radicals who did not appreciate his libertarian socialism, his aristocratic style of life and his support of the Polish uprising of 1863. But in one important respect Herzen had a vital influence on later Russian radicals. He drew their attention to possibilities latent in the Russian peasant commune. It is ironic that Karl Marx, who later took seriously the possibility that the peasant commune might be the seed of a socialist order in Russia, dismissed Herzen's writings on the subject out of hand as the ravings of a "half-Russian and full Muscovite ... belle-lettrist" who had "made his discoveries on 'Russian' communism not in Russia, but in the work of the Prussian Privy Councillor Haxthausen."[44]

Proudhon's experience of the Second Republic was of course different from that of Hugo, Herzen and Marx because he spent much of this period in prison. Thanks, ironically, to reforms introduced by Thiers in the 1840s, the conditions he had to face were hardly onerous. Except for brief periods in the Conciergerie or at Doullens, he spent his term at the

---

[43] Herzen, *Past and Thoughts*, IV, 1688.

[44] This derisive reference to Herzen appears in the first German edition (1867) of *Capital*, cited in Gareth Stedman Jones, *Karl Marx: Greatness and Illusion* (Cambridge, MA, 2016), 580–581. Marx dropped this reference in the second (1873) German edition. In the meantime he had learned Russian, read Nikolai Chernyshevsky's writings on Haxthausen and communal land ownership in Russia, and had come to believe, with Chernyshevsky, that Russia might possibly proceed straight from the village commune to socialism. For full discussions see Stedman Jones, *Karl Marx*, 568–586; Teodor Shanin, *Late Marx and the Russian Road: Marx and the Peripheries of Capitalism* (New York, 1983); and James D. White, *Marx and Russia: The Fate of a Doctrine* (London, 2018).

prison of Sainte-Pélagie in Paris, where he was allowed to receive visitors and correspond with friends, to keep books and papers in his cell, and even to leave prison one day a week. This enabled him to write three books, to marry, and to father a child during his incarceration. He continued to oversee the publication of two more journals. But he was removed from the day-to-day responsibilities of an editor, and he could write in July 1851 that "while the government, in breaking my journalist's pen, has cut me off from daily polemics, my revolutionary soul has taken to wandering in the land of ideas."[45]

On December 2, 1851, Proudhon had permission to leave the prison. He spent the day walking around the capital, observing the response of Parisians. That evening, near the Place de la Bastille, he encountered Victor Hugo whom he tried to discourage from seeking to organize resistance. "You are creating illusions for yourselves," he said. "The people have been taken in. They won't stir. Bonaparte will win them over ... He has power on his side, canons, the peoples' blindness, and the follies of the Assembly." Hugo rejected this advice and later remembered it bitterly, as if it had been a betrayal.[46]

In retrospect, many republicans were unhappy about Proudhon's unwillingness to join the resistance to Louis-Napoleon's coup. They were even more unhappy about the book – really a long pamphlet entitled *La Révolution sociale démontrée par le coup d'état* – that Proudhon published in August 1852. In this book Proudhon called on Louis-Napoleon to take over leadership of the social revolution that neither the Provisional Government nor the National Assembly nor the republican opposition wanted. Unlike his fellow democrats and republicans, and unlike Victor Hugo whose *Napoléon le petit* appeared the same month, Proudhon claimed to take a constructive position, recognizing that the demise of the Republic was a *fait accompli*. The point now was not to curse the victor but to persuade him to embrace the "democratic social revolution" whose time had come. This social revolution, asserted Proudhon, was a necessary stage in the process that would lead to "the levelling of classes, the emancipation of the proletariat, the freedom of labour the freedom of thought; in a word, the end of all authority."[47]

Proudhon's book was attacked from all sides. Conservatives found it insulting and even "satanic." Bonapartists were confused by it.

[45] Pierre-Joseph Proudhon, *L'Idée générale de la Révolution au XIXe siècle* (Paris, 1924), 96; Dédicace, July 10, 1851,

[46] Pierre Haubtmann, *Pierre-Joseph Proudhon, sa vie et sa pensée, 1849–1865*, 2 vols. (Paris, 1988), I, 139.

[47] Pierre-Joseph Proudhon, *La Révolution sociale démontrée par le coup d'état du deux décembre* (Paris, 1936), 177, 191.

Republicans and socialists denounced it as a "panegyric" of Louis-Napoleon which was treasonous to the republican cause, unrealistic, and also totally inconsistent with Proudhon's longstanding hostility to reforms imposed from above.[48] Proudhon denied the charge of inconsistency. But he soon recognized that his hopes for Louis-Napoleon were indeed unrealistic. By the fall of 1852, he was arguing that Louis-Napoleon had identified himself with the old financial elites and that his concessions to the working class were mere window-dressing.

Proudhon's mind never stood still, and during the Second Republic he rethought his positions on politics and social change. His experience of 1848–1851 led him to appreciate the tenacity of political traditions. He questioned his earlier demands for the total elimination of politics and came to believe that political decision-making required the development of organizations and institutions representing the economic base of society and establishing federative links between communes, trades, and professional associations. He always remained critical of the "top-down" Jacobin socialism epitomized by Louis Blanc. But he came to recognize the need to include professional and communal organizations within a federally structured network that would eventually encompass all of France.[49] Finally, the most significant consequence of Proudhon's experience of 1848 was the discovery that he could speak to – and for – workers. After December 2, he no longer had a journal of his own. But thereafter he knew he could reach a working-class audience. He also became convinced of the need to educate this audience. Much of his subsequent work, culminating with *De la Capacité politique des classes ouvrières*, was an attempt to do just this.

Marx's experience of 1848 was the opposite of Proudhon's: the failure of revolution distanced him from the working class. For five years prior to his expulsion from France in August 1849, he had been actively involved in political organizing and political journalism, first in Brussels and then in Cologne. In England, he initially tried to revive the *Neue Rheinische Zeitung* and to revitalize the Communist league. He continued to hope until the summer of 1850 that a working-class uprising in France would spark a revolutionary upheaval that would engulf Europe. But by the fall of 1850, he had given up on France and had become convinced that the

---

[48] Marxists continued well into the twentieth century to mock Proudhon's "coquetry" with Louis Napoleon. See Georges Cogniot, *Proudhon et la démogoguerie bonapartiste: Un socialiste en coquetterie avec le pouvoir personel* (Paris, 1958).

[49] K. Steven Vincent, *Pierre-Joseph Proudhon and the Rise of French Republican Socialism* (New York, 1984), 209–228; Robert Hoffman, *Revolutionary Justice: The Social and Political Theory of P.-J. Proudhon* (Urbana, 1972), 283–308.

economic prosperity of England and the United States would spread to the continent. A new revolution would only be possible, he wrote in October 1850, "in the wake of a new crisis." For the time being there could be "no talk of real revolution."[50] The coup d'état of Louis-Napoleon on December 2, 1851, the creation of a Second French Empire a year later, and the consolidation of authoritarian regimes throughout Europe only served to reinforce Marx's desire to withdraw from active political life. In October 1853 he wrote Engels of his intention "to declare publicly that I have nothing to do with any party. I no longer feel inclined to allow myself on so-called party grounds to be insulted by any old party jackass." He never issued such a declaration but, as Jonathan Sperber observes," "he certainly lived out its principles, giving up any engagement with the German artisans and European political refugees in London."[51]

It was in this state of mind, that Marx returned to the study of economic questions that he had embarked on in Paris in 1844. Already, in 1845, Engels and other friends had urged him to finish his "book on economics," parts of which were to appear in the manuscripts comprising *The German Ideology*. Once settled in London and provided in June 1850 with a reader's card to the British Museum, he threw himself into reading and writing on political economy. He saw this as a retreat from, but not an abandonment of, his political activity of the 1840s. His project was to prepare himself intellectually for the next revolutionary outbreak by demonstrating that capitalism was destroying itself.

The Texts Compared: The June Days, Blanqui, Thiers

In the preceding chapters we have often found our protagonists running into each other – arguing, observing, criticizing, complimenting, colliding. We have seen George Sand engaged in a long entanglement with Marie d'Agoult, in deep conversation with Lamartine and Tocqueville, and in affectionate dialogue with her "vieux troubadour," Gustave Flaubert. We have seen her defending Bakunin against baseless charges by Marx, serving as a moral mentor to Herzen, and visiting Proudhon in prison. Similarly, Herzen has appeared as a comrade of Proudhon and Hugo, an admirer of Sand, a critic of Lamartine's oratory and d'Agoult's

---

[50] Karl Marx, "Review" (May–October 1850], *Neue Rheinische Zeitung. Politisch-ökonomische Revue* (1850) MECW, X, 509–510.
[51] Marx to Engels, October 8, 1853, MECW, 39, 386; Jonathan Sperber, *Karl Marx: A Nineteenth-Century Life* (New York, 2013), 292.

History, and an antagonist of Marx. We have also noted Herzen's unpleasant encounter with Tocqueville during the June Days when he was arrested as a "foreign rioter." One could chart the personal relations of most of our writers with each other. For a few years in the 1840s, they lived in close proximity: they had Paris in common, and at times they belonged to the same intellectual world. Even Marx, who might be considered the outlier, was in 1844 close to Proudhon and, through his friendship with Herwegh, moved in a circle of German emigrés in which Marie d'Agoult was at home.

I want now to prolong the conversation by comparing the ways in which our writers responded to particular events and wrote about particular themes. This involves a certain amount of editorial license because not all of them took (and held) "positions" on particular issues. They wrote in different genres, and their presence in their works varies. Whereas Flaubert wished to write "like God in the universe, everywhere felt but nowhere seen,"[52] his friend George Sand never lets one forget her desires and opinions. In Lamartine's History of 1848, everything is framed within the story of his achievements, his courage, his feats of valour. Proudhon's Confessions d'un révolutionnaire is simultaneously the story of the collapse of the revolution and his own making as a revolutionary. With Herzen on the other hand, personal and political failure go together and reinforce each other. Hugo's massive ego is often not in evidence in the notes and jottings that make up his choses vues, but one is constantly reminded in reading Tocqueville's Souvenirs that he felt he was living in a world of fools. Marie d'Agoult's voice is cautious; she asks us to follow her as she seeks confirmation for her insights and ideas. Marx, on the other hand, overwhelms us with his verbal pyrotechnics as he exposes the emptiness of the old language and the old symbols.

This said, one is often struck by the congruence of their views. Most strikingly, all our writers build their accounts of 1848 around the contrast between the hopes of February and the carnage of June – in Marx's words, the "*beautiful* revolution" and the "*ugly* revolution."[53] The good revolution in February is marked by minimal violence, and power virtually falls into the hands of the insurgents. Marie d'Agoult concludes her first volume by paying tribute to the "generosity," the "naïve fraternal enthusiasm," the "proud disinterestedness," and the "delicate *courtoisie*" of the people of Paris in their triumph.[54] Even Tocqueville marvels at the composure and the lack of anger on the part of the "gentle" crowd which

---

[52] Flaubert to Louise Colet, December 9, 1852, *Correspondance*, II, 204.
[53] Marx, *Class Struggles in France*, 57, quoting *Neue Rheinische Zeitung*, June 29, 1848.
[54] Daniel Stern, *Histoire de la Révolution de 1848*, 3 vols. (Paris, 1850–1853), I, 270.

suddenly found itself in control of Paris.[55] The one account of the February Revolution that strikes a more critical note is Flaubert's. In *L'Education sentimentale* the taking of the Tuileries Palace and the occupation of the Palais Royal are described as scenes of mayhem on the part of a bad-smelling and destructive *canaille* made up of crooks, hooligans, and prostitutes.[56] There is, of course, a reason for the negative image: the crowd is seen through the eyes of the affluent Frederick and Hussonet, whose language tells us more about them than about it. Still, this is the only account of the February Revolution offered by Flaubert.

All our writers see something unprecedented and terrible about the June uprising and the killing it provoked. Even Marx and Tocqueville, who deride the revolution of 1848 as a farcical replay of 1789, argue that beneath the comic exterior, something significant was happening. In Tocqueville's words, the imitation was "so visible that the terrible originality of the facts remained hidden."[57] What was this? For both Marx and Tocqueville, the originality of 1848 lay in the fact that the conflict in June was a class war. It was not, writes Tocqueville, a conflict over "the form of government" but a conflict over "the order of society." It was "not a political battle, but a class struggle, a sort of servile war." Likewise, for Marx the June insurrection marked "the first great battle between the two classes that split modern society."[58]

Several of the most powerful accounts of the June Days focus on a particular moment at the end of the fighting: the arrival in Paris of volunteers from the provinces – bourgeois National Guard units, royalist landowners, wealthy peasants – to help round up and guard prisoners. For Flaubert, this moment, which culminates in Roque's shooting of a helpless, unarmed prisoner, illustrates the savagery of the repression. It is the only moment of the June Days that Flaubert discusses directly. Almost everywhere else in the novel we see people, places and events through the eyes of Frederick Moreau, but in this passage there is no hint of Frederick's perspective. Roque's killing of the young man is framed

[55] Alexis de Tocqueville, *Souvenirs* (Paris, 1978), 123–126.
[56] Gustave Flaubert, *L'Education sentimentale*, Edouard Maynial (ed.) (Paris, 1961), 290–292.
[57] Tocqueville, *Souvenirs*, 100.
[58] Ibid, 212–213; Marx, *Class Struggles*, 56. For the range of views held by modern historians see Charles Tilly and Lynn H. Lees, "The People of June 1848" in Roger Price (ed.), *Revolution and Reaction: 1848 and the Second French Republic* (New York, 1975), 170–209; Mark Traugott, *Armies of the Poor: Determinants of Working-Class Participation in the Parisian Insurrection of June 1848* (Princeton, 1985), 168–190; Laurent Clavier, Louis Hincker and Jacques Rougerie, "Juin 1848. L'insurrection" in Jean-Luc Mayaud (ed.), *1848: actes du colloque international du cent conquantenaire* (Paris, 2002), 123–140.

within a hallucinatory account of the improvised prison in the cellars of the Tuileries – an account in which cries of fear and rage are mixed with smells of excrement and dead bodies. The ferocity of the guards is succinctly evoked: these are people who wished to "avenge themselves all at once for the newspapers, the clubs, the threatening crowds, the doctrines, for everything that had been exasperating them for three months."[59] The killing itself is described in just three short sentences, and in language so condensed and so opaque that the reader is forced to visualize exactly what has happened and how fragments of the young man's skull and brain became stuck on the rim of the prison bucket.[60]

Flaubert's narrative of this episode is based, we know, on an article in the radical journal *La Commune de Paris*, describing the shooting of an "innocent provincial property owner" by a member of the National Guard in the Tuileries cellars. But there is a fuller account of the prison shootings in a long article originally published in *La Vraie République* in May and June 1849. The author was a young law student named François Pardigon who joined the insurgents on June 23 only to be arrested that evening.[61] Pardigon spent six days in a series of prisons including the Tuileries cellar where he was held from noon on June 25 until the evening of June 26. His account of conditions in the prison, which is just as grim as Flaubert's, concludes with the story of "a poor madman" who, disobeying the prison guards, was drawn to the cellar window "as a butterfly is drawn towards a flame," and shot. Pardigon himself emerged unscathed from his two days in the Tuileries cellar, but the next day, while being transferred to another prison, he was caught in a crossfire. A stray bullet hit him in the face and tore off his lower jaw, leaving him disfigured for life.[62]

Pardigon's story was to live on in the writings of European radicals. Alexander Herzen, who met Pardigon in London in the 1850s, tells the story in his memoirs, altering it so that the shooting of Pardigon takes

---

[59] Flaubert, *L'Education sentimentale*, 338.

[60] See above Chapter 10, p. 390. See also Tony Williams, "From Document to Text: the 'terrasse au bord de l'eau' episode in *L'Education sentimentale*," *French Studies*, 47 (1993), 156–171; and Pierre-Marc de Biasi, *Gustave Flaubert: Une manière spéciale de vivre* (Paris, 2009), 349–352. Other contemporary accounts of the prison shootings include Louis Ménard, *Prologue d'une révolution, février-janvier 1848* (Paris, 1849), 269–286; and Norbert Truquin, *Mémoires et aventures d'un prolétaire à travers la révolution* (Paris, 1977), 81.

[61] In 1850, Pardigon joined the ranks of French *proscrits* in London, where in 1852 he published an enlarged edition of his *Episodes des journées de juin 1848*. In 1858 he emigrated to the United States, found work as a journalist for the *Richmond Enquirer*, and served as a lieutenant in the Confederate Army during the Civil War. See the Introduction by Alix Héricourt to her edition of *Episodes des journées de juin 1848* (Paris, 2008), 7–45.

[62] Pardigon, *Episodes des journées de juin 1848*, 179–195.

place in the Tuileries prison and under circumstances much like those described by Flaubert.[63] And during the ferment of 1871 that led up to the Paris Commune, Jules Vallès evoked the shootings in the Tuileries prison in terms that recall both Flaubert's novel and the article that was Flaubert's source: "In the cellar of the Tuileries, beneath the barracks, in the Panthéon, the prisoners were swimming in blood and excrement. Sometimes they were asked through a skylight, 'Who wants bread?' And when a pale face appeared, it was blown apart by a rifle shot."[64]

Proudhon spent the morning of June 26 in the Faubourg Saint-Antoine, watching the taking of the last barricades. That evening he noted in his *Cahiers* the shooting of unarmed and wounded prisoners, and later he wrote a friend: "The triumphant bourgeoisie are as fierce as tigers."[65] Unlike Proudhon, Marie d'Agoult could write enthusiastically in June about the "fraternal zeal" of the provincials who "flew to the aid" of Paris.[66] But in time she came to see the movement in a harsher light: her History of 1848 depicts provincial National Guard units making up for their tardy arrival by tormenting the prisoners placed under their guard. In language that Flaubert was to borrow, she describes the scene at the makeshift prison created in the cellar under the Tuileries. Fifteen hundred people were packed into the "fetid sludge" of an improvised prison, she writes. As the prisoners fought for places near the vents that let in air and light, the guards on sentry duty took aim and fired at these helpless "wretches."[67] D'Agoult goes on to describe in terms that Flaubert was to transpose to a different context, the "retrospective terror" of the bourgeoisie and the wild rumours that circulated around Paris weeks after the crushing of the insurrection concerning the insurgents' plans to blow up the whole Faubourg Saint-Germain or to cut gas lines and to massacre Parisians in the darkness.[68]

[63] Herzen, *Past and Thoughts*, III, 1097–1098.
[64] Jules Vallès, *Le Cri du Peuple*, February 22, 1871; Robert Gildea, "1848 in European Collective Memory" in Dieter Dowe, et al., *Europe in 1848: Revolution and Reform* (New York, 2001), 922.
[65] Proudhon to Maguet, June 28, 1848, *Correspondance*, II, 337–338. See also Proudhon, *Cahiers*, III, 66–67 and Chapter 8.
[66] Daniel Stern, "Lettres républicaines," VI, "Les Trois socialismes," *Courrier français*, July 8, 1848.
[67] Stern, *Histoire*, III, 271. Another witness of the "hécatombes des prisonniers" committed by the National Guards in the Tuileries was the young Ernest Renan. See his letter to Henriette Renan, July 16, 1848, in Pierre Michel, *Un Mythe romantique: Les Barbares, 1789–1848* (Lyon, 1981), 238.
[68] Stern, *Histoire*, III, 271–273. In Flaubert's *Education sentimentale* (340–344) the Dambreuse dinner party is the setting in which wealthy Parisians exchange stories about the insurgents' plan to blow up the whole Faubourg Saint-Germain and their

The most fascinating, and most disturbing, account of this final phase of the repression is Alexis de Tocqueville's. We have seen that a distinction between the high-minded and the petty, between grandeur and greed, runs through the *Souvenirs*.[69] The work is full of examples of pettiness, vanity, myopia, selfishness, stupidity and greed. But there is in the *Souvenirs*, I have noted, one moment of collective behaviour that Tocqueville regards as marked by grandeur. This is, precisely, the arrival at Paris by train and by foot at the very end of the insurrection of thousands of provincials eager to "save" Paris from the insurgents. Tocqueville praises the "resolution and vigour" of this heroic movement of national unity; and in celebrating the arrival on June 26 of 1500 volunteers from his own department of La Manche, his language becomes positively lyrical. He is "touched to recognize among them landowners, lawyers, doctors and farmers, my friends and neighbours" and nobles great and small who "remembered at this moment that they had once belonged to a warlike ruling class."[70] This lyric celebration of the provincials who rushed to Paris to rescue the Republic stands in stark contrast to the much darker pictures painted by our other writers.

Significantly, in Tocqueville's extensive account of the June Days there is no reference to the shooting of prisoners. And while Tocqueville evokes vividly the climate of fear that prevailed among affluent Parisians, before, during and after the June Days, he does not mention the absurd rumours that circulated in the wealthy quarters of the capital. The story he has to tell is the story of "the delivery of the French nation from oppression by the Parisian labourers." Greed and envy are the principal motives of the insurgents, and Tocqueville's tone in describing the role of provincials of all classes in the common effort to defeat the insurrection is lyrical and elegiac.

If Tocqueville stands apart from our other writers in his celebration of the descent on Paris of provincials bent on finishing off the insurgency, his dramatic portrait of Auguste Blanqui is also in a class by itself. Almost every contemporary narrative history or memoir of 1848 included a portrait of Blanqui. Most of these portraits are one-dimensional. Blanqui is sometimes presented as the evil genius of revolution – as a

---

ability to pass messages to each other by means of coded melodies played on the barrel organ.

[69] See above Chapter 6, pp. 228–229.

[70] Tocqueville, *Souvenirs*, 251. Not all members of the Party of Order shared Tocqueville's positive assessment of this final phase of the repression. Odilon Barrot writes in his memoirs of the "horrible massacre" of "the unfortunate people who were crammed into the cellars of the Tuileries." See *Mémoires posthumes de Odilon Barrot*, 4 vols. (Paris, 1875–1876), II, 273–274.

perpetual conspirator who never failed to attract followers. George Sand came to adopt this view.[71] There is the heroic Blanqui epitomized by Alexander Herzen as "a concentrated, nervous, gloomy person, exhausted and ill from terrible imprisonment" who nonetheless "preserved an improbable energy of spirit" and who "shook the masses" with "a completely original eloquence."[72] Then there is Proudhon's dark, fatalistic Blanqui: "a pessimist and a misanthrope, always expecting the worst," appalled by his own judgments. "He believes the Republic lost, the revolution aborted, the proletariat forever in chains, mankind irredeemable."[73]

More nuanced portraits of Blanqui appear in the writings of Marie d'Agoult, Hugo, and even Lamartine. In d'Agoult's portrait, discussed in Chapter 6, Blanqui is pale and sickly, but he owes his influence to his personal magnetism and to his sheer intelligence and finely developed "political tact."[74] Lamartine depicts Blanqui as an actor – a refined individual whose gestures, attitudes and statements are always calculated: "Blanqui himself enjoyed the fear that his name inspired, and affected anger more than he felt it."[75] In *Choses vues*, Victor Hugo treats Blanqui as a problem to be solved: "Deeply shrewd, no hypocrisy. The same in private as in public. Harsh, severe, serious, never laughing, replying to respect with irony, to admiration with sarcasm, to love with disdain and inspiring extraordinary devotion."[76]

Tocqueville's Blanqui is totally different. He appears just once in the *Souvenirs*, in a single unforgettable paragraph describing the chaos in the National Assembly on May 15:

I saw a man approach the rostrum, and although I have never seen him since, the memory of him has filled me with disgust and horror ever since. He had sunken, withered cheeks, white lips, and a sickly, malign, dirty look like a pallid, mouldy corpse. He was wearing no visible linen; an old black frockcoat covered his lean,

---

[71] Writing Mazzini in 1852, Sand said she had never read a line of Blanqui's writings and could not pass judgment on him, *Correspondance*, XI, 185. During the Paris Commune she described him as the embodiment of the violent and destructive impulses that had fatally compromised the socialist movement.

[72] Alexander Herzen, *Letters from France and Italy*, tr. Judith E. Zimmerman (Pittsburgh, 1995), 154–155; Marc Vuilleumier, "La Rencontre Herzen-Blanqui. Fribourg, 16–17 Octobre, 1866," *Revue des études slaves*, LXXXI(1) (2012), 219–225.

[73] *Carnets de P.-J. Proudhon*, Pierre Haubtmann (ed.), 4 vols. (Paris, 1960–1974), III, 358–359 (May 7, 1850).

[74] Stern, *Histoire*, II, 35–36. See Chapter 6 above.

[75] Lamartine, *Histoire de la Révolution de 1848*, II, 149–150.

[76] Victor Hugo, *Choses vues. Souvenirs, journaux, cahiers 1830–1885*, Hubert Juin (ed.), 2nd ed. (Paris, 2002), 648.

428   Aftermath: Themes and Conclusion

emaciated limbs tightly. He looked as if he had lived in a sewer and only just emerged. I was told that it was Blanqui.[77]

Not a word about Blanqui's views; just two sentences on the content of his speech; and all the rest on Tocqueville's visceral reaction to the appearance of this "pallid, mouldy corpse."

At the other end of the ideological spectrum from Blanqui stands Adolphe Thiers. Here our authors seem to be of one mind. For some of them, Thiers serves as the negative pole in an antithesis. Marie d'Agoult's History is built in part around the contrast between the generous, idealistic and ineffective Lamartine and the vulgar, cynical, calculating Thiers. For four authors (Herzen, Marx, Sand and Flaubert) Thiers is the quintessential bourgeois – a comic figure, the butt of jokes. Marx calls Thiers a "monstrous gnome" and a "mischievous abortion."[78] Herzen's Thiers is "a little old man with a round belly" who "looks like "a thieving butler or a Figaro" and is "a typical expression of bourgeois France."[79] In their correspondence, Flaubert and Sand compete to concoct ever more comical descriptions of Thiers. When Flaubert asks, "Can anyone find a more triumphant imbecile, a more abject old scab, a more turdlike bourgeois?" Sand replies that "turdlike" is just the word to characterize this "shit-shaped vegetable," this "clown without an idea."[80] Even the prim Tocqueville turns the fearful Thiers into a ludicrous hysteric when on February 24, after wandering distraught around Paris, "he took me by the hands" and "told me that he was going to be massacred by the people unless I helped him escape."[81]

It's worth recalling that many of the writers who ridiculed Thiers in 1848 eventually offered him grudging respect. The elderly George Sand applauded Thiers' leadership in the establishment of the Third Republic and the annihilation of the Paris Commune.[82] Others, closer to the French radical tradition, still appreciated Thiers' role in guiding the first steps of the Republic after the trials of the war and the Commune. In 1872, Marie d'Agoult thanked Thiers publicly for his contribution to the establishment of republican institutions.[83] And both Hugo and Flaubert

---

[77] Tocqueville, *Souvenirs*, 189.
[78] Marx to Liebknecht, April 6, 1871, in Karl Marx and Frederick Engels, *Selected Correspondence* (Moscow, n.d.), 317.
[79] Herzen, *Letters from France and Italy*, 178.
[80] Flaubert to Sand, December 18–19, 1867 and Sand to Flaubert, December 21, 1867, in Flaubert, *Correspondance*, III, 711, 713.
[81] Tocqueville, *Souvenirs*, 106.
[82] Sand to Henry Harisse, July 6, 1871, *Correspondance*, XXII, 450. See Chapter 3 above.
[83] Marie d'Agoult, Open letter to Littré in *Le Temps*, November 14, 1872. See Chapter 4 above.

joined the thousands of marchers in Thiers's funeral cortege in 1877. "I didn't like this King of Prudhommes," wrote Flaubert. "No matter! Compared to those around him, he's a giant. And he had a rare virtue: Patriotism."[84]

The Language of 1848: Religiosity, Theatricality, the Image of the People

Most broad studies of the revolution of 1848 – both those written by modern historians and those by contemporaries – have something to say about the style or idiom of the *quarante-huitards*. High-minded, sentimental, generous, hyperbolic, extravagantly hopeful, full of references to Providence, the will of God and the sublime good sense of the People, this was the language of Lamartine in his loftiest mode. It was also the language of Lamennais, Pierre Leroux and George Sand. One can find characterizations of this style, appreciative if sometimes with an edge of irony, by historians from Georges Renard and Jean Cassou to Maurice Agulhon and Quentin Deluermoz.[85] One can also find critiques of it in the writing of Flaubert and Proudhon and (in a calmer voice) Tocqueville.

Proudhon and Flaubert held opposing views on most questions, but both detested what they regarded as the flood of sentimental idealism that suffused radical thought in the 1830s and 1840s. Both writers celebrated irony, and both admired Voltaire because they saw in him the antithesis of romantic sentimentality. Tocqueville's views were more soberly stated: one cannot imagine him writing the boisterous outbursts of Flaubert's letters or the extraordinary paean to the goddess of irony with which Proudhon's *Confessions* concludes. But Tocqueville's insistent criticism of the "overblown language" and "crude colours" of Lamartine's *Histoire des Girondins* and, more generally, of the "literary spirit in politics" places him among the critics of the romantic radicals.[86]

---

[84] Flaubert to Edma Roger des Genettes, September 17, 1877, *Correspondance*, V, 297. See also Peter Brooks, *Flaubert in the Ruins of Paris*, 148.

[85] Georges Renard, "L'Esprit de 1848," *La Révolution de 1848 et les révolutions du XIX⁰ siècle*, XXVII(134) (1930), 140–158; Jean Cassou, *Quarante-huit* (Paris, 1939); Maurice Agulhon, *Les Quarante-huitards* (Paris, 1975), 238–239; and Quentin Deluermoz, *Le Crépuscule des révolutions, 1848–1871* (Paris, 2012), 20–23. For a critique of the notion of an "esprit de 1848" see Jean-Yves Mollier, "La Culture de '48" in Sylvie Aprile et al. (eds.), *La Révolution de 1848 en France et en Europe* (Paris, 1998), 127–178; and "Les Cultures de 1848" in Hélène Millot and Corinne Saminadayar-Perrin (eds.), *1848: une révolution du discours* (Paris, 2001), 47–60.

[86] Tocqueville, *Souvenirs*, 100, 119, 128.

The critique of sentimental idealism was central to the thought of Flaubert. His favourite target was Lamartine.[87] But his critique was general, and he even invented a word – *le sentimentalisme* – to try to grasp the "radical defect of imagination" that he saw at work among his contemporaries. He once characterized this malady as a "taste for excess, too much sensuality, the lack of coherent thinking, too much dreaming."[88] A succinct definition of sentimentalism as Flaubert understood it might be this: the refusal to see things as they are, the insistence on embellishing, sugar-coating. Something like this appears to be what Flaubert understood by "sentimentalism" in 1862 when he wrote in an early notebook for *L'Education sentimentale*: "Show that sentimentalism (its development since 1830) follows politics and reproduces its phases."[89]

One manifestation of sentimentalism that Flaubert found particularly troubling was the blending of Christian language and imagery with democratic and socialist ideologies. This was a prominent feature of the writing of Buchez, Leroux and Lamennais. Among our authors it appears most often in the work of George Sand, and especially in her journalism. Take for example this excerpt from Théophile Thoré's, *La Vraie République*:

Where is God? He is not shut up in a gold or silver chalice. His spirit floats freely in the vast universe and every republican soul is its sanctuary. What is the name of religion? Its name is *Republic*. What is its slogan? *Liberty, Equality, Fraternity*. What is its doctrine? The *Gospel*, stripped of the additions and deletions of the Middle Ages; the Gospel, freely understood and interpreted by the good sense and charity of the people. Who are its priests? We all are.[90]

By 1850, with the passage of the Falloux Laws, which gave the Catholic Church control of primary education in France, this kind of language had disappeared from Sand's writing and from that of most French democrats. Nonetheless, it was pervasive before and immediately after the February Revolution.

Flaubert's correspondence is full of tirades against the "deplorable" influence of Christianity, especially Catholic Christianity, on the

---

[87] One could easily compile a little anthology of Flaubert's derisive comments on Lamartine, the "eunuch" who "lacks balls" and can only "piss clear water." Not all of it is translatable. For example: "C'est à lui que nous devons tous les embêtements bleuâtres du lyrisme poitrinaire."

[88] Flaubert, "*Carnets de travail* for *Education sentimentale*" in Tony Williams (ed.), *Flaubert, l'Education sentimentale, les Scénarios* (Paris, 1992), 332.

[89] Flaubert, *Carnets de travail*, 332.

[90] George Sand, "Le Dogme de la France, La Vraie République, May 11, 1848" in *Politique et polémiques (1843–1850)*, Michelle Perrot (ed.) (Paris, 1997), 459.

socialists and republicans in the run-up to 1848. This became an obsession with him in the late 1860s as he was dutifully reading French
socialists; and ironically it was to George Sand that he unburdened
himself most often. "All the Christianity I find in socialism appalls
me!" he wrote Sand in 1868. "I think that a part of our evils comes from
republican neo-catholicism," he wrote Jules Michelet, adding that "from
Saint-Simon to Proudhon they all start out from religious revelation."
And to Sand again: "Neo-Catholicism and socialism have rendered
France stupid. Everything is either Immaculate Conception or workers'
lunches."[91]

What particularly disturbed Flaubert about the mixing of Christianity
with socialism and republicanism – the invocations of Jesus Christ the
first republican and communism as "true Christianity" – was the intellectual confusion that this sort of syncretism revealed. For Flaubert, the
facile identification of socialism and Christianity was a distinctive feature
of 'forty-eighter radicalism, a major cause of the failure of the Republic,
and a clue to the underlying authoritarianism of so many socialists. The
radicals of 1848 want to enroll all of humanity into a system, he kept
repeating. At bottom they were authoritarian religious believers who
stood at the opposite pole from genuinely critical thinkers like Voltaire.

Flaubert was not alone among our writers in deploring the penetration
of the language of the left with religious images, metaphors and
preoccupations. Proudhon often criticized the recourse to religious language and imagery on the part of his socialist contemporaries; and, like
Flaubert, Proudhon regarded Voltairean skepticism and irony as an
antidote to the facile identification of socialism and Christianity.
Nevertheless, Proudhon was deeply ambivalent about Christianity and
its relation to socialism. On the one hand, he carried on a lifelong quarrel
with God, pronouncing God an "evil" being who "merits eternal dam-
nation"[92] and mocking the Christian socialists as overstimulated by
romantic religiosity. "Socialism and romantic literature have put our
generation in heat," he thundered. "A thick fog of religiosity weighs
today on the heads of all reformers."[93] On the other hand, he venerated
Jesus the man – not Christ the Messiah – as an inspiration to a suffering
and striving humanity. Proudhon could also write eloquently, and with a
kind of Pascalian intensity, about the predicament of human beings

[91] Flaubert to Sand, July 5, 1868, Flaubert, *Correspondance*, III, 771; Flaubert to Michelet,
February 2, 1869, Flaubert, *Correspondance*, IV, 13; Flaubert to Sand, September 19,
1868, Flaubert, *Correspondance*, III, 805.
[92] Proudhon, *Système des contradictions économiques, ou Philosophie de la misère*, 2 vols. (Paris,
1923), I, 384, 381.
[93] Proudhon, *Système des contradictions économiques*, II, 381, 302.

whose sense of limitless potential is belied by paltry achievements and who experience an "incomprehensible emptiness" when they reject God.[94] As he said of himself in 1849, "The author is more religious than he claims and, above all, than he wishes to be."[95]

Alexander Herzen sometimes used conventional quasi-religious romantic language to describe his own hopes and ideals – his "religious" belief in individuals and "the religion of the coming revolution."[96] But there was a critical edge to his writing on the religiosity of the French left. One of his chief complaints against French socialists and republicans was that they were unable to free themselves from Christian habits of mind:

> The French are not at all emancipated from religion. Read George Sand and Pierre Leroux, Louis Blanc and Michelet: their work is full of Christianity and romanticism adapted to our ways; everywhere there is dualism, abstraction, abstract duty, formal conventional virtue without any connection to practical life.[97]

Herzen's language here resembles that of Flaubert's correspondence. But unlike Flaubert, Herzen was fascinated by the "social religions" and "political religions" of his time. He could speak of an idealized aristocracy whose "social religion" was founded on honour, courage and love of country.[98] He described republicanism as "an ardent faith, a religion" and Louis Blanc as "the high priest and preacher of the new temple" of socialism.[99]

Marie d'Agoult's attitude toward radical religiosity evolved. Prior to 1848, she showed a propensity for the kind of unrestrained religious language that Flaubert deplored. But this didn't last. In the first volume of her *Histoire de la Révolution de 1848* she explicitly rejected the identification of socialism and Christianity:

> If it is true to say that at first glance socialism seems to be an extension of the principle of fraternity brought to the world by Jesus Christ, it is also and above all a reaction against the central dogma of Christianity: the fall and the expiation. One might, I think, more accurately consider socialism as basically an effort to give *materiality* and *immediacy* ... to the spiritual paradise and the future life of the Christians. That may be fulfilling the law, but it is fulfilling it by abolishing it.[100]

---

[94] Ibid, 174.

[95] Proudhon, *De la Création de l'ordre dans l'humanité* (Paris, 1927), 74n. Note added by Proudhon to the 1849 edition. On Proudhon and Christianity, see Pierre Haubtmann, *Pierre-Joseph Proudhon: genèse d'un antithéiste* (Paris, 1969); and Henri de Lubac, *Proudhon et le christianisme* (Paris, 1945).

[96] Herzen, *From the Other Shore*, 4.

[97] Herzen, *France and Italy*, 161. Translation slightly modified.   [98] Ibid, 29–30.

[99] Ibid, 169, 151.   [100] Stern, *Histoire*, I, xxxv–xxxvi.

This comment was buried in a footnote on the Saint-Simonian religion. But there was nothing buried in d'Agoult's reaction in December 1850 to the religious language of her socialist correspondent, Ange Guépin: "Your word *révélateur* exasperated me. I can't bear this tendency of socialism to think itself a revealed religion."[101] The nineteenth century, she argued, was an age of science, and it "will not follow you in your superstitions." Accordingly, in preparing a second edition of her History, d'Agoult cut out some of her own religious language.

As for Marx, he had had his say on religion in the mid-1840s; and in 1848 he saw no reason to call into question his earlier characterization of religion as "the sigh of an oppressed creature, the heart of a heartless world ... the opium of the people."[102] Indeed, *The Communist Manifesto* included an explicit rejection of the effort to reinforce socialism by showing its parallel with Christianity. "Nothing is easier," Marx wrote, "than to give Christian asceticism a socialist tinge ... Christian socialism is but the holy water with which the priest consecrates the heart-burnings of the aristocrat."[103]

So, five of our writers criticized the mixing of social radicalism and religion. Only Sand and Lamartine regularly employed this sort of language after February 1848. But other socialists and republicans remained convinced that their arguments could only be strengthened by the appeal to Jesus Christ, the first socialist. In his first electoral profession of faith Ledru-Rollin celebrated Jesus Christ who "preached equality and fraternity to men," and he continued to use this language in 1848. Although Louis Blanc advocated a secular socialism, he inveighed against the "insolence" of Voltairean skepticism: "To continue Voltaire today," he wrote in 1840, "would be dangerous and puerile. Each era has its own task! That of our time is to revive religious sentiment." In 1849 in his *Catéchisme des socialistes* he could still describe socialism as "the Gospel in action."[104] Similarly, in November 1849, Pierre Leroux fiercely attacked Proudhon's "atheist" manifesto "against God and socialism," and in 1850 Leroux observed that the word "socialisme," which he had helped coin, had now come to refer to "religious democracy."[105]

---

[101] "D'Agoult to Ange Guépin, December 13, 1850" in Jacques Vier (ed.), *Daniel Stern: Lettres républicaines du IIe Empire* (Paris, 1951), 24.

[102] Marx, "Contribution to the Critique of Hegel's Philosophy of Law: Introduction," MECW, III, 175–176.

[103] Marx, *The Communist Manifesto*, Gareth Stedman Jones (ed.) (London, 2002), 246–247.

[104] Ledru-Rollin, Profession de foi électorale (1841) and Louis Blanc, *La Revue du progrès* (1840), I, 246: both cited in Weill, *Parti républicain*, 186n; Louis Blanc, *Catéchisme des socialistes* (Paris, 1849), 3.

[105] Pierre Leroux in *La République*, November 18, 1849, in Haubtmann, *Proudhon: Vie et pensée*, I, 43; and Leroux's Note of 1850 on his 1834 article "De l'individualisme et du

A second recurrent feature of our texts is the repeated recourse to theatrical language to describe both the course of events in 1848 and the tendency of the revolutionaries to mimic the words, deeds and gestures of the leaders of the first French Revolution. The topos of the world as a stage and politics as theatre was of course hardly new in 1848.[106] It had flourished in Shakespeare's time and again during the French Revolution when Robespierre claimed that "the eyes of Europe" were fixed on "the theatre of our revolution" and Marat could speak menacingly of "the same actors, the same masks, the same plots" concealed "behind the curtain" of "the theatre of the State."[107] During the Bourbon Restoration, debate in the Chamber of Deputies once again assumed a theatrical character.[108] And the theatre became a site from which critics could offer carnivalesque parodies of religious revival meetings and mount assaults on the intrigues of "the Jesuits" and the "Tartufferie" of both clerical and civil authorities.[109] Under the July Monarchy, with the rise of small popular theatres along the Boulevard du Temple, Parisian audiences became more diverse and the theatre offered fertile ground for social commentary and criticism. Novels by Eugène Sue, Frédéric Soulié and Balzac were adapted for the stage, giving audiences vivid images of the Parisian worlds of crime, poverty and prostitution. And in the social melodramas of Emile Souvestre and Félix Pyat, and the vehicles of the immensely popular actor Frédéric Lemaître – Robert Macaire, Vautrin and Le Chiffonnier de Paris – the villains were bankers and aristocrats and sometimes society itself.[110]

socialisme" in David Owen Evans, Le Socialisme romantique: Pierre Leroux et ses contemporains (Paris, 1948), 223.

[106] See E. R. Curtius, European Literature and the Latin Middle Ages (New York, 1963), 138–144; and Frances Yates, Theater of the World (Chicago, 1969).

[107] Maximilien Robespierre, "Speech of January 11, 1792" in Textes choisies, Jean Poperen (ed.), 3 vols. (Paris, 1973–1974), II, 150–152; Jean-Paul Marat, L'Ami du Peuple, 667 (July 7, 1792) in Paul H. Beik (ed.), The French Revolution. Selected Documents (New York, 1970), 217. For a rich overview, see Joseph Butwin, "The French Revolution as Theatrum Mundi," Research Studies, 43(3) (September 1975), 141–152.

[108] James R. Lehning, The Melodramatic Thread: Spectacle and Political Culture in Modern France (Bloomington, 2007), 24–30.

[109] Cheryl Kroen, Politics and Theater: The Crisis of Legitimacy in Restoration France 1815–1839 (Berkeley, 2000); Alain Corbin, "L'Agitation dans les théâtres de province sous la Restauration" in Le Temps, le désir et l'horreur. Essai sur le XIXe siècle (Paris, 1991), 53–79. Denise Z. Davidson, France after Revolution: Urban Life, Gender and the New Social Order (Cambridge, MA, 2007), 73–128.

[110] John McCormick, Popular Theatres of Nineteenth-Century France (London, 1993); Philippe Vigier, "Le Mélodrame social dans les années 1840," Europe: Revue littéraire mensuelle, 703–704 (November–December, 1987), 71–81; and Frederick Brown, Theater and Revolution: The Culture of the French Stage (New York, 1980), 83–131.

Theatrical imagery was current in journalism and historical writing throughout the July Monarchy. It became commonplace to describe contemporary history in theatrical terms – as comedy, tragedy, melodrama, or farce. After the February Revolution the use of such imagery exploded. In Dolf Oehler's words: "In 1848 the theatrical metaphor became the privileged means of characterizing the present moment."[111] Readers and writers could see themselves as actors or spectators in the revolutionary drama, and the great question was to determine what act was about to begin. Thus Marie d'Agoult asked in her *Lettres républicaines*, "Is this the last act of a political revolution?" or "Is it the tragic prologue to a social conflict?"[112] Alexander Herzen announced in *From the Other Shore* that "the fifth act of the tragedy began on February 24th", and Proudhon declared in his *Confessions* that with Cavaignac's declaration of a state of siege on June 23 the curtain had fallen on the fourth act of the revolution.[113] Finally, Marx could write after the fall of Vienna that "the second act of the drama has just ended. The first was played out in Paris under the title 'June Days.' ... We shall soon see the third act performed in Berlin."[114]

Sometimes theatrical imagery was used descriptively in the literature on 1848 without strong negative connotations. Proudhon could playfully address his readers: "You know, reader, the characters who ... are going to play the principal roles, you know the subject of the performance. Now listen attentively to what I am going to tell you."[115]

More often the theatrical metaphor was negative, and the revolution of 1848 was seen as an inept replay of the first French Revolution. This view of 1848 as bad theatre was widely held at the time: it made its way into cartoons and popular novels. Well known today are the derisive comments in Tocqueville's *Souvenirs*:

The men of the first revolution were alive in everyone's mind, their acts and words present in everyone's memory ... It seemed to me that they were acting out the French Revolution rather than continuing it ... It all looked to me like a vile tragedy performed by provincial actors.[116]

In Tocqueville's view, the theatricality of the principal actors in the revolution of 1848 was manifest above all in their preoccupation with models drawn from the first French Revolution. This was not only a

[111] Dolf Oehler, *Le Spleen contre l'oubli. Juin 1848* (Paris, 1996), 142.
[112] Stern, *Lettres républicaines*, VI, "Les Trois socialismes," July 8, 1848.
[113] Herzen, *From the Other Shore*, 79; Proudhon, *Confessions d'un révolutionnaire*, 166.
[114] Karl Marx, "The Victory of the Counter-Revolution in Vienna," *Neue Rheinische Zeitung*, 136 (November 7, 1949); MECW, VII, 505.
[115] Proudhon, *Confessions d'un révolutionnaire*, 85.   [116] Tocqueville, *Souvenirs*, 100.

matter of gestures, poses and dress – Ledru-Rollin imitating Danton; Marc Caussidière, the self-appointed police chief in 1848, dressing like a Montagnard of 1793. Institutions and rituals were also mimicked. On May 15, the insurgents seeking to set up a new Provisional Government marched to the Hôtel de Ville, imitating the conduct of the revolutionaries in February, who had themselves been imitating the revolutionaries of 1792. Five days later, on May 20, the Fête de la Fraternité was a direct imitation of the revolutionary festivals of 1789–1794. In all this, Tocqueville argued, the veneer of theatricality concealed from the 'forty-eighters "the terrible originality of the facts."[117] It blinded them to the need to take the steps necessary to secure liberty.

Marx's opening to *The Eighteenth Brumaire of Louis Bonaparte* makes an indictment of the theatricality of the 'forty-eighters that is even more famous than Tocqueville's:

Hegel remarks somewhere that all great world historical facts and personnages occur, as it were, twice. He has forgotten to add: the first time as tragedy, the second as farce, Caussidière for Danton, Louis Blanc for Robespierre, the Mountain of 1848 to 1851 for the Mountain of 1793 to 1795, the Nephew for the Uncle ... The Revolution of 1848 knew nothing better to do than to parody, in turn, 1789 and the revolutionary tradition of 1793 to 1795.[118]

The difference between the first French revolutionaries and the 1848ers, according to Marx, was that the former had invoked the Roman republican past in order to destroy feudalism. But the revolutionaries of 1848 were invoking 1789 to conceal from themselves the modesty of their goals. Far from seeking to overthrow capitalism, they only sought to widen the suffrage and to introduce republican institutions.

Marx and Tocqueville's critical use of the theatrical metaphor was hardly unique. The metaphor was common coin in 1848 and most often used to underline the limitations of the 'forty-eighters. Marie d'Agoult has harsh words for "the general mania, after February 24, to relate everything to our First Revolution." The metaphor was prominent in Proudhon's *Confessions d'un révolutionnaire* and also in his journalism which includes a critique of the "monkeys of the Mountain" whose brains are "encumbered" by "images and words from the past" and who "spill their blood for the useless pleasure of re-enacting a warmed-over farce of 1793."[119] Lamartine likewise describes Blanqui's club as a kind of "historical theatre" presenting "the dramas and parodies of another time performed by actors in outdated costumes."[120] Nobles

---

[117] Ibid.   [118] Marx, *Eighteenth Brumaire*, 13.
[119] Stern, *Histoire*, III, 56–57; Proudhon, *Confessions d'un révolutionnaire*, 13.
[120] Lamartine, *Histoire de la Révolution de 1848*, II, 149.

and bourgeois could attend the meetings of this club out of curiosity, knowing that there was nothing to fear from the "wailing" of these latter-day Babeufs and Marats. But the most elaborate literary treatment of this theme comes in *L'Education sentimentale* where the 'forty-eighters – starting with Sénécal, the "future Saint-Just" – are depicted as mimics of actors in the first French Revolution. Flaubert's narrative reaches a climax with Frédéric Moreau's visit to the misnamed Club de l'Intelligence in which "each person based himself on a model, one copying Saint-Just, the other Danton, another Marat," and yet another "trying to look like Blanqui, who was himself imitating Robespierre."[121]

All of these illustrations are examples of what Dominica Chang has aptly described as the "discourse of revolutionary mimicry," which she defines as "the predominantly negative critique that revolutionaries mindlessly imitated events from a scripted and therefore inauthentic and untrustworthy past."[122] This critique appears in the writing of both revolutionaries and counter-revolutionaries. We find it not only in Marx but also in Victor Hugo who, as he distanced himself from the Party of Order, was increasingly put off by the posturing of the Left. A favourite target for Hugo was Ledru-Rollin whom he described as "a kind of bastard Danton ... leaning on the podium with his fat stomach buttoned in," and mimicking Pétion's voice and Mirabeau's gestures without the eloquence.[123] Hugo returned to the subject often to register his disgust at revolutionary mimicry: "We can fall below Marat, below Couthon, below Carrier. How? By imitating them. They were horrible and grave. We'll be horrible and ridiculous. What, the Terror parodied! The guillotine plagiarized! Is there anything more hideous and more stupid? ... Ninety-three had its men. Now, fifty-five years later, it will have its monkeys."[124]

Sometimes revolutionary mimicry is contrasted explicitly with a call to serious revolutionary action. In Proudhon's words: "The democrats, seduced by memories of our glorious revolution, have wished to restart in 1848 the drama of 1789. While they are acting out a comedy, let us try to make history ... From my seat in the audience, I will leap on stage as a new actor."[125] Usually, the call to action is implicit. In any case, the

[121] Flaubert, *Education sentimentale*, 374.
[122] Dominica Chang, "Reading and Repeating the Revolutionary Script: Revolutionary Mimicry in Nineteenth-Century France" in Keith Michael Baker and Dan Edelstein (eds.), *Scripting Revolution: A Historical Approach to the Comparative Study of Revolutions* (Stanford, 2015), 181.
[123] Hugo, *Choses vues*, May–June 1848, *Oeuvres complètes Histoire*, Laffont, 1118.
[124] Hugo, *Choses vues*, May–June 1848, *OC Histoire*, Laffont, 1044.
[125] Proudhon, *Confessions d'un révolutionnaire*, 171.

result of the ridicule repeatedly heaped on the 'forty-eighters for mimicking 1793 was to discredit romantic conceptions of revolution.[126]

An issue confronting everyone who wrote about the revolution of 1848 was how to characterize "the people" in whose name the revolution had been made. Paeans to *le peuple* came easily to the 'forty-eighters. Marie d'Agoult was not at all exceptional in celebrating the people as "an eternal poet," nor was George Sand in writing shortly after the February Revolution: "I have seen the people great, sublime, naïve, generous!"[127] Still, our writers recognized that the concept was deeply problematic. They regarded the people as the ultimate source of democratic legitimacy. But who were *le peuple*? Did the term refer to the whole population? Or just the poor? Were the people actors in history or acted upon? Were the people defined by what they were, or by what they might become? Who did *not* belong to the people?

No contemporary took these issues more seriously than Jules Michelet. His hugely influential *Le Peuple* (1846) is a searching, deeply personal, and at times exasperating exploration of the effects of the social dislocations of the post-revolutionary period on peasants, artisans, shopkeepers, bureaucrats, and the rest of France. His aim was to specify the common impulses, instincts and forms of association that might bring together a divided society. Michelet is anything but consistent in his use of the concept of the people. Often, he argues that the great division in French society is between the bourgeoisie and the people."[128] But he sometimes speaks of the people as constituting the whole society.[129] In any case, there is one quality that Michelet's *peuple* indisputably possess: *chaleur vitale*. This vital warmth or energy distinguishes them from the cultured upper classes.[130]

In the formal histories by Lamartine and d'Agoult, the term *le peuple* usually refers to the lower classes. In her Introduction d'Agoult describes the proclamation of a democratic republic on February 24 as the result of an "involuntary accord of the bourgeoisie and the people." This, she says, was the "logical consequence" of the efforts of the educated classes (*classes lettrées*) to obtain freedom of thought and the struggle of the

---

[126] Dominica Chang, "Revolutionary Mimicry," 181.

[127] Stern, *Histoire*, I, 141; Sand to Charles Poncy, March 8, 1848, *Correspondance*, VIII, 330.

[128] Jules Michelet, *Le Peuple* (Paris, 1965), 146: "Ancient France was divided into three classes; the new France has only two – the people and the bourgeoisie."

[129] Michelet, *Histoire de la Révolution française*, 2 vols. (Paris: Pléiade, 1961), I, 77: "The convocation of the Estates general of 1789 was the true moment of the birth of the people. It summoned the whole people to the exercise of its rights."

[130] Michelet, *Le Peuple*, 71.

"laborious classes" to gain freedom of action.[131] Three years later, in her third and final volume, d'Agoult substitutes "proletariat" for "people" The February Revolution was "provoked," she writes, "by the common action of the proletariat and the bourgeoisie."[132] Lamartine's conception of *le peuple* is more opaque. In the long run, he argues, the story of the people is a success story: it is the story of "the emergence of the masses" as an autonomous political force. But what is essential in Lamartine's telling of this story is his account of his own role in guiding and moderating the people and encouraging them to follow the leadership of "a few men" (like himself) willing to risk "calumny, exhaustion and death for the salvation of all."[133]

George Sand's writing on and for *le peuple*, which lacked the self-promoting asides and the underlying narcissism of Lamartine's, has already been discussed. Suffice it to say that Sand's admiration for the people, boundless in February, underwent a series of shocks between April and June. Initially, she believed in the transparency of democratic politics. If the people had their say through elected representatives, a consensus would emerge around the best idea. But after June she concluded that "we were not ready for the Republic" and "the people were not with us."[134] When the people voted massively for Louis Napoleon Bonaparte on December 10, 1849, she made a public confession:

Of all the men and all the political parties that I have observed over the past forty years, I confess that I have not been able to identify myself exclusively with any of them. Apart from all these men and parties, there was always an abstract and collective being, *the people*, to whom I could devote myself unreservedly. Well, even if the people act stupidly, I will do for them in my heart what political people do for their party through their acts: I will endorse their follies and accept their errors.[135]

For the rest of her life Sand remained convinced that in 1848 she, like many others, had failed to understand the extent to which "the people" – both peasants and city dwellers – were caught up in their daily struggles and unable to respond to the leadership of writers and intellectuals like herself. In her autobiography she presents herself as sadder and wiser: "I have witnessed a campaign in the world of action and am no longer the same as before. I have lost the youthful illusions that my privileged life of reclusive contemplation had allowed me to hold longer than one reasonably should."[136]

---

[131] Stern, *Histoire*, I, ii.   [132] Stern, *Histoire*, III, 263.   [133] Lamartine, *Histoire*, I, 388.
[134] Sand to Marc Dufraisse, July 4, 1848, *Correspondance*, XXV, 579.
[135] Sand, *La Réforme*, December 22, 1848, in *Politique et polémiques*, 566–567.
[136] Sand, "*Histoire de ma vie*" in *Oeuvres autobiographiques*, Georges Lubin (ed.), 2 vols. (Paris, 1970), I, 465.

The concept of the people looms large in the work of both Hugo and Proudhon. Each of the four journals published by Proudhon during the Second Republic includes the word *peuple* in its title; and in *L'Idée générale de la Révolution au XIXe siècle* (1851) he declares: "The people is the god that inspires true philosophers."[137] The word occurs often in the *Confessions d'un révolutionnaire* in passages in which Proudhon calls on the "disinherited, wounded, proscribed people" to reject promises of salvation coming from higher authorities in church and government.[138] But there are also passages in which Proudhon writes as a seeker rather than a preacher and appears to be inspired by Michelet to work out his own conceptions of collective instinct and popular spontaneity. "All revolutions," he writes, "have been accomplished by the spontaneity of the people." Change comes not from above by governments but from an "immanent and perpetual motivating force" that is rooted in the instincts of the people. Sometimes this force provokes a revolutionary explosion, and experience shows that "any revolution, to be successful, must be spontaneous and must emerge from the entrails of the people and not from above."[139]

The people are everywhere in Hugo's writing, and there is never any doubt as to who they are. They are eternal victims. Hugo tells and retells their story – from *Claude Gueux* and *Ruy Blas* to *Les Misérables* – and it is always more or less the same story. Ground down by circumstances, the people are driven to crime or prostitution, and more often than not, they end badly. In the hands of an inflexible policemen like Javert, the law becomes the instrument of their downfall: it drives them deeper into criminality. If they ever discover the way out, it is too late. Hugo's people endure their own history: they do not make it. He could write in *Les Misérables* that June 1848 was "a revolt of the people against itself."[140]

Four of our writers reject or ignore the cult of the people: Tocqueville, Marx, Herzen and Flaubert. For the political liberal and social conservative Tocqueville, the rule of the people was not to be celebrated but feared. There are numerous indications of this in the *Souvenirs* – Tocqueville's account of his relations with his porter, for example, and the chapters on the role of the people in May and June – and his pages on

[137] Proudhon, *Idée générale de la Révolution au XIXe siècle*, 286.
[138] Proudhon, *Confessions d'un révolutionnaire*, 166.
[139] Ibid, 82, 94, 118. See also Simone Bernard-Griffiths and Alain Pessin (eds.), *Peuple, mythe et histoire* (Toulouse, 1997), 65–76 and 77–91.
[140] Hugo, *Les Misérables*, II, 409. In *Les Misérables* Hugo writes that it is mistaken to treat the bourgeoisie as a class because "the bourgeoisie is quite simply the contented portion of the people." See *Les Misérables*, II, 12.

"the tyranny of the majority" in *La Démocratie en Amérique*.[141] As for Marx and Herzen, each saw a different locus for the hopes that others invested in the people. For Marx it was the economically defined proletariat that carried the hope of the future and not the amorphous people. For Herzen, the future belonged not to the people in general, but to the Russian people.

Flaubert detested the cult of the people. Although he appreciated Victor Hugo, he scoffed at the "childish" celebration of the people in *Les Misérables*.[142] The idea of the people is as dead as that of the monarchy, he wrote Louise Colet, adding that he would like to see both "thrown down the toilet."[143] In *L'Education sentimentale* the people are represented either as an unruly mob, or as an object of mixed curiosity and fear. Consider the passage (discussed in Chapter 10) in which Frederick and Hussonet watch the people racing up the stairs of the Tuileries Palace on February 24 "in a bewildering flood of bare heads, hats, red caps, bayonets, and shoulders."[144] Here the people are a faceless and "bewildering" collection of body parts and articles of clothing driven forward by a process as blind as a spring tide or the flowing of a river. Natural imagery is used throughout the novel to characterize the interventions of the people; their revolution is portrayed as a natural upheaval, and its main consequence is to unleash wild, uncontrollable forces. The people, when caught up in revolution, become such an elemental force.

If our writers did not speak with one voice about what went wrong in 1848, it is clear that the revolution of 1848 was not the turning point, the opening of a new world, that most of them had been looking for. What is also clear, however, is that 1848 was a turning point in their lives. For all of them, as we have seen, the experience of 1848 was life-changing. It drove three of them out of politics altogether. In 1849 Lamartine still had twenty years to live, but his political career was finished. Sand's withdrawal came earlier: even before the June Days, she had retreated to Nohant. Subsequently, she continued to correspond with political friends. But her days as an activist were over. As for Tocqueville, he remained active in politics until the end of the Second Republic. But his

---

[141] Tocqueville, *Souvenirs*, 238–240; André Gain (ed.), *De la Démocratie en Amérique*, 2 vols. (Paris, 1951), II, 430–439. [II, iv, 6]

[142] Flaubert to Edma Roger de Genettes, July 1862, *Correspondance*, III, 235–237: "This book is made for the catholico-socialist scum [*crapule*], for all the philosophico-evangelic vermin."

[143] Flaubert to Louise Colet, May 26, 1853, *Correspondance*, II, 336.

[144] Flaubert, *L'Education sentimentale*, 289–290. For the full passage, see Chapter 9 above.

tenure as Foreign Minister in 1849 was anything but glorious, and the coup d'état of Louis-Napoleon drove him back to his study.

For the others 1848 was a life-changing experience in a more positive way. It brought Hugo into republican politics and made a democrat of him. He took to exile as a duck to water, and from his battle station on the Channel Islands, he made himself into a living symbol of the republican ideal. The revolution brought Marie d'Agoult into moderate republican politics and political journalism and launched her career as a *femme de lettres*. 1848 enabled Proudhon, initially a critic of the February Revolution, to find a voice, first as spokesman for the workers of the Parisian faubourgs and eventually for workers all over France. And in making London exile permanent for both Herzen and Marx, it launched them both on new careers. It was in London that Alexander Herzen became the voice of "Free Russia," the theorist of a native Russian socialism, and the author of a great *European* autobiography. It was also in London that Karl Marx became the author of *Capital*.

Then there is Flaubert. At first glance, it might seem that the Second Republic simply passed him by. In 1848 he had other priorities. But if in the short run 1848 was not the life-changing experience for him that it was for our other writers, it was an experience that he felt he had to understand. For the collapse of the illusions of the 1840s – and of the *sentimentalisme* that underlay the illusions – defined the world that he entered as a writer. He came to see the revolution of 1848 as the formative experience of his generation, and it was in an effort to make sense of that experience that he wrote *L'Education sentimentale*. One can argue that Flaubert never got out of the shadow of 1848. His lifelong disgust with politics, his cult of art, his attempt to write like an unseen God – all this can be seen as an effort to carve out for himself a realm of meaningful activity in a world disfigured by the compromises and vulgarity of the new age of mass politics.

Conclusion

Among French revolutions, 1848 enjoys a modest reputation. The Great French Revolution of 1789–1794 continues to provoke arguments among the general public as well as historians, and the Paris Commune of 1871 remains an inspiration to political activists. Even the revolution of July 1830 may be better remembered than 1848, if only because of Delacroix's magnificent painting, *Liberty Guiding the People*. T. J. Clark has written a fascinating essay exploring the reasons for the failure of the Second Republic to produce a remotely comparable image, and Marie d'Agoult was already reflecting on the problem when she wrote in

1851 of "the absolute incapacity of the arts to create the image, the tangible form, of an idea which is no longer, or not yet, alive in the minds of ordinary people."[145] Indeed, the one memorable image to come out of the Second French Republic was not an image of the Republic but rather the image of the Bonapartist con man, Ratapoil (see Figure 9.3).

The French have always been fond of anniversaries, and over the years three French republics have diligently celebrated anniversaries of 1848. A Société d'histoire de la Révolution de 1848 was founded in 1904 to keep alive the memory of the revolution. Its journal, originally called *La Révolution de 1848*, flourishes, though now under the broader title of *Revue d'histoire du XIXe siècle*[146]. But until late in the twentieth century, the most widely read general study of the revolutions of 1848 may have been Lewis Namier's entertaining but tendentious screed, *1848: The Revolution of the Intellectuals* (1944) in which intellectuals, and especially Polish intellectuals, are presented as unhinged dreamers. Even today, insofar as 1848 is remembered by a wider public, it is probably not through any academic study but through extracts from works that we have been discussing here – notably those by Tocqueville, Marx and Flaubert.

In the academic world, the image of the French Revolution of 1848 has been transformed in the past fifty years. The impetus for this transformation was provided by Maurice Agulhon. I have already observed that most historians now accept Agulhon's view of the Second French Republic as a period of "apprenticeship" in which the ideal of a democratic republic acquired a significant following and lessons were learned that made possible the creation of lasting democratic institutions after 1870. The secularization of the Third Republic, the emphasis on education as the key to the development of republican consciousness, the desire to make a place in politics for the hopes and needs of the working poor – in these and other respects the republic of Gambetta and Jules Ferry is now seen as the heir to the republic of Ledru-Rollin and Louis Blanc.

But when one considers the representations of 1848 in the texts we have considered, a different picture emerges. There is a pervasive sense

[145] T. J. Clark, *The Absolute Bourgeois: Artists and Politics in France 1848–1851* (Greenwich, CT, 1973), 31–71; Stern, *Histoire*, II, 348.
[146] For valuable historiographical surveys, see Francis Démier and Jean-Luc Mayaud (eds.), "Cinquante ans de recherches sur 1848," Special Issue of *Revue d'histoire du XIXe siècle*, XIV(1) (1997); and Jean-Luc Mayaud (ed.), *1848: Actes du Colloque Internationale du Cent Cinquantenaire* (Paris, 2002). For a fascinating, highly personal review of recent approaches to 1848 written with an eye to the resonance of the historian's present, see Edward Castleton, "Introduction" to special issue on 1848 of *Revue d'études proudhoniennes*, V (2019), 5–33.

444   Aftermath: Themes and Conclusion

of disappointment with the people, events and institutions of the Second
Republic. And the overall assessment is uniformly devastating. Marx's
characterization of 1848 as a farcical and involuntary parody of 1789 is
echoed not only by Tocqueville but also by Flaubert, Hugo, Proudhon,
Herzen and Marie d'Agoult. The key difference is that while contemporaries saw 1848 as a failure, modern historians have had more to say about
the accomplishments of the revolutionaries. They have done this by
shifting the focus from Paris to the provinces, from politics to social
and cultural history, and from the first four months to the whole four-
year history of the Second Republic. They have studied the development
of the democratic-socialist movement in a coordinated campaign for the
legislative elections of May 1849 and the spread of a network of democratic clubs and workers' associations from the cities to the countryside.[147] Some of these studies have focused on national trends; others
on particular regions. Margadant has shown how and why significant
resistance to Louis-Napoleon Bonaparte's coup d'état of December 2,
1851, came not from Paris but from peasants and artisans in two dozen
scattered rural departments, whereas Agulhon's *La République au village*
is a meticulous study of the process by which the intertwining of republican politics with popular culture served to radicalize ordinary people in
a single *département*, the Var.[148]

This work leads in important directions. In retrospect, it is evident that
French political life was transformed by the emergence of the *démoc-soc*
movement after June. But for contemporary intellectuals, the history of
the Second Republic was above all a history of disappointment, defeat,
and exile. To be sure, Lamartine's vision of a conservative republic could
be seen as an anticipation of the Third Republic, and Marie d'Agoult
concluded her history by arguing that the experience of the Second
Republic had brought France nearer the democratic and republican
ideal. There are also moments in *Napoléon le petit* when Hugo looks
forward to a parliamentary republic that would draw on the experience
of the Second Republic. But none of our writers grasped the long-term
consequences of the emergence of "Red France." For all of them, the
experience of 1848–1852 was primarily an experience of failure and loss.

---

[147] Berenson, *Populist Religion and Left-Wing Politics*, 74–224. See also McPhee, *Politics of
Rural Life*, 106–259.

[148] Margadant, *French Peasants in Revolt*; Agulhon, *La République au village: Les populations
du Var de la Révolution à la IIe République* (Paris, 1970). Also important here are
numerous books and articles by John Merriman, from *The Agony of the Republic: The
Repression of the Left in Revolutionary France* (New Haven, 1978) to *History on the
Margins: People and Places in the Emergence of Modern France* (Lincoln, NE, 2018).

Why should we care about attempts to explain a failure? One reason is that in their efforts to understand 1848, our writers posed, sometimes eloquently, questions about politics and history that continue to engage us. First, there is the question of the role played by memory in both constituting and stunting movements for change. Can those who seek to change the world ever escape the weight of the past? Under what conditions can the appeal to the past reinforce or cripple movements for change? As we have seen, Marx was famously concerned with such questions. So was Herzen, whose critique of French radicals cantered around their inability to emancipate themselves from inherited traditions. And so was Flaubert, for whom memory, whether individual or collective, repeatedly appears in *L'Education sentimentale* as an instrument of deception, and generally self-deception.[149]

There is also the question of the pervasive role of fear in 1848. As Gareth Stedman Jones has observed, memories of the Terror, persistent nightmares about "dangerous classes," and the "spectre of communism" haunted the political imagination in 1848.[150] In her 1848 writings we find George Sand constantly striving to allay fears – the fears of the rich, the peasants, the city-dwellers. In almost every case the fear is for the loss of property. D'Agoult's *Histoire* includes an extensive section on the "retrospective terror" of the bourgeoisie in the aftermath of the June Days; and a discussion of the fears of "the lettered and wealthy class" stands at the centre of her analysis of the fragility of democracy throughout the Second Republic.[151] Flaubert was fascinated by the seemingly limitless capacity of the affluent to believe the most absurd rumours concerning the lower orders. Both *L'Education sentimentale* and *Bouvard et Pécuchet* are full of stories of imagined plots and of panic attacks on the part of people who actually have nothing to fear. Tocqueville has much to say about rumour and exaggeration – especially among his friends and relatives. But his *Souvenirs* also include vivid details about his own fears. Finally, references to fear are ubiquitous in Lamartine's *Histoire*. He justifies the rejection of a regency and his initial support of the right to work as necessary given the threat of popular violence at the outset of the revolution. And he returns often to the danger posed by criminal elements in the Paris crowd – the "ignorant, rootless and disoriented" rabble.[152]

---

[149] Frederick's escapist fantasies at Fontainebleau are a case in point, as is the facile bonding that takes place at the end of the novel as Frederick and Deslauriers console each other for their wasted lives. The mindless evocation of a revolutionary past by self-styled radicals like Sénécal is just one more example of the deceptive use of memory.
[150] Stedman Jones, *Karl Marx*, 312.   [151] Stern, *Histoire*, III, 271–273 and II, 13.
[152] Stern, *Histoire*, III, 271–273; Flaubert, *L'Education sentimentale*, 340–344; Tocqueville, *Souvenirs*, 239–240; Lamartine, *Histoire de la Révolution de 1848* I, 208–209, 339,

But the most pressing questions confronting our nine writers concerned politics. In their writings we can watch them testing and questioning the shibboleths of liberal constitutionalism. They were intensely eager to understand the nature, forms and limits of the democratic republic, and they sought ways to introduce a concern with social issues into the discussion of political problems. The fundamental question was how to give substance to popular sovereignty. For a few weeks in 1848, Michèle Riot-Sarcey writes, "insurgents believed they had it in their power to put into practice the idea of the sovereignty of the people."[153] When, and how, would the people be able to govern themselves? This question, which underlay our writers' seemingly endless appeals to "the people," was asked repeatedly by George Sand in the spring of 1848. Her initial response was positive. But after May 15, she lost hope. "The people are not ready to govern themselves," she wrote Mazzini on June 15.[154] She made the same point, in slightly different words, in a dozen letters written in the aftermath of the June Days.

Then there is the related question of universal suffrage. This was a revolutionary idea in 1848. It inspired extravagant hopes and was hailed as marking the dawn of an era of class harmony. Lamartine could even declare in March that with universal suffrage there would be "no more proletarians in France."[155] Of course, "universal" suffrage was not universal. Women were denied the right to vote. There were in 1848 groups of French feminists who created their own clubs. journals and schools and argued eloquently for women's suffrage.[156] But they got no support from either George Sand or Marie d'Agoult. Both Sand and d'Agoult maintained that the important issues for women at the time had to do with marriage and the family and the legal rights of wives, not with the suffrage.

Universal suffrage was contested on other grounds as well. Prior to the voting, Proudhon could already assert that the influence of provincial elites and "the priests" guaranteed a conservative outcome; and after the results were in, he fastidiously analyzed "the mystification of universal suffrage."[157] Critics of universal suffrage focused on its links to two ideas

---

[153] Michèle Riot-Sarcey, *Le Procès de la liberté. Une histoire souterraine du XIXᵉ siècle en France* (Paris, 2016), 20.

[154] Sand to Mazzini, June 15, 1848, *Correspondance*, VIII, 513.

[155] *Bulletin de la République* 4 (March 19, 1848) in Pierre Rosanvallon, *Le Sacre du citoyen: Histoire du suffrage universel en France* (Paris, 1992), 286.

[156] Michèle Riot-Sarcey, *La Démocratie à l'épreuve des femmes: Trois figures critiques du pouvoir 1830–1848* (Paris, 1994).

[157] Proudhon, "La Réaction" and "Mystification du Suffrage universel," April 29 and 30, 1848, in *Mélanges: Articles de journaux 1848–1852* (Paris, 1868) I, 11–22.

that were not at all revolutionary. First, a concept of *representation* which marginalized the sovereign people once an election was over. Could the people be adequately represented by an elected national assembly? The issue became urgent on May 31, 1850, when the conservative majority in the Assembly, frightened by radical electoral successes, passed a new electoral law that disenfranchised three million citizens.[158] Also linked to universal suffrage was a concept of *citizenship* which made the right to vote the most sacred right of the citizen and the full and complete expression of the citizen's power. Most of our writers, like the vast majority of newly enfranchised voters, subscribed to such a purely electoral view of citizenship. They believed that to attack a representative assembly elected by universal manhood suffrage was to place one's self above the law.[159]

But the question of how to give substance to popular sovereignty was inescapable. Weren't there other ways to participate in government beside voting? And didn't the February Revolution offer something more than the vote to all adult males? Didn't it also offer the right to work? Popular sovereignty was seen by members of the working class as including the recognition of this other right, more sacred than the right to vote. But what was actually entailed in the right to work? What did this term mean? And how could it be translated into practical terms? Did its proclamation constitute a recognition, on the part of the Provisional Government, of the need to confront the problem of endemic poverty and unemployment among the urban working class? Was it a guarantee of employment? Did its recognition entail a denial of the rights of property? As Thomas Bouchet has shown, there was no agreement about these issues, even among the socialist supporters of the right to work.[160] Whereas Louis Blanc favoured a state-based political program, Proudhon argued that the implementation of the right to work must be realized by the workers themselves through their associations. Finally, the right to work might best be seen in Françoise Mélonio's terms as "less a clear-cut juridical concept than the legitimation by a constitutional text of a kind of utopia, the desire felt by workers for a better life."[161]

[158] Pierre Rosanvallon, *Le sacre du citoyen: Histoire du suffrage universel en France* (Paris, 1992), 302–307.

[159] Anne-Sophie Chambost, "Socialist Visions of Direct Democracy: The Mid-Century Crisis of Popular Sovereignty and the Constitutional Legacy of the Jacobins" in Moggach and Stedman Jones (eds.), *The 1848 Revolutions*, 102.

[160] Thomas Bouchet, "Socialist Vicissitudes on the Right to Work in France, 1848–1851," *French History*, XXXIII(4) (2019), 572–586.

[161] Françoise Mélonio, "Le Droit au travail ou le travail de l'utopie" in *La Constitution du 4 novembre 1848: l'ambition d'une république démocratique* (Dijon, 2000), 204. See also

The key moment at which questions of popular sovereignty and the rights of citizens came to a head was the June insurrection, which was touched off by the decision to suspend the National Workshops. These National Workshops were understood by many Paris workers as a means of guaranteeing the right to work and creating a "democratic and social republic." But for most members of the Provisional Government, they were simply a short-term expedient, a means of buying time.[162] Neither Marx nor Proudhon – nor Louis Blanc – regarded the National Workshops as a serious effort to guarantee the right to work: Proudhon told the Paris workers that the Provisional Government "tricked you" by making "a promise that it was unable to keep."[163] But Marx and Proudhon were almost unique among European radicals in standing together with the insurgents in June. They saw the insurgents as in some ways misguided but as defending their conception of a democratic and social republic in which the right to work mattered even more than the right to vote.

Proudhon's most dramatic gesture of solidarity with the insurgents came shortly after the June Days. He never fully approved of the June revolt. But, as we have seen, his public support of the insurgents provoked the comment "It's June 23rd at the rostrum" and made him the object, on July 31, of a formal vote of censure.[164] Karl Marx's gesture of support for the June insurgents was less spectacular than Proudhon's, but it separated Marx from radicals throughout the German-speaking world. While they saw the June revolt as an appalling attempt to overthrow a democratically elected assembly, Marx praised it as the work of "plebians tormented by hunger." "It is the *right* and the privilege of the democratic press," he concluded, "to place laurels on their dark, threatening brows."[165]

How did our other writers respond to the June revolt? Tocqueville's response was brutal. For him "the insurrection was of such a nature that

Francis Démier, "Droit au travail et organization du travail en 1848" in Mayaud (ed.), *1848, actes du colloque*, 159–183.

[162] Mark Traugott, "Les ateliers nationaux en 1848" in Mayaud (ed.), *1848, actes du colloque*, 185–202; Donald McKay, *The National Workshops: A Study in the French Revolution of 1848* (Cambridge, MA, 1933), 11–13.

[163] Proudhon, *Confessions*, 167.

[164] See above Chapter 7, p. 257. Earlier, on June 28, the Assembly had already passed a resolution condemning Proudhon's "savage doctrines" as a cause of the June insurrection. See Proudhon, *Carnets*, III, 66. (June 25, 1848); Pierre Haubtmann, *Pierre-Joseph Proudhon, sa vie et sa pensée, 1809–1849* (Paris, 1982), 896, 918–920; Edouard Dolléans and J.-L. Puech, *Proudhon et la révolution de 1848* (Paris, 1948), 52–60.

[165] Karl Marx, "The June Revolution," NRZ 29 (June 29, 1848); MECW, VII, 144–149.

any understanding with it became impossible immediately, and from the first it left us with no other choice but to destroy it or perish."[166] Such blunt language would not have been used by Lamartine or Hugo. But they too condemned the insurrection as an attack on the authority of a democratically elected republican government. In their eyes, it was an attempt to overthrow the Republic. For them, as for most republicans, the exercise of popular sovereignty began and ended with the casting of a vote. They had little interest in the right to work and did not support its inclusion in the constitution.[167]

It is striking, however, to note the ambivalence and uncertainty, even bewilderment, displayed by some of our writers in their later comments on the June Days. Hugo, the only one to take arms against the insurgents, was later deeply ambivalent about his own role in June. He never ceased trying to make sense of the insurrection and to answer the question of its legitimacy. But his attempts at a conclusive assessment are contorted: "What at bottom was June 1848? A revolt of the people against itself."[168] In the end, Hugo's response seems not unlike that of Flaubert's Dussardier who joined his National Guard unit in June to put down the insurrection but was later "tormented by the idea that he might have been fighting against a just cause."[169] Marie d'Agoult's doubts were similar.. She believed at the time that the insurrection had to be put down. During and after the June Days she gave Cavaignac her full support. But in writing the final volume of her History, she could describe the insurrection as an attempt on the part of "the proletariat" to "reclaim" a right given and then taken away: "What gave the June insurrection its power and its incredible duration ... is that at its origin and until the very end it had, in the minds of many, the character of a just protest against the violation of a right."[170]

Much more could be said about the issues raised by our writers. But I want to conclude with a comment on the language and tone of the texts. What makes these commentaries on 1848 worth coming back to, I think, is not only the brilliant originality of a few of them but the sense of the *immediacy* of the experience of 1848 that one finds in *all* of them. Except

[166] Tocqueville, *Souvenirs*, 223.
[167] In the debate on the constitution in September 1848, Tocqueville attacked the right to work as a step toward socialism; Lamartine defined the right to work in terms so vague as almost to identify it with the right to public assistance; and Hugo did not participate in the discussion or vote on the right to work. Tocqueville, "Discours sur la question du droit au travail," September 12, 1848, *Ecrits et discours politiques*, III, 167–180. On Lamartine and Hugo see Thomas Bouchet, *Un Jeudi à l'Assemblée: Politiques du discours et droit au travail dans la France de 1848* (Québec, 2007), 73–82, 159–167.
[168] Hugo, *Les Misérables*, II, 408. [169] Flaubert, *L'Education sentimentale*, 337.
[170] Stern, *Histoire*, III, 155–156.

of course for *L'Education sentimentale*, these writings on 1848 were written during the course of events, as the future was still unfolding. The
views of our writers were not yet shaped by later perspectives. Their
hopes and fears were near the surface. Even Lamartine seems to have
been imagining a new life in politics as he wrote his History of 1848.
Marie d'Agoult was torn between her realistic observations and her
hopes for a lasting republic. And Tocqueville was still too close to the
situation to resist discharging "pints of accumulated bile" in his
Souvenirs.[171]

The events of 1848–1851 led some of our writers to question their
most cherished views. Consider Marx's thinking about revolution. In
February 1848 Marx believed that a process had been set in motion that
would culminate in proletarian revolution.[172] But the "lesson" that he
was eventually to draw from 1848 and its aftermath was that many more
years of industrial growth would be necessary before there could be any
talk of revolution. Still, as late as March 1850, with the victories of three
radical candidates in Parisian bi-elections, Marx could write that "the
moral influence of capital is broken" and that the bourgeois republic had
"entered the phase of its dissolution."[173]

Four of our other writers underwent major intellectual transformations
in the years 1848–1852. In the correspondence of George Sand, the
articles of Proudhon, the speeches of Victor Hugo, and the essays of
Alexander Herzen, we have watched intellectual identities being tried on
or rejected. We have witnessed the collapse of George Sand's faith in
"the people" and the growth of Proudhon's identification with the cause
of the artisans of the *faubourgs*. Similarly, we have observed both
Herzen's rejection of the republican ideal and the protracted process by
which Hugo came to inhabit the role of the quintessential republican. In
each of these cases, the revolution of 1848 initiated a process of self-
criticism and self-discovery that was life-changing.

Neither Lamartine nor Tocqueville went through major intellectual
changes during the Second Republic. But their stories contrast in
important ways. After 1848 Lamartine lapsed into a state of intellectual
somnolence that persisted until his death two decades later. Tocqueville,
on the other hand, was forced by 1848 to bring into sharper relief his
reflections on the necessary moral and cultural foundations of democratic self-government and to try to understand the root cause of the
inability of the French to create a viable liberal polity. After 1848 he
became increasingly convinced of the need to understand the

---

[171] Brogan, *Tocqueville*, 488.   [172] See above Chapter 9, p. 344.
[173] Marx, *Class Struggles*, 127–129; MECW, X, 128–130.

revolutionary mentality. But in the end, and despite the remarkable achievement of *L'Ancien Régime et la Révolution française*, he could only attribute the "immoderate, violent, radical, desperate, audacious, almost crazy but powerful and efficacious" character of modern revolution to "a *virus* of a new and unknown kind."[174]

Do these texts speak to us today? Lamartine's History may be primarily interesting for what it reveals about its author. But George Sand's correspondence, Hugo's speeches, Proudhon's articles, and Herzen's memoirs open up whole worlds. In their very different ways, Marx, Flaubert and Tocqueville have made 1848 alive for modern readers. If Marie d'Agoult is not widely read now, her work was a source for other accounts, starting with Flaubert's. All these works explore suggestively the causes and consequences of the failure of the democratic republic in 1848–1852. And most of them have, at moments, a startling contemporary resonance. There are worse places to go, I think, if we are to begin to understand the failures of democratic politics in our own time.

---

[174] Tocqueville to Louis de Kergorlay, May 16, 1858, *Correspondance Tocqueville-Kergorlay*, 2 vols. (Paris, 1977), OC XIII, ii, 337.

Glossary

Banquet Campaign:	Protest against suffrage restrictions of the July Monarchy which took the form of banquets in order to avoid laws against political meetings.
Committee of the rue de Poitiers:	The heart of the Party of Order. Conservative grouping of Orleanists, Legitimists and Bonapartists, which gained two-thirds of the vote in legislative elections of May 13, 1849.
Constituent Assembly:	Elected on April 23, 1848 to draw up a constitution for the Republic. Replaced by the *Legislative Assembly* in May 1849.
Démoc-socs:	Democratic socialists. Coalition of left-wing groups that took shape at the end of 1848 with the formation of a national federation of radical political clubs. Through their newspapers, clubs and pamphlets, they created a movement that brought peasants, artisans and professional people together around an ideology that fused socialism and democratic politics.
Dynastic Opposition:	Group of Orleanist deputies led by Odilon Barrot who constituted the "official" (sanctioned) opposition to Guizot under the July Monarchy. After the repeated rejection of their proposals for a wider suffrage, they organized the "banquet campaign" that, contrary to their intentions, brought down the July Monarchy

Elysée Palace:	Residence of the President of the Republic.
Executive Commission:	Short-lived governing body, replacing Provisional Government May 10, 1848 but forced to resign on June 24 with outbreak of the workers' insurrection.
Journée:	A day of revolutionary protest
July Monarchy:	The constitutional monarchy of Louis Philippe (1830–1848), so named for its origin in the insurrection of July 1830 against the Bourbon monarchy of Charles X.
Legitimists:	Royalist supporters of the senior branch of the Bourbons, headed by le comte de Chambord.
Luxembourg Commission:	Created February 28 to consider plans for the organization of work and to regulate labor disputes. Led by Louis Blanc. Dissolved May 16.
Luxembourg Palace:	Site of the Chamber of Peers, then of the Luxembourg Commission.
Mobile Guard:	A full-time, fully mobilized force of (mostly) young men of working-class origin, designed to supplement the police and the National Guard in maintaining order.
Mountain, montagnards:	Radical republicans who sat high up on benches of Convention in 1792–1794. This tradition was revived in 1848, and during the Second Republic the Montagnards became the most outspoken representatives of the democratic left.
National Guard:	Citizen's militia, founded in 1789. Originally limited to relatively wealthy, opened to all adult males in 1848.
National Workshops:	Program created by the Provisional Government to provide work for the unemployed. Presented as a means of guaranteeing the "right to work," but

regarded by moderates in the Provisional Government as a temporary expedient. The announcement of its suspension on June 21 touches off the workers' insurrection.

Orleanists: Supporters of the Orleanist dynasty of King Louis Philippe and the constitutional monarchy of 1830–1848.

Palais Bourbon: Meeting place of the National Assembly.

Party of Order: Coalition of conservative groups and movements claiming to stand for three principles: Religion, Family and Property and united by their opposition to the democratic and socialist left.

Provisional Government: Assumes power during the February Revolution and organizes elections for a Constituent Assembly. Replaced by Executive Commission May 10, 1848.

"Red France": Portion of rural France (especially in the Centre and the East) that voted for radical republican and démoc-soc candidates in the legislative elections of May 13, 1849. These areas were to remain radical well into the history of the Third Republic.

Representatives of the People: Members of the National Assembly.

Républicains de la veille: Republicans prior to February 1848.

Républicains du lendemain: Republicans after February 1848.

Society of December 10: Both a support group and a fighting force for Louis-Napoleon Bonaparte during his tours of the provinces in 1850 and 1851. Marx saw it as constituting a Praetorian Guard for the would-be emperor.

Index

Page numbers for illustrations are in *italics*, and for glossary entries are in **bold**.

siege (cont.)
  Marx on, 357
  prolongation of, 185
  Tocqueville and, 214, 238
silkweavers (*canuts*), 26, 28–31, 83–4, 257, 336
Simon, Antoine, 53
Sismondi, Jean Charles Léonard de, 128
skepticism, 306–9
slavery, abolition of, 175
Sobrier, Joseph, 64–5, 247
social class. *See* class, social
social question, 2–3, 30, 33, 248–9
socialism, 33–6, 142, 402–3
  as cause of revolution, 234
  and Christianity, 35–6, 430–3
  collapse of, 270
  criticism of, 248
  feminist, 34
  fictional representation of, 394–6
  history of, 405–6
  libertarian, 270–1
  opposition to, 61, 64
  repression of, 5
  romantic, 33–5
  Russian, 278–9, 417–18
  Sand's support for, 84–7
  state, 248
  Tocqueville and, 207–8
Société d'histoire de la Révolution de 1848, 443
Society of December 10, 356, **454**
solidarity, 229
  cross-class, 94–5, 148–9, 237
  lack of, 10
Soulié, Frédéric, 434
Souvestre, Emile, 434
sovereignty
  national, 24–5
  popular, 445–8
Sperber, Jonathan, 333, 336, 421
Speshnev, Nikolai, 257
state
  Marx on, 344
  rational, 321–3
  socialism, 248
Stedman Jones, Gareth, 318, 321, 445
Stern, Daniel. *See* Agoult, Marie d'
strikes, 28–30
style, 429–42
  allegories, 386–9
  allusions, 343
  characterization, 73
  chiasmus, 351, 357
  dialogues, 306–9

free indirect (*style indirect libre*), 368
immediacy, 449–50
mock-heroic, 351
narrative, 368, 381–3, 422, 430
pathetic fallacy, 388
people (*le peuple*), characterization of, 438–41
personification, 351
portraiture, 156–8
religiosity, 430–3
sentimentalism, 429–30
symbolism, 285, 360–3
tableaux, 225–6, 309, 311–12
tenses, use of, 368
theatricality, 230–2, 433–8
vignettes, 389–96
Sue, Eugène, 6, 191, 340, 434
  Le Juif errant, 37
  Les Mystères de Paris, 37
suffrage, 3, 25, 63
  extension of, 25, 170, 244–6
  opposition to, 145, 246, 250–1, 446–7
  reduction of, 190–1, 221, 341
  universal male, 25, 35, 197, 446–7
    effects of, 10, 153, 210, 345–6
    introduction of, 1–2, 62
    Roman Constituent Assembly, used for, 10
  women's, 98–9, 163, 446
surveillance, 407
Switzerland
  Geneva, 290–2, 294
  political refugees in, 407
symbolism, 285, 360–3

tableaux, 225–6, 309, 311–12
taxation
  increases, 44, 97, 347
  opposition to, 43
  strikes, 334
tenses, use of, 368
Teste, Jean-Baptiste, 168–9
theaters, 434
theatricality
  of language, 230–2, 433–8
  of politics, 355–6
  of revolution, 73, 230–2, 268–9, 272, 345–6
Thierry, Augustin, 147–8
Thiers, Adolphe, *143*, 428–9
  on Agoult, 161
  Agoult on, 428
    criticism, 79, 144
    recognizes achievements of, 79, 160, 165–6, 428

For EU product safety concerns, contact us at Calle de José Abascal, 56–1°,
28003 Madrid, Spain or eugpsr@cambridge.org.

www.ingramcontent.com/pod-product-compliance
Ingram Content Group UK Ltd.
Pitfield, Milton Keynes, MK11 3LW, UK
UKHW020404140625
459647UK00020B/2636